GETTING IT RIGHT

A Power-Packed Resource for Adventist Youth Leaders

GENERAL CONFERENCE OF SEVENTH-DAY ADVENTISTS
YOUTH DEPARTMENT

REVIEW AND HERALD® PUBLISHING ASSOCIATION
HAGERSTOWN, MD 21740

Bible texts credited to Amplified are from *The Amplified Bible,* Old Testament copyright © 1965, 1987 by the Zondervan Corporation. The *Amplified New Testament* copyright © 1958, 1987 by The Lockman Foundation. Used by permission.

Texts credited to Clear Word are from *The Clear Word,* copyright © 2000 by Jack J. Blanco.

Scripture quotations marked NASB are from the *New American Standard Bible,* copyright © 1960, 1962, 1963, 1968, 1971, 1972, 1973, 1975, 1977, 1994 by The Lockman Foundation. Used by permission.

Scriptures credited to NCV are quoted from *The Holy Bible, New Century Version,* copyright © 1987, 1988, 1991 by Word Publishing, Dallas, Texas 75039. Used by permission.

Texts credited to NEB are from *The New English Bible.* © The Delegates of the Oxford University Press and the Syndics of the Cambridge University Press 1961, 1970. Reprinted by permission.

Texts credited to NIV are from the *Holy Bible, New International Version.* Copyright © 1973, 1978, 1984, International Bible Society. Used by permission of Zondervan Bible Publishers.

Texts credited to NKJV are from the New King James Version. Copyright © 1979, 1980, 1982, Thomas Nelson, Inc., Publishers.

Bible texts credited to Phillips are from J. B. Phillips: *The New Testament in Modern English.* Revised Edition. © J. B. Phillips 1958, 1960, 1972. Used by permission of Macmillan Publishing Co., Inc.

Bible texts credited to RSV are from the Revised Standard Version of the Bible, copyright © 1946, 1952, 1971, by the Division of Christian Education of the National Council of the Churches of Christ in the U.S.A. Used by permission.

Bible texts credited to TEV are from the *Good News Bible*—Old Testament: Copyright © American Bible Society 1976, 1992; New Testament: Copyright © American Bible Society 1966, 1971, 1976, 1992.

Verses marked TLB are taken from *The Living Bible,* copyright © 1971 by Tyndale House Publishers, Wheaton, Ill. Used by permission.

This book was
Edited by Shirley Mulkern
Electronic makeup by Shirley M. Bolivar
Text: 11/14 Times New Roman

PRINTED IN THE U.S.A.

09 08 07 06 05   1 2 3 4 5

R&H Cataloging Service
Getting it right: a power-packed resource for
    Adventist youth leaders.

    1. Youth—Religious life—Seventh-day Adventists.   2. Seventh-day Adventists—Youth.
I. Seventh-day Adventists. General Conference Youth Department.

                    268.43

ISBN 0-8280-1805-7

To order more copies of this book, call 1-800-765-6955.
Visit us at www.reviewandherald.com for information on other
Review and Herald® products.

FOREWORD

This youth ministry resource book will help you, the reader, to get the right resource information to build a strong youth ministry in your local church—the right theology, the right history, the right motivation for youth, and many other ideas to put you on the right tract of conducting youth ministry.

For the first time we have a comprehensive resource book for youth leaders written by internationally experienced youth professionals.

Getting It Right suggests power-packed ways to minister to the new generation of the twenty-first century.

ACKNOWLEDGMENTS

How do we begin to thank all the men and women who have helped us see this project come true? This resource book is the culmination of five years of much research and writing. It is written with a global background.

Special thanks to Robert Conway, who untiringly edited the entire project; and Baraka Muganda, Robert Holbrook, and Alfredo Marenko for coordinating the project. Thanks to Betty Brooks, administrative secretary with several years' experience in the Youth Department, who offered proofreading insights on all chapters.

Thanks to all world youth directors around the globe who have been the source of *Getting It Right* in youth ministry.

Praise to God, who inspired all the writers to come up with the content for aiding youth leaders around the Seventh-day Adventist world to getting the right resources for a youth ministry that focuses on salvation and service.

CONTENTS

SECTION 1 • FOUNDATIONS FOR YOUTH MINISTRY

1. Why the Church Should Minister to the Youth   11
   Johann Gerhardt

2. Philosophy of Adventist Youth Ministry   17
   Trudy J. Morgan-Cole

3. Religious Education   22
   Steve Case

4. A Brief History of Seventh-day Adventist Youth Ministry   30
   Trudy J. Morgan-Cole

5. Beyond the Obvious   35
   Baraka Muganda

SECTION 2 • PARAMETERS FOR YOUTH MINISTRY

6. Youth Leadership   41
   Kim Allan Johnson

7. Developmental Psychology and Youth Ministry   48
   Trudy J. Morgan-Cole

8. Moral Development in Youth Ministry   54
   Dave Allen

9. Models of Youth Ministry   60
   Jennifer Morgan

10. Leadership in the Adventist Youth Movement   66
    G. T. Ng

11. Understanding Young People—Why a Special Youth Ministry?   76
    Barry Gane

12. Biblical Models for Youth Ministry   91
    Trudy J. Morgan-Cole

13. Religious Education in Youth Ministry   97
    Udo Worschech

SECTION 3 • EFFECTIVE TOOLS FOR YOUTH MINISTRY

14. Youth Inreach   105
    Neil Thompson

15. Youth Outreach   110
    David M. Parks

16. Campus Ministries   116
    Trudy J. Morgan-Cole

17. Youth Evangelism   122
    Kerry Schafer

18. Strategies for Successful Youth Evangelism   128
    Alfredo Garcia-Marenko

19. Public Relations in Youth Ministry   132
    Trudy J. Morgan-Cole

20. The Youth Sabbath School   137
    N. J. Enang

21. Youth Involvement   145
    Trudy J. Morgan-Cole

22. Youth Evangelism   152
    James Wu

23. Youth Ministry and the Church   159
    Michael Peabody

24. Foundation and Transmission of Ethical Instructions in the New Testament   167
    Bernhard Oestreich

25. In or Out of Shape?   178
    Delyse Steyn

26. Youth and Health   193
    Michael Peabody

27. Youth Leaders' Frequently Asked Questions   199
    Trudy J. Morgan-Cole

SECTION 4 • CHALLENGES AND OPPORTUNITIES IN YOUTH MINISTRY

28. Growing Up Faithful: Faith Development and Youth Ministry   209
V. Bailey Gillespie

29. Catching God's Grace: Youth Ministry and Spirituality   216
V. Bailey Gillespie

30. Maintaining an Attitude of Grace in Youth Ministry   224
Michele Deppe

31. How to Create a Family-centered Youth Ministry   230
Patricia Humphrey

32. Current Social Issues   237
Trudy J. Morgan-Cole

33. More Current Social Issues   244
Trudy J. Morgan-Cole

34. Youth Ministry in Colleges and Seminaries   250
Errol H. Thomas

35. The Impact of Social Pressures on Youth Ministry   258
Antonine Bastien

36. Urbanization and Adventist Youth Ministry   265
Gladwin Mathews

37. Youth Apostasy and Recovery of Backslidden Youth   272
Barry Gane

38. Helping the Wounded Adventist Youth   285
Kerry Schafer

39. Ministry to Those Who Are Divorced—Broken Hearts in the Body of Christ   292
Jennifer Jill Schwirzer

40. Ministering to Young Singles   298
Regina Reaves Hayden

41. Cyberia: Youth Ministries' New Frontier   304
A. Allan Martin

42. Crisis Counseling   312
Marianne Dyrud

SECTION 5 • RESOURCES FOR YOUTH MINISTRY

43. Visionary Leadership 321
   Jennifer Morgan

44. Missions 327
   Kerry Schafer

45. Nature and Camping Programs for Seventh-day Adventist Youth 332
   Gary Thurber

46. Nature and Youth Ministry 339
   Robert Holbrook

47. Effective Delegation 346
   Kim Allan Johnson

48. The Role of the Pastor in Youth Ministry 352
   Jennifer Morgan

49. Communication With Youth, Peers, and Parents 358
   Trudy J. Morgan-Cole

50. Sports in Youth Ministry 364
   Manfred Woysch

51. Small Groups in Youth Ministry 369
   Hiskia I. Missah

SECTION 6 • FACING THE TWENTY-FIRST CENTURY YOUTH MINISTRY

52. Youth Ministry in the Twenty-first Century—Finding the Lost Generation 377
   Jennifer Jill Schwirzer

53. Meeting the Needs of the Twenty-first Century Youth 383
   Paul Tompkins

54. Preaching to Twenty-first Century Youth 389
   Siegfried Wittwer

55. AIDS Education in Developing Countries 398
   Rick Ferret

REPRODUCIBLES 403

SECTION 1

Foundations for
Youth Ministry

CHAPTER 1

Why the Church Should Minister to the Youth

by Johann Gerhardt

WHEN SEARCHING FOR A THEOLOGICAL rationale for youth ministry, one is startled by the fact that there is neither an expressive theology of youth nor a theology of youth ministry. Apparently it has not been urgent to give special attention to a theology of the youth. The time of youth has been considered a period of transition from childhood to adulthood, the adult being the real entity, the ultimate goal of all education and personal development. Consequently, the youth have been described as the "church of tomorrow." Although this is still true in one sense, the world church has come to realize that the youth also are the church of today.

The reasons for a theology of youth ministry can be listed along the following lines:

- There is a growing recognition of the youth as an important segment of society.
- The Adventist world church is a church of the younger generation.
- Adventist youth are highly educated.
- The belief system of the church has to be plausible for the next generation.
- Adventist socialization of the younger generation cannot be taken for granted.
- The "do's and don'ts" of youth ministry must come from a reflection on the relationship between the youth, the church, and our biblical faith.

"It is the task of theology to reflect upon the principles and implications of the existence of Christ in today's world. These principles—as facts of revelation—should be recognized as already existent in the communication and in the experiences of men in the church and in society, or as still lying in the future demanding actions of conversion."*

In our approach to developing ideas for youth ministry and of finding principles that may lead to action, we will concentrate our thinking on four theological motifs that are at the center of Adventist biblical understanding.

The Anthropological Motif

The most important message in the biblical account of the creation of humanity is that we have been created in the image of God (Gen. 1:26; 9:6). This means that human beings have their origin in the self-decision of God to create them out of freewill. Humans receive their identity from God speaking to them. Like other creatures, they receive God's blessing, but unlike other creatures, they are made capable of taking on responsibility for their actions and to make intelligent decisions (Gen. 2:15-17). Humans are able to listen and to answer (verses 19, 20), and they are even free to say no (Gen. 3:1ff.).

God has made humanity as male and female, thus from the beginning bringing humans in relation to one another. The world around individual human beings comes, like themselves, from God. How humans relate to their fellow beings, whether human or animal, tells something about their own relation to their Creator.

Humans have been called to rulership, but unlike the old Oriental kings, they have no power to rule in their own right; they are only the image of God, the representative of God. Rulership is given, not to a single individual, but to humanity: "Let us make *adam* that **they** may rule." As soon as somebody starts to dominate somebody else, the image of God is destroyed and needs special protection. Rulership according to God is possible only in solidarity with one another.

Although having come perfect from God's hand, humans are able to grow, to develop, to build, to invent. They are made open for the future with an inner, onward thrust, in each single stage bearing the image of God.

The story of the fall of humanity (Gen. 3) adds another side to the image of human beings: humans have lost their integrity and unity. They suffer from their broken identity and from the unresolved tension between what they believe and what they do. From then on human beings are doomed to search for meaning and identity. Life asks questions, and humans have to find the answers, even among contradicting options. From then on, not only development, but also restoration, are the goals of life the individual person has to find meaning in life and meaning in faith, both interrelating with one another.

Implications for Youth Ministry
- The youth, like the adult, bears the image of God.
- The state of the youth is of equal value to the state of the adult.
- Dominion over the youth is destroying the image of God.
- The need for maturity and development belongs to every stage of human life.
- Responsibility is an asset not only of the adult but of every life stage.
- Search for meaning and identity is one of the most important tasks of the youth.
- Broken identity is the experience of young people, especially during adolescence.
- Personal faith, not the religion of a church, is the restoring power in one's life.

The Christological-Soteriological Motif
In the writings of the New Testament, Christ is not, in the first case, the Big Brother of humanity in our lost condition. He is the New Man. The image of God may have been distorted. Yet it has become fully alive again in the person of Jesus of Nazareth. He "is the image of the invisible God" (Col. 1:15). He is the Savior from slavery, from the bondage to one's self and the destructive forces of life. He puts human beings right with God and gives them a new identity as His children, symbolized through the act of baptism. Whoever and whatever a person may become in the passages of time, he or she is safe, because by faith he or she has taken part of the identity of Christ.

Atonement is the result of Christ's ministry (2 Cor. 5:18ff.). Human beings are "at one" with God, "at one" with themselves, and "at one" with their fellow humans. This reality has to be realized and put into action by humans. It is because of the unconditional acceptance of God in Christ that humans can accept the truth about themselves without always trying to excuse themselves and to blame others. It is because of the unshakable confidence of Christ in sinners and in their deep desire for repentance that human beings are able to repent and to change their lives. It is the overwhelming experience of acceptance and trust that draws people into the presence of Christ and abolishes the feelings of fear and of lack of self-worth. Individuals, irrespective of sex, age, and status, experience the power of hope, love, and personal value. Thus, through faith, the image of God in humanity is restored until its full realization in the world to come.

Through conversion the new human being is a partaker of the power of the Holy Spirit. The human efforts are combined with the forces of the heavenly world. By this power individuals can transcend themselves, transcend the barriers of race, sex, culture, life conditions, guilt—even death.

Christ, in the first place the Savior of humanity, is also our model, a model of real self-worth, of human dignity combined with kindness and loving care, a model of confidence and belief in people, a model of self-control and responsibility.

Implications for Youth Ministry
- No one is born a Christian, not even our children.
- Each single person is born under the condition of guilt and grief.
- Each single person has an inner desire for good.
- Young people especially suffer from the experience of lack of self-worth.
- The experience of unconditional acceptance is the most powerful source for conversion.
- The teaching of righteousness by faith is the door to a personal belief system.
- The developmental needs of the youth are unconditional faith, hope, and love.
- The development of a personal relationship with Christ is more important than consent to a belief system.

The Ecclesiological Motif

Like the human body the church is the creation of God, being the living body of Christ (1 Cor. 12:12ff.). The individual believers count as members of this divine creation, visible in human and mundane affairs. There is no church without a flock of believers. Social interrelations, family structures, are characteristics of this body. There is no head except Christ. All structures must be in harmony with this Christocentric prestructure. There is no exertion of human power because of sex, status, influence, age, or money. On the contrary, the seemingly least important and least valuable deserves the highest esteem from all.

Fellowship of the believers, proclamation of the gospel, and loving service to the world are the three all-encompassing principles of any Christian congregation. In this endeavor the church is the obedient servant of the Lord, fulfilling His commission until He comes. The goal is to set people free from their bondage, from any suppression by evil powers, and to call them into the kingdom of God.

The church, sent into the world as a mediating agent, is not the noble club of the spiritual elite, but the advocate of the oppressed, of the suffering, of the fear-stricken, of those who try and fail, of those who need the life-creating power of hope and reassurance, of confidence and forgiveness. The church is a symbol for, and an institution of, the ongoing atonement of God with the human race.

Its relevance depends on how plausible the belief system becomes for the life affairs of believers and nonbelievers alike. In the attempt to transmit contents of faith and values, it has to evangelize not only nonbelievers but also its own youth.

In a segregated world the church demonstrates unity in variety. It unites people of different cultures, characters, and individual lifestyles under general biblical values and principles, thus nurturing personal growth and calling to responsibility and solidarity with others at the same time.

Implications for Youth Ministry
- The young are members of the body of Christ.
- The church understands the developmental tasks of the youth.
- The church helps the youth in the search for meaning.
- The church is a nurturing group for the social and spiritual needs of the youth.
- The church invests time and material resources in the youth.
- The church calls on the youth for service and involvement.
- The church fosters personal faith.
- The church rethinks its plausibility structures in the light of the life experience of the youth.
- The church tries to win the youth by convincing, not by coercing.

The Eschatological Motif

In the eschatological motif (Matt. 28; Rev. 21) Jesus is not only Lord of the *kairos* at the time of the saving acts of God, but is now Lord of the *chronos,* of the historical periods of time. He is the one in the beginning and in the end of the history of the world. The climax of all eschatological thinking is not the end as destruction, but the new beginning. It is the fulfillment of all individual and social growth through God's intervention by overthrowing the conditions of the old aeon and establishing their everlasting kingdom of peace, righteousness, and justice.

Christ's return is also the climax of all individual time. The goal of hoping, believing, and loving has been reached. Humans are transformed into the likeness of God (1 John 3:1, 2). Human beings are real again. The brokenness of identity resolved, no tensions between the inside and outside, no fear and anxiety, no lack of self-worth, no need for defense mechanisms, for coping strategies. Finally, the tension between "already—not yet" dissolves. There is no promise but reality.

The eschatological motif is the motif of the future. When hope dies, humanity dies. Eschatological thinking surpasses the limits of human perspectives of the present and the future. It is a remedy for despair and for blind optimism. It encourages humans to engage in the affairs of this world, to better the circumstances of life, to work for peace and justice, to relieve the burdens of war and crime, to interfere in problems with the power of Christian love and care. It prevents having a fatalistic approach to life. It demonstrates that God still is, and forever will be, the God who cares for this planet. Under this horizon of hope human beings can do their part.

Since the church has a future, it takes the present seriously. The church is not only a change agent but also under constant change in order to proclaim the gospel as present truth. Special needs of society demand biblical understanding. In order to remain faithful to the fathers of the church, the church must always be up-to-date, bringing together the quest of the time with the answers of the everlasting gospel.

Implications for Youth Ministry:
- The church celebrates hope in the future as center of worship.
- The credibility of the church depends on its actions as a relief system.
- The church encourages youth to discover their personal gifts (charismata).
- The church encourages youth to develop professional skills.
- The church upholds an educational system that transmits knowledge and values.
- The church demonstrates to their youth that they are needed for the present and the future of the church by laying responsibility in their hands.
- The church encourages change in order to keep its identity.

Conclusion

The time of youth is in many respects a special time: the clear identity of childhood has passed away; there are developmental tasks ahead, such as reaching sexual maturity, gaining a new personal identity, finding professional perspectives, experiencing love and partnership, finding a place in society, finding answers to the questions of meaning, building a sound biblical basis for faith. Many dangers lurk along the roads. But life offers even more possibilities. It is the task of the church to accompany its youth on their way, enabling them to find a place in the church and in society (understanding the sometimes-rebellious attitude as a time of probing), nurturing personal growth, fostering an atmosphere of acceptance and respect. There is no more important task than to draw its own children to God. Service to the youth is mission in its real sense. Rethinking the theological motifs gives a meaningful rationale for action. It has to be done again and again.

---

* Ottmar Fuchs, *Prophetische Kraft der Jugend?* (Freiburg: Lambertus, 1986), p. 16.

Selected Bibliography

Biemer, Günter. *Der Dienst der Kirche an der Jugend. Handbuch kirchlicher Jugendarbeit Bd. 1.* Freiburg: Herder, 1985.

Dalferth, Igolf et al. (Hrsg.). *Person und Gottebenbildichkeit. Christlicher Glaube in moderner Gesellschaft, Bd. 24.* Freiburg: Herder, 1981. S. 57-99.

Dudley, Roger L. *Passing On the Torch.* Hagerstown, Md.: Review and Herald Publishing Association, 1986.

———. *Why Teenagers Reject Religion.* Hagerstown, Md.: Review and Herald Publishing Association, 1978.

————. *When Teenagers Cry Help.* Washington, D.C.: Review and Herald Publishing Association, 1981.

Fuchs, Ottmar. *Prophetische Kraft der Jugend?* Freiburg: Lambertus, 1986.

Lechner, Martin. *Pastoraltheologie der Jugend.* München: Don Bosco, 1992.

Raffelt, Albert, und Karl Rahner. *Anthropologie und Theologie. Christlicher Glaube in moderner Gesellschaft, Bd. 24.* Freiburg: Herder, 1981. S. 8-55.

Schweitzer, Friedrich. *Die Suche nach dem eigenen Glauben.* Gütersloh: Gütersloher Verlagshaus, 1996.

White, Ellen G. *Education.* Mountain View, Calif.: Pacific Press Publishing Association, 1903.

————. *Evangelism.* Washington, D.C.: Review and Herald Publishing Association, 1946.

CHAPTER 2

Philosophy of
Adventist Youth Ministry

by Trudy J. Morgan-Cole

WHY DO WE NEED YOUTH MINISTRY? Why does the Seventh-day Adventist Church operate ministries specifically aimed at young people? If you're involved in a youth ministry, you may feel too busy with your individual "trees" to step back and look at the whole forest, but it pays to have a sense of context. To understand why we're doing this work and how it came about helps put into perspective our day-to-day struggles as youth ministry leaders.

The Bible is filled with examples of children and young people who were faithful to God and active in His work—think of Naaman's slave girl, of young David, of Joseph, Daniel and their friends, Timothy, and Jesus Himself in the Temple as an earliteen, amazing the rabbis. Yet the Bible doesn't explicitly say much about youth ministry as distinct from other ministries. That's partly because the concept of youth was different in biblical times.

In those days—and, indeed, until quite recently in human history—children left childhood behind and assumed adult responsibilities almost immediately upon reaching puberty. The "teenage" years, that prolonged period in which people have adult bodies and many adult abilities but remain dependent on their parents, simply didn't exist in Bible times. Mary, Jesus' mother, may have been as young as 14 when she was visited by the angel Gabriel, but she was more concerned about her upcoming marriage to Joseph than about Saturday night socials and Pathfinder camporees.

Although the Bible doesn't directly address the subject of youth ministry as we know it, God's Word does recognize that young people—both children and those newly come to their adult status—have special needs. Most of the advice in Scripture about young people is directed at their parents, since the primary responsibility for raising children to know and love God rests with them. Counsels such as "Train a child in the way he should go, and when he is old he will not turn from it" (Prov. 22:6, NIV) and "Fathers, do not exasperate your children; instead, bring them up in the training and instruction of the Lord" (Eph. 6:4, NIV) instruct godly parents to pass their values on to their children.

Religious Education in the Old Testaments

God's instructions to Israel after He brought them to the Promised Land include admonitions to teach their children about what He has done for them. After reminding parents that

17

"your children were not the ones who saw and experienced the discipline of the Lord your God: his majesty, his mighty hand, his outstretched arm. . . . It was not your children who saw what he did for you in the desert" (Deut. 11:2-5, NIV), He then tells them to "fix these words of mine in your hearts and minds. . . . Teach them to your children, talking about them when you sit at home and when you walk along the road, when you lie down and when you get up" (verses 18, 19, NIV). Clearly it has always been God's plan for young people to learn about Him in their homes.

Does the Bible outline a role for the church in training young people? Ellen White tells us that "God had commanded the Hebrews to teach their children His requirements. . . . This was one of the special duties of every parent—one that was not to be delegated to another." She goes on to add that "further provision was made for the instruction of the young, by the establishment of the schools of the prophets."[1]

The Scriptures make brief references to the "sons of the prophets," who apparently gathered in schools during the time of Elijah and Elisha. Elijah, just before being taken up to heaven in a chariot of fire, visited the schools of the prophets at Gilgal, Bethel, and Jericho. During Elisha's ministry he performed the miracle of the floating axhead while helping the sons of the prophets expand their living quarters (see 2 Kings 6).

In *Patriarchs and Prophets* and *Prophets and Kings* Mrs. White expands our picture of these institutions of religious education, suggesting that they were first established by the prophet Samuel. "Samuel gathered companies of young men who were pious, intelligent, and studious. These were called the sons of the prophets. As they communed with God and studied His Word and His works, wisdom from above was added to their natural endowments." She adds that "the chief subjects of study in these schools were the law of God, with the instructions given to Moses, sacred history, sacred music, and poetry. . . . In those schools of the olden time it was the grand object of all study to learn the will of God and man's duty toward Him. In the records of sacred history were traced the footsteps of Jehovah."[2] These schools of the prophets expanded on the family's role of training the young in God's service by showing how He had led in Israel's past.

Throughout Israel's history the community, as well as the home, continued to play a part in educating the young. "After the return from Babylon," Ellen White writes in *The Desire of Ages,* "much attention was given to religious instruction. All over the country, synagogues were erected, where the law was expounded by the priests and scribes. And schools were established, which, together with the arts and sciences, professed to teach the principles of righteousness."[3] This continued in Jesus' time. "In the days of Christ the town or city that did not provide for the religious instruction of the young was regarded as under the curse of God."[4]

Religious Education in the New Testament

Mrs. White goes on to point out, however, that by the time of Christ these schools had become ineffectual, focusing on ceremony and tradition rather than on the truth of Scripture. The comment made during Jesus' ministry that He had "never learned" (John 7:15) suggests that Jesus did not attend the synagogue schools of His day; Mrs. White tells us that the instruction of His mother and His own study of Scripture prepared Jesus for His life's work.

We do know, however, that during His visit to the Temple at age 12, Jesus was found "in the temple courts, sitting among the teachers, listening to them and asking them questions" (Luke 2:46, NIV). "At that day an apartment connected with the Temple was devoted to a sacred school, after the manner of the schools of the prophets. Here leading rabbis with their pupils assembled, and hither the child Jesus came."[5] It was in this setting of religious education that "everyone who heard [Jesus] was amazed at his understanding and his answers" (verse 47, NIV).

Though the synagogue schools did not always fulfill their God-appointed purpose, the tradition to which they belonged, going back to the ancient schools of the prophets, clearly indicates that the Jews recognized the role of the community of believers in educating the youth. They believed in and practiced the equivalent of what we call "Christian education": an education that does not simply prepare young people for a career and for citizenship in the secular community, but that passes down spiritual values and leads the young person to a knowledge of God.

So the Bible, by precept and example, indicates that both the home and the faith community have a part in training young people to know and love God. The Bible writers also make it clear that young people, even children, have an active role to play in sharing God's love with the world. The examples mentioned above of young people who stood firm for their faith through difficulty and temptation show that clearly; so do the ringing words of Paul to the young adult Timothy: "Don't let anyone look down on you because you are young, but set an example for the believers in speech, in life, in love, in faith and in purity" (1 Tim. 4:12, NIV).

Adventist Youth Ministry Begins

Seventh-day Adventist youth ministry has historically focused not just on leading young people to God, but on training them to take an active part in the Lord's work. Although the church has not always put this into practice as we should have, it is clear from the history of Adventist youth ministry, from the Bible, and from the writings of Ellen G. White that this has always been the goal toward which we should work. Adventist youth were never meant to be spectators or pew warmers; they were not meant to be entertained or amused; they were not intended to spend years preparing for missionary work they might do someday when they were old enough. The goal of Adventist youth ministry has always been to engage young people in active work for the Lord as soon as they accept Him as their Savior.

In the very earliest days Seventh-day Adventists had no specific youth ministry; young people were as active and involved in the church work as older ones were. Indeed, the original Advent movement was very much a youth movement, led by people like James White, who began preaching at 21, Ellen White, who received her first vision at age 17, and John Loughborough, who began preaching when he was 17. These young people needed no one to minister to them; they themselves were the ministers, sharing the exciting truths they had discovered in God's Word.

Soon after the Adventist Church was organized and began to grow, people recognized the need for a work specifically directed at young people. And from those earliest days the emphasis was on youth who would be workers for God. Ellen White's best-known statement about youth makes this emphasis quite clear: "With such an army of workers as our youth, rightly trained, might furnish, how soon the message of a crucified, risen, and soon-coming Savior might be carried to the whole world!"[6]

Throughout Mrs. White's inspired writings there is a twofold message about youth: the church must make every effort on behalf of youth, and youth themselves must become active in God's work. "Let not the youth be ignored; let them share in the labor and responsibility. . . . Let the overseers of the church devise plans whereby young men and women may be trained to put to use their entrusted talents," she wrote in volume 6 of *Testimonies for the Church*. "Let the older members of the church seek to do earnest, compassionate work for the children and youth. Let ministers put to use all their ingenuity in devising plans whereby the younger members of the church may be led to cooperate with them in missionary work." [7]

The same burden for youth is evident in other passages from the Spirit of Prophecy: "Very much has been lost to the cause of truth by a lack of attention to the spiritual needs of the young. Ministers of the gospel should form a happy acquaintance with the youth of their congregations. . . . Why should not labor for the youth in our borders be regarded as missionary work of the highest kind? . . . When the youth give their hearts to God, our responsibility for them does not cease. They must be interested in the Lord's work, and led to see that He expects them to do something to advance His cause. . . . Youthful talent, well organized and well trained, is needed in our churches." [8]

Adventist Youth Ministry Expands

But even before Ellen White penned these words, Seventh-day Adventist youth ministry was already on the move—and it was a youth-led movement from the start. Many lifelong Adventists are familiar with the story of 14-year-old Luther Warren and 17-year-old Harry Fenner, who in 1879 knelt under a tree in their hometown of Hazelton, Michigan, to ask God's guidance in how to win other young people to Christ. Inspired by that prayer, the two teenagers formed the church's first young people's missionary band, with a charter membership of nine boys.

That Hazelton prayer meeting soon expanded into a young people's society that included both boys and girls and involved not only religious services but such popular nineteenth-century social events as taffy pulls, sleigh rides, and sugaring-off parties. Though parents and other adults in the church became involved, leadership was still very much in the hands of the youth, particularly of young Luther Warren, who went on to a lifetime of youth ministry and evangelism within the Seventh-day Adventist Church.

Within a few years of the formation of that first young people's society, similar groups sprang up in Adventist churches all over the United States. The first such society outside North America was organized in Adelaide, Australia, in 1892. Ellen White encouraged the growth of Adventist youth ministries, suggesting that the church should set up an organization modeled on the Christian Endeavour Society, a youth organization active in many Protestant churches during that time, which emphasized missionary activity.

Steps Toward Organizing Youth Ministry

At the General Conference session in 1901 the Seventh-day Adventist Church took the first steps toward organizing its youth ministry. A recommendation was passed to organize young people's societies and appoint a committee to plan their organization. For the first time youth ministry began to move forward at the denominational level.

By 1905 Adventist youth work was growing, not just in the United States, but in Australia, Germany, England, Trinidad, Jamaica, Canada, and other countries. In 1907, at the Sabbath school and young people's convention in Mount Vernon, Ohio, the name "Seventh-day Adventist Young People's Society of Missionary Volunteers" was chosen. Usually short-ened to "Missionary Volunteers," or simply MV, this name served the denominational youth work for many years and highlighted the emphasis on youth as active participants in soul winning. From that meeting also came the resolution that "the primary object of young peo-ple's societies is the salvation and development of our youth by means of prayer, study, and personal missionary effort." [9]

In the years immediately following the 1907 convention Adventist young people's soci-eties sprang up in Africa, Tahiti, Singapore, Fiji, Portugal, Bermuda, Japan, the Philippines, and Central America. Missionary volunteers were truly becoming a worldwide army. Junior MV societies for younger children, incorporating hiking, camping, and arts and crafts, be-came popular after the first world war. JMV societies led to the development of junior youth camps and eventually to the formation of the Pathfinder Club in 1950.

The first Seventh-day Adventist youth congress was held in Germany in 1928, and was attended by 3,000 youth and youth leaders from all over Europe. Twelve thousand youth at-tended a North American youth congress in San Francisco in 1947, and 6,000 youth from 25 countries gathered in Paris, France, in 1951. As youth congresses grew and spread, the em-phasis on youth sharing their faith with others remained constant.

Though the name of the church's official youth ministry department was eventually changed from Missionary Volunteers to simply Youth Department, the emphasis in Seventh-day Adventist youth work is still, and should always be, on salvation and service—training youth to share their love of Jesus with others. Over the years, activities such as the student missionary program for college students, short-term mission projects and outreach programs within the local community all train young people to be aware of and concerned about the needs of others, and to begin meeting those needs with God's love and His last-day message.

---

[1] Ellen G. White, *Patriarchs and Prophets* (Mountain View, Calif.: Pacific Press Pub. Assn., 1890), pp. 592, 593.

[2] *Ibid.,* pp. 593, 594.

[3] White, *The Desire of Ages* (Mountain View, Calif.: Pacific Press Pub. Assn., 1898), p. 29.

[4] *Ibid.,* p. 69.

[5] *Ibid.,* p. 78.

[6] White, *Education,* p. 271.

[7] White, *Testimonies for the Church* (Mountain View, Calif.: Pacific Press Pub. Assn., 1948), vol. 6, pp. 435, 436.

[8] White, *Gospel Workers* (Hagerstown, Md.: Review and Herald Pub. Assn., 1915, pp. 207-211.

[9] Nathaniel Krum, *The MV Story* (Washington, D.C.: Review and Herald Pub. Assn., 1963), p. 39.

CHAPTER 3

Religious Education

by Steve Case

HAVE YOU EVER PLANTED A GARDEN? Virtually all gardeners know it's foolish to expect a worthwhile harvest without preparing and tending the garden. Occasionally you may discover a patch of tasty berries in the wild or watermelons that sprouted from leftover picnic rinds by the river. But those would be the exception rather than the norm. When you faithfully prepare and tend the garden, you significantly increase the chances for a good harvest. However, you have no guarantee that all will go well. While a number of things are up to you, some things simply are beyond your control.

The same could be said about a person's spiritual development. It would be sheer foolishness to do nothing to influence, train, teach, correct, encourage, model, discipline, or celebrate the many facets that shape a person toward godliness. Although guarantees can't be made, and the power of choice repeatedly gets exercised, you can certainly influence a person in a favorable direction.

The Role of Religious Education

Seventh-day Adventists believe God created human beings in His image, but because of Adam and Eve's rebellion in the Garden of Eden, humans now come into this world with a natural bent to evil in spite of being made in the image of God. This "bent to evil" continues to be a force we are unable to resist apart from the power of Jesus Christ. This is the purpose of religious education—to lead people to accept Jesus Christ as their Savior and then to live for Him in service.

Religious education has specific emphases in various denominational settings. For Seventh-day Adventists, the following components should be included in reference to religious education:

- Christ-centered with a gospel focus
- Empowered by the Holy Spirit
- Based on Scripture
- Character-transforming
- Spiritually wholistic (includes physical, mental, social, emotional)
- Integrates faith into life, including one's home, community, work/school, and leisure
- Leads to worship
- Results in reaching out to others—in fact, to the whole world

- Sustains one's heritage (remembering God's actions in the past)
- Continues throughout life

In a sense religious education started in the Garden of Eden, and it continues through the restoration of a new earth. One could trace it through Scripture, with a family locus of instruction, with schools of the prophets added by Samuel. By the time Jesus came to earth, the religious instruction actually sidetracked people to the point they missed the Messiah. But with the special revelation of Scripture, people needed to be able to read, so education was integral for religious training. Many universities today that may be secular in their emphasis had religious education as their original impetus for existence.

Seventh-day Adventists and Religious Education

Even before formally organizing in 1863, Seventh-day Adventists started Sabbath schools, in which participants recited memory verses, answered questions posed by teachers, and participated in times of singing and prayer. Eventually curriculum for various age groups became standardized, and Flora Plummer headed up a Sabbath school department for the denomination for nearly 35 years. Sabbath schools became characterized by biblical instruction, prayer, and a mission emphasis with mission offerings and mission stories.

With the development of an Adventist school system, religious instruction took place each school day during a "Bible class," in addition to potential religious instruction in other disciplines, plus special chapel periods, daily worship times, and school outings. When it is well developed, religious instruction in a school setting often takes a more dominant role than the Sabbath school.

At the same time a Sabbath school forged an existence, young people formed their own missionary society. Initiated in 1879 by Harry Fenner (17 years old) and Luther Warren (14 years old), and further spurred by Meade MacGuire, these Sunshine Bands sometimes received opposition from adults. By 1907 the General Conference had started a youth department and named it the "Seventh-day Adventist Young People's Department of Missionary Volunteers." Its programs became "MV meetings," and the aim throughout the years has been "the Advent message to all the world in this generation."

What and How

Seventh-day Adventists see themselves as a movement of destiny with an end-time message for the entire world. Doctrinal statements define what is "truth," and an official book published in 1988 further expounds on these doctrines so believers will know what is truth. Some place a special emphasis on values, claiming that values run deeper than doctrinal statements, with core values functioning as essential building blocks for beliefs and behaviors.

But knowing WHAT is true in no way guarantees or necessarily motivates a person to live the truth. Learning a set of doctrinal statements or a series of texts or memorizing answers to Bible trivia games doesn't mean a person will come to Jesus or live for Him. To truly be experienced, faith must go beyond WHAT (content) to HOW (process).

Some have memorized a set of behaviors and may actually live by them, yet fail to make the linkage between what they live and how it relates to deeper callings God has placed on them. Such a lifestyle typically lacks integrity and is bereft of joy.

The rest of this chapter is devoted to sharing seven key processes for transmitting the content for religious education. It gives the HOW, so the WHAT takes hold internally. Each process will also call forth implications for youth ministry.

Seven Key Processes for Religious Education

1. Modeling

"Follow me even as I follow Christ" is one way to describe modeling from a biblical passage. Sometimes people express that they would "rather see a sermon than hear one any day." When referring to character instruction and development, modeling fits into shaping a person more by what is "caught" than by what is "taught." A person may teach the principle that service is the norm for the Christian life, but unless that person also models service, it isn't likely that service will be inculcated by the student.

It's possible to intensify modeling. Here are seven elements that increase the likelihood that modeling will actually occur:
- frequent, long-term contact
- a warm, loving relationship
- exposure to the inner states of the model
- observation of the model in a variety of life settings and situations
- consistency and clarity in the behavior and values of the model
- correspondence between the behavior of the model and the beliefs and standards of the community
- lifestyle of the model explained conceptually, especially through shared experiences

The home environment seems best suited for each of these elements. However, the majority of teens usually look for additional models beyond their parents, even when parents have been excellent role models throughout a teen's childhood. For youth ministry to make a positive impact, it needs to be relational—relationships must be foundational. Obviously 30 minutes a week won't make much of an impact. It's the youth leader who invests significant time and vulnerability with young people who will become a model they emulate. Scan over the previous seven enhancers of modeling and ask yourself to what extent you implement these with the youth you serve. How potent is your modeling?

In recent years mentoring has come into vogue as an intense relational approach to ministry. It requires a tremendous investment of time and a commitment to the individual and the process. The rewards vary from utter disappointment and frustration to tremendous growth, satisfaction, and even celebration.

2. Teaching

Although people often bemoan the educational system and highlight other forms of instruction, actual teaching forms part of the religious education matrix. It's not just experiencing a fun or caring environment; there is content to discover, to analyze, and to evaluate. Although modeling emphasizes what is "caught" over what is "taught," there is still a need for what is "taught."

In the 1960s Ronald Goldman rocked the religious education community by suggesting that since a child's thinking isn't capable of abstract thought, many religious topics and lessons that have been introduced early in life should be withheld until adolescence or adulthood. Others have rebutted Goldman, and there's no question that children and youth do need some amount of content. According to Deuteronomy 6:7 parents are to teach their children about God and what He has commanded. The Hebrew word utilized, *shanan,* refers to sharpening or whetting; to stimulate or heighten by constant and repetitive instruction.

If we apply this to youth ministry, one must ask where the instructional components are in the overall youth ministry program. While some people operate as if the only useful evaluation tools might be "good time was had by all," there must be much more to it than that. Don't misunderstand this to mean that drab and boring lectures are medicine we have to take. It simply means that a body of information does need to be communicated in a way and to the extent that it is *taught.* What curriculum do you use in your youth ministry, and what methods do you employ for instruction?

3. Internalizing

If you had a choice, would you rather:

A. Have people act right on the outside even if they didn't have it right on the inside? or

B. Have people be right on the inside even if they don't act right on the outside?

What's your vote—A or B? Wouldn't it be nice to have it right on the inside *and* on the outside? But that's not one of the options! Some might argue that if you have it right on the inside, then it will be right on the outside. Nice try, but it rarely works that way in practice. What's your choice—A or B?

If limited to those two choices, most people throughout history say they would prefer B, but they live as though A is more important. Perhaps that's because we can see (and judge) the outside and then infer what is inside. Maybe it's because we aren't very good at reading the heart. Because "man looks at the outward appearance, but the Lord looks at the heart" (1 Sam. 16:7, NIV), Samuel picked Jesse's oldest son, rather than the baby of the family, David, to be the next king. Certainly we can think of times when we have done the same type of thing.

But repeatedly God tells His people that He wants the inside to be right. Although He provides external behaviors of correctness, God always goes for the heart. "Stop the forms of religion; love and obey me from your heart" formed the keystone of the messages from the prophets before and during the Israelite captivity. Jeremiah put it this way: " 'This is the covenant I will make with the house of Israel after the time,' declares the Lord, 'I will put my law in their minds and write it on their hearts. I will be their God, and they will be my people' " (Jer. 31:33, NIV).

This creates profound implications for youth ministry. It means we will go for the hearts of the young people far more than we'll focus on their clothing and hairstyles. It means we'll probe for what is behind their actions rather than jumping to conclusions when we first become aware of their actions. It means we will push the "good kids" to have a heart relationship with Jesus instead of assuming that outward niceness (or being "politically correct" in the religious realm) guarantees that the heart is right.

4. Disciplining

Occasionally confused with punishment, discipline refers to reinforcing positively what is good and ignoring or extinguishing the negative. It also includes enhancing the good to make it better, and it won't neglect the fine points. It's a process, not an isolated moment. Disciplining looks forward toward self-control.

In contrast, punishment is limited to a negative consequence in response to a given action (or lack of action). It sometimes causes pain and attempts to motivate different behavior when faced with a similar situation in the future. You must have some type of leverage in order to administer punishment. You must be big enough or strong enough or powerful enough to follow through in a meaningful way. In a sense the punishment or the person endorsing the punishment provides the control.

Because discipline continues to move toward self-control, it features an internal locus of control. Scripture refers to discipline for parents with their children, for God with His people corporately, and for God in dealing with us individually.

Youth leaders often see discipline only as punishment, or they may shy away from it if the atmosphere becomes potentially negative. Perhaps the desire to be liked as a youth leader has superseded the desire for the young people to be self-disciplined. How unfortunate! The more you invest in young people, the more likely you will need not only to implement discipline but to actually make it one of your methods for transmitting religious education.

Instead of banning the class clown from your youth group, find a way to direct those energies into something positive for the group. The clown also needs to develop some self-control to learn when clowning enhances things and when it detracts. Discipline includes discovering the reasons behind people's actions instead of responding only to their behavior. By asking "Why?" you shape their awareness that they do have the power to act on their own volition.

5. Serving

Because we inherit a sinful nature, we naturally are selfish. The antidote is giving, and service provides a multitude of avenues to give. Service can be an isolated event, or it can be an attitude that leads to repeated events. Once again, the motivation plays a crucial role. It's possible to serve from completely selfish motives (helps my reputation; may result in a favor for me; I had to do this in order to graduate).

Ideally the motivation springs from a response to God's gift to us. The last phrase of Matthew 10:8 reads, "Freely ye have received, freely give." *The New English Bible* presents it this way: "You received without cost; give without charge." Not only did God create us, but He also has redeemed us. If we were to keep score, that would mean that each one of us owes our life to God at least twice! If we need a role model, consider the Son of God Himself. According to Matthew 20:28, "the Son of Man did not come to be served, but to serve, and to give his life as a ransom for many" (NIV).

But even those who lack a heartfelt inner motivation to serve receive certain benefits from service. When you help or serve someone else, your own self-worth increases. This happens whether or not the person serving has religious motivations. It's like a universal principle: by helping others you help yourself.

Service activities have the potential to enhance the self-worth of young people and to combat their natural selfishness. Sometimes service gets limited to one or two pet activities, and young people make the mistake that they have nothing to offer or that service has a narrow avenue for implementation. Encourage the young people to expand the possibilities for service based on the simple principle that we are saved to serve.

Young people who attend churches with active youth programs sometimes make the mistake of thinking that others should forever provide programs for their participation. References might be made to "the church" as some type of nebulous and inadequate sponsor. Especially during the teen years the young people need to be led to see that *they are the church* and to respond accordingly. Actually they are *part* of the church. The church doesn't revolve *around* them, but they should jump on board so it revolves *with* them.

Those who complain that their church doesn't do enough for them need a wake-up call to action. Those who prevent or hinder young people from being involved in the church should be disciplined, because surely they wouldn't purposely exclude young people or try to erect an artificial hierarchy and discriminate against young people. This can be handled on a one-to-one basis, but occasionally, when done publicly, it must be corrected in an equally public manner.

6. Celebration

God's people in Old Testament times took celebrating quite seriously! Each year the people adjusted their lives to fit into three annual celebrations. And these weren't one-day holidays. They didn't lose the spiritual root of the festivals, and yet, with a full week to celebrate, there certainly was still time to play, too.

The Passover commemorated God's deliverance from Egyptian slavery. Whether it was crossing the Red Sea at the beginning of the journey to Canaan or crossing the Jordan River at the end of their sojourn, the result always seemed to be celebration.

From the start of this earth's history the Sabbath has been set as a celebration each week. And at Sinai God gave a reminder about the seventh-day Sabbath, a celebration for everyone—family, friends, slaves, foreigners, and even animals. Rarely do we party with such inclusiveness and abandon. In fact, we rarely party at all. If someone mentions partying we usually think of shallow socializing that often relies on alcohol to break the ice and too often results in superficial sex. It's time to reclaim celebrating with the joy, intensity, and expressiveness God designed from the beginning.

When it comes to youth ministry, let the party begin! At one time it didn't seem politically correct even to use the word "celebration," because it made people think of an alternative worship style. Some think that God approves of only one worship style. They quote the end of Psalm 46, "Be still, and know that I am God" (verse 10), but somehow miss the start of the very next psalm, "Clap your hands, all ye people; shout unto God with the voice of triumph" (Ps. 47:1).

But the celebration isn't just for the sake of celebrating. The depth comes from the purpose of the celebration—God's deliverance, God's provision, God's goodness. On an earthly level we could think of wedding anniversaries and birthdays as celebrations with a cause. Luke 15 contains three stories of lostness—a lost sheep, a lost coin, and a lost son. Each story concludes with celebration. How could it be any other way?

The implication seems obvious. Don't neglect the celebration opportunities already in place; and keep your eyes open to celebrate additional ones. It's not only OK; it's desired and even commanded.

7. Covenanting

Some confuse this with celebrating. The two can go together, but covenanting deals more with decision-making. Joshua's shout pierces the air afresh today: "Choose for yourselves this day whom you will serve. . . . But as for me and my household, we will serve the Lord" (Joshua 24:15, NIV). Elijah made a similar call on Mount Carmel as he challenged the Israelites to choose between Baal and Yahweh. Even Queen Esther's last-minute call to prayer dealt with a covenant in terms of making a decision for her life.

For those who grow up in the church, especially if parents are active, being a Christian requires little more than "going with the flow." As adolescents individuate from their parents, one way to be different is to be apathetic or even reject religion. Roger Dudley's classic youth ministry volume addresses this very dynamic.

Religious educator Horace Bushnell's often quoted statement, "The child is to grow up a Christian, and never know himself as being otherwise," has meaning in response to the expectation in his day that people would grow up as horrid sinners and then have an incredible conversion story. But when the expectation is that a person is growing up Christian and, therefore, must always stay that way, there is a tendency to ignore the fact that people do have choices and they aren't guaranteed to be just like their parents.

Covenanting can give a young person an anchoring point that provides personal meaning. This may come outside of the regular family setting. That is why young people need significant others in the church to mentor them outside the cocoon of a good family (if they're fortunate enough to have that). The key element is being able to make a decision for oneself.

Potent settings for covenanting include short-term mission trips, Pathfinder camporees, summer camps, Weeks of Prayer, Bible camps, evangelistic series, and retreats. Boarding academy teens, because they already are outside of their home, are more susceptible to covenanting than day academy students.

The most typical form of covenanting centers on an altar call following a passionate sermon. Sometimes a baptism becomes the starting point for a covenant experience. We need far more forms for covenanting as a congregation, as families, and as individuals. Beyond the Communion service, many never encounter any type of covenanting experience.

Because "God has no grandchildren" (He has only children), we have no guarantee that the next generation will also follow Christ. That's why each generation and each person within each generation needs to come face to face with a decision regarding who Jesus Christ is and how they will relate to Him. Don't be surprised if those who are baptized prior to adolescence want a rebaptism when they're in the thick of adolescence. Both baptisms are valid, but an early baptism is more like a community covenant, and most adolescent baptisms tap into the individual stand for Jesus.

We need to take young people seriously. Without our coercing them, they need opportunities to covenant individually and with groups. After all, God does call each one to be part of the family of faith.

Summary

If you leave a garden to itself and you plan to live off of it, you will probably starve to death. The same could be said regarding the religious development of people of all ages. We have recognized the importance of good *content* when it comes to religious education. Our current need for improvement is in the *process*.

CHAPTER 4

A Brief History of Seventh-day Adventist Youth Ministry

by Trudy J. Morgan-Cole

I N ITS VERY EARLIEST DAYS the Seventh-day Adventist Church had no specific youth ministry; young people were as active and involved in the work of the church as older ones were. Indeed, the original Advent movement was very much a youth movement, led by people like James White, who began preaching at 21, Ellen White, who received her first vision at age 17, and John Loughborough, who began preaching when he was 17. These young people needed no one to minister to them; they themselves were the ministers, sharing the exciting truths they had discovered in God's Word.

Early Beginnings

Soon after the Adventist Church was organized and began to grow, people recognized the need for a work specifically directed at young people. And from those earliest days the emphasis was on youth who would be workers for God. Ellen White's best-known statement about youth makes this emphasis quite clear: "With such an army of workers as our youth, rightly trained, might furnish, how soon the message of a crucified, risen, and soon-coming Savior might be carried to the whole world!"[1] Ellen White strongly advocated youth work within the church, but the work she envisioned was not one in which youth would be passive recipients of adult-directed programs. She foresaw a youth work in which youth would be trained and equipped for evangelistic work that they themselves would carry out—a true "army" to finish God's work in the world.

Appropriately the credit for actually starting Adventist youth ministry goes to two teenagers who felt a need and sought God's help in meeting it. Many lifelong Adventists are familiar with the story of 14-year-old Luther Warren and 17-year-old Harry Fenner, who in 1879 knelt under a tree in their hometown of Hazelton, Michigan, to ask God's guidance in how to win other young people to Christ. Inspired by that prayer, the two teenagers formed the church's first young people's missionary band, with a charter membership of nine boys.

That Hazelton youth meeting, which included prayer, hymn-singing, election of officers, a report on mission work done, and an offering to purchase literature, soon expanded into a young people's society that included both boys and girls. Their activities involved not only religious services but such popular nineteenth-century social events as taffy pulls, sleigh rides, and sugaring-off parties. Though parents and other adults in the church became involved, leadership was still very much in the hands of the youth, particularly of young Luther Warren, who went on to a lifetime of youth ministry and evangelism within the Seventh-day Adventist Church.

A group similar to the Hazelton missionary band was formed in 1891 in Antigo, Wisconsin, by Meade MacGuire. Looking back on the experience in later years, MacGuire said, "I was but a youth, and had no one to counsel with; but I felt that something ought to be done to help and inspire the young people. I had never heard of any young people's organization among our people, but acquaintances of mine attended meetings of the local Christian Endeavour Society and the Epworth League, and I felt that our own young people needed something of this kind as much as did those of other denominations. I proposed holding a young people's meeting, but my proposal was met with almost universal disapproval. However, the elder, a saintly old man . . . placed his hand on my shoulder and said, 'My boy, you go right ahead. You may have the church for your meeting, and I will stand by you.'"[2]

The Antigo young people's society had 30 members, and their meetings were similar to the ones Luther Warren had organized in Hazelton. Along with singing, Bible study, and prayer, there was time for personal testimonies. Participation was wholehearted; MacGuire recalled that there was intense disappointment if even one member failed to testify, but that this hardly ever happened. Reflecting on the success of that early society and the initial reluctance of the church to support it, he commented: "I believe God restrained the enemy because He wanted this work to go forward, and the people were not sufficiently in favor of it to stand by us if mistakes were made."[3]

Within a few years of the formation of the first young people's societies, similar groups sprang up in Adventist churches all over the United States. The first such society outside North America was organized in Adelaide, Australia, in 1892. Ellen White encouraged the growth of Adventist youth ministries, and, like Meade MacGuire, she suggested as a model the Christian Endeavour Society, a youth organization active in many Protestant churches at that time, which emphasized missionary activity.

The Youth Work Is Organized

At the General Conference session in 1901 the Seventh-day Adventist Church took the first steps toward organizing its youth ministry. A recommendation was passed to organize young people's societies and form a committee to plan their organization. Luther Warren, at that time the most active youth worker in the Seventh-day Adventist Church, chaired the committee. For the first time youth ministry began to move forward at the denominational level.

The Sabbath School Department of the General Conference was given responsibility for encouraging young people's work, and that responsibility was enthusiastically taken up by the department's secretary, Mrs. L. Flora Plummer, another pioneer of Adventist youth ministry whose name deserves to be remembered. By the summer of 1901 the tireless Mrs. Plummer had contacted church leaders all over the United States, "agitating the organization of young people's societies everywhere."[4] When confronted with the fact that only three of the 50 conferences were able, or willing, to appoint young people's secretaries to be responsible for this work, Mrs. Plummer simply wrote to all the Sabbath school secretaries in the remaining 47 conferences and informed them that until a youth secretary was chosen in their conference, *they* would be regarded as leaders of the young people's work. Her ploy worked, and the Sabbath school secretaries added youth work to their agendas.

By 1905 Adventist youth work was growing, not just in the United States, but in Australia, Germany, England, Trinidad, Jamaica, Canada, and other countries. In 1907, at the Sabbath school and young people's convention in Mount Vernon, Ohio, the name "Seventh-day Adventist Young People's Society of Missionary Volunteers" was chosen for the new Youth Department of the General Conference. Usually shortened to "Missionary Volunteers" or simply MV, this name served the denominational youth work for many years and highlighted the emphasis on youth as active participants in soul winning. From that meeting also came the resolution that "the primary object of young people's societies is the salvation and development of our youth by means of prayer, study, and personal missionary effort."[5]

In the years immediately following the 1907 convention, Adventist young people's societies sprang up in Africa, Tahiti, Singapore, Fiji, Portugal, Bermuda, Japan, the Philippines, and Central America. Missionary volunteers were truly becoming a worldwide army. Familiar elements of the Missionary Volunteer program, which older church members today will recall from their youth, began during these early years. These included the *Morning Watch* devotional calendar, the Missionary Volunteer Leaflet Series, the Reading Course, and the Bible Year reading plan.

During these years separate Junior MV societies for younger children also began to spring up in Adventist churches around the world. At first the JMV societies were very similar in structure to the senior MV societies, incorporating a Junior Reading Course and Junior Bible Year. But in the years following the first world war, many Adventist youth leaders became convinced that junior youth needed a different approach. JMV societies began to include storytelling, hiking, camping, arts and crafts—a more "hands-on" approach to suit the more active learning style of juniors. Many leaders used the Boy Scouts and Girl Scouts program as a pattern for these junior youth societies. This new direction in junior youth ministry naturally led to the development of junior youth camps in the 1920s.

The Junior Missionary Volunteer Society was formed as a separate branch of the Missionary Volunteer Department during these same years. The JMV Society, which in 1950 became the Pathfinder Club, was a tremendous success in attracting junior youth and helping them to become active in God's church. Today the work of the Pathfinder Club continues around the world, channeling the energies and interests of youth in their preteen and early teenage years.

Youth Congresses and Camporees

The first Seventh-day Adventist youth congress was held in Germany in 1928, and was attended by 3,000 youth and youth leaders from all over Europe. Twelve thousand youth attended a North American youth congress in San Francisco in 1947, and 6,000 youth from 25 countries gathered in Paris, France, in 1951. As youth congresses grew and spread, the emphasis on youth sharing their faith with others remained constant.

Today, youth rallies and conventions are held all over the world at the local, national, and international level, sometimes with special emphases such as Bible study, prayer, or drug-abuse prevention. Pathfinder camporees, also organized on every level from the local up to the international, have become another effective way of drawing Adventist youth together. An amazing 22,000 young people gathered in Oshkosh, Wisconsin, U.S.A., in August 1999 for the "Discover the Power" Pathfinder Camporee. For Adventist young people, especially for the many who attend small churches and small church schools in isolated communities, gatherings like camporees and youth rallies do indeed help them to "discover the power"— the power of the Holy Spirit in their lives first and foremost, but also the power of belonging to a worldwide movement of young people.

Youth Publications

Another aspect of Adventist youth work that has always been central to the movement is the publication of youth-oriented magazines. The Seventh-day Adventist Church has always been a church that believes in the power of the printed word, as evidenced by the avalanche of books and periodicals produced by our publishing houses over the years. A paper for young people, the *Youth's Instructor,* was being published long before Adventist youth work was formally organized; it was started by James White in 1852. For many years the *Youth's Instructor* was the staple of Adventist youth work, aided by other materials such as the *MV Program Kit* (renamed *Youth Ministry Accent* in 1975) and the Sabbath school lesson quarterlies.

In 1970, after 118 years, the *Youth's Instructor* was given a fresher, more contemporary look under the new title *Insight. Insight* magazine continues to minister to the high school-aged youth of the church, but it is no longer alone in the field of Adventist youth publications. In 1953 the *Junior Guide* (now *Guide* magazine) was launched, "packed with stories, pictures, games, puzzles, campcraft, Junior Sabbath school lessons, and interesting Pathfinder activity."[6] *Guide* has changed its appearance and format many times over the intervening years, but it still appeals to its target audience of 10- to 14-year-old readers, perhaps because it is still "packed" with many of the same features it advertised back in 1953.

Recent Developments

Seventh-day Adventist youth work has grown so much and in so many ways since Luther Warren and Harry Fenner first knelt together in 1879 that the movement we are a part of today would probably have astounded those first pioneers. Let us hope, though, that it would not have disappointed them. The focus of Adventist youth ministry—preparing youth for service in God's work—has remained the same in more than a century of growth, and is manifesting itself in new and exciting ways each year.

The General Conference department responsible for youth work changed its name in 1978. "Missionary Volunteers" was cherished by generations of Adventists, but it carried unfortunate connotations in some parts of the world. At a time when many countries had won their independence from their former colonial masters, the *missionary* carried echoes of centuries of colonial domination by Western nations. The more widely acceptable term "Youth Department" replaced the old name. But the focus on service to God and others has not changed. Programs such as the college student missionary program, which began in the 1950s, and the short-term mission projects for high school and college students that became so popular in the 1980s and 1990s, continue to give young people the experience of serving God outside their own countries. Local youth programs involve young people in service and outreach within their own communities in a variety of ways. The "Missionary Volunteer" spirit marches on.

As youth leaders we often focus so much on the day-to-day aspects of our ministry—teaching the Sabbath school lessons, planning the weekend retreat, hosting the Saturday night social—that we lose sight of the "big picture." A glance back at the long and proud history of Seventh-day Adventist youth work helps put our work into perspective. And the most important part of looking back is recognizing that this youth ministry has always been about leading youth to know Jesus and then training them to share Him with others. We are still training that army of youth Ellen White dreamed about—and they are accomplishing His work. Through the Spirit's power they will soon finish it.

---

[1] E. G. White, *Education,* p. 271.

[2] Nathaniel Krum, *The MV Story,* p.11

[3] *Ibid.,* p. 12.

[4] *Ibid.,* p. 25.

[5] *Ibid.,* p. 39.

[6] *Junior Guide,* Oct. 7, 1953, p. 10.

CHAPTER 5

Beyond the Obvious

by Baraka Muganda

SINCE THE INCEPTION OF THE youth department, youth directors in the Seventh-day Adventist Church have always exceeded the obvious of their times. As we approach the second advent of Jesus Christ, this thrust becomes of paramount importance. We need to build up our ancestors' visions by looking beyond the obvious as we enter the third millennium. Our current programs are great, yet we must not relax. It is essential that Adventist youth be challenged to finish the work of the gospel.

Facing the future with such a mentality requires us as youth leaders to shift our paradigm from program to people, and from past to future. Business as usual must stop. It is obvious we have youth camps. It is obvious we have many youth activities. It is obvious we have outstanding Pathfinder programs, and it is obvious that we have an energetic Adventurer program. If we want to prepare our youth to face the future, we must move beyond the obvious and come up with programs that are issue- and need-driven. There is nothing wrong with the obvious: uniforms, parading, or insignias. However, we are losing too many young people despite the excellent programs we have. They are looking for more than the obvious. Let us build a youth ministry that meets the needs and issues affecting the spirituality of the youth.

Meeting the Needs of Youth

Recent studies within the Seventh-day Adventist Church have shown increased at-risk behavior among our youth. Many times some of these behaviors are not being addressed by the programs that are in place. We have taken everything within the obvious contexts. The programs we run must be built on our current strength and stretched beyond the obvious traditional boundaries. In the past, youth ministries have concentrated their efforts on producing quality spiritual products and services for youth leaders. It is becoming increasingly clear that such efforts, while necessary, are not sufficient in themselves. Moving beyond the obvious calls for us as youth leaders to inform and persuade not only the youth but also those that deal with youth leaders, church administrators, parents, and church members.

Our focus and priorities have changed with the societal problems that are endemic in the society in which our youth live. Aids, poverty, street kids, secularism, postmodernism, New Age, drugs, single-parent families—all force us to see farther than our own perceptions. Society is constantly changing. In order for our ministry to be successful, we must respond to the political, social, and economic challenges that affect and influence our youth.

Cooperative Ministry

"Beyond the obvious" calls us as spiritual youth leaders to move away from working above as a department to working together with other departments within the church. This includes youth administrators, pastors, educators, and ministries throughout the world church structure. Those involved in the youth ministry of the future must expand their vision of ministry.

For too long we have been isolated by the church or have isolated ourselves from the church. Youth ministry has been seen by many to be just dealing with youth and running their programs. This has been a very unfortunate approach. To reach young people, we reach those who work with them. We must not be simply specialists in providing programs, but specialists in ministry. The youth department must be a vehicle for the church to accomplish its mission. Spiritual youth leaders must be specialists in communicating the mission of the church to youth and communicating the needs of youth to the church.

The department, with such focus, will increase the spiritual emphasis of its approach to ministry rather than concentrating on only the mechanics of the programs. Faith development, conversion, commitment, training, and the development of a lifestyle of service by our youth to accomplish the mission of the church will be the priorities of the department as we take up the challenge of moving beyond the obvious: Preparing our youth for eternity. "The youth in our day may be workers with Christ if they will; and in working their faith will strengthen and their knowledge of the divine will will increase."[1]

Centered on the Word

"Beyond the obvious" calls for youth leaders, pastors, and church elders to challenge the young people with the Word of God. Many times those who work with young people say, "Youth are bored by church stuff." Contrary to this statement, when one asks youth what they are bored with at church, they say, "We are bored with leaders who do not challenge us."

Youth want to be challenged. Give youth more than entertainment. As youth leaders with an ear tuned to "beyond the obvious," we are admonished to hear the cry of our youth. Youth are crying to our church, saying:

- We want to find real answers.
- We want to find hope.
- We want to be challenged.
- We want to know God.
- Please give us more than concerts, parades, insignias, uniforms, and other mechanics within the various youth ministry activities.
- Show us how in God's Word to find answers to our questions.

Youth ministry has one goal—to save its youth and involve them in the mission of the church. Youth ministry is not babysitting or entertaining. Many youth leaders try the following approaches:

- Hold young people in the youth society or club so they do not leave the church or join another church.
- Hold young people in the youth society or club so that they do not go places or do things we don't approve of—to keep them entertained under our control. (We are

suggesting not that youth should not be entertained, but that entertainment should not be used as a long-term goal for youth ministry.)

- Hold young people until they are old so that we can give them some positions in the church and teach them the Christian faith.

Youth leaders whose goal is to hold young people usually end up catering to those who are most likely to leave—at the expense of committed young people. Our business should always be to mold the character of youths into the image of Jesus Christ. That is our ministry.

The objective of "beyond the obvious" is to place emphasis on salvation and service. Paul's goal in ministry was to present every person mature in Christ (see Col. 1:28). The goal of Adventist youth ministry should be to present every young person mature in Christ. The goal is not to run programs or use methods, because they are merely tools we use to achieve the goal of leading young people to maturity. When the goal is maturity in Christ, the youth leader is set free to use any method that achieves that goal. Neither is the goal to hold young people within the fellowship of the church; that is a by-product of leading young people to maturity in Christ.

"Beyond the obvious" challenges the way we think about youth ministry, because youth ministry is not only happening where there is a youth program. It is quite possible to have a Pathfinder or senior youth/young adult program in which hundreds of young people attend smoothly organized activities and yet no one is led to maturity in Christ. On the other hand, a church may lack an organized youth group, so that people say it has no youth ministry, yet through personal relationships, young people are led to maturity in Christ that is beyond the obvious.

A Challenging Faith

"Beyond the obvious" challenges our youth to move out of comfortable faith in challenging faith. It might be more of a sin to suggest to young people that the Christian life is always fun and never boring. Christian faith may begin on the mountaintop, but Christian character is formed in the crucible of pain. Mature Christian adults, then, are those people who no longer depend on bells and whistles or mom and dad to motivate them to live out their faith.

Young men and women become proactive Christians—not reactive. When young people grow up to be reactive Christian adults, they are constantly waiting for someone, or something, to attract them—to involve them, to impress them. A reactive Christian youth puts the responsibility for his/her spiritual life on someone else. Could it be that our church youth programs and publicity may, in fact, be moving teens away from, rather than toward, mature Christian adulthood?

Today we are fighting for young people, including the small young ones of the church. "Youth ministry" has to be reinvented for the needs and wavelengths of a whole new youth world. Some basics have not changed, and they never will. In other areas today's youth leader needs fresh thinking, plowing a new path where the old "young people's group" used to sit. The "beyond the obvious" mentality recognizes that the youth society is "base camp" for the Adventist young people who are the frontline soldiers in the battle for their generation. It is a "field hospital" for the many wounded kids. And it must be the redeeming place where Satan's prisoners of war are attracted and set free. Ellen White rightly said it: "We have an army of youth today who can do much if they are properly directed and encouraged. We want our children to believe the truth. We want them to be blessed of God. We want them to act a part in well-organized plans for helping other youth. Let all be so trained that they might rightly represent the truth, giving reason for the hope that is within them, and knowing God in any branch of the work where they are qualified to labor."[2]

Prayer-driven Ministry

The Bible clearly shows the need of prayers in the lives of youth leaders. In the story of Moses, Aaron, and Hur, the Jews prevailed against the Amalekites as long as Moses could hold up his arms. But he couldn't keep them up all day, so Aaron and Hur walked with him and held his arms up (see Ex. 17:10-12). Every youth leader needs an "Aaron and Hur Club" around him—this is war.

We cannot afford to have a ministry that is program-driven or idea-driven or even goal-driven. It must be a prayer-driven ministry, or we will only see results humans can produce. In "beyond the obvious," fervent focused prayer will give us what God can do for our young people. "The prayer of a righteous man is powerful and effective" (James 5:16, NIV).

A youth leader with the "beyond the obvious" burden will challenge the young people to be what they would like the church to become. Young people can catch a vision that says, "If it starts here, maybe it could spread throughout the church."

Adventist young people need to realize their potential to be spiritual examples for their church and beyond. They could be God's instruments to lead the church into something more loving, more evangelistic, more exciting, more real than many adult believers are experiencing.

Ellen White, in her "Appeal to the Young," says: "If they would elevate their thoughts and words above the frivolous attractions of this world and make it their aim to glorify God, His peace, which passeth all understanding, would be theirs."[3] She also says that "our young people need to be helped, uplifted, and encouraged, but in the right manner; not, perhaps, as they would desire it, But in a way that will help them to have sanctified minds. They need good, sanctifying religion more than anything else."[4]

God has commissioned us as leaders to "pump up the volume" of Adventist youth ministry for the salvation of our youth! Let the message of salvation sound above the noise of the world through the Adventurer, Pathfinder, and senior youth/young adult programs, resources, and leadership. Time is running out. We must move "beyond the obvious" to save our youth.

---

[1] Ellen G. White, *Testimonies,* vol. 3, p. 370.

[2] White, *Testimonies to Ministers and Gospel Workers* (Mountain View, Calif.: Pacific Press Pub. Assn., 1923), p. 32.

[3] White, *Testimonies,* vol. 3, p. 371.

[4] White, *Fundamentals of Christian Education* (Nashville: Southern Pub. Assn., 1923), p. 547.

SECTION 2

Parameters for Youth Ministry

CHAPTER 6

Youth Leadership

by Kim Allan Johnson

YOU HAVE ACCEPTED THE NOMINATING committee's invitation to become youth director of your local church. Perhaps you feel both excited and scared stiff. One minute you picture all the possibilities, and the next minute you worry about all the challenges. Such a reaction is entirely normal. Success will not come, however, by simply hoping for it. There are certain principles that need to be followed to be effective. This chapter will attempt to prepare you to wear that weighty mantle of leadership. It will explore various leadership issues that can help make your ministry a success. We will look first at the role of youth director and then discuss building a leadership team.

The Youth Director

When we think of the word "leader," we often get a mental image of such powerful personalities as the apostle Paul, Martin Luther, Abraham Lincoln, Winston Churchill, or Nelson Mandela, to name a few. That's very unfortunate, because we can feel that unless we are a gifted speaker, brilliant scholar or spiritual giant, we cannot lead. Nothing could be further from the truth. In fact, one of the best definitions of a leader is simply someone who has followers. In that sense, many people can be leaders.

"Leonard Ravenhill . . . tells about a group of tourists who were visiting a picturesque village. As they walked by an old man sitting beside a fence, one tourist asked in a patronizing way, 'Were any great men born in this village?' The old man replied, 'Nope, only babies.'"[1]

The truth is that leaders are made, not born. Leadership skills can be developed just like any other ability. There are Christians who have the spiritual gift of leadership, which enables them to develop leadership skills more readily. But people can be leaders to varying degrees within their own sphere. Whether you teach quilting to five women in your home or conduct a Sabbath school class, you are, to a certain extent, a leader, because at its root, leadership boils down to influence. When we influence others to actually change the way they think or act, we are exerting leadership. There are areas of our life where we lead and other areas where we follow. Who can estimate the influence of a mother or father? Who can measure the influence of teachers and countless caring people we meet along the way? Whether their impact was brief or lasted over many years, they all helped lead us along life's journey.

You can have confidence in God's ability to work through you as a leader, not because of your unparalleled abilities, but because you are willing to utilize your influence to accomplish His purposes. Just as God employed Moses' plain wooden staff to deliver the Israelites, He can use your life to direct youth toward the heavenly kingdom.

Inner Qualities of a Youth Director

Love. The two most vital qualifications for youth leadership are to love the Lord and to love young people like crazy. No amount of programming resources, technical expertise, or financial support can substitute for these essential, bedrock characteristics. In order to share Christ with teenagers, He must be at the center of our own lives. In order to attract youth to the Savior, His genuine, unconditional love needs to permeate every aspect of our ministry. As has often been stated, the youth will not care how much we know until they know how much we care.

Integrity. Dwight D. Eisenhower taught, "In order to be a leader a man must have followers. And to have followers, a man must have their confidence. Hence the supreme quality for a leader is unquestionably integrity. Without it, no real success is possible."[2]

Servanthood. Jesus taught, "Whoever wishes to be first among you shall be slave of all" (Mark 10:44, NASB). God's kingdom is built upon the greatness of humility and service. The question is not what is best for the leader, but what is best for the young people.

Positive Attitude. "Leadership has less to do with position than it does with disposition."[3] "I believe that a leader's attitude is caught by his followers more quickly than his actions."[4] What level of influence we reach is determined to a large degree by our attitude. Optimism, hopefulness, and a cheerful smile are priceless leadership traits.

Styles of Leadership

The three basic styles of leadership are authoritarian, laissez-faire, and democratic. An authoritarian leader is dictatorial, telling everyone else what to do, how to do it, and when. The followers have no input at all in decision making. This would be appropriate for an army sergeant or police officer, but not for youth ministry, unless the church building is on fire. A laissez-faire leader, on the other hand, lets things drift along without giving any direction. This is useful for a mother and her children at the beach on a hot summer day, but not very helpful for teenagers. A democratic leader is the middle ground between those two extremes. He or she gives guidance where appropriate, allows the entire group to participate and shares leadership with others.

While emphasizing the principles of democratic leadership, effective youth leaders will lean toward being either more directive or more open and "hands off" according to the needs of the group and each individual at the time. They will shape their style according to the situation. At first the group will need more direction. Later, shared leadership will hopefully be the rule.

Leadership Roles

Coordinator. A local church that cares about its youth will not let the responsibility for the nurture of its young people fall on the shoulders of the youth director alone. An adequate number of associate youth directors should be gleaned from the adults. Every department and ministry of the church should also have their youth awareness sensors tuned in and active.

The development of teenagers is the responsibility of everyone, young and old, from the social committee to the church board.

Barry Gane, author of *Building Youth Ministry: A Foundational Guide,* believes that "youth ministry is enabling and mobilizing the gifts of many people, to touch with the truths of the gospel the lives of youth in every realm of their being. . . . Youth ministry strives to touch youth with a myriad of positive experiences . . . because every different experience presents the truths of the gospel in a slightly different setting."[5] Helping to create those varied experiences is the privilege of the entire church. One congregation has built into its vision statement the phrase "valuing youth" to indicate its centrality to church life. The youth director should be given opportunity to solicit and coordinate the input and assistance of the whole church. Barry Gane suggests establishing a "youth coordinating council" to continually assess the needs of the youth, provide feedback, and recommend strategies and support.

It is particularly important for the director to draw parents of teens into the discussion about youth ministry and make them feel part of the overall process. They can be an invaluable source of information about the needs of the youth and the effectiveness of the church's ministry.

Visionary. The book of Proverbs tells us, "Where there is no vision, the people perish" (Prov. 29:18). Youth need to catch a vision of what God can do through them today.

"He [Satan] well knows that there is no other class that can do as much good as young men and young women who are consecrated to God. The youth, if right, could sway a mighty influence. Preachers, or laymen advanced in years, cannot have one-half the influence upon the young that the youth, devoted to God, can have upon their associates."[6]

"An elevated standard is presented before the youth, and God is inviting them to come into real service for Him."[7]

The youth director needs to keep his or her eye on God's big-picture priorities and continually seek to sensitize the young people to His intense desire to build Christlike disciples and save the lost.

Atmospheric Engineer. We are not talking about the temperature of the room, but the climate in people's hearts. The youth director is responsible for creating a friendly, creative, uplifting atmosphere within the youth group. There needs to be a place where young people can feel safe, where they can fail without fear of rejection, and ask any question without fear of criticism. The spirit of the group should ideally be one of mutual respect, caring and support. The youth director sets the tone by modeling the values he or she wants the group itself to exemplify. Life begets life, and love begets love.

Leadership Builder. This is undoubtedly the most important role the youth director plays and will be explored further in the following section. Building a leadership team is at the very core of an effective youth ministry. Ray Johnston hits the nail on the head when he writes, "Most youth ministries go in one of two directions—they either entertain students or they *equip* students. Each route leads to a different destination. The results are dramatic. When we major in *entertaining* students, we will most likely produce spectators. If we take on the challenge of *equipping* students for leadership, we will produce *servant leaders.*"[8] When adults do for the youth what the young people can be trained to do themselves, they ironically create the very apathy they are striving to avoid.

The youth are a wonderful, often untapped, source of leadership within the church that the youth director cannot afford to ignore. "What is the main responsibility in ministry with young people?" One word: *equipping*. It is your job to find leaders, train leaders, develop leaders, encourage leaders, and to set leaders free to do greater things than you can accomplish."[9]

The Leadership Team

Youth as Leaders

Every youth can exert "informal" leadership among their peers, to varying degrees. That should certainly be cultivated. In this section, however, we will be emphasizing the more "formal" role of leadership that certain youth can assume within the group. They would be officially chosen and acknowledged as having authority to plan and organize.

The Scriptures record, "The Lord called Samuel: and he answered, Here am I" (1 Sam. 3:4). About the tender age of 12, Samuel was selected by God to be His spokesman to Eli.[10] Though only a boy, Samuel was chosen by Heaven to enter the early stages of a vital leadership role within Israel.

The giant Goliath bellowed defiance, and the Israelite soldiers cowered in fear. David, a member of the local youth group, stepped forward in faith and gained a great victory. God later call David to be anointed king while he was "yet a lad."[11]

God delights in calling youth to leadership. Ellen White observed, "[God] is waiting to inspire the youth with power from above, that they may stand under the bloodstained banner of Christ, to work as He worked, to lead souls into safe paths, to plant the feet of many upon the Rock of Ages."[12]

Discovering Potential

How would you feel if the first time you visited a church the greeter said, "Welcome. Your name is Frank, but from now on it will be Harry." Wouldn't you scratch your head and think that person was just a little odd? Well, that's exactly how Jesus greeted Peter the first time He met the burly fisherman. John records, "'You are Simon, Jona's son,' [Jesus] said. 'You will be called Cephas.' *Cephas* is the same name as *Peter* and means a *rock*" (John 1:42).[13]

In *effect,* Jesus looked Peter squarely in the eye and said, "Nice to meet you, 'rock man.'" The truth is that all throughout the Gospels the apostle is anything but a rock. "He is impulsive, volatile, unreliable. But that was not God's last word for Peter. Jesus' words point to the change that would be wrought in him by the power of God."[14]

Christ focused more on the future possibilities than present failings. Jesus specialized in discovering people's potential. He always saw the oak in the acorn. John Maxwell observes, "There is something much more important and scarce than ability: It is the ability to recognize ability. One of the primary responsibilities of a successful leader is to identify potential leaders. It's not always an easy job, but it is critical."[15]

An effective youth director will need to look beneath layers of adolescent immaturity to find the leadership qualities that could be developed for the Lord. I will never forget the time I was elected president of our local "youth fellowship." Suddenly people looked to me for advice and direction. Overnight I was at the center of planning sessions, interacting with adults I had only seen up front during worship. I felt a mingled sense of humility and satisfaction I had never known before.

Advantages of Developing Student Leadership

When we give teenagers genuine leadership roles, the benefits are many. Because the church takes them seriously, they will, in turn, take the church seriously. They discover the thrill of seeing God use them personally. They learn how to develop realistic plans and make effective decisions, to set goals and achieve them. They gain invaluable insights into their own spiritual gifts and abilities. They develop self-confidence and understand the deeper meanings of the word "commitment." By investing, they have a real sense of ownership. These teenagers are best able to win the support and involvement of their friends, both inside the church and out. They develop attitudes and skills that will benefit the church for years to come. Last, but not least, they enable the adult leaders to avoid burnout.

Hindrances to Developing Leaders

By placing real leadership in the hands of young people, you may encounter criticism from those who are wary of teenagers taking on weighty responsibilities. Don't let flak undermine your own commitment to following God's counsel. Listen long enough to the critics to glean whatever positive lessons may be available, but stay focused on what you know to be best. Initiate regular communication with parents and key church members in order to clear up misunderstandings and win their support. Gain the adults confidence by periodically seeking their advice. Let them hear from the young people who are benefitting from your emphasis.

Ironically, the youth director himself or herself can be one of the greatest hindrances to leadership development. Relinquishing control and letting others take over fulfilling roles and ministries can be difficult. To paraphrase the words of John the Baptist: "The adults must decrease so the youth may increase." It can also be very tempting to step in and rescue teens instead of letting them learn from their mistakes. Adults tend to forget that they, too, had to stumble before learning how to walk in life. Personal time pressures can be a hindrance, as well, by pushing the director toward quick-fix programming and away from the patient training that is necessary for youth leadership to eventually emerge.

The Selection Process

If you want the youth to take their leadership roles seriously, you will have to develop a meaningful selection process. The easier it is to get into leadership, the easier it will be to get out. One of the worst things you can do is to simply have the teens vote on their peers. Popularity, good looks, and an outgoing personality will usually determine the winners. Quiet, competent teens often get overlooked.

In his book *Developing Student Leaders* Ray Johnston recommends creating leadership application forms on which students are asked to get references, describe their experience and abilities, and indicate what areas of ministry interest them most.[16] You will also need to write out detailed job descriptions. The clearer you are at the beginning about expectations and commitments, the fewer disappointments will occur later. You may informally have to solicit names of potential leaders and personally encourage shy teens to step forward. You can survey the youth group itself for names. Johnston goes on to suggest the development of a selection committee of various ages to interview the students and make choices. Set terms of service for specific periods. Conduct the recruitment process two or three times a year to glean new applications and allow for transfers to different ministries. Most of all, invest in prayer for wisdom and the special moving of God's Spirit.

Training and Accountability

Jesus set the example of spending most of His time with a few core leaders and developing others on a less-intense level. The "Pareto Principle" suggests that you will best accomplish your goals by spending 80 percent of your time with 20 percent of the youth. Personally get to know their skills and limitations, background and personality, frustrations and dreams. Take time to study about the development needs of teenagers. Find adult mentors for youthful leaders who will use Christ's four-step discipling method: (1) I do it and you watch, (2) we do it together, (3) you do it and I watch, (4) you do it. All training should be loaded with encouragement.

Training will require regular leadership development meetings where you can spend time discussing leadership skills, set goals and objectives, do problem solving and solicit reports for accountability. Periodic leadership retreats are a great way to give concentrated instruction.

Let the student leaders plan the leadership retreats, the regular monthly meetings of the entire youth group, and periodic social events to which everyone can invite their non-Christian friends.

Types of Responsibilities

The youth director should primarily minister to the youth through the youth. Let all the young people brainstorm regarding what ministries they feel are important, both for the group itself and for the community. From that list of potential areas of service, leaders and other group members can select their area of interest. Ministries can range from preparing refreshments for monthly meetings to helping the elderly to giving Bible studies. Student leaders should find a meaningful job for every willing teen.

Ministry to youth can, without doubt, be very challenging and yet also intensely rewarding. The full results of loving, Christ-centered leadership to young people can only be measured in the eons of eternity.

---

[1] John G. Maxwell, *Developing the Leader Within You* (Nashville: Thomas Nelson Publishers, 1993), introduction.

[2] Fred A. Manske, Jr., *Secrets of Effective Leadership* (Columbia, Tenn.: Leadership Education and Development, 1990), p. 32.

[3] Maxwell, p. 98.

[4] *Ibid.,* p. 106.

[5] Barry Gane, *Building Youth Ministry: A Foundational Guide* (Riverside, Calif.: Hancock Center Publications, 1997), pp. 64, 65.

[6] Ellen G. White, *Messages to Young People* (Nashville: Southern Pub. Assn., 1930), p. 204.

[7] *Ibid.,* p. 24.

[8] Ray Johnston, *Developing Student Leaders* (Grand Rapids: Zondervan Pub. House, Youth Specialties, 1992), p. 15.

[9] Gane, p. 87.

[10] *Seventh-day Adventist Bible Dictionary* (Washington, D.C.: Review and Herald Pub. Assn., 1960), vol. 8, p. 952.

[11] *The Seventh-day Adventist Bible Commentary* (Washington, D.C.: Review and Herald Pub. Assn., 1954), vol. 2, p. 530.

[12] Ellen G. White, *The Ministry of Healing* (Mountain View, Calif.: Pacific Press Pub. Assn., 1905), p. 405.

[13] William Barclay, *The Gospel of John* (Philadelphia: Westminster Press, 1975), p. 88.

[14] Leon Morris, *The Gospel According to John* (Grand Rapids: Eerdmans, 1971), p. 161.

[15] Maxwell, p. 37.

[16] Johnston, pp. 81-87.

CHAPTER 7

Developmental Psychology and Youth Ministry

by Trudy J. Morgan-Cole

HUMAN BEINGS GO THROUGH certain typical life stages as they grow and develop. Yes, every individual is unique, but we all recognize certain behavior, from the "terrible twos" to the "midlife crisis," as being normal for people of certain ages. Perhaps during the adolescent years more than at any other time of life, "It's just a phase they're going through" is uttered by parents, teachers, and church leaders as they attempt to deal with the crises of adolescent development.

You don't need to have taken a psychology course to be an effective youth leader, either. But, just as most of us are already aware of the tremendous physical changes teenagers are going through, and we understand how these changes affect them, so it also helps to be aware of the changes happening in the minds of youth. A basic knowledge of human development, especially of the developmental issues young people deal with, can help you understand and appreciate the struggles of your youth. It can also help you recognize and capitalize on their strengths.

Psychosocial Development: Erik Erikson

There are many theories of human development, but the most widely recognized and influential is that of Erik Erikson. Erikson's theory, which was first published in the early 1950s and which he continued to refine over the following decades, suggests that there are eight major stages of development through which a person's personality passes throughout life. He identifies the major conflict that the individual must struggle with at each stage. Briefly, Erikson's eight stages of life development are:

Stage	Psychosocial Crisis
Infancy (0-18 months)	Basic trust versus basic mistrust
Early childhood (toddlers)	Autonomy versus shame and doubt
Play age (preschool)	Initiative versus guilt
School age	Industry versus inferiority
Adolescence	Identity versus identity confusion
Young adulthood	Intimacy versus isolation
Adulthood	Generativity versus stagnation
Old age	Integrity versus despair[1]

Dealing with crises, or conflicts, is a central theme in Erikson's theory. We sometimes tend to think of conflict as a bad thing in our lives, but, in fact conflict is necessary for growth and development. If we do not deal with the key conflicts in each phase of our lives, we may be unable to mature and move on. The adolescent struggle with identity and identity confusion may be painful not just for adolescents, but for the adults who care about them. But it is a necessary struggle if the young person is to develop into a mature adult.

Cognitive Development: Jean Piaget

Another influential thinker in the area of developmental psychology is Jean Piaget, who studied cognitive development in children and adolescents. Piaget's theories focus on how the mind develops, how people learn to think. Piaget divided childhood and adolescence into stages very similar to Erikson's, and for each stage he described how the ability to reason developed. As a young person enters adolescence, he or she moves, in Piaget's terms, from the "concrete operations" stage of the elementary school years to the "formal operations" stage, the final stage in cognitive development. "Individuals in this stage are able to make use of more complicated systems of classification, deal with hypothetical situations, understand and use concepts involving probability, and deal with other complex problems involving logic and reasoning."[2]

It's important to remember that the age boundaries Piaget suggests, like those Erikson suggests, are not hard and fast. They will differ from one individual to another. Not everyone enters the formal operations phase as soon as they turn 12 years old. A very abstract discussion about a concept such as God's grace may be too difficult for a 13-year-old in your earliteen group to follow, while an 11-year-old in the same class may have no difficulty following and contributing to the discussion.

Moral Development: Lawrence Kohlberg

Lawrence Kohlberg expanded on Piaget's work, beginning in the 1960s, when he conducted an in-depth study of moral reasoning in adolescents. (His research was confined to young males, which has led to some criticism from women, who feel that his theories do not adequately represent both genders.) Kohlberg described six stages of moral development through which a person may pass. Unlike Piaget and Erikson, he did not assign these stages to specific age groups, but his understanding was that as the person matured from early childhood through adolescence to adulthood, he would pass through these stages, though not everyone would reach the highest levels of moral development. Kohlberg's stages of moral reasoning were:

Preconventional morality
> Stage 1: Avoid punishment
> Stage 2: Seek rewards

Conventional morality
> Stage 3: Gain approval/avoid disapproval, especially with family
> Stage 4: Conformity to society's rules

Postconventional morality
> Stage 5: Principles accepted by the community
> Stage 6: Individualized conscience[3]

It is even harder to apply Kohlberg's moral stages to a particular age group than it is

Piaget's moral stages. The development of moral reasoning is a very individual thing, and there are even some adults in society who have never progressed beyond the very lowest stages—their only motivation is to avoid punishment for breaking the law. But an adolescent who is developing normally should have left the preconventional morality stage behind with childhood and be moving through the conventional morality stage, perhaps beginning to develop a post-conventional morality, where laws are obeyed for internal reasons rather than external ones.

There is plenty of room to criticize and disagree with Kohlberg's theories—they can be shown to be strongly influenced by cultural bias and, as we have seen, by gender bias. But they do provide one useful guideline for exploring how human beings make moral choices, which is a subject of great interest to Christian educators and leaders.

Some people might argue that a Christian can never reach the highest level of Kohlberg's stages, since the Christian is always obeying an external law (God's Ten Commandments) rather than his or her individual conscience. But the ideal for the Christian is to obey not just because "the Ten Commandments tell me to" but because we have internalized God's law; we have allowed Him to write it in our hearts and live it out in us through His Holy Spirit. From that perspective, a truly mature Christian would have arrived at Kohlberg's stage 6, because they would be following the dictates of their conscience—an inner voice that has been shaped and molded by God's Word and His indwelling Spirit. This is the highest level of moral development we should hope to see in our young people.

What This Means for the Youth Leader

Depending on your own educational background, names like Erikson, Piaget, and Kohlberg may roll off your tongue like the alphabet, or they may be entirely new to you. Your knowledge of psychology isn't going to determine how effective you are as a youth leader. What matters is how you apply the knowledge you do have. Knowing what you know about how human beings develop and grow, how will that affect the way you work with youth?

First, it's important to remember, as pointed out above, that any guidelines regarding the "typical" age at which young people pass through developmental stages are just that—guidelines. Just as the physical changes of puberty hit every young person at a different age and in a different way, so young people differ in when and how they mature psychologically. It's not impossible for a 10-year-old to struggle with issues of identity, nor is it at all unusual for a person in his or her mid-20s to still be dealing with identity issues. These "stages" are generalizations, nothing more.

But these generalizations can help you see that while a group of nine-year-old Pathfinders may not spend a lot of time worrying about who they are, a group of 15- and 16-year-olds will probably all be dealing with the question "Who am I?" at some level. And this "identity crisis" will affect every aspect of those teenagers' lives—their schoolwork, their relationships with family, their relationships with friends, and their religious lives.

For some young people, questions of identity are resolved much more easily than for others. Every young person faces and resolves this conflict in a different way. Seventeen-year-old Debbi may seem to have passed through adolescence entirely untroubled by conflicts; her biggest crisis may be deciding in her senior year of high school that she would like to attend a different college than the one her parents are encouraging her to go to. Seventeen-year-old

Paul, on the other hand, may be rebelling against every rule and value his parents have ever taught him. He may be failing in school, fighting with other boys, dating the wrong kind of girls, experimenting with alcohol and drugs, breaking the law, constantly arguing with his parents, and questioning everything about religion, including the very existence of God.

It's tempting to conclude that Debbi is a "good" young person, while Paul is a "bad" one (or that Debbi's parents did a "good" job of raising her and Paul's did a "bad" job). In fact, both are dealing with Erikson's basic conflict of identity versus identity confusion. And everyone else in your youth group probably falls somewhere on the spectrum between Debbi and Paul in terms of how severe that conflict is for them, and how they choose to deal it.

As a youth leader, your responsibility is not to condone or approve of everything a young person may do in his or her struggle for identity. Adolescents can make some very harmful choices as they seek to find out who they are, and they need to be aware of the consequences of those choices. But it helps greatly if you can keep in mind that they are going through a struggle, a very important and necessary struggle, and that with love and support they can emerge stronger and more mature as a result. If they deal with this conflict successfully, they will develop their own identity—separate from that of their parents, but hopefully incorporating the best of what their parents have taught them.

Your job is to provide some of that love and support. All adolescents need significant adults in their lives, beyond their own immediate families, who care for them and can help them as they move through their identity crises. For young people whose search for identity takes the form of openly rebelling against their parents, creating constant conflict at home, the support that a loving youth leader, pastor, or teacher can provide is especially important.

Understanding Moral Development

At the same time, knowing a little about how cognitive and moral reasoning develops can help you, both in your individual relationships with youth and in planning more formal programs such as how to teach a Sabbath school lesson. Be sensitive to where your youth are in developmental terms. Are they able to deal with abstract concepts in discussion? Will they be confused or disturbed by situations that challenge their moral reasoning?

Very small children learn what Kohlberg called "preconventional morality" at home—they learn to obey because they will be punished if they don't and rewarded if they do. We see this level of morality in some of our Christian education materials for young children as well—think, for example, of the classic *Uncle Arthur's Bedtime Stories,* in which good behavior was always rewarded, and bad behavior inevitably received punishment. This is very appropriate for young children; it is the only way in which they can understand right and wrong.

As children move through Christian education, through our kindergarten and primary Sabbath schools, we seek to move them into the conventional morality stage, where they see that good behavior earns them approval—not just from their families and society, but from God. "Jesus loves me when I'm good, when I do the things I should; Jesus loves me when I'm bad, even though it makes Him sad" is good theology for children at this age—God's love is unconditional, but when we do what's right, it makes Him happy. Disobedience makes Him sad.

With teenagers, we can begin to challenge them to think on a higher moral level. Do they believe in doing what's right because those are society's laws? Challenge them to think about *why* those laws exist—to understand the reasons behind them. *Why* does it make God happy when we do good? Remember that the ultimate goal is for them to follow their own conscience—but a conscience that has been sharpened by a relationship with God, rather than dulled by sin.

Many people in the church are a little frightened of adolescents. Even some of us who love them and work with them are sometimes uneasy and disturbed by the changes we see them going through. When they question the moral reasoning they were taught at home, it makes us—and them—uncomfortable. When they challenge authority and struggle to define who they are on their own terms, we get scared—not just scared of them, but scared for them and how they might hurt themselves in the struggle. Understanding human development helps us to see that change is natural and positive. People have to change in order to grow.

The smiling little girl or boy you remember seeing up in front of church with the other primaries may have changed into a sullen teenage girl who talks to nobody but her best friend, or an argumentative young man who questions every statement that comes out of your mouth. But if young people never passed through these stages, never questioned what they had been taught or attempted to figure it out for themselves, they would remain forever in a state of arrested development. The unquestioning, simple trust and obedience that is so charming and appropriate in a small child is pathetic in an adult—adults who are truly "child-like" in that sense can be victimized by any evil or unscrupulous person who tries to take advantage of them.

We want to see young adults who follow God, love their families and participate in church because they have thought through the issues surrounding those commitments and made those choices freely. But we will never see them reach this stage if they do not deal with the psychosocial, cognitive, and moral development conflicts of adolescence. Our role is to support, help, and guide them on that journey.

Development in Young Adults

Theories of human development tend to focus very heavily on children and adolescents, and have much less to say about development during the adult years. Carl Jung, writing in *The Stages in Life* in 1931, was the first to suggest not only that human development continued in adulthood, but that those years—especially the years after midlife—were some of the most important in human development. In spite of Jung's powerful influence, developmental psychology still tended to focus mainly on the early life, and, in fact, "it wasn't until the late 1970s that adult developmental theorists emerged and showed that human development, rather than ceasing after adolescence, is instead a lifelong struggle."[4]

People don't reach adulthood with their twenty-first birthday and suddenly stop developing. The young people in your youth group are dealing with developmental conflicts, but so are their parents and even their grandparents—and so are you. Being sensitive to some of the changes people go through later in life can help you as you work with families and other church members in your ministry; it can also help you understand yourself and your own needs and conflicts better.

What about those who are making the transition from adolescence to adulthood—our young adults? Those of us who minister to college students and others in this age group are aware that the boundaries of adolescence are by no means carved in stone. The identity crises of the teen years often linger on long into the twenties—particularly for young people who had a very difficult time dealing with those issues in their teens, or those who never really confronted and dealt with questions of identity at all when they were teenagers. It's a mistake to look at a room full of college-age young people and assume that their identity crises are all behind them.

At the same time, we should be aware that while young adults may still be resolving the identity conflicts of adolescence, they are also moving on to cope with new conflicts and challenges. They are facing the major life choices: deciding on further education, choosing a career, learning to live independently, and choosing a life partner. They need special support and guidance as they navigate these choices.

Erikson described the major conflict of the early adult years as "intimacy versus isolation." Young adults, who are often away from home and its comforts and securities for the first time, may indeed feel isolated from that family environment that supported and defined them in their early years. They are choosing whether they will create new bonds of intimacy to replace or to supplement their family ties, and they are choosing the people with whom they are going to forge those bonds. The most important of these is the choice of a marriage partner, but that is not the only important relationship formed during the young adult years.

This stage is a very important one in terms of young people and their relationship to the church and to God. Many young adults, looking for a supportive community to belong to and a partner with whom to share their lives, find neither within their church. It's very easy for them to drift away from active involvement in church—and that may also mean drifting away from God, especially if they haven't yet formed an intimate relationship with Him. If you minister to young adults, you should be aware of this intimacy-versus-isolation conflict. Help Christian young adults to create and find communities of faith in which real intimacy can flourish. Most important, help them discover a personal friendship with God as the most significant relationship in their lives.

---

[1] Frank A. Nugent, *An Introduction to the Profession of Counseling,* 2nd ed. (New York: Macmillan Pub. Co., 1994), p. 51.

[2] Robert I. Watson and Henry Clay Lindgren, *Psychology of the Child and the Adolescent,* 4th ed. (New York: Macmillan Pub. Co., 1979), p. 83.

[3] Nugent, p. 55.

[4] *Ibid.,* pp. 48, 49.

Moral Development in Youth Ministry

by Dave Allen

TWENTY-FIRST-CENTURY YOUTH ARE worth saving for Christ, and if youth leaders in the twenty-first century are going to be successful in the ministry entrusted to them, they will need to make a significant difference in the way they prepare youth for salvation and service. One aspect of this ministry relates to the way we accompany youth in effective moral decision-making. The following references include important principles in this work of building God's kingdom:

Principle 1. "With eyes wide open to the mercies of God, I beg you, my brothers, as an act of intelligent worship, to give him your bodies, as a living sacrifice, consecrated to him and acceptable by him. Don't let the world around you squeeze you into its own mould, but let God re-make you so that your whole attitude of mind is changed. Thus you will prove in practice that the will of God's good, acceptable to him and perfect" (Rom. 12:1, 2, Phillips).

Principle 2. "Every human being, created in the image of God, is endowed with a power akin to that of the Creator—individuality, power to think and to do. . . . It is the work of true education to develop this power, to train the youth to be thinkers, and not mere reflectors of other men's thought."[1]

Grace Orientation

The Seventh-day Adventist Church is not wrong to place importance on the behavior of Christians. What the young people of our church do does matter. But it is more important to place our behavior in the correct context. We have underemphasized the fact that there is nothing we can do to make God love us more and there is nothing that we can do to make God love us less.[2] Our youth need to know this and see it clearly placed as foundational to all youth ministry, to both individuals and groups.

Choices and Motives

Moral issues are those that have to do with whether we are thinking or doing right or wrong. The choices that our youth are making between good and evil are of concern to youth leaders. But the motives behind the choices are of more importance to us than the resultant action. Although we are inclined to judge what the young person does by what we observe, it is the reason behind that choice that is more important—especially to God (1 Sam. 16:7;

John 7:24). Therefore, it behooves us to seek as accurately as is possible to find out what motivates our youth decision-making and explore more why they have done this or not done that rather than to be so focused on the act itself.

Models of Moral Development

One way to think about what motivates moral decision making is by means of an (over)simplified version of Kohlberg's *Theory of Moral Development,* which categorizes motives for moral decisions into three levels:

3. I decide on the basis of principle.
2. I decide in order to protect or establish a good reputation.
1. I decide in order to gain a reward or avoid a punishment.

As one progresses up this hierarchy, the reasons for one's actions move from external sources to internal ones.

To illustrate, a single young man may choose to sleep with his girlfriend (presumably a wrong moral decision) for reasons of pure pleasure (level 1: reward), or he could be socially pressured to have something to report to his buddies and be able to say, "I also did it! I have arrived!" (level 2: reputation). He could even attempt to use the "principle" of "If you love me, you will prove it" or "I want to show my love for you this way." (Most would question whether this is indeed level 3, or perhaps manipulation.) In each case it is the same wrong act but for different reasons. On the other hand, the same young man may choose not to sleep with his girlfriend before marriage (presumably the correct moral decision), because he wants to avoid an unwanted pregnancy (level 1: it is sad that pregnancy is considered a punishment) or because he has just been appointed a deacon in his local congregation and deacons will not do that (level 2: reputation). One would hope that he has decided not to sleep with her on the basis of principles (level 3) that he has internalized and inculcated into his lifestyle, and one would hope that these principles are Bible-based.

The task of youth leaders is to help their young people to do a self-analysis of the motives behind their moral decisions. When honestly done, most youth (and adults) will find themselves on the upper edge of level 1 and the lower edge of level 2. We need to realize that in any individual's life, certain behaviors at various times are motivated by lower-level reasons, while others can be identified as sources at higher levels. Kohlberg maintained, however, that a person could grasp or use lower-order reasoning, but they would be hard pressed even to understand more than one stage above the level where they were currently functioning.

It then becomes the responsibility of youth leaders to assist the youth to improve the generally identified level of moral decision-making. One is able to accomplish this by means of exposing the youth to levels of decision-making slightly higher that the level on which they are currently operating.

Problem: How does a youth leader (who is operating on level 1) assist young people in their group who need to be exposed to level 2 or 3 operations?

This problem manifests itself in the form of a youth leader who struggles to handle the "outrageous utterances" of young people under their care. Another common situation is that of a youth leader using an external authority, such as biblical sources, who, because of the way they approach the group or the topic, could be seen as functioning on level 2 to "protect God's reputation" when they intended a level 3 principle.

One does not have all the answers to these problems, except to appeal to and encourage openness in thinking and creating a sense of genuine freedom of thought and questioning without judgment.

The Effective Use of Discussion About Moral Dilemmas

One of the best means to this end is to involve young people in discussion around situations of so-called moral dilemma during which they explore all the possible motives behind the issues portrayed in the hypothetical or real-life dilemma. Then attempt to focus "level 1" youth on "level 2" motives and "level 2" youth on "level 3" motives. The inevitable sharing of different motives in a group discussion of a moral dilemma brings the youth into conflict with their existing moral reasoning (because of the inadequacies it demonstrates) and to an awareness of other (perhaps better, higher) levels of reasoning, which can then be internalized. These higher levels will be experienced as encompassing more demands.

Youth Specialties has compiled a number of publications that systematically use moral dilemmas to process a number of youth issues. Among its first releases were a series of "tension getters," in which they use a number of strategies designed to "create a dilemma or situation with conflicting issues that require young people to think through all possible alternatives and consequences before arriving at a moral decision."[3] The tension is revealed in the overlap of values that make a simple black-and-white response impossible. For example, when asked by a friend to help him cheat on a test, a teen is torn by the tension between loyalty to his friend and the value of honesty. For one person the overlap is minimal or even clearly nonexistent. For another the overlap is vast. This tension becomes fertile ground for fruitful discussion and, if directed by responsible and skilled youth leadership, yields effective moral decision-making.

An obstacle to the effective spiritual growth of young people is the perception that the church has provided all the correct answers or is perceived as being unwilling to allow for exploration of other options. In this area of youth ministry there is need for much open-ended discussion and freedom for youth to speak their minds without fear of judgmental put-downs. We are to enquire honestly and genuinely of our youth: "What do you think?" And then we need to provide the opportunity for them to do just that and share their opinions. Thus, we, as respecting listeners, enable them to explore their world with the God-given skills of thinking, evaluating, and choosing.

The desired openness of the church is often revealed in the way we ask questions and what type of questions we ask our youth. Herein lies a test as to whether we are prepared to risk giving the type of freedom to choose that God Himself grants all humanity!

Higher-Order Questions

Samples of higher-order questions to ask during group discussions of dilemma situations include the following:
1. What are Bill's options?
2. What would you advise him to do? Why?

3. How do you feel about Sally's statement (five-point scale from "strongly agree" to "strongly disagree")? If you agree, what would you add to her statement? If you disagree, why?

4. Rank the characters/persons in the situation described as to who is most responsible for the problem that occurred. Provide reasons for each ranking.

5. What Bible text would provide the most relevant principle to give guidance in this situation? Explain your choice.

The Emotional Side

But to look only at moral development from this rather intellectual perspective does not tell the whole story. What a person feels about a moral decision is equally important in the process of developing an effective decision-maker. Thus it is that the moral decision making done in an atmosphere of perceived warmth and acceptance will be more effective. And when someone has made an inappropriate or wrong moral decision, that person needs to experience the church, the youth group, or youth leader as a place/person of acceptance and compassion and as people of kindness and forgiveness. Of course, emotions underlie more than merely the times when we do wrong. The point here is that all decisions, good or bad, are made in an atmosphere of feelings about the decision and its corresponding actions. Moral decisions have more than an intellectual basis. The emotional basis plays a more significant role than we realize.

With this in mind, Roger Dudley points out that youth leaders need to approach their ministry through a framework of relationships. First (and central) is a relationship with God as a loving Father and Friend (the "first and great commandment" of Matthew 22:37, 38). From this primary relationship, religion and development of moral decision-making operates on our own interior relationships, eliminating anxiety and stress and bringing harmony and peace of mind (John 14:27).[4]

Dudley continues to explain that out of this twofold relationship with God and ourselves comes a new (and perhaps renewed) relationship with our fellow humans. The second great commandment of Matthew 22:39, to "love thy neighbour as thyself," gives the mandate that Christianity uniquely brings to relationships—that they should be characterized by compassion and concern for other people. This is then the basis for the essential climate of warmth and acceptance that must characterize our congregational and youth ministry activities designed for effective life-learning experiences.[5]

Youth leaders, together with their youth, need to be encouraged to develop compassion and empathy in their relationships. This leads to more mature moral decision-making and the ability to integrate justice and mercy, as Micah 6:8 describes. Dudley adds this significant comment: "We best learn about and accept grace through warm, supportive, interpersonal relationships with grace-filled people. A major task in the coming years is to instruct our teachers and congregational leaders in how to become that kind of people."[6]

Emotional Intelligence

Though this is a relatively new science, youth leaders need to seek opportunities to help our youth develop skills to regulate their own emotions, bringing them to be more in control of the feelings on which so many actions are based. This type of emotional literacy would help youth manage anger, frustration, loneliness, etc., in ways that also positively develop people skills such as empathy and graciousness, making them better suited to accomplish the building of God's kingdom on earth and developing characters fit for eternity. This would include providing opportunities to identify, talk about, and take responsibility for their own individual feelings and emotions in general.

There is, of course, the danger that this kind of focus ends up being a purely humanistic science, and the best way to avoid this is to focus on the character traits Jesus manifested, particularly on the gospel of grace revealed in His ministry on earth. Ask, "What would Jesus do here?" Add to this the attempt to seek out many examples of grace in human living, especially encouraging each young person to find such examples experienced in their own life, and you have a Christian context for a new and vibrant youth ministry designed to prepare the church for the second coming of Jesus. (Phillip Yancey's book *What's So Amazing About Grace?* is an example of stories of grace.)

Freedom to Choose

One of the amazing characteristics of God is the fact that He has granted humanity freedom of choice—particularly in the area of moral decisions. From the Genesis account of the fall of Adam and Eve into sin, through the millennia to the predicted conclusion of the history of man, God has proved how seriously Heaven respects this freedom granted to men and women. Dare we, as leaders in His church and entrusted with the challenge of building His kingdom on earth, act in any way other that to reinforce this attitude as we deal with youth in their life situations? It is our task to hold high this principle of freedom to choose in our approach to young people, particularly those in trouble.

While we rejoice with those who have demonstrated responsible decision-making, we also sincerely weep with those who have chosen the wrong way. God grant us the genuine sorrow He must experience when people turn their backs on Him. It is a for-better-or-for-worse commitment we make with those we lead in youth ministry. God also grant us the grace to continue to show interest, love, and compassion for those in our charge who have wavered and the ability to show that we are still there for them.

Youth leaders are, then, challenged to walk with their youth through the consequences of their decisions (especially the negative ones), helping them not to despair but to see the light at the end of the tunnel.

Absolutes

While we lead youth through thinking experiences that explore many options, even those we may not fully approve of, it is the responsibility of youth leaders to prominently refer to the pillars of principles that still exist in our Seventh-day Adventist truth structures. These beacons must be clearly positioned in our discussions, as well as in our church life and Christian practice. Exploration of options in an atmosphere of freedom to choose shows the essential respect for the human dignity we acknowledge in our youth. At the same time, reference to clearly spelled-out parameters in youth ministry experiences gives youth a sense of security.

Modeling

Youth leaders are then challenged to evidence this freedom of choice in their leading of youth. But while we give options for them to choose from, they are also looking up to us to model appropriate choices in our own lives. After exploring various avenues with a group of youth in a dilemma situation, the youth leader does well to demonstrate his/her personal choice in the matter. This is a revelation of the leader's own decision, while at the same time genuinely leaving it to the youth to make up their own minds and honestly respecting that decision without prejudice one way or the other.

Conclusion

God help all those involved in the education of Seventh-day Adventist youth—parents, pastors, teachers, youth leaders and others—to so conduct our ministries that, by His all-sufficient grace, we may be actively involved in preparing a church that manifests principled thinkers and individual moral decision-makers who clearly side with what is right and true.

---

[1] E. G. White, *Education,* p. 17.

[2] Philip Yancey, *What's So Amazing About Grace?* (Grand Rapids: Zondervan, 1997).

[3] *Youth Specialties,* 1988, p. 12.

[4] Roger L. Dudley, " Understanding the Spiritual Development and Faith Experience of College and University Students," *Journal of Adventist Education,* April/May, 1998, p. 16.

[5] *Ibid.*

[6] *Ibid.*

CHAPTER 9

Models of Youth Ministry

by Jennifer Morgan

The School-based Model

S EVENTH-DAY ADVENTIST CHURCH A HAS BEEN supporting youth ministry for years. It has assigned fund-raisers who remind the church how important our youth are. Private members give behind-the-scenes donations to help individual young people. Church A is the conference's most loyal supporter of youth ministry. The members just don't call it youth ministry. They call it Christian education.

Church A is a faithful supporter of its conference's "worthy student" fund, and a sizable percentage of the church budget goes to support the local academy. Many students from Church A's Sabbath school class leave every September for the closest boarding academy, and when parents are willing to carpool, some attend an Adventist day academy in the next conference. During the school year the local day academy students are very involved in school weekend obligations and rarely attend Sabbath school in the local church. Parents support the school with tuition as well as fund the bands, choirs, senior trips, and mission trips sponsored by both schools. Church A sees its youth developing into talented, active teenagers with a lot of leadership and extracurricular options that do not cause Sabbath problems. In addition, parents are impressed with the God-fearing teachers in their local academies and feel that their choice has given their child a safe environment in which to grow up.

"Children are like rare tropical plants," explains one grandmother. "They need to be raised in a greenhouse and slowly acclimated to the outside world. You can't expose them to the elements all at once. They will die. But you can't keep them in the greenhouse, either."

On June 3, 1872, when Goodloe H. Bell opened the first official Seventh-day Adventist school for 12 students in Battle Creek, Michigan, he had no idea what a greenhouse system he was starting. Adventists today are proud of having the largest Protestant school system in the world.

Advantages of the School-based Model

School-based youth ministry has many advantages. Adventist day and boarding high schools bring together teenagers and talented professionals. Instead of many overworked youth leaders trying to minister to separated church-based youth groups, the Adventist school provides a center of activity for all the area youth. Adventist postsecondary schools return well-educated teachers with fresh ideas and newly minted skills to the local church. Church schools also offer a relatively safe place for Adventist youth to study and explore their faith in this world.

Disadvantages of the School-based Model

The disadvantage of our emphasis on school-based ministries is that they consume a lot of the time and financial and energy resources of the local congregation. Boarding schools and colleges drain young people from the local church. When students graduate, their allegiance can be to their school and not to the local church. Local churches often do not offer services geared to young people and disappointed teenagers may opt out of church attendance after high school. The biggest losers in this scenario, however, are the public school students, for whom there is no ministry.

The Youth Church Model

The youth pastor of Adventist Church B found that she had a great high school youth program going. But as soon as Sabbath school was over the kids headed for the parking lot to hang out with their friends for the church service. Pastor B also felt that she lost a lot of her senior youth and college-age members. When they graduated from youth Sabbath school, they often stopped coming to church. Attempts were made to make the church service more "relevant," but when contemporary music was introduced, the congregation complained that it was too noisy for them to worship.

Church B's senior pastor suggested that the young people start an alternative "contemporary" service. To begin with, it would be once a quarter. But if it took off it could be offered as a regular option to the 11:00 worship—"so long," warned the senior pastor, "as the main sanctuary attendance doesn't drop off!" There was no danger of that. The Generation Xers who have arranged the band have made sure that only a very youthful audience would enjoy this music. But those students who enjoy coming to church in casual attire and going straight from the singing to the message or a drama find this a place that meets their needs. The first Sabbath is standing room only, and Pastor B is excited.

Asian young people were the first to experiment with holding alternative church services. First-generation Asian-Americans were more comfortable worshiping in English than in the language of their parents or grandparents and, after holding English Sabbath school classes, requested permission to hold alternative English-language churches. The alternative churches often included a youth-style worship format and music as this approach spread to other churches.

Advantages of Youth Church

Youth churches flourish in congregations with an unusual balance between a vocal minority who are unwilling to adapt to alternative worship methods and an open-minded pastor and church board who support innovation and youth ministry. In these alternative services, young adults can be mentored into running their own churches and offering contemporary services that non-churched youth feel comfortable attending. They are good outreaches, also, for some of our lost Adventist young adults who have left boarding schools and haven't found any worship alternative that fits their needs.

Disadvantages of Youth Church

Youth churches create a lot of controversy. Sometimes they grow bigger than their parent organization envisioned and become an expensive institution on their own. Like the school-based model, they consume a lot of time and financial and emotional energy. They can also be a way of keeping youth from integrating fully with the parent church. Young adults are so busy with the youth church that they don't get involved in the church choir or other ministry opportunities in the main sanctuary. Likewise, the "adult" congregation does not benefit from the challenges and change that come from adapting to and trying to incorporate youth into the main worship service. And smaller churches with limited leadership do not have this option.

The Meta Model

Adventist Church C is really proud of its youth group—not that you often see their youth group in action. Most of the action occurs off church grounds. This evangelistically based church has trained its youth to reach the community with small-group ministry. Throughout the week adult mentors meet with youth Bible study groups in members' living rooms. Each group always keeps one empty chair in the circle, to remind members of an unchurched friend they need to invite next week.

Once a week the youth pastor of Church C meets with his adult mentors. There are also weekly youth meetings that all the youth come to. But the aim of these youth is to reach people for Christ. Their small groups grow until they are too large, and then they split, amoeba-like, into new outreach groups.

In some parts of the world small groups were piloted as a reaction to the institutionalized programming of large Adventist youth meetings. Throughout Adventism, Friday night programs were replaced by group meetings where teenagers met in home Bible studies. In an indirect way these teenagers were being influenced by the nontraditional worship styles of the Jesus movement.

The *Voice of Prophecy* radio program circulated "The Way Out" curriculum material. Guitars replaced pianos, and wide-ranging discussion was encouraged. By the 1980s the small group curriculum was formalized and institutionalized in Lyman Coleman's *Youth Ministry Encyclopedia* and the *Serendipity Bible.* In Coleman's model the small-group discussion is used to create community for the larger group by building koinonia (fellowship) first in small "c group" cells.

The meta model does not intend to build a long-term support group. It is a church-building model based on the Central church of Seoul, Korea. This church built a membership of 200,000 using the meta group model. The goal is to reach a community that is not familiar or comfortable with Christian churches. Some youth ministry experts feel that the meta model worked very well in South Korea because of the authoritarian style of leadership in that country. The small group leaders were very loyal to Seoul's Central church, and believed in integrating their new converts into the church as a whole.

However, as we approach a new generation of nonchurched youth, Central church's model looks very attractive as a means to reach Generation Xers. These teenagers might never enter a church door, but will come to a friend's living room. The relaxed atmosphere can help leaders answer questions a nonchurched youth would not feel safe asking in a church setting.

The Advantages of the Meta Group Model

This is a good outreach tool. It offers a nonthreatening environment for non-Christians to explore Christianity. Living rooms of friends are safe places in our society. While churches have an obvious agenda, the living-room meeting provides a good place to explore ideas. Like many successful commodities that are sold in "home parties," Christianity can be offered through friends and relationships in this manner. Churches carry a lot of cultural expectations of dress, rite, and behavior that Christians are comfortable with but which further alienate the non-Christian. If we make friends first, meta groups can be a stepping-stone leading to church attendance. This is also an exciting way to mentor our youth into leadership with their own Meta groups.

The Disadvantages of the Meta Group Model

There are problems that youth leaders have encountered with this model. Meta groups can become too intensely supportive of each other and refuse to split when the group grows. Often they will reach a maximum size and then stay there. These groups require a lot of time investment from the adult leader, especially for individual counseling and mentoring outside of meeting time. A problem all small groups face is that leaders with unsound theology can turn their group into a small faction of extremists. Group leaders need to be accountable to the church body as a whole and their own adult support group.

The Family-based Model

Adventist Church D has a radical model for their youth Sabbath school class. They closed it down. Instead, there is a parent-teen class. One quarter the fathers meet with their teens; the next quarter the mothers meet. Parents who do not meet in the parent-teen Sabbath School class meet for a weekly parents prayer meeting, "A bunch of beggars meeting to tell each other where to find bread," they laughingly describe their support group.

The parent-teen Sabbath school was kicked off with a father-teen trip to a local climbing wall, where teens learned to belay and dads learned to trust their teens. After the trip, sitting around a pizza, the pastor asked them what biblical principals they learned from their activity. In January the four families are planning a ski trip: a Saturday night singing vespers and then board games and Sunday on the slopes—although, as one mother said, "I'll probably be praying on the slopes on Sunday, too."

If most youth leaders were honest they would prefer to separate youth members from their parents. While parents are useful when it comes to fund-raising and transportation, we often fear any parental involvement in planning or program execution. However, a revival of family-based youth ministry is in effect in North America. Inspired by James Dobson's radio broadcast *Focus on the Family,* and encouraged by rallies like Promise Keepers, this model represents a formalized return to the informal family-centered Christian education that existed before the Industrial Revolution.

Families have always been the underpinning of any successful youth ministry, but family-based ministry centers on this resource. In family-based ministry the parent-leaders meet in weekly prayer and support groups. Activities are structured to improve parent-student interaction and include the whole family. Parents, youth leaders, and teachers network to provide encouragement and support to families. Parents determine the direction of Christian education. Time with family is paramount.

Advantages of Family-based Ministry

Traditional youth ministry creates a youth division in an organization somewhat separate from the church. When the youth graduate, they often are not mentored into church life, but wander around looking for something they can identify with. Some of these "church orphans" become youth ministers themselves, to prolong the involvement they had in their academy days or in their youth churches. But the best way to mentor youth into a long-term relationship with a church is to mentor their whole family into church attendance.

Overworked church youth leaders can rely more on parent talent and natural interest, and take more of a mentoring role than a leadership role. Today's young people, when surveyed, have shown a desire to increase their time with their families, not to decrease it. The family-based model allows parents to be the primary role models they always were, and removes the church from competing with the family as God's chosen institution for educating the youth.

Disadvantages of the Family-based Model

Not all Adventist parents think alike, and not all parent the same way. Some would not have any problem with certain types of recreation on Saturday, while others would find them offensive. Careful preplanning sessions are needed to make sure that everyone's Sabbathkeeping beliefs are protected and that parents respect each other's viewpoints. This discussion is not a bad thing, by the way. It happens all the time throughout Adventism, but seldom with parents and their teens in the same room.

Another concern with this model is that not all kids have traditional two-parent homes. However, children of divorce need to spend more quality time with their parent, and the church should foster these times, not hinder or replace them. Those students who do not have parents willing or able to mentor them can have "adoptive" parents from the church: grandparents, senior youth, people who love them and are willing to spend time with them.

Implication for Youth Ministry

The direction of youth ministry in the new millennium is back to the grass roots. Like the Internet, our society is becoming less institutionalized, more diverse, and less centralized. Old structures and programs are not working because, lament youth leaders, "the kids are not showing up!" Generation X is famous for being skeptical of formal, institutional-based ideas. This is a legacy they inherited from us, the boomer generation. We questioned and tested all these institutions, and we did not leave our children with a lot of structure behind.

Adventist schools have experienced dropping enrollments, most boomers don't attend the adult Sabbath school, and divorce is more common now than for any previous generation in Adventism. As a result, we produced a generation of young people whose loyalties are not to organizations, such as schools and churches, and, sometimes, not even to their families. Instead, their loyalties are to their peers, and they show up where their friends are. Information sources are not large formal meetings, but informal communication links, such as e-mail and telephone calls. Community is not based on geographical limitations, but can be global in nature.

As Adventism enters the twenty-first century, individual members rely less on the institution and turn more toward nontraditional and noninstitutional models of youth ministry. The rest of Christianity has used parachurch models for a long time. The Young Men's Christian Associations were first started to offer safe places for rural youth looking for jobs in big cities during the Industrial Revolution. Today this concept is being revived in the inner city for at-risk youth. Mall ministries offer drug-free places for teens to mingle, with the permission of security guards. Some youth leaders have their boards invest in athletic equipment or arrange after-school tutorials, so that their church can became a teen hangout. Other people feel called to go to where the teenagers are.

Christian adults with a passion for the Lord and a talent in one area of youth culture meet teens and form community working on their shared interest. Skateboarders trust an adult who perfected boarding. Computer nerds are comfortable talking to adult computer nerds. Drama buffs will bend over backward to perform for a talented director. In the process of building relationship, Jesus Christ is introduced to many nonchurched teens.

To match this new generation, many Adventists, along with their fellow Christians, are creating Web-based ministries. An example of this is dre*am vision ministries. Youth ministers Deirdre and Allan Martin have made a Web page their meeting place. They communicate with members through Internet links and e-mail (dream_VISION_ministries @CompuServe.com), and they also offer workshops—offline. Like the Internet, these parachurch ministries may not have a central organizing force, but they benefit from the stability of an institutionalized church with reliable programming and dedicated leaders.

The models mentioned in this chapter range from one of the oldest in Adventism to models that are rarely tried. These are models only. Assess your local context, consider your own talents and interests, and observe how the Holy Spirit works in your environment. If nothing fits, create your own model! If we are to meet the challenges of these last days, we need to meet the individual needs that exist rather than relying on a one-size-fits-all ministry.

For Further Reading

Daily, Steve. *Adventism for a New Generation.* Portland, Oreg.: Better Living Publishers, 1993.

Barker, Steve, et al., *Good Things Come in Small Groups.* Downers Grove, Ill.: InterVarsity, 1985.

Benson, Warren S., and Mark H. Senter III, eds. *The Complete Book of Youth Ministry.* Chicago: Moody, 1987.

DeVries, Mark. Family-based *Youth Ministry.* Downers Grove, Ill.: InterVarsity, 1994.

Dunn, Richard R., and Mark H. Senter III, eds. *Reaching a Generation for Christ.* Chicago: Moody, 1997.

Senter III, Mark. *The Coming Revolution in Youth Ministry and Its Radical Impact on the Church.* Wheaton, Ill.: Victor Books, 1992.

Smith, Glen C., ed. *Evangelizing Youth.* Wheaton, Ill.: Tyndale, 1985.

Welty, Lavon J. *Side by Side: Mentoring Guide for Congregational Youth Ministry.* Newton, Kans.: Faith & Life, 1989.

CHAPTER 10

Leadership in the Adventist Youth Movement

by G. T. Ng

THE BELIEVERS WERE EXCITED! In fact, they were electrified when they learned that Jesus, the high priest, would complete the cleansing of the sanctuary on October 22, 1844. The prophecy of Daniel 8:14 would be fulfilled. The Bridegroom would come back to earth to take His waiting bride. With gratitude, tears flowed freely. "We are almost home! Glory hallelujah!" they cried. Adventists sold their land, businessmen closed their shops, farmers left their farms idle. Potatoes remained in the ground unharvested. Apples rotted in the orchards. "Yours in the blessed hope," many signed their letters. The message went from city to city, town to town, village to village, to the farthest part of the land. Every Millerite waited with joyous longing for Jesus to return to Planet Earth.

As October 22, 1844, dawned, believers assembled in their homes, tents, and churches praying, praising, and waiting. *It won't be long,* they thought. *The Bridegroom will return!* But the Bridegroom did not appear. The day had ended, and Jesus hadn't come! What had happened? What had gone wrong? Their hopes dashed, they wept unashamedly till dawn the next day.

As it turned out, William Miller was correct in his calculation of the end of the 2300-day prophecy. But he was mistaken about the event that fulfilled the "cleansing of the sanctuary." As Millerites continued searching the Scriptures, they realized that 1844 was the time Jesus was beginning His final work of atonement in the Most Holy Place of the heavenly sanctuary. It was not to be the Second Advent, as they had expected!

The Great Disappointment of 1844 prompted many to leave the Millerite movement. But a small cluster of believers remained, and out of it arose a great religious movement—the Seventh-day Adventist Church.

Young Pioneers

What is noteworthy among the pioneers of the Seventh-day Adventist Church is the fact that most of them were young. A casual survey of Adventist history reveals an unmistakable and significant role young people played at the inception of the church. Almost without exception Adventist pioneers were young people. The Great Disappointment experience of October 22, 1844, was a shock to the early Adventists. Many became disillusioned and eventually left the Millerite movement. A group of Adventist young people, however, encouraged the disappointed ones to keep their faith and stay on course.

Ellen Harmon recalled the bitter experience: "It was a bitter disappointment that fell upon the little flock whose faith had been so strong and whose hope had been so high. But we were surprised that we felt so free in the Lord, and were so strongly sustained by His strength and grace. . . . We were disappointed, but not disheartened."[1]

James White started preaching the second coming of Christ in 1842 at the age of 21. He was ordained to the Christian Church at the age of 22. Full of zeal, he was prominent in encouraging the group of disappointed Adventists who later became members of the Seventh-day Adventist denomination.

John N. Andrews, the first overseas missionary of the Adventist Church, began preaching and writing at the age of 21. At 22 he was named to the publishing committee supporting the work of editor James White. He became the third president of the General Conference at the age of 38.

John Loughborough was known as the "boy preacher"; he began preaching at the age of 17. He was the first historian of the Seventh-day Adventist Church and the first minister sent to England.

Uriah Smith, a coworker of James White for 30 years, began 50 years of editorial service to the denomination at the age of 21. Much of that time he served as the editor of the *Advent Review and Sabbath Herald.*

Stephen Haskell was a youth of 19 when he accepted the Adventist message, and in a matter of weeks he was preaching the message. He became the father of the Tract and Missionary Society, which has since developed into the Adventist Book Centers. He pioneered Adventist work in England, South Africa, New Zealand, and Australia.

Ellen Harmon was only a teenager of 17 when she began her long ministry as the prophet of the Seventh-day Adventist Church. From a humble background she emerged as God's messenger in a most forbidding era. In 60 years Ellen White, as she was later known, wrote about 25 million words. That is equivalent to three to four typewritten pages (1,100 words) a day for every day of those 60 years!

The pioneers were dedicated, they were young, and they contributed greatly to the formation of the infant church. But they have gone to their rest. Nearly 160 years have come and gone since 1844. The pioneers died in the faith, as did a large number of early Adventist Christians. They thought they would see Jesus come in their generation, but Jesus did not come. The mantle from the pioneers must now pass on to the younger generation. Leaders must be raised to take hold of the challenges that face the church.

Why Develop Youth Leaders?

Leadership development is important because youth leaders are needed today more than ever before, especially in areas where church membership is 50 to 75 percent youth. Affluent churches have the advantage of youth pastors, complete with huge budgets, full-time secretaries, and the latest electronic equipment capable of producing state-of-the-art programs. Most churches around the world, however, do not have the luxury of hiring a youth pastor. Local church youth ministry must depend on young people themselves. Since the church relies on volunteer leaders, youth ministry depends on volunteer youth leaders to carry out its functions and mission. Obviously leaders do not appear from nowhere. They have to be developed, and leadership development should be an ongoing process; it should not be left to chance.

Leadership development helps to eliminate the problem of burnout. The nominating committee selects the new youth leader. He accepts the challenge and starts out enthusiastically. He has to be at every meeting. He carries all the responsibilities on his shoulders. He practically runs a one-person show, wearing himself to the bone. Before he knows it, he has suffered burnout. He vows never to accept the same job again! If the church has been developing new youth leaders on a regular basis, the burnout phenomenon can largely be avoided.

Assumptions About Leadership in Youth Ministry

In order to focus on the significance of leadership in Adventist youth ministry, we need to recognize the following assumptions.

1. Each Young Person Has Gifts for Ministry. (See 1 Cor. 12; Rom. 12; Eph. 4.) Spiritual gifts are given so that the body of Christ may be edified and enriched. In the kaleidoscope of God's family, there is room for every gift. Effective youth ministry is a collective ministry of the community of faith. It is not the sole prerogative of a few exclusive ones. Those who are gifted in leadership should be encouraged and opportunities given them to exercise their gift in youth ministry.

2. The Success of Youth Ministry Depends Largely on Quality Leadership. Hence, dedicated and responsible leadership is imperative. The story is told of a man who had been elected as the president of a mission. Someone asked him, "Tell me, just how did you happen to be chosen for this high honor?" He replied, "Well, they wanted me to be the secretary, but I can't write. Then they wanted me to be the treasurer, but I can't count. So they elected me the president!" Quality leadership does not come accidentally. It is cultivated and developed, and it makes a difference between success and failure in an organization. Hence, strong youth work may be attributed, to a large measure, to competent leadership.

3. Adventist Youth Leaders Can Be Equipped for Ministry. Equipping the saints for the work of ministry constitutes the purpose of the giving of spiritual gifts (see Eph. 4:11, 12). A lack of trained leaders in youth ministry is self-evident in most countries. Rather than decrying the scarcity of youth leaders, we should be in the business of producing them on a regular basis. The church must place a high premium on the recruitment and development of youth leaders.

4. Youth Ministry Involves Youth in Mission. Youth ministry facilitates nurturing, worship, and fellowship among young people. The tendency in the past, however, has been to confine youth ministry to these three objectives, giving it a warped view of what youth ministry is all about. Authentic youth ministry must be mission driven. It should become part and parcel of the overall objective of the church in obedience to the Great Commission, bringing the gospel to the world.

Youth Leadership

There are two kinds of leadership in youth ministry: adult leadership and youth leadership. Adult leadership lends stability and credence and provides leadership training for young people.

Adult leadership is needed to guide young people toward spiritual maturity. "Till we all come to the unity of the faith and the knowledge of the Son of God, to a perfect man, to the measure of the stature of the fullness of Christ; that we . . . may grow up in all things into Him who is the head—Christ" (Eph. 4:13-15, NKJV). The function of adult youth leaders is to provide leadership to young people until spiritual maturity is achieved. Thus, an adult leader working with youth is a guide, a counselor, and friend.

Young people are often at the crossroads of life: they are not sure where they are heading and are not sure of themselves. The trauma of growing up, the rebellion of the teenage years, the choices of young adulthood, give rise to a need for guidance. A recent survey among the brightest teenagers in the United States found that nearly a fourth of them had considered committing suicide, mostly because of general depression and school pressures.[2]

Qualifications of Youth Leadership

What type of person can become a leader of young people? What are the basic qualifications one should look for?

Availability

Everyone is busy these days. Even with the convenience of the latest timesaving electronic gizmos, we still don't have time to do the things we wish we could. Time has become a tyrant rather than a servant. Every passing day seems to enslave us further in the relentless circle of busyness. "Where in the world can we find time to help young people? We don't even have time for ourselves" seems to the off-repeated refrain.

Have you thought of the ways the Lord called leaders to serve His cause? God never looked among idle people when He needed men and women for His service; God called busy people: Moses was busy with his flock at Horeb, Gideon was busy threshing wheat by the winepress, Saul was busy searching for his father's lost beast, Elisha was busy plowing with 12 yoke of oxen, David was busy caring for his father's sheep, Amos was busy following the flock, Nehemiah was busy bearing the king's wine cup, Peter and Andrew were busy casting a net into the sea, James and John were busy mending their nets, and Jesus was busy about His Father's business.

In similar ways, God calls dedicated adults today who have a burden for young people and who are willing to step out of their comfort zone in order to take on the task of youth ministry. If not now—when? If not me—who?

Authenticity

During the Gulf War a newly promoted colonel had just arrived and moved into a makeshift office. He was getting things organized when he saw a private walking toward his office. Wishing to look more important then he really was, he picked up the phone and said, "Yes, General Schwarzkopf, yes, yes, of course, I think that's an excellent idea. You have my support. Thanks for checking with me, Norm. 'Bye." As he hung up the phone, he asked the private, "And what can I do for you?" The private answered, "Sir, I am here to hook up your phone!"[3]

Pretense abounds in the world, but an adult leader in youth ministry must be an authentic Christian. Young people know adults are not perfect, and they do not expect to see perfection in adults. But they do care if adults are real and sincere about their religion. They want to know if adults are serious about their faith. They detest hypocrisy, which is one of the greatest stumbling blocks for youth leaving the church.

Adult leaders should model the values and dedication they seek to develop in youth. Stone believes that the spirituality of youth is largely dependent on adults modeling their faith. "Youth have a need to belong and to be accepted. They are leaning toward spiritual fulfillment. They want models. Those of us who work with youth need to offer a setting that meets their personal, social, and spiritual needs. We must provide role models that are authentic in both practice and spirit."[4]

Living up to one's faith is often a challenge, and it is more so in adults modeling their faith before young people. Unfortunately, not many adults provide good models for young people to follow. Richards warns, "Too often in the contemporary church youth and adults come together only within the church walls, or on occasions where they talk about the Christian life—not live it. And so very often we develop young people who can talk a good faith, but who have no capacity to express faith through their life in the world. We have such young people in large measure because they have had opportunity to hear adults talk about their faith—not to live it in the real world."[5]

Richards maintains that modeling is the primary means of Christian education. He equates modeling with discipling, as Jesus modeled for His disciples. Modeling needs authenticity. While adults cannot model perfection, they should model transformation and humility, and perhaps, repentance. And when they do, it gives young people the courage to commit their lives to Jesus in authentic relationships.

Identity

Identity is the ability to regard oneself as sharing the characteristics of someone. The apostle Paul was a master of identity in the early church. "For though I am free from all men, I have made myself a servant to all, that I might win the more; and to the Jews I became as a Jew, that I might win Jews; to those who are under the law, as under the law, that I might win those who are under the law; to those who are without law, as without law . . . that I might win those who are without law; to the weak I became as weak, that I might win the weak. I have become all things to all men, that I might by all means save some. Now this I do for the gospel's sake, that I may be partaker of it with you" (1 Cor. 9:19-23, NKJV). By the same token, today a youth leader may say, "To the youth, I become as a youth, that I may win the youth."

Understanding is a key ingredient in identifying with the youth. Swiss psychiatrist Carl Jung once said, "If one does not understand a person, one tends to regard him as a fool." One of the most common recurring complaints of youth about adults is "But you don't understand!" Why is it that young people think adults don't understand them, or have a hard time understanding them? Wayne Rice believes he has the answer.

According to Rice, the best youth workers are the ones "who can identify with young people—that is, who can understand what it's like to be a young person. Most adults just can't do that. To those who can't, young people seem incredibly strange—moody, noisy, unreasonable, disrespectful, irreverent, lazy, and just plain crazy most of the time. But to the junior higher, there are very good reasons behind all those idiosyncrasies that adults don't like, and they desperately want someone who will try to understand. Without this understanding, communication becomes almost impossible.

"Every adult has one good point of identification with junior highers: He or she was once upon a time a junior higher too—and not too many years ago. And since, in reality, the problems that young people face today are not that different from the problems we faced when we were that age, it seems logical that we would have a certain amount of empathy almost automatically.

"But psychologists tell us that normal adults have a problem remembering what it was like to be an adolescent. They call it 'repression,' which is something like amnesia. Repression is defined as the 'rejection from consciousness of painful or disagreeable ideas, memories and feelings.' It is something that the mind does to make life more endurable—it automatically tries to forget, or at least block from memory, painful experiences of the past. Those painful experiences are never lost completely from consciousness; they are just pushed back into the recesses of the mind and never recalled. It's common for therapists to use hypnosis or some other method to help people recall and deal with repressed events.

"What does all this have to do with working with young people? Simply that psychologists also tell us that some of life's most painful experiences occur during our adolescent years. Consider the embarrassment and humiliation of the struggle with parents for independence, the times when one was not accepted by the peer group, guilt feelings brought on by new awareness of one's sexuality, puzzling questions from a developing mind, love triangles and broken hearts—the list goes on. No one wants to go through life with all that on his mind. So it is repressed. And that accounts for the average adult's inability to understand young people very well. They just don't remember."[6]

The adult leader should overcome this selective amnesia by getting into the world of young people. He should spend time with them and get to know them personally. He should be well versed with their hobbies, recreational interests, choice of career, and other personal interests. One of the leader's responsibilities is to visit their parents and get acquainted with them, and get their support and understanding. Young people know if the leader is genuinely interested in them. They are quick to detect a phony, so the attempt to identify with them should be an authentic effort.

Destiny

Youth leaders are people of destiny. They have a strong sense of calling. They know they are in youth work because God has called them to be there. They are like John Knox when he said, "Give me Scotland or I die!"

People of destiny are not easily discouraged. They know they are there for a purpose, and no obstacles are too great to overcome. Neither are they naive in thinking youth ministry is a bed of roses and destiny equates plain sailing. Youth leaders are realists. They are aware that youth ministry can be convoluted with pains and sacrifices, yet a sense of destiny prevails. Obstacles serve to galvanize them into greater partnership with God and greater dependence on Him for success.

Having a sense of destiny does not mean slaving to the point of burnout. Youth leaders must prioritize the nurturing of their own souls, lest after caring for youth, they themselves should become disqualified (see 1 Cor. 9:27). Daily devotions and a close relationship with

Christ are not an option but an obligation. Contemporary society is not exactly conducive to Christian growth and development, as Christians are caught up in the rat race, too. Someone remarked that the trouble with the rat race is that even if you win, you are still a rat at the end of the day.

Synergy

Synergy is "interaction of two or more agents or forces so that their combined effect is greater than the sum of their individual effects."[7] The word comes from its Greek origin *synergia,* which means "cooperation," and *synergos,* which means "working together." A synergistic youth leader is one who is a team player. He recognizes he does not have all the expertise there is to develop a youth ministry, and that he is dependent on the team to make it work. He does not feel a strong compulsion to dominate the scene, realizing that a person's efforts are at best inadequate. Rather, he fosters esprit de corps in every aspect of his leadership.

Youth leaders are teachable. They are aware they do not know all there is to know, but they want to learn all they can so as to be on the cutting edge. They know they have not arrived and thus see the need of attending seminars and workshops to sharpen their tools. They are like Apollos, who "began to speak boldly in the synagogue. When Priscilla and Aquila heard him, they invited him to their home and explained to him the way of God more adequately" (Acts 18:26, NIV). Imagine, two laypeople expounding the Scriptures to a preacher! What an example of humility and teachability! Youth leaders would do well to ask counsel from their pastors, elders, and even young people themselves.

Youth leaders should be team players. They recognize the danger of being lone rangers. Many youth leaders are gifted people having enormous energy and charisma, which, ironically, leads them to believe they can do all and be all. Wallowing in pride, their success is short-lived, and soon they fade out of the picture. Synergetic leaders are different. They emphasize the significance of team spirit. They recognize the pitfall of a one-person show. Hence, each member of the leadership team is important, and the leaders are the first among equals. They plan together and move together as a unit.

Connectivity

A major problem of young people is apathy. One youth leader asked a group of adolescents, "How would you define apathy?" The response was predictable—"Who cares?" Apathy can easily be detected during worship service or youth meetings. It is said that the crew and passengers on board the great ocean line *Titanic* were concerned neither about the fate of the ship nor their safety. After all, the *Titanic* was built to be unsinkable! Each compartment was watertight, and even if two compartments were filled with water, the ship would still be safe. Consequently, the ship carried too few lifeboats. Of the 2,208 passengers on board, only 705 survived!

One of the pitfalls of youth ministry has been in the area of programming. Living in a spectator age, young people are accustomed to being entertained. Often, youth programs are designed to entertain rather than to equip young people to be connected with each other and to the world. If youth programs take the direction of entertainment, invariably we will produce spectators, and spectatorship leads to apathy.

Getting indifferent young people to be connected to the reality of life is the challenge of every youth leader. Jean Rostand, French biologist and writer, said, "One must either take an interest in the human situation or else parade before the void." Given that idleness is the devil's workshop, connectivity is the answer to the problem of apathy. To be connected is to be involved in the lives of others and in the services of the church. Too often we underestimate the willingness and ability of young people.

If approached correctly, young people can be challenged and trained to handle responsibilities well. John Howard's comment is well taken: "Having spent a career trying to understand and help young people, I am convinced that the one primary cause of the tragic self-destruction of so many of our youth is that they do not know the work and satisfaction of living for something larger than themselves. The human psyche cannot stand up against moral neutrality. If nothing is truly good, right, and worthy of striving and sacrificing for, life is meaningless and no course of action can build a sense of one's own self-worth. Without large goals, life is barren, life is a burden."[8]

James Steward echoes the same sentiment for greater connectivity and involvement of young people when he says: "In my estimation, the greatest threat to Christianity is not Communism, not atheism, and not cultism. . . . In my estimation, the greatest threat to Christianity is Christians who are trying to sneak into heaven incognito, without ever sharing their faith or becoming involved."[9]

To the apostle Paul, every Christian is an agent for connectivity to the world. "Therefore, if anyone is in Christ, he is a new creation; old things have passed away; behold, all things have become new. Now all things are of God, who has reconciled us to Himself through Jesus Christ, and has given us the ministry of reconciliation" (2 Cor. 5:17, 18, NKJV). As far as Paul is concerned, every person who is born into the kingdom of Christ is born as an ambassador (see verse 20). Each is to be connected to the world through the ministry of reconciliation. "The spirit of Christ is a missionary spirit. The very first impulse of the renewed heart is to bring others also to the Savior."[10] "Everyone who is added to the ranks by conversion is to be assigned his post of duty."[11]

It is one thing to challenge young people to get on with the task of evangelism; it is quite another to mobilize them. Herein lies the weakness of youth ministry. Mobilizing youth for evangelism takes preparation, and this is where youth leaders come in. Ellen White outlines the responsibilities of youth leaders for the newly baptized: "When the youth give their hearts to God, our responsibility for them does not cease. They must be interested in the Lord's work, and led to see that He expects them to do something to advance His cause. It is not enough to show how much needs to be done, and to urge the youth to act a part. They must be taught how to labor for the Master. They must be *trained*, disciplined, drilled, in the best methods of winning souls to Christ."[12]

Postbaptismal training of youth for missionary activities should become a priority for youth leaders. After all, Adventist youth have been described as an army of God in the oft-quoted words from the pen of inspiration, "We have an army of youth today who can do much if they are properly directed and encouraged."[13]

Writing from the background of a senior churchman, Elton Trueblood makes the following observation on connectivity in the traditional sense of the word: "Millions are merely backseat Christians, willing to be observers of a performance which the professionals put on, ready to criticize or to applaud, but not willing even to consider the possibility of real participation. Here is the fundamental weakness of the contemporary church. Millions claim to have some sort of connection with the church, but it is not a connection of involvement."[14]

The parallelism of Christians with the military is common in Christian culture. The Apostle Paul speaks of putting on the armor of God (see Eph. 6:10-17; 1 Thess. 5:8). Christian hymnwriters often utilize military language in such songs as "Onward Christian Soldiers," "Marching to Zion," and "We're in the Lord's Army." Yet the similarity ends there. Trueblood laments the fact that the army of God is ill prepared for warfare: "There is no real chance of victory in a campaign if 90 percent of the soldiers are untrained and uninvolved, but that is exactly where we stand now."[15]

Youth specialist Doug Fields believes that youth ministry should be purpose-driven. The five purposes are worship, ministry, evangelism, fellowship, and discipleship.[16] Contemporary youth ministry as he sees it, however, presents an unbalanced picture. Fellowship tends to be very strong while evangelism tends to be weak. Evaluating contemporary youth ministry against the five purposes, Fields believes most youth ministry would get the following letter grades: Fellowship, A; Discipleship, B; Worship, C+; Ministry, C—; Evangelism, D+.[17]

Good youth leaders do their job well. Better youth leaders involve and equip young people in leadership and the mission of the church. Youth must be connected to the church as well as to the world. Indeed, it is well said that the church is not an agency to be served, but a work force to be deployed! Now, that's real connectivity!

Conclusion

Edward Everett Hale once said, "I am only one, but I am one. I cannot do everything, but I can do something; and what I can do, that I ought to do; and what I ought to do, by the grace of God I shall do." Today God is looking for men and women who have a burden for the salvation of our young people. If you have a passion for youth, God will give you the grace to be a youth leader.

Dedication is crucial in the business of youth ministry. God is looking for dedicated leaders. The great Methodist John Wesley devoted his life to service for lost humanity. He said, "If I had three hundred men who feared nothing but God, hated nothing but sin, and were determined to know nothing among men but Jesus Christ and Him crucified, I would set the world on fire!" Youth ministry is the future of the church, and youth leaders are crucial to successful youth ministry. May commitment be the hallmark of Adventist youth leadership in this new millennium.

---

[1] Ellen G. White, *Life Sketches* (Mountain View, Calif.: Pacific Press Pub. Assn., 1915), p. 61.

[2] The annual poll by the publishers of "Who's Who Among American High School Students" reported on InfoBeat e-mail service, Nov. 12, 1998.

[3] Bill Hybels and Mark Mittelberg, *Becoming a Contagious Christian* (Grand Rapids: Zondervan, 1994), p. 57.

[4] Stone (1985), p. 20.

[5] Lawrence Richards, *Youth Ministry: Its Renewal in the Local Church* (Grand Rapids: Zondervan, 1972), pp. 123, 124.

[6] Wayne Rice, *Junior High Ministry* (Grand Rapids: Zondervan, 1978), pp. 28-31.

[7] "Synergy," Microsoft Bookshelf, 1996-1997 edition.

[8] John Howard, *In Touch Newsletter,* September 1990, p. 2.

[9] James Steward, *In Touch Newsletter,* September 1990, p. 1.

[10] Ellen G. White, *The Great Controversy* (Mountain View, Calif.: Pacific Press Pub. Assn., 1911), p. 70.

[11] White, *Testimonies,* vol. 7, p. 30.

[12] White, *Gospel Workers,* p. 210. (Italics supplied.)

[13] White, *Testimonies to Ministers,* p. 32.

[14] Elton Trueblood, *The Company of the Committed* (New York: Harper & Row, 1961), p. 57.

[15] *Ibid.,* p. 38.

[16] Doug Fields, *Purpose-driven Youth Ministry* (Grand Rapids: Zondervan, 1998), pp. 46ff.

[17] *Ibid.,* p. 50.

CHAPTER 11

Understanding Young People— Why a Special Youth Ministry?

by Barry Gane

THIS CHAPTER WILL ENDEAVOR TO answer these often-asked questions: "Why should we consider a separate and special ministry for youth? Can't they just do everything with the rest of the church family? Aren't they, after all, a part of the church anyway?" We certainly should consider the youth to be a part of the church. However, they are that part of the church that is moving through a particularly sensitive period of personal development. They are faced with a set of issues, problems, and tasks that younger or older members do not face with the same intensity. As a result, they have a range of needs that require a distinct ministry that is especially directed toward meeting those needs.

It is very easy for us to consider that all young people are the same and for us to make sweeping generalizations about their needs, psychology, beliefs, and hence build some type of program to meet all of them. Tony Campolo counsels us that "there is no single youth culture in the technological urban industrialized societies of the Western world. Instead, there are a variety of subcultures existing side by side, each with its own language, value system and world view."[1]

There are, however, some common elements in all young people who make up the group whom we call teens and young adults. There are a series of social forces that have impacted the lives of all teenagers, and to look at this, we need to review the history of how the teenage phenomena came about.

The Impact of the Industrial Revolution

Before the Industrial Revolution (about the later part of the eighteenth-century) the majority of people lived in rural settings.[2] Families worked either on small holdings or in cottage industries. They had big families, not just because there was no birth control, but because children were needed to make sure the work of the cottage industry or the farm was done. They were an economic necessity, but they also had a sense of being needed and wanted. The father was very much the head of the home, the authority figure. There were no problems of the father being away for many hours, for he and his wife worked side by side on their small holding or in their cottage industry, and he was at home all the time. The extended family was within close reach, and many people lived and died within a few miles of their place of birth.

With the advent of steam and the Industrial Revolution, many of these factors began to fall apart. People moved away from the rural environment and entered the fast-growing towns and cities, the new urban environments. For the most part this meant that they were removed from the extended family. Not only did the father go out to work, but he would be absent for up to 16 hours a day, leaving most of the child rearing and discipline with the mother. Children were also sent out to work—in many cases at the age of 8.

During this time, because of the lack of birth control, children began to sense that they were a drain on the family economy, rather than being needed to hold the family together. In the years of the Industrial Revolution the exploitation of children and workers was very common. The family started to disintegrate, and many of the social problems we are now acutely aware of find their roots here. Children were not needed. They knew it and felt unwanted. The camaraderie and bonding between father and son, and mother and daughter, began to be eroded, and in time gave rise to the generation gap.

Youth in the Twentieth Century

A brief survey of modern history reveals that for the vast majority of young people in the western world prior to the second world war, education ended in the early years of secondary school. Young people were sent out to work in order that their earnings might supplement the united family budget.

Children became responsible working people while they were still in early adolescence; they were often sent out to work alongside their fathers. They worked long hours, six days a week. The family devoted most of its free time to the church, with Sunday kept as the Sabbath. The drift toward the towns and cities accelerated, until today 85 percent of Australia's population live in urban centers.

After the second world war the Western world began to change, as families became smaller and compulsory education for all children brought more years of school. Expectations changed. Fathers were rarely at home, and young people were made to feel that they contributed nothing to the family. They were there as objects of love, at best, and derision, at worst. Fathers were technically still the head of the house but were no longer home enough to be involved in child rearing. Discipline began to break down, becoming more of a threat than a reality. The roots of permissiveness were sown as mothers sought to be friends rather than tackle the hard task of disciplining.

With young people spending more time at school than at work, they had more time for leisure, time to think, and time for fun. People began talking about time in different terms: pastime, mark time, spend time, take time, waste time, kill time. This extra time gave way to boredom.

In the early 1950s rock and roll music gave relief to boredom, and early motion pictures took youth into the world of fantasy. Such stars as James Dean and Marlin Brando set the pace in lifestyle, dress, and speech. The culture of a new society was beginning to evolve.

It was in 1949 that the word "teenager" appeared for the first time, and about the same time gangs of youth with nothing to do evolved. Teenagers' heroes were rebelling against the status quo—the society of their parents, their dress, their attitudes, their politics, and their world. Rock and roll was about rebellion. It was listening to Elvis Presley when they were supposed to be listening to Pat Boone. Presley was described as "white, greasy, with the sullen good looks of a successful hubcap thief."[3] He fast became the symbol of antiauthority and anti-parents.

The new pattern of counterculture among youth was established and is still with us. The most noticeable of these countercultures was born in the sixties, when youth felt that they had an alternative, that they had the power to change the world, and there was a concerted effort to do just that—change the world. It was the Age of Aquarius; flower power; make love, not war; ban-the-bomb sit-ins; demonstrations; and protests. Bob Dylan, the Beatles, the Who, the Rolling Stones, and others were the prophets of a new age. But the sixties ended with a whimper. Optimism gave way to despair and hopelessness; nothing really changed. Still, that age left us some legacies, and it continues to influence much of what happens today. The nihilism, the despair, the search for meaning, have brought us through the nineties and to the mess we are now in.

The Youth of Today

To a great extent, the media have shaped the values of young people today. Adult knowledge, the type of thing we wished to keep from our children until they were mature enough to cope, is shown on the news in graphic detail. More than 14,000 acts of sexual intercourse—or implied intercourse—were broadcast on prime-time television last year in the United States, and Australia tends to mirror her big Western cousin. Teenagers listen to four hours of rock music per day and watch MTV for up to 10 hours per week—60 percent of which contains sex or violence.

David Breskin describes what life has become for many Western teenagers. "First off, chances are an adolescent's parents are divorced. Suicides come disproportionately from broken homes, and the increase in young suicides parallels the giddy divorce rate, now over 50 percent and the highest in the world. Married or divorced, the adolescent's mother works outside the home. She prides herself on how quickly she goes back to work after he/she is born. (That the father is absent or away at work is a given.) His parents subcontract responsibility for raising him/her to day-care surrogates, nurses, and sitters, and to Johnny himself. . . . There's no extended family around for him, not with the geographic mobility for which Americans are famous. The moving is hard on him. He must keep readapting to new environments.

"American parents spend less time with Johnny than any other parents in the world. While he's a teenager, they spend an average of 14 minutes a week communicating with him. By the time Johnny graduates from high school, he'll have spent more time with his blue, flickering electronic parent than doing anything else but sleeping; he'll have seen 20,000 hours of TV, 350,000 commercials, about 18,000 killings. The family doesn't talk; they watch. On TV, problems resolve themselves in 30-minute spans. It's his only problem-solving role model, and it's unrealistic.

"That his life is not as exciting as the life on TV may come as a disappointment. His pain comes as a nasty shock, and he'll learn to escape rather than cope. He has far more access to booze, dope, pills, coke, than any previous generation of kids, and at an earlier age. He also has easy access to the genitals of the opposite sex, and the sooner he scores, the more difficulty he'll have with intimacy later on. Chances are increasing that he will be sexually or physically abused by an adult at an early age.

"Competition is tremendous. If he is middle or upper-middle class, his parents have already told him he had better start running, and fast, because the pie is shrinking. The number of his peers has doubled in 20 years, but the opportunities haven't. There are only so many spots on the basketball team or in the law firm. He feels pressure to be perfect. This 'cohort effect' means he lives in a downwardly mobile, increasingly Darwinian world. It's called, trendily, the end of childhood. Johnny quickly learns that good grades and other tangible achievements are the currency in which he trades for his parents' approval and concomitant permissiveness. The parents see the equation differently: They provide material well-being; he delivers good grades in return. His parents are permissive because it's easier to say yes than no. Besides, they don't know what rules are valid anymore. Everything in this world is negotiable now: Everything is shades of gray, and all that matters is green. They treat the kid like a little adult because they want him to be a little adult. They seek his friendship and fear his disapproval. When they give him too much freedom, he secretly desires rules; but they don't want to tell him about sex, about values, pain, problem-solving, living with limitations. All is uncertain, nothing is shocking, everything is tolerated.

"All told, Johnny lives in a bizarre warp of freedom and pressure at a stage of his life when neither is appropriate: when pressure makes him brittle and freedom's just another word for everything to lose."[4]

The Changing World of Today's Youth

Prior to the second world war there were certain pillars that supported the adolescent into adulthood. These were the family, moral certainty, respect for authority, protection from some adult knowledge, and a sense of community. It is fair to say that this support structure has all but crumbled in the late twentieth century. These pillars once reduced stress and supported the adolescent into adulthood. Now he is pushed earlier, and the stress level grows. Let's examine these factors:

Family. The traditional refuge the place of acceptance. However, 60 percent of all marriages end in divorce. Instability is the result.

Moral Certainty. Society doesn't appear to know what is right anymore. We are told that there are "no longer moral choices but personal choices." Relativism has arrived—"It's right if I choose to do it." We live in a multiple-option society.

Authority. Kids don't look to adults to receive their norms; they look to their peers. Respect for age and knowledge is disappearing. Every corrupt police officer or politician makes an impression. It seems that adults don't know what is right or wrong.

Protective Knowledge. Some things we waited to tell children until they were ready. Now society loads it all on them—"Tell them everything." As a result, kids are carrying more stress; they don't know what their parents believe in many areas that are important to a balanced lifestyle.

Community. Pragmatism rides high—"What's in it for me?" people ask. The Western culture has moved into isolation, into unstable little units.[5]

All of this has produced a generation of young people who are, to a large degree, apathetic and self-centered. This apathy doesn't stem from a lack of knowledge about the world, for they are better educated than any previous generation. The media has made them aware of the big issues—the global problems that humanity faces. They do not have the optimism of the youth of the sixties or even the blasé "couldn't care less" attitude of the seventies and early eighties, but rather, they believe that they can make very little difference. There is still a crisis over identity, the lack of a sense of belonging. They search for meaning through secularism, materialism, and humanism. Many of them struggle under a burden of fear.

Teenage magazine surveyed youth to find their greatest fears: number one was nuclear war; two, the death of a parent.[6] The fear element seems to have given rise to a new conservatism. The destructive and unsettling factors that sexual freedom and promiscuity have brought to families and children in the past 25 years have led many youth to a greater desire for security. There is even an interest in monogamy and a real hunger for a caring relationship. Every day in Australia a young person ends his/her own life. This figure, horrendous though it is, doesn't tell the full story, because every year there are 50,000 others who try but are unsuccessful![7]

For a number of reasons, the most dominant being the sense of failure, there are 40,000 children who skip school on any given day. For far too many there is a feeling of hopelessness; they ask, "What's it all about, anyway?" "What's at the other end of all this study if you aren't all that bright?" "Is this all there is?" And so begins the struggle to blot out reality. Many begin to experiment with substances that are a substitute for hope but that soon become an everyday trip into oblivion.

More and more children are leaving home. When they leave home, what are they trying to escape? For many it is verbal and physical abuse, incest, and other sexual aberrations. So many young people, even as young as 7, leave home to join the growing number of 40,000 homeless kids.

Over the past five years 600,000 teens have dropped out of school believing that with work they will find life better. But their search ends at the unemployment line. There are more than 250,000 young people—that's half of the official 500,000—who are currently unemployed. In the sixties there was only one in 20 who could not find a job; now the figure is one in five.

Is it any wonder that the two dominant characteristics of youth of the Western world are conservatism and apathy? Sadly, these characteristics are dominant in the church's youth, too. There is a conservatism among our youth that leads them to protect those things they feel underpin their security as Seventh-day Adventist Christians. There are, however, a growing number who are concerned about their fellow inhabitants on this planet and wish to bring them the gospel that has changed their lives.

Sadly, there are a large number of apathetic youth who fail to see relevance in the religion of their fathers, since it makes no impact on the problems of the world in general or their own private world. These youth often lose themselves temporarily in sheer hedonism (the pursuit of pleasure), which, given time, turns to despair. Let's look at the developmental stages through which the Adventist youth passes.

Postmodernism: The Biggest Paradigm Shift in 200 Years

For most of the history of the Adventist Church we have successfully used the modernist approach to finding meaning. This approach has been based on logic and revolves around the preacher's ability to logically construct a case or an argument using empirical evidence. For many people this proved to be an overwhelming argument for truth, to which they responded positively. After presenting the scriptural evidence that the seventh day is the Sabbath of the Bible, we expected people to accept it, and in many cases they did. But today the postmodernist would say, "OK, but so what?"

There has been a reaction against the long, dry reign of rationalism. Many young people today see themselves as spiritual but not necessarily religious. They believe there are more ways of "knowing" than just cognitively, and they would point to intuition and emotion, just to cite a few. The postmodernist is aware of different ways of processing information and making sense of it. Doctrine must have meaning for them personally. It has to make a difference in *their* world. The following points may help us understand this line of thinking:

- The postmodernist would assert: Things and events do not have intrinsic meaning. There is only continuous interpretation of the world.
- Continuous examination of the world requires a contextual examination; we ourselves are part of the context.
- Interpretation depends not on the external text or its author, but on the relative viewpoint and particular values of the interpreter.
- Language is not neutral, but relative and value-laden. Language conveys ideology.

It is not hard to see how threatening this thinking is to a church so long locked in modernism. Reaching the current generation of youth and young adults requires a shift in our thinking, as well. The educational system, the popular media, and the entertainment industry are saturated with postmodernism. Adventist youth are not immune to its effects. And although this is not the chapter to deal with the topic, this brief introduction puts us on notice that everything we do in our church services and youth programming needs to preach—the architecture, music, fellowship, prayer, even the smell of the place will say something. This area demands a chapter of its own.

The Life Stages of an Adventist

The baby Adventist progresses through cradle roll or beginners and kindergarten and on to primary Sabbath school. He eagerly participates in thirteenth Sabbath programs in front of Mom and Dad, brothers and sisters. Memory verses, finger plays, and coloring form a delightful part of the child's life. Sabbath and church are synonymous with activity, fun, and learning about Jesus. For the little child, this age of infant adoration is one in which the church plays an important part in a happy, secure world.[8]

About 10 years of age the child begins to make the transition into adolescence. With it there is often a desire to make a real "grown-up" spiritual commitment. Most young Adventists are baptized between the ages of 10 and 14. Although peer pressure sometimes prompts this step, there is usually a genuine and personal desire to make a public commitment to Jesus.

Moving from early adolescence into middle adolescence, there often comes a time when spiritual interest diminishes and takes a secondary place to the much stronger developmental aspects of physical and social growth. This is often a superficial spiritual barrenness and begins to balance out again in late adolescence. Those who formerly sat near the front of the church move to the back (or the last row of the balcony). It is "uncool" to sing hymns, and only older people carry Bibles.

Not every teenager experiences this time of "turnoff," and one would hardly recommend that those who seem to be missing out pray for it to happen to them. Youth leaders and parents should be aware that if it does surface, it is a stage (hopefully a brief one), and to overreact is "overkill." It should also be remembered that the spiritual experience of the early period doesn't usually die. Rather, it goes underground and, if nurtured, will surface a little later when the young person gains more self-confidence.

Toward the end of the teenage years, in the late adolescent period, youth are likely to examine critically the belief structure of their parents and the church. They may question the existence of God, the validity of recommended standards of behavior, or the relevance of certain doctrines of the church. In this review and assessment time, two critical areas of development take place: a review of the individual's personal systems of belief and moral values. The direction of life is determined. This, of course, does not mean that either of these factors is set in concrete, but societal expectations and internal psychological pressures drive the late adolescent to make decisions in these areas at this time.

Later, young adults who have successfully passed through this stage become faithful supporters of the church, offering their time, energy, and means to assist in the running of the church.[9]

There is little doubt that the adolescent period is a most critical stage of development. During these years families and the church must, therefore, assume the heavy responsibility of nurturing the youth in such a way that they will emerge from adolescence with a mature faith and relationship with Jesus. A separate and distinctive style of church ministry is usually necessary if this is to happen. This should take the form of a balanced youth ministry plan that includes the four basic elements of worship, nurture, fellowship, and mission.

Areas of Adolescent Development

Physical Development

Puberty heralds the release of a whole range of hormones that radically change the young person. Physically, he/she is now moving into adulthood and experiences rapid growth spurts. Muscles and bones do not always grow at the same pace, and hence, many adolescent boys have trouble with coordination and often look and feel awkward. This is not so obvious in girls. The change in body shape brings with it a new self-awareness, and young persons can be very sensitive about how they look and concerned about whether or not they are normal. This concern can sometimes turn to anxiety, especially if the youth perceives that these changes are occurring before or after the rest of his/her peer group. It must be remembered that there is a wide variety within age groups, and every child is different. The hormonal changes can also bring a change in the skin, and acne is something that many young people are very sensitive about.

With the release of the sex hormones, the adolescent becomes increasingly more aware of his/her sexuality and often acutely aware of the opposite sex. The early teen often seems to dwell on sex, and this is a time when many learn and tell dirty jokes and use a lot of "double talk."[10]

Adolescents can suffer wild mood changes and often do not know why they react the way they do. Many go through fad stages with food and clothes, and what they liked or enjoyed today they may have no interest in tomorrow. This is a confusing time for the adolescent and can be very irritating for their parents and also their leaders. This is a time when leaders need to be very supportive and understanding.

Emotional Development

Human development can be seen as a series of crises or conflicts that, if successfully resolved, lead to growth and healthy development. Adolescence sees the onset of a crisis of identity. At this stage there is a new sense of self-consciousness. This is the time when the young person starts to break away from the family and traditional ties in an attempt to establish his/her own identity. The stages are not totally clear-cut, and even before identity is satisfactorily established the youth will enter the next crisis period in the search for intimacy. He/she may fail in the attempt to form a special closeness with another human being if still deeply involved in their own search for identity. Hence, they need to be placed in an environment where they are given an opportunity to establish a belief in themselves. Youth ministry also needs to supply occasions for young people to meet prospective life partners.[11]

Cognitive Development

Adolescence marks the onset of the ability to think abstractly. But a significant body of research has shown that almost 50 percent of adults in a Western culture never fully attain the ability to think in this manner. In the context of youth ministry it is significant to note that the application of abstract thinking in relation to religious matters appears to occur later than for some other fields of learning. This is accentuated if the individual does not have an aptitude for religious issues. Rather than an abstract or theoretical approach to learning in matters of faith and religion, we see again that youth ministry should attempt to relate biblical truth and principles to the practical issues, experiences, problems, and needs of the youth.

Moral Development

Since many youth have not achieved the ability to think abstractly, it is unlikely that they will naturally develop the ability to exercise mature moral judgment and develop mature moral values. Therefore, in attempting to influence moral development, youth ministry should avoid forms of communication and programming that consistently depend upon propositional or abstract modes of thinking. In other words, devotional modules, discussion of issues, sermons, prayers, songs, etc., should as often as possible reflect a more concrete thought form and relate biblical concepts to the life situation in which youth exist.

The program content should sensitively encourage youth to face issues and guide them in the decision-making process without making the decision for them. Youth should be led to submission to God and revealed truth, for here is where faith takes root. It is crucial to nurture them so that their mature ideological stance is that which they have thought through and made their own.

Research has shown that significant changes in the level of commitment to a system of moral values occurred during the sixties. This relativism, which characterizes current attitudes to ethics and morality, poses a threat to the "automatic" adoption of religious values by adolescents. However, it does allow, and in fact should provide, a stimulus for a new focus in religious education and youth ministry in which there is a distinct attempt to be practical and relevant.

Faith Development

The noted psychologist Erik Erikson suggests that ideology is the "guardian of identity." That is to say, a belief system is the guide that helps the developing adolescent shape his or her life. "Without some ideological commitment, however implicit in a 'way of life,' youth suffers confusion of values." The Christian religion offers a way of life in which ideological commitment is paramount. It is the perfect vehicle to assist the young person shape his or her life.

V. Bailey Gillespie, a Christian psychologist, emphasizes the close relationship between identity formation and religion: "Religion tells man who he is—a child of God; what he is—one in need of saving; where he belongs—in the family of God; how to belong—through commitment to God; how to relate to others—in loving, caring responses; and what man's future is—identity with God."[12] In the movement toward maturity, adolescence is the optimum age for identity formation; it is also the optimum age for the development of a belief system and for the adoption of a personal set of values; it is the stage of faith in which an individual sees deep meaning behind faith issues.

John Westerhoff III has identified the adolescent period as the time when the faith and value system of the parents is questioned and when youth begin to own their own faith.[13] He sees faith developing much like the growth rings in a tree. The earliest stage he calls experienced faith. This is where the child experiences God through their parents or other caregivers. The adult stands in the place of God and gives a picture of Him, faulty though that may be. The second growth ring is seen in affiliate faith. This is where the young person, usually around the age of 10-12, has an urge—even a drive—to belong, to affiliate. It is significant that more young people seek baptism in their twelfth year than at any other time. Many pastors, knowing this, will say, "Sally, your friend is going to be baptized. How would you like to join her?" And more often then not, the answer will be positive.

It is in the middle adolescent years that youth move into the next growth ring, or what Westerhoff would call *searching faith.* This is the period of their lives when they are trying on a number of new identities and are prepared to question whether or not the parents' belief system works for them. If the youth leader or parent is supportive and helps the young person discover answers, then the chances are that the youth will progress to what Westerhoff sees as the final stage or growth ring, and that is *owned faith.* It is the role of youth leaders to support and guide through the difficult years when identity is being formed and faith tested and tried.

Youth is a critical age in the development of faith. A child accepts literally the beliefs and values of those that they regard as significant. In adolescence there is a tendency to review the meanings of these beliefs and values and attempt to apply them in their widening sphere of experience. Beyond adolescence the individual engages in a critical assessment of these previously held beliefs and values.

Ignoring the faith development stages of youth, which can be a creative age, may well result in alienation. If youthful creativity encounters resentment because it appears to challenge the traditional view, youth will often regard it as suppression of personal identity and individuality. The most natural consequence of this is counterconversion and negative identity reaction.

If youth ministry is to be successful for those in these transitional stages, it must provide a sheltered environment for discussion of these issues and must provide an intergenerational context for faith building. James Fowler has been applauded for his work in the area of faith development, and although space will not permit us to discuss his work in depth, we should include a summary of the stages that he says most often coincide with adolescence.

Fowler has given titles to his stages, which in and of themselves have little or no meaning to the laymen. Stage three is the *synthetic-conventional*. It's during this stage that the adolescent has a greater insight and experience of the larger world beyond himself and his immediate surroundings. His/her faith at this time plays a meaningful role in helping the individual relate and interpret a more complex spectrum of people and ideas. It provides a basis for identity and outlook, and faith is in the process of synthesizing values and information.

Fowler tells us that faith during the adolescent period is still basically "unowned," as adolescents continue to look to significant others and still have the tendency to conform to their views of God and the world. He asserts: "Values, commitments, and relationships are seen as central to identity and worth, at a time when worth is heavily keyed to the approval and affirmation of significant others."[14] The individual does not yet have a secure hold on his or her identity or confidence in personal judgment to the place where they can construct and maintain an independent view. Fowler sees this sort of activity taking place in stage four, which he calls individuating-reflexive.

In Fowler's view it's not until toward the end of adolescence that a young person comes to the place where they seriously begin to look at concepts of the world, that they begin to consider a commitment to a lifestyle, a belief system, that will affect their attitudes and behaviors. The strength that is beginning to emerge toward the end of adolescence involves a capacity for reflecting on their own identity—who they are, where they stand in the scheme of things, where they are heading, and their world view in relation to others and to God. It's at this time that they begin to individuate or form perspectives that are truly internalized and made their own.

Adolescent Developmental Tasks

As a child approaches adulthood, a number of developments will occur. Social scientists call these developmental tasks. A balanced adult will have successfully dealt with each of these tasks. A representative list of these includes the following:

- achieving new and more mature relations with age-mates of both sexes
- achieving a masculine or feminine social role
- accepting one's physique and using the body more effectively
- achieving emotional independence of parents and other adults
- achieving assurance of economic independence
- selecting and preparing for an occupation
- preparing for marriage and family life
- developing intellectual skills and concepts necessary for civic competence

- desiring and achieving socially responsible behavior
- acquiring a set of values and an ethical system as a guide to behavior[15]

Each of these developmental tasks forms a part of the basic task of identity formation (who I am and what I am going to do, what I am going to behave like, and who or what will I believe in). Though all of this may appear rather theoretical, it is important to understand, for now we can more easily show how faith and religion should play a significant role in identity formation, which we have said is the primary developmental task of adolescents.

STAGES OF DEVELOPMENT

AGE	SOCIO-EMOTIONAL (Erikson)	COGNITIVE (Piaget)	MORAL (Kohlberg)	FAITH (Fowler)	FAITH (Westerhoff)
0-1	Trust Versus Mistrust	Sensorimotor			
2-3	Autonomy Versus Shame/Doubt	Preoperational (Preconceptual)	Punishment and Obedience Orientation		Experienced Faith
4-6	Initiative Versus Guilt	(Intuitive)		Intuitive-Projective	
7-11	Industry Versus Inferiority	Concrete Operations	Instrumental Relativist Orientation	Mythic-Literal	Affiliate Faith
12-18	Identity Versus Role Confusion	Formal Operations	Interpersonal Concordance Orientation (good boy/nice girl) Law and Order Orientation	Synthetic-Conventional	Searching Faith
18-30	Intimacy Versus Isolation		Social Contract Legalistic Orientation	Individuating-Reflexive-Conjunctive	Owned Faith
30-50	Generativity Versus Stagnation		Universal Ethical Principles Orientation	Universalizing	
50+	Ego Integrity Versus Despair				

Characteristics of Adolescents

	INTELLECTUAL	EMOTIONAL	PHYSICAL	SOCIAL	SPIRITUAL
9-11 YEARS OLD	• They're concrete thinkers, leaders — should use nonsymbolic objects. • They think in terms of facts, not feelings. • They're in the golden age of memorization power.	• They like nonmushy touching. • They enjoy obvious, concrete humor.	• They're energetic and active. • They express awareness of sexuality with dirty jokes.	• They like competition, team games, clubs, and "mysterious" activities. • They express affection through attention, both positive and negative. • They're eager to please whomever they're with. • They don't have a strong internal sense of right and wrong.	• They want Christian heroes to look up to. • They make spiritual decisions based on facts only.
12-14 YEARS OLD	• They enjoy nonverbal creative expression. • Their verbal skills aren't fully developed. • They need structure and limits; they can't handle too many choices. • They have an odd sense of humor. • They like to explore what's funny.	• They have mood swings. • They need successful experiences and achievements. • They hibernate in self-preoccupation.	• They experience rapid, uneven growth. • They are self-conscious about appearance and have ravenous appetites. • They enjoy vigorous activity but sometimes are lethargic. • They express confusion over sexuality with false bragging and conversations about sex.	• They test authority but still want it. • They need to belong to a group to help to define who they are.	• They're ready for more personal faith. • They look for meaning in Bible stories, and can identify with Bible characters.
15-17 YEARS OLD	• They organize, evaluate, and make choices. • They have verbal skills and talk well in small groups. • They want to use their talents, creativity, and imagination. • They're curious. They want to know who, why. • They enjoy oddball ideas. • They look for recognition.	• They're independent and don't want to always "do what they are told." • They may be intense with emotional outbursts. • They want acceptance, so they adopt the hairstyles, dress, and habits of friends. • They're forming personal identity and may try on new identities or values to see how they feel.	• They're curious about sex, especially pornography and masturbation. • They experience rapid physical growth, ravenous hunger, and exhaustion.	• They're more independent. • They want more freedom. • They want to share themselves and develop friendships. • They're loyal — even to unusual friends. • They need to practice Christian principles in a nonthreatening atmosphere.	• They branch out and serve on their own. • They can apply skills learned in Bible study. • They're defining their beliefs and convictions.
18-25 YEARS OLD	• They're interested in social issues. • They want to develop knowledge and skills. • They're making initial career choices. • They're becoming more expressive, more open to newness. • They think more deeply, clarifying their beliefs.	• They want intimacy with others. • They're more expressive in relationships.	• They're looking for their sexual identity. • They want to adopt sexual values that reflect their value system.	• They want autonomy. • They've moved from dependence to independence, but they're still interdependent. • They make friends with different types of people. • They want to learn about romantic commitments: "When should I marry? What can I do to become a successful spouse?"	• They're developing and implementing values and sorting out values they've been exposed to. • They're learning how to use leisure time in light of their values.

Youth Needs

In discussing the needs of youth, needs that arise because of the special set of circumstances that they find themselves in, we should recognize that needs assessment and meeting those needs is a complex matter. Consider the following:

- Needs change from year to year and from place to place.
- Needs may be conflicting.
- Needs may arise from external or internal pressures.
- Needs may be impossible to meet fully.
- Needs may be temporary or permanent.
- Needs may be imagined or real.[16]

Youth Problems

As adolescents face the business of living there are a variety of experiences and situations that confront them. Somehow they must cope with these if they are to be equipped to move successfully into adulthood and independence.

- school
- interpersonal relationships
- maturation expectations
- emotional highs and lows
- work and marriage options
- sport and recreational choices
- acceptance of personal health and appearance
- ethical and moral problems
- religion
- family life
- personal habits
- finances[17]

This list of items is interesting because it is a summary of the responses to a survey of adolescent problems. They are shown here in order of descending importance as adolescents view them. It is significant that career and interpersonal relationship matters are more intense types of problems than ethical, moral, religious, family life, or personal behavior concerns.

Youth ministry should relate directly to the major problem areas or it will be viewed as irrelevant to youth. This should be done by showing how one can cope with these problems better as a young Christian. Faith and religion should be shown to relate to the major specific problems that adolescents face.

Building a Ministry to Meet Contemporary Youth Attitudes

In shaping a pattern of ministry that is suited to today's youth, consideration of typical youth attitudes is important.

Flexibility. Youth will respond to that which appeals without the cluttering effect of traditional hang-ups.

Creativity. Youth of this generation particularly appreciate and respond to the creative—a consequence of being second-generation "TV kids."

Impatience. Youth tend to be impatient with what appears to them to be irrelevant and obsolete.

Intolerance. Youth tend to be intolerant when issues have a negative impact on them. In the area of religion, youth appear to withdraw rather than do battle with authorities, ie., they will leave the church because of harsh criticism, hypocrisy, perceived irrelevancies, etc.

Idealism. Youth are typically idealistic and are particularly perceptive when inadequacies or irrelevancies exist, or hypocritical attitudes are persistently held.[18]

Youth Ministry—A Special Ministry

In the church family, all have needs, but we must recognize that because of the transitional stage that youth are passing through, they are most vulnerable to societal pressure, which they are often ill-equipped to handle. To assist our precious youth through this period we should do all that is possible through the union of divine and human agencies. Ellen White sums up a basic approach to youth ministry when she said that "in our work for the youth, we must meet them where they are, if we would help them."[19]

A young person, writing of the effort of older members of the church to operate an effective ministry to youth, said that "older people should not attempt to take the youth to where they are, nor go with them to where the youth are, but to move in faith to a place where neither have yet been."

In view of all that we have said regarding a special ministry for youth, it should be characterized by a leadership style, program format, content, and approach that provides the following:

- fellowship
- lifting of spirits
- sense of participation/involvement
- a sense of enjoyment
- change/variety
- relevant religion so that youth are able to:
  - (a) gain youth-oriented insights into religious beliefs and traditions
  - (b) see and accept the relevance of religious beliefs and traditions
  - (c) understand the relationship between a Christian and the world
  - (d) understand the role and real mission of the church
  - (e) be brought face to face with a realistic representation of God's ideal for humanity
  - (f) be challenged to establish/maintain a relationship with Christ through His Spirit, which brings direction, joy, and genuine peace of mind to the individual's life

Youth is an age of wide horizons and great possibilities. In times past the Holy Spirit has worked marvelously through the lives of committed youth. May our insights into the need for a special youth ministry in twenty-first-century Adventism help to allow that same Spirit to work in and through the youth of our church in our day.

---

[1] Anthony Campolo, "The Youth Culture in Sociological Perspective," *The Complete Book of Youth Ministry,* ed. Warren S. Benson and Mark H. Senter III (Chicago: Moody Press, 1987), p. 37.

[1] R. Julian Hafner, *Marriage and Mental Illness: A Sex Roles Perspective* (New York: The Guildford Press, 1986). Chapter 1, "The Changing Institution of Marriage," gives a good description of the changing family from before the Industrial Revolution through to the twentieth century.

[3] See Mick Farren and Edward Barker, *Watch Out, Kids* (London: Open Gate Books, 1972). This book contains a lot of history on the youth counterculture.

[4] David Breskin, "Dear Mom and Dad," *Rolling Stone,* November 1984.

[5] Mike Yaconelli, lecture notes from Youth Specialties, Australia Conference, 1987.

[6] *Survey in Teenage,* 1986.

[7] Statistics taken from ABC television documentary on Sydney's street kids broadcast in 1990.

[8] Some sections in this chapter are taken from notes supplied by Glenn Roberts in "Why a Special Youth Ministry," *Youth Ministry: Leadership Training Manual,* ed. Alva Barry Gane (Sydney: South Pacific Division of Seventh-day Adventists, 1989).

[9] Adapted from William G. Johnsson, "The Seven Ages of Adventist," *Insight,* July 26, 1983, p. 12. (Johnsson borrowed this idea from William Shakespeare.)

[10] See the section on sex and dating in chapter 33, "Current Social Issues."

[11] James W. Fowler, *Stages of Faith: The Psychology of Human Development and the Quest for Meaning* (Blackburn: Collins Dove, 1987). See Part Two, "Windows on Human Development."

[12] V. Bailey Gillespie, *Religious Conversion and Personal Identity: How and Why People Change* (Birmingham, Ala.: Religious Education Press, 1979), p. 156.

[13] John H. Westerhoff III, *Will Our Children Have Faith?* (East Malvern, Australia: Dove Communications, 1976), pp. 96-99.

[14] James Fowler, in *Faith Development* and Fowler, ed. Craig Dykstra and Sharon Parks (Birmingham, Ala.: Religious Education Press, 1986), p. 29.

[15] R. J. Havighurst, *Human Development and Education* (New York: Longmans, 1953), cited by Elizabeth B. Hurlock in *Adolescent Development* (New York: McGraw-Hill, 1967), p. 7.

[16] Adapted from Jan Johnson, "Kids' Developmental Needs," *Group,* March 1990, pp. 26, 27.

[17] Denham Grierson, David Merrit, Patricia Baker, Margaret Yates, *Discovering the Needs and Interests of Young People* (Melbourne: Joint Board of Christian Education of Australia and New Zealand, 1977), pp. 86, 87.

[18] Lawrence O. Richards, *Youth Ministry* (Grand Rapids: Zondervan, 1985), p. 51.

[19] E. G. White, *Gospel Workers,* p. 209.

CHAPTER 12

Biblical Models
for Youth Ministry

by Trudy J. Morgan-Cole

A S CHRISTIAN YOUTH LEADERS, most of us have probably read dozens, if not hundreds, of books and articles about youth leadership: ideas for youth activities, theories about youth leadership, suggestions on how to motivate youth for service, or how to lead them to Christ. We have attended workshops and seminars on youth leadership; we have discussed our youth ministry with other leaders, teachers, and parents.

As Seventh-day Adventist youth leaders, many of us have also consulted Mrs. White's writings for further guidance on how to lead young people. All these are excellent sources of inspiration, assistance, and ideas. But we do ourselves and our youth a disservice if we ignore the Bible as a source of youth ministry training. If the Bible is really the only rule of faith and practice for the Christian, then it surely must provide guidelines and a model for the Christian youth leader, also.

Though the Bible has little to say specifically on the subject of youth leadership, its pages are filled with examples of how God's people led others, those chronologically younger than themselves or younger in the faith, to follow Him. By studying some of these models we can find valuable guidelines to apply to our work with young people.

Our ultimate example is, of course, Jesus Christ. The leadership He showed to His disciples over His three years with them is a perfect guideline for those of us who seek to make "disciples" of our youth. Along with Jesus' example, this chapter will focus on Elijah's relationship with Elisha, Paul's relationship with Timothy, and Barnabas' relationship with John Mark, to build a model of Christian youth ministry.

Nurture and Mentoring

As we examine how our Bible heroes trained their would-be disciples, one theme emerges clearly and consistently: they spent time together. Building relationships, often referred to as "nurturing" or "mentoring" our youth, is absolutely essential in our youth ministry. Too often we concentrate most of our time and effort on developing impressive programs rather than on building relationships, spending time with our young people, and getting to know them as individuals. But real spiritual growth can only occur in an atmosphere of love and acceptance, and we cannot create that atmosphere with someone we do not know.

When Elijah called Elisha to become his successor as a prophet, Elisha "set out to follow Elijah and became his attendant" (1 Kings 19:21, NIV). From that time until the Lord carried Elijah to heaven in a whirlwind, the two were constant companions; Elisha was able to observe and participate in everything Elijah did. Though the Bible gives us few details about their lives together, we know that by the time Elijah went to heaven, their bond was so close that although Elijah tried three times to leave Elisha behind, Elisha loyally replied, "As surely as the Lord lives and as you live, I will not leave you" (2 Kings 2:2, 4, 6, NIV).

When Elijah was carried off in the chariot of fire, Elisha's parting cry was "My father! My father!" (verse 12, NIV). His bond with his mentor had become as close as that of a father and son, and it was this relationship that had prepared Elisha to ask for, and receive, a double portion of the Holy Spirit power with which Elijah had been blessed.

A similar relationship existed in New Testament times between the apostle Paul and his young convert Timothy, whom Paul refers to as "my true son in the faith" (1 Tim. 1:2, NIV). Their friendship began in Lystra, where Timothy's family lived; from there Paul decided to bring this young man along on his missionary journey (Acts 16:1-4, NIV). As they traveled together, preaching and sharing the challenges and hardships of evangelism, Timothy took Paul as his model for the Christian life. Later, when Paul wrote to the Corinthians, urging them to imitate his own Christian lifestyle, he was able to say, "For this reason I am sending to you Timothy, my son whom I love, who is faithful in the Lord. He will remind you of my way of life in Christ Jesus, which agrees with what I teach everywhere in every church" (1 Cor. 4:17, NIV).

Everyone learns from and imitates those with whom they spend most of their time. Jesus invested huge amounts of time in training His disciples, not only attending religious services and sharing in God's work, but living beside them, eating together, traveling together, going together to social events like the wedding at Cana and the feast at Simon's house. Jesus truly nurtured those 12 men! At times it must have seemed to Him that His mentoring was having little effect; after three years of daily contact with Jesus, the disciples were still quarrelsome and self-seeking.

Youth leaders may be able to relate to this feeling. It may seem that no matter how much quality time we spend with our young people, they still act immature and unchristian. But Jesus had patience; so must we. After Jesus had returned to heaven and his disciples, filled with the Holy Spirit, were fearlessly preaching the gospel despite opposition, observers "were astonished and they took note that these men had been with Jesus" (Acts 4:13, NIV). It took time for Jesus' patient nurture to bear fruit, but in the end, even His enemies could see the results of the time His disciples had spent in His presence.

As we seek to obey His command to make disciples of our youth, we can never overlook the importance of spending time together.

Teaching

Though much of Jesus' time with His disciples was spent in the business of day-to-day living, He did take a great deal of time, over the course of the three years they spent together, directly teaching them about God's kingdom. The disciples, of course, had "front-row seats" for all Jesus' great public presentations—the Sermon on the Mount, the parables, His discourses in the Temple. But in addition to this, His disciples received deeper, more personalized instruction in the time they spent together with Jesus. Many of His recorded statements were for their ears alone.

He took time apart from His public teaching to concentrate on training the disciples; for example, Mark tells us, "They left that place and passed through Galilee. Jesus did not want anyone to know where they were, because he was teaching his disciples" (Mark 9:30, 31, NIV). Often, after He taught the crowds, the disciples came to Him privately for a further explanation of His parables (see Mark 4:10-20, NIV). He used everyday experiences, even their quarrels about who would be greatest in His kingdom, as an opportunity to teach them more about His plan (see Matt. 18:1-9, NIV). When He sent them out to teach and heal in His name, Matthew's Gospel records an entire chapter of instruction He gave them (Matt. 10, NIV). When the disciples asked Jesus to "teach us to pray, just as John taught his disciples" (Luke 11:1, NIV), He gave them what we now know as the Lord's Prayer as a pattern for their own private prayers.

Jesus' method of teaching His disciples should form part of our model for youth leadership. Spending time with our young people is tremendously important, but if in our time together our conversation never rises above the level of trivia, we are not really nurturing. Though young people don't like it when adults constantly "lecture" them, we should be aware of opportunities for teaching that will flow naturally out of our interaction with them.

Like Jesus' public sermons, much of the teaching we do as youth leaders will be in a formal setting through a Sabbath school class, a Sabbath morning sermon or Friday night worship talk, a Bible class or a Pathfinder devotional. But, important as these are, they aren't enough. We must do as Jesus did and use our day-to-day interaction with our youth for further teaching that will enlarge upon what we've taught them in a public setting.

We can use everyday events, even their mistakes (or ours!) to draw lessons about biblical values. And on those rare and special occasions when young people seek us out with a question, as the disciples did with Jesus when they wanted to learn to pray, we must be eager to seize the moment. Never be too busy to talk to a young person who wants to learn more about God. Without pressuring or being pushy, you can look for those moments that provide opportunities to teach.

Paul doubtless did the same with Timothy during their years of traveling and working together. Once Timothy was established in a ministry of his own, Paul's work of teaching him did not stop. He penned the letters of First and Second Timothy to his protégé, filling them with valuable guidelines for a young pastor beginning his ministry. A similar letter to another of Paul's young friends, Titus, is also preserved in the New Testament. Who knows how many other such letters Paul may have written that did not survive to the present time?

Like Paul, we need to take opportunities to instruct our youth, not just as a group but as individuals. As we get to know them, and we recognize the special challenges they face in their Christian life and work, we can offer them the same kind of loving, personalized instruction that Paul gave to Timothy and Titus.

Missions and Service
We must never lose sight of the fact that when we are training Christian youth, our goal

is not merely to see them saved but to see them serve. As soon as our young people accept Jesus, we need to help them move toward sharing His love with others. Even youth who have not yet accepted Jesus as their Savior can grow in their knowledge of Him and become more open to spiritual things by serving others. A teenager who has given his life to the Lord may be ready to start learning how to pray with people and give Bible studies. A teenager who is still skeptical about religion and its role in her life might grow spiritually if she's given an opportunity to help feed homeless people at a city soup kitchen.

"The only way to find God is through service," says Cheri Peters, author of *Up From the Streets* and host of *Teen Pathways.* "Any other way is like trying to learn how to swim through a correspondence course."*

Every one of the biblical models we have looked at in this chapter was primarily a training for service. Elijah took Elisha under his wing, bringing him along as he did the work of a prophet, with the express purpose of training Elisha to take over that work (see 1 Kings 19:16, NIV). Jesus sent His disciples out in pairs to minister very soon after He chose them to be His disciples. His instruction to them was "Preach this message: 'The kingdom of heaven is near.' Heal the sick, raise the dead, cleanse those who have leprosy, drive out demons. Freely you have received, freely give" (Matt. 10:7, 8, NIV). As we help our young people to see that they can "freely receive" God's love and salvation, we should at the same time guide them toward learning to "freely give" to others.

Paul, as we have seen, invited Timothy along as a partner on his missionary journey soon after he met this promising young man. But perhaps an even more inspiring example is that of Paul's former partner, Barnabas, who seized an opportunity Paul missed to help a very *unpromising* young man. Just before Paul met Timothy in Acts 16, we learn that Paul and Barnabas, who had traveled and worked together successfully for a long time, had a "sharp disagreement," so much so that "they parted company" (Acts 15:39, NIV).

Why this sharp disagreement between two committed gospel workers? On an earlier mission trip, Barnabas' young cousin, John Mark, had joined them, but left part way through the voyage, perhaps discouraged with the hardship involved (see Acts 12:25; 13:5, 13, NIV). Sometime later, when Paul and Barnabas returned to Jerusalem, John Mark again wanted to accompany them, "but Paul did not think it wise to take him, because he had deserted them in Pamphylia and had not continued with them in the work" (Acts 15:38, NIV).

Paul's attitude is perhaps understandable and certainly would be shared by many church leaders today: the work they were doing was of vital importance, and anyone who showed as little commitment to it as John Mark had would only slow them down and hinder their efforts. Paul was unwilling to jeopardize his important ministry for the sake of a young man who had already proved unreliable.

But Barnabas' attitude is the one that a youth leader needs to cultivate. Barnabas had earlier risked his own popularity among the apostles to befriend Paul when the believers found it hard to trust the former persecutor-turned-convert. Now he showed that same spirit in standing up to his friend and partner Paul, being willing to "go out on a limb" for John Mark. Though Barnabas knew the risks of taking on a partner who had once proved unreliable, he was willing to give up his own position as half of the Christian church's most successful evangelistic team ever to team up with the young man who needed a second chance.

We may encounter a few Timothies in our careers as youth leaders, but we are likely to meet many more John Marks, young people who try to do God's work but fail, become discouraged, give up, or make mistakes. When they are ready and willing to try again, many adults in the church may not be prepared to trust them. Our call is to be "Barnabas," to take a chance on the young person with the unpromising track record, to give them opportunities to minister even when they have failed in the past. We are to be their greatest cheering section.

John Mark's story has a happy ending. "Barnabas'" faith in him paid off, as will our faith in many of our "slow starters." John Mark succeeded in his career as a missionary and went on to develop a close mentoring relationship not only with Barnabas but also with one of the most influential of the original twelve disciples, Simon Peter. In Peter's First Epistle he sends the believers greetings from "my son Mark" (1 Peter 5:13, NIV). Mark went on to author the Gospel that bears his name, probably the first written account of Jesus' life. Most scholars believe it is based largely on Peter's memories of Jesus, which the older apostle shared with his young friend.

Even Paul was convinced of John Mark's value in later years. He refers to him as a "fellow worker" (Philemon 24, NIV), and in his Second Letter to Timothy, when he is alone in prison and asking Timothy to come to him, Paul adds, "Get Mark and bring him with you, because he is helpful to me in my ministry" (2 Tim. 4:11, NIV). Paul was originally unwilling to give Mark a second chance, but because Barnabas had a more forgiving and encouraging spirit, Paul later discovered a young man who was a valuable asset to his ministry. Each of us should remember to be a "Barnabas" as we train young people for service to the Lord.

Worship and Fellowship

None of the leaders we have looked at—Jesus, Elijah, Paul, Barnabas—trained their disciples in a sterile vacuum, apart from other believers. Each was part of a community of faith, and they took part in corporate worship and fellowship with other believers. Elijah and Elisha went together to visit and, no doubt, to worship with the "[companies] of the prophets" at Bethel and at Jericho (see 2 Kings 2:2-5, NIV).

Jesus, although His teachings and His sacrifice were ultimately rejected by the Jewish leaders of His time, did not separate Himself and His disciples from the Jewish faith. Together Jesus and His followers attended the synagogue on Sabbath, went up to Jerusalem for religious festivals, worshiped in the Temple, and met together to eat the Passover meal. Corporate worship was a regular part of the lives of Jesus and the disciples.

Paul and Barnabas were active members in the early Christian church, and brought their young protégés along with them on their missionary work, planting churches and building up those already begun. Everywhere they went they met with believers on Sabbath, both Jews and Gentile converts, in synagogues, in homes, and on riverbanks. They trained their followers to be part of a community of believers.

In our work as youth leaders, we should not lose sight of the fact that we are a part of the community. Everyone in the church is involved in our youth work, because every church member can influence a young person. And we need to train our young people to be an active part of the worshiping community, not to separate themselves from the church.

Important though corporate worship is, we can see from the models we have looked at that it is not enough in itself. Though we know that Jesus and His disciples attended worship services, very little is said about these occasions in the Gospels, compared with the time Jesus spent nurturing His disciples, teaching them, and training them for service. Too often we as youth leaders think that if we succeed in getting our youth to attend church services regularly and plan good worship experiences for them, our work is done.

But the biblical model shows us that youth leadership is so much more than that. We "make disciples" not just by planning exciting youth services that all our young people attend, but by spending time getting to know our youth and becoming their friends. Discipleship is built out of a relationship in which we are able to teach and to train the young people who have become our friends.

---

* Interview with Céleste perrino Walker, Oshkosh, Wisconsin, for *Pathfinder Today,* Aug. 12, 1999.

CHAPTER 13

Religious Education in Youth Ministry

Udo Worschech

RELIGIOUS EDUCATION IN YOUTH ministry today faces many challenges for dedicated teachers in that field and also for those who feel commissioned to reflect a Christian attitude while teaching nontheological subjects. Since adolescence does not stop when young people leave school, and since religious convictions are, hopefully, carried into adult life, it is necessary to lay a solid foundation for Christian convictions during both the early and later school years. While endeavoring to do that, the teacher is confronted with a secular environment; when not in school, the youngster is either at home or on the streets with his friends, who may not share his ideals or those held by his parents. This complex situation is difficult to deal with. The following observations and suggestions are meant to help those involved in youth ministry to find ways to adapt to the various and dynamic aspects of youth education today.

Youth as Individuals

There is usually a noticeable gap between the religious socialization of young people and the subjective construction of their own personal religious biography. Their religious behavior may not always correspond to their inner subjective religious convictions, which are beyond dogmatic considerations. Religion is not necessarily expressed by outward actions (i.e., churchgoing) but may find expression in a unconventional and nonliturgical context.

For this reason it is the challenging task of the religious educator not to label this behavior as secular but rather to *sense* the religious mind in the individual expression. Further, it is important to *acknowledge* this behavior as an expression of the religious biography of the youth with regard to age, maturity, and social relations. It is therefore necessary to *allow room* for this religious expression and to *guide* and *accompany* the youth on their way to spiritual maturity.

Another area that involves careful guidance is the challenge for young people and adults alike to find their way in the religious diversity of today. Here the religious educator has the responsibility to educate and help the youth to develop and strengthen the mind to examine and judge critically religious ideas. It is helpful for the youth to be informed about the origins, contents, and results of the diversity that religion offers. Since we talk about the individual at this point, it is important that the teacher not only point to the church teachings or to social expectations in order to find answers, but also consider the individual mind and convictions of the pupil, and find ways and criteria for the students to react to and answer questionable religious movements. The Christian goal must be to help the young find meaning in Christian values in ethics and beliefs and Christian lifestyle.

The individual's religious socialization while still an adolescent presents another challenge to the religious educator. The early steps of child and adolescent development carry the chances of laying the basis for religious and, thus, Christian values well beyond later childhood. Many adults lost their religious socialization in early adulthood. This is because faith and religion are generally linked with one's childhood and early adolescence, and is usually not regarded as necessary and helpful in adult life. Here religious education in youth ministry meets its greatest challenge: helping the young people to move from a simple childhood faith to a critical, and yet positive, adult faith, which is meaningful for one's own religious needs and also mediates Christian values for everyday-life situations.

Finally, it is to be recognized by the religious educator that the young person is usually regarded by society as an "object" without autonomy. This is actually the reason for the conflict between the ages. Childhood and adolescence represent life at an early stage in which the definition of life goals are not clear—the young appear to be socially not important. However, Christian values must overcome the generation gap, because the child and the young adult is seeking guidance that only the mature adult can give.

This presupposes, however, that the adult has Christian values of his own and acts responsibly with the young people. Hence, religious education in youth ministry must always consider the parents of the ones to be educated as part of the educational process. First and foremost, it is necessary, therefore, to consider the young people as individual subjects with their own biography, which must be carefully shaped in order to live out Christian values.

Illustrative Application. The story to contemplate is found in Mark 10:13-16, where Jesus takes the side of the children, to whom belongs "the kingdom of God" (NIV). The acceptance of the children without any knowledge on their part of dogmatics and ethical foundations indicates that Christ is receiving man on the basis of openness and trust in Him. While the disciples regarded the children as too immature to have contact and understanding for the Rabbi's teachings and ways of life, Jesus accepts them as they are and the way they see and interpret their lives. Accepting the youths and meeting them on their own grounds is the secret of successful religious education.

Youth in Society

The most important task in presenting religious convictions to the young people is to outline and interpret religion as relevant for, and in, society and the public. If young individuals have accepted religion for themselves as an important concept for their personal lives, the great danger is that they might lose this conviction because it does not seem necessary or plausible in their public and everyday lives.

The fact is that almost all areas of society do function without any kind of cooperation with religious or church institutions or the consideration of traditional virtues. From this, one may also conclude that personal religious convictions or the finding of meaning for one's own life is irrelevant and superfluous. It becomes increasingly important in religious education, therefore, to help the youth not only to see the value of religious convictions for their own lives but also for and in society, without hiding one's own convictions.

Another aspect with which the educator is confronted is the fact that in a pluralistic society individual convictions are generally accepted, but it is increasingly difficult to have religion communicated to those who need to be reached. If there is no communication about religion anymore, religious convictions become a mere matter of one's own privacy and are taken out of the perspective of society. Religion becomes a taboo.

Psychology and sociology agree in demanding that in the transition from childhood to adolescence and adulthood ideals, values and virtues that help to make possible the peaceful relationship of people in society need to be acquired and developed. Here the church has great responsibilities in conveying her ethical values and laying the foundations for virtues furthering living and working together in society. The task is the transmission of ethical values and the education in virtues in order to help the youth to find a basic orientation in society and realize the importance their Christian values have in shaping a peaceful and tolerant society.

The protests of the youth against the establishment is, as far as society is concerned, a cue for acts of violence and destruction of common values. For the youth, however, the protests are the articulation of rightful requests and matters (i.e., peace movement, ecology), which actually also express the concern of society. One may want to call it a "prophetic" matter, since the protests are diagnostic of present-day shortcomings that exist on various levels in society, the church, and everyday life. And like the prophet, the youth are convinced that they have to expose these shortcomings. For the Christian educator the challenge lies in the task of making himself an advocate of the youth's concern and at the same time leading the youth to realize that there is a Christian answer to the problem. It is important to see that the generation gap must also be closed by taking the concerns of the youth seriously.

Illustrative Application. Again, the example of dealing with others is Christ's dealings with His disciples. The society in His day was as diverse and pluralistic as today, if not even more pluralistic than we want to admit. Religious movements all concentrated in Palestine, which had become a melting pot of Mediterranean and Oriental religions. Judaism was itself divided into many sects with various expectations, hopes, and convictions. It is remarkable that Christ does not get involved in any basic theological discussions but is always pointing to and developing ethical and moral issues. Even on the Mount of Blessing He does not try to convict people of His understanding of Judaism but presents an extensive account of Christian values that were to shape society and have influenced society ever since (see Matt. 5). It is noteworthy that even people from different nations seemed to agree to this presentation of His values.

It is a challenging task of the Christian educator to study and apply Christ's values to the educational principles of today. Christian principles as outlined in the Sermon on the Mount need to be applied in the education of the child and the youth, not as adhering strictly to some abstract values but as part of the individual's religious biography the parents and the educator share with the young adult. The basic idea must be to make Christian values plausible to the youth as a meaningful way of life. This includes the definition of a Christian concept of humanity and a Christian definition of human dignity. The prophets' and Christ's critique of society, whether religious or profane, was always from the standpoint of the revealed will of God. The love of God to humans and humans' love for others is the basic principle from whence any kind of social and religious criticism of society and the individual must begin: the "golden rule" is the Heaven-assigned way of educating the youth to find their Christian way in society.

Youth in the Church

The relationship of Adventist youth to their church is in most cases not problematic when compared with the situation of the larger state-related churches. However, the reservation that some have against the church is not unimportant to consider here. For the Christian educator it is of great help to realize that at a certain age youths may dissociate themselves from the church because they are parting from the faith of their childhood. However, this should not lead the educator to give up on the youth, but rather to see this reservation as an expression of their entry into adulthood and to religious autonomy. The question now is What does the church have to offer to the young adult? If the above-mentioned foundation has been laid, there is a good chance that the youth will continue in the ways of their religious convictions. In any case, during this transitional stage it is not a problem of the youth but rather of the church if it is not aware of the needs of the young adult.

When young adults leave their families and enter the world in which they have to live and establish themselves, they find themselves confronted with a modem society character-ized by pluralism and a great complexity of life. If even older adults need help in this soci-ety more so do the young people. It is of utmost importance for the Christian church to find its position in the horizon of the religious pluralism of today. This has to be done in such a manner that young adults find a plausible position for their church and in their church. It is therefore also of vital importance for the Adventist Church to have interconfessional dialogue with other churches; otherwise her own position will become more and more meaningless for the youth.

Finally, while the world and society are constantly changing, the church is, for the youth—and not only for them—a homestead where to return is to seek peace with God and humanity. At the same time, the church, the pastor, and the educator have to ask themselves in what way the spiritual and religious food the church is offering applies to the needs of the youth themselves, who are part of a pluralistic society, working in it and establishing them-selves there. Here lies the greatest challenge of the educator, the pastor, and the church: to be and to serve as a center of calming influence and yet be modem enough to answer sensibly to the needs of today's youth.

Illustrative Application. The biblical record of the dealings of God with humanity pre-sents a colorful picture of an Israelite society in constant change under the influence of for-eign nations and right-and-wrong prophets in Israel. A detailed study of the Old Testament will show that the messages of the prophets set different accents at different times, but always answered to the needs of the people. God's love is so immense that He will bless and protect the liar and betrayer Jacob on his flight to Haran (see Gen. 28). But He will also ask for con-version, which Jacob experienced decades later (Gen. 32). God's history of dealing with people is not always straightforward; rather, there are bends, disruptions, and one-way streets. And yet He is overruling humanity's efforts. When dealing with the salvation of the youths, one has to keep in mind that a life span may pass before a person responds to the love of God. It is the responsibility and the challenge of the Christian educator to seek ways and means to answer to the needs of today's youth and to lay the foundation for the continuous working of the Holy Spirit on the mind and the heart of the young people.

SECTION 3

Effective Tools for Youth Ministry

CHAPTER 14

Youth Inreach

by Neil Thompson

THE GROWTH PATTERN OF THE Christian can be expressed in two distinct directions: inreach and outreach. The word "inreach" is not used as often as "outreach." However, its meaning becomes clearer when it is considered in contrast to outreach. Outreach generally denotes evangelism—the act of reaching out to others with the goods news of salvation. It implies service on behalf of those who have not responded to the divine invitation.

Inreach, on the other hand, depicts an "inner" experience in the life of the believer; in other words, a personal growth or development process. This connotes allowing God to "touch" your life and prepare you for salvation. Inreach involves the work of nurturing the individual believer to grow spiritually in the faith.

Youth inreach could be understood as the act of leading young people into full commitment to Jesus Christ. It is stimulating our youth to develop their full potential. It also provides a means of holding the youth in the church. In short, youth inreach focuses on strengthening the faith of the young people in the church based on their relationship with Jesus Christ. The apostle Paul summarized it all as "Christ in you, the hope of glory" (Col. 1:27).

Purpose of Inreach

Youth inreach is essential for the survival of the young believer in the church. It provides opportunities for growth and development. The purpose of youth inreach may be considered as follows:

1. **Assurance of Salvation.** As enshrined in our mission statement, the main objective of our ministry is the salvation of our young people. Young people may be drawn into the church through various avenues, including family ties and parental influence. Yet if they are not helped to focus their attention on Jesus Christ, "the author and finisher of our faith" (Heb. 12:2), and His assurance of salvation, they could be disappointed or discouraged or even misled by what they see and hear within and outside church circles.

2. **Help Youth Discover Their Self-worth.** Youth is a critical time of searching for self-identity. Questions such as "Who am I?" "Am I loved?" "Can I make it?" and "Am I needed?" are commonly asked at this age. Answers to such questions can be self-discovered when there are inreach programs and activities in the church conducted by these very young people. The youth must be helped to see themselves as Christ sees and loves them, so much as to die on the cross of Calvary on their behalf (John 3:16). Youth inreach can awaken and enlighten each youth's concept of his or her personality.

3. Opportunity for Nurturing. Youth inreach programs and activities offer great opportunities for the nurturing of the young Christian. As young people plan, organize, and conduct inreach programs, they cultivate interest in church-oriented activities that they might have ignored. Through such programs they learn to be disciplined disciples of Jesus Christ, making their faith stronger, their love greater, and their hope surer in the service and promises of Christ.

4. Sustain a Revival. Whenever there is spiritual reawakening among believers, there is always a need to sustain that renewed interest with soul-inspiring inreach programs that will enhance a personal and practical relationship with the Master.

5. Teach Standards of Christian Living. In these times of vigorous evangelism, many young people enter the church from different cultural and social backgrounds with opinions and ideas that may be inimical to Christianity. These persons must be taught how to live a victorious Christian life, how to surrender one's views and position to that of Christ. They must know what the Lord expects of them and how they can fulfill that expectation in spite of their shortcomings. Such training and direction come alike through inreach activities.

6. Counteract External Attractions. Young people everywhere are easily attracted to the things they often see and hear, such as negative peer-group activities, indecent mass media presentations, and popular fads and fashions. We need to help them focus their attention on things of eternal value rather than mundane ones. When there are well-planned, thought-provoking inreach programs in the church, the influence of such distractions will be minimized.

7. Empower Youth for Leadership. In recent times youth empowerment has become a social demand. Many young people feel they are not being used by the church and their energies are underutilized. When they are involved in inreach activities, they become sensitized and groomed for leadership in both the church and the community. Young people must not be made to see themselves as observers of today and leaders of tomorrow, since tomorrow begins at sundown today.

8. Unearth Talents. By way of exposure, youth inreach provides opportunity for dormant or hidden talents to be activated or unearthed. Through their participation in such activities, they gradually discover their capabilities, interests, and hidden potentials. These discoveries help them serve God better.

9. Keep Church on Track. Setting the objectives of the youth organization on the church, the Spirit of Prophecy identifies one of the objectives as to assist "those who profess to be Sabbath keepers."[1] In the church there are some who merely profess but do not practice the faith. Much as the youth need the church, the church, as well, needs the youth to inject life and fun into it. It is the responsibility of the youth through their programs to help redirect the attention of the church should it shift from its course because of the pressure on it. For instance, sometimes the focus of the church shifts to programs instead of people, or to the organization instead of God. In such instances the youth should help the church to stay on course.

10. Prepare a People for Heaven. It could be said that the main purpose of youth inreach programs and activities is to help young people to know and serve God. To prepare a people ready for the risen and returning Lord—a people ready for heaven. This should be the ultimate goal of all programs, not only of the youth department but the entire church.

Inreach Provides Affirmation

Many people yearn for affirmation. It costs nothing, is invaluable, and builds relationships and confidence at no cost. Spouses rarely affirm each other, and parents scarcely affirm their children, or vice versa. The absence of affirmation may account for some of the problems in our society. Affirmation gives a sense of belonging, a sense of need and identity. Youth inreach provides affirmation to many struggling young people in the church. This includes:

1. Affirmation of Divine Love. Despite their conversion, many young Christians are haunted by their past. Perhaps they have not really forgiven themselves and therefore cannot *fully* accept God's forgiveness. They often hesitate to participate in most church activities, but when they are challenged and involved in inreach programs, they suddenly become aware that God can use them. They then experience the love of God in spite of themselves and their past. The feeling of God's acceptance gives the assurance that they are not beyond the reach of God's love.

2. Affirmation of Worth. In every person there is a fundamental human drive to be needed. This drive draws us closer to places where we feel wanted and useful. When young people generate and implement programs to strengthen their faith, they end up enhancing their personal values and affirming their self-worth.

3. Affirmation of Care. Some of the young people in the church today are from broken homes. Others have emerged from homes in which they hardly experience love and care. The effect of these situations places an expectation on the church. As these young people participate in inreach activities, they are assured of the care and love of the church.

4. Affirmation of Hope. The worry of most of our adult membership today is whether the youth can really maintain the principles and standards of this church in the years ahead. However, if the youth of today can conveniently handle programs and activities that will ensure their spiritual growth and development, then we can be assured that they have the capacity to manage and maintain the church tomorrow. The ability of the youth to conduct inreach programs affirms that there is hope for the future.

Inreach Provides Celebration

The word "celebration" means different things to different people. However, youth inreach provides celebration based on the premise of what God has done and is still doing in the lives of our youth. There are many types of youth inreach programs, ranging from personal Bible study to group interactive activities such as youth congresses. However, some common youth inreach programs are:

1. Youth Week of Prayer. It is usually conducted on the last week of the first quarter of every year in churches, schools, and colleges. (The date may vary for schools and colleges so as to fit into the academic program.) The Youth Week of Prayer is normally accompanied by spiritual revival and rebirth. It must therefore be prayerfully planned and presented to ensure great success.

2. Commitment Celebration. "This is a time when the church celebrates the faithfulness of its youth. A time when youth join the church by baptism and participate in a great celebration for the whole church family. A day of commemoration and rededication for baptized young people in the church."[2] Youth Commitment celebration is in June in the Northern

Hemisphere and in September in the Southern Hemisphere.

3. Bible Conference. Bible conferences are special meetings that can be conducted in the form of a retreat and may be held for several days at a camp, or they may be conducted as one-day meetings. The objective of Bible conferences is to get youth to study their Bibles regularly. It is the time when, through Bible study, we can help give answers to our youth. The main purpose is to help youth who are not attending church-operated schools to strengthen their faith. However, youth in Adventist schools should be made welcome.

4. Morning Watch. The Morning Watch is our appointment with our Friend and Savior. As surely as God called Moses to meet Him in the mountain, so He wishes to meet every youth and every youth leader in the secret place of prayer. The Morning Watch period needs to be undisturbed. Jesus gave the first instruction concerning the Morning Watch: "But when you pray, go into your room and shut the door and pray to your Father who is in secret; and your Father who sees in secret will reward you" (Matt. 6:6, RSV).

From the teachings and examples of the Lord Jesus, we learn that there can be three definite parts to the Morning Watch plan: (a) prayer, (b) Bible study, and (c) meditation. Bible study is the practical link in the Morning Watch. Without it, prayer may become formal and meditation may drift into vague dreaming. It is also good during the Morning Watch period to memorize the text for the day or another portion of scripture.

5. Prayer Groups. The AY Society executive committee of the local church is primarily a prayer group seeking for the power of the Holy Spirit. One of the first messages from the Lord calling for the organization of Adventist young people linked the youth organization with a prayer group: "Cannot you form a band of workers, and have set times to pray together and ask the Lord to give you His grace, and put forth united action?"[3]

A youth organization for the young people of the church, as well as for nonchurch members, is doomed to fail its God-given task unless the young people of that organization are men and women of prayer and "have set times to pray together." The AY Society committee of the church is not like a secular business that may be operated efficiently without reliance on the Lord for guidance and direction in every detail.

6. Bible Reading Plan. Systematically reading the Bible is another devotional feature that dates back to the very beginnings of our youth organization. Names of the plans have changed over the years, but the basic principle of reading the Bible only or reading it along with the Spirit of Prophecy books has remained unchanged. When we remember that "none but those who have fortified the mind with the truths of the Bible will stand through the last great conflict,"[4] we realize the vital importance of this devotional feature.

7. Youth Retreats. Youth retreats are the devotional assembly of youth at a given location in a youth-camp atmosphere. Evolving around a specific theme, youth retreats provide spiritual encounter and revival to a group of young people away from home for a while. It is a response to Christ's invitation "Come ye yourselves apart . . . and rest a while" (Mark 6:31). Being apart with Jesus is always rewarding and refreshing.

8. Youth Day. Youth Day is a Sabbath set apart for the young people of a church. They take charge of all the activities of the day, from Sabbath school session through the divine service until sundown. In some places Youth Day is the last Sabbath of the Youth Week of Prayer. In other places it is scheduled at a time when most of the students are home on vacation for maximum participation. Youth Days can serve as youth baptism days as well. When properly planned, Youth Days can be memorable days for the young people.

9. Youth Profile. Testifying of one's conversion or encounter with Jesus can be challenging and inspiring. When young people testify of their experiences with Christ in the presence of their friends, it goes a long way toward reinforcing their faith and encouraging others. Youth Profile creates a forum during which young people can give testimonies of encounters in their spiritual journey.

---

[1] Ellen G. White, *Christian Service* (Washington, D.C.: General Conference of Seventh-day Adventists, 1947), p. 34.

[2] *Youth Ministry Handbook* (Silver Spring, Md.: General Conference Youth Department).

[3] White, *Christian Service,* p.34.

[4] White, *The Great Controversy,* p. 593.

CHAPTER 15

Youth Outreach

by David M. Parks

WE HAVE ALL SEEN MAGAZINE advertisements featuring an attractive model with a luxuriant growth of hair. These ads suggest that beauty is found in a bottle of shampoo. The ads must be effective, because people spend billions of dollars annually on products and accessories in an attempt to make themselves look more attractive.

Are you concerned about your appearance? Do you want to look good? If you're like the rest of us, I'm sure you do! The prophet Isaiah describes a surefire method to make ourselves attractive so we will be welcomed by others: "How beautiful on the mountains are the feet of those who bring good news, who proclaim peace, who bring good tidings, who proclaim salvation, who say to Zion, 'Your God reigns!'" (Isa. 52:7, NIV).

And it's not just our feet! The people who share God's last message of mercy with their neighbors and friends all have beautiful faces, as well. "Servants of God, with their faces lighted up and shining with holy consecration, will hasten from place to place to proclaim the message from heaven. By thousands of voices, all over the earth, the warning will be given."[1] The key to being attractive and making our message attractive is to remember that it's good news we are sharing—good news for us and good news for others.

Several reasons for the importance of outreach activities by young people are found in the Scriptures.

1. To Spread the Gospel to All the World

The command of Christ to go and make disciples of all nations (Matt. 28:18-20) applies in a special way to the youth in the church. The Lord desires to use the time, talents, and energies of the entire church to spread the gospel, but young people have a special role that no one else can fill. "The Lord has appointed the youth to be His helping hand."[2]

The fresh zeal and courage of young people are crucial to the forwarding of God's work. "Through keen thought and vigorous action they [will] bring glory to Him and salvation to their fellow men."[3]

As Elijah approached the end of his ministry, he was told to anoint Elisha to be his successor as the prophet in Israel. "Then Elijah passed by him and threw his mantle on him. . . . Then he arose and followed Elijah, and became his servant" (1 Kings 19:19-21, NKJV). And when Elijah was translated to heaven in a chariot of fire, a double portion of his spirit fell upon Elisha.

His example has a special lesson for the youth of today. "The standard-bearers are falling, and [the] young . . . must be prepared to take the places left vacant, that the message may still be proclaimed. . . . Those who have youth and strength are to go into the dark places of the earth, to call perishing souls to repentance." [4]

Elisha also worked carefully to train other young men to take up the work of God. "Faithfully, untiringly, throughout his long and effective labors, Elisha endeavored to foster and advance the important educational work carried on by the schools of the prophets. In the providence of God his words of instruction to the earnest groups of young men assembled were confirmed by the deep movings of the Holy Spirit, and at times by other unmistakable evidences of his authority as a servant of Jehovah." [5]

2. To Strengthen and Build Up the Church

The counsel of the apostle Paul to his young associate Timothy was "Let no one despise your youth, but be an example to the believers in word, in conduct, in love, in spirit, in faith, in purity" (1 Tim. 4:12, NKJV). The youth in the church today have this same responsibility. As they exhibit the power of practical Christianity, many around them will be blessed and encouraged. [6]

Paul told Timothy that if he followed this counsel the result would be to "save both yourself and those who hear you" (verse 16, NKJV). The youth have a special influence and can reach hearts that others cannot. God's work suffers when young people refuse to accept this responsibility.

Paul mourned the loss of another of his young associates: "Demas has forsaken me, having loved this present world" (2 Tim. 4:10, NKJV). But he rejoiced that the young man Mark, who also had forsaken him once, had reconsecrated himself to the work of God. He wrote to Timothy, "Get Mark and bring him with you, for he is useful to me for ministry" (verse 11, NKJV).

Jesus also was disappointed with the decision of the rich young ruler when he refused the invitation to work with Christ because he was unwilling to give up the idols in his life. And in so doing he turned his back on the one opportunity for true happiness. "He went away sorrowful: for he had great possessions" (Matt. 19:22).

But when young people are willing to be used by God, amazing things occur. When the Lord set about to establish His last-day church He used youth, for the most part. Ellen White was only 17 when she had her first vision. James White was 21 when he began preaching the Second Advent message. Uriah Smith was also 21 when he joined the editorial staff of the *Advent Review and Sabbath Herald.* To be sure, some of the pioneers were older people, such as Joseph Bates, but mostly the work went forward on the shoulders of the youth.

3. To Represent the Principles of God's Kingdom Before the World

At 17 years of age Joseph was sold by his brothers into slavery in Egypt. Overnight his circumstances changed dramatically. But he determined to be true to his father's God. So when Potiphar's wife tried to coerce him into an adulterous relationship, he declared, "How then can I do this great wickedness, and sin against God?" (Gen. 39:9). He clearly recognized his responsibility to represent the God of heaven. And the Lord blessed his loyalty by elevating him to a position of great authority.

The experience of Daniel was similar in many respects. As a teenager he too was taken as a captive to Babylon. But even as an exile in a foreign land, he decided to be true to the

Creator-God and to follow the principles of well-balanced living he had learned in his God-fearing home. The Lord rewarded his fidelity and that of his companions. "And at the end of ten days their features appeared better and fatter in flesh than all the young men who ate the portion of the king's delicacies" (Dan. 1:15, NKJV).

Eventually Daniel also assumed positions of great responsibility in the governments of both the Babylonian and Medo-Persian empires and was an influence for good on all those around him. Worthy of special notice is his lifelong habit of prayer three times a day.

At one point his enemies used this allegiance to God to get Daniel thrown into a den of lions, but the Lord delivered his faithful servant. The lesson is for us. "Consecrate yourself to God in the morning; make this your very first work. . . . Surrender all your plans to Him, to be carried out or given up as His providence shall indicate."[7]

4. To Strengthen the Youth by Giving Themselves in Service for God

The experience of the apostle John is a good example of the change that occurs in the life of a young person who gives himself or herself to the service of God. Along with Peter, Andrew, and his brother James, John willingly responded to the invitation of Jesus to leave their fishing business on the Sea of Galilee (and even a net full of fish) and become His disciples. Jesus said to them, " 'Do not be afraid. From now on you will catch men.' So when they had brought their boats to land, they forsook all and followed Him" (Luke 5:10, 11, NKJV).

John was the youngest of all the disciples, and a special relationship developed between him and the Savior. But John had a lot to learn before he would be able to fill the role that the Lord intended for him. John was naturally proud, ambitious, and combative; his character needed to be softened and subdued. But as he learned to love Jesus and took Him as the model for his life, he was changed. And eventually some of the Savior's deepest spiritual teachings were communicated to the world through John.

The experience of Jeremiah is another example of personal growth through service. He was just a young man when the Lord called him to deliver the unpopular message of impending doom to the unrepentant nation of Judah. How inadequate he felt! And he nearly decided that he couldn't do the job at all. He said to the Lord, " 'Behold, I cannot speak, for I am a youth. . . . Then the Lord put forth His hand and touched my mouth, and the Lord said to me: 'Behold, I have put My words in your mouth' " (Jer. 1:6-9, NKJV).

So Jeremiah began to deliver God's message, but he was mocked, derided, and finally put in the stocks as a traitor against the nation. And again Jeremiah nearly gave up. "Then I said, 'I will not make mention of Him, nor speak anymore in His name,' But His word was in my heart like a burning fire shut up in my bones; I was weary of holding it back, and I could not" (Jer. 20:9, NKJV). Through adversity and trial Jeremiah was learning that God's biddings are enablings.

5. To Utilize Everyone's Spiritual Gifts

Through the Holy Spirit, Jesus has bestowed gifts on His church. Every member has at least one gift that is to be used for the advancement of God's cause. Paul's counsel to every Christian is "Having then gifts differing according to the grace that is given to us, let us use them" (Rom. 12:6, NKJV).

Certainly young people are included in the group who have useful spiritual gifts. As a mere boy, Samuel was given the gift of prophecy: "So Samuel grew, and the Lord was with him and let none of his words fall to the ground. And all Israel from Dan to Beersheba knew that Samuel had been established as a prophet of the Lord" (1 Sam. 3:19, 20). His spiritual leadership, even as a youth, was a stabilizing factor for God's people, Israel.

The disciple Andrew is another example of a young man who discovered his spiritual gifts and used them. He was younger than Peter and was often in the shadow of his older brother. Undoubtedly his gifts were less spectacular than Peter's. Evidently his talents were for personal work, because nearly every time his name is mentioned in the gospel narrative he is introducing someone to Jesus. He is the one who brought Peter to Jesus (see John 1:40-42). He also brought the lad with the lunch to Jesus which the Savior used to feed 5,000 people (John 6:5-13). He brought the Greeks to Jesus a few days before Calvary (John 12:20-23).

"The Lord has a place for everyone in His great plan. Talents that are not needed are not bestowed. Supposing that the talent is small. God has a place for it, and that one talent, if faithfully used, will do the very work God designs that it should do."[8]

Like Andrew, our gifts may not lead us to positions of prominence. Nevertheless, they are important and will bring glory to God's name if we use them well. Jesus denied the request of the healed demoniac to be one of His band of disciples, but he could do a special work for God, nonetheless. Jesus said to him, "Go home to your friends, and tell them what great things the Lord has done for you, and how He has had compassion on you" (Mark 5:19, NKJV).

That is still good counsel for Christian youth today. "Our confession of His faithfulness is Heaven's chosen agency for revealing Christ to the world. . . . That which will be most effective is the testimony of our own experience."[9]

6. To Reach Other Young People for God Effectively

"There is no other class that can do as much good as young men and young women who are consecrated to God. The youth, if right, could sway a mighty influence."[10]

Young King Josiah of Judah was only 8 years old when he ascended the throne. And in direct contrast to his father, Amon, and his grandfather, Manasseh, he faithfully served the Lord. When he was 26 years old he had a unique experience. As the temple in Jerusalem was being repaired, a long-lost scroll containing the law of God was found and read to the king. He immediately recognized how far Judah had wandered into transgression, and he called a solemn assembly of all the men of Judah to hear the law of God.

Through the influence of the repentant king, many others in Judah, including other young people, were led to renew their dedication to the Lord. This is a courageous example for the youth in the church today. "Never be ashamed of your colors; put them on, unfurl them to the gaze of men and angels."[11]

Certainly it is clear that the youth have a special influence with their peers, for good or evil. A clear biblical example of the latter is the case of King Rehoboam. He rejected the counsel of the elders and listened instead to the advice of the young men who were his contemporaries. However, this counsel was extremely unwise and led to a revolt and ultimately to the divided kingdoms of Israel and Judah. Like all other Christians, the youth must use their influence wisely. Therefore the responsibility of the church is to "educate the youth to help the youth."[12]

7. To Help Finish God's Work

Nearly all the biblical signs of the end of the world have been fulfilled, but one remains. "And this gospel of the kingdom will be preached in all the world as a witness to all the nations, and then the end will come" (Matt. 24:14, NKJV). The Lord designs to use Christian young people to accomplish this task. "And it shall come to pass afterward that I will pour out My Spirit on all flesh; your sons and your daughters shall prophesy, your old men shall dream dreams, your young men shall see visions; and also on My menservants and on My maidservants I will pour out My Spirit in those days" (Joel 2:28, 29, NKJV).

The time has some for the final fulfillment of Joel's prophecy. "With such an army of workers as our youth, rightly trained, might furnish, how soon the message of a crucified, risen, and soon-coming Savior might be carried to the whole world! How soon might the end come—the end of suffering and sorrow and sin!"[13]

It is a daunting challenge. Young people are needed who can face trial, persecution, and death without flinching. As we approach the end of time, the religious persecution depicted in Daniel 3 will be reenacted. The three young Hebrew men refused to worship the king's golden image and were thrown into the furnace of fire, but the Lord protected them from harm.

Courage, my young friends; this is the time to stand up for the Lord! "Now is the time for God's people to show themselves true to principle. When the religion of Christ is most held in contempt, when His law is most despised, then should our zeal be the warmest and our courage and firmness the most unflinching. To stand in defense of truth and righteousness when the majority forsake us, to fight the battles of the Lord when champions are few—this will be our test. At this time we must gather warmth from the coldness of others, courage from their cowardice, and loyalty from their treason."[14]

8. To Bring Praise and Glory to Our Heavenly Father

Most young people today consult only their own pleasure and have forgotten the ways of the Lord. But to the young people of His church, God says, "You are a chosen generation, a royal priesthood, a holy nation, His own special people, that you may proclaim the praises of Him who called you out of darkness into His marvelous light" (1 Peter 2:9, NKJV).

At the end of time the most important issue of all is worship. Will we really bring honor to God's name? When the shepherd boy David brought provisions to his brothers in the army and heard the challenge of the Philistine Goliath, he was indignant. "For who is this uncircumcised Philistine, that he should defy the armies of the living God?" (1 Sam. 17:26, NKJV). His only concern was for the honor of God's name, and because of his faith the Lord wrought a great victory.

One of the most sublime statements in all the Scriptures was uttered by John the Baptist. As a young revivalist John was having great popular success—until he met Jesus. Then he said, "He must increase, but I must decrease" (John 3:30, NKJV). His attitude was, "Let me get out of the way so that all eyes can be fixed on the Savior."

Which brings us finally to the perfect example of youth ministry—Jesus Himself! Even as a boy of 12 he had a clear-eyed vision of His purpose in life. He said to His mother, "Did you not know that I must be about My Father's business?" (Luke 2:49, NKJV).

Throughout His brief sojourn in this world He never lost sight of that purpose. As He came to the close of His ministry He said to His Father, "I have glorified You on the earth. I have finished the work which You have given Me to do" (John 17:4, NKJV). So the young people of today must learn the secrets of soul winning from the Great Teacher. The one essential for success is a knowledge of Christ and His methods for reaching hearts.

As we seek to fulfill the gospel commission and to reach out to others, let's turn our gaze to Jesus. Then "the countenance is changed. Christ abiding in the heart shines out in the faces of those who love Him."[15] Then surely we will fit the apostle Paul's description of God's young people: "that you may become blameless and harmless, children of God without fault in the midst of a crooked and perverse generation, among whom you shine as lights in the world" (Phil. 2:15).

---

[1] E. G. White, *The Great Controversy,* p. 612.

[2] White, *Testimonies,* vol. 7, p. 64.

[3] White, *Gospel Workers,* p. 67.

[4] *Ibid.,* p. 104.

[5] White, *Prophets and Kings* (Mountain View, Calif.: Pacific Press Pub. Assn., 1917), p. 240.

[6] See White, *Messages to Young People,* p. 200.

[7] White, *Steps to Christ* (Mountain View, Calif.: Pacific Press Pub. Assn., 1956), p. 70.

[8] White, *Testimonies,* vol. 9, p .37.

[9] White, *Christian Service,* p. 16.

[10] White, *Messages to Young People,* p. 204.

[11] *Ibid.,* p. 28.

[12] *Ibid.,* p. 203.

[13] White, *Counsels to Parents, Teachers, and Students* (Mountain View, Calif.: Pacific Press Pub. Assn., 1913), p. 555. See also *Messages to Young People,* p. 196.

[14] White, *Testimonies,* vol. 5, p. 136.

[15] White, *Christ's Object Lessons* (Washington, D.C.: Review and Herald Pub. Assn., 1900), p. 102.

CHAPTER 16

Campus Ministries

by Trudy J. Morgan-Cole

WHEN YOU'RE ASKED TO PICTURE "the youth of the church," what springs to your mind? A semicircle of teenagers in a Sabbath school class? Young adults leading worship in church? Pathfinders squealing with excitement at a camporee? All these images are accurate, but they're only a small part of the picture. They're images of youth in church. In reality Seventh-day Adventist young people spend only a small part of their time at church and church-related activities. Most of their "real lives" occur at home, in the neighborhood, and in the place they spend many hours a day for most of the year—school.

That's why it's so vital that our vision of youth ministry not be confined to youth in church. We need to reach the youth of the church in other places if they are to see Christianity as relevant to their whole lives and not just a Sabbath-morning ritual. Campus ministries is the branch of youth ministry that strives to reach young people in their high schools and colleges.

Typically we think of campus ministry as a program offered on a Seventh-day Adventist academy or college campus, under the direction of a campus chaplain, pastor, or Bible teacher. But the campus ministries department on a Seventh-day Adventist campus is only one part of the picture. Many Seventh-day Adventist young people attend public high schools and colleges. A vision of campus ministries that is restricted to Seventh-day Adventist schools excludes thousands of our young people. Secular campus ministry providing support for Adventist students in public school and outreach to non-Adventists is a vital part of youth ministry.

Christianity becomes relevant to young people when they see it working outside the walls of the church in the corridors and classrooms of their schools. That's equally true for students on Adventist and public campuses.

Campus Ministry in Adventist High Schools and Colleges

Virtually every Seventh-day Adventist school offers some programs to meet the spiritual needs of students. In some day academies, this may be limited to Bible classes and an annual Week of Prayer, as teachers may rely on the local church to provide Sabbath schools, socials, and outreach activities. In such situations it's ideal if the local pastor and/or youth leader can cooperate with the school staff, perhaps becoming a volunteer or at least a frequent visitor at the school. In this way, students will see that the school and church are working together to make Jesus real in their daily lives.

Most colleges and boarding academies (as well as many day academies) offer much more extensive campus ministry programs, sometimes in cooperation with a local church. These campuses usually have at least one chaplain or pastor on staff whose role includes coordinating campus ministries activities and providing counseling services to students.

The chaplain usually works with a staff of student leaders to plan the campus ministries program. These student leaders are key to the success of campus ministries. Perhaps even more than in church youth ministry, campus ministry programs will fail if they are imposed from the "top down" so that young people view them as the faculty's concern, not the students'. "Our most effective programs are always the ones that are student-driven," says Traci Sawyer, of the chaplain's office at Columbia Union College. "The students are what make the programs. . . . The faculty and staff only take on a sponsorship role, if that," agrees James Johnson, assistant chaplain at Southern Adventist University.

Although high school-level programs may require more hands-on involvement from faculty because the students are younger, student leadership is just as important in high school ministry as it is at the college level. In the school as in the church, young people need to take ownership of the program in order to feel that it's meaningful to them.

Campus ministries includes programs aimed directly at the student body, such as Sabbath services, dorm worships, chapel programs, Sabbath afternoon activities, praise and testimony services, Weeks of Spiritual Emphasis, and small-group Bible study and prayer groups, which often become popular on campuses after students attend a retreat or prayer conference. Programs such as these can be anything from a token nod at spirituality on campus to a vital, exciting part of student life, depending on the level of involvement and commitment that both student and faculty leaders bring to them.

One disgruntled ex-academy student complains that the school she attended "didn't have a chaplain or any ministries program. . . . Once a year they got some person in for 'spiritual week'. . . where we had to go to a room and listen to that person preach once a day. Which, in my opinion, didn't help any of the students." Another student who transferred from an Adventist academy to a public school and eventually to a self-supporting academy says that in the academy she attended first, "I found it to be a very dead school. . . . I felt spiritually deprived there. . . . They had no programs to reach out to others in the community. . . . They would have their Week of Prayer, and the staff would say that there was a revival, but if there was, nobody ever saw it, or else it was short-lived."

Clearly it's important for Adventist schools not only to make spiritual programs a priority on campus, but to involve students and get their feedback to find out whether these programs are really effective. A "revival" that only the faculty can see isn't a revival at all.

What most students do find rewarding and spiritually enriching is the second branch of campus ministries-outreach programs. The same student who felt her campus was "dead" now enthuses about the self-supporting academy she attends: "On Sabbaths we go out to the community; on Friday we do community service. . . . We go to public schools and do temperance talks, and we go to surrounding SDA churches to revive them. . . . I have found a fulfilled spiritual life."

Sometimes a successful on-campus program can lead directly to outreach, as in the case of the Scripture memory teams started by Dan Vis at Weimar College in 1998. From a small group of a dozen young men committed to memorizing Scripture and applying it to every aspect of their lives, revival spread throughout the campus and into the community—as far as Romania, where some of the team members went to give seminars in Scripture memorization and discipleship.

Active outreach programs are central to the success of campus ministries. Young people generally enjoy getting involved in service and find it meaningful, even if they aren't interested in Sabbath services or Bible study groups. Many Seventh-day Adventist academies and colleges worldwide are running lively, creative outreach programs that include conducting Weeks of Prayer in smaller Adventist schools and worship services in area churches; serving in soup kitchens for the homeless; doing literature evangelism; building and painting houses for low-income families; tutoring underprivileged children; leading out in Pathfinder clubs; visiting nursing homes and prisons; hosting Christmas parties for area children; volunteering at women's and children's shelters; and participating in clown ministries, puppet ministries, and drama ministries. Many campuses make community outreach part of the school program on a regular weekly basis, encouraging as many students as possible to participate.

Lack of participation is often a problem even in successful campus ministry programs. "The one thing that I wish I could change is that there is usually an awesome core group of students getting involved," but the same ones get involved with everything," says James Johnson of Southern Adventist University. "I would like to see a broader cross-section of students get involved." Whether a campus ministries program is large or small, the students who participate are the ones who grow spiritually.

One popular outreach program is the short-term mission trip. Many academies offer a yearly mission trip; some offer more than one. Laurelwood Academy, in Oregon (U.S.A.), offered five different mission trips during the 1998-1999 school year. Students were able to go to the Philippines, Kenya, Arizona, Norway, or Poland to participate in everything from holding evangelistic meetings to building churches. "The group came home on fire for God and changed forever," says one Laurelwood student of the Philippine's mission trip. Though short-term mission projects are extremely popular in North American schools, they are not exclusively a North American phenomenon. For example, students at Sydney Adventist College in Australia travel annually to Fiji for their "Fly and Paint" project, in which they build, repair, and paint classrooms at Navesau Junior Secondary School.

The focus of Seventh-day Adventist youth ministry is to train young people for service to the Lord. This is as true on our school campuses as it is in our churches. We are not here to preach to our students, but to work beside them in doing God's work for the world. When that happens, the gospel will not only be spread to the community, but it will catch fire in the hearts of our young people, too.

The chaplain has a central role in all this—a role that can sometimes be overwhelming. One person can't carry the load of planning religious activities for an entire school and also be available to serve as a counselor and mentor. Student leadership is essential, and so is the involvement of other faculty members. If other teachers in a school are not supportive of campus ministry programs, not only will the programs flounder for lack of leaders, but students will get the message that "religious stuff isn't really that important; it's just the pastor's thing."

This support is crucial, because the chaplain's role goes far beyond just planning worship services and outreach programs. A school chaplain is like any other youth minister in that his or her job is not just to put on programs but to build relationships. Students who know that they can talk to their campus pastor about their problems and relate to him or her as a friend are seeing God's love in human form. Chaplains, like all other youth leaders, have a responsibility to get to know the students in their care, to offer them unconditional love and acceptance, and to model the values and behavior they hope students will develop as growing Christians.

Campus Ministry in Public Schools

The programs described above can be excellent for students in a Seventh-day Adventist school, but what about the thousands who don't attend our schools? Too often Adventist students on public campuses feel like second-class citizens; not only do they not fit in with the lifestyle of their secular campus, but the local church often ignores their needs, sometimes overtly suggesting that they are inferior to students who have chosen an Adventist education.

Public Universities

On the university level many programs are in place to attempt to solve this problem. In 1992, delegates attending the Annual Council of the General Conference voted to implement secular campus ministries programs to meet the needs of the 60,000 Adventist young people attending non-Adventist colleges and universities. Around the world, organizations such as AMICUS (Adventist Ministry to College and University Students), Adventist Christian Fellowship, Campus Advent, Adventist Students Association, and many others are active on public university campuses where Adventist students attend.

A primary goal for secular campus ministries is to provide Seventh-day Adventist students with opportunities for fellowship. When you're attending a public university "sometimes it is rather lonely," says Nathaniel Bardell, who attends Oregon State University. "You sense that there is no one else who shares the same beliefs and morals that you do." University of Colorado at Boulder student Faith Clauson shares her need "to read and study the Scriptures, to hear what others have to say about spiritual issues, and to establish lasting friendships that will extend into heaven." Activities such as Friday night discussion groups, small-group Bible studies, Saturday night socials, and gym nights allow Adventist students on public campuses to get together and meet some of those needs.

Some of these programs are very successful; others struggle. The success of any secular campus ministry program depends on the number and dedication of Adventist students involved, support from faculty (if any), and support from the local church and conference. "This support is crucial, because students themselves have such packed schedules," says Christine Zinner, a student leader of the Campus Advent group at the University of Alberta in Canada. She says that secular campus groups need "financial support, and a part-time church employee who can spend at least half a week as chaplain and codirector of the group on campus."

Paul Krueger, who was actively involved with the Adventist student group while attending the University of California at Berkeley, agrees. "It is imperative that the local SDA conferences get involved with students who are trying to form SDA student groups on their campuses. Indeed, the conference needs to be proactive in this duty (students won't always come to the conference for help). The most important resources the conference can provide are support from clergy and financial support."

But though support from the local church or from Seventh-day Adventist faculty members is crucial to running a successful program with busy college students, student leadership is still vital. "Campus ministries must be student-driven. . . . If it is not, it becomes just another one of the pastor's responsibilities, molded after his/her own ideas. Our ideas are the only ones that will really work," says Faith Clauson. Faith also points out that the Adventist student group at her university "is not as successful as it could be because it is more church-based than campus-based. People from church invite us over and we leave campus for all our activities." Unless a campus ministries program is student-driven and is active on campus, it will not be effective in meeting the needs of the college community.

What are those needs? University students need fellowship and social activities; they need an outlet from the stress of their studies; they need encouragement and friendship; they want to explore serious questions about life, nature, humanity, and God. All these needs provide an opening for Christian students to share their faith with others on campus. Some Adventist students may feel that, compared with large interdenominational groups like Campus Crusade for Christ or University Christian Fellowship, their small Seventh-day Adventist group has little to offer in the way of outreach. "They have so many programs, so much support, so much money," says Faith Clauson. "How could we ever possibly compare?". . . I was intimidated by the other large Christian groups on campus and felt that we really had no place. I created God as small as I felt."

Seventh-day Adventist groups do have a unique role on public campuses, small though their numbers may be. Adventists have a special message, which is just as relevant on a university campus as it is anywhere else in the community. Many Adventist student groups in public universities are involved in outreach programs that include concerts, health fairs, vegetarian restaurants, seminars, and evangelistic series. However, most agree that Adventists on their campus could be doing more to reach out to the unchurched student body. Secular campus ministry is an area of youth ministry that is growing fast in our church. It has tremendous potential, and should be a priority for those involved in youth leadership in the local church.

Public High Schools

If the church is just beginning to meet the needs of students in public universities, it has even further to go to help students in public high schools. In most places, no organized campus ministry exists to reach public high school students. Adventists in public school often feel particularly left out, especially if a majority of youth in their local church attend church school. "Just recently it seems that it is hard for me to go to church," says one Adventist teenager. "I go to a public high school, and the rest of my friends attend the private church school. At times I find that hard, because [church] seems to be more geared to those who went to the private school and had all their verses memorized from classes. I feel excluded."

Local church youth leaders need to be especially sensitive to the needs of public school students. These youth often feel tremendous pressure to take part in activities such as school dances, proms, and Friday night and Sabbath sports, even though these may be against their personal standards. A church youth program that provides lots of social activities will help meet some of these students' needs.

Some churches provide a formal dinner or other social activity for youth who are graduating from public high school. This provides a "prom alternative" for those who feel that attending the school's graduation celebration would violate their beliefs; it also lets public school students know that the church values them and recognizes their accomplishments. Activities such as these will go a long way toward helping Adventist students in public school feel that the church includes them in its youth ministry.

As for outreach in public high schools, we have a huge and almost unentered mission field waiting for us. As with all other forms of campus ministry, strong adult leadership must be balanced with active student involvement. Barry St. Clair and Keith Naylor, writing in the interdenominational journal *YouthWorker,* suggest that youth leaders seeking to start a ministry to public school students adopt Paul's visit to the city of Athens (see Acts 17:16-34) as a model. "Paul observed that environment as he walked around. In the same way, you can walk around and observe your school. . . . Put yourself in situations that give you exposure to the school."[1]

Get to know the school's culture and its students, they suggest, so that you can meet them on their own ground, as Paul did with the Athenians. Just as Paul found the altar to the "Unknown God" in Athens and used it as an opening, youth leaders can learn what public school students" needs are and look for ways to fill them, perhaps by volunteering to help out with a school's sports or music program. "Our goal is to infiltrate the campus with Spirit-filled leaders who can move among the lives of hurting students. We can position ourselves to develop relationships that allow us to introduce Christ."[2]

Whether in high schools or universities, in public or private schools, youth are waiting. Adventist youth are waiting to see their faith become meaningful and relevant. Unchurched youth are waiting for us to reach out to them with the message of Christ's love. Campus ministries is a field of service that no youth worker can ignore.

---

[1] Barry St. Clair and Keith Naylor, "Laying the Groundwork: Preliminaries to Campus Ministry," *YouthWorker,* Summer 1993. Online: www.youthspecialties.com.

[2] *Ibid.*

CHAPTER 17

Youth Evangelism

by Kerry Schafer

EVERY YOUTH LEADER DREAMS of working with a group of young people who are spiritually on fire and constantly growing in faith. Yet many leaders find their youth groups apathetic and spiritually immature. Some young people come to church because of parental pressure, some to visit with friends, a few because they are spiritually thirsty and come seeking God. Sadly, far too many churches have little to offer their own young people and nothing to offer the young people in the world outside.

At the same time, today's young people have an overwhelming need for meaningful religion. As a group, they have grown up with absent parents, their value systems shaped primarily by the media. They are open-minded to a fault; all ideas and beliefs come in shades of gray, and it is difficult for them to believe in and accept absolute truth in any form. They expect to be entertained and are easily bored. Our time-honored systems of religion and evangelism are failing to reach them.

Graeme Codrington, in "Methods of Evangelistic Contact," [1] asserts that it is essential to use a variety of methods to reach young people today. He believes that although it is necessary to proclaim, or teach, the gospel, the act of modeling and explaining the Christian message is much more effective with today's generations. This is really nothing new; it is a method that arose with the very foundation of Christianity.

Ellen White depicts Christ's way of reaching people: "Jesus saw in every soul one to whom must be given the call to His kingdom. He reached the hearts of the people by going among them as one who desired their good. He sought them in the public streets, in private houses, on the boats, in the synagogue, by the shores of the lake, and at the marriage feast. He met them at their daily vocations, and manifested an interest in their secular affairs." [2]

Relational Evangelism

Various forms of relational evangelism have proved to be highly effective with adults and young people alike. Friendship evangelism, small groups, and mentoring are all ways of presenting the love of God to others through the lives of Christians. When those who are seeking God are able to witness how He lives and works in the lives of His people, the desire to have Him in their own lives is deepened. When young people actively take steps to lead others to Christ, the impact on their own spiritual lives is tremendous. Youth groups (and entire churches) have been energized and rejuvenated by youth evangelism for youth and by youth.

The need for relational evangelism does not mean that more traditional methods are no longer important. Proclamation, or preaching the Word, will always be an integral part of evangelism. In recent years, the youth services at a number of churches have taken a new and exciting turn with the creation of weekly services specifically designed for young people. Outreach projects and relational evangelism make contact with people out in the world. The church service provides a place where those seeking Christ can gather to learn more about Him.

Friendship Evangelism

Friendship evangelism is just what the name implies: making friends for Christ. There is a tendency for Christians to associate predominantly with other Christians. Many Christians fear unbelievers, perhaps misunderstanding the biblical command to not be unequally yoked. It is easy to forget that Christ also commanded that we be in the world, not of the world. Befriending somebody who does not know Christ is an opportunity for Christianity in action. As an unbeliever watches the work of Christ in the life of another, they often come to the realization that there is an emptiness in their own life.

There are some essential principles to keep in mind if this type of evangelism is to be a success, however. The friendship must be genuine. Friendship evangelism is not pretending to be a friend to somebody solely for the purpose of converting him. It is effective only when there is a genuine interest in the other individual as an individual. A relationship established solely for the purpose of finding opportunities to discuss religion will almost always be ineffective. In a real friendship there will be many opportunities to discuss Christ without having to resort to pressure tactics of any kind. Questions about lifestyle and values will arise spontaneously, and can be answered when asked. Conversion is the work of the Holy Spirit; the Christian is only the sower of the seed.

Mentoring

A related form of relational evangelism is mentoring. Although this is primarily a way for adults to reach young people, older youth could develop mentoring relationships with younger teens and children. A mentor is somebody older and more experienced who guides and teaches a less-experienced person, or as the *Oxford English Dictionary* puts it, an experienced and trusted advisor. Any mature person with a love for Christ can be a mentor who makes a profound difference in the life of a young person.

Mentoring can be as simple as meeting regularly for a weekly shopping expedition or a chat over lunch. Or it can become as involved as providing support and a positive example to a teen parent struggling with the complexities of raising a child. Many young people are in desperate need of somebody who can model the love of Christ for them. The mentor does not need to (and, in fact, should not) preach. Positive love and acceptance plant seeds that will later reap a rich reward.

Outreach Activities

Many young people are at a stage of spiritual development where they would like to do something to share Christ but are not quite ready to engage in an intensive witnessing experience. There are a wide variety of outreach activities involving more impersonal contact to help them get started.

Random Acts of Kindness

A number of churches have become involved in a project called random acts of kindness. On a given day the entire church or youth group hits the streets of their city in order to engage in helpful activities. These projects vary from traditional activities such as mowing lawns and cleaning windshields, to more unconventional methods, like volunteering to clean gas station restrooms and cleaning up after people's dogs. Other ideas include handing out free soft drinks outside grocery stores or sports events, and offering doughnuts during the morning traffic rush. This is an opportunity to say "We are demonstrating the love of Jesus today" and extend an invitation to visit church.

Some organizations hand out "connection cards" with their services. These are cards explaining that the service is done as an act of love in the name of Christ, and include the address and phone number of the sponsoring church.

Campus Evangelism

Random acts of kindness has also been successfully tailored for use in campus evangelism. Postcards and stamps, photocopying cards, and free pizza on move-in day at the dormitories are ways of letting college and university students know that the church is interested in them and their needs. Other ideas for this population, which could lead to opportunities to chat and develop a relationship, include bicycle fix-up stations, nonalcoholic beverages at parties, and free tutoring.

A number of organizations provide support in creating a campus evangelism program. Campus Crusade for Christ, InterVarsity Christian Fellowship, Baptist Student Union, Fellowship of Christian Athletes, and Navigators all strive to develop Christian groups on secular campuses. Adventist Campus Evangelism ministries can also be expanded to reach out to those who do not know Christ.

Creative Ministries

Young people also tend to be drawn to creative ministries both from the inside as team members and as an audience. Drama and street theater have been used by some groups to present Christianity both in and out of a church setting. Young people with computer skills can put their talents to work to help create Internet websites informing the community about the services and ministries offered by their church. Clown ministries and puppet groups are other great ways to reach a variety of people.

Puppet groups are usually focused on children, where the appeal is obvious. Performances can take place in hospitals, on the street, in schools—the options are many. Children inevitably respond enthusiastically to the visual impact and humor of puppet shows. Somewhat less expectedly, the puppets can be effective in reaching youth also, as Go Tell Productions discovered.

This dedicated group has been operating for eight years now, targeting the issues and concerns of teens. They have performed all over the United States, including at the 1990 General Conference session and on the *Breath of Life* telecast. Their success illustrates the benefits in thinking creatively and creating unique ministries to meet the needs of the community.

Youth-oriented Church Services

In Richland, Washington, a weekly nondenominational youth service called "The River" takes place every Thursday evening. Every week the building is packed with young people of all ages and backgrounds, from the clean-cut girl next door to the young man with multiple body-piercing and blatant tattoos. The message is clear: Jesus Christ has the power to work in your life, and we are here to celebrate Him. Although there is adult leadership, the visible presence on stage is heavily dominated by young people. They celebrate Christ boldly and with contagious enthusiasm. This is not only a place of worship for those who have committed their lives to Christ; it is a place to bring non-Christian friends where they can experience Christ without danger of judgment.

A number of Seventh-day Adventist churches across North America are instituting similar services targeted to reach the youth population. The Thousand Oaks church in California is one of these; their service is called "The Place." A new building was recently opened in which to hold these services, but the building is already full. There are plans to have a larger building ready within the next three years.

The service itself is relaxed and informal. The pastor and the congregation dress casually; suits and ties are definitely not required. The message is presented in a multimedia format, incorporating music and video/movie clips to illustrate points. For example, a recent sermon used a scene from the movie *Patch Adams* to illustrate a point. Pastor Dan Savino does not do all the preaching; in fact, the young people speak at least twice a month. It is an exciting, safe place, where young people can bring friends who are not Christian and expose them to the gospel.

Although the service is innovative, Dan believes that the small-group program is also largely responsible for the enthusiastic spirituality. The groups are called D teams (D is Greek for change) and are composed of around 10 young people per group. The D teams meet for one hour, once a week. The young people share significant things happening in their spiritual lives as well as favorite Bible texts. Then they study a topic related to the upcoming sermon.

Intensive Evangelistic Experience

For spiritually mature young people who desire to be involved in active evangelism there are more spiritually intensive witnessing projects. Monte Torkelson, the associate director of youth ministries in the Oregon Conference, took a group of young people to the 1996 Olympics in Atlanta to pursue one-on-one evangelism. Their agenda was simple: to meet people on the street and bring them to Jesus.

The goal was to strike up a conversation with somebody and bring it around to the question "So why are you here?" The answer: "I am here to tell people about Jesus. Have you heard about Him?" If the walls went up at this point, the young person would back off and drop the subject. However, if the contact expressed an interest in learning more about Jesus, the conversation went on. Many young people had the opportunity to pray with others and lead them to Christ.

Monte believes that this type of witnessing is more difficult for young people to practice locally in the streets of their own city, at the mall, or on a college campus. They are self-conscious and worried about the reputation they will gain if they encounter other young people they know while engaged in witnessing. A trip to another city gives them an opportunity to participate in intensive witnessing with less risk. Although this type of witnessing is a step out of their comfort zone no matter where they do it, it is easier to take the risk in a place where they feel anonymous. If they are successful, their spiritual courage increases and they are more likely to take the greater risk of witnessing to other young people in their immediate environment.

Of course, the drawback to this method is that there can be no follow-through. The prayer is prayed, a recommendation is made to the new Christian to seek out a church and spiritual community, and that is all that can be done. A similar program done locally would allow for follow-up and the development of a relationship.

Northwest Youth Challenge

During the summer of 1999 approximately 2,000 youth across the United States and Canada were involved in the Northwest Youth Challenge. This program also operates during the school year, when anybody who is interested is welcome to be involved. During the summer, however, the program is more intensive, and young people are asked to submit applications before being accepted. They are selected on the basis of several criteria: task commitment, good work ethics, and positive recommendations.

Young people may be involved in three different aspects of the program: Bible studies, magabooks, and Revelation seminars. Group homes are created in target cities with volunteer houseparents. Young people who live elsewhere then have a safe place to stay. On Mondays all of the young people within a particular region worship together as a group, spiritually preparing to share Christ with others. They also study the Bible independently for six hours every week in preparation for the Revelation seminars.

1. Bible Studies. The young people find their own contacts for the Bible studies and Revelation seminars. Some groups follow up on requests to *It Is Written,* or contact people who have subscribed to *Signs of the Times.* Some of the brave conduct door-to-door surveys, asking people if they would like to study the Bible. One of the most effective methods is direct mail, but it is also the most expensive. Children are located by pulling out the names of reading-age, non-SDA children from Vacation Bible School lists.

Although many young people might feel intimidated by the idea of teaching the Bible to somebody else, a specific format makes the Bible study much easier. The program uses Discover Bible lessons to work with adults. For children's Bible studies Good News for Kids, by Marge Grey, is used.

2. Revelation Seminars. Many Revelation seminars involve an impersonal setting such as an auditorium, where the role of the learner is to listen to a sermon by a professional evangelist. These Revelation seminars are different—they are put on exclusively by young people, and bear more resemblance to a group Bible study than the traditional evangelistic meeting. The youth handle the direct-mailing campaign, from creating the list to stuffing the envelopes. They also teach the seminars. They go through the lesson with guests, then follow up with a video presentation, usually by Doug Batchelor.

According to Cindy Tutsch, of the Washington Conference, the program has the effect on young people of changing their priorities from a focus on worldly things to being more connected with God. She also believes that studying the Bible in preparation for both the studies and the seminars leads to a thorough understanding of the uniqueness of the Adventist Church.

3. Selling Magabooks. The third aspect of the program is selling magabooks. In addition to the witnessing experience involved in literature evangelism, young people have the opportunity to earn money for school or college. Youth go door to door selling vegetarian cookbooks, children's books, and a special edition of selected writings by Ellen White. These books are designed to look more like magazines, and have more visual appeal than the more traditional bindings.

At every door the young people ask if they can pray with the people who live there. They ask for special prayer requests. John Weigley, an 18-year-old in his third year with the program, reports that the young people in his group have had many inspiring moments, as well as some rather strange ones, including praying with a Buddhist and having a woman involved with witchcraft attempt to share energy. The young people are inspired by miracles: they often find that they are able to help somebody with a problem just when that individual has been praying for help.

John says that during his first summer with the program as a 16-year-old, the idea of teaching adults was intimidating. By the time he taught four classes he was over it, however, and he has continued with the program and is now a group leader. He believes that "this program has made God more real to me; I can see His power working through the kids in my group." Cindy Tutsch reports that the young people return to their homes spiritually empowered and on fire, ready and able to share Christ with others in their schools and communities.

There is no one way to reach youth for Christ, or to involve them in reaching out to others. The possibilities are virtually endless. The most important common ingredients to successful programs are a relational element, sincere interest in others, an open mind, and, of course, a close partnership with the Holy Spirit.

---

[1] Available online: www.tomorrowtoday.biz/generations/xpaper1002.htm.
[2] E. G. White, *The Desire of Ages,* p. 151.

CHAPTER 18

Strategies for Successful Youth Evangelism

by Alfredo Garcia-Marenko

ACCORDING TO A STUDY by Roger Dudley, two important areas of youth ministry have been neglected—youth involvement and youth witnessing. Young people indicated that they want to be involved in mission projects, community service projects, Youth to Youth seminars, and other youth discipleship programs. Young people want to be involved in their local churches, and we need to put them to work!

We need to keep alive the Adventist Youth Society. Other senior youth and young adult programs need to be introduced to the local church organization with youth representation and involvement in the leadership, programs, and mission of the church.

IAD Adventist Youth on Mission for God

Adventist youth in many world divisions are overwhelmingly involved in church leadership and missionary activities through our youth organizations: Adventurer, Pathfinder, Master Guide, and AY Leader clubs, AY societies, AY federations, and university Student Associations. Wherever I go, I find our precious youth on fire for God, willing to be involved in the leadership and mission of the church.

In the Inter-American Division, under the leadership of the 12 union youth directors and the 60 conference/mission youth directors, more than 15,000 youth and child preachers have done exploits for God. It began in 1989 when the Inter-American Division celebrated the 110th anniversary of the Adventist Youth Society with an evangelistic plan known as AY Maranatha 10,000 Project. During the Month of Youth Evangelism, more than 10,000 youth and child preachers preached simultaneously in an unprecedented chain of 10,000 Voice of Youth and Junior Voice of Youth programs in Inter-America, resulting in baptisms of more than 20,000 persons.

In 1993 a more ambitious plan was launched, the AY Maranatha 30,000 Project, which brought to the church more than 50,000 precious souls through more than 15,000 youth programs and other missionary projects; these were part of the Year of Youth Evangelism proclaimed by the General Conference. Encouraged by the positive results, the Inter-American Division executive committee voted "AY Maranatha 30,000 II Project" for 1994 and "AY Maranatha 30,000 III Project" for 1995, with a yearly goal of 15,000 AY missionary projects and 30,000 baptisms, involving all youth organizations in every church or company of the division, again with resounding success. During the 1900-1995 quinquennium more than 150,000 persons were baptized as a direct result of the missionary efforts of our courageous youth.

Strategies and Logistics

The following are some tested strategies for successful youth evangelism at division, union, and conference levels.

1. Set Youth Evangelism as the Number One Priority of Our Ministry. This strategy is in harmony with the aim of the Adventist Youth organization: "The Adventist Message to All the World in This Generation." If we lead our youth in service for God and man, our whole youth program will be strengthened and will receive a new meaning. The administration on every level of our church will provide natural support to youth ministry. In addition, our youth will grow in spirituality.

The Spirit of Prophecy says: "Let ministers teach church members that in order to grow in spirituality, they must carry the burden that the Lord laid upon them—the burden of leading souls into the truth. . . . In thus working they will have the cooperation of heavenly angels, and will obtain an experience that will increase their faith, and give them a strong hold on God."[1] That's why we keep youth evangelism as the number one priority in our youth organizations.

2. Lay Broader Plans to Accomplish a Greater Work for God. Young people like challenges. They enjoy action, surprise, color, sparkle, variety, and beauty, and they love to participate in great and uncommon things. We must think big and challenge our youth with great ventures for Christ. Ellen G. White says: "We are altogether too narrow in our plans. We need to be broader minded. . . . We must get away from our smallness and make larger plans."[2] She also encourages our positive thinking with the following: "A great work is to be accomplished; broader plans must be laid."[3] Young people enjoy being part of a great plan with large objectives, in large activities, and feel happy to know that many other peers are involved in the same task they are performing, preferably at the same time. They enjoy being part of a winning team with great results for God.

3. Take an Official Action. Channeling your plans through the appropriate committee will strengthen your efforts, communications, and materials, as well as the efforts of your counterparts, in the implementation of the evangelistic program all the way down. Before this official action, your plan is only your plan; after an official action, your plan becomes the plan of our organization, the plan of our church.

4. Organize Our Youth to Do a Larger Work for God. Let's consider this important item in relation to youth evangelism. The Spirit of Prophecy declares: "Time is short, and our forces must be organized to do a larger work."[4] In order to be sure that we have an effective organization of our forces for youth evangelism, we must answer the following five questions, which can be represented by the five figures of a hand: What? Who? When? Where? and How? This includes the materials to be used and the financial implications (see strategy 5). Be sure that your plans specifically answer these five questions. Many good ideas don't work because of lack of organization or because the leader has the wrong concept of organization. Indefinite plans answer the same five questions as follows: Whatever, Whoever, Whenever, Wherever, and However. And that's why nothing ever! We youth leaders would rather perform a "larger work" for God. Let me use the following contrast to illustrate this important concept:

Effective Organization: What, Who, When, Where, How = Larger Work

Ineffective Organization: Whatever, Whoever, Whenever, Wherever, However = Nothing Ever

5. Provide Appropriate Training to the Youth and Child Preachers. In order to train the young people, a special training meeting should be called by the conference or mission youth director one or two months before the beginning of the programs, inviting at least two delegates from each church—the youth preacher and the coordinator of the youth program. Suggested classes to be taught during this training course are:

1. How to get more decisions.
2. How to preach evangelistic sermons.
3. How to give Bible studies.
4. How to organize an evangelistic program (including the responsibilities of the service committees).

Training must be one of the top priorities of youth ministry.

6. Provide the Evangelistic Materials to be Used in the Entire Field. A division may encourage unions and local fields to publish materials of their own election, granting them some financial appropriation. Whenever the church provides specific materials for a plan, it is easier for everybody to press together to get the best results. The training meeting is the right time to distribute such materials as Bible courses, posters to promote baptism, handbills, and the book of sermons to each youth preacher, allowing them enough time to study and adapt the sermons. Sometimes, because of lack of funds, some local fields may provide only the book of sermons and the poster promoting the baptismal ceremony at the end of the youth programs. Experience shows that this still brings good results.

7. Use an Effective System of Communication and Reporting. As soon as the plan is voted by the division committee, communicate to the field through circular letters, posters to be placed in every church, the official magazine of programs, and sermons for the churches, as well as the official magazine with programs and leadership ideas for the Youth Societies. Promote it in the division's special edition of the *Adventist Review* and the division newspaper. If possible, talk about this Youth Evangelism Plan in interviews on our radio stations, in workers' meetings, and in all youth events, such as youth congresses, Pathfinder and Master Guide camporees, youth camps, youth ministry, and Pathfinder leaders' training courses, and university student retreats. Put a report system in place to receive the information from your local fields and unions. Use this information in regular statistical reports.

8. Recognize Adventist Youth Ministry as "Missionary Work of the Highest Kind." All youth organizations of our church are soul-winning agencies on behalf of our precious youth and the unchurched youth. In spite of criticism, lack of support, opposition, or misunderstanding, we must keep on and persevere in the accomplishment of our ministry, having in mind that we are doing a great missionary work for the Lord. Ellen White states: "Why should not labor for the youth in our borders be regarded as missionary work of the highest kind? It requires the most delicate tact, the most watchful consideration, the most earnest prayer for heavenly wisdom. The youth are the objects of Satan's special attacks; but kindness, courtesy, and the sympathy which flows from a heart filled with love to Jesus will gain their confidence, and save them from many a snare of the enemy."[5]

As an integral part of the philosophy, organization, curriculum, and activities of all our youth organizations, we are performing an evangelistic task "of the highest kind"!

Success, Success, Success

Since the 1900 General Conference session in Indianapolis, I have been part of the 6:15 Worldwide Prayer Chain for the outpouring of the Holy Spirit. In our home, in our office, and in all our youth activities we pray for the outpouring of the Holy Spirit. He is the main source of our success. I am convinced that God wants our young people to be involved in youth evangelism, and He is more than willing to bestow His Spirit upon us.

In addition, I have discovered the following declarations from the Spirit of Prophecy, which have been followed as divine philosophy in our youth evangelism endeavors: "The secret of our success in the work of God will be found in the harmonious working of our people. There must be concentrated action. . . . We must press together against obstructions and difficulties, shoulder to shoulder, heart to heart."[6]

On the same page I underlined the following related phrases: "harmonious working," "concentrated action," "press together," "to act in concert," "moving forward as one," "under the direction of one Power," "for the accomplishment of one purpose," "harmonious action," "work in unison," "union of action."

This is God's philosophy for successful youth evangelism.

---

[1] E. G. White, *Gospel Workers,* p. 200.

[2] White, *Evangelism,* p. 46.

[3] White, *Testimonies,* vol. 5, p. 187.

[4] *Ibid.,* vol. 9, p. 27.

[5] White, *Gospel Workers,* p. 207.

[6] White, *Christian Service,* p. 75.

CHAPTER 19

Public Relations in Youth Ministry

by Trudy J. Morgan-Cole

HOW OFTEN HAVE YOU, as a youth leader, planned a program that took the best of your time, energy, and creativity—and had only half the attendance you expected, or less? And how often have young people come up to you afterward and said, "Oh, that program Saturday night—I forgot all about that," or "I never heard about it until it was over"?

"Your program may be the very best in town, the spiritual goals you've set for your kids may be exactly what your church needs, but if nobody knows about it—nobody will be there to support your program."[1] Public relations is an essential part of a successful youth ministry. As a youth leader you must learn to communicate effectively about what you are doing in your work. The message has to get out to the youth themselves, their parents, the church, and the community if you are to expect support from all these sources.

Get the Message Out to Youth

The authors of the book *7 Principles for Youth Ministry Excellence* suggest the "Seven Time Rule" as a guideline for public relations in your ministry: "Tell people about your event in seven different ways to guarantee adequate communication."[2] Repeating a message seven times may seem excessive, but when you think of all the messages and information bombarding your youth from school, home, and the media, you'll quickly realize that your message needs to shout to be heard over the clamor. If you plan a Friday night youth meeting at your home, you could announce it in Sabbath school, put a note in your youth newsletter, place an announcement in the church bulletin, put up a poster at church, mention it to youth when you see them during the week, assign a group member to phone the others and remind them and send out e-mail reminders (if your youth have e-mail). You've fulfilled the Seven Time Rule—and you'll probably have good attendance at your program!

Other ways to communicate with your youth might include mailing out messages in letters, flyers, or postcards; sending personal invitations to an event; distributing a calendar of upcoming events, and assigning a few members of your group to be responsible for spreading the news by word of mouth.

Timing is also important when it comes to public relations. Events need to be announced far enough ahead of time so that people can plan for them, but youth (and adults, too!) usually need to be reminded shortly before the event. These reminders are probably best done by telephone a day or two before the planned activity. If you have a large youth group and, like most youth leaders, a busy schedule, you can simplify this task by assigning a few members of your youth group to phone the others with announcements, or by organizing a "phone chain" in which each group member is responsible for calling one or two others. Teenagers love to spend time on the phone, so this task is much less of a burden for them than it is for you.

Newsletter

Printing up a regular publication such as a newsletter is well worth the time and effort it takes—and again, it will take a lot less of your time and effort if you can recruit some of your young people into doing the work for you. A newsletter not only can keep youth and their parents informed about upcoming events; it can include news items about your youth group members and their accomplishments and activities. This will help to build a sense of community. A more elaborate newsletter might include photos, cartoons, and articles of general interest to Christian youth and their families. Many resources exist to help prepare such newsletters—an excellent one for those with access to the World Wide Web can be found at www.cm-online.net/ym/.

Web Page

Also, for those with Internet access, it's worthwhile building and maintaining a youth group Web page. Once again, a group member who's talented in this area will probably enjoy taking on this challenge. A Web site, particularly one that's regularly updated with new information and photos, will give your group an identity within the church and the community, and will provide one more way for members to keep up-to-date on events. Youth group members who have gone away to academy or college can even use the group Web site to keep in touch.

But no matter how high-tech the public relations aspect of your ministry becomes, with a polished Web site and full-color newsletter, remember that there's no substitute for the personal touch. If you see one of your young people in a shopping mall during the week, don't assume, "He must know about the Saturday night social, since we announced it in church and it's been in the newsletter." Take the time to say, "Remember, we're going to the gym Saturday night—can you be there?" Even if the young person already knows about the scheduled event, the fact that you took the time to invite him or her personally will mean a lot. It may make the difference between showing up and staying home.

Get the Message Out to Parents

"Adolescents can never be trusted to pass on information to their parents. It is up to the youth worker to communicate to parents."[3] This unfortunate truth, voiced by veteran youth leaders Mike Yaconelli and Jim Burns, may come as a surprise to some youth leaders, but it's a secret that elementary and high school teachers have known ever since the first "Important Notice" was sent home. "Important Notices" lie crumpled in the bottom of book bags; they wither on the floors of lockers. In a church setting, they may become paper airplanes before they ever leave the Sabbath school room, or become scribbled with notes passed in church, then abandoned in the pew. Young people generally do not remember to pass on information to their parents, whether in written form or by word of mouth. It simply isn't a priority for them.

Your job is to make sure that the parents of your youth are not only informed about the program but made to feel included and wanted. There are several effective ways of doing this, and one of the best is a parents' meeting. "At least twice a year, invite parents to attend a meeting that will provide information about scheduling for the coming year, the costs of activities, dates for camps, and a short explanation of your goals," suggest Yaconelli and Burns.[4] At a meeting like this, parents will also have the opportunity to ask questions and make suggestions. And it's the perfect time to enlist their help and support.

"I'm not convinced that parents think that teenagers or young adults want them around," writes Pat Wick in *Let Me Be a Window,* "so if you want to get parents involved, you are going to have to give them something specific to do."[5] She suggests asking parents, during a planning meeting or via a letter, how they would like to be involved in your ministry to their youth. Suggest options: They could provide transportation, offer their home for social functions, help with food for group outings, assist with decorating events, or serve as a sponsor for youth activities. "You will be surprised how many parents would love to help *if they knew they were not locking themselves into a permanent commitment,"* add Yaconelli and Burns. "There are many legitimate ways parents can perform on a one-time basis, and many parents who would be willing to give their time once."[6]

After you have had a meeting with parents to give them an overview of your program and enlist their support, continue to keep them informed. You can use many of the same methods you use to communicate with the youth themselves: telephone calls, word of mouth, a newsletter. "Mail your youth newsletters directly to parents," suggest the authors of *7 Principles for Youth Ministry Excellence.* "They'll appreciate their own copy, especially when the kids don't bring it home."[7]

Get the Message Out to the Church

"The name and activities of the youth group should be in front of people every time they pick up a piece of literature published by the church. . . . By printing notes in the bulletin and articles in a youth or church newsletter, the youth department is seen as a vital part of the church."[8] Even if you feel you've communicated your message adequately to the youth and their families by phone, word of mouth and the use of your youth newsletter, still put an announcement in the church bulletin, if for no other reason than to let church members know that the youth are active. "This is one way the church knows there is some life in your department."[9] The more you make an effort to keep church members informed and involved in your youth ministry, the more supportive they will be.

The authors of *7 Principles for Youth Ministry Excellence* also point out that your communication to the church, as well as being consistent, should always be positive. "There's a big difference between reporting that 'Portland's youth gathered last Sabbath to continue their help-the-elderly project' and 'only two members of the Portland youth group were present last week for their meeting.' The first example promotes the project and the group in a truthful and . . . extremely positive light. The second example, although definitely truthful, has a negative slant to it ('only two') and tells nothing about what has been or is being done. Promote well, and members of the group as well as members of the congregation will begin believing, 'We have a great youth group.'"[10]

Besides using the church bulletin, you can get your message out by inviting youth to report on their activities in church or in adult Sabbath school. You can involve church elders, church board members, and the pastor in your youth programs from time to time. See if one of them would be willing to open their home for a youth meeting or social activity. And if you produce a youth newsletter, make sure your pastor and other church leaders receive a copy.

Society's message that teenagers are mostly lazy, irresponsible criminals-in-waiting has seeped into the church, to the point that many church members, especially those who aren't and have never been parents of teenagers, look suspiciously at all young people. It's up to you and your youth department to portray a different image of the church youth. As well as letting them know what activities the youth are doing, and giving them the opportunity to interact with the young people, you can use your communication tools—newsletters, bulletins, announcements—to introduce them to the youth as individuals. When a young person has done something praiseworthy within the church, their school, or the community, make sure your whole church knows about it and has an opportunity to celebrate that young person's accomplishments. Just using your church newsletter to introduce one member of the youth group a month, or setting up an "adopt-a-teen" program where church members agree to pray for and get to know a specific young person, can help the whole church feel more interest in the young people. This will do immense good for the youth involved; it will also do a great deal of good for your youth program, since more church members and leaders will be supportive of your ministry.

"Never underestimate the importance of gaining the prayerful, emotional, and financial support of your local leaders that comes through simple, honest communication." [11]

Getting Your Message Out to the Community

Every successful youth ministry needs to impact the community in some way. If service is to be at the heart of our youth work, then our youth should be found out in the streets and shopping malls of our cities and towns. Whether they're performing street drama, repairing houses for senior citizens, tutoring children, or inviting people to an evangelistic series, they have work to do in their community!

But this work won't be successful unless the community knows about it. Whenever your youth group plans an activity that targets the community or is open to the public, make sure you use every means available to advertise it. Use posters, signs, press releases in the local newspaper, public service announcements on radio and TV. Not only will you ensure that particular events are a success, you'll tell the community, "Here is a group of Christian young people who are doing something to make the world a better place." As well as promoting upcoming activities, use the media to report on good things your group has done. When a group of teenagers goes on a mission trip, not only the church but the whole town should know what they've done.

Types of events that might be worthy of a news item in your local paper include church events such as celebrations, anniversaries, or special observances; graduation; special lectures or classes; special groups visiting your church; youth groups on tour; youth receiving an award or honor; youth church services; service projects; mission trips, or completion of a long-term project. [12]

In *The ABZs of Adventist Youth Ministry* Stuart Tyner shares four steps to follow in writing a successful press release.

Step 1. Identify your audience and objectives: be sure you know what section of the newspaper your item would be suitable for. Contact the reporter or editor of that section before you send the release.

Step 2. Write the release: "Have all your facts straight, and lead with the piece of information you think is the most important or attention-getting."

Step 3. Mail or fax your release to the same reporter you have already contacted. Follow it up with a phone call within a day or two.

Step 4. Build relationships with local reporters and editors for the future.[13]

"No one can read your mind," the authors of *7 Principles for Youth Ministry Excellence* remind us. "You've got to let them know about your program, your philosophies, your events, your dreams, and your needs. . . . Use as many methods as possible, but don't forget the most effective method of all, face-to-face communication."[14] Effective communication—to the community, to the church, to families, and to young people themselves—is a vital tool for a successful ministry.

---

[1] Jim Feldbush, William Hurtado, and Ron Whitehead, *7 Principles for Youth Ministry: Practical Strategies to Turn Yourself and Your Youth Into Leaders* (Riverside, Calif.: Center for Youth Evangelism, 1999), p. 99.

[2] *Ibid.,* p. 98.

[3] Mike Yaconelli and Jim Burns, *High School Ministry* (Grand Rapids: Zondervan, 1986), p. 72.

[4] *Ibid.,* pp. 72, 73.

[5] Pat Wick, *Let Me Be a Window: Building a Relational Youth Ministry* (Silver Spring, Md.: North American Division Church Ministries Department, 1990), p. 51.

[6] Yaconelli and Burns, p. 76.

[7] Feldbush et al., p. 101.

[8] *Ibid.,* p. 99.

[9] Wick, p. 52.

[10] Feldbush et al., p. 99.

[11] *Ibid.,* p. 102.

[12] Stuart Tyner, *The ABZs of Adventist Youth Ministry* (Riverside, Calif.: John Hancock Center for Youth Evangelism, 1999), p. 183.

[13] *Ibid.,* p. 182.

[14] *Ibid.,* p. 105.

CHAPTER 20

The Youth Sabbath School

by N. J. Enang

T HE YOUTH MINISTRY, WITH ITS salvation and service emphasis, poses great challenges to the church, especially in these closing scenes of earth's history. For these challenges to be met, every available opportunity needs to be explored to reach the young people, win them to Christ, and prepare them to serve the Lord.

Much time will be required to do this work. Youth ministry therefore should not be limited to designated periods for youth programs. It should extend to the youth's church life, home, school, and the community at large. The sixth chapter of Deuteronomy presents a model to be followed.

It is in this light that the youth Sabbath school offers another opportunity for the youth of the church to be reached. The aspects of making disciples, baptizing, and teaching, as found in the Great Commission of Jesus in Matthew 28:18-20, would become relevant to the youth Sabbath school program.

History of Youth Sabbath School

As far back as the early Reformers, such as Martin Luther and John Knox, to Robert Raikes, who started the modern Sunday school movement in England, the target had always been the young people and how to reach them for Christ. The Sabbath school started by the Seventh Day Baptists at Ephrata, Pennsylvania, in 1739, had the same goal. When James White introduced the idea of the Sabbath school in the Seventh-day Adventist Church, his concern was also on the young people—how the children of believers could be established in the Advent faith.[1] Elder White launched the *Youth's Instructor* in 1852, a journal that contained a series of Sabbath school lessons. In 1853 he started a Sabbath school at Rochester. Many early Adventist Church leaders accepted the idea of establishing a Sabbath school. Some were slow to the call to establish one in their churches. With much promotion and demonstrations in camp meetings, the number of Sabbath schools increased. The focus was still on the young people—how to establish them in the faith.[2]

Today Seventh-day Adventist churches worldwide have Sabbath schools. Presently the Sabbath school is designed to serve all age groups, but the youth are still expected to receive much attention.

The *Youth's Instructor,* in which the Sabbath school lessons were contained, was not always in supply. At such times each school decided on what to study. Lessons included studies on the books of the Bible, prophecies of Daniel and Revelation, and the Sermon on the

Mount. Some of these lessons, especially the prophetic books, might have been difficult for the young minds to understand.

Adelia Pattern in 1863 began lessons for children in the *Youth's Instructor,* while G. H. Bell went one step further by publishing separate lessons for children and youth in 1869. These lessons were in use for the next 25 years.[3]

Each class was made up of six to eight "scholars." The program consisted of Bible study that lasted for almost an hour. The teaching method consisted of drilling and quizzing members on assigned lessons. This was to ensure that the seeds of truth had been planted in the young minds.[4] The General Conference Sabbath School Department was organized in 1902,[5] and in 1910 the department started a special training course for Sabbath school teachers.[6]

The early Sabbath schools initially were primarily concerned with their internal organization, but by 1885 members started to take interest in missions. Weekly offerings collected helped to establish Adventism in other parts of the world. The work in Australia and Africa were the earliest beneficiaries, in 1885 and 1887, respectively.[7] Today missions have become an important and regular feature in Sabbath schools worldwide, and as a result, important evangelistic projects are being accomplished in different parts of the world.

Objectives of Youth Sabbath School

Mrs. L. Flora Plummer, leader of the General Conference Sabbath School Department from 1902 to 1936, had a "special burden" for the Sabbath school, calling it a "recruiting station where volunteers are enlisted in the army of the Lord." She concluded that it was a privilege and the responsibility of the Sabbath school teacher to help develop the members of their classes into strong fruit-bearing Christians. This objective was to be achieved through careful Bible instruction, prayer, and personal appeals to the members of the class to be involved in soul-winning projects.[8]

This objective is in line with the salvation and service emphasis of youth ministry. The objective of the youth Sabbath school is to win, hold, and train our youth for the service of our Lord Jesus Christ. This objective is to be carried forward through the two-pronged ministry of salvation and service.

Salvation Emphasis. Making the saving gospel of Christ central in all youth Sabbath school programs, giving the youth opportunities for their personal expression of their love for Jesus, and challenging the young people to a life of daily Bible study and prayer.

Service Emphasis. Encouraging the young people to enjoy fellowship with one another, training and challenging the youth to be involved in witnessing activities, and placing before the youth the mission of the church and their part in fulfilling that mission.

Purpose of Youth Sabbath School

The youth Sabbath school is designed to meet the needs of our young people in fellowship, nature, worship, and mission. This is to be done under the supervision of dedicated and God-fearing leaders and teachers.

Fellowship. Introduce programs and activities that will help the young people to develop and strengthen their relationship with Christ and one another through love and acceptance. This would be seen more in deeds than in words.

Nurture. The young people should be encouraged to study their Bibles and pray. Youth Sabbath school leaders and teachers should be available to provide counsel to the young people, answer their questions and help them find solutions to their problems, based on God's Word. Programs should be relevant to the spiritual, physical, mental, and social needs of the young people.

Worship. The young people should be taught to approach God in the spirit of praise and adoration. This comes as a result of a personal experience of God's goodness and greatness.

Mission. With a saving relationship with Christ established and spiritual gifts affirmed, the young people will now "go on God's errands," using these gifts in serving others.

Organization of the Youth Sabbath School

The fact that young people love to move with their peers in groups prepares the ground for the youth Sabbath school units. The Adventurer/Pathfinder unit pattern can be useful for churches with either small or large youth membership. A church with small youth membership may consider the following arrangement:

Adventurer	(ages 6-9)	primary division (one unit)
Pathfinder	(ages 10-12)	junior division (one unit)
Pathfinder	(ages 13-15)	teen division (one unit)
Master Guide	(ages 16-19)	youth division (one unit)

(In the above grouping, each division could contain up to four units.)

Churches with a large youth membership may consider organizing the divisions as follows:

Adventurer (ages 6-9)	
Busy Bee—age 6	primary division, unit 1
Sunbeam—age 7	primary division, unit 2
Builder—age 8	primary division, unit 3
Helping Hand—age 9	primary division, unit 4
Pathfinder (junior, ages 10-12)	
Friend—age 10	junior division, unit 1
Companion—age 11	junior division, unit 2
Explorer—age 12	junior division, unit 3
Pathfinder (teen, ages 13-15)	
Ranger—age 13	teen division, unit 1
Voyager—age 14	teen division, unit 2
Guide—age 15	teen division, unit 3
Master Guide (ages 16-19)	youth division

In this arrangement the primary division can have four units, the junior division three units, the teen division three units, and the youth division three units or more. Master Guides should be given the opportunity to teach or assist in teaching the youth Sabbath school classes. This will assist in their leadership training, which is part of their class requirement. Those not involved can remain in the action units under the youth division.

The organizational structure indicated above ensures that the youth ministry is maintained in the Sabbath school with the following advantages:

- The young people will enjoy the fellowship in the Sabbath school units because they are grouped with friends.
- They will find it easier to do assignments together.
- The youth class requirements to be met in the Sabbath school setting will be relevant to most of the unit or class numbers.
- The Sabbath school division structure is maintained and does not pose any problems to the leaders.
- The recommended unit size of six to eight members agrees with the number in the Adventurer and Pathfinder Club units.

Youth Sabbath School Leaders

The youth Sabbath school leaders have the responsibility to plan and direct activities and programs for the various divisions involved in the youth Sabbath school, i.e., the primary, junior, teen, and youth divisions.

The task of planning programs to meet the spiritual, physical, mental, and social needs of the young people is challenging, especially so in the face of the dramatic breakthrough in technology that has turned our world into a global village. It is in this setting that our young people must be saved for Christ.

Leaders of the youth Sabbath school should bear in mind the following:

- Youth Sabbath school leaders must have a burden for the salvation of the young people.
- The focus of all youth Sabbath school programs and activities should be on salvation and service.
- All youth Sabbath school leaders should seek to understand the "youth culture" so that they can offer a meaningful and relevant ministry to the young people.
- Youth Sabbath school leaders should seek to employ all available resources to offer an effective ministry to the young people.
- Youth Sabbath school leaders should create a conducive environment that will help the youth to grow in Christ and love the church.

(See the *Sabbath School Manual* for details regarding duties for leaders.)

The Youth Sabbath School Teacher

More attention will be given to the youth Sabbath school teacher, since he or she comes in closest contact with the youth in the unit or class. The teacher's responsibilities can be compared to that of the Adventurer/Pathfinder counselors and teachers. Because of this, great care should be taken in choosing them.

Qualities

- Must be a converted and dedicated Christian.
- Must have an enduring love for young people.
- Must set good example in behavior.
- Must love to teach.
- Must have a desire for self-improvement.

- Must be diligent, creative, and enthusiastic.
- Must know how to interact with young people.
- Must be interested in soul winning and other missionary activities of the church.

Responsibilities

- Establish contacts with individual youth both in and out of the Sabbath school class.
- Should win the confidence of the young people so that they could be led to Christ.
- Should be present in all church-planned youth programs, participate in as Pathfinder/Adventurer achievement classes, camping, congresses, etc.
- Must visit homes of the young people and maintain close contact with their families.
- Encourage the young people to study their Bibles, follow the daily lesson study plan, read available devotional books and relevant magazines, and have a consistent prayer life.
- Be a companion to the youth, ready to give counsel when necessary.
- Must create leadership opportunities for the young people in the classes.
- Must ensure that order and proper decorum is maintained in the class.
- Should manifest love, courtesy, sympathy, and understanding for the young people.

The Spirit of Prophecy has this to say of the diligent youth Sabbath school teachers: "The Lord will recognize and bless the humble worker who has a teachable spirit, a reverential love for truth and righteousness, wherever such a worker may be. If you are thus, you will show a care for your scholars [class or unit members] by making special efforts for their salvation. You will come close to them in loving sympathy, visiting them at their homes, learning their true condition by conversing with them concerning their experience in the things of God, and you will bear them in the arms of your faith to the throne of the Father."[9]

Teaching the Youth Sabbath School Class

There are three major steps in the teaching process of the youth Sabbath school teacher: preparation, presentation, and evaluation.

Step 1. Preparation. The following steps should be considered:

- Prayer—ask God for guidance and wisdom as you prepare to reach out to the young people.
- Give careful study to the lesson to be presented.
- Determine how you will make the lesson interesting and appealing to the young people. This is where creativity skills need to be applied.
- Be sure that the lesson would be covered within the allotted time.
- Topics could be assigned to class members in advance for study and investigation. This will enhance better participation and understanding of the lesson.

Step 2. Presentation

- Relevant information should be presented through talks, readings, audiovisual aid discussions, demonstrations, etc.

- Participation that will lead the young people to discover the truth for themselves should be encouraged. Truth learned through discovery is not easily forgotten and will enrich their spiritual experience.
- Reports on assigned topics, discussions, questions, demonstrations, drama, mime, debates, forums, and quizzes are some of the methods that could be used for effective participation.
- Lessons should address the problems youths have in today's world. Examples of how such problems could be handled should be sought from the Bible. For example, the story of Joseph (Gen. 37; 39-45) can address: how to handle sex problems; reward for diligence and honesty; forgiveness; the evils in jealousy (Joseph's brothers); God's plan for us unhindered by initial setbacks; falsehood and its consequence (Joseph's brothers).

Step 3. Evaluation

The teacher needs to know if the principles in the lesson were understood, appreciated, and ready to be applied by:

- Giving room for self-expression by the young people.
- Asking questions about the lesson.
- Making an appeal for commitment by surrendering to Christ.

The Youth Sabbath School Program

The youth Sabbath school program should provide for the following facets of ministry to the young people: fellowship, nurture, worship, and mission. Below is a suggested program for the youth Sabbath school divisions.

Fellowship Module (9:00-9:20)

Opening prayer	Short, offered by teacher, a leader, or a class member.
Song service	Spiritually uplifting. Use songs or choruses from the church hymnbooks.
Special feature	Audiovisual, invited guest speaker, etc. Creativity is needed to generate the interest that will bring the youth back every Sabbath.
Welcome	Teacher welcomes guests and regular members; special gifts or cards given out. Should be brief, warm, and enthusiastic. Class records. Care for missing member and visitation plan.

Worship Module (9:20-9:45)

Song of praise or special music	
Testimonies	Encourage the young people to recognize God's goodness and care. Let them share with others.
Prayer session	Either pray in groups or appoint someone or persons to pray.

Nurture Module (9:45-10:25)

Church heritage or discussion	An opportunity for the youth to see God's leading in His church on doctrine in the past, which gives confidence for the present and hope for the future.
Music/expense offering/ lesson study	Lesson discussion, application, and appeal.

Mission Module (10:25-10:45)

World mission report/ outreach	Challenge the youth to see their role in missions. Collect offerings. Witnessing reports, training in outreach methods, assignment on outreach for next week with materials given out.

Closing Exercises (10:45-10:50)
Closing song
Benediction

Youth Ministry Requirements to Be Met in Sabbath School

The youth Sabbath school provides an opportunity for some youth achievement class requirements to be met. It is best to assign teaching of the youth Sabbath school classes to youth leaders, especially the Master Guides. Where it is impossible to do so, the Adventurer/Pathfinder counselors and/or teachers should work closely with the class teachers so that these requirements could be met. Below is a chart showing the youth achievement class requirements and how they could be met in the Sabbath school.

Adventurer Requirement: Story Charts. *Primary Division:* The church heritage or discussion on doctrines slot or lesson study period may be used. Making the charts could be part of class activities or a take-home assignment after they have been shown how to make one.

Friend Requirement: Show Christ's Care in Old Testament Story. *Junior Division:* Could be done during discussion on doctrine or lesson study. Christ's loving care before His incarnation should be stressed.

Friend Requirement: Prepare a Time Chart Showing From Christ's Ascension to 1844. *Junior Division:* The presentation should lead the youth to see the events that led to the establishment of the remnant church.

Friend Requirement: Invite Two Visitors to Sabbath School. *Junior Division:* This could be an outreach assignment in the Sabbath school program.

Companion Requirement: Participate in a Presented Activity About a Story of Jesus. *Junior Division:* A drama, mime, etc., could be on a story of Jesus. For example, Jesus and the Samaritan woman at the well. A special feature or lesson study slot can accommodate such a topic.

Companion Requirement: Prepare a Time Chart Showing From the Midnight Cry to Establishment of the Seventh-day Adventist Church. *Junior Division:* Establish that the Adventist Church is the remnant church of Bible prophecy. The church heritage slot can be used. (A follow-up from the Friend requirement.)

Companion Requirement: Participate Two Hours in Community Expressing Companionship. *Junior Division:* Assignment and report during witnessing activities.

Companion Requirement: Tell How Jesus Saves From New Testament Story. *Junior Division:* Could be discussed during study or discussion on doctrines. A topic for study and investigation in advance.

Companion Requirement: Draw a Time Chart Showing 1844 to J. N. Andrews. *Junior Division:* During the church heritage period this chart could be done. Emphasize God's leading in the early development of the Seventh-day Adventist Church to its beginning of missions.

Companion Requirement: Enroll Member in Sabbath School or Pathfinders. *Junior Division:* A series during the discussion on doctrine will help meet this requirement. The discussion should lead to challenging the young people to live a Christian life. Those not yet baptized should be encouraged to take that step.

Voyager Requirement: Doctrine—Holy Spirit. *Teen Division:* This could be done during the slot on discussion on doctrines. Challenges the young people to yield to the Holy Spirit's control of their lives.

Voyager Requirement: Doctrine—Second Advent. *Teen Division:* Encourage the youth to prepare for Christ's second coming.

Guide Requirement: Doctrine—Gift of the Spirit. *Teen Division:* Discuss during the discussion on doctrine slot. Emphasize the discovery and use of spiritual gifts for ministry by youth.

Guide Requirement: High-priestly Ministry of Christ. *Teen Division:* Show that Christ cares and is interested in the young people's salvation. Show how each person benefits from this high-priestly ministry of Christ.

Master Guide Requirement: Teach in the Sabbath School Class for at Least a Quarter. *Youth Division:* Teaching and leadership opportunities should be given to the youth leaders. They can begin as assistant teachers and with more experience can be made teachers.

Master Guide Requirement: Help Conduct a VBS Program. *Youth Division:* Encourage the young people to participate in the church's vacation Bible program.

The program and activities in the youth Sabbath school should be evangelistic. It should result in young people surrendering to Christ. It should help the young people to appreciate the church and its mission to the world and encourage them to play an active role in this mission. That way the youth are fully involved in the work, and more souls are won for Christ. At the same time, their salvation needs are being met.

---

[1] Richard W. Schwarz, *Light Bearers to the Remnant* (Mountain View, Calif.: Pacific Press Pub. Assn., 1979), pp. 159, 160.

[2] *Ibid.,* pp. 160, 161.

[3] *Ibid.,* p. 160.

[4] *Ibid.*

[5] *Seventh-day Adventist Yearbook* (1998), p. 21.

[6] Schwarz, p. 378.

[7] *Ibid.,* p. 161.

[8] Schwarz, p. 379.

[9] Ellen G. White, *Counsels on Sabbath School Work* (Washington, D.C.: Review and Herald Pub. Assn. 1938), p. 76.

CHAPTER 21

Youth Involvement

by Trudy J. Morgan-Cole

A S WE LOOK AT THE ROLE of young people in the Bible, it's clear that youth were never intended to be spectators, sitting on the sidelines while the adults do God's work. From Naaman's slave girl to the boy Samuel, from the boy Jesus in the Temple to the youth Timothy working beside Paul, young people and even children were always a part of God's plan. His plan for the Seventh-day Adventist Church is no different. Ellen G. White's vision of an "army of youth" who would bring God's last-day message to the world inspired our pioneers to include young people in an active way in the work of soul winning. This is what Adventist youth ministry was always intended to be—a means of training young people to take their own place in God's work—now, not in the nebulous future.

Sometimes we wonder if that vision is still alive today. In some of our churches, youth and young adults may be barely active at all. Perhaps you look around and see youth taking no real interest in outreach and service, or young adults eager to serve but being given no opportunities for leadership in the church. Certainly we have a long way to go to reach the divine ideal, in which every Christian young person works side by side with older Christians, taking an active role in the work.

Although we may see many examples of churches where youth ministry falls short of the ideal, there are many more where young people are doing their part with Spirit-led enthusiasm. Thousands of young people serve as missionaries overseas and in their own countries, volunteering a summer, a year, or even more. And in schools and churches around the globe, youth leaders and young people themselves are catching the vision of youth involvement and making it a reality in hundreds of creative ways. Here are just a few stories of youth around the world who are responding to God's call to become involved in ministry.

Brazil: A Bible Two Miles Long

Nearly 3,800 Seventh-day Adventist youth attending a "Bridge of Hope" convocation in Florianópolis, Brazil, in October 1999, chose an unusual outreach to catch the attention of people in that city. On a piece of paper stretching two miles (three kilometers) along a waterfront boulevard, they wrote out the entire Bible by hand. The Bible-writing event, which took only 25 minutes, caught the attention of the national media.

The young people, who came from four southern states of Brazil, "came to build a human 'bridge of hope' in the community," said Udolcy Zukowski, communication director of the South Brazilian Union of Seventh-day Adventists, who was in charge of the event. "We wanted to do something more than just meet, play, and study together. The plan is to show our Christianity in practice, as members of the community in which we all live," he explained.

Florianópolis was an ideal site for the Bridge of Hope convocation, since the island city is famous for the bridge that connects it to the mainland. "The bridge metaphor was important for us," Zukowski explained. "No matter where you come from, it's the community in which you live that challenges you to share who you are and be practical. So we came to show our religion in practice in Florianópolis. Our young people will now return to their own local communities and be inspired to build bridges wherever we come from."

Local government officials, including the state governor and the mayor of Florianópolis, participated in the Scripture-writing project and had warm words of praise for the Adventist young people. Mayor Angela Amim said he was overwhelmed by the young people's dedication, "mainly because it is a work done with love."

The organizers of the youth convocation and the young people who participated wanted the weekend to be more than just an inspiration to the youth themselves; they wanted it to make an impact on the community. Besides writing the entire Bible out by hand, the young people participated in many other practical outreach activities. They developed and participated in about 20 different community projects, including cleaning city streets and local beaches.

"There is always more to do. It was exciting to see us make a contribution, though always only symbolic. We have much to do where we are living. That's the challenge," said Alexandre, a 20-year-old student from Santa Catarina.

As Alexandre's comment indicates, the most exciting thing about an event like this is the young people's commitment to make it more than a one-time experience. They hope to carry their eagerness for outreach back to their home churches and communities. "We will continue our witness with the enthusiasm we are seeing this weekend," said one local pastor.*

Australia: A Growing, Active Youth Group

When Michael Worker became associate pastor of the Seventh-day Adventist church in Clarkson, Perth, Western Australia, in 1995, the youth group was virtually nonexistent. About four young people "floated in and out," Worker says, but during his first year he made them a priority. "I had discussions with a couple of them with regard to making their church a place where they wanted to be, rather than visiting other churches for uplifting services for them."

Fortunately, the Clarkson church was open and enthusiastic about having their youth more involved. "Things just blossomed," Worker reports. One of the members of the struggling youth group, a university student, invited some of his friends from the university to join him at church. His friends were singers, and a music ministry began. Soon the youth began to take charge of a church service every quarter, and the Sabbath school preliminaries once or twice a quarter, as well. At first "they were spoon-fed and hands-held through the whole planning process," says Worker, but soon they progressed to the point where they were organizing and producing the whole program themselves. Four years later, not only were the young people actively leading out in church services and programs, but four of them were serving on the church board. "They hold offices in the church such as Sabbath school superintendent, youth leaders, music coordinator, Pathfinder director, personal ministries, cradle roll leader, social committee leader, and assistant treasure," Michael Worker says.

By 1999 this church of about 80 members had a group of 20 young adults between 17 and 24 years of age. At least half the group are new Adventists, won to the church by the genuine friendship and evangelistic efforts of the handful of original youth who "floated in and out" until someone decided to make a commitment to keeping them "in." As Pastor Worker says: "The key to all of this was someone who believed in them, and the church's willingness to give them responsibility."

From the U.S.A. to Romania: a FAST Journey

At the beginning of the 1998-1999 school year at Weimar College in Weimar, California, Professor Dan Vis gave a short dorm worship on the importance of memorizing Scripture and asked if any would be interested in learning how to do it effectively. He had developed a Discipleship/Scripture memorization program called FAST Basic Training, which built Scripture memory into every key area of discipleship—prayer, study, obedience, witnessing.

In response to the worship talk, about a dozen young men agreed to meet at 5:00 a.m. once a week. "They became committed to sharing the program with others," says Vis, "and most of them started teams of their own. The second quarter we had five new teams going. Major changes had taken place in the lives of the original dozen men—and lots of people wanted to know what was going on."

FAST continued to grow across campus and in area churches throughout that school year. Soon, people all over the United States who had heard about FAST program were requesting the Scripture memory-training materials, and several people were translating them into other languages. A campus revival began, fueled by the Spirit-led excitement of the FAST Team members, who were receiving speaking invitations on- and off-campus.

But FAST's most far-reaching result came when two students, Richard Constantinescu and David Currier, decided to spend their spring break in Romania, giving seminars on Scripture memorization and discipleship. "The response was tremendous," Vis says. On the second day of their trip the bus broke down just outside the Seventh-day Adventist conference headquarters—where they happened to meet the youth director, Daniel Delcea. Delcea took an interest in the FAST program and invited the Weimar students to a youth conference, where they were able to speak to about 500 young people.

David and Richard returned to Romania in the summer of 1999, planning to start some FAST Basic Training teams and train leaders to continue the work. Their plans were ambitious, says Vis, "especially considering we didn't even have the materials translated yet!" But, he adds, "God blessed and they were able to start six teams in six different cities—translating the materials just a week or two ahead as they went." They were also invited to attend two youth leadership training camps. Overwhelmed by the interest, David and Richard invited Dan Vis to join them.

"The response of the kids was fantastic," says Vis. "But the pastors who conducted the camps were even more excited—really catching the vision for spiritual multiplication through the life-changing power of the Word."

David and Richard's summer was an intensive one—traveling on buses and taxis to different locations every day of the week, leading teams, speaking at churches, getting materials translated, edited, formatted, and printed. "They were rushing around on four to five hours of sleep a night most of the summer," Dan Vis says. But the response made it all worthwhile. Pastor Delcea pledged to get FAST Basic Training materials—now finally translated—into the hands of every youth leader in his conference.

In the year following that summer visit, FAST continued to grow throughout the church in Romania. Young people, as well as adults who had caught the vision, formed Scripture memorization teams in churches and on campuses. Meanwhile, the Scripture memorization concept also caught on back in the U.S., with the FAST program spreading to other Adventist colleges and even to secular campuses. Back at Weimar College, where it began, "we have 11 teams in progress," reported Vis in the fall of 1999. The first FAST Field School in discipleship, an intensive-training program in disciple-making also began at Weimar in 1999. College students not only led the FAST teams but also conducted two major evangelistic series during the 1999-2000 school year. (You can find out more about FAST and the Scripture memorization program at their Web site www.fast.st.)

"I wish I could somehow describe the electricity that is in these meetings," says Dan Vis, of the growing FAST movement. "There is something about the Word of God, that when it really takes center stage in the life, things begin to happen."

South Africa, Part I: An Adopted Orphanage

The Seventh-day Adventist Student's Association (SDASA) in South Africa is an organization for Adventist college students, most of whom are studying on secular campuses. Each of the 18 SDASA chapters around the country not only provides fellowship and support for students, but also looks for a way to be involved in the community.

In 1997 the West Rand SDASA Chapter in Soweto decided to focus on one of the many orphanages in Soweto—the Edemeni Home for Abandoned Children. Like most Soweto orphanages, it was in great need, and the SDASA students chose to adopt and support it. The first step was to visit the orphanage and get to know the children. "Since they come from very terrifying circumstances in their homes, the development of trust was necessary," says SDASA president Nikelo Bangisi. Next the students started an informal worship program with the children. "No formal type of church worship would make sense to them," Bangisi says, so they would gather at the orphanage, sing choruses with the children, teach them how to pray and read the Bible, and provide food. Since the congregation was composed of children between 8 and 17 years old, these "church services" were always short.

The following year, SDASA secured a sponsorship from a local sports company to provide sports shoes for all the children at the orphanage. They also launched a fund-raising program, with the support of their local churches, in order to send the children from the Edemeni home orphanage to youth camp. The program was a success and they planned to repeat it the next year.

West Rand SDASA students visit the Edmeni Home once a month as a group, but individual group members also visit the home on their own time. "We are also allowed to take the children for a weekend in our own homes," says Bangisi.

South African SDASA students sponsor many other projects, including a bursary fund to allow Adventist young people from disadvantaged backgrounds to continue their education . A planned SDASA conference for the end of 1999 was expected to bring together about 800 students and professionals, who would not only camp and worship together, but also conduct a 10-day evangelistic program in a nearby village. There's no doubt that Adventist young adults in South Africa understand what it means to be part of the Lord's army.

South Africa, Part II: Teens Making Connections

High school student Brenda-Louise Pretorius was attending camp meeting when she decided that young people her age needed to be more active in the church. She responded by starting a youth group called New Connection. A year and a half after it began in 1998, New Connection had eight regular members and was busy with a variety of outreach programs. Group member Landi Fourie says, "It was always a dream of mine to be a part of a Christian youth group. I was extremely excited about the idea, but I wasn't sure if God would use a 14-year-old girl for His work. The moment I arrived at the group's first meeting, all my doubts disappeared. There was a special closeness between the members of the group and I could feel God's presence among us."

The central focus of New Connection's program is a puppet ministry for children, but the group has also done programs for youth, performed at youth ministry seminars, and run the children's department at camp meetings. They have brought their outreach to schools, orphanages, hospitals, and even prisons. "The kids find it educational, the teens find it interesting, and the adults find it cute and entertaining," says group member Donald Virgin.

When New Connection takes charge of a children's program, Brenda-Louise says, "We do all sorts of crafts with them. We do programs with morals varying from washing your face before bedtime to acceptable behavior in church. We usually start with a song service, then we do a story, and we like to do mini discussions with them, to make them feel actively involved. We find it works very well to have the kids play an active part in the program."

When they perform for youth their own age, they also use music, along with skits and discussions on topics such as peer pressure, self-image, drugs, and Christ's second coming. "With the teens," says Brenda-Louise, "our main focus is to bring across the message that no matter how worthless they think they are Jesus still loves them, and that He can do a lot with their lives. We encourage them to give their problems to God completely."

Some of New Connection's favorite outings are to orphanages. They collect presents for the children, do a program for the children, and then hand out the gifts and treats. "Those children were so hungry for a little love and affection; they loved the programs and the dolls, and every last one of us left there feeling completely touched by these tiny persons," Brenda-Louise says.

New Connection's commitment to outreach extends beyond their own community. In 1998 they collected about 175 pounds (80 kilograms) of Christian literature to send to the Philippines, Ghana, and Nairobi. The following year they began to collect Bibles and copies of *Steps to Jesus* (an abridged version of *Steps to Christ*) to send to missionaries in Japan.

New Connection's ministry is living proof that a group of teenagers can take a dream and make it reality for God. "Everywhere I go with New Connection, I receive countless blessings," says Landi Fourie. "God has really touched my life. He's changed me from a shy, quiet girl into a young woman who's not afraid to stand up for what she believes in. I so much enjoy going out and telling people about His love and praying with them."

North American Division: The eXtreme Road Trip

When Brian Yeager was a junior in college, he started a group called "Salt and Light" that was intended to be a traveling summer ministry. "Salt and Light" never made it on the road, but when Yeager talked about it with Ron Whitehead, who later became the associate youth director of the North American Division, Whitehead shared his dream of starting a full-time traveling youth revival team.

About the same time another young adult, Danny Houghton, dreamed about a young adult evangelistic team. That idea reached the ears of NAD youth director José Rojas, and the process of making it a reality began. When Brian Yeager heard that a traveling ministry was in the works, he was eager to be involved. Originally hired as drama director, Yeager eventually became codirector of the YouthNet eXtreme Team, which began its youth revival ministry in June 1998. Since then, the eXtreme Team has traveled with their truck and trailer across the United States and Canada presenting God's Word through music, drama, and inspirational speaking.

The team consists of five young adults, most of whom sign on for a one-year term. In the 1999-2000 year the team's youngest member was 19, while the oldest was 26. All eXtreme Team members are college students or recent graduates with a wide variety of backgrounds. What they have in common is a strong love for God and a passion for ministry.

The eXtreme Team has performed at youth rallies, camp meetings, academies, public school assemblies, local churches, a youth detention center—they even do street ministry in shopping center parking lots. The youth to whom they minister are not just passive spectators at their programs. "We encourage youth to become involved in outreach by getting them actually doing it," says Yeager. They include teenagers in their street drama programs, or take them door-to-door offering to pray for people in their neighborhoods. The results are always exciting—the teenagers come back amazed at what God has been able to do in and through them.

Youth are sometimes reluctant to get involved, Brian Yeager says, because they are used as free labor when the church needs a job done. "We need copies of *The Great Controversy* passed out; let's make the youth do it. They have no ownership. But it's different when they have something that they have a passion for and they believe in. Once they do something that is real to them, they see God work—then they get excited."

The same could be said of the young adult eXtreme Team members themselves. Their ministry is one that kindles their passion for God and for youth—a ministry they believe in completely. And as one teenager who attended an eXtreme Team event wrote to the team members afterward, "Thanks for coming to our campus and sharing Christ with us. I appreciate your enthusiasm and dedication. I don't think I will ever forget this week of prayer; I came seeking a blessing, seeking to grow closer to God, and I have."

For the members of the YouthNet eXtreme Team, responses like that are a dream come true.

* * *

As you read these stories, your response may be: "I could have written one of those! The Adventist youth and young adults in my community are doing things just as exciting as that!"

If so, then you know the truth—that the dream of Adventist youth forming an army to bring the message to the world is alive and well, all over the world. It's your privilege as a youth leader to be part of keeping that dream alive.

But if your response is "I wish something like that would happen in my community! Our youth are so uninvolved!" then take heart. All of the leaders of these ministries counsel church members, pastors, and youth leaders to encourage youth involvement by letting youth take the lead. Find out what their gifts are, and let their strength and interests determine how they will serve the Lord. With their energy and His Holy Spirit, your battalion may soon be ready to join the lord's army on the march.

---

* All information and quotes in this section taken from Ray Dabrowski, "Brazilian Youth Write Out Three-Kilometers-Long Bible in 25 Minutes," Adventist News Network: *This Week's News,* Oct. 12, 1999. Online: www.adventist.org/issues/data/939763264/.

CHAPTER 22

Youth Evangelism

by James Wu

YOUTH IS THE SYMBOL of life and energy. A church with active youth evangelism means a church with vitality. A living church, similar to a living organism, will grow and reproduce.

Evangelism is important to prepare youth for salvation and service. Faith in Jesus needs action. Sharing the gospel message with others helps our youth to exercise their faith. Involvement in youth evangelism can mean caring for others' salvation. Caring is the best service our youth can provide for others. We will first look at some of the common factors for successful youth evangelism before we go into the different types.

Common Factors for Successful Youth Evangelism

Clear Vision: We Want Good Results

Why do we conduct youth evangelism? Clear vision and clear mission aimed toward real results should be considered carefully. A clear vision for results is basic for good leadership. Look into the future, a year or months from now. What do we see as the result of conducting youth evangelism? We see two groups of young people, one group helping the other group. They pray together, study the Bible together, sing songs, worship God, and play games and have fun together. Soon the two groups become one in Christ. They become members of the body of Jesus.

To be more specific, this vision becomes a mission to act. We want to see at least 20 of our young people involved in the coming youth evangelism. We want to see at least 20 youth attracted to come and join us. These numbers become our goals and objectives—something that can be measured and counted to show that we are successful. The first factor for successful youth evangelism is to look for a leader with a vision.

Planning: We Put Our Brains Together

A good leader does not work alone. We will help our visionary youth leader to call a brainstorming meeting, inviting a few representative youth. During the meeting everyone is allowed to speak freely, without others questioning the suggested ideas, and we encourage the free flow of ideas. We will put all the ideas on the blackboard, then organize by different categories, and place in order of importance.

Planning is an exercise of determining all the things that we need to do in order to see results. There are things that we need to do in sequence, one after another. There are things we need to do independently, with a specific date and time. Good planning needs youth who can work with details. These people become good executives or managers.

We will put the plan into a written form, with specific place, date, time, and programs. We call it the first draft of a successful youth evangelistic plan. It is now ready for more input of ideas and suggestions before the final draft is ready for approval and action.

Work Committee: We Go for Teamwork

We must get as many of our youth as we can to be involved in the evangelistic plan. There are many specific jobs that need to be done; closely related jobs are assigned to different working committees. Job descriptions for all committees, with specific timing and procedures, should be clearly written on the evangelistic plan. Some of the working committees that are common to many types of youth evangelism are listed below:

Advertising Committee. Main function: To make our target group(s) aware of our evangelism and want to participate in our program. Main jobs: To design and prepare all handouts, posters, invitation letters, and promotional materials; to work out the schedule for advertising; to estimate the amount and budget for different advertisements needed.

Prayer Committee. Main function: To solicit wisdom and power from God. Main jobs: To arrange specific timing and schedule for regular prayer sessions before, during, and after the evangelism; to prepare a list for prayer requests; to help all the members of the prayer committee to pray in faith for good results.

Program Committee. Main function: To prepare quality program contents for the evangelistic meetings or outreach. Main jobs: To arrange the details of the program contents; to assign persons to carry out all specific programs; to remind and supervise all persons responsible for the programs.

Usher Committee. Main function: To give a warm welcome and good direction to guests coming to the evangelistic meetings. Main jobs: To assign different persons to take care of all the posts of welcoming; to make a roster of assignments and to give supervision; to train all ushers for protocol.

Record Committee. Main function: To keep track of all participants. Main jobs: To record all target groups being contacted by all advertising methods; to record all participant attendance; to analyze all data; to give meaningful statistical reports to show results.

Technical Committee. Main function: To prepare and maintain all equipment needed. Main jobs: To make a list of all equipment needed and get ready for the programs; to operate and maintain the equipment in good order; to prepare for emergencies and spare parts; to keep security for the equipment.

Small Group Committee. Main function: To care for all individuals. Main jobs: To assign small group leaders and members to the different small groups; to train group leaders how to care for their group members; to prepare forms and handout materials for small group activities.

Finance Committee. Main function: To receive funding and to manage an income and expense statement for the evangelistic program. Main jobs: To keep record of all income and expenses with proper receipt and authorized signature; to distribute funding for activities by preparing a balanced budget; to supervise the use of the budget; to make periodic finance reports.

Human Resource Committee. Main function: To involve all church members with different gifts from God. Main jobs: To identify all the talents and gifts of church members, particularly the youth; to encourage full participation of church members in the evangelistic plan; to give training for specific skills and services.

Planning and Steering Committee. Main function: To coordinate and to implement the evangelistic plan. Main jobs: To call regular meetings for all leaders of working committees; to monitor the progress of all committees; to evaluate the outcome of the plan in different stages and to make necessary adjustments.

Budgeting: We Have Financial Resources

Successful youth evangelism needs ample resources. Good budgeting from the beginning of planning is important. We must list all the items needed for the outreach program with costs attached. Then we estimate the total financial obligation for the outreach program.

Next, we should make a list of all the possible income or appropriation that we can find. For example, special church offering, appropriations from higher church organizations, funding from humanitarian or government organizations, donations from individuals or companies, fund-raising projects, etc. Let the church members know the financial and budgeted needs for the youth evangelistic plan. Pray and trust that God will provide.

The finance committee should work closely with the church treasurer. All income and expense should be recorded clearly. Two persons should be responsible for all accounting procedures to ensure internal control. Regular balanced reports should be posted on the church bulletin board. A strong and sound financial budgeting plan will enhance the success of youth evangelism.

Needs of Youth: We Know What They Want

During Jesus' ministry on earth He mingled with the people. He knew the needs of the people and ministered to their needs. To be effective in youth evangelism, we must know the needs of our target groups. Whether we plan to reach high school or college students, the youth in the inner city, or the youth in the neighborhood, we must find out their felt needs or their immediate needs—in simple words, what they are interested in.

There are methods to find out the needs of our target groups. We can conduct interviews. Train and assign a few of our youth to do the job. Prepare an appropriate questionnaire and go to meet the target group to collect responses. Or we can do focus group interviews by inviting a group of youth that can represent a sample of our target group.

Another method is to assign a few mature youth leaders to do observation. Go to meet the target group. Observe their lifestyle, recreation, interests, activities, environment, food and drink, music, dress, etc. The youth leaders meet together after completing their assignment. The observers will share their reports and discuss their findings. Suggestions will be drawn from the findings regarding the needs of the target group.

The use of a questionnaire survey is more complex and time-consuming. Designing the questionnaire, finding the sample group at random, collecting data, doing data analysis, and drawing conclusions from the findings require knowledge and skills. In this way, the results could be more objective.

People: We Have Human Resources

Successful youth evangelism depends on good leadership. One spiritual and energetic youth leader will get things going. The church pastor plays an important role here, too. He or she should search out and affirm our youth leaders, helping to involve them in youth evangelism. How to get our young people involved in youth evangelism? Our youth are looking for friendship, meaning, fun, and adventure. Let us plan our outreach programs with these elements. The gospel of Jesus can be exciting and fun.

Training for youth evangelism is important. Every person has his or her apparent and hidden talents. We must discover the talents of our youth and give proper training to help them reach the apex of self-actualization in Christ.

Group Dynamics: We Are Not Alone

Teamwork is the road to success. We must get our youth to plan in teams, work in teams, pray in teams, and fellowship in teams. Jesus had a smaller team of four and a larger team of 12. There are many successful examples of small group ministry. Friendship and mutual support give our youth the strength they need for perseverance. Our youth will not give up easily when they have group support.

We must select and train small group leaders. They will be assigned to take care of six to eight group members. We can call them care groups, cell groups, support groups, or any name our young people would prefer.

Regular group fellowship materials should be prepared for the care groups. Bible study outlines, prayer requests, action plans or projects, and simple activity report forms should be available for the proper function of small groups. When a local church has youth groups functioning properly, any youth evangelism effort will be almost a guaranteed success, because we have a mechanism to absorb and nurture new friends.

Follow-up: We Make Sure They Come to Christ

We should put more energy in the follow-up work when we plan for youth evangelism. We tend to concentrate on the preparation and are almost exhausted when we come to the end of the youth evangelistic meetings or outreach. Then we lose interest in the harvesting part of evangelism because we are not ready for it. Let us put our heart and mind on the young we come into contact with during the evangelism. Get to know the individuals. Try to become friends with as many as we can. Meet others with the love of Jesus and with the wisdom of His Spirit. Youth will be attracted to sincere people.

We can plan for camping, games, interest groups, special projects, and Bible studies to enhance the youth evangelism. These follow-up activities should be announced early, and group leaders should invite newcomers to join. Good follow-up plans will give good results.

Types of Youth Evangelism

We have discussed some of the factors that will affect the outcome of youth evangelism. These factors should be considered in general. They might not be applicable to every type of youth outreach program. However, they are important elements for effective evangelism.

We are now ready to examine the various types of youth evangelism. We will first look at the regular way we conduct the various types of outreach, then follow with some special way of looking at the types. Some suggestions might not be appropriate for some cultural backgrounds or practices in some countries. Church pastors should help our youth leaders to make careful consideration and selection of programs.

Voice of Youth

Regular. Youth speakers preaching like evangelists in the church or meeting hall. One or a group of youth speakers are selected for the job. Usually a few to 10 days or nights of meetings are arranged for the Voice of Youth. Each night the program will be well planned. This will include song service, welcoming chairperson, special music, gifts to encourage attendance, and well-selected topics for the speaker(s) that will make up a theme.

Invitation through handbills, letters, posters, and personal invitations should be used to get other youth to come for the meetings. Most of the working committees discussed in the first part of this chapter would be appropriate for Voice of Youth. We strongly encourage the use of small groups to work closely with Voice of Youth. Thirty minutes of fellowship and discussion in responding to the topic presented by the speaker has proved effective.

Special. Voice of Youth evangelistic outreach can be presented as drama or play. Gospel themes or topics can be written in drama scripts and acted out by our talented young people. We can try the idea of meeting our young people in the form of coffee shops. Arrange the meeting hall like a coffee restaurant. Serve the youth with healthy soft drinks or fruit juices. Musical programs and discussion topics can be presented by our youth or a casual discussion period, just like friends chatting around the tea table.

Try the idea of holding a debate for our youth in the form of evangelism. We can arrange a sequence of topics with a central theme and assign debate teams to participate. At the end of every debate, a speaker can give a thought from the biblical standpoint as conclusion.

Today's youth like to look at movie stars and sports stars as their idols. We can try to contact successful Christian sports stars for experience sharing, interviews, and discussions.

Campus Evangelism

Regular. Students are our main target group. There are day students and dormitory students. The usual outreach for our students includes Bible study groups, prayer groups, and care groups. However, we can use the Voice of Youth evangelism ideas to make contacts.

Special. Consider the needs of our students, it would be profitable to hold academic support groups to help those in need of improving their school work. Good camping trips during term breaks led by mature leaders are effective evangelism for our students. Family camps and field trips are similar activities that our students are likely to join. Students like to meet new friends. Interschool activities for faith sharing, fellowship, fun, and games are attractive to students.

Personal Witnessing

Regular. One-to-one personal witnessing usually goes with literature sharing and personal testimony. Good and attractive Christian literature will make personal witnessing easier. Door-to-door visitation in some areas is an effective way to do personal witnessing.

Enrollment for Voice of Prophecy Bible lessons is usual in some parts of the world.

We need to train our youth to share Jesus more directly. Personal witnessing is not an invitation to church or to youth evangelistic meetings. Neither is personal witnessing what the literature says about Jesus. Personal witnessing is sharing what Jesus has done for the individual—how one life was changed after knowing Jesus personally.

Special. Try doing personal witnessing by writing letters and cards. It is easier to share with others by writing. Many can use electronic mail to write and to share what Jesus has done for them.

Music Evangelism

Regular. Singing is the most common form of youth evangelism. Either vocal or instrumental music together with personal testimony can be very effective in sharing the gospel. We can plan for a regional youth religious concern. Send invitations to local churches, schools, and community youth organizations. We can involve more youth in music groups, make more friends, and have more opportunity to share Jesus.

Special. There are many talented youth in our community. We must discover their talents. Try to organize a youth song composer and music festival. Get people to donate prizes to honor the winners. Welcome students to participate. Welcome them to church.

The art of listening to music can be considered a way of evangelism. Select classical and contemporary religious music, folk music, even jazz and rock music, and let the professional music teacher guide our youth in how to distinguish and listen to good music that will enrich their lives.

Vocational Evangelism

Regular. The most effective way to evangelism is to live out the life of Jesus. We can let our working youth witness about Jesus in their work places. Train them to form Bible study groups and prayer groups with their coworkers. We should provide study guides to them.

We must find out the needs of the workplaces. Why do some of the youth need to work? Do they have enough opportunity to study? Can we provide on-the-job training or night school for education? We should consider career safety and health for our youth workers. Christian caring will bring people to Jesus.

Special. Vocational training classes can attract young people to our services. Some examples are language study for the workplaces, accounting and secretarial courses, computer courses, and sales and marketing skills. Bible studies and small group fellowship can be arranged as part of the vocational training classes.

Metropolitan Evangelism

Regular. We can use almost every evangelistic method in the big cities. The common factors regarding the youth or adults in the cities can be summed up as too busy, too many secular choices, too many people, too crowded, or too lonely.

It is not easy to invite the youth to church. We have to reach them where they are. We can use good and appropriate literature to do visitation in the streets or out in the parks. Friendship evangelism has proved successful for our youth in the big cities. Also, we can work along with TV evangelists and radio broadcasters to reach youth in their homes.

Special. The church can operate a social youth center for our young people. In the center we can provide many services where our youth can find a safe place to make friends, play games, read, and socialize together.

Inner-city Evangelism

Regular. Social services and community development can meet the needs of some of the youth in the inner city. Medical and health services can make contacts with the families. Meeting the material needs and providing care for the poor will make friends. Building trust and relationships will lead people to Jesus. Our youth can be good volunteers in many of these outreach programs.

Special. We can try educational and vocational training classes in the inner city. Field trips for inner-city youth to national parks and interesting historical sites can be friendship-building and educational. Let our more fortunate youth meet the less fortunate ones and let them learn from one another.

For Further Reading

Cho, Yonggi Paul. *Prayer: Key to Revival.* (Taiwan: Word Books, 1989).

Deville, Jard. *The Psychology of Witnessing.* Silver Spring, Md.: Ministerial Association, General Conference of Seventh-day Adventists, 1996.

Dudley, Roger L., and Des Cummings, Jr. *Adventures in Church Growth.* Hagerstown, Md.: Review and Herald Publishing Association, 1983.

Eims, Leroy. *The Lost Art of Disciple Making.* Grand Rapids: Zondervan Publishing House, 1980).

Knowles, George E. *How to Help Your Church Grow.* Silver Spring, Md.: Ministerial Association, General Conference of Seventh-day Adventists, 1997.

Mueller, Walt. *Understanding Today's Youth Culture.* Wheaton, Ill.: Tyndale House, 1994.

Patton, Michael Quinn. *Qualitative Evaluation Methods.* London: Sage Publications, 1986.

Ro, Bong Rin, and Marlin L. Nelson, *Korean Church Growth Explosion.* Taiwan: Word of Life Press, 1985.

Spotts, Dwight, and David Veerman. *Reaching Out to Troubled Youth.* Wheaton, Ill.: Victor Books, 1987.

Van Dolson, Leo. *How to Get the Most Out of Bible Study.* Silver Spring, Md.: Ministerial Association, General Conference of Seventh-day Adventists, 1996.

White, Ellen G. *Christian Service.* Washington, D.C.: Review and Herald Publishing Association, 1947.

————. *Evangelism.* Washington, D.C.: Review and Herald Publishing Association, 1946.

CHAPTER 23

Youth Ministry
and the Church

by Michael Peabody

SOMETIMES IN THE LIFE of each youth within the church, there needs to be a transition from "Isn't that just special?" to "That's a good idea; let's do it." Ellen White recognized this when she wrote that "if the youth will consecrate mind and heart to the Lord's service, they may reach a high standard of efficiency and usefulness."[1] Unfortunately, in many churches, the mantra of "we-need-to-get-the-youth-involved" dissolves somewhere between special music and collecting the offering.

Battling Tokenism

"In the near future many children will be endued with the Spirit of God, and will do a work in proclaiming the truth to the world that at that time cannot well be done by the older members of the church."[2]

Experience is the teacher that guides a youth through adolescence and into adulthood. While there may be a place for doing things for the express purpose of showing that "we have youth, and we let them do certain things in church," youth should be given an opportunity to develop their own identity by participating in the week-to-week operation of the local congregation. This goes beyond simply filling slots in a weekly church service to welcoming the fresh perspective that they bring to the table. Youth need to "own" their identity, not merely be younger clones of their more experienced counterparts.

From your vantage point as a youth leader, you have the ability to search for places in the church where youth can participate in the life of the congregation. As part of the transition from the "gimme" mentality of children to the "let me help you" concern of mature adults, youth need to have the opportunity to render meaningful service to the church.

For instance, when nominating committee season comes around, work to make sure that a young person is able to participate on each key committee of the church. Participation in these committees will give youth firsthand knowledge of the ways the local church operates—both positively and negatively. The committees, in turn, can benefit from the perspective of a young person who isn't jaded by past experience, and who is willing to ask the difficult questions.

Many churches have begun inviting youth to be members of their church boards. In these churches youth representatives are recognized as full members of the church boards, with all

159

the rights and responsibilities of their older counterparts. As a result, these church boards have benefited from an increase in intergenerational dialogue, and youth have been given an unprecedented opportunity to be heard and to influence church policy.

Although there is a place for tradition, in most churches the youth have developed a more progressive concept of worship. As members of the congregation, youth need to be encouraged to participate in the planning and act of worship, not only to fill in blank slots in the traditional worship order, but also to play a role in shaping the services so modern styles of worship and ministry are welcome, as well.

Many churches set aside a week each month or quarter for young people to present the worship service. In recent years some churches have begun to feature a separate church service each week that caters to the new generation. Still others provide a hybrid contemporary and traditional worship in a combined worship service.

These churches have caught a vision of what is possible when young people are given the opportunity to participate fully in worship. Many of the churches that offer a contemporary service have realized increased attendance as a result. However, of these approaches, the combination of contemporary and traditional worship is preferable, because it gives a broader range of age groups an opportunity to work together and experience a wider spectrum of worship.

Initially, it may be difficult for some of the "senior saints" to warm up to electric guitars and high-tech presentations in the sanctuary service; however, the combination of lively praise music and the classic hymns can create an unparalleled worship experience that can touch old and young hearts together.

These are just a few examples of the many ways in which your church can give its younger members a voice. The possibilities are as endless as their imaginations.

As in many aspects of church life, from choosing the color of carpet to redesigning the bulletin, making the changes necessary to integrate young people in the life of the congregation will draw an assortment of naysayers. The best advice in times like this is simply what Paul told Timothy: "Don't let anyone look down on you because you are young, but set an example for the believers in speech, in life, in love, in faith, and in purity. . . . Be diligent in these matters; give yourself wholly to them, so that everyone may see your progress. Watch your life and doctrine closely. Persevere in them, because if you do, you will save both yourself and your hearers" (1 Tim. 4:12-16, NIV).

The Administration of a Youth Program

An effective youth ministry is a costly investment for any congregation, and youth leaders often find themselves spending a considerable amount of time and energy pulling together enough money to achieve their ministry objectives.

The Difference Between Youth and Adult Ministry

Youth ministries are virtually defined by the ability to remain dynamic, vibrant, and flexible as they reach out to the current generation of youth. Youth ministry magazines feature the "ideal" youth room as decorated with the latest color scheme and featuring the latest multimedia equipment. The youth are in touch with the trends in contemporary music and popular culture. While youth ministries remain focused on the unchanging principles of the Word of God, they are often in a constant state of flux.

On the other hand, the classic "adult" church is defined by its tradition. The peaked ceilings and stained glass of the "ideal" sanctuary is designed to portray a feeling of security and stability. Although they appreciate progress to a certain extent, the "senior saints" pride themselves on their ability to remain rock-solid in their tradition in the midst of the turbulence caused by the MTV generation. Thus, the youth leader's task is twice as difficult, because he or she does not only need to raise the necessary funds but must also convince skeptical church members that the contemporary youth program will not send young people down the "primrose path."

Why Some People Are Reluctant to Give for Youth Ministry

One reason that people are reluctant to give to youth ministry is that they have been burned in the past by youth who never seemed to appreciate fully or even use the donation. For instance, there are stories of youth groups who have begged and pleaded for money for a boat (or something similar) that sits in disrepair behind the church, where it has been ever since the youth took it to the lake one time 20 years ago.

Other members ask, "If the youth really need this so badly, why don't they earn the money and buy it for themselves?" A good question, especially when the item is something within easy reach of the youth members. If there is, for instance, an upcoming weekend camping trip that will cost $10 for each youth member, there is reason that the youth, with enough work and planning, can't come up with the money themselves. Potential donors may see this as laziness, and they may very well be right.

So what does it take to put your youth ministry on the road to financial success? Simply stated, you need to plan ahead. There is a distinct advantage in developing a long-term strategic plan.

The Budget

Businesses know the importance of the yearly budget. Your church probably has one with a small slice cut out for your youth group. However, knowing the total amount of money that your youth group will have for a given period of time is not enough.

A couple of months before the start of the new fiscal year, it would be a good idea for the leadership of your youth group to spend some time developing a specific budget for the upcoming year. Include all the money you need to spend on materials, supplies, food, activities, etc., and balance it with the income you hope to receive from the church budget and fund raising. Be sure also to include a savings line for projects or large expenses that you plan on purchasing later in the year or even the following year. Be as realistic as possible. It is better to err on the conservative side in terms of fund-raising.

Prepare the budget so that it is responsible. You may wish to show the budget to the church treasurer and ask him or her to check it out to see if it makes sense. Once you've ironed out the wrinkles, present the budget to the finance committee of your church and request that your budget be calculated into the church's budget for the youth program. Once the budget is in place, stay within it as much as possible so you do not have to run to the church board for emergency funding later on for things that you could have planned for.

A Basic Primer on Church Politics

"Peacemakers who sow in peace raise a harvest of righteousness" (James 3:18, NIV). Whether you like it or not, as a youth leader you'll spend a great deal of time and energy dealing with your congregation's political situation. While the ideal congregation would be "pure . . . peace-loving, considerate, submissive, full of mercy and good fruit, impartial and sincere" (verse 17, NIV), the cold, hard reality in many churches does not quite reach these standards. Your job, then, is to combine the biblical admonition to be a peacemaker with your duty to be an advocate for the youth program.

If you have an understanding of church politics, your chances of succeeding will be much greater than if you blindly walk into a political trap much like an unwary soldier marches onto a land mine. In the midst of congregational politics, always keep Christ and His will central to your plans. Do not fall into the equally dangerous trap of making poor choices for your youth ministry because they appear politically expedient.

The central aspect of church politics is that, as in any other type of organization, each person has a goal that they wish to achieve. Each thing a person says or does is designed to take steps toward achieving this goal. In a church most people have a goal of promoting church growth and fostering an atmosphere in which people can grow closer to God. The way a person reaches toward the goal is influenced by a variety of suppositions and experiences, as well as the individual's psychological makeup and temperament. The key to "winning" at church politics is to determine what goals people are trying to achieve and convince them that you are interested in their goal and aspirations. Most of the time you will find that you fully agree with what the person is trying to achieve, but the disagreement exists over the methods.

So how do you apply this principle in real life? Imagine that you wish to take the youth on a kayaking trip, where they can be in nature and have an opportunity to get to know Christ in a more personal way. Unbeknown to you, for some reason kayaking is a taboo activity for some members of your church. As soon as you announce plans for the trip, a well-meaning church member approaches you and tells you that kayaking is "of the devil." The member produces an extensive document linking the modern sport of kayaking with an ancient pagan ritual of Nimrod.

You explain your overall vision for the youth of the church. As you discuss your shared goal of seeing the youth come to a saving relationship with Christ, you can slowly make the transition from a general discussion to the issue at hand. Although the concerned member may not fully agree with you, at least he or she will gradually be able to realize that you are on the same team and sharing the same goals. The key is to remain as peaceful and calm as possible. Be diplomatic.

Oh, the People You'll Meet!

In addition to those who have various fanatical viewpoints that may conflict with your ministry, there are other personality types to be aware of. This list is by no means exhaustive.

The Rah! Rah! "Poof." Soon after you begin your ministry, you will see these people being welcomed by other members as superheros returning from their latest adventure. After the initial greetings with their long-lost friends, they will make it a point to approach you and tell you how much better you are than your predecessor was. They will be strong cheerleaders for your program and are indeed valuable to have around at first, because the rest of the church will see that they have returned and will say to themselves, "Wow! This new youth leader must be doing an excellent job. People who have been gone for ages are now returning to church." Be glad that they are around when they are, but be wary about giving them too much responsibility initially. They will show up every week for a month or two and vanish when they find greener pastures elsewhere.

The Faithful Pain. This is the kind of person you can depend on to attend every week and help with your program. However, this person may or may not like you. In fact, they may think that you're actually doing a pretty lousy job and that they are doing a gallant job just trying to keep you from falling over the cliff. The best way to work with the faithful pain is to integrate them into the planning process and give them complete responsibility for some aspect of your program. The faithful pain will be much less likely to complain when they are responsible for a considerable part of the program and may actually appreciate your confidence in their "superior" abilities.

The Drill Sergeant. Sometimes people view the youth program as a boot camp designed to keep a bunch of "brats" in line. Their goal is to "teach these kids a lesson," rather than demonstrate a loving Savior. A fundamental qualification of a youth leader is missing—they must first of all love the youth and enjoy being around them. "They must love the children because they are the younger members of the Lord's family. . . . In educating the children and youth, teachers should not allow one passionate word or gesture to mar their work, for in so doing they imbue the students with the same spirit which they themselves possess."[3] This type of individual should not be given a position of responsibility over youth.

The *Church Manual* Thumper. On the church board the *Church Manual* thumper is usually an older member who has a firm grasp of the mechanics of church policy but does not necessarily have a great understanding of the underlying reasoning behind the policy. When you propose a concept that is not "traditional" in every sense of the word, the CMT pulls out a copy of the *Church Manual* and a collection of previous board meeting minutes to see whether or not you are violating the *Church Manual* or precedent. The CMT's interpretation of precedent and policy is respected because the rest of the board members often have no idea what they voted for several months ago and therefore have no basis on which to challenge the pronouncements.

It is, however, a good idea to get to know your board's CMT so you can run your ideas past them before the board meeting—once you've secured their support, your ideas have a much better chance of succeeding. Be careful never to make the CMT think that you are trying to bribe or sweet-talk them into sharing your viewpoint—the CMT has a reputation to retain as a respected person of principle.

The Wind Sock. Similar in many ways to the rah! rah! "poof," the wind sock's failing is that they do not disappear when they inevitably find greener pastures elsewhere. When you first arrive as a youth leader, it is easy to get the feeling that they think you are the salt of the earth. But as time progresses, you get the sense that you are not living up to their blimp-sized expectations. When the rah! rah! "poof"s disappear, the wind sock places a barely perceptible target of blame directly on your forehead.

You can identify them from their comments, such as "Have you noticed that the youth aren't as 'spiritual' as they were before?" or "Somebody—I won't give you their name—told me that they are bored in Sabbath school." They rarely admit that they are the originator of these rumors, but instead purport to report the way that the wind is blowing. These little bombs of doubt are planted all over the church until a large number of people slowly get the idea that you are not doing your job well enough. One day some small thing sets off all these little bombs, there's a big explosion, and you find that you've landed somewhere in the middle of the wilderness.

The wind sock is probably the most difficult personality type to deal with, since it is virtually impossible to figure out what they are thinking. They'll seem to be "supportive" of what you are doing but will often say something totally different to other people. They will often approach the *Church Manual* thumper and convince him to twist church policy to favor their position. Continue to be the best leader you can be without sacrificing principle for their favor.

The Experienced Unconditional Supporter. Worth more than gold to your ministries, the experienced unconditional supporters are people who have led out in ministry in years past and share your passion for the gospel of Christ. They are the ones who will pray for you, whether or not you ask them to, and will speak in support when others talk behind your back. They will show their confidence in your ministry by example—never criticizing you in public, but rather expressing their concerns to you privately. When they offer you words of advice, treasure them and take them seriously, because they understand your situation and also understand the politics you are dealing with. Although they prefer to work in the background, they are the strongest members of your ministry team. As Aaron and Hur held up Moses' arms in the midst of the battle, experienced unconditional supporters will hold up your arms in ministry.

Working With the Board and Other Committees
One Word: Attend

A wise person observed that people vote for things in a committee that they would never consider doing personally in their wildest dreams. As a youth leader, you have received a vision, but most boards and committees will do all they can to "help" bring you back to "reality." In short, church boards and committees are highly political organizations that you must deal with diplomatically.

Board meetings are where the "movers and shakers" of your congregation assemble to make the decisions that will govern your church's direction until, perhaps, the next board meeting. Although board meetings are not usually very exciting, it provides the only opportunity many people get to influence decisions that will affect people other than themselves, so they relish this opportunity to "impact" the ecclesiastical process. If these people are willing to put aside a couple hours a month to spend time listening to financial reports and making decisions, they expect you, as a leader, to be there too. And when you go, look interested.

How to Get Things Done

If you have a proposal that you are presenting to the board, there are two fates that you need to avoid. The first is having your proposal "tabled" or postponed until some later date in the ethereal future. The second is having your proposal sent off to an ad hoc committee, where it will be studied and dissected and then brought back to the board, which may at that point either pass, deny, or table the proposal. The truth is that ad hoc committees are often formed simply for the purpose of turning down a weak proposal while avoiding the embarrassment of placing board members in the position of voting it down in front of the person making the proposal.

Preparation is the key to success. Although your idea may make perfect sense to you, it is vital that you be able to explain it to the members of the board, who will be much more critical and studious during board meetings than they are as individuals in church. Do your research ahead of time.

For instance, if you need a new sound system for your youth room, ask the questions that the board would ask. Find out what type of systems your room needs, what other youth groups are using, and how much the system will cost. Look at the church calendar and see if this is a good time to ask for the funding. Make a simple chart listing the type, price, and features of the four or five systems within the price range of systems most likely to fill your needs. In your presentation, don't include systems that may fill your needs but are of questionable quality.

With your research done, talk to key board members individually (preferably those who also serve on the finance committee) and enlist their support about two weeks before the meeting at which you will make your presentation. Make it a special point to speak to those who will be willing to speak in your favor at the board meeting. Avoid speaking with those who will probably vote against your proposal, because they may speak to others against your proposal ahead of time and "poison the well." If you find that those who have supported you in the past privately counsel you against presenting the proposal for certain reasons, it may be best to postpone your presentation yourself rather than have the board table or send your presentation off to an ad hoc committee. As in any proposal, it is best to minimize the amount of negative history associated with your idea.

When the board meeting time comes, confidently extol the virtues of your proposal. Remember, even if you think you have previously secured the support of the people you have spoken with, there is no guarantee that your proposal will pass. There may have been subsequent conversations that "covered" your conversation with them. You must absolutely avoid the pitfall of whining or sounding overeager. If you do, even your most ardent supporters will be reluctant to speak in your favor.

Do not disparage the equipment you are going to replace, because chances are that somebody sitting in front of you purchased it several years ago. Rather, describe the many years of service the old equipment has given and how your successful youth group has simply outgrown its capabilities.

In your presentation, it is important to disassociate your desire for success from your ego. If a board member speaks against your proposal, do not "shoot them down" with "logic," but rather try to appreciate their viewpoint. Be objective throughout your presentation. If you attack a member's concern as completely invalid and indeed loony, it is an insult. If the board votes against your proposal or tables it indefinitely, thank the board for giving you the opportunity to serve as the youth leader.

The Five-Minute News Show

Board meetings also give you the opportunity to let the board know what is happening in the youth program. Members of the board are often too busy in their own ministries and careers to be aware of your ministry, so take every opportunity you can to talk about what the youth are doing. Also be sure to invite board members and others to participate in youth events and activities.

Some youth leaders prepare a newsletter that they distribute each month outlining the latest youth news and upcoming events. It would be a good idea to have a member of the youth group edit this newsletter, which can include articles by youth, short bits of trivia, and anything else that the youth find interesting. The newsletter can be printed or posted on the Internet. For the church board, you may wish to put together a monthly spreadsheet outlining how the youth budget is coming along.

When the congregation begins to see that things are happening in the youth department, they will get excited, and the way will be opened for the church to support the youth program even more.

---

[1] E. G. White, *Messages to Young People,* p. 199.

[2] White, *Counsels to Parents, Teachers, and Students,* pp. 166, 167.

[3] *Ibid.,* p. 170.

CHAPTER 24

Foundation and Transmission of Ethical Instructions in the New Testament

by Bernhard Oestreich

IN HIS LETTERS THE APOSTLE Paul not only teaches theological dogma but also instructs the churches on how to live as Christians. The questions examined in this chapter are: How does Paul transmit ethical values? How does he encourage the readers of his letters to live according to his instructions? The main concern is not the content of Paul's instructions but rather the methodology of transmission.

The importance of Paul's methodology becomes obvious if we ask ourselves: How are we to transmit ethical values? What are the most effective ways of teaching ethical conduct? These questions are especially relevant for all who work with youth.

One salient feature of Paul's ethical instructions is his use of arguments. They are an important means to help the members of his churches live according to Christian ethical values. Which arguments does Paul use? First we will investigate his theological arguments; next we'll turn to the arguments of the consequences of Christian conduct; then we'll deal with Paul's authoritative arguments; and finally we'll come to the arguments of tradition.

Theological Arguments

Christological Argument

We can discern three main arguments. First, Paul's ethical argumentation is basically a Christological one. The foundation of Paul's ethic is our salvation in Christ's death and resurrection. What Christ has done not only justifies men but also determines the daily life of the believer. They are drawn into the Christ event so that Christ lives and rules in them (Gal. 2:20). They live no longer for themselves but for the one who for their sake died and was raised (2 Cor. 5:15; cf. Rom. 14:9).

Christian believers are under the government of the resurrected one, the *jyrios*. They live according to the saving righteousness of God (2 Cor. 5:21; Titus 3:8) and in a manner worthy of the gospel of Christ (Phil. 1:27). This means that the Christians' behavior is not an extra that is added to their salvation in Christ. By their moral lives human beings do not supplement or complete what God has done in Christ. Rather, what the believers do is also initiated, moved, and accomplished by God's actions (Eph. 2:10).[1]

In keeping with the Christological foundation of his ethics, Paul constantly refers to Christ in his instructions (Rom. 12:1; 15:2, 3, 7; 1 Cor. 5:6-8; 6:15, 20; 7:23; 2 Cor. 5:15; 8:9;

Gal. 5:24, 25; Eph. 5:2; Col. 3:9-11, 17). Christ is more than an example or ethical ideal whom the Christian has to follow. He and His salvation work is the foundation and orientation (Phil. 2:5-8). He is the realm in which the Christian, being "in Christ," can walk in the newness of life (Rom. 6:4). Baptism (Rom. 6:2, 3) and the Lord's Supper (1 Cor. 10:14-17) direct the conduct of the believers. The call of God becomes an important argument for ethical instructions (1 Thess. 4:7; 5:24; Col. 3:12, 15).

The fact that Paul bases his ethical instructions on the salvation of Christ results in optimism and confidence concerning his readers' moral conduct and growth. God will come to His goal with them (1 Cor. 1:8, 9; Phil. 1:5; 2:13; 3:15; 1 Thess. 5:23, 24). They are cleansed (1 Cor. 6:11); even the children and the unbelieving spouse are holy (1 Cor. 7:14). Paul has great confidence in the members of his churches and praises them everywhere (2 Cor. 7:4, 16). He expresses his appreciation for the fact that the readers already live according to the principles of which Paul reminds them (Phil. 2:1, 12; 1 Thess. 4:1, 9, 10; 5:1, 4), and he urges them to hold on to what they have (Phil 2:15) and live according to what they are (Rom. 6:11-14; Phil. 3:16; Col. 3:8-10).

Eschatological Argument

The second argument Paul uses in his exhortation is the Christian conviction of living in the end-time and moving forward toward the end of this world. Is this a theological argument in the sense that it argues with the cause and consistency of the Christian life? Or is it an argument that refers to the eternal effect of the Christian conduct, i.e., reward or punishment? Of course, this does not seem to be an exclusive alternative. But we must be clear that for Paul the emphasis is on the former. The eschatological argument is related to the Christological one, because in Christ the eschatological time has come and in him the believers have the foundation of their hope.

In most cases the eschatological argument expresses encouragement and confidence. The believers belong to the new world (Phil. 3:20) and will certainly be held firm until the day of the Lord (1 Cor. 1:8; Phil. 1:6; 1 Thess. 5:23, 24). Therefore they are admonished to live according to their hope (Rom. 13:11-14; 14:10-13; 1 Cor. 4:5; 6:2, 3, 14, 15; 7:26-31; 2 Cor. 5:9, 10; Col. 3:1-5; 1 Thess. 5:1-11; Titus 2:11-15). The eschatological hope strengthens the responsibility in this world before the end (1 Tim. 4:7-11). Because of the nearness of the Lord's coming the Christians can live in joy and expectation and without fear and sorrow (cf. Luke 21:28), and at the same time can encounter their fellow humans with gentleness (Phil. 4:4-6).

Even the reference to God's judgment in 1 Corinthians 6:9, 10 and 2 Corinthians 5:10 is a threat only in a qualified way, because in the immediate context Paul speaks about the change the Christians have experienced that made them justified in the name of the Lord Jesus (1 Cor. 6:11 and 2 Cor. 5:14, 15; similarly Phil. 3:18-21; Gal. 5:19-26; 6:7-10; Col. 3:6, 7; cf. the qualification of the judgment theme in 1 Cor. 10:13; 11:32; 1 Cor. 3:17 might also be an encouragement).

This does not mean that the Christian does not need to take the judgment seriously. But when Christians stand in the final judgment the basic question will be about the acceptance of God's grace, i.e., if they have accepted Christ's offer of salvation completely and consistently, including the new way of life the apostle Paul encouraged.[2]

Creation Order Argument

Third, besides the Christological and the eschatological argument we find, however scarcely used, the argument of the creation order. It occurs only (always together with other arguments) in passages dealing with the relationship of man and woman (1 Cor. 11:7-9; 1 Tim. 2:13, 14; cf. Eph. 5:31). In other places the argument of creation is absent.

Values Growing Out of the Theological Arguments

Ethical decisions are often decisions in conflicts of values. We must decide what is more important in a given situation. For this reason ethical values form a hierarchy. Which ethical values correspond to the Christological and eschatological arguments in Paul's admonitions?

As a substantiation and rationale for Paul's instruction he often refers to the ethical value of altruism. The Christian is to take care of his fellow humans (cf. Matt. 25:35-46), he is concerned about the weaker brother (Rom. 15:1, 2; 1 Cor. 8:9, 12, 13), and he sacrifices his rights or his advantage for the sake of others (1 Cor. 9:15, 19-23; Phil. 2:4-11). This behavior can be summarized in the commandment of love (Rom. 13:8-10; 14:15; Gal. 5:13, 14; Col. 3:12-14; cf. John 13:34, 35; 15:12). Love is the basic command (cf. 1 Cor. 13) for Christian ethics.[3] The foundation of this ethical value is Christ who loved us and gave Himself for us (Rom. 5:5, 8; 2 Cor. 5:14; Gal. 2:20; cf. John 15:13).

Related to the commandment of love is the value of *humility*. Paul admonishes his readers not to think highly of themselves but to be humble (Rom. 12:10, 16; Gal. 5:26; 6:3, 4; Eph. 4:1, 2; Phil. 2:3; cf. Matt. 23:11, 12; Luke 14:10, 11; 1 Peter 5:5). The reason for this is found again in Christ, who humbled Himself in order to save us (Phil. 2:6-8).

Another important value can be found in Paul's exhortations. He calls the Christian believers to strive for *peace and oneness* (Rom. 14:19; 2 Cor. 13:11; Phil. 1:27; 2:2; 4:2; Col. 3:13, 15; 1 Thess. 5:13; 2 Tim. 2:24, 25; Titus 3:2; cf. 1 Peter 3:11; Heb. 12:14), to have peace in the church and, if possible, with unbelieving spouses (1 Cor. 7:12-15) and people outside the church (Rom. 12:18). To the ethical value of peace belongs the value of unity of the church (cf. John 17:21), which functions as foundation for many admonitions of Paul. The unity of the church is again substantiated with Christ Himself (Rom. 12:5; 1 Cor. 1:13; 12:12; Eph. 4:5).

The fact that Paul includes these ethical values in his arguments indicates that they rank high in his value system and thus can be used to deduce Christian conduct in certain cases. On the other hand, he substantiates these values with Christ Himself, more specifically with the salvation act of Christ. That means that these values are not an end in themselves. Christians follow not a moral system but their Savior. Their moral conduct is a consequence of their salvation.[4]

Conclusions for Ethical Instruction of Youth

What can we conclude about the instruction of youth from these facts? First, ethical teaching needs arguments. It is important that Paul argues at all.[5] Paul's ethical reasoning and his goal indicates that he is aware of the fact that there is not a direct command of Jesus for all decisions of life. He applies the general rules and values for the concrete situation. Application is the lasting task of the believers. For Paul to gain understanding of the will of

God is equivalent to growth in love. To follow moral rules without insightful application can result in bad results.[6] In the name of the law and also in the name of a misunderstood love humans have done much harm to others.

Arguments are one way to learn the task of application. If the instructions make sense for individuals, if reasons are given, individuals learn to decide for themselves. Paul wants his readers to come to their own ethical decisions. This is his goal: "to learn what is good and pleases God" (see Rom. 12:2; Eph. 5:10, 17; Phil. 1:9, 10).

For the instruction of our youth it is important that we not only teach values but that we teach them to value. Our society is pluralistic: there is no uniform value system. This fact causes uncertainty in young people. They have to find out what is right. They must be enabled to come to their own ethical decisions about "what is good and pleases God." This is to be done in discourse with other convictions and presupposes a readiness to listen to others and to be challenged, but also the ability to assert and prevail. Ethical arguments are an important means to developing this ability. If we give orders without reasoning we give the impression that we want to keep the younger generation in dependence. This will not be accepted. Arguments, however, indicate that we want the youth to decide for themselves.

Second, Christian behavior finds orientation in Christ. No other theological argument is of equal importance. The argument of eschatological hope grows out of the Christology. Paul's ethical values have their foundation in Christ. It is noteworthy that the creation order plays a minor role in Paul's ethical argumentation.

Our ethical reasoning should have the same Christological consistency. Youth seeks for consistency, for a correspondence between what we are and what we do. A large number of unrelated arguments are suspected as opportunism or manipulation. Youth will accept (at least rationally) Christian moral admonition if it can be legitimized from Christ's work for us.

Third, Paul's ethical admonition is very optimistic. He assumes that his readers belong to Christ. He encourages them to continue in their Christian ethics. He is optimistic that they will realize that his teaching is according to the Lord's will (1 Cor. 14:37; Gal. 5:10; cf. 1 John 4:6). This positive view of his readers grows out of his faith. Because Christ has begun the good work he will bring it to completion (1 Cor. 1:8; Phil. 1:6).

People who teach ethical values today also need a positive attitude toward the receivers of the instruction. Youth are sensitive to attitudes and will reject ethical admonition if it comes from the viewpoint that youth are basically depraved. A negative view is a negation of the Christian faith.

Arguments of the Consequences

Besides theological arguments Paul advances arguments that build on the consequences of Christian conduct. First, we must mention again the eschatological judgment (1 Thess. 4:6; Rom. 14:4, 10-12; Gal. 5:21; Col. 3:25). Paul, however, when mentioning God's judgment does not threaten the members of His churches with the eschatological outcome of their lives. We have already seen that he speaks mainly in an encouraging or affirming way after mentioning the eschatological judgment (e.g., Gal. 5:22-25). After the traditional eschatological image of harvesting with the warning not to be deceived about God's judgmental consistency

(Gal. 6:7, 8) Paul continues with the positive outlook to the harvest of the good works of the believers (verses 9, 10).

More important, Paul argues with the positive effect that the Christian conduct will have for believers and also for other people. The reputation of the Christian church is an especially often used argument. The objectionable practice of some members of the church in Corinth is reproved with the argument that it is even unheard-of among non-Christians (1 Cor. 5:1), or that it is done in the presence of unbelievers (1 Cor. 6:5, 6). In these cases the non-Christians are mentioned in order to demonstrate the gravity of the misconduct.

Another argument of the believer's reputation is presented in 1 Corinthians 11:6, 13: it is a shame for a woman to cut her hair or for a man to have long hair. In general Paul warns against doing anything that would diminish the respect of the unbelieving people for the church, e.g., lawsuits of church members before unbelievers (1 Cor. 6:4-6), hasty liberation of women in the church (1 Cor. 14:34, 35; 1 Tim. 2:11, 12), the slaves' disobedience (1 Tim. 6:1), abuse of spiritual gifts (1 Cor. 14:23), living at the expense of others (1 Thess. 4:11, 12; 2 Thess. 3:6). Similarly Paul admonishes the Christians not to give offense to anyone (1 Cor. 10:32; cf. Rom. 14:16, 18), but to live respectably before the society (1 Thess. 4:12; cf. Phil. 4:8; Col. 4:5; 1 Tim. 3:7; 5:10; Titus 2:3, 5, 8, 10) in order to shine as a light in the world (Phil. 2:15).

This moral argument reveals an ethical value that plays an important role in Paul's admonitions. Christians are expected to live quietly (1 Tim. 2:2) and independently (1 Thess. 4:11, 12), and seek the best for society (Rom. 12:17).

Sometimes Paul argues with the consequences that the person who does not live according to apostolic advice suffers. Unmoral conduct (1 Cor. 6:18) or selfishness while celebrating the Lord's Supper (1 Cor. 11:17) does harm to the Corinthians. Paul gives advice for the reader's own benefit (1 Cor. 7:35). These consequences are not a divine punishment that comes superficially upon the disobedient Christian. They are rather the natural outgrowth of the unfavorable behavior.

Conclusions for Ethical Instruction of Youth

The argument of the consequences is important for the ethical teaching also today. Youth asks for the practical relevance of ethical instructions. What good will it do for me? What advantage do I have if I live according to these admonitions?

However, it is important that the consequences are shown to be the natural result of the behavior. Even divine judgment of sinful conduct is not God's strange reaction but grows out of His character and correlates to His destination for the world. If a person does not understand the connection of behavior and consequences, the argument of negative consequences becomes a threat and of positive consequences becomes a bribery. If the young person has not yet found a firm personality, he or she might follow the advice because of self-interest or fear of the consequences. This, however, will not lead to maturity of the person. If, on the other hand, the young person has developed a strong personality, he or she will reject all advice that seems to lead to dependency by way of reward or punishment.

Of special interest are the consequences of social acceptance. In today's individualistic society people are still concerned about what others think of them. But it seems that they are interested only in the view of the members of the various groups to which they belong. This is often a selfish interest. Paul, with his concern for the reputation of the church, teaches us to be open for society on a larger scale. The believers of Christ and the church in general is responsible for people who are not yet known to its members, who only have heard something about the church. They might later come into contact with the church, and then it is of relevance what view they have. Christians are responsible for their impact on society far beyond their own social groups. Ethical instruction for the youth includes to teach social responsibility, because everybody lives in a social network broader than usually thought.

Arguments of Authority

Paul underlines his ethical admonitions by referring to authorities. These arguments presuppose a certain acceptance of the authorities in the church. The first to which Paul refers is Christ (1 Thess. 4:1, 2; Col. 3:13). His self-humiliation and self-sacrifice are the basic orientation for the Christian life (Phil. 2:5-11; 2 Cor. 8:9; Rom. 15:3, 7). The law of Christ (Gal. 6:2) is the command to deny one's own interests and carry the burdens of the brother in the same way as Christ did.[7] This basic orientation is meant with the formula of imitation of Christ (1 Cor. 11:1; 1 Thess. 1:6). The authority of Christ is the background of Paul's reference to the words of Jesus (1 Cor. 7:10; 9:14). The words and the teaching of Jesus are the foundation of a moral life (1 Tim. 6:3-5).

Of course, also God Himself and His Holy Spirit is the authority whom the Christians have to follow. Their sanctification is the will of God (1 Thess. 4:3, 7, 8; cf. 1 Thess. 5:18), God himself taught the believers to love one another (1 Thess. 4:9). God's authority is clearly distinguished from human authority.

Another authority to which Paul refers is Scripture. It is written to encourage the Christians (Rom. 15:4). Paul mentions the commandment of love (Gal. 5:14). He refers to the negative example of Israel's conduct (1 Cor. 10:1-11) and to the law of Deuteronomy 25:4 (1 Cor. 9:9; 1 Tim. 5:18) or alludes to the command of holiness Leviticus 11:44 (1 Thess. 4:3). First Timothy 1:8-10 seems to be shaped according to the Ten Commandments. However, it is surprising that Paul in his ethical instructions uses Scripture only occasionally. In the parenetic sections of 1 Thessalonians 4:1–5:24; Colossians 3:1–4:6 and Philippians 1:27–2:18; 3:1–4:9 there are no explicit Scripture references. And when Paul refers to the law then he gives very broad admonitions and general rules, only seldom he comes to specific commandments.[8] He indicates this way that his main authority is Christ Himself. He reads Scripture in the light of the Christ event and thus selects what is applicable for the church (e.g., 1 Cor. 9:9). Scripture is for him not simply a law but first of all a testimony of God's love in Christ (Gal. 5:14). This love leads necessarily to a certain conduct of the believers, to the obedience of faith (Rom. 1:5).

The Christ event also leads to other important authorities of the church. These are the apostles, eyewitnesses, and founders of the church. However, their authority is derived from Christ; thus Paul admonishes "in the Lord" and the believers should respect their leaders "in the Lord" (1 Thess. 4:1; 5:12; Gal. 6:6).

An argument of authority is the reference to the community of churches. The believers should respect the consensus of the community of churches (1 Cor. 4:17; 11:5). Paul praises certain churches in order to encourage others to follow their example (e.g., Rom. 1:8; 15:26; 16:19; 2 Cor. 7:14; 8:1-5; 9:2; 1 Thess. 1:7, 8; 2:14).

An often-used argument is the authority of the apostle Paul himself and in most cases the founder of the churches he addresses. The church members should accept his advice and thus contribute to his joy (Phil 2:2; 4:1) and make sure that his work was not in vain (Phil. 2:16; Gal. 4:11, 19, 20; 2 Cor. 11:2, 3). He connects also his confidence that the believers will live according to their faith with his as a person, e.g. being present or absent (Phil. 1:27; 2:12). He utilizes his personal relationship to the members of his churches in order to strengthen his ethical instructions. He has a positive attitude toward them (e.g., Phil. 1:7; 2 Cor. 6:11-13). He trusts that they respect him and confronts them with high expectations of their willingness to follow him.

Other authorities include the coworkers and commissioners of the apostle whom he sends to the churches and whose respect he requires (e.g., Timothy: 1 Cor. 4:17; 16:10; Phil. 2:19, 20; Epaphroditus: Phil. 2:29; Epaphras: Col. 1:7; Titus: 2 Cor. 8:23, 24; Phoebe: Rom. 16:1, 2). They transmit the doctrinal and ethical tradition of the church. Paul admonishes the believers to accept and honor their leaders (1 Cor. 16:15-18; 1 Thess. 5:12; 1 Tim. 5:17).

Paul also supports the authorities of society by instructing the believers to submit to husbands (1 Cor. 11:2, 3; Eph. 5:22-24; Col. 3:18), parents (Eph. 6:1-3; Col. 3:20), masters (Eph. 6:5-8; Col. 3:22-25; 1 Tim. 6:1, 2; Titus 2:9, 10), government (Rom. 13:1-7; 1 Tim. 2:1, 2; Titus 3:1). However, these authorities receive admonitions as well and are reminded that they have the Lord's authority above them (Col. 3:19, 21; 4:1).

Paul not only introduces authoritative persons in his ethical advice; he presents persons as examples and models for his readers (Rom. 16:1; Phil. 2:29). Paul again and again emphasizes the importance of models (Phil. 3:17; 1 Tim. 4:12; cf. Heb. 6:12; 13:7). More, Paul himself is a model (Phil. 1:30; 2 Tim. 3:10-12). Often he admonishes his readers to follow his example (1 Cor. 4:16; Gal. 4:12; Phil. 3:17; 4:9; 1 Thess. 1:6; 2 Thess. 3:7, 9). His example, however, is not independent from Christ, since he himself follows Christ (1 Cor. 11:1; Gal. 2:20; 1 Thess. 1:6). Paul serves like a mediator who transmits the example of Jesus to the churches.[9]

Conclusions for Ethical Instruction of Youth

The first conclusion we have to draw relates to the importance of authorities in general. Of course, the structures of our society and its authorities are different from those in the time of Paul and the first churches. We have today different roles of political leaders, church leaders, husband and wife, employer and employee, and other authorities. But what has not changed is the fact that authorities are necessary for the society. Ethical values of society are confirmed and supported by persons and groups who function as institutional or informal leaders of the society.[10] Therefore the society needs authorities, which are marked by competence and experience, in order to maintain and transmit ethical values to the next generation. Young people have difficulties to develop their own value system if they are left without authorities that give the necessary orientation.

Ethical instruction needs models. If we teach abstract principles and values, the effect will be marginal. Especially the youth learns and internalizes values from persons who live out these values. The best substantiation of values is the living model.[11] They need transmission of Christ's teachings through tangible persons.[12] Although these models can be persons of history or remote heroes of faith (Heb. 11), of greatest impact are models that are approachable for youth, persons who live together with, or close to, youth. This is one reason that for Paul it is not enough to present Jesus in His incarnation and salvation work as a model for Christian conduct but refers to his own conduct and to other Christians. Today youth will follow the example of authorities of church and society which they know personally. Youth leaders who want to have influence must of course teach morale and values, but at the same time they must be ready to reveal the way they live in order to make young people know what they mean by saying Do the same as I do.

Paul's authority was always a derived one. He is a servant of Christ and follows Christ. Today's leaders of youth, and of the church in general, need to make clear that they have no authority of their own but that they follow Christ. More, the foundation of their conduct is the authority not of a law but of a loving personal God and Savior, Jesus Christ, from whom all rules are derived. The fear to violate a set of rules leads youth to dependence from human interpreters of the law. Youth leaders are called to help the youth to grow to a loving relationship with Christ and to live happily according to His principles instead of getting into the fearful and slavish dependence of rules.

Arguments of the Tradition

Paul refers often to the tradition of the church. It consisted not only in the truth about Jesus and His work for human salvation. Ethical instructions were part of the tradition that the apostle received and handed down to new converts (1 Thess. 4:1, 2, 6; 1 Cor. 4:6).[13]

In Paul's ethical teaching history plays an important role. The members of the churches in the Hellenistic cities should realize that they became part of a history that goes beyond the time of their own Christian life. Paul reminds the Thessalonians (1 Thess. 2:14), the Corinthians (1 Cor. 14:36), and the Romans (Rom. 11:18) that not from them Christianity or faith originated. They belong to a history that manifests itself in cherished memories, in values and practices of the church.

But it is not only the history of the church as a whole to which Paul refers. He reminds the readers of his letters of what he has taught them in the beginning of their Christian life (1 Cor. 11:1; 1 Thess. 4:6). He reminds them of their willingness and their zeal at these days (Gal. 4:14, 15). This means that the ethical values have also a history in the lifetime of the believers and their immediate social group.

In any case, the recalling of ethical tradition establishes continuity of values for the readers of Paul's letters. Continuity provides orientation (cf. 1 Tim. 4:16). Thus the believers can hope to find the right decisions in their daily life situations.

It is important to see that Paul introduces the history of Christian ethical values in a positive way. This reasoning could be called the reasoning by positive experience. He reminds the readers of what they already know and what they already practice. He commends them for their faithfulness and admonishes them to continue in their way.

Conclusions for Ethical Instruction to Youth

In our most differentiated and pluralistic world every day we have to make decisions that include ethical aspects. To be able to decide is part of human freedom, but at the same time it makes people feel insecure, because every decision includes the potential to mistakes. Ethical values reduce the stress of freedom by providing orientation and guidance for the individual to come to decisions more easily.[14]

In order to fulfill this role, ethical values must have duration.[15] What constantly changes cannot provide orientation. In other words, values are manifestations of long cherished convictions and experiences. They have a history in the individual, in society, in religious groups, and in the culture. They offer a mental and spiritual "homeland." Society gains stability if ethical values have some continuity and are handed down from one generation to the next.[16]

What does this mean for the transmission of values? First, to teach values needs consistency. The more basic a value the more firmly it should be held. Especially youth cannot develop a helpful value system if it is confronted with inconsistent value education.

Second, to teach values is closely connected with the teaching of history. Because a value system belongs to a social community and necessarily has duration, an individual who is to internalize a value system needs to accept that he or she is part of a history that embraces more than one's lifetime. This is especially true for young people or new converts. Therefore it is necessary to get informed about the history of the social community in which the value system is current and develop a sense of belonging, a feeling of being part of this history. This way the newcomer or youth can share in the continuity which is part of values.

Third, the historical aspect requires that the teaching of values includes repetition and assurance. In order to have duration values need to have continuing attention. As long as society speaks about them, reflects on them from many different sides, verifies them and substantiates them, these values matter in society. When society does not constantly deal with their values they lose meaning and effect. Therefore it is important that church members get reminded and assured, they need to encourage and confirm each other to do right in applying their values.

Oftentimes, today's youth reject traditional values. If ethical instructions are supported with traditional arguments ("we have always done it this way"), the young people react with reluctance or openly refuse. The reason is not the traditional argument as such because in some instances the youth acts very traditional. The reason is often that traditional values are not presented in such a way that the youth had a chance to accept them as part of their own history.[17]

To do this, youth instructors have to bear in mind two important principles. First, ethical instruction must be accompanied by historical information and the development of the feeling of belonging to a social entity that has a history and a tradition, of which ethical rules and values are only a part. And second, an individual internalizes values by developing his or her own history with them. This needs time. An educator who wants to help young people to establish their own value system according to the Christian values must give them opportunity to try out these values, to make them the foundation for their own decisions. This calls for a certain freedom in the application of traditional basic values.

This also needs a "social room," in which the individual can have his or her own experiences. We learn to value by means of concrete cases where we have to take a stand. General teaching of "love for all" alone is not effective. Therefore the transmission and education of values functions best in the smaller social groups of which the individual can be an active partner.[18] If this small group is experienced as part of the larger community, as representative of the church in general, the individual's experience is connected with the whole.[19]

---

[1] Cf. Wolfgang Schrage, *Ethik des Neuen Testaments* (Berlin: Evangelische Verlagsanstalt, 1985), p. 129.

[2] *Ibid.*, p. 151; cf. Ulrich Luz, "Eschatologie and Friedenshandeln bei Paulus," *Eschatologie und Frieden,* ed. Gerhard Liedke (Heidelberg: Forschungsstätte der Evangelischen Studiengemeinschaft, 1978), pp. 278f.

[3] Karl Kertelge, "Freiheitsbotschaft und Liebesgebot im Golaterbrief," *New Testament und Ethik,* für Rudolf Schnachkenburg, ed. Helmut Merklein (Friburg: Herder, 1989), p. 337.

[4] Compare the discussion of ethical values in Eberhard Jüngel, "Wertlose Wahrheit: Chrisliche Wahrheitserfahrung im Streit gegen die Tyrannei der Werte," *Wertlose Wahrheit: Zur Identität und Relevanz des christlichen Glaubens, Theologische Erörterungen 3, Beiträge zur evangelischen Theologie* 107 (München: Kaiser, 1990).

[5] Compare Wolfgang Schrage, "Zum Verhältnis von Ethik und Vernunft," *Neues Testament und Ethik,* für Rudolf Schnackenburg, ed. Helmut Merklein (Freiburg: Herder, 1989), pp. 504-506.

[6] Rudolf Ginters, *Werte und Normen: Einführung in die philosophische und theologische Ethik* (Göttingen: Vandenhoeck and Ruprecht, 1982), pp. 168f.

[7] Cf. Gal. 2:20; cf. Heinz Schürmann, "'Das Gesetz des Christus' (Gal. 6:2): Jesu Verhalten und Wort als letztgültige sittliche Norm nach Paulus," *Neues Testament und Kirche,* für Rudolf Schnackenburg, ed. Joachim Gnilka (Freiburg: Herder, 1974), pp. 282-300; Schrage, *Ethik des Neuen Testaments,* p. 171.

[8] Wolfgang Schrage, *Die konkreten Einzelgebote in der paulinischen Paränese: Ein Beitrag zur neutestamentlichen Ethik* (Gütersloh: Gütersloher Verlagshaus Mohn, 1961).

[9] Cf. Otto Merk, "Nachahmung Christi: Zu ethischen Perspektiven in der paulinschen Theologie." *Neues Testament und Ethik,* für Rudolf Schnackenburg, ed. Helmut Merklein (Freiburg: Herder, 1989), pp. 172-206.

[10] Hans-Jürgen Fraas, "Religionsspädagogik und Ethik. Zur ethischen Dimension religiöser Erziehung," *Jahrbuch für Religionspädagogik* 9 (1992): 24.

[11] Leopold Neuhold, *Wertwandel im Christentum, Soziale Perspektiven,* (Linz: Veritas, 1988), vol. 4, p. 120.

[12] Ginters, p. 134.

[13] Heinz Schürmann, "Die Gemeinde des Neuen Bundes als der Quellort des sittlichen Erkennens nach Paulus," *Theologisches Jahrbuch* (Leipzig: St. Benno, 1973), p. 42.

[14] Neuhold, p. 18.

[15] *Ibid.,* p. 19.

[16] Hans-Jürgen Fraas, "Religionspädagogik und Ethik. Zur ethischen Dimension Religiöser Erziehung," *Jahrbuch für Religionspädagogik* 9 (1992): 130.

[17] Neuhold, pp. 92-97.

[18] Helmut Anselm, "Virtuelle Ethikgemeinschaften und Werteerziehung heute," *Zeitschrift für Evangelische Ethik* 41 (1997): 134.

[19] Neuhold, p. 120.

Bibliography

Anselm, Helmut. "Virtuelle Ethikgemeinschaften und Werteerziehung heute." *Zeitschrift für Evangelische Ethik* 41 (1997): 129-136.

Fraas, Hans-Jürgen. "Religionspädagogik und Ethik. Zur ethischen Dimension religiöser Erziehung." *Jahrbuch für Religionspädagogik* 9 (1992): 11-29.

Ginters, Rudolf. *Werte und Normen: Einführung in die philosophische und theologische Ethik.* Göttingen: Vandenhoeck and Ruprecht, 1982.

Jüngel, Eberhard. "Wertlose Wahrheit: Christliche Wahrheitserfahrung im Streit gegen die Tyrannei der Werte." *Wertlose Wahrheit: Zur Identität und Relevanz des christlichen Glaubens. Theologische Erörterungen 3. Beiträge zur evangelischen Theologie* 107. München: Kaiser, 1990.

Kertelge, Karl. "Freiheitsbotschaft und Liebesgebot im Galaterbrief." *Neues Testament und*

Ethik. Für Rudolf Schnackenburg. Ed. Helmut Merklein. Freiburg, Basel, Wien: Herder, 1989. Pp. 326-337.

Kress, Harmut. *Ethische Werte und der Gottesgedanke: Probleme und Perspektiven des neuzeitlichen Wertbegriffs.* Stuttgart: Kohlhammer, 1990.

Luz, Ulrich. "Eschatologie und Friedenshandeln bei Paulus." *Eschatologie und Frieden.* Ed. Gerhard Liedke. Heidelberg: Forschungsstätte der Evangelischen Studiengemeinschaft, 1978. Pp. 225-281.

Merk, Otto. "Nachahmung Christi: Zu ethischen Perspektiven in der paulinischen Theologie." *Neues Testament und Ethik.* Für Rudolf Schnackenburg. Hrg. Helmut Merklein. Freiburg, Basel, Wien: Herder, 1989. Pp. 172-206.

Neuhold, Leopold. *Wertwandel im Christentum.* Soziale Perespektiven 4. Linz: Veritas, 1988.

Schrage, Wolfgang. *Die konkreten Einzelgebote in der paulinischen Paränese: Ein Beitrag zur neutestamentlichen Ethik.* Gütersloh: Gütersloher Verlagshaus Mohn, 1961.

————. *Ethik des Neuen Testaments.* Berlin: Evangelische Verlagsanstalt, 1985.

————. "Zum Verhältnis von Ethik und Vernunft." *Neues Testament und Ethik.* Für Rudolf Schnackenburg. Hrg. Helmut Merklein. Freiburg, Basel, Wien: Herder, 1989. Pp. 482-506.

Schürmann, Heinz. " 'Das Gesetz des Christus' (Gal. 6:2): Jesu Verhalten und Wort als letztgültige sittliche Norm nach Paulus." *Neues Testament und Kirche:* Für Rudolf Schnackenburg. Ed. Joachim Gnilka. Freiburg: Herder, 1974. Pp. 282-300.

————. "Die Gemeinde des Neuen Bundes als der Quellort des sittlichen Erkennens nach Paulus." *Theologisches Jahrbuch.* Leipzig: St. Benno, 1973. Pp. 217-237.

CHAPTER 25

In or Out of Shape?

by Delyse Steyn

THERE IS A GENERAL POLARITY of thinking about what health and healing are. The various perspectives on the Seventh-day Adventist "health message" run along a continuum from "What is in shape?" to "What is out of shape?" To many, these ideas have nothing more than nuisance value, while to others they are a recipe for righteousness by roughage. This dichotomy is reflected in youth's choices of lifestyle. Unhealthy living in the context of strict health laws may be a means of rebellion by some. Others choose to be healthy, in spite of the values of their home. The question "In or out of shape?" raises issues confronting those in youth ministry.

In this chapter we will examine the ideas of three youth who represent three groups of young people today.

(AB) Autobiographer. Bachelor of Arts, major in English and communication. A thoughtful, compassionate 21-year-old, born a Seventh-day Adventist, parents are church workers. Reads widely, lived recklessly, serious about individuality and freedom of choice.

(CE) Communication Expert. Bachelor of Arts, major in communication and psychology. A serious-minded 25-year-old, born a Seventh-day Adventist, disruptive family life. Enjoys philosophy, experienced, serious about overcoming.

(TM) Transformed "Mary." Health Promotion (two-year diploma) graduate. Born Presbyterian, disruptive family life, older sister died while a young teenager. Baptized a Seventh-day Adventist in 1998.

The profiles of these three were shaped in weekly meetings during the past year. The "how" becomes "wow!" when the young person is personally convinced of his/her responsibility for the shape that he/she is in and the shape that God empowers him/her to imagine. This shape is not a mold. It has to do with formation and reformation (the key ideas in Philippians 2 and Romans 12 about the Christian mind). The educational principle that youth must learn to think and not merely reflect the thoughts of others undergirds this chapter and is the method recommended to any leader.

This discussion is not a definitive statement on health, but rather the beginning of an adventure for the youth, their leaders, and God as Wonderful Counselor. The subheadings form a curriculum comprising significant topics for discussion at youth meetings. Issues must be raised; questions beg answers.

God's Shape for Healthy Living

This shape is expressed in 3 John 2: "that thou mayest prosper and be in [good] health." Moses' training in the Wilderness School included primary health care, water resources, and sanitation. It was directly related to his divinely appointed mission. Exodus 16:26 reminds us that the Lord is the Physician that heals, but that the command to live according to His laws is reinforced by the promise "I will not punish you with any of the diseases that I brought on the Egyptians" (TEV). A lifestyle of prevention through wise choices of the natural remedies listed by Ellen White[1] is currently being supported by research. It is too bad that these ideas are often mocked in the church while gaining general acceptance elsewhere.

Rational therapy (originally used by Dr. J. H. Kellogg and Ellen G. White) requires a confrontation with biblical principles, scientific facts, heart-searching, and informed decision-making. It assumes the role of reason, the right use of the will, God's power, and the law of cause and effect. The choices are based on an understanding of anatomy, physiology, and health. A prohibitive legalistic approach denies the power of choice.

Change is a biblical principle. Prescription breeds resistance. What are the biblical principles of health living? How can one evaluate the prevailing ideas bombarding the youth and their leaders?

The Shape of Society

The ideas of popular culture have been drummed into the minds of the youth! "A friend in need's a friend indeed, [but] a friend with weed is better," sung by Placebo, offers a way of life and is a challenge to tradition and authority. Heavily influenced by hallucinogens and amplification, the youth are driven by nihilism to find altered states of consciousness and virtual reality is more real! John Fahey said that his angry music encourages people to commit suicide.[2]

This is the diet they are fed. Whole foods are not the menu choice for a fast-food generation. Just as one's taste has to be reoriented, humanity's myths have to be debunked. Ecstasy and heightened spiritual experience are enticing. A healthy life promising longevity lacks appeal when the statistics show that 40 percent of 90-year-olds have Alzheimer's. Who wants to be in that shape?

The crisis of confidence in science, medical science, and technology as progress has resulted in a rise of spirituality with a "new worldview." The vacuum left by the inadequacies of Christian thinking is being filled by deeply religious philosophies. Jacob Needileman says that the youth are "demanding courses in Buddhism, Hinduism, and mysticism, often forming their own 'free universities' to study these subjects, [and] that psychiatrists, psychologists, and clergymen of all faiths are joining the younger generation in this pursuit."[3]

The distinct Cartesian line between science and religion is fading. Health and religion share the same metaphysical ideas of the miraculous, energy, and healing. A health message, in the context of the great controversy and the third angel's message, would call to question Satan's attempts to fog the issue of true healing. There is an urgent challenge to the youth to confidently restate a biblical position on health and healing.

Materialism, consumerism, the deification of self, and hedonism—typical of the media-constructed subculture—impact heavily on the youth. Glamorized images and picture-perfect models devastate one's personhood. Body image is measured against pornographic images and body doubles, who stand in for unacceptable legs of a star with the face and status of a celebrity. Our inadequacies make us sick with worry. The images of the techno-body are unrealistic, but we try to squeeze it to be acceptable to unreal people, thus making ourselves spectacles. We are offered plastic shapes to emphasize, to extend, and to shape our shapeless forms. The multimillion-dollar fashion and beauty industry and plastic surgery shape us into the image of our choice—but at a price.

Rodin suggests: "The quest for physical perfection is the up-to-date way we barter with the uncertainty of life. Like a set of worry beads, we always have our calories to count, our minutes of aerobics to execute. If everything else in our lives seems out of control, we at least have our diet and exercise regimens. In the chaos called modern life, ordering the body to do what we want it to may give us a much-needed illusion of control."[4]

The grungy look at Generation X signifies their criticism. There is a paradox in the spiritualistic reaction of the "god within" movements against the idolization of self (see 1 John 5:21). Christian churches are numbered by their enculturation. The answer to Jeremiah's question at the end of the twentieth century: "Is there a doctor in the house?" (see Jer. 8:15, 18, 22) is answered by David: "[God] forgives all [my] sins and heals all [my] diseases" (Ps. 103:3, NIV). A significant test of a worldview is Does it offer me a Savior who heals holistically? How do I think when I become the source of truth, reality, and meaning?

The Shape of Self

Samson was dedicated to be the ultimate image of health and strength. The recipe was God-given and detailed. But he made narcissistic and sensory rather than integrity choices. Ultimately, Samson was out of shape with Israel and in shape with the Philistines. Daniel and his friends lived among highly intelligent youth. Their integrity choice versus appetite resulted in a power of intellect 10 times superior.

"In physical strength and beauty, in mental vigor and literary attainment, they stood unrivaled. The erect form, the firm, elastic step, the fair countenance, the undimmed senses, the untainted breath—all were so many certificates of good habits, insignia of the nobility with which nature honors those who are obedient to her laws."[5] Mom's home cooking was chosen above the rare foods on the king's table that could become addictive.

What are the lifestyle choices being made by the youth? Is health a personal, private choice, or is there an element of social responsibility? What is the relationship between a reckless lifestyle and a wrecked future? The slogan used by *Details* magazine is "Once a cult, now the culture."[6] How do I see myself when the mirror reflects a mainstream of alternative lifestyles? How can I cope when I don't fit in?

Shape Up

The WHO strategy for health for all by the year 2000 has identified the role of lifestyle. The current health crisis includes medical care costs and startling facts about cancer (one third of Americans will contract the disease, most of whom will die of it), heart disease (accounts for half of all deaths in U.S.), viruses, the reemergence of "controllable" diseases and the spread of uncontrollable ones, for example, AIDS.[7] The problems of holistic health—the techniques, the intrusion of the occult, spiritualism, and New Age thinking—are compounding the confusion. Acceptance of these health philosophies is accelerating. The fact that a counterfeit uses the same ideas with subtle twists actually reinforces the truth of the original idea. For example, a total vegetarian way of living is becoming popular, but Adventists are moving away from the ideas that made them unique.

A call for "health reform" is not an idiosyncratic appeal by a church. What an indictment that we have been sitting on some of the foremost health knowledge for more than a century! God gave health-care instructions to His chosen people so that while they wandered in an unfriendly wilderness, with compromised immune systems, they would be divinely protected from becoming ill. There was no 911 team, no trauma units. Health was a priority; it had to do with their mission.

A rational being needs to have facts to give an account of the decision made. *Proof Positive,* by Neil Nedley, reflects commitment to God's message that is scientifically founded and timely. However, in representing these concepts, the youth leader needs to be sensitive to peer pressure, stereotyping, conformity, and inability to think critically.

In-Shape Youth

The Creation story was a reminder to the Jews exiled in Babylon of their freedom and destiny. Living in an alien culture requires that we constantly remind ourselves of the abnormality of it. A distorted relationship between the creature and the Creator, as described in Romans 1:24-32, results in broken people and an unhealthy society. Inconsistency is a problem of integrity.

Freedom is not one element in the Christian life; it is the Christian life. Hope is a counterreality to despair, and manifests itself in the desire for purity from the strains of the world. The Christian mission is a lifestyle of freedom and apocalyptic hope. The essence of lifestyle education is the story lived, not told.

Self-critique is accomplished by a search for an alternative view of health. Walsh suggests that "we need to know deeply and intimately the *wisdom* of God . . . if we are to both diagnose our present disease and prescribe healing redirection."[8]

The continuum of ideas on health represents the following variations:

    health + beauty = success
    beauty + success = health
    success + health = beauty

Out-of-Shape Youth

The images of "healthy" vary from the pumped-up "jock" with muscles bristling, the ultimate advertisement for steroids, and the victim of ill-health, to the "sickly" nerd who has endless stamina and runs on water and soybeans. Holistic health gurus live and eat naturally. Health, as body control, will energize so that we may reach unknown spiritual heights where unconscious, repressed desires will be actualized. Tranquility and inner harmony will be restored to the cosmos of the inner world, which will ripple through the greater cosmos to save nature. (CE)

The "healthy" image adorning the fashion magazine is an anorexic female body, fed salads, mineral water, diet pills, and vitamin supplements. Fashionable clothes today are small and revealing; tomorrow, large and baggy. One is never well-dressed. (CE)

"At night we go clubbing, pulsating in a tribal trance that revives the spirit of gods in us. We drink firewater to relieve our stress. We rave for days in ecstasy and fall in a heap, totally dehydrated. We abandon our inhibitions but awake feeling awkward and violated in a stranger's bed. We have bacon and eggs to line our arteries before we jump on the last 'stress express to success.' Then we wake up to the need for change but face the cruel reality of breaking addictive habits. Where do we go in our desperation for support?" (CE)

Need to Shape Up

"The youth long for acceptance in a therapeutic community where caring adults understand what the youth experientially know but offer true freedom." (CE)

"As I reminisced, it suddenly struck me that from the age of 12 (10 years ago) my desires had been controlling my actions. I was merely a puppet doing what everyone else said was cool. Freedom of choice! My body had been my master while my mind was in neutral. I realized that the physical being has a natural inclination toward self-destruction.

"In the midst of a divorce, my mother did not notice either the blue haze or my absence. The awakening of physical desires drove me to sexual involvement with anyone game. Involvement in sports hid the ill effects, but I became increasingly alarmed by a cough and weight gain. While working and touring abroad, I reveled in free drugs and sex. But I ran away—to home! I reached out to adults, but they didn't notice.

"Then I did something that was stupid but amazing. I registered for the Health Promotion course at Helderberg College in South Africa. I was introduced to rational therapy. I kicked against the spiritual context of health, but the information was convincing. The lecturers were caring. The first in renewal was that I have a mind to choose. I am responsible for my life, my health. I don't have to use self-destructive behavior when I don't cope.

"I needed to discover God. This meant that I had to unlearn and relearn ideas and habits. If my health is damaged, it will dull my mind, rendering it incapable to choose so that my desires again rule. This discovery has changed my life. I now understand what God is talking about when He wants us to be free. My response is 'Wow!'" (TM)

Living a healthy life talks louder than telling. God positioned Israel at the crossroads of the world (with the injunction of Deuteronomy 4:5-8) to acknowledge by their lives that "no other nation . . . has a god who is so near when they need him as the Lord our God is to us. He answers us whenever we call for help" (Deut. 4:7, TEV). "Christians . . . are called, to create a new style of life, a style at odds with the expectations of the earthly city because they are 'living at the intersection between this world and the New Jerusalem.'" [9]

What Shape Are You In? (Parable)

A young man, John, left home. He pointed his dingy downstream. With no destination in mind, he went with the flow. He visited alluring places and people, but remained restless. Snaking down the river, John tasted "freedom." All-night, no-holds-barred parties deprived him of sleep. Exotic fragrances and sounds assaulted his senses. Appealing images flashed on and off at him. He worshiped his body, but didn't admire it—he was constantly on the lookout for blemishes, yet he was immortal!

John's health deteriorated. He was tired, but couldn't sleep. Fevers gripped him in alternately icy, then hot, clutches. A dry cough rattled his bones. He couldn't think clearly as his body battled against the self-inflicted damage of unrestrained appetite.

One day he drifted by a tiny island. A deranged old man was shouting at him.

"Don't . . . further . . . lies . . . Listen . . . us . . . them . . . STOP! . . . confuse you . . . there is . . . and hope!"

John was delirious. He needed someone to cure him of his life-sucking illness, not a madman.

He spent his remaining energies on "experts" who professed to take away his pain. His searches led him down unfamiliar tributaries of the river. Other inquiries were dead-ends. In a hut in a thick forest, a healer offered from the palm of his hand, "Here, eat this root. It will cure your sickness." Staggering up steps of a stone temple, a resident priest explained, "That root you ate was heathen. Here, say this prayer." John visited a friendly medicine man living on the banks of a stream. "That prayer is superstitious. Here, drink this potion."

A signpost beckoned him: HOSPITAL ⇨. The remedies he had tried did not deliver as promised. The burning sensation in his chest became unbearable. Uniformed nurses paraded down hospital corridors smelling of chemicals. Dr. Feelgood laughed at his story. "That potion must have been snake oil or something. Here, swallow this pill."

Beautiful neon girls from the sprawling city with glittering lights offered him quick fixes. Cars roared by, and in dingy basements people gyrated to a throbbing, primal beat for exercise and pleasure. Freaky virtual reality superstars leered at him, alluring him into their three-dimentional world. In a towering skyscraper he found Dr. Newman busy at a computer: "I know Dr. Feelgood well. His pills are ineffective. Here, take this antibiotic."

With aching limbs and raw feet, John encountered a meditating guru in the wasteland. He dug into a pouch, producing something from its dark interior. "That antibiotic you took was artificial. Here, eat this root!"

Full of despair and hopelessness, John continued until, without warning, a whirlpool sucked him in. Driftwood and rubbish crashed against the dingy, spinning it in circles until it was dashed to pieces on a submerged rock. As the angry water wrestled with John, he realized that he was in mortal danger. He recalled the words: "lies . . . STOP! . . . hope . . ."

John lost consciousness . . . Blinking his eyes, he discovered that he was home with the mad old man. He saw sadness in his eyes, not madness. The old man understood. He too had journeyed down river as a youth. Seduced by images, he acted on sensory pleasure and polluted reasoning. It led to cancer. For years he chased elixirs. Then he stopped chasing shadows and turned to face the sun. Hope displaced despair, and gradually he tasted the fruits of true freedom. His cancer had been reversible.

He tended to John as a son, preparing nourishing meals. Fresh water was in constant supply. The practical results of the old man's adherence to basic health principles were astounding. John's spirits were lifted by optimism and his storytelling was enlightening. John recovered some of his long-lost strength. He knew that the disease had not yet fully released its grip, but he felt alive and was ready to go.

Traveling in the opposite direction, he had the feeling that deep within him and his surroundings, life was different. When he stopped to pick berries, he could hear birds singing. He inhaled the fresh air deeply and gazed at the river water sparkling in the sun. As John scooped up water, he noticed for the first time that the water was clear enough for him to see the pebbles at the bottom. (AB)

A healthy, vibrant youth group reaches beyond their own eating and drinking to the support of those who are trying to kick bad habits but feel so alone. Maybe you can begin by unpacking the levels of meaning in the parable above and share the journey of life and hope, just as the four of us have. It will be good for the health!

Resources and Discussion Topics

The subheads in this chapter serve as topics for exploration and discussion. What is applicable to one group may not be to others. The ideas presented in this section serve to highlight the topics raised as points of current and relevant interest to youth. The author is not suggesting that the resources recommended should be accepted without discussion, because it is in the process of discussion that the youth hear and understand how they fit into current trends and what God intends for each one of them. The Holy Spirit is the teacher. For the youth to make an informed decision on their approach to a healthy lifestyle, they should be alerted to the relevance of health to one's personal life and one's mission and the relationship between health and the gospel, i.e., What is God's good news for humankind?

In the introductory paragraphs of this chapter, the issue of the diversity of ideas on health within the Adventist Church was raised. The history of the health message should serve to reaffirm its importance with reference to its uniqueness at a time in which many are becoming increasingly interested in health living and wholesome lifestyles. An understanding of the biblical health principles illuminated by the writings of Ellen White can facilitate a very contemporary, yet sound and rational, approach to good health and healthy living.

In addition to the topics and resources listed below, you'll want to request a catalog from the Health Connection, 55 West Oak Ridge Drive, Hagerstown, MD 21740 (or call 1-800-548-8700). This material from the Health and Temperance Department of the General Conference includes wonderful resources and information. You won't ever run out of ideas, and actually there won't be time to deal with any other topics. Look carefully through the contents of this resource book and see how many of the topics are related to health. Integrate the topics, as man is a whole being and the restoration process that is God's ideal for His children has to do with balance and a symmetrical development of the physical, the mental, the intellectual, the emotional, and the spiritual.[10]

The History of the Adventist Health Message

The Story of Our Health Message, by D. E. Robinson (Nashville: Southern Publishing Association, 1965), is one of the best resources on this topic. Others include Arthur White's biography of Ellen White and the specific books on health written by Ellen White. Videos that can be used are *The Search* and *The Adventist Health Study.*

Contact the Ellen White research center that is closest to you for information on articles and books that affirm Ellen White's ideas on health topics—such as vegetarianism and a whole-food diet—from a scientific perspective.

Discussion Questions: The fact that science often affirms the ideas that she presented much later than when she first wrote them is an interesting topic of discussion. Does science have to affirm her ideas for them to be credible? Why is it that her ideas on temperance and the rejection of the use of tobacco, coffee, and alcohol are only being propagated?

Research which countries have taken the problems, both on personal and societal level, that are tobacco-related so seriously that advertising is banned and all public areas are designated as smoke-free. Why does France not host the Formula 1 Grand Prix car race? Will research on the effects of alcohol lead to similar reactions in the future? Although drinking and driving are believed to be fatal, observe the defiance of this fact in magazines that advertise cars and drink, etc. The youth come to some interesting conclusions when these topics are tackled from a discussion and research approach.

The Current Emphasis on Healthful Living

The growing interest in health, especially by those interested in complementary and alternative perspectives on health and healing, requires a critical approach. Look at current popular health journals and discuss any of the health ideas from a biblical and scientific perspective; this is an interesting way to establish and reinforce these principles. Health ideas are often based on New Age thinking, which introduces confusion that is relevant to the rise in spirituality, spiritism, and the miraculous. Health and "religion" are combined and the ideas are very convincing but need critical thinking. Because of the eclectic approach, not every idea is "healthy"! Our youth need to develop skills in discernment.

An awareness of the basic ideas of postmodernism and New Age thinking is important. *Dialogue* magazine is published for students in secular educational institutions and has good articles to assist with this. Understanding the assumptions of current philosophies is important in searching for truth.

Scientific Proof

It is important to introduce youth to the scientific proof that supports the Adventist message of health as well as reaffirms the currency and credibility of Ellen White's writings from a century ago. Refer especially to Appendix X of *Medical Enlightenment: A Century in Advance.* It is interesting to note that the principles of living in the Pentateuch were not directly connected to health. However, freedom from disease, productivity, and prosperity are promised both as a natural consequence and with miraculous intervention. Discover how a health ministry conveys vital truths of the gospel better than miracles. A holistic perspective must underlie a discussion of spiritual maturity to the glory of God, the Great Physician, Healer, and Savior. (You may also wish to contact Pastor Gary Strunk, who presented a paper to the General Conference Theology of Health Conference in 1993.)

God's Shape for Healthy Living

A significant aspect of this topic is What was God's original health plan? The true remedies identified in *The Ministry of Healing,* by Ellen White (p. 127), can be found in Genesis. This is an opportunity for a "treasure hunt" on a cold winter's afternoon/evening youth meeting. A discussion could include the abilities and capabilities of a "fit" person. What is the lifestyle of a physically well-functioning person?

Many of the current ideas on health and healing reflect the ideas of ancient Egypt. Moses' education in Egypt no doubt included the arts of healing as practiced by the priests. He had to undergo a reorientation process in his ideas of health and healing from what he learned in the "universities" of Egypt to what he learned in the Wilderness Training School about primary health care, including knowledge about water resources, plants that "heal," sanitation, etc., which equipped him to be the leader of God's people from enslavement to the Promised Land. God's ideal was that His people would not get any of the lifestyle diseases of the Egyptians.

A study of the contrast between these ideas of health and healing are very enlightening, especially with reference to the crisis of confidence in orthodox medical science (the biomedical approach) and the consequent emergence of holistic healing arts and various approaches that bombard us with a mixture of credible and questionable ideas.

In 1873 scholars discovered a collection of medical texts at Luxor and gave them the name of the Ebers papyrus, which is 60 feet (20 meters) in length, and consists of 110 pages with 2,289 lines of hieroglyphics. They are housed today in the University of Leipzig. They contain 850 prescriptions. A study of these makes one wonder how anyone survived a visit to the doctor. Here are some "choice" examples:

- For baldness: make an intelligent use of a pomade compounded of equal parts of the fats of the lion, hippo, crocodile, goose, serpent, ibex.
- For embedded splinters, the physician applied worm's blood and asses' dung.
- The most common ingredients were lizard's blood, swine's teeth, putrid meat, stinking fat, moisture from pet's ears, animal fats, etc.

In extreme contrast, Moses recorded health laws given to him by God with the promise: None of these diseases (of the Egyptians) will come upon you. While some used human excreta on their wounds, he instructed that the toilet should be outside the camp. The Hebrews were the most hygienic of Eastern people. The laws of quarantine were specific. Ironically, they were rediscovered 3,000 years later and integrated into public health again. There were laws about the use of animal fats with reference to heart disease. The interesting point is that Moses was using different health principles and was not copying the medical authorities of the day. Is this still God's plan for His people today? These topics could be illustrated and an outreach program prepared.

The Shape of Society for Healthy Living

The influence of the media on the youth's ideas of health and healing must be noted. These ideas (myths) are not "black and white." In pop music there are antiestablishment ideas that sensitize youth to the problems human beings have caused for themselves, but most of the ideas are anarchic, advocating self-destruction, individualism, and defiance of authority. Sex, drugs, and pornography are idolized as the way of life. And popular music is popular. It may not be acceptable to you, but it is important for the youth to discuss what is important to them. Discussion of the lyrics and what is actually being said, in addition to the music and its influence, is important—it helps youth see their world as it really is. The fact that this is a topic of discussion does not mean that it is condoned as being acceptable, but youth are so besieged that they cannot hear it for what it is and what it is actually recommending to them.

The question of image, the problems of peer pressure, the tendency to conformity, the negation of integrity, and the power of choice are key issues that touch on the whole life of the youth. There are many divesting consequences of the power of the image from a health perspective. Two of the important values of the youth are beauty and money. Being attractive and acceptable are critical. But the problems faced in sacrificing health and, ironically, contributing to the decline in physical attraction must be discussed.

The unreality of the picture-perfect models held up as images of beauty are myths. A very useful video for discussion of these important issues is *The Famine Within*. What are some useful, positive methods for dealing with the "uncertainties of life"? These could form the basis of an outreach program for youth by youth on stress management.

"Partying" is the norm for a happy life, but, some of the activities of partying are unhealthy and self-destructive. A typical sitcom episode in which these ideas are presented could serve as the basis for discussion of "fun."

Charles Shulz expressed concerns about fun, and any one of the Peanuts cartoons can be used as a platform for healthy discussion.

AIDS and Current Ideologies

The reality about AIDS is blurred in the media, as sexual promiscuity and alternative sexual preferences are not only tolerated, but extolled. AT the same time, there is great support for AIDS movements from the celebrities. These contradictory ideas must be confronted and the myths debunked.

The media reflect the current ideologies, i.e., of the New Age on life after death, after-death experiences, etc. The rise in spirituality is very topical. Many of the celebrities and stars are New Age thinkers and/or have become involved in Eastern religions. Their influence on the values of the youth cannot be underestimated. The importance of achieving spirituality is the basis for a healthy lifestyle in many of the Eastern religions. This approach underlies many of the articles and books written on health. The shape of society must be identified and its shaping power must be withstood, by God's grace.

Our Health Message

The multilayered meanings of the parable in the section "What shape are you in?" are worth many hours of discussion on the various topics that it raises as interesting points of discussion. It is not merely a reflection of many of the lies and experiences of contemporary youth, but it gives a short history of medicine, which is also an interesting and current topic of interest. How do Ellen White's ideas fit into this move toward "Here, Eat This Root"?

What about the story of Moses and the bitter water at Marah? Ellen White comments in letter 65a, 1894: "When Moses presented before the Lord the sad difficulties of the children of Israel, He did not present some new remedy, but called their attention to that which was at hand; for there was a bush or shrub which He had created that was to be cast into the water to make the fountain sweet and pure. When this was done, the suffering people could drink of the water with safety and pleasure. God has provided a balm for every wound. There is a balm in Gilead, there is a physician there."[11]

The contrast between the abundance of water at Elim and the problems of a lack of water and then the discovery of bitter water and God's solution are relevant topics about faith and providence and miracles (see Ex. 15:22-27). The topic of "natural remedies" (true remedies) is worth exploring. *Doctor, What Can I Do?* by Herald Habenicht and Helen Rhodes (1962), is useful, especially if one is looking for natural ways to keep healthy. Prevention is better than cure!

Use of Charcoal

Discover magazine, July 1998, contained this interesting report entitled "A Briquette a Day."

"The human population of Zanzibar, a Tanzanian island off the East African coast, doubles every 15 years or so. The island's red colobus monkeys, however, are dwindling as their habitats are destroyed for firewood and timber. But some monkeys have found a way to co-exist with humans: they snack on charcoal.

"Thomas Struhsaker, a zoologist at Duke University, has been studying the effects of selective logging on rain forest wildlife in eastern Africa. A Tanzanian biologist told him about the monkeys' charcoal habit in 1981. Over the years, as the human population grew, Struhsaker noticed that the monkeys ate more and more charcoal. 'Each animal,' he says, 'eats about five grams a day.'

"Monkeys live in an area with almond, mango, and other exotic fruit trees. The leaves of these trees are rich in protein but also contain toxic compounds like tannic acids. Most animals avoid the leaves. But charcoal has a well-known ability to absorb toxins—it is used as a poison control agent, and in Europe people use it in liquid form as a digestive aid. When a monkey eats charcoal after chomping on leaves, its meal goes down a little easier. The charcoal selectively holds on to large tannic acid molecules, allowing them to pass through the body while nutritious proteins are absorbed by the gut.

"The monkeys snatch charcoal from kilns and also nibble on charred wood and tree stumps. Struhsaker isn't sure how they acquired the habit. 'There must be a quick effect so they can learn by association,' he says. Baby monkeys, at least, learn from imitating their mothers, and the mothers themselves may have learned from eating soil containing charcoal particles.

"'These are pretty clever animals,' says Struhsaker. 'They've picked up a habit that allows them to exploit a resource to an extent that was not possible before.' Despite this adaptation, red colobus populations are still shrinking in Zanzibar, even in nature reserves, where speeding cars take a large toll. 'If they put the potholes back in the road, or built speed bumps, I think the reserve animals would be fine.'"[12]

The marvels of charcoal are a very interesting topic of discussion. Its properties are worth investigating, as well as its use in dealing with many common ailments. The Thrashes from Yuchee Pines Institute have developed a booklet on the uses of charcoal. Check with your local poison units and ask what their first-line treatment is for poisoning. Ask relevant people or organizations why charcoal is not commercially freely available.

Usage of and training in the use of charcoal in needy communities is an excellent outreach project. This is a practical way to overcome the enculturation of the church and to answer in a practical way the question "Is there a doctor in the house?" A large proportion of the time Jesus spent was in ministering to the health needs of the community. Besides offering the marvelous healing properties of charcoal to one's neighborhood, one can in a practical way, point to Jesus as Savior and Healer in the context of "salvation." There is a growing movement toward the use of household "remedies." Develop a resource file to collect scientifically proven ways of health and healthy living. Setting up criteria for selecting this information can help the youth to sift through the "alternative," the questionable, and that which is credible from a rational perspective.

The Shape of Self

The contrasts between the narcissism of Samson and the integrity of Daniel (and his friends) need to be discovered by reading the biblical account, Ellen White's comments and Bible commentaries. Their choices with reference to lifestyle are an important aspect of their mission, God's intentions for their lives and their influence in the history of humankind. The role of Daniel in our understanding of where we are in the scheme of things and the great controversy is significant. What relationship is there between his health habits and his great intellect (How could he be 10 times wiser than his counterparts, who were definitely not "dummies"?), his ability to understand, and God's trust in him to deliver prophetic messages that had an immediate bearing on the history of God's people, as well as on God's people in the end-time? An important issue is that of wisdom and foolishness. First Corinthians 1:20 suggests that what man believes is wise is often foolishness to God. The ideas of a life of foolishness and one of wisdom from a study of Psalm 78 and Proverbs 1; 9; 14 (as well as many other relevant passages) are a base from which to discern what current ideas are merely a dead end. Develop a drama, skit, or TV documentary—involving these two characters—that could then be used as an outreach program with a powerful message relevant to contemporary youth. Write some newspaper reports.

Cooking schools can be useful methods of sharing ideas of healthy eating. These can emerge out of a "Daniel's feast" evening in which the taste of junk foods and "unhealthy" eating habits can be challenged and the taste buds tantalized by an alternative way of eating in a whole-foods diet. Tasting is believing. "O taste and see that the Lord is good" (Ps. 34:8). What is the best diet for health, the original diet, and the importance of nutrition? Start with an inreach program before you advocate this lifestyle as an outreach project! A vegetarian barbecue engenders great interest!

An interesting challenge to the youth is what they can contribute to the WHO strategy of the relationship between lifestyle and health for all. The importance of the uniqueness of the Seventh-day Adventist health message, which takes lifestyle into consideration, is gaining impetus. Uniqueness can be both positive and negative to a youth. Being different is a challenge. However, if being "different" is seen in a positive light, then belonging to those who are the same is exciting and acceptable. The emphasis is on the right use of the will, commitment to God and a rational approach to making decisions about one's health. A significant consequence is the healthy image of a youth that gives glory to God, who is omniscient and omnipotent.

In-Shape Youth and Out-of-Shape Youth

There are very interesting paradoxes in these sections. This could take the form of a dress-ing-up evening in which various images of "health" are illustrated. A discussion of these stereotypes could have a number of implications: dealing with the power of the stereotype (the media thrives on the use of the stereotype) and our prejudices and bias toward certain groups of people that we judge and/or emulate, based on the ideas that we have been given to think about them. The youth are easily "fooled" by external appearance and make choices about friends based on "looks." The influence of the fashion and beauty industry can be identified.

The desperate need addressed in the last paragraph of this section raises issues about raving and addictive behavior. This is a realistic description from someone who knows! The appeal is for support. A challenge to any youth group is for them to set up a support group for other youth and typical youth problems. This type of involvement will be a challenge to the whole church, as the youth arriving for support might appear unacceptable (back to the influence of stereotypes!) to many in leadership positions. How does God see a soul? The story of the prodigal son and his pig-pen appearance could have a powerful influence on a change of heart, and the perfume of empathy and support could infuse the lives of all.

There is an interesting topic of discussion on the interrelationship between mental and physical health (and spiritual) in the following statement by Dr. John Zachary Young: "Human beings are . . . especially programmed to be indoctrinated."[13] From a brainstorming session, youth can identify the factors that influence one's freedom to choose.

In a very revealing article David Grossman explains that the same tactics used to train soldiers are being used by media and entertainment to train our children to kill.[14] His job includes making people aware of the magnitude of killing, as well as dealing with incidents such as the Jonesboro, Arkansas, schoolyard shooting incident in which a teacher and four girls were shot, 10 were injured, and two boys, ages 11 and 13, were charged with murder and jailed. His expertise in killology includes post-trauma in the military, but this was a new experience. His insight on the magnitude of the virus of violence need to be communicated.

The increase in the rate of killing and attempted killing has gone from 60 per 100,000 in 1957 to 440 per 100,000 by the middle of the 1990s. If it were not for the increase in the imprisonment rate of violent offenders (prison population in the U.S.A. quadrupled between 1975 and 1992) and the improvement of medical technology, the statistics on violence would be much higher. There are always multiple factors involved in statistics, but Grossman suggests that there is a significant common factor, and that is media violence presented as entertainment for children and interactive video games.

Part of Grossman's expertise is the technique of killing. He suggests that it does not come naturally, and humans have to be taught by conditioning how to kill with safeguards. He explains: "Vasoconstriction, the narrowing of the blood vessels, has literally closed down the forebrain—that great gob of gray matter that makes you a human being and distinguishes you from a dob. When those neurons close down, the midbrain takes over and your thought processes and reflexes are indistinguishable from your dog's. . . . The battlefield and violent crime are in the realm of the midbrain responses."[15]

By the time a young child goes to school he or she has been exposed to 8,000 murderers and 10,000 acts of violence (CNN report, November 1998).

Neil Nedley, in the book *Proof Positive,* deals with the factors affecting the optimal functioning of the frontal lobe in the chapter "The Frontal Lobe: The Crown of the Brain." He identifies lifestyle factors that damage this vital area. It is therefore critical in understanding the power of choice that is God-given but possibly usurped, thus leaving the human being vulnerable to indoctrination. He lists the following factors: "Impairment from drugs, nicotine, alcohol, caffeine, a toxic chemical. Effects of diet and nutrition on the function of the frontal lobes, e.g., sugar, meat. Effects of hypnotism, TV, and music on the frontal lobe."[16]

Nedley's recommendations of seven actions to take for enhancing the function of the frontal lobe are worth exploring and making some choices about. Explore the world of the youth to illustrate these assumptions.

The youth in my classes were horrified that they were vulnerable and that both their individuality and their power of choice were possibly at stake. After lengthy discussions based on useful credible information, they began to understand that the first choice they probably have to make is to claim back their power of discernment and their freedom to choose.

Need to Shape Up

Change is dependent on the recognition of need. Change is a biblical principle. Christ offers the package of change as a gift. The prodigal son's story evidences this. The levels of meaning of the father's patient waiting behavior is an object lesson for everyone where youth are trying to find their feet and establishing a value system apart from what the church says they should do and not do. This individual move toward maturity needs to be supported. Many youth do not have parents who can support them, and the church can play an important role in this discovery. The story of TM in this section is one that can be used as a "testimony" that is believed to be typical of many of the lives of the youth. The interesting point is that the message of health, although TM kicked its spiritual overtones, was ultimately what helped her become aware of what God intends for the youth. This changed her life.

What Shape Are You In?

There are a number of issues implicated in this question. First, it is on a personal level, with reference to health and rational choices for a healthy lifestyle. Second it raises the issue of one's mission and relationship to others and the good news that we have to share. Third, it is an SDA problem. Laodicea is in a bad way. What is the importance of the unique health message to a postmodern, New Age generation? What is the relationship between the three angels' messages and "medical missionary" work? What are the "remedies" that Christ prescribes?

"There is a great work to be done. How shall we reveal Christ? I know of no better way . . . than to take hold of the medical missionary work in connection with the ministry. Wherever you go, there begin to work. Take an interest in those around you who need help and light. You may stand and preach to those here who know the truth; you may preach sermon after sermon to them, but they do not appreciate it. Why? Because they are inactive. Everyone who is able to go out and work should bring to the foundation stone, not hay, wood, or stubble, but gold, silver, and precious stones."[17]

"Seventh-day Adventists are to be represented to the world by the advance principles of health reform which God has given us."[18]

"Seventh-day Adventists are handling momentous truths."[19]

My daughter became desperately ill during her last year in academy. The specialist's prognosis was five to 15 years in bed. I decided to apply Ellen White's health message, and with God's help and His healing, my daughter is 100 percent well. Maybe in the exploration through the narrative of each youth member in your group there will come a revelation of the power offered by God to restore His image. This brings us back to the original topic of God's shape for healthy living.

[1] E. G. White, *The Ministry of Healing,* p. 127.

[2] Edwin Pouncy, "John Fahey," *The Wire,* 1998, p. 27.

[3] Richard J. B. Willis, *Holistic Health, Holistic Hoax?* (Watford, United Kingdom: Pensive Publications, 1997), p. 264.

[4] Judith Rodin, "Body Mania," *Psychology Today,* January 1992.

[5] White, *Prophets and Kings,* p. 485.

[6] Keff Gremillion, "The Cultural Evolution," *Details,* March/April 1998, p. 117.

[7] Donald S. McAlvany, *The McAlvany Intelligence Advisor,* November 1997, pp. 1, 2.

[8] Brian J. Walsh, *Subversive Christianity* (Bristol, United Kingdom: The Regius Press, 1992), p. 36.

[9] Jacques Ellul, *The Ethics of Freedom* (Grand Rapids: Eerdmans, 1976).

[10] See White, *Education,* pp. 15, 16.

[11] In White, *Selected Messages* (Washington, D.C.: Review and Herald Pub. Assn., 1958), book 2, p. 273.

[12] "A Briquette a Day," *Discover,* July 1998, pp. 14, 15.

[13] John Zachary Young, *Programs of the Brain* (Oxford: Oxford University Press, 1978), p. 216, quoted in Willis, p. 23.

[14] David Grossman, "Trained to Kill," *Christianity Today,* Aug. 10, 1998. Online: www christianitytoday.com.

[15] *Ibid.*

[16] Neil Nedley, M.D., *Proof Positive* (Ardmore, Okla.: Neil Nedley).

[17] White, in *General Conference Bulletin,* 1901, Extra, no. 18. In *Medical Ministry* (Mountain View, Calif.: Pacific Press Pub. Assn., 1932), p. 319.

[18] White, *Medical Ministry,* p. 187.

[19] White, *Testimonies,* vol. 9, p. 158.

CHAPTER 26

Youth and Health

by Michael Peabody

THROUGHOUT THE BIBLE, GOD makes good health a top priority for His people. From the health laws introduced under the hot Sinai sun to His own healing touch as he journeyed through Palestine, God demonstrates that good health goes hand-in-hand with spiritual health. "Beloved, I pray that in all respects you may prosper and be in good health, just as your soul prospers" (3 John 2, NASB).

Good health is important to everyone, though it is never fully appreciated until it is lost. We cannot function at our peak—physically, emotionally, or spiritually—if we are sick or malnourished due to poor dietary choices. Through casual disregard for the laws of good health we place ourselves in grave danger of losing our health to sickness or disease. God gave us stewardship over our bodies and minds, and it is important that we learn how to best take care of both.

Youth, particularly, are going through tremendous changes in their lives. As a youth director, you have a unique opportunity to address health issues and concerns youth have about health. Although this chapter is by no means comprehensive, it is designed to provide a general overview of some specific areas.

Exercise

Exercise is perhaps the most talked about method for achieving good health. In their early years children effortlessly spend a large amount of time involved in sports and moving their bodies through active play. But as they grow older, youth find that they must make an effort to devote time to exercising. Many teens participate in sports programs or physical education classes in school, but those who do not may not be taking adequate time to enjoy the benefits of exercising.

Research shows that every day a person should spend 30 minutes or more in moderately intensive physical activity, such as brisk walking, hiking, bicycling, or similar activity. Often, even simple activities that individuals participate in anyway, such as taking the stairs instead of the elevator, or just walking around school, can count toward this time.

As your youth group's "coach," you can incorporate many exercise activities into your youth program. You can take youth hiking or bicycling on Sabbath afternoons, go canoeing, or meet for a Sunday afternoon baseball game.

There is one caveat, however. If you decide to play sports games, be careful about using the "captain" approach to choosing teams, in which two youth members get to pick the people they perceive to be the "best" in the sport first. This is incredibly hurtful to the self-esteem of those chosen last, and makes competition the main thing instead of just having fun. Although sports are a good activity, care must be taken to make sure that it does not just become a competition, in which the second-place team members are made to feel like "losers."

This can effectively negate the positive value of teamwork that can be carried over into other areas of service. Also, do not allow youth to make fun of those who do not perform well athletically. The point, again, is to have fun without having hurt feelings.

Nutrition

Advertisers would have us believe, and our taste buds sometimes agree, that there's nothing quite like the pure chocolate of a Hershey's bar, that few foods can compare with a Taco Bell quesadilla, and a Dr. Pepper can make your day. But it doesn't take a gastrointestinal engineer to tell you that this stuff can't be good for you.

The nutritional guidelines for healthy adolescents are quite different from those for children or adults, because they're going through massive changes in their lives. The following chart outlines the minimal nutritional requirements for adolescents, which obviously will vary, depending on the age, gender, and activity level of the youth.

Food Group	Servings Per Day
Milk, yogurt, cheese	3 or more
Meet substitutes, dried beans, eggs, nuts	2-3
Vegetables	3-5
Fruit	2-4
Breads, cereals, grains	6-11
Fats, oils, sweets	Use sparingly

Adapted from www.drkoop.com.

It is important, as youth leaders, not to send mixed messages to youth about nutrition. The truth that pure, natural, and unprocessed foods are the best for our bodies quickly becomes meaningless when we don't follow that advice ourselves. This is not a "Do what I say, not what I do" area.

Neither should we become so rigid that we can't pull the bus over for pizza. There is a major difference between our *diet* and what we eat occasionally. While we should never consume things that are bad for us, most food we avoid is not good for us on a regular basis, but eaten occasionally will not harm us.

Vegetarianism

Although Adventists have been expounding the benefits of a vegetarian lifestyle for years it's only been recently that the medical community has begun to agree. Because of the increase in health-conscious diets, recent statistics show that more than 12 million people in the United States now practice some form of vegetarianism, which is twice the number of vegetarians in 1985.[1]

There are many reasons a person may wish to adopt a vegetarian lifestyle. Lower blood pressure; lower risks of cancer, obesity, and heart disease; and a higher-fiber, lower-fat diet are key benefits. The problem youth run into is their reliance on fast foods and snack foods that are high in fat and have little nutritional value. Skipping breakfast or other meals because they are too busy is bad for anyone, but particularly devastating to youth, who need balanced diets with adequate protein and vitamins to meet the requirements of their growing bodies.

A vegetarian diet is the most sensible and the healthiest, but it can't be adopted recklessly. Teens who are not responsible concerning their nutritional requirements are headed for disaster, physically and mentally. When blood sugar levels surge erratically, concentration is nearly impossible. Physical activity is impaired. Also, the Holy Spirit can't be heard easily by someone whose mind is on food because they are starving, or sluggish because they've pigged out on fat-saturated food. A poor diet affects all areas of life.

As temples of the Holy Spirit, we should be careful what we put into our bodies. Even some vegetarian food isn't healthy. Nutrition must be considered before any food is eatern.

Eating Disorders

Obesity

In this fragile time of life, youth are the most susceptible to the pressures associated with the ideal body shape. They believe that looks are everything. They compare themselves to TV stars or models, and even average-sized individuals come up short. Overweight teens are at an extreme disadvantage, socially as well as healthwise.

With so many ways to exercise and lose extra pounds, it seems that weight loss would be an easy proposition. However, in the United States 55 percent of the population is considered to be medically obese. Obesity has been linked to diseases that can short-circuit a person's life. In addition, society associates beauty, intelligence, and success with being thin, so it's not uncommon for overweight individuals to experience severe psychological stress, reduced income, and other forms of discrimination.

Youth are susceptible to these pressures, and often obesity leads to poor self-esteem and other psychological problems. If a young person's body image is severely limiting his or her ability to enjoy life fully, it may be helpful for them to talk to a professional counselor or therapist. The importance of approaching this recommendation with tact and genuine concern cannot be overemphasized.

It is important for you to foster positive, supportive relationships with these youth especially. Because a young person's self-worth should be based on the fact that they are children of God, this should be reflected in your eyes.

Anorexia and Bulimia

Anorexia nervosa and bulimia nervosa are serious eating disorders. Those with anorexia intentionally starve themselves, when they are already below optimum weight because of a prevailing fear that they are becoming fat. The medical definition of anorexia involves those who are 15 percent or more below their recommended body weight as determined by a standard height-weight table. Females with anorexia often stop having their menstrual cycle for several months, a condition called amenorrhea.

On the other hand, those with bulimia nervosa eat large amounts of food during "binge" episodes, in which they feel out of control of their eating. After they have eaten, they try to prevent weight gain through purging by vomiting their food, using laxatives or diuretics, dieting, and/or exercising aggressively. To be medically diagnosed as having bulimia nervosa, an individual must engage in binging and purging at least two times a week for three months. However, an individual experiencing even less frequent episodes may require professional assistance.

Young people with eating disorders are often very reluctant to admit that they have a serious problem, and in many cases, especially with anorexia, family or friends must persuade the individual to seek treatment. Both of these disorders are considered psychological disorders that manifest themselves physically. They are brought on by worries that an individual has too much body fat. However, they are most prevalent when an individual wishes to meet society's stick-figure ideal as portrayed in the popular media, where even undersized models bemoan their figure flaws.

Although eating disorders can be prevented through programs that emphasize a healthy diet, positive self-esteem, weight acceptance, and participation in athletic activities that produce positive feelings about one's body and fitness, it is advisable to seek professional advice when these situations arise.

It is important for youth leaders to emphasize the biblical view of beauty—it "should be that of your inner self, the unfading beauty of a gentle and quiet spirit, which is of great worth in God's sight" (1 Peter 3:4, NIV). Our bodies are temporary things. *Health* should be our goal, not looking like a cover model. God doesn't care what our outside looks like. It's our inside that counts with Him.

Facing an Unplanned Pregnancy

Most teenage girls do not know where to turn for help if they discover that they are pregnant. You may be the only person that they can reliably turn to for support. A pregnant girl may initially feel as though she is a failure and that there is no hope for her. There is comfort for her in the grace of Jesus Christ, whose love continues through this situation.

In the United States and many other nations, there are three fundamental ways to deal with this situation. First, the girl can give birth and raise the child with the help of her family. Second, the girl can legally obtain an abortion early on in the pregnancy. This option, however legal, presents serious ethical and moral problems. The third option is presenting the baby for adoption. There are many people who are unable to have children of their own and are praying for this opportunity to raise a child.

Often, the girl bears the brunt of church sanction, while the boy who brought her to this position is unaffected. It is a tragedy when a young woman in this particular situation is ostracized by the church, which may be the only remaining vestige of hope. Whatever happens, let her know that you will do all you can to support her as she goes through this time. If she decides to keep the baby, plan a baby shower to buy gifts that she will need to help raise the child

As far as church discipline for this action is concerned, it is wise to remember Christ's words when He was presented with a similar situation: "Whoever among you has not sinned, let him be the first to throw a stone at her." When the crowd that had lusted for her blood slowly dispersed, Christ asked, "Where are your accusers? Didn't anybody condemn you?" I imagine her looking to the ground as she replied, "No one." Jesus' response exemplifies the response the church should give in these situations: "I don't condemn you either. You are free to go now. But don't do this again" (John 8:7-11, paraphrase).

Sexually Transmitted Diseases (STDs)

In spite of the movement to increase the availability of contraceptives and safe-sex products, sexually transmitted diseases are very common. In the United States, STDs are the most common contagious diseases, second only to the cold and the flu, and more than 12 million Americans contract a sexually transmitted disease each year.[2]

STDs are transmitted during unprotected sexual contact and can cause a host of problems including infertility, heart disease, blindness, permanent damage to newborn babies, cancer, and even death. There are more than 20 different types of STDs that can spread through close contact with the genitals, mouth, or the rectum. The only sure way of preventing STDs is complete abstinence or a monogamous relationship, ideally within a marriage.

If a member of your youth group suspects that he or she has contracted an STD, refer them to a physician. This is a matter of utmost confidentiality. Within the United States, you can contact the Centers for Disease Control and Prevention's National STD Hotline at 1-800-227-8922 for confidential counseling and referrals to testing locations.

Teens who have contracted an STD are probably facing more shame and condemnation from themselves than from anyone else. STDs are not glamorous illnesses; they are painful, shameful, scary diseases. Teens may feel as though anyone who knows about their disease will ostracize them, not only socially, but physically, because they are "unclean." It is important to demonstrate love, not only verbally, but to reinforce that love with a kind touch as Jesus did with the lepers.

Drug/Alcohol Abuse

The worldwide epidemic of drug use is a very real threat to youth whether they are Christians or not. Recent studies reveal that 35 percent to 50 percent of Adventist academy students and 55 percent of college students "used alcohol in the last year," while only 13.9 percent of the adult membership admitted to doing so. Adventist young people who do use alcohol are more likely to abuse it than young people in the general population.[3]

At first glance the Bible seems to be contradictory about alcohol, praising it in some instances and condemning it in others. The contradiction occurs because the assumption is made that the Bible speaks only of fermented wine, writes Samuele Bacchiocchi, the theology professor at Andrews University and author of *Wine in the Bible.* "The Bible knows both fermented wine, which it disapproves, and unfermented grape juice, which it approves. This conclusion becomes clear when we examine the reasons for the biblical disapproval of fermented whine and approval of unfermented grape juice."[4]

"From a biblical and Christian perspective, to impair our mental and moral judgment by the use of alcohol means to destroy the very discriminatory sense of right and wrong God has implanted within us, the fundamental reason the Bible prohibits the use of alcoholic beverages, namely, because they impair our mental judgment."[5] Teens who have a problem with alcohol need help. Alcoholics Anonymous is a nationwide group started by alcoholics that gives support and unconditional acceptance to all alcoholics.

If one of your teens is struggling with alcohol, volunteer to attend meetings with them. AA meetings can be incredibly religious experiences, but they are also attended by rough people whose everyday life is probably much different than your teen's. It helps to have a friendly face and emotional support. Offer to give the teen a ride to the meeting and back. Be their sponsor, a person they can call and talk to when they are facing rough times. Don't assume that AA will "cure" them and that you don't have to do anything else. Get involved. Show that you care. Build a relationship with your teen that will weather the storms that will come.

Another potential problem in the area of alcohol and drugs is that you may learn that members of your youth group are using illegal drugs at home, school, or somewhere other than church. Initially, speak to each involved young person individually, and discuss the various ways that they can get help with the problem. Refer teens to the appropriate support group where they can get necessary counseling and interdiction, as well as a positive peer environment. Let the youth know that you have their best interest at heart. You may also need to check with a local attorney in your jurisdiction to see if you are required to report the situation since you work with the youth.

If you find out that some people are using your church as a convenient place to sell or distribute drugs, it is your responsibility to contact authorities immediately, because the safety of all youth in the program is at risk, both from the threat of drug addiction and also the violence that inevitably accompanies it.

Body Piercing and Tattooing

A rather new phenomenon in pop culture, these ancient expressions of personality are back in style, even in Adventist youth groups. Because body modification and tattooing involves breaching the skin, it can cause infection if done improperly.

Documented risks include hepatitis, tetanus, and even the contraction of HIV. These risks are so real that the American Red Cross has named it as a disqualifying factor in screening potential blood donors. Under American Red Cross guidelines, donors must wait one year from the time of piercing before they may donate blood.[6]

Once a person has a tattoo, it is very difficult, if not impossible, to have it removed. Piercing and tattooing also bring along other risks, such as a social stigma that can lead to the loss of employment opportunities later in life, and may identify a youth with a criminal part of society.

Adventists have historically been strong advocates for healthy living. As our teens test their wings and prepare for leadership of the Adventist Church, it is important that they realize how good health determines, to a large degree, their ability to lead and make sound decisions for the future. And that the future is built on decisions made and habits cultivated now.

[1] Sharon Howard, "Vegetarianism Facts." Online:/ www.drkoop.com. July 1, 1999.

[2] "Sexual Health." Online:/ www.drkoop.com.

[3] Steven Daily, *Adventism for a New Generation* (Better Living Publishers, 1993), p. 304.

[4] Samuele Bacchiocchi, *"The Bible and Alcohol: Moderation or Abstinence—Part 2,"* Endtime Issues, No. 26, Aug. 25, 1999. This e-mail newsletter is also available on Bacchiocchi's Web site: www.biblicalperspective.com.

[5] *Ibid.*

[6] "Body Piercing: It's More Than Skin-deep," *Mayo Clinic Health Oasis,* Mar. 24, 1997.

CHAPTER 27

Youth Leaders'
Frequently Asked Questions

by Trudy J. Morgan-Cole

MANY INTERNET WEB SITES include a page called the FAQ—frequently asked questions. On this page, those who maintain the site briefly list and answer the questions that are most often asked about their topic. This is a useful resource for anyone researching that topic, and it ensures that the people maintaining the site don't get bombarded with e-mails asking the same question again and again.

This chapter is intended to be an FAQ for Seventh-day Adventist youth ministry. Local youth leaders in several different countries were invited to respond with their most common questions. Though the handful who found time to respond came from different backgrounds, their questions were for the most part very similar. Whether in Croatia or Canada, those who work with teens and young adults worry about the same things. How do we get our youth to come to church? How do we keep them there? How do we teach them to really love Jesus?

The questions, when compiled, were sent back to the same youth workers for comments, as well as to several people who are leaders within the field of youth ministry. As you read the questions and responses, you may find answers to some of your own frequently asked questions.

1. **How do we build a youth ministry that is effective in introducing young people to Christ, not just entertaining them?**

Grant Misseghers, youth director for the Alberta Conference in Canada, has a ready answer for this question. "The most effective form of youth ministry I have engaged in was mentoring-based youth ministry," he says. Misseghers tells of how, as the leader of 80 earliteens in a large church in the United States, he focused his time and energy on building one-on-one relationships with about 14 of them. "I found that the more I focused my attention and efforts on this small core group of leaders, the more they were empowered to minister to their peers."

Mladen Kuzminski, a church leader in Croatia, agrees. "I found out that the best way is to hang around with them and to share your experiences with them. I listen to them, answer their questions, and share my experiences in life with them. I challenge them to trust the Lord and commit their ways to Him."

A key to success in this area is "having a real connection with God yourself," says Brian Yeager, director of the YouthNet eXtreme revival team. "What you do in your ministry will reflect what's going on in your own life."

A. Allan Martin, cofounder of dre*am vision ministries, has focused his research and ministry on the so-called "Generation X"—today's young adults. He offers three tips—A, B, and C—for reaching youth and young adults. "A. Activate Their Assets." "If I make authentic efforts today to identify and implement Xer talents, skills, and, most important, their passions, our church will find itself not only retaining a generation, but moreover, mending the spiritual leaks that have crippled our ability to live and share the gospel in the contemporary youth setting," Martin writes. B stands for "Build Relational Bridges." Like Grant Misseghers and Mladen Kuzminski, Martin recognizes the importance of personal relationships with youth. "Recently we took a serious look at the needs of Xers in our community through surveys and dialogue with our youth and young adults. It surprised me that the primary need they expressed was the desire to have significant adults more relationally involved in their lives." Finally, C stands for "Cultivate Communities of Character." "Creating communities of character in the church, the home, and the school, where we tell rightly the story of Jesus, will draw an alienated generation of Xers into the very core Christian community," Martin writes.[1]

Activating our young people's assets, building relationships in which we honestly care and honestly share what God is doing in our lives and creating a sense of community for our youth—all these are key to a youth ministry that goes beyond entertainment.

2. How do we make our programs interesting and attractive to youth and get them motivated to be involved?

"In my experience, I have discovered that when a group of young adults is made to feel like they can make a difference, and they begin to pray together and see answers to their prayers, they will become addicted to following their Savior. To bring a youth group together, give them the reins," says young adult leader Shasta Burr, "tells them that they are not only being trusted, but counted upon to help our church minister, you will begin to watch as kids feel needed, and they will want to come."

"The best thing you can do for Sabbath morning," says Brian Yeager, "is to have interaction with them during the week, in your house on Friday night, Wednesday night—whatever. That way your programs are more hanging out with friends than coming to hear an adult they have no connection with."

Leaders worry not just about attracting young people to "youth programs," but about their involvement in the life of the church as a whole. Allan Martin describes watching teenagers "zone out" in church on Sabbath morning. As he wondered about this, he writes, "I noticed that most of the participants in our worship service were male elders in the church. . . . In addition, I found that most of the worship service was geared toward Adventist adults talking to Adventist adults. No wonder our teens tuned out of our services! They didn't want to eavesdrop on the conversations we adults were having among ourselves."

Rather than taking youth out of the regular worship service and planning programs exclusively for them, Martin says: "My challenge to youth leaders is to spend some of your ministry energy integrating youth and young adults into the very core of the church life. Inoculate your "main worship service" with youth and young adult participation. Place the cloak of mentorship on church elders and adult leaders, calling them into relationships with your teens and collegians."[2]

3. How do we get youth out (on time!) for Sabbath school and AY meetings?

Several of the respondents suggested that when you answer questions one and two—when you have developed a close relationship with youth and let them take ownership of the program, attendance will cease to be a major problem. "I never pressured any of my teens to participate in Sabbath school," says Grant Misseghers. "Actually, it was quite the opposite; they consistently hounded me to give them opportunities to minister!"

Brian Yeager suggests the problem of tardiness can be addressed if you "start on time and have something interesting happening at the beginning. Sometimes it's hard, because they are dependent on their parents [for transportation]."

Stuart Tyner, in the book The *ABZs of Adventist Youth Ministry,* has some additional suggestions for building attendance. Along with knowing who's in your group, personally inviting them, and planning fun events, Tyner suggests a warm greeting to each young person as they arrive, letting them know you're happy to see them there. "If your attendance problem is tardiness," he adds, "begin to build some early bonuses into your program. For example, serve hot chocolate and doughnuts 15 minutes before your Sabbath school begins. Or plan a bring-your-favorite-song time before the program. Play the songs and find out why each song is a favorite." Follow-up after the program, perhaps in the form of a short note to each one who attended, also helps. Tyner agrees with other respondents that "poor attendance sometimes indicates you're doing too much of the work yourself. Involve the kids in all aspects of the programming. Let the ministry become theirs, not just yours."[3]

4. What do I need to know or do to be a more effective leader and understand youth better?

The authors of *7 Principles for Youth Ministry Excellence* recommend that youth leaders first take time to define their mission (why their ministry exists) and vision (what they want the ministry to become). "Determining a mission and vision for your group provides a direction and helps determine if you are staying on course. They're like a map and compass that helps chart the course of your programs, calendar, budget, and everything else involved in your ministry."[4]

Stuart Tyner suggests taking time to think about the philosophy behind your youth ministry by exploring the answers to 10 questions:

1. What kind of God do you serve?
2. How does that God get in touch with us? This answer will help you see the place of Bible study and devotional practices in your ministry.
3. How do youth learn?
4. What is ministry all about? Here, studying the life of Jesus is most helpful.
5. How do adolescents grow?
6. What do you hope will be the outcomes of your ministry? Some time must be spent in visioning what you want to accomplish in six months or one year or, for that matter, five years down the line.
7. How should other leaders be involved in your ministry?
8. What kinds of programs are consistent with our mission and understanding of youth ministry?
9. What does your church think of youth ministry?

10. How do you understand your own gifts for youth ministry?[5]

Once you have developed an understanding of the philosophy and purpose driving your ministry, some essential skills you need to develop include:

- Counseling: Know how to help youth with their problems.
- Discipline: Teach your kids to take responsibility for the consequences of their actions.
- Facilitating small groups: Learn to get your youth talking.
- Understanding the normal growth and development of teenagers.
- Programming ideas.
- Understanding and teaching about spiritual gifts.
- Knowing youth culture: Understand the world your kids live in.
- Resourcing: Make use of the best that's available in the world of youth ministry.[6]

Grant Misseghers adds that "the best way to understand youth better is to spend lots of time with them! Read magazines that they read; watch some movies that are popular with them. Immerse yourself in their culture!"

"The lasting enthusiasm and life change that we pray for can only be discovered when prayer and God are present," Shasta Burr reminds us. "Do more than plan a Sabbath school—plan to change lives."

5. If "youth ministry is a ministry of presence" (a quote one youth pastor shared from NAD youth director José Rojas), how much time do you need to put into spending with young people? And how do you do that if you're swamped by other responsibilities?

This can be a difficult challenge for busy youth leaders. Volunteer youth leaders usually hold down full-time jobs in addition to their ministry, and paid youth pastors are often loaded with additional church responsibilities. Yet every respondent agreed that spending time with youth is vital to a successful ministry—even if it means rearranging your priorities. "If you have tons of other responsibilities, you may need to get rid of some," says Brian Yeager. "Sometimes we need to cut back and say the rest of the things can fall apart. Develop a team of volunteers around you even if they don't *do* everything with the youth, they can provide food or help with transportation. The key is not to do it all yourself." Free up as much time as possible to spend building relationships with your young people.

Grant Misseghers agrees. When he worked as a earliteen leader, Misseghers says, "almost all my spare time went into my teens." He too suggests that overburdened youth leaders need to rethink their priorities.

Along with paring down your to-do list, you can find ways to include young people in some of your other responsibilities. Can you take a teenager along as you run errands? Invite youth to your house to play with your preschoolers or help you paint your porch. Bring them along as you visit elderly church members.

A. Allan Martin, in his essay "The Gift Hour," shares fond memories of weekend visits to the flea market with Mr. K, his academy work supervisor. "Mr. K . . . had a passion for finding trinkets and bargains. He shared that passion with me by inviting me each Sunday to join him on his adventures. It was not so much the secondhand treasures that stay in my mind, but rather the hour or so that we had to talk together about anything and the relationship that developed. . . . Beyond being my work supervisor, Mr. K was my friend and a wonderful support during the turbulent years of adolescence. His simple gift hour to me was a vivid reminder that I was not alone." Martin challenges adults in the church to follow Mr. K's example, spending one hour a week with a young person. "Your gift hour may be as simple as having lunch with a young person; it may be window shopping with a young adult, or running errands with a young parent. Walk your pets together; have them over for a barbecue. You may even opt to check out a local flea market. The key is to ensure that the time is spent in conversation and relationship building."[7]

Remember that it's OK to focus your mentoring time on a handful of youth (as long as this doesn't open you up to charges of favoritism). A few will influence others. Grant Misseghers says, "I found that the more I focused my attention and efforts on this small core group of leaders, the more they were empowered to minister to their peers. The result was that I (indirectly) touched and ministered to more people than I ever could have done alone." It may also help to recruit other caring adults in your church to spend time with some of the youth. You can't be a mentor to every one of them personally: not only time, but individual personality differences, makes that impossible. But you can help everyone find a mentor!

6. How do we motivate youth to stay in church and not leave?

A. Allan Martin, in his essay "Martin's Millstone: How I Killed a Youth Ministry," tells of his first job as a youth pastor when, as an overly enthusiastic "professional," he took over leadership of the youth program from the college-age volunteers who had been handling it. Though the youth program flourished, the sidelined young leaders drifted away from active involvement in that church. "I robbed them of their sense of value and importance," he confesses. "I trampled over their special place of involvement to do my model ministry. . . . As a minister, an adult, and a fool, I fell into the same trap many adults in the Adventist Church seem to be caught in: *Since we are older, our ideas are better, and therefore, we are more important.*[8]

Other respondents agreed with Martin's conclusion: when youth are involved in the church in a meaningful way, when they feel that their ministry is important and needed, they will stay. "Give them ownership," Brian Yeager says. "We must move beyond ministry of entertainment and into ministry of empowerment. By the time they're in the youth department, they need to realize that they are the church, not served by the church."

7. How do we motivate youth for service?

"Find out what they can do that is fun and is a part of who they are," Brian Yeager says. "Get them involved in service that fits their spiritual gifts." When you spend time getting to know your youth well, you'll know their strengths and their interests. You can help guide them into service activities that will make use of their gifts.

Most youth enjoy service projects even when they don't respond to other kinds of activities and events. The best way to get your youth motivated to serve may be simply to plan a service event "within the church or the community, or a project that impacts the wider world such as a short-term mission trip" and let youth see for themselves how much fun it can be. And don't be afraid to try *their* ideas, rather than yours, for service projects.

"They like to do radically different mission stuff than we typically think about," says Sherry Reinbold, who has served as her church's family life director in Michigan. "For example: a *free* carwash, telling people they are doing it free, just like God's love is free, and praying with people if the opportunity presents itself. The things they think up will blow the lid off what we think about doing as service to God. A fresh new approach—that is what they will offer us."

8. **How do we attract youth and young adults from outside the church, and how much "spirituality" should such a program include? How quickly should spiritual themes be introduced?**

If we hope to share Jesus' love with unchurched youth, our programs will certainly have to be spiritual in nature, "but a more important question is How do you present your spirituality?" says Mladen Kuzminski. "As old-fashioned saints with long faces? We must make spirituality something interesting. Crowds were always around Jesus because He knew how to attract them."

What methods will make His message attractive to secular youth and young adults? Allan Martin discusses ways the church can reach out to Generation X—today's young adults. He suggests prayer is the essential starting point, along with genuine renewal and revival from within the church. "Young adults," he writes, "are not drawn to programs or events as much as they're drawn to people with passion." Research these young people, their world and their needs, and "relate realness . . . build relationships of integrity with them." He points out that research shows today's young adults want honesty and integrity; they seek community; they are attracted to the arts, and they want diversity.[9]

As you reach out to youth and young adults in your community, remember to find out who they are and meet them on their own ground—but never lose sight of Jesus.

9. **How do we relate to youth who are being abused at home? What procedures are we to follow when we face this situation?**

This topic is dealt with in more depth in the chapter "Helping the Wounded Adventist Youth" in this book. Briefly, when a young person first mentions the possibility of abuse, "if [the youth] even hints in a vague way that abuse has occurred, encourage him or her to talk freely," says Stuart Tyner. "Take the report seriously. . . . Assure the individual that he or she did the right thing in telling."[10]

It's important to note that in many countries (including the U.S. and Canada) the law requires you to report any suspicion of physical or sexual abuse to the authorities. If you have told your young people that any secrets they confide in you will remain confidential (as you should do), it's important to note this exception up front, so that they will not feel betrayed when you do report abuse. In addition, if you are not a professional counselor yourself, you should do everything possible to see that the victim of abuse (present or past) talks to a trained counselor. You can continue to be a supportive, listening friend and advocate even after you have referred the person to a counselor.

This FAQ probably underlines for you the truth that there are no simple, pat answers in youth ministry. Everyone who responded shares a love for Christ and for youth, and a desire to bring the two together. Use these opinions and suggestions to build a youth ministry that will help you do just that!

---

[1] Allan A. Martin, "The ABCs of Ministry to Generations X, Y, and Z." Online: www.tagnet.org/dvm/ABCs.html.

[2] Martin, "Involve Me and I Will Understand." Online: www.tagnet.org/dvm/InvolveMe.html.

[3] Stuart Tyner, *The ABZs of Adventist Youth Ministry,* p. 35.

[4] J. Feldbush, W. Hurtado, R. Whitehead, *7 Principles for Youth Ministry Excellence: Practical Strategies to Turn Yourself and Your Youth Into Leaders,* p. 36.

[5] Tyner, pp. 175, 176.

[6] Feldbush et. al., p. 38.

[7] Martin, "The Gift Hour." Online: www.tagnet.org/dvm/mentor.html.

[8] Martin, "Martin's Millstone: I Killed a Youth Ministry." Online: www.tagnet.org/dvm/millstone.html.

[9] Martin, "Generation X in NET '98." Online: www.tagnet.org/dvm/neXt98.html.

[10] Tyner, p. 2.

SECTION 4

Challenges and Opportunities
in Youth Ministry

Growing Up Faithful:
Faith Development and Youth Ministry

by V. Bailey Gillespie, Ph.D.

ONCE I MET A NEWLY elected youth leader in a local congregation. She had been asked to lead out in the teen program. Well, not really. She was begged to help. She had fears and frustration about the ministry in her church during the whole year. In fact, she was troubled that the teens sat in the back of the church, seldom participated in worship, and grouped together after church outside the front door of the sanctuary.

She was certain that something could be done, but she also was certain she was not the one to do it. After all, she didn't know much about teens and knew even less about how faith could be shared. But she did have one thing going for her. She loved the children and youth of her church. So she took the job, knowing it would be for only one year. And she knew that God loved each young person in her church.

The first thing she did was to research faith development theory. She discovered that it was not as complicated as some would make it to be. In fact, understanding how people learn about God can provide clear insights into faith growth and maturity. Let's begin at the beginning, just as she did.

Biblical Models of Faith Development

God's Word provides us with some important models of faith growth. People learn about God through the following.

1. Rebirth and Conversion (John 3). Often God breaks into people's lives with a revelation of His grace and goodness. It might be sudden, as a result of crisis, emotional stress, or a profound sense of distance from God, but more often it is gradual and comes during the process of growth and commitment. John 3:16 says that whoever believes in Jesus has eternal life. Rebirth comes from God and from our acceptance of Jesus as our Lord and Savior. The process is really a miracle and often comes at moments when we are surprised by God's grace. C. S. Lewis calls it "surprised by joy." But belief in Jesus, according to John, is called the new-birth experience. Conversion describes our turning back to God, while new birth establishes our ownership.

2. Nurture (1 Cor. 3:1-10). The apostle Paul suggests that through caring and compassion people learn about God. By participating in acts of service and care we learn something unique about the nature of God. Jesus' mission on earth was one of nurture. He cared about and healed others as a sign that the God of the universe cared for them and understood their needs. As Christ's church learns to help others, they participate in Jesus' mission. Others come close to God and actually see in us what God is like. And just as Jesus represented God in His actions, we do the same.

3. Ministry (Rom. 12:4-8). The Bible talks about the gifts of the Spirit that are left with the church. As those gifts of ministry are enacted, people grow closer to God. That is why the church focuses on ministry. We, with God's help, target ways to help others. Through teaching, evangelism, sharing, and preaching we use the gifts of ministry to reach others' lives.

4. Assent to Truth (2 Thess. 2:13-15). In the New Testament we learn that understanding God's message in the Scriptures, presented clearly with the power of the Holy Spirit, provides insight into what one should believe. Believing the truth helps us understand correctly just what God is like. That is why we want to have clear, accurate biblical doctrines. The more clearly we understand God's will, the better picture of God we have.

These classic biblical means for finding God provide the first look at faith development. However, we can understand more about how people learn about God from research about faith development.

Situations of Faith

We could model faith experience in a number of ways. I want to focus on seven major generic faith situations that roughly correlate with the life-cycle concerns of most religious people. These situations of faith often define or explain the kind of significant features of the faith experience during the transition from children to youth and young adults and, finally, adult faith itself. And on the practical side, once we understand how people at different ages or stages experience faith in God, we can respond to their needs appropriately. We then become better ministers of God's grace.

The nurturing models described below will provide help to youth pastors, children's ministers, Pathfinder leaders, pastors, or parents. (I am not postulating a formal stage theory; rather, I am attempting to describe what I have observed, with a view toward the nurture of faith experience itself.) None of these steps is better than the others; they are simply descriptive in nature and hint at an educational/ministerial basis for our understanding of children's, youth, and adult ministries. We suggest the following situations of faith.

1. Borrowed Faith—Early Childhood. Here, within an active faith environment such as the home or family unit, basic trust gradually becomes established. Parents provide the relationships here; yet faith as an experience is observed externally—the child's faith is the parent's faith modeled, borrowed by the child. It is the other's faith, trust, and reliability that are seen. This situation teaches God's trustworthiness.

Children learn how to trust during this situation. Parental love models, it and the caring and compassion children feel illustrate it. It is the basis of any religious growth. As stages five and six approach, there is a different experience, which identifies faith. This is why spiritual parenting is so crucial.[1]

2. Reflected Faith—Middle Childhood. In this stage we notice a sense of becoming and individuation. The child realizes that he or she is a member of many communities of faith—family, friends, church, Sabbath school division, grandparents, etc. Family life has been the major reflector of faith before, and now these "others" become the teachers of faith. Reflected back from the caring group of churchgoers, the young child finds God as one who cares and loves and has attributes much like those of the caring group itself. Feelings of acceptance and fit are the basic religious experience during this age. Faith is seen as acceptance now. The actual experiencing of a faithful sense, a faith feeling, and a faith sensation in the affective domain is more present than ever before. While the faith experience has both cognitive and affective significance, its primary feeling tones are beginning to be understood.

Heroes become important faith guarantors now. Preadolescents love heroes. Jonah, Noah, Jesus, and John the Baptist provide role models now, so choose stories that reflect a positive role model. Don't dwell on the violent side of the stories; rather, share God's care, His love and friendliness. While faith is first experienced inactively, "it is next experienced in images and stories. Learning the community story is, therefore, an essential for faith."[2]

3. Personalized Faith—Early Adolescence. The faith experience now moves into a third, personalizing stage. This is the age of the teenager. But remember, all faith experience, whether or not it is in the natural growth cycle or happens late in life, usually goes through these stages. Some of the qualities of this situation during early adolescence are searching, questioning, committing, and examining one's faith. Doubt is the means of finding faith during this situation. Reflection and reasonableness are needed in the teen years as faith is experienced now for the first time in a personal, meaningful way.

Perhaps a characteristic of this period is the rapid change and reordering of the world view that goes on. Conversion can take an extreme look, with sudden enthusiasms, deep contemplation, action, and commitment. And often faith is rejected just as quickly as it is found.

But the new faith found in this situation is a personal one. Theological processes are beginning, and abstract thinking is ready to give meaning to the words that before were only memorized but now bring real understanding. So during this time, take care to give reasonable explanations to their theological questions. Take care to offer real answers rather than quick ones. If, for example, you want to instill a love for Ellen G. White, don't use her during this time to end discussion; rather, share her insights into the Bible and open a discussion with her.

4. Interior or Established Faith—Later Youth. The faith journey now comes to a time that can be called established faith. This fourth situation comes after the personal sorting and questioning period. It contains a desire to testify as to what one believes. For some, witness only is witness when first it is deeply believed. Established faith is perfect for this time period. New concerns are in the offing. These concerns often try to crowd out religious reflection. It is a good time for people to learn about giving their testimony. I like to call it "faith talk." Here, people share what God has done for them. They don't spend time telling others what is right, nor do they try to correct others. Simply sharing the good news in their own lives is enough. As people in this faith situation do so, they become more committed to seeing God in all of their lives and experience the joy of beginning to follow God.

5. Reordered Faith—Young Adult. Later in young adulthood another situation emerges that nurtures this faith experience. It now reinterprets personal faith. Theological reflection again comes to the front with its cognitive focus, but experientially there is a lifestyle focus on relationships and future that shapes the description of faith now. This remythologizing and reinterpretation fashions faith response and form. Young adults sort out what is important, what worship meets their needs, and to what degree involvement fulfills their life of faith. Every pastor knows that young adults who are turned on to God's grace in their lives are both active and enthusiastic about their newfound friend, Jesus. Churches can capitalize on the kinds of ministry that these young people can provide if they are careful to nurture and help them reorder their faith experience.

6. Reflective Faith—Middle Adult. As age begins to creep up on people, things get sorted out. This happens in their faith life as well. Middle-aged adults prioritize God, future, integrity, and hopefulness as they age. Life and religion are often seen in a broad perspective now. Helping these adults share what has meant so much to their lives is a crucial activity that can benefit children's and teen ministry. After all, this age group sees God as real and has a rich history of God's leadings, so they can be asked to talk about their own faith history. Sharing the actions of God in their lives with others strengthens their own faith and enriches everybody else.

7. Resolute Faith—Older Adult. Some resolution during this time is exhibited. The decisions made earlier are often tolerated now, and faith reaches beyond the here and now into the future. God is seen more as "comforter" than "unsettler." God is known in reality. God is felt in personal comfort. This group shares God's actions now, knowing they can change little as they make sense out of their lives. They can be a great help to other adults as they share hope.[3]

So What?

It is clear that people go through these situations as they discover God in their lives. Ellen White struggled with the health message later in her ministry. As she matured, she was able to write some of her greatest books. For example, *Steps to Christ* was a product of an older, more reflective understanding of God's leading. If we look at King David, we see a man growing two steps forward and often one backward. He is crowned king, yet he has problems later on in his life. One would think that finding God would solve all his problems. That is not the case, and as we watch David live his life we see him sort out what is central for his life in the long run.

One question that I always ask my students to answer after a lecture on a difficult theological subject is "So what?" What is theory must be made practical. So let's look for a moment at the implications of this theory in the actual life of the youth professional or the local church youth leader, parent, or religious worker.

1. Knowing how people learn about God helps us in the following three ways: People grow up in stages, and these stages present unique opportunities for faith development.
2. The situations people find themselves in suggest some methods of helping people discover faith in its richest form.
3. Those who are aware of the nature of faith growth can be more effective youth leaders, youth professionals, or guarantors for the faith of others.

Stages Present Unique Opportunities for Faith Development

As children grow, there are ample opportunities to assist them in their quest for God. For example, children borrow faith experience from the significant parental figures in their home.

It may be a single parent, a stepparent, grandparent, or guardian. Any and all parenting figures provide role models for faith.

Youth leaders should capitalize on these situations and provide parenting classes and information for parents about spiritual life in order to assist them in their challenge of leading their children to God. Provide the following types of resources: (1) materials that enrich family worship; (2) resources that change passive parent-led worship into interactive, creative, blended, or shared worship experiences; (3) videos, tapes, sermons, or reading material about parenting and being a mentor for faith experience.

One can assist parents in their religious experience with a view to making them better models of faith life. And it is important to share stories from the Bible of people that struggled with problems and through reliance on God found victory. Help parents in your ministry become faithful guarantors of faith.

We want our children to learn in the early situations of faith that they can rely on God for everything. In fact, this is one crucial truth everyone needs to learn. Make God first, think about God during the day, and remember God when problems come are first priorities for any family ministry. Youth leaders, youth directors, youth ministry professionals, and parents can explore their roles in these early situations of faith.

Later, as children begin to experience the power of others in their lives and see the church as a new kind of family, the church members can make it a point to keep children front and center in worship and programming. Don't let the church have worship services without special bulletins for growing children. Try to encourage the church to use children in the worship service so they begin to feel needed and a part of the whole congregation. Be creative; soon you'll recognize the power of having children be seen and heard in the church. The more they feel a part of it, the more they will see the importance of God in their lives. So involve them in prayer, in teaching, in Scripture lessons, and give them jobs that help the church. Give them real ministry to do. They are full members in the church, and the church benefits by nurturing in them loyalty and orthodoxy. And by all means, don't forget to talk about the children from the front of the church.

Teens going through the challenge of personalizing faith present a special gift to the church. Not only do they wear their identity on the outside through their clothes, music, and public presence; they are forming their identity through the interaction they see with those that have already learned about God. The church is a crucial place for teens to see if Christianity works or not. So remember the following:

- Do a climate check in your church to see if it is both *warm* and *open to new ideas.* This is especially crucial for church members to understand. It is through these two climates that teens understand the nature of the kingdom of God.
- Find adult mentors who can provide models of the values we want our teens to internalize. Forming relationships early on with adults who live their values and want to spend the time it takes to build meaningful relationships with teens best prevents at-risk behavior.
- Make sure that programming in your church is not just for the older members. Youth feel alienated anyway just because of their age. Don't let the church encourage this distance by not taking the time to provide meaningful and frequent programming for teens. Remember, youth ministry does make a difference.

- Keep the ministry active. Personalize faith situations; blend action and reflection in a learning loop. Remember the Gospel of Matthew—Jesus sent His disciples out to do ministry and then to talk about it. He told parables and then explored their meaning. He healed and then taught. Actions always preceded Jesus' teaching.

What More Can We Do?

Explore faith in the now, not the hereafter. Don't let teens and young adults feel that they can wait to become Christians. Stress their involvement in the church now, that their commitments can be made while they are young, and stress how much God desires their friendship.

Establish relationships first. Your ministry must be relationship-oriented. Jesus spent His years teaching truth through His work with people. Take the time to build close relationships with teens and young adults. It pays off in big dividends later in life when they come back to you with their questions and challenges.

Watch for moments for "faithing." Think of faith as a description of the way we feel about God. The Bible calls it a gift. And it is in the give-and-take of daily living that it is seen, explored, and received. Those teachable moments during crisis or moments of reflection can be some of the most important moments for God to break through our worldly view and give us a glimpse of heaven.

Avoid These Barriers

Make sure you are not modeling a works-oriented approach. Keep everything grace-full! Barry Gane, in his book *Building Youth Ministry: A Foundational Guide,* says, "If youth ministry is to be successful for those in these transitional stages, it must provide a sheltered environment for discussion of these issues, and must provide an intergenerational context for faith building."[4]

Don't give a false picture of the church at work in the world. Make sure the activities your church provides in children's, youth, and young adult ministry are creative, exciting, and explosive. Why would anyone want to join a church that's dull, introverted, and boring?

Don't let your ministry marginalize youth and young adults. Keep them at the very center of your ministry and your church's mission. Youth tend to be impatient with what appears to them to be irrelevant and obsolete, and are even intolerant when issues have a negative impact on them. It is natural for youth in a personalizing situation of faith to seem to be withdrawn rather than to fight authorities. It is because youth and young adults are basically idealistic and perceptive when inadequacies or irrelevancies exist or if they see a hypocritical attitude.

Faith development theory, while often theoretical, has a basic practical conclusion. Do what is right at the right time. Provide the proper content at the right moment. Give the needed care and concern when the time is right. Build ministry that meets personal needs when faith is emerging. And by all means, take the time to build relationships with children, youth, and young adults if you want ministry to make a difference.

---

[1] For detailed resources to help parents with spiritual growth, see V. Bailey Gillespie and Judith Gillespie with Tim Gillespie and Cheryl Webster, *Keeping the Faith: A Guidebook for Spiritual Parenting* (Lincoln, Nebr.: AdventSource, 2001).

[2] G. W. Allport and J. M. Ross, "Personal Religious Orientation and Prejudice," *Journal of Personality and Social Psychology* 5 (1967): 434.

[3] For a complete look at the faith development experience, see V. Bailey Gillespie, *The Experience of Faith* (Birmingham, Ala.: Religious Education Press, 1992).

[4] Barry Gane, *Building Youth Ministry,* p. 42.

CHAPTER 29

Catching God's Grace:
Youth Ministry and Spirituality

by V. Bailey Gillespie, Ph.D.

MIKE ACCEPTED JESUS WHEN HE was 16 years old. It was after he heard a terrific sermon by Pastor Tim, his youth pastor. He was convinced that his life was not quite right. He heard about the wonderful gift of God's grace given to us by Jesus, and it finally sank into his heart. He personally accepted this God/man who loved so much and was willing to give the ultimate gift for others. He died for Mike.

Catching God's Grace

Mike thought long and hard about that gift. He felt down deep inside that he didn't deserve it. But after long, silent hours sitting up on the rock behind his house, looking down the valley, thinking about some of his friends who were angry with their parents and the church, and just feeling that big, empty feeling inside his heart, he looked up at the stars one night and just said, "Jesus, I need You; I can't do it by myself," and accepted Jesus. At that moment he knew he had made a wonderful choice. He felt free for the first time in years. "The truth will make you free indeed." He was ready to face his problems with some new power and attitude. He was beginning to believe the verse that says, "I have come that they may have life, and have it to the full" (John 10:10, NIV). The texts he had learned in Pathfinder Club really did make sense.

He had just been born again. He opened up his Bible and read a verse that has become his favorite text. It was Revelation 21:5: "He who was seated on the throne said, 'I am making everything new!'" (NIV). He knew he had a fresh new start now. He understood forgiveness.

But Now What?

Now Mike faced another challenge. He had accepted Jesus' gift for his life, recognized he couldn't do anything to deserve it, but wanted to know more. He had never been the best student, and he knew that "good Christians" always studied their Bibles and prayed. Somehow they focused on Jesus most of the day. He could hardly focus on his required schoolwork—which brought immediate consequences. Once he even forgot his algebra assignment. How could he ever be a truly religious person? He saw his need in an entirely different light now that he had found Jesus.

He had never wanted to build a relationship with God before. Now he was determined to try. Something was different this time. What he did to meet Jesus now was because he understood the wonderful gift Jesus had given him. He never wanted to forget that gift. And he had so much more to learn.

Mike was beginning to understand how to be a Christian. He understood how to live with his wonderful new gift from God.

A Spiritual Quest

Mike was coming face to face with the challenge of spirituality. His challenges are the same ones that every Christian faces almost every day. He was thinking about spirituality and wanted to do something about it.

By spirituality, I mean *our inner experience of the sacred and our living out of that experience.* Notice the twofold quality of spirituality as we have defined it: (1) *spirituality is something we experience,* feel, react to, and understand; and (2) *spirituality is the way we live out that experience.*[1]

The work of Charles Shelton, a Catholic religious educator, emanates a deep compassion for children and youth. His seminal work, *Adolescent Spirituality: Pastoral Ministry for High School and College Youth,* is a monumental work. In it he defines what the spirituality of an adolescent might be. He identifies four specific dynamics: (1) it is a Christ-centered spirituality; (2) it is found to a great extent in the context of community; (3) it is future-oriented because it impacts hopes and attitudes about life that have yet to be lived; (4) it is developmental. You see, it is shaped and impacted by the various intellectual, social, and physical changes that impact adolescents' lives on a day-to-day basis.[2]

In this chapter we want to do three things that relate to understanding the spiritual life:
 • Explore the nature of the spiritual journey itself.
 • Examine how youth ministry can aid others on this journey.
 • Identify some challenges in the youth professional's life of faith.

The concern over spirituality comes out of an understanding of the life and ministry of Jesus. As we discover Jesus and begin to explore the way He lived for His Father, we will see Him at prayer in the Garden of Gethsemane, we will listen to Him tell about His intimate life with God—so close that when we have seen Him we have actually seen God! We see Jesus caring for the sick and the needy and marvel at His teachings on the importance of caring for our neighbors as He shares the story of the good Samaritan.

Early on in His life He did battle with Satan and we see His victory through reliance upon God and not on His own ability. We see Him choosing not to use His own power as God for victory. Later in His ministry we notice Him living empowered by the Spirit of God and hear His teaching about the strength that comes through the Holy Spirit.

In the synagogues, the churches of His day, He reads the Words of his Father and learns the importance of hearing plus doing. From His life we can identify five distinct areas of spirituality that can become models for youth and young adults.
 • personal devotion to God
 • compassion toward all people
 • evangelism toward the lost
 • virtue in thoughts, words, and actions
 • Spirit empowerment in His ministry

These five areas in Jesus' life provide a basis for understanding our own walk with Jesus. And they give us a picture or outline of a curriculum for youth ministry in the local church or conference.

Spirituality is not only a personal, deep, almost mystical encounter with God. While it might include this, it also involves compassion for others, evangelism toward those who have not yet found God, the challenge of making life-affirming choices and excluding life-denying choices in our lives, as well as seeking the Holy Spirit for empowerment in what we do for God. The gift of grace Jesus gives us called "salvation" not only motivates us to grow in our relationship with Him; it inspires us to live like Him too. And the good news is that as we live our life with Jesus, His love makes up the difference in our own lives, covers our sins, and, best of all, forgets them every day as we live with Him.

How Does Youth Ministry Help on This Journey?

The power of youth ministry is clear. If there is a high degree of ministry perceived by young people, a number of things are understood as better. For example, youth like sermons more, see their church as more loving and accepting, and are more committed to God; and their loyalty to the church increases at a deeper level than does the loyalty of those who experience only low or no youth ministry at all.[3] Likewise, when youth feel accepted by God, understand that Jesus loves them, and know they are a part of His kingdom through the gift of His grace, they too benefit in their spiritual lives.

Youth ministry assists in another way, too. Good youth ministry has as a part of its curriculum educational insights of how to do good Bible study, how to enrich your prayer life, how meditation assists our understanding of God, and how community service, mission involvement, and making good choices helps one's personal experience with God. In fact, youth ministry can be the basis for young people understanding how Christians grow and cope in a world that has so many choices.

When people try to find God, there are not very many ways in which this can be done. Let's make a list:
- We learn about Jesus through the witness of people that know Him.
- We sense His presence in times of greatest need.
- We learn objective things about Him by reading the only Book written to tell us about Him.
- We live in a world where if we look carefully enough we can see glimpses of His presence.
- We sense His presence in quiet moments of reflection.
- We are touched by His grace when we take time to talk and listen in prayer.

There aren't many more options out there!

Competent youth ministry provides all six of these options during the regular course of ministry. When people criticize youth ministry as simply "entertainment," they really don't know the depth and scope of competent youth ministry. Whether the youth professional is working with a group of five young people or is responsible for whole conferences and unions, ministry with young people covers a spiritual curriculum that is often unwritten but just as real.

Youth pastors provide a wonderful model of what the Christian life might be like for their youth. That is why their own personal experience with God needs to include the spiritual dimensions identified above, too. After all, we learn much of what we know about God from important others. Youth pastors provide that model in a significant way. In our research about youth ministry and those things that are important to young people as they build their own faith life, youth ministers ranked in the top five of more than 20 choices.

How Does the Youth Ministry Impact Others' Spirituality?
1. We Hear God Through the Voice of Others Who Know Him.

When you want to hear Jesus, you have to listen to all of His voices. Sometimes He talks to us through others' experiences. If you have a friend who knows God, take some time to talk about it. All too often we are afraid to share our experiences because we think that others will judge us, especially if we are new in our feelings about God. But religious experience is best understood when we can see how it works in another person's life. This sharing is part of any balanced youth ministry approach.

Don't be afraid to be honest. Talk about the failures you are experiencing. Be open to talk about the feelings you have and how distant you feel sometimes. Everyone has feelings. Everyone has many of the same feelings you do. Christians must learn that sharing their doubts, frustrations, feelings of distance, and experiences of closeness with Jesus are the best way to understand the nature of the religious life. Even the most religious person you know has the same feelings you do. Everyone must start at the same place.

Find a friend to talk to about your decision and spiritual life. Be bold. After all, one thing that comes with accepting Jesus is a new boldness to share exactly what is on your heart. Here are some guidelines you can share with young people that may help them share their experience with God.

a. Find a friend who has had a new experience with God, or is struggling to find Jesus anew.

b. Be the first to open up the conversation by saying, "I want to tell you something that has just happened to me." Be free and honest about your fears and doubts about sharing. You might be surprised how much that friend needs to talk too.

c. Try to meet regularly and talk together. In this cyberspace world there are all kinds of ways to talk. Use your e-mail, write a computer journal, use the phone anytime, or meet face to face once in a while. But be sure you talk to someone. There are all kinds of people who care. Your parents might be delighted to talk to you, your brothers or sisters, some near relative you trust. Your best friend or your teacher or counselor are always there for you when you need them. Your pastor is a good reflector, too. Try sharing and see if you don't feel close to Jesus because you can now hear how Jesus is working on somebody's life.

d. Begin to ask personal questions. Talk about your feelings, not about your beliefs. Talk about your failures, not about theology at first. Talk about your "experience" with God. There are many ways to experience God. Sometimes the experience seems almost too real to believe; other times they simply are a soft warm feeling that you have made a good decision. Share these feelings with someone else, and see what kind of experience they have had with Jesus.

2. We Hear God in Moments of Crisis

Don't be surprised if some of the most intense experiences of God come to you during or after moments of intense struggling and crisis. A crisis is a chance to change rather than a moment of catastrophe. Crises comes to us because we sense conflict in our lives or we find ourselves trapped in a unique problem. Think how Jesus might respond in that situation and then claim the power of Christ to help you. Here's a Bible text you can trust: "Cast all your anxiety on him because he cares for you" (1 Peter 5:7, NIV).

Often the problems we have are problems we have created. Check to see if you are responsible for the crisis. Did you initiate the crisis by forgetting about others in your family? Look at yourself—have you been careful to be kind to others.[2]

Some crises are completely beyond your control. Sickness in the family, a death of a family member or good friend, the loss of a boy or girl friend—those bring the world crashing down around you.

Suggest that young people read Romans 5 over and over. "Therefore, since we have been justified through faith, we have peace with God through our Lord Jesus Christ [the battle is now over between us and God], through whom we have gained access by faith into this grace in which we now stand. [We don't have to get more grace; we stand in it right now!] And we rejoice in the hope of the glory of God. [He's coming back, so let's be happy about it.] Not only so, but we also rejoice in our sufferings [here comes the hard part], because we know that suffering produces perseverance [that's a good thing]; perseverance, character [character's good too]; and character, hope. [I sure need it at times like this.] And hope does not disappoint us, because God has poured out his love into our hearts by the Holy Spirit, whom he has given us [we aren't alone anymore; God's Spirit is always here!]" (verses 1-5, NIV). This text can really help you feel God's closeness to our problems.

3. We Hear God's Voice by Reading the Book That Shares God

When you want to learn about something, you go to the library or to the Internet to find out what's been said on the topic. I did that as I was researching this chapter. When we want to learn anything, we usually have to put in some hard study time.

You know the analogy. If you want to find out about the God who saved you, you have to go to the source. The Bible is the best story of salvation that exists. Remember, the pages of your Bible contain stories written by people who experienced God in a very personal way. The way they tell their testimony about God can help us understand Him and grow even closer to Him. And the more information we have, the better equipped we are to make some correct choices when the going gets tough and decisions are hard to sort out.

Here's one helpful hint. Don't read just any Bible. Read one that is your own. Find the translation that talks just to you and make it your own. Put your name in the front and mark it up as you read. You will be amazed at what you underline and highlight. And later, when you go back and see what you marked, you will learn how God helped you in that unique text.

Here's another tip. Don't feel guilty if you don't spend hours with your Bible. People don't become saints instantly. It takes time. So pace yourself as you begin to study the Bible. Take only one verse, study it, and pray about its meaning and try to apply it to your life. It's just a beginning, but you have to start somewhere—so take it easy, take it slow, but don't forget to do something with God's Word.

4. We Hear the Voice of God in the World Around Us.

When you look at a flower, what do you see? Now, this is not a biology or botany experiment. There is no trick answer. What do you see? Let me give you some hints. Do you see hints of a Creator who puts things together? Do you see evidence of love in the order and perfection of the flower's parts? Whatever you see, it is not very specific, but you can't be impressed with the detail and beauty you hold in your hands.

Many religious people find peace and solitude in the quiet of God's creation. If you want to build a spiritual life, learn to take time in the middle of the creation and let it softly speak of God to your heart. Here's some practical suggestions:

- Take a walk outside in nature; look around and learn to wonder at what you see.
- Sit for a time with a small object of nature in your hand; hold it, feel it, smell it, use all of your senses to experience it in a real way. Then think about what it says to you about God.
- Clean up a spot that has beauty but that people have neglected. Get involved in an ecological movement; start collecting flowers or even butterflies or bugs. In the study you will come to appreciate the details of God's wonderful world.

Pathfinder ministry may provide an excellent model here for older teens and families. For years they have understood the power of weekend outings, camping trips, walks in nature. Encourage your youth to get out into nature and discover God.

5. We Feel God in Quiet Moments of Reflection, Prayer, and Meditation

When we think of spiritual people, we often think of holy men and women who can spend hours focusing on some aspect of truth and meditating for hours. We have heard stories of Simeon Stylites, who, after deciding to be religious, climbed a pole for years in order to be close with his Lord. Once when traveling to Israel, I met a young student only 21 years old who was going to a monastery in the Sinai desert in order to get away from the world's pressures, and he had pledged that he would not come out until he found God. The history of the world is filled with stories of holy people who had to get away in order to sort out their religious lives. The Bible contains a number of stories too.

- Paul, after he met Jesus on the road to Damascus, spent some time in Arabia in order to get his head straight.
- Moses was always wandering in the wilderness! Forty years wasn't enough. He did it for more than 80.
- Jesus had to get away too. His sojourn in the wilderness helped Him formulate His mission and gave Him a chance to see God and His role in the saving of the world in a different light. So don't be ashamed if you need an occasion to take some time by yourself, alone, where you and God can touch each other.

Traditionally, meditation was seen as the best way for people to get close to God. Western minds have a difficult time focusing on anything that lasts more than a half hour. And often we channel-surf rather than focus on the few minutes of commercials that break up the stream of the story we are watching on TV. But meditation is a discipline that many have used to get in touch with God and to reorder their lives. The word "discipline" sounds so boring that we usually don't try to do it at all. But in Bible times, with no distractions around, with only the wilderness cluttered with sheep and goats, it may have been easier to learn this skill. Here is something you can try that will help you learn how to meditate.

- Find a Bible text you like.
- Take a minute to read the text and think for another minute what it is about, what it says to you.
- Now read the text 10 times. After each reading, think of a word that pops into your head that relates to the text. For example, you may select John 3:16, an old familiar text. The first time you read it you might think of the words "unbelievable love"; the next, the word "gift-love"; and so forth for 10 tries.
- Close your eyes and think what the text means to you today.
- Here's the hard part. Give yourself 10 minutes to read, think, ponder, and wonder about the text. Time yourself so you don't cheat on the short end!

You just meditated on God's Word. The more you try it, the easier and more refreshing it becomes to your heart.

Another form of meditation is to use a journal to organize your thoughts. Keep it handy and try to write for 10 minutes a day. Don't make it sound like a diary. Try not to make such entries as "John met me today at the cafeteria!" Instead, talk about your spiritual quest. Ask yourself questions you need answered, write down insights gained from meditation, and be very specific. Teach your youth to journal. Their spiritual life will grow as yours will as you learn to journal God's love.

Some journals are poetic; others are abstract. But when you write regularly, you build up a routine that will benefit your personal religious life. And remember this bit of theology: you read your Bible, pray, and meditate because God has given you such a great gift in Jesus. You don't do it to get religion or to make God like you better. You are learning to worship, and prayer, meditation, and Bible study are ways you respond to God's love in your life.

Let's Take Inventory

Nothing is more important than your youth ministry professionals and their young people to have a close, rich walk with God. This spiritual journey is central to any ministry or growth in grace. So this chapter is directed to anyone wanting a deeper understanding of God's will in their lives—youth directors, youth leaders, or youth and young adults themselves.

As you all grow spiritually, you will have choices to make: You can choose to build a close relationship with Jesus, or you can choose to neglect it. The problem with neglect is that eventually you might lose most of your interest altogether. That is why these spiritual activities are so helpful. They keep you in touch with the God that has saved you. They build some good skills that can benefit you in other areas of your life. Youth often find that their grades get better because they have learned to concentrate better because of the discipline they are learning with God. And prayer, meditation, journaling, and Bible study get you in touch with the sources of your spiritual energy.

You test the strength of a rope by pulling against it; you test the strength of the wind by walking against it; and you test your spiritual strength by never giving in to the temptations that are around you. Look at these disciplines and activities as ways to keep in touch with someone you love, ways to understand what's in God's mind. They inspire you, motivate you, and instruct you in the ways of salvation. And that's not such a hard thing to do, especially if you love the one you are learning about.

---

[1] V. Bailey Gillespie and Judith Gillespie with Tim Gillespie and Cheryl Webster, *Keeping the Faith: A Guidebook for Spiritual Parenting,* p. 26.

[2] For a complete discussion of adolescent spirituality, see Charles Shelton, *Adolescent Spirituality: Pastoral Ministry for High School and College Youth* (Chicago: Loyola University Press, 1983).

[3] Barry Gane, *Valuegenesis Project Report No. 3: Youth Ministry and the Transmission of Beliefs on Values* (South Pacific Division Youth Department, 1997), pp. 69-97.

CHAPTER 30

Maintaining an Attitude
of Grace in Youth Ministry

by Michele Deppe

What Is Grace?

"GRACE AND PEACE TO YOU" (Rom. 1:7, NIV). In his letters Paul greeted fellow believers with these awe-inspiring words. This special Greek terminology indicates that accepting God's grace in your soul gives you peace throughout your life. This grace and peace come from the knowledge that God has forgiven us. Isn't this knowledge worthy of our personal experience? Certainly the lifestyle that this greeting represents is what we want our children to adopt. Meditate on what God has for you to do as you prepare to communicate grace and peace as your greeting to the following generation.

Grace is at once simple to define and nearly impossible to comprehend. Grace is best illustrated by Jesus' sacrificial death on the cross to save us from our destructive, disobedient nature, done in order to reinstate our relationship with Him. Ellen White observed, "As soon as there was sin, there was a Savior."* To imagine that God, the awesome Creator of the universe, has made a way to be intimately acquainted with us, despite the shameful clothing of our sin, is an extraordinary concept to internalize.

Even before we sinned, the "Word" was with God, and would later come to earth to be a man and provide atonement for our sins. Every parent knows that their newborn baby will grow up to disappoint them at some time in the future; but parents are already prepared to love their child no matter what.

The dictionary defines grace as God's loving mercy displayed toward human beings for the salvation of their souls. The biblical definition of grace is both passive and aggressive. It is a message that motivates us to fall on our knees to receive its goodness as we realize that only God could give us such a precious gift, a gift that we don't deserve.

At the same time, there is a challenging aspect to grace when we are impressed to circulate the mercy that God has shown us. To follow the example of Jesus, we must reciprocate where grace is concerned: "Each one should use whatever gift he has received to serve others, faithfully administering God's grace in its various forms" (1 Peter 4:10, NIV).

Representing Christ to young people is to reciprocate grace in a very meaningful way. Paul, in 2 Timothy 3:14, reminds us of the everlasting impact that we can have on youth. Not only are you investing God's love in the lives of the kids that you have the privilege to minister to, but you're helping them to build a strong foundation that can influence generations to come. Remember the folks who took the time to invest in your life. Taking the time to be there for someone will probably motivate them to disciple someone else in need later in their lives. And 2 Timothy 2:2 reminds us that those who learn go on to share with others. Kids who are taught grow up to be teachers.

Cheap Grace Versus Biblical Grace

Here's a bit of "heavenly humor." A man dies and goes to heaven. Of course Peter meets him at the pearly gates. Peter says, "Here's how it works. You need 100 points to make it into heaven. You tell me all the good things you've done, and I give you a certain number of points for each item, depending on how good it was. When you reach 100 points, you get in."

"OK," the man says. "I was married to the same woman for 60 years and was always faithful to her, even in my heart."

"That's wonderful," says Peter. "That's worth five points!"

"Five points?" he says. "Well, I attended church all my life and supported its ministry with my money and my talents."

"Terrific!" says Peter. "That's certainly worth at least three points."

"Three points?" I was a youth group leader and worked in a shelter for homeless people."

"Fantastic; that's good for three more points," Peter says.

"Three points!" the man cries. "At this rate the only way I can get into heaven is by the grace of God."

"Exactly! One hundred points! Come on in!"

Cheap grace might be described as a real tongue-in-cheek response to being forgiven. Cheap grace might consist of doing patronizing works without letting the gift change your heart. Biblical grace must be qualified as everything that we can't do by ourselves with our own motivation and good intentions. To really accept the gift of grace in our hearts, we need to grasp the notion that no matter how "good" we can be, we can't be good enough to deserve God's grace. That is, in fact, what makes it a gracious act of love from our heavenly Father. We can never really be worth our redemption by our own merit, but only through Christ's payment for our sins. Remember, God is not mocked; we reap what we sow. Live by God's grace, and it will multiply.

A prideful attitude can block the gift of grace from working its power in our lives. Isaiah 64:6 says that all of our righteousness is as filthy rags. People today have so much pride in their filthy rags! Owning things and being a success is the main goal in life for many. Our young people are encouraged to define who they are by their education, paychecks, and the Calvin Klein on their backs. We are a "self-made" society that believes that as long as you are a good person you're not hurting anyone, then you'll be set for eternity. When you're too full of self, you can't experience grace. After all, you're too good to need it, right? Encourage the youth in your care to be humble and to know God, instead of being rag collectors.

Another thorny weed that inhibits grace from growing in our lives is unforgiveness. The people that surround us, Christians and nonbelievers alike, often hurt us by what they say or by unloving actions toward us. In Matthew 5:44 Jesus said to operate in grace, even admonishing us to love and bless people who mistreat us. In our current vernacular: when someone does something wrong, get over it! Let it go. Let's not be so self-centered that we illustrate touchy immaturity in front of our youth.

As we drink the cup with Jesus, we're guaranteed some discomfort and opposition. Remind kids that biblical grace is powerful and that Jesus can soothe whatever wounds the world inflicts upon us. We have mighty weapons in prayer and in exercising love and grace in our dealings with others. A benchmark of gracious living is not to indulge in self-pity over the small darts that piece our thin skin. Romans 12:17 and 18 tells us to live graciously and at peace with everyone.

One of the most powerful lessons that we can imprint on the hearts of our young people is that nothing that God offers is cheap, instant, or selfish. God has put you in the position to point young people to God, and to encourage them to discover who He really is. They need to retain the ability to have childlike faith, letting pride fall by the wayside and keeping their eyes on things of eternal value.

The Cost of Discipleship

The United States was founded on biblical principles, and sometimes it is easier to sort of blend in. Basically this government is supposed to uphold the Ten Commandments. As a result, a lot of our churches may focus on missionary work elsewhere as a means of saving souls. Let's not forget what is happening here at home; move back to discipleship.

Our world is becoming more accessible, and all along that was Jesus' concept of how things would become. He told us in Matthew 28 to go out over the globe and make disciples. Our kids need to have a strong Christian foundation and a sense of a world vision. When we disciple our kids, let's remind them that we're not the only Christians. Our global view needs to include people of different countries. Some of us need to give some thought to the concept that Jesus isn't an American!

Grace is given to us freely, and that is how we should express it to others. God wants only those who have opened their ears to listen, although He desires everyone to hear. When young people seem too distracted to listen, gracious leaders don't grab them by the hair and force them to listen. Discipleship will take place when their hearts are open to God and your spirits can commune on biblical truth together.

Pray for your young charges; God will work in their hearts when we pray without ceasing. Part of the price of discipleship will be time spent on your knees. Ask several trusted intercessors to pray for you and the youth group, making way for the Holy Spirit to draw kids into the kingdom. The main battle in winning souls is in the spirit realm, so go on the field with the weapon of prayer.

Jesus said, "If you hold to my teaching, you are really my disciples" (John 8:31, NIV). Kids today are grasping for things to hold on to. As youth leaders we can help them to hold fast to God's Word. The cost of discipleship is actually the cost of being obedient to the Word. We can't afford not to be obedient! How well do you model biblical grace? Have you studied the Word and have it upon your lips to have ready answer to youngsters who need the truth? The Old Testament teacher Ezra devoted himself to knowing the Word and teaching it (Ezra 7:10). Our kids deserve no less.

The youth that you'll minister to are not the only ones who are growing. We all are. Paul notes that we keep growing until we become mature and attain "the whole measure of the fullness of Christ" (Eph. 4:13, NIV).

Teens mess up. Unfortunately most of us learn by doing things the wrong way on occasion, instead of complying with what we have been taught. Your influence with the youth that you encounter is built on relationships. When young persons make mistakes, show them grace. Forgive them as Christ forgave you. Remind them: "In the past you were slaves to sin—sin controlled you. But thank God, you fully obeyed the things that you were taught. You were made free from sin, and now you are slaves to goodness" (Rom. 6:17, 18, NCV).

What does being a slave to goodness mean? Does it mean cracking the whip over kids' backs and making them toe the line? Or does it mean being used of God to expose kids to His love, so that they feel His sweetness and want to be just like Him? Teenagers, like the rest of us, are works in progress. Grace is showing young people how to be like Jesus. His whole life was lived in the message of grace and love. When you feel as though you have no patience left, when you cannot cope with an egocentric youth an instant longer, remember that "my grace is sufficient for you, for my power is made perfect in weakness" (2 Cor. 12:9, NIV).

The teen years can be devastating if a young person experiences bondage to unhealthy habits or suffers guilt over a transgression of their conscience. As a young leader, try to remember that our Master came to be a physician to those who need care, not to kids who are perfect. Love them through their crisis, apply tough love, and help them to switch tracks. Years of hurt can follow someone through adulthood if problems such as drinking, taking drugs, or engaging in premarital sex begin to establish roots in a young person's life. Teenagers think that they've learned all there is to know; so remind them how young they really are and that Jesus has a lot of plans for them.

Discipleship can involve being a defender, a shield to a kid who is being mistreated. Kids can suffer secretly in a number of ways at the hands of their parents, guardians, or even other youth leaders. If you become aware of a youth who is being violated, take action immediately to stop the abuse. This book and others are chock-full of what to do when you discover that a child is being abused. Don't be afraid to get involved.

Don't give up on young people when you think they are living beneath their potential and need to "straighten up." Once I had a job that I liked a lot, but I decided that it was a big hassle. I was new in my field, but at least I had some experience on my résumé. I told my boss, who had hired me right out of school, that I was ready to move on. I believed that it was time to get out there and really stretch to my true potential. I quit my job, and my boss did not question my decision in the least. She patiently endured my telling her that this job had been a stepping-stone and that I was grateful, but that I felt that I'd learned enough to see what else might be available to me. Obviously, with a prideful attitude like mine, my boss was not motivated to creatively meet my craving for advancement. She probably knew that I'd made up my mind and that discussion would be futile.

I quickly found that the grass is not always greener working for another business across town. In fact, my new job chewed me up and spit me out within a month's time. Like the prodigal son, I went back to my previous boss and asked if I could have any job that she had available. She kindly welcomed me back to my old job. Wow! That was gracious of her, but God's grace toward us would rival hers. He knows everything about us and still wants us to work for Him. God wants more than anything else to reconcile us with Him. Romans 3:22 explains that it doesn't really matter who we are, where we've come from, or what is on our résumé. He wants us to be forgiven through the sacrifice that Jesus has made for us.

Applying Grace in the Lives of Youth

Paul instructs, "Don't let anyone look down on you because you are young, but set an example for the believers in speech, in life, in love, in faith and in purity" (1 Tim. 4:12, NIV). God believes in the innocence and ability of young people to grasp His love for them. They are able to glean the richness of God's gifts from the Word and apply them to daily life. As youth ministers, let's not be ageist! Paul's instruction is: "Treat younger men as brothers" (1 Tim. 5:1).

Our kids have amazing challenges in the area of self-esteem. In this age of divorce, drugs, violence, and teen pregnancy there are plenty of places for kids to bury themselves in negative behavior. The old saying "misery loves company" is very true. Grace, the intimate love of our personal Savior and friend flowing through you, can help keep kids on the straight and narrow by helping them to like the person they see in the mirror. Discipleship can play a strong role in raising a kid's self-esteem to a healthy level, as any Big Brother or Big Sister program will attest to.

Express your expectations that kids look for ways to invest grace in others. Have them keep an eye out for circumstances in which to do "random acts of kindness." This guarantees that the seed you're attempting to plant in their lives gets a fair chance at spreading into the fertile soil of a youth who is a "doer of the Word," and not a hearer only. Just as you are acting out God's will for your life, kids need to start developing a pattern of gracious acts too. A friend told me his 6-year-old wants to save aluminum cans to earn revenue for a needy family that she learned about at kindergarten. Imagine! A 6-year-old taking the initiative to make kindergarten an environment in which grace abounds.

One of the most exciting aspects about grace is the future life that a young person will experience. God wants not only to rescue us, but also to continue down the road of life as our constant companion, helping us every step of the way. God has exciting plans for each young person. It is thrilling to think of the potential that each life has for displaying God's love and individual care for His children. Encourage youth to think about who God made them to be and the talents they possess as individuals. God's mercy will follow us when we go to college, pursue relationships with the opposite sex, and discover our ministry goals for reaching our world with the gospel.

Applying grace in the lives of youth also includes grace expressed from youth to youth. When we think back to our younger years, it is easy to remember that the thoughts and actions of our friends had a great impact on us. One kid who is really turned on to Jesus can drastically affect a peer group. That youth, who understands that people will know we're Christians by our love for humanity, has the ability to enrich the lives of his or her peers in ways that we cannot. When you communicate grace to the young people in your group, pray that the harvest will spread to include their friends.

Friendship witnessing can evolve into a decision for Christ, resulting in another soul for you to disciple. If the kids in your group feel shy about sharing Jesus, tell them to challenge their friends to "come and see." Christian youth may best reach their friends by letting you do the ministering at first!

A Final Thought to Help You Maintain an Attitude of Grace Toward Young People

Remember this acronym when applying grace in the lives of young people: God's Reaching Acceptance Cultivated Eternally! God yearns for young people and reaches out to them through us. We need to accept each young person where they are, for who they are, and cultivate truth in the soil of their hearts. Eternal consequences are at stake, and we're laying up our treasures in heaven when we invest in the lives of our youth.

---

* E. G. White, *The Desire of Ages,* p. 210.

CHAPTER 31

How to Create a
Family-centered Youth Ministry

by Patricia Humphrey

What Is Family-centered Youth Ministry?

YOUTH MINISTRY IN THE Adventist Church has come a long way since the days of Henry Fenner and Luther Warren back in the late 1800s. Fenner and Warren were revolutionary leaders whose role in the establishment and growth of Adventist youth ministries is unparalleled. But any ministry, in order to remain effective, must continue to grow and mature if it is to meet the challenges of the times. Youth ministry is no exception. As youth ministry evolves to become more relevant to youth in the twenty-first century, we as leaders must respond lovingly and sensitively to those who are entrusted to our care.

For example, if you're a typical youth leader, you probably minister to youth who come from a wide range of family backgrounds, such as two-parent homes, single-parent families, and teens who live with an extended relative, such as an aunt or grandparent. Each family circumstance presents its own unique needs and challenges for the youth, their families, and those who minister to them. Recognizing that no one lives in a vacuum, we as youth leaders cannot respond effectively to the needs of youth unless we reach them within the context of the family, where ideas, values, and attitudes are shaped.

It took us a while to reach this point, but somewhere along the line we finally recognized that youth ministry encompasses much more than reaching out to youth as individuals. Gone are the days when a youth leader's only contact with parents and relatives was when they dropped off their kids or picked them up from a youth meeting. Youth ministry, as defined today, is about meeting the needs of the whole person, and that includes not only youth but also those with whom they live and learn.

As one author puts it: "Family ministry is a total approach to families—an outlook. The essence of family ministry is an attitude toward the family that must be integrated into every aspect of church life. . . . The church is more like a family than anything else."[1]

"Family ministry includes any services provided by a church or church agency, whether by a helping professional or by a nonprofessional volunteer, which aim to strengthen the relationships between family members."[2]

If the thought of a family-centered youth ministry is a little overwhelming or if the concept is a new one to you, there's no need for anxiety. Becoming family-oriented is a growth process, and as you read on, you'll see that getting there is simply a matter of planning, organizing, and implementing. The first step to making changes is knowing why change is necessary.

Why Your Church Needs a Family-centered Youth Ministry

Probably the greatest reason youth ministry should be family-centered is that family involvement in the lives of youth is a biblical mandate. "These commandments that I give you today are to be upon your hearts. Impress them on your children. Talk about them when you sit at home and when you walk along the road, when you lie down and when you get up. Tie them as symbols on your hands and bind them on your foreheads. Write them on the doorframes of your houses and on your gates" (Deut. 6:6-9, NIV). No matter how much we as youth leaders want or try to reach and win young people for Christ, we must always remember that God has entrusted parents with the first and most important role in that process. Granted, not all parents are motivated or equipped to fulfill that role; nevertheless, youth leaders must always remember that their job is to support, but never usurp, the role of parents.

Fred Cornforth, in *The Family and Youth Ministry,* cautions us, describing the process of taking over the role of parents as the "cardinal sin." He relates the following scenario youth leaders often face: "Jimmy, who can come to us from a broken or healthy home, experiencing the throes of adolescence, identifies his parents as his major problem in life. We listen to him (without having to live with him), and identify with him. He senses our support and returns to us repeatedly. The bond that develops between us and Jimmy personally warms us. He might even tell us that he wishes we were his parents—we might even agree with him in our minds.

"But we must remember that our relationship with Jimmy cannot be developed at the parents' expense. Rather than helping Jimmy to see situations from his parents' perspective, well-intentioned and sometimes weak-egoed youth volunteers or pastors will take advantage of normal and abnormal stresses and strains parents and adolescents go through, resulting in alienation between parents and their youth. This is not youth ministry. In fact, it is the cardinal sin of many youth leaders. The damage done to relationships between parents and their children is cataclysmic. If anything, youth leaders should support families—the good, the bad, and the ugly—assuming the youth are not in danger of abuse."[3]

Here are some thoughts to consider as you ponder the question of why your church needs to become family-centered. According to Doug Fields, author of *Purpose-driven Youth Ministry,* the need for a family-centered ministry is a must, not an option. "Youth workers are becoming increasingly aware that a student-only youth ministry is less effective than a family-friendly youth ministry. Because we rarely see students in their family context, we often underestimate the power of the family. Each student in our youth ministry is the product of a unique family system, a system responsible for forming beliefs, values, and actions. If we plan to effectively minister to students over the long haul, we must sincerely desire to minister to entire families, because a youth ministry that excludes parents is about as effective as a Band-Aid on a hemorrhage."[4]

Now do this little exercise: Picture in your mind each of the youth in your congregation. Write down their names, leaving half a page of space under each name. Describe their family situation. With whom do they live? What unique challenges do each of these families face (illness, economic hardship, lack of education, single parenthood, nonchurched family, etc.)? How does the family situation impact the youth who attends your Sabbath school (behavior, attendance, participation, motivation, interest, Bible knowledge, etc.)? Finally, considering these factors, jot down some ideas about what you could do to reach out and meet the needs of each of these students and their families better. Once you've completed this exercise, you're on the way to adding an exciting new dimension to your youth ministry.

Establish a Model That Works for Your Church

According to Chap Clark, author of *The Youth Worker's Handbook to Family Ministry,* there are three perspectives on family ministry in our culture. In short, these are the:

1. Therapeutic/Counseling Perspective

This model, says Clark, seeks to address "the specific emotional and relational needs of a congregation." A church that bases it ministry on this perspective would emphasize educational programs, such as parenting seminars, marriage-enrichment seminars, and programs to help parents understand and get along better with their teens.

2. Nuclear Family Perspective

Churches that operate from the nuclear family perspective have as their major goal the purpose of strengthening and equipping the family to fulfill their God-given role in nurturing and giving spiritual instruction to their children. Proponents of this model view the family, not the church, as the primary discipling entity of youth.

3. Church-as-a-Family Perspective

Just as its name implies, people who take this perspective think of the church as a family. Clark says that "according to this model, the church's primary function is to be such a close-knit faith community that individual nuclear families will be encouraged to draw together and not separate themselves." In a church that operates on this philosophy, you would find programs that focus on intergenerational activities and that involve participation from a wide segment of the church body, rather than a single department.

Steps Toward Family-centered Ministry

Now that you're aware of the different paradigms on family ministry, it's time to raise your church's awareness of the need to focus its ministry from a youth-centered one to a family-centered one. The following are some suggested steps to follow in initiating this process.

1. Establish a Visioning Committee

This committee will not only explore ways to make your church more family-friendly, but help to guide the church in exploring the purpose for, and philosophy behind, doing so. When selecting committee members, be sure to include a wide segment of the church's membership in terms of gender, age (don't forget to include teens), nationality, and family types (not just nuclear). The committee should also include representatives from as many church departments as possible, but whose interests include the "big picture" rather than just their own departmental needs. It is also important that members of this committee be sensitive to and understand the developmental needs and characteristics of adolescents.

Hand out the agenda in advance of the meeting so that people can allow their ideas to "percolate" before the meeting. By all means, begin each session with prayer, allowing the Holy Spirit to guide you in your discussions and in formulating a plan for your church.

2. Formulate a Statement of Purpose for Your Church's Family-oriented Youth Ministry

Ask such questions as Where are we now in terms of being family-oriented? Where are we going? Why do we want to do this? Whom are we trying to reach? What would God have us to do? What aren't we doing that we should be? What are we doing that we should not? What kinds of things can we do to help families connect? What resources (both human and physical) do we have available to help us achieve our goals? What other resources will we need to make our church more family-friendly?

Allow the group to brainstorm and come up with ideas. Jot them down and then use these as fodder to begin formulating a written statement. Begin with a list of objectives (e.g., to minister to the emotional needs of families within our congregation) and then expand these into a mission statement or statement of purpose.

3. Set Some Achievable and Measurable Goals

For example, you might say, "Each quarter our church will host one cross-generational social activity," or, "Our church will sponsor an annual parenting seminar." Include a time line, making sure to set a date for accomplishing each goal. Design a plan for evaluating whether your goals are met. At least once a year the visioning committee needs to reconvene in order to assess how well you've done and whether or not you've achieved your goals.

4. Put Your Plan Into Action

The best way to begin the action is to develop a master church calendar that includes family-friendly activities. Make sure that specific, reliable people are assigned the task of coordinating and implementing the activities, or all your planning efforts will go to waste.

Establish a Family-friendly Youth Ministry

Now that you've developed a plan of action, it's time to implement. Below are four key steps to follow:

1. Build Relationships With Parents

If you truly want a family-friendly youth ministry, the first and most important job is to develop a relationship with the parents of your teens. And what's the key to any good relationship? Communication, of course.

Communicate. Make a special effort to have casual contact with parents and family members of your youth. When parents drop their teens off or pick them up from Sabbath school or other events, take time to talk with them. A quick question or comment such as "We've missed seeing Jennifer lately" or "I've really noticed that Justin is maturing spiritually" can open the door to building a relationship.

Other ways to keep parents informed include a monthly or quarterly newsletter. You could even solicit a parent with desktop publishing or writing skills for help with the newsletter production. Another way to get information out in a hurry is to set up a "telephone tree" among the parents. Hand out a list of phone numbers identifying specific parents as callers and the names and numbers of other parents they are to call whenever information needs to be distributed.

Visit and Call Family Members. Another way to establish relationships is to visit, and it doesn't always have to be at home. One youth worker tries to have lunch periodically with the parents of teens in his youth group at their place of work. When you make visits to the home, try to get to know siblings as well as parents and other extended family members. This will give you a lot of insight into the teens' lives.

In this busy age, visits aren't always possible. But the next-best thing is a telephone call. If a brother or sister answers the phone when you call, don't just ask to speak to the parent. Introduce yourself, address the child by name, and ask how he or she is doing.

Invite Parents to Events and Programs. At least once a quarter, try to plan an event that you invite parents to attend along with their teens. Make sure they are informed well in advance of the event, and try to call and remind them personally during the week before it happens. Let them know that their support and participation are both welcome and wanted.

Hold Regular Meetings With Parents. Once a quarter, meet with parents to inform them of your youth program's progress and plans, and allow them to give their input and feedback as well. Ask for their ideas on the kinds of activities (for youth and parents) they would like to see planned, spiritual topics they would like to have addressed, and ways they could be of support to your overall program. Let parents know that they are part of your team, and remind them that everyone can offer something, even if it's only a simple task such as transporting teens to a social outing.

Affirm. As we all know, the job of parenting isn't easy. As a youth worker, you can affirm parents in their role by complimenting their kids in their presence every opportunity you get, or occasionally sending a card, letting parents know how much you appreciate their good work in raising their kids. Or what about a Parent Appreciation Night planned by you and your teens to honor their parents? With a little creativity you can probably come up with lots of ideas and ways to affirm parents.

2. Provide Support for Families

Be Sensitive to Needs of Nonnuclear Families. Remember that every family does not fit the ideal model, with both mother and father present in the home. Single-parent households are on the rise, but even though they are more common today, that doesn't make the job of single parenting any easier. In your parent meetings and in casual talks with parents, try to find out how the church can make the job of parenting easier for these parents.

Do a Family Needs Assessment. To find out what specific needs families with teens have in your congregation, you could design a survey that asks questions about their family status and gather information about family size, family members, church affiliation, areas of concern, etc. An example of a family needs assessment can be found in *The Youth Worker's*

Handbook to Family Ministry, by Chap Clark, on pages 99-103. such a survey could be very helpful in determining how and where to begin when designing a ministry to meet the needs of families.

Educate. Another way to support parents is to invite knowledgeable people to host seminars on parenting topics of interest, such as "How to Communicate With Your Teenager" or "10 Things Teens Wish Their Parents Knew." If local experts aren't available, there are many Christian video resources available. Check with your local Adventist Book Center, conference Family Ministries Department, or even your local library.

Start a Parent Support Group. This would be a group of parents who meet regularly to pray, support one another, discuss common issues parents face, and come up with creative ways to handle the challenges of parenting teens. The group should be moderated by someone who is knowledgeable in the area of parenting and family life.

Establish a Parent Resource Library. Begin to gather a collection of resources such as books, videos, and periodicals that deal with parenting topics and make them available to parents on a loan basis.

3. Encourage Family Participation

Before you begin to solicit the help of parents, it is important to know why you should get parents involved in youth ministry. Here are a few reasons:

- Parent involvement in the youth program helps parents to be more sensitive to the youth leader's role. Involvement helps them understand the challenges youth leaders face, and appreciate the youth leader more.
- When parents are involved in the youth program, they get to know and understand their teens better. They see their teens in a different role, and the experience allows more opportunities for a growing relationship with them.
- Having the involvement of parents also expands your ministry. It allows you to utilize the skills, gifts, educational and work background, and parenting experience of the parents of your teens.

Maybe you're wondering *What can parents do? How can I involve them in my ministry?* The book *130 Ways to Involve Parents in Youth Ministry* lists 39 different tasks parents can do to enhance a youth ministry program. Here are a few: bulletin board caretakers, calligraphers and artists, child-care providers for youth workers, drivers, family picnic organizers, fund-raisers, hosts for home parties, lay counselors for teenagers, parent Bible study leaders, parent-teenager retreat coordinators, supply purchasers, and trip sponsors. The book outlines specific instructions for implementing these and other ideas.

There Are Some Cautions to Be Aware of When Soliciting Parental Involvement:

- Some teens may object to their parents getting involved. Always be sure to approach the subject with teens first before inviting their parents to participate.
- You or the parents may feel they aren't cut out for the job. Solution: find something they can do. Maybe a particular parent isn't good at counseling or relating to teenagers. But he or she might have a gift for fund-raising or organizing. They key is to utilize the skills they do have to everyone's best advantage.
- Some parents don't want to be involved or say they don't have the time. Youth lead-

ers can help them to fill their God-given role better by encouraging them, being supportive and understanding, and offering training and assistance whenever possible.

4. Plan Family-centered Activities

Now the real fun starts. You choose and plan the fun, creative activities your church will engage in. The following resources are chock-full of activity ideas, such as service projects, retreats, socials, communication exercises, and fun and games for teens and their families: *Family-friendly Ideas Your Church Can Do* (Group Publishing); *130 Ways to Involve Parents in Youth Ministry* (Group Publishing); and *The Family and Youth Ministry,* by Fred Cornforth (AdventSource). As you, your teens, their parents, and other supportive church members work together to create a family-friendly youth ministry, you'll not only have fun—you'll find yourselves growing closer to God and to one another!

---

[1] Royce Money, *Ministering to Families,* quoted in Chap Clark, *The Youth Worker's Handbook to Family Ministry* (Grand Rapids: Zondervan Pub. House, 1997), p. 20.

[2] Diana Garland and Diane Pancoast, *The Church's Ministry With Families,* quoted in Clark, p. 14.

[3] Fred Cornforth, *The Family and Youth Ministry* (Lincoln, Nebr.: AdventSource, 1995), p. iii.

[4] Doug Fields, *Purpose-driven Youth Ministry,* p. 251.

For Further Reading

Freudenburg, Ben, and Rick Lawrence, eds. *Family Friendly Ideas Your Church Can Do.* Loveland, Colo.: Group Publishing, 1998.

130 Ways to Involve Parents in Youth Ministry. Loveland, Colo.: Group Publishing, 1994.

Up the Creek With a Paddle: Building Effective Youth and Family Ministry. Minneapolis: Augsburg Fortress, 1998.

CHAPTER 32

Current Social Issues

by Trudy J. Morgan-Cole

T HE YOUTH TO WHOM WE minister live in a culture that is increasingly complex and demanding. Rather than sheltering them from the "real world" and its challenges, we have to help prepare them to face that world with a strong foundation of biblical truth. This chapter will explore some of the issues that youth and youth leaders have to grapple with today.

Dating and Sexuality

"Sexual desire and sex-related decisions are as much a part of adolescence as homework and parents."[1] This is true partly for biological reasons—the young people with whom we work are in the ever-widening span of years between puberty and marriage, a time when sexual curiosity and desire are present but have no biblically approved outlet. It's even more true now than it was 50 years ago, as we live in a society in which increasing media focus on sex and disintegrating family structures are leading young people to become sexually active at an earlier age than ever.

"Young people have always been troubled by sexual temptations . . . and have always been preoccupied with sexual concerns," write Christian author Tony Campolo. "However, there is something that has changed and changed dramatically—behavior. The revolution in sexual behavior among American youth is awesome to behold. While the church has maintained, for the most part, its traditional positions on sexual morality, the proportion of the teenage population violating those norms has increased significantly."[2]

A study in the mid-1980s found that 50 percent of sexually active 19-year-old males first had sex between the ages of 11 and 13. Sexually active high school boys reported losing their virginity at an average age of 13.2 years; the average age for girls was 14.6. Some sexually active middle school students reported losing their virginity at age 11.[3]

Clearly, by the time young people arrive in earliteen Sabbath school class, it's high time to begin addressing the question of sexuality from a biblical perspective. Older youth and young adults will almost certainly have begun making choices about sexual activity.

Traditionally, our church, like most conservative Christian denominations, has always taught that sexual intimacy is reserved for the marriage relationship. In today's society our challenge as youth leaders is to make that standard meaningful to young people whose culture is sending them a radically different message. We also have to deal with questions about how we define "sexual intimacy"—how far is "too far" to go before marriage? And as well as passing along negative messages about what not to do, we have to teach young people about healthy dating and marriage relationships.

Since the beginning of the AIDS epidemic in the 1980s, public education and media have been pushing for a "safe sex" agenda as the best way to protect young people from sexually transmitted diseases and unwanted pregnancy. The safe-sex message acknowledges that many young people are going to choose to have sex, and focuses on encouraging them to use protection in the form of a condom, which guards against both STDs and pregnancy. Many Christian educators have always been uncomfortable with the safe-sex message, feeling that it virtually condones adolescent sexual activity; and recently more and more mainstream educators have begun to question its effectiveness. Sex education programs that emphasize abstinence are now being given more serious consideration.

Condoms, which are only about 87 percent effective in preventing pregnancy, are even less effective in reducing the risk of HIV transmission (the virus that causes AIDS)—only 69 percent effective, according to researcher Susan Weller.[4] As used by teenagers, who often do not use such devices regularly or correctly, the condom's effectiveness can be as low as 45 percent.[5] Even safe-sex advocates are now beginning to use the term safer sex to indicate that condoms are only a partially effective form of protection.

There's no doubt that complete abstinence from sexual intercourse until marriage is 100 percent effective in preventing both sexually transmitted disease and pregnancy. But how do we share the Bible's message of purity with today's youth? Marriage and family counselor Mary Ann Mayo, writing in the Christian journal *YouthWorker,* makes a strong case for sex education in the church that is straightforward and honest, talking openly about sex, sexual temptation, and the consequences of intimacy. "The more fuzzy a church makes its teaching on sexuality, the less impact church involvement will have on a teenager. In other words, youths will be less susceptible to cultural influences if they clearly understand the alternatives and the reasons for them. . . . A values-laden sex education is the only approach that really does what it says it does: actually change behavior instead of merely instruct. Kids avoid becoming involved sexually because they see meaning and purpose in not doing so."[6]

Miles McPherson, who works with inner-city youths in a program called Project Intercept, agrees. "One of the devil's weapons in the sex-ed battle is secrecy." He challenges those who work with youth to become well informed about teen sexuality and ready to discuss openly such issues as condoms, masturbation, and oral and anal sex. "Until you can discuss these things without getting sick to your stomach or making faces, kids won't come talk to you," he says.[7]

Use panel discussions, expert speakers, visits from married couples or single parents, parent-education workshops, classes, and discussion groups about sex—use whatever means you can to ensure that your youth are well informed and have a sound biblical basis for abstaining from premarital sex, one that they can apply to their everyday lives. Don't be afraid to explore those difficult "gray areas." As Youth Specialties leaders Mike Yaconelli and Jim Burns point out, "there may not be specific [Bible] verses regarding French kissing, but there are a lot of verses about moderation (1 Peter 4:7, for instance), putting others' interests ahead of our own (Phil. 2:3-5), and putting ourselves in situations in which we are tempted beyond our capacity (1 Cor. 10:13)."[8]

Many youth are attracted to such programs as True Love Waits, a sexual purity campaign started in 1993 by Southern Baptists in the United States. The youth-led True Love Waits program invites teenagers and college students to sign a covenant card stating: "Believing that true love waits, I make a commitment to God, myself, my family, my friends, my future mate, and my future children to be sexually abstinent from this until the day I enter a biblical marriage relationship." Since 1993 hundreds of thousands of youth have signed the cards, often displaying them at national and international celebrations. The campaign has spread to more than 150 countries and has been used in churches of many different denominations (including the Seventh-day Adventist Church).[9] The strength of this type of program is that it uses "positive peer pressure," sending the message to youth that many others support them in their decision to remain pure.

"Helping high school students deal with their sexuality doesn't mean that we only tell them what they shouldn't do. We should also give them suggestions about what they *should* do," writes Yaconelli and Burns. "The church can help high school students understand that dating can be great fun."[10] We need to help young people have positive relationships with the opposite sex as they grow up. This is the time for them to learn more about themselves and about what they want in a future marriage partner. As youth leaders, we can provide plenty of social activities to allow teenagers to interact with the opposite sex in a fun, nonthreatening way. We can give them guidelines to help them avoid unhealthy relationships that may lead to abuse, premarital sex, or unhappy marriages. This will also include dealing with the difficult issue of "unequally yoked" relationships, and helping youth see why it is better to date someone who shares their beliefs and values.

Another issue that becomes important as youth become young adults is that of those who *don't* date and eventually get married, for whatever reason. Although in some ways the lifestyle of young singles is glamorized in the media, neither society nor the church provides much support or affirmation for the person who doesn't eventually settle down and get married. And our teaching on sexuality has almost nothing to say about the struggle of the single adult. We direct our abstinence message at teenagers, saying "Wait till you get married!" What do we say to the young adult who doesn't plan to marry?

Youth and young adults need to be taught that the single life is not a "second-best" option; it is a biblically honored lifestyle chosen by Jesus Himself and praised by another single adult, the apostle Paul. We need to work toward creating an environment in our churches in which single people are included and honored, and in which their sexual questions can be dealt with honestly.

Teen Pregnancy and Abortion

The inevitable consequence of teenage promiscuity is that more and more young girls become pregnant each year. As single parenthood becomes more acceptable in society, more girls choose to have and raise their babies. Others choose to terminate their pregnancies through abortion.

As you teach your young people about sexuality, you will naturally mention unwanted pregnancy as a consequence of premarital sex and discuss the options of single parenthood and abortion, exploring why neither fits God's ideal plan for the family. But what should your response be when an unwanted pregnancy has already occurred—when a young woman grapples with the decision to keep or terminate her pregnancy?

Unlike most mainstream churches, the Seventh-day Adventist Church has not spoken out strongly on the abortion issue. Most evangelical churches are strongly opposed to abortion, and speak out clearly on the "pro-life" side of the issue. In the Seventh-day Adventist Church, though many members personally believe abortion to be a sin, many others support the "pro-choice" view. While the church's 27 fundamental beliefs contain no statement about abortion, the General Conference Annual Council in 1992 responded to the abortion question by releasing the statement "Seventh-day Adventist Guidelines on Abortion."

These guidelines affirm the sanctity of human life, including prenatal human life. "Abortion is never an action of little moral consequences," these guidelines state. "Thus prenatal life must not be thoughtlessly destroyed. Abortion should be performed only for the most serious reasons." The statement goes on to point out that "the church should offer gracious support to those who personally face the decision concerning an abortion. Attitudes of condemnation are inappropriate in those who have accepted the gospel." It affirms that "abortions for reasons of birth control, gender selection, or convenience are not condoned by the church," but also allows that "women . . . may face exceptional circumstances that present serious moral or medial dilemmas, such as significant threats to the pregnant woman's life, serious jeopardy to her health, severe congenital defects carefully diagnosed in the fetus, and pregnancy resulting from rape or incest. The final decision whether to terminate the pregnancy or not should be made by the pregnant woman after appropriate consultation. She should be aided in her decision by accurate information, biblical principles, and the guidance of the Holy Spirit."[11]

Since our church, while affirming the sanctity of human life, allows for individual choice in the area of abortion, what you teach your youth about abortion will probably grow largely out of your own beliefs and your understanding of the Scriptures. As with all issues, it's vital that you encourage them to search the Bible for themselves and have a firm basis for their beliefs.

Your personal beliefs will also determine whether you would be comfortable recommending abortion as an option to a young woman who came to you for counsel, or whether you would do everything in your power to dissuade her from such a course. No matter what your convictions or the young person's decision, remember that your role is always to model God's unconditional love and acceptance. And in the case of someone suffering guilt because she has already had an abortion, assure her of God's absolute loving forgiveness.

Unconditional love and acceptance should also be the keynote of your response to a young woman who chooses to keep her baby. Some church members feel that activities such as hosting a baby shower for a single mother are inappropriate, because they send the message that we condone premarital sex. This view certainly will do nothing to convince the young mother that God loves and accepts her as she is! While we should never glamorize the single-parent lifestyle as the media sometimes does, single parents themselves should always receive Christlike love and affirmation.

Homosexuality

The Seventh-day Adventist Church's official position on homosexuality is that it is a phenomenon caused by sin, in contravention of God's original plan. "Scripture condemns homosexual practices in strongly negative terms (Gen. 19:4-10; cf. Jude 7, 8; Lev. 18:22; 20:13; Rom. 1:26-28; 1 Tim. 1:8-10). Practices of this type produce a serious distortion of the image of God in men and women."[12] Most young people will not have difficulty accepting this church standard; in fact, unlike many issues in which leaders struggle to get youth to accept the Bible's teaching, most teenagers tend to take a far harsher view of homosexuality than the Bible does. Homophobia, gay-bashing, and even hate crimes against homosexuals are all too common among teens—even Christian teens. It may be more of a challenge for leaders to point out that the denomination's official statement on the subject goes on to say: "Christians will deal redemptively with [homosexuals]."[13]

A young person who comes to you for counsel because he or she is attracted to people of the same sex is facing an extremely difficult struggle. It's important to reassure the young person that having these feelings does not make him or her a "bad person." Feelings "are not 'good' or 'bad'—but what you do with them is," writes psychologist Ron Coffen in an article directed at Christian youth who feel homosexual desires.[14] Reassure the youth of God's love, grace, and acceptance. If you don't feel you know enough about the problem to counsel the person, help him or her find a trained Christian counselor who can help.

As a Christian leader you probably will not want to affirm and encourage young people in pursuing a homosexual lifestyle. Instead you may want to help them discover whether they really are gay or lesbian, bearing in mind that, especially in the early teen years, when sexual feelings are new and confusing, many young people are unsure about their orientation. One study "found that 25.9 percent of 12-year-olds and 17.4 percent of 13-year-olds were unsure of their sexual orientation. . . . In most cases, those who are unsure resolve their uncertainty in the direction of heterosexuality." This article, from a Web site maintained by a Christian support group, goes on to say that "it is important to reassure these teenagers that uncertainty about sexual orientation is a normal part of growing up. They do not have to rush to decide or take on a label." Misinformation, unmet emotional needs, or unsuccessful relationships with the opposite sex might also lead some teenagers to wonder whether they are homosexual, even if they are not really attracted to people of the same sex. These young people need help to clarify what their desires really are.[15]

If a young person is consistently attracted to people of the same sex, "affirm the young person and assure them of their worth and value regardless of the direction of their sexual attraction."[16] If they ask your advice, you can share your own understanding of the Bible's perspective on homosexuality, but remember that in this issue, as in all others, young people are free to make their own decisions. The Christian young person who is gay or lesbian will have to choose one of three options. The first of these is to attempt to change the homosexual orientation. Many Christians believe that this can be done through the Holy Spirit's power, just as we would attempt to overcome any sin in God's strength. Organizations such as Exodus International, a worldwide Christian support organization, provide help for those who wish to change their orientation and testimonials of those who have successfully done so.[17]

Others believe that "change ministries" are unsuccessful and offer a false hope. For Christians with homosexual orientation who do not believe that change is possible but who wish to live by biblical standards, celibacy is the natural choice. Though our sex-saturated society leaves little room for celibacy as a lifestyle choice, it is in fact a perfectly acceptable and achievable lifestyle for Christians who do not marry—both heterosexual and homosexual. A lifelong commitment to celibacy is by no means easy, but it was Jesus' choice, and it can be the choice for many successful young Christians.

There are also many homosexual Christians, including many Seventh-day Adventists, who believe that the Bible's statements against homosexual behavior apply only to promiscuous homosexual behavior. They believe that their homosexual relationships can be blessed by God if they live in a committed, monogamous relationship just like a heterosexual marriage. Support groups (such as Kinship) also exist for those who choose this option. While the church does not endorse this view, remember that young people are free to make their own choices, and our attitude toward those who live in homosexual relationships should never be one of hatred or condemnation. It is always the Holy Spirit's job to convict people of sin, and any gay or lesbian person has probably already experienced enough condemnation to last a lifetime.

Your greatest challenge as a youth leader will probably not be to deal with gay or lesbian youth (of whom you may meet only a few, if any, during the course of your ministry), but rather to help your heterosexual young people lose their prejudice against homosexuals. Some Christians seem to see homophobia as the only "acceptable" form of hatred. In fact, all hatred is evil and is directly contrary to the loving spirit of Jesus. Help young people to see that Jesus loves everyone, including homosexuals, and calls us to love everyone too.

Pornography

The problem of pornography is given far less attention than it deserves in our churches and schools, especially now when it has become so much more readily accessible through the Internet. Like all issues related to sexuality, pornography needs to be discussed openly and honestly in Christian circles. Christian youth (especially boys, since pornography is much more of a problem for men than for women) need to understand clearly that whether they're renting X-rated movies, reading pornographic magazines, or looking up X-rated Web sites on the Internet, it's a sin and it violates their purity as Christians. They should also be aware of the consequences of getting involved in a habit that can lead to a dangerous and destructive addiction in later life.

Part of the appeal and the danger of pornography is that it is secret—a private act that many think "doesn't hurt anyone." The secrecy extends to the church or youth group, where we feel that if we don't talk about pornography, it may go away. Taking away the cloak of secrecy makes it possible to talk about the dangers openly. "A mother's teenage boy was secretly reading pornographic magazines," says former youth pastor Miles McPherson. "When she asked me what she should do, I suggested (among other things) that she take the secrecy out of the problem by laying out all the magazines on his bed when he was out and then preparing herself to be vulnerable and ready to really talk when he came home." While you may not want to invite the boys in your youth group to bring all their pornographic magazines to Sabbath school, this attitude of openness to the subject will help "Open discussion in which kids explain their views exposes teenagers in a healthy way to their peers—and often to the faulty logic or naïveté upon which their views are based," says McPherson.[18]

As we learn to talk openly about the sexual issues and questions our youth face, we will be able to help them meet temptation with a sound biblical basis for their beliefs. In the world in which they have to live, they'll need it.

In the next chapter we'll discuss some other issues facing today's young people and how we can help them deal with those issues.

---

[1] Mike Yaconelli and Jim Burns, *High School Ministry,* p. 48.

[2] Tony Campolo, "Christian Ethics in the Sexual Wilderness," *YouthWorker,* Winter 1985.

[3] Josh McDowell and Dick Day, *Why Wait? What You Need to Know About the Teen Sexuality Crisis* (Nashville: Thomas Nelson, 1994), p. 23, in Grant Misseghers, "Youth in Contemporary Culture: Promiscuity and Safe Sex." Online: www.telusplanet.net/public/gkm.

[4] Marilyn Morris, "How Do You Spell PROTECTION?" *Tips on Encouraging Sexual Purity.* Online: www.aim-for-success.org/tips/9603.html.

[5] Ray E. Short, *Sex, Love, or Infatuation: How Can I Really Know?* (Minneapolis: Augsburg Pub. House, 1990), p. 136.

[6] Mary Ann Mayo, "The Safest Sex Education Isn't Safe," *YouthWorker,* Fall 1994.

[7] Miles McPherson, "Answer Their Hard Questions," *YouthWorker,* Fall 1994.

[8] Yaconelli and Burns, p. 48.

[9] "Frequently Asked Questions About True Love Waits." Online: www.truelovewaits. com/faq.htm.

[10] Yaconelli and Burns, p. 51.

[11] "Seventh-day Adventist Guidelines on Abortion: A Report From Annual Council, 1992," *Journal of Adventist Youth Ministry,* 1993.

[12] *Seventh-day Adventists Believe: A Biblical Exposition of 27 Fundamental Doctrines* (Washington, D.C.: Ministerial Association, General Conference of Seventh-day Adventists, 1988), p. 303.

[13] *Ibid.*

[14] Ron Coffen, "Two Sides," *Insight,* Dec. 12, 1998.

[15] "Free to Be Me." Online: www.freetobeme.com.

[16] *Ibid.*

[17] Contact Exodus International at P.O. Box 77652, Seattle, Washington 98177-0652, U.S.A. Online: www.messiah,edu/hpages/facstaff/chase/h/exodus/.

[18] McPherson.

CHAPTER 33

More Current Social Issues

by Trudy J. Morgan-Cole

T HE ADOLESCENT AND YOUNG adult years have always been a time of change, choice, and decision-making. But today's youth live in an even more challenging world than their parents and grandparents did. They are faced with an alarming array of temptations to sins that have become more socially acceptable than ever before. And they are being challenged to take stands on some very complex social issues. How can we help them face these tough questions?

Substance Abuse

Substance abuse—particularly the abuse of alcohol—has always been a problem in society. Today, though, it's becoming more prevalent and more alarming among teenagers—and more frightening, as new and more dangerous drugs seem to appear on city streets each year. Despite our church's traditional strong stand against substance abuse, Seventh-day Adventist young people are not immune to this epidemic. Both the Valuegenesis study and studies conducted by the Institute for Prevention of Addictions indicate that, at least in North America, substance abuse is a problem for Seventh-day Adventist teenagers. These surveys, conducted in the late 1980s, showed that 3 to 5 percent of 12- and 13-year-olds were using alcohol, and 4 to 6 percent had used marijuana. By twelfth grade the numbers increased to 13 to 15 percent using alcohol and about 11 percent using marijuana. By age 14, 23 to 27 percent had tried alcohol, and 22 percent had tried tobacco.[1]

Simply telling kids to "just say no" doesn't begin to meet their needs. We need to give them reasons they should "say no," and skills that will enable them to say it when peers and media are pressuring them to say yes.

Tobacco

In the United States almost 5 million youth ages 12 to 17 are smokers. And every day nearly 3,000 more youth under age 18 join their ranks. Decades have passed since we learned that smoking is the single greatest preventable cause of illness and premature death; yet in most countries the number of young smokers is rising, not falling. By 2020 the World Health Organization predicts that 10 million people worldwide will die as a result of smoking each year.[2]

Those facts alone aren't enough to convince children and teenagers not to smoke: if they were, smoking would have been wiped out long ago. It's difficult for young people to focus on something as far in the future as their own death; in recent years it has become something of a fad for young people to defy adults' predictions of doom and gloom by smoking, despite the health risks. Your young people need to know the facts about smoking, but don't expect those facts alone to keep them from smoking.

Alcohol

Who consumes the most alcohol? People in their late teens and young adult years. "The ages 18 to 21 are the period of heaviest alcohol consumption. By the time they finish high school, 64 percent of teenagers have already used alcohol."[3]

The health risks associated with alcohol use, like those associated with smoking, are well known. It contributes to 100,000 deaths annually in the United States alone. Alcohol kills and injures people through driving accidents, drownings, and violent crime. It affects babies still in the womb. It is involved in more than half the cases of domestic violence in the United States.[4]

If anything, the pressure on young people to drink is even greater than the pressure to smoke. Drinking is central to most teen and young adult social activities—as it is to many activities in the adult world. One of the functions of a church youth group is to provide a place in which young people can socialize without being pressured to drink.

Drugs

We tend to think of drinking and smoking as "mainstream" temptations that most of our youth will face at some point. Unless we minister in inner-city areas, we may be less aware of the dangers of drug use, or believe that it will affect only "bad" kids. But consider these 1994 U.S. statistics from the National Household Survey on Drug Abuse:

- Between 1992 and 1994, marijuana use among youth ages 12 to 17 almost doubled.
- 1.1 million youth said they had smoked marijuana in the past month.
- 13 million Americans (6 percent of those 12 years old and older) used illicit drugs.
- 10 million Americans (four fifths of current illicit drug users) used marijuana.[5]

Among teenagers, marijuana use is becoming as accessible and acceptable as cigarette smoking or drinking alcohol. And it seems that every day's news brings reports of a new drug that hits the streets and destroys the lives of more and more young people.

Prevention

Since tobacco, alcohol, and narcotics are all addictive drugs, it makes sense that the most effective strategy for dealing with them is to prevent youth from ever experimenting with them. Many young people feel "it's not going to hurt me to try smoking just once," but in fact "nearly one third of everyone who tries a single cigarette develop a dependence on tobacco."[6] A good prevention program will help youth build the determination and skills to decide in advance that they will not be drawn into these addictions.

One good prevention program is the Youth to Youth model (Y2Y), which became very popular in North America during the 1980s and 1990s. Youth to Youth is a drug-prevention program based on peer support and leadership. "Youth to youth focuses on four areas of emphasis within its comprehensive approach: drug education and information, personal growth and decision-making, environmental change, and drug-free fun."[7] Whether your youth are involved in a formal Youth to Youth program or you just want to incorporate these elements into your own drug prevention program, the Youth to Youth model is a good one to follow.

Drug education and information gives teens the facts about alcohol and other drugs. Personal growth and decision-making skills will help them feel self-confident enough to take a stand on the issue. Environmental change connects the young person to a peer group that will support a drug-free lifestyle, and drug-free fun activities will help the teen learn how to spend his or her time in healthy and fun ways.

One reason this type of approach is effective is that it focuses on complete abstinence from all drugs. Messages about the "responsible use" of alcohol can be vague and confusing to teenagers; the abstinence approach sends a stronger and clearer message.

We sometimes believe that simply providing young people with plenty of positive, healthy alternative activities will keep them from needing to try drugs and alcohol. While these "alternative highs" do have their place, Peter Bell, president of the Minnesota Institute on Black Chemical Abuse, offers a warning about this approach. Many young people, he says, will choose to go on your camping trip or to your baseball game—and get drunk or stoned during or after the event. "Kids don't necessarily choose one or the other. There is a high likelihood to choose both. I think that we set kids up when we don't help them acknowledge the reality that part of the human condition is feeling hurt, lonely, bored, frustrated, anxious, and inadequate. And we don't always have to fix it."[8]

As Christian leaders, we need to help our youth look to Jesus as the ultimate answer rather than using the "quick fix" of drugs and alcohol, but at the same time we need to help them realize that even Christians experience bad feelings at times, and it's all right to have those feelings. They don't need to be driven away by drugs.

The Seventh-day Adventist Church promotes Adventist Youth to Youth (AY2Y) conferences especially for its young people, using the Y2Y model. Along with the general principles of Youth to Youth, the Adventist program emphasizes a biblical perspective and a growing relationship with God as part of its drug-prevention strategy. "Commitment to a drug-free lifestyle is a spiritual decision. Therefore, nurturing spiritual growth is a key goal of Adventist Youth to Youth."[9] The AY2Y program, which began in the Asia-Pacific and North American divisions of the church, has now spread to the Southern Asia, Inter-American, and Euro-African divisions, says Kathleen Kuntaraf, of the General Conference Health Ministries Department, and updated training materials are available in English, French, and Spanish. Kuntaraf is excited about the program because, as she says, young people who feel discouraged and alone will be tempted to use drugs. "The only thing that can make them feel connected is the power of Jesus Christ. The Youth to Youth program is very scripturally based."[10]

We need to inform our young people about the dangers of substance abuse and support them in making healthy lifestyle choices. As we do so, we must always remember the importance of presenting God's grace in our message. Stuart Tyner, author of *The ABZs of Adventist Youth Ministry,* offers a warning to the youth leader about presenting issues of substance abuse to youth. "Whatever you do, don't connect it with salvation! This is . . . not an entrance requirement for heaven. Never make the mistake of telling a young smoker that Jesus won't love them if they keep smoking."[11]

Treatment

No matter how successfully you teach prevention, you will encounter young people who have already tried tobacco, alcohol, or drugs. If they have only experimented with substance abuse, use the same methods you use in prevention to encourage them to quit before they become addicted.

Young people who are already "hooked" on drugs, alcohol, or tobacco don't need condemnation; they need help. If they have come to you for help, they have already taken the first and most important step in breaking free of their addiction. Affirm them for taking that step and then help them find the resources that the church or community offers to assist them. For smokers, many Adventist churches offer Breathe Free programs. Other organizations, such as your local Cancer Society, may offer similar programs.

Alcoholics and drug addicts may find help through 12-step programs such as Alcoholics Anonymous or Narcotics Anonymous. (These programs are often offered through local churches, even Adventist churches in some areas.) For others, individual counseling or even a residential treatment program may be needed. If you have young people who need this kind of help, make every effort to become their advocate—find out and access whatever resources are available in your area. And always remind the struggling youth that God's grace is sufficient to meet every need and overcome every sin.

Equality

Prejudice exists in every society—racial discrimination, gender discrimination, class divisions, religious prejudice, prejudice against those with disabilities. Young people, who are strongly influenced by their peers and by their need to be accepted, can easily fall into the trap of looking down on those who are "different" from the mainstream. However, youth also have a strong sense of justice once it is awakened, and when young people are made aware of the evils of prejudice, they often become wholehearted crusaders for equality.

Youth need to be taught the message of Galatians 3:28: "There is neither Jew nor Greek, slave nor free, male or female, for you are all one in Christ Jesus" (NIV). Help them to understand that God calls us to treat every human being with equal dignity and respect. Remember to model the acceptance and equality that you preach. For many young people, this will be enough to start them thinking about treating others equally.

For youth in some settings, especially in areas in which racial tensions run high, you may have to tackle the problem of prejudice, particularly that of racism, much more aggressively and directly. Author Graeme Codrington suggests that youth leaders addressing the problem in a church setting first help youth to identify the problem—discuss what racism is and how our racist attitudes develop. Then create goals and "homework assignments" to help solve the problem. These might include encouraging students to study and experience another culture. Lead students into what Codrington calls "narrative interaction . . . a deliberate desire to get to know each other's histories and futures." He tells of showing a slide presentation to an American high school class with "47 African-Americans and three Latino students. The images included lynchings and police and police beatings of Mexicans and other Latinos, and many years of resistance. At the end one Black student asked, 'Seems like we have had a lot of experiences in common—so why can't Blacks and Mexicans get along better?' No answers, but there was the first step: asking the question."[12]

Codrington goes on to point out that the Christian leader can include biblical support for the message of equality. "Although this problem can be dealt with on a purely social and psychological level, Christian counseling is unique in its reliance upon the Holy Spirit. The Holy Spirit is intimately involved in helping people become more Christlike, and this will involve removal of sins and barriers. Racism is a sin."[13] The sin of racism, and of all forms of discrimination, is one that God is eager to free us from.

The Environment

Concern for the earth's environment has become a popular cause among many young people today—and with good reason! As we look at the frightening world picture—exploding population, increasing pollution, a shrinking ozone layer, ever-expanding landfill sites, and scores of other problems—it's clear that we human beings haven't been doing a very good job of taking care of the world God made for us.

Teens are often attracted to environmental causes; they can see that the world that previous generations have ruined is the world they have to live in. Environmentalism is taught in schools and promoted through activities such as recycling programs.

But many Christians are uncomfortable with the environmental movement and don't encourage young people to become involved in it. They may be uneasy with the New Age connections of some in the environmental movement (some extremists promote a reverence for nature that borders on pantheism) or with the extreme tactics some environmentalists are willing to use. Or they may simply reason, "The Lord is coming back soon anyway, so why worry about the future of the planet?"

But there's plenty of biblical evidence to suggest that Christians should be the most ardent environmentalists of all—not because we worship nature for its own sake, but because we recognize that this earth is the gift of a loving, wise Father who expects His children to care for His gifts. Humanity was given "dominion" over the earth (Gen. 1:28); this dominion was not intended as a harsh totalitarian regime but rather as a wise stewardship, as is clear in Genesis 2:15, when Adam is commanded to "take care of" the Garden of Eden (NIV). Revelation 11:18 reminds us that when God does return, His task will include "destroying those who destroy the earth" (NIV). Yes, we believe He is coming soon, but when He comes back we hope He will find us taking care of the resources He has given us.

With this biblical perspective in mind, we should encourage our youth to be active in caring for the environment—while warning them about some of the dangerous extremes within the environmental movement. Among our community service projects we can include those that nurture the natural world, such as cleaning up a local park or river, or helping to care for animals. When you point to nature as "God's second book," revealing His character and Creatorship, remind youth of our responsibility to take care of His creation.

---

[1] "Substance Use Among Seventh-day Adventist Youth: A North American Division Leadership Briefing Paper Prepared by the Institute for the Prevention of Addictions." Online: www.cs.andrews.edu/IPA/research/sda_youth.html.

[2] Stuart Tyner, *The ABZs of Adventist Youth Ministry*, p. 234.

[3] *Ibid.,* p. 26.

[4] *Ibid.,* p. 27.

[5] *Drug Abuse Update,* Winter 1995, as reprinted in Dateline Dream, February/March 1996. Online: www.teenchallenge.com/main/stats/1994surv.htm.

[6] Tyner, p. 27.

[7] "What is Y2Y?" Online: mbx.pd.sk.k12.ri.us/y2y/What_is_y2y.html.

[8] "Prevention." Online: mbx.pd.sk.k12.ri.us/y2y/prevention.html.

[9] "What Is Adventist Youth to Youth?" Online: www.andrews.edu/IPA/y2y/ay2ywhat.html.

[10] For more information about Adventist Youth to Youth, contact Kathleen Kuntaraf at the Health Ministries Department, General Conference of Seventh-day Adventists (phone: 301-680-7602).

[11] Tyner, p. 27.

[12] Graeme Codrington, "Racism." Online: www.pix.za/atd/graeme/racism.html.

[13] *Ibid.*

CHAPTER 34

Youth Ministry in College and Seminaries

by Errol H. Thomas

THE SEVENTH-DAY ADVENTIST CHURCH is indeed a "youth church," in that more than half of its baptized membership is made up of young people 30 years old and younger. The report of the 1993 General Conference Commission on Youth indicated that in the world church approximately 60 percent of the membership is age 30 and under.[1] It further concludes that when youth who regularly attend Sabbath services, baptized and unbaptized, are factored in, the percentage is as high as 70 percent. In eight divisions of the world field youth membership ranges from 60 to 80 percent.

Of great concern is the youth-loss rate to the church. The report indicates that 20 to 40 percent of Adventist youth leave the church—in one division it is as high as 50 percent.[2] A 1995 review of youth ministry in the Adventist Church revealed that 70 percent of the world church was 30 years of age and under. Of the youth who regularly attend church:

- 70 percent are baptized
- 30 percent are lost through nonbaptism
- 20 percent are lost through apostasy after baptism[3]

This indicates a 50 percent loss of young people. If we did not have this hemorrhage, this loss of youth to the church, the youth membership percentage would be higher. The church cannot be at ease with this frightening loss of 50 percent of its young people, whether they grew up in the church or came into the church through outreach programs and other means. It is true that some will be lost by their own choice, indifference, and carelessness, or as a result of yielding to the tremendous and unprecedented pressures that confront young people today, but the church can never feel at ease with this youth-loss reality.

Against the background of such considerations, the focus of youth ministry in the Seventh-day Adventist Church has to be how to win, reclaim, revive, nurture, keep, and involve youth in the life, ministry, and mission of the church. There is need for introspective evaluation, a new philosophy of mission, new strategies and programs, and a new and renewed plan of action if the church would bring about positive change for the salvation, preservation, and empowerment of its young people. To be out of touch with the youth of the church is to be out of touch with the church itself and the prospects and possibilities for the future. Their spiritual nurture, growth, and development are essential. Youth ministry must target youth who grew up in the church, youth who came in with their parents/guardians or who came in without them, and youth of the community at large, all of whom are heirs of the kingdom of God.

The emphasis of youth ministry on an ongoing basis has to be: how to attract youth to Christ in ways that would lead them to accept Him as their personal Savior and Lord, and how to create and maintain a youth-friendly church. Being sensitive to the needs of youth at their respective age levels, the local church would be the primary setting, with trained youth leadership of an effective and dynamic ministry "for, with, and by young people."[4]

Because youth ministry is most effective at the local church level, pastors need to be exposed to, sensitized concerning, and trained to minister effectively to the youth of the church. The pastor will be able not only to minister directly to the youth, but also to work with youth lay leaders for the best good of the youth. With adequate preparation, exposure, and experience, he could be a good youth pastor and possible youth director. This is why it is necessary for prospective pastors to be prepared for youth ministry as an integral part of their overall training if they expect to have a meaningful pastoral ministry. As pastors are adequately prepared they will be able to minister for the saving of twenty-first-century youth for Christ within the church and from the wider community.

To achieve the primary goals of ministry for, with, and by young people for their salvation and service for Christ, youth ministry in and of the Seventh-day Adventist Church must seek to provide an effective dynamic, and Bible-based program for:

- leading youth to Christ
- facilitating young people's spiritual nurture and development
- helping youth to prepare for life and to deal positively with the demands and challenges of everyday living
- training youth for community and evangelistic outreach

Youth ministry targets youth who grew up in the church, youth who come into the church with their parents or guardians, youth who come without family connections, and youth of the community at large—all who need Christ and the joy and power of His salvation. It will not only seek to win youth of all ages to Christ, but equally so to keep them for God's kingdom. It will empower them to understand that they are special to the Lord, that they are "more than conquerors" (Rom. 8:37) through Christ who loves them, and that they can and will achieve the best that the Lord intends and has designed for them to be. It will create and maintain the climate in which youth will be encouraged to have a personal, living, growing, and joyous relationship with Christ in preparation for His soon return.

Youth ministry's approach takes into account and provides for the physical, mental, social, and spiritual needs of each young person at the respective age levels, thus providing a total ministry to and for youth. It will work toward building, strengthening, and enriching family/parent-youth and church-youth relationships; and where there are church schools, it will maintain positive youth-benefiting connections. Youth ministry will achieve its God-designed purpose as it assists with the concerns of the very young, the preteens, the teens, the young singles, and young married couples. Only a Spirit-empowered ministry for young people can effectively counter the prevailing evil that is set against them. Under the Holy Spirit's leading, youth ministry will aim at creating and maintaining a youth-friendly church at the local and field levels.

Youth ministry in our universities and seminaries will, among other things, help the students who are preparing for pastoral or lay leadership ministry to:

- understand the importance of and need for ministry to youth
- appreciate youth, their world, and their needs in order to reach them for Christ and to secure them for His kingdom
- become acquainted with the dynamics of effective youth ministry
- develop skills that will enable them to be a resourceful, creative, and effective youth leader
- facilitate the conversion processes, the faith-strengthening experiences, and the witnessing endeavors of the youth of the church
- look at the youth ministry of the Seventh-day Adventist Church and be able to develop programs and strategies for ministering effectively to youth

The basic presuppositions of youth ministry are:

- that God desires and has made every provision to save all lost humanity, including the very young and youth (1 Tim. 2:3-6; 2 Cor. 5:19; 1 John 2:1, 2, 12-14; John 3:16, 17; Heb. 7:25; Matt. 18:1-14)
- that the Lord understands youth, their circumstances, their needs, and their aspirations, and offers them meaning and purpose to life and living (Jer. 1:5-8; John 10:10; 21:15; Matt. 10:29-31; 6:33; Ps. 16:11)
- that despite the prevailing negative pressures, conditions, and circumstances, youth will triumph in Christ to live with Him in His kingdom (Rev. 12:11; 7:13-17; Eph. 6:10-18; Rom. 8:31-39)
- that the Lord can and will use youth leaders and an effective Bible-based youth ministry program to lead youth to Christ and into a living and preserving relationship with Him (John 21:15-17; *Testimonies for the Church,* vol. 1, p. 187; *Education,* p. 259)
- that youthful talents and potentials can be harnessed and channeled for effective, Spirit-empowered ministry for fellow youth and others (1 John 2:14; 1 Sam. 16:17; 1 Tim. 4:12; *Messages to Young People,* pp. 7, 20, 47, 197, 198, 207, 217; *Gospel Workers,* p. 211)
- that the Seventh-day Adventist Church has been and is being led of the Lord in the development of a dynamic youth ministry for winning, nurturing, and training youth for the Lord[5]

Youth Ministry Curriculum

To prepare the student adequately for youth ministry, the curriculum should include the following:

Theology of Youth Ministry

- The Lord and His people through the ages: Abraham, Isaac, Jacob, the children of Israel, the Christian Church, the Reformation/Protestant Church, the Seventh-day Adventist Church—highlighting the Lord's leading of and special blessings on His people through the ages.

- Youth and firsthand, durable faith:[6] Jesus Christ is Savior and Lord of youth, meeting all the needs of youth for salvation, acceptance, restoration, and empowerment; conversion and strengthening processes; overcoming and victorious realities; faith development and denominational loyalty; salvation assurance and the joyous Christian experience.
- Six presuppositions of youth ministry.
- The four-module approach to youth ministry: Revival, recovery, evangelization, and nurture.
- The critical age of 12 (Eccl. 12:1). Young people make their decisions best before they have passed age 12.

Survey of Youth Ministry

- The three cycles of youth ministry with their primary agencies and strategies.
- The predictable crises of youth ministry and the strategies for dynamic and effective youth ministry.[7]
- Beginnings, development, structures, and functions of youth ministry in the Seventh-day Adventist Church: 1879 to the present.
- Current structures and ministry: the three levels of youth ministry to Adventurers, Pathfinders, and senior youth.

Understanding Today's Youth

- Overview of developmental psychology with emphasis on children, teens, and young adults to age 30.
- Youth needs and meeting those needs with emphasis on helping youth move toward maturity—independency and self-sufficiency.
- Helping youth to develop, maintain, and enhance positive self-esteem.
- Empowering youth to manage positively the stresses and challenges of the times.

Christian Youth Leadership

- Qualities, perspectives, styles, and functions of Christian youth leadership.
- Incarnational, relational, and redemptive youth ministry: Christ is the leader who is in touch with today's youth for the salvation of youth; reaching youth for Christ and discipling them for Him.
- Dynamic, innovative, and effective ministry to and for youth for the salvation of youth and their involvement in the life ministry and mission of the church.
- Youth leaders connected in ministry with Christ: as soul winners/evangelizers of youth; role models; mentors; trainers/disciplers; empowerers; intercessors.
- Facilitating *youth connectedness* for nurture and evangelization: significant relationships (ultrapersonal, the supreme relationship between God and the individual; intrapersonal; interpersonal [Mark 12:33]); family connections; church-family connections, youth-friendly church; youth-to-youth connections; peer counseling.

Youth Counseling
- Understand and be able to put into practice the principles of counseling young people.

Youth Evangelism
- Reaching youth for Christ and equipping them to reach fellow youth for Christ.
- Employing various means and methods that are in harmony with biblical principles for winning and keeping young people for Christ.
- Youth evangelism imperatives: (1) know Christ and His Word; (2) understand today's youth; (3) get close to youth; (4) model Christianity; (5) share biblical teachings in ways youth will understand and be led to accept and follow Jesus Christ; (6) follow-up by nurturing youth to experience "durable faith" in Christ;[8] (7) empower and provide opportunities to share Christ with peers and others.
- Strategies and programs for reaching youth for Christ: hikes, outings, games, socials, camps, camporees, retreats, congresses, Festival of the Word/Bible conferences, youth rallies, youth revivals, youth evangelistic crusades/programs, singles ministries, youth federations, AMiCUS.
- The student is required to conduct one four-week youth revival or youth evangelistic program.

Christian Youth and the New Millennium
- The millennial generation: the times, the setting, and the prospects; Christian youth today, tomorrow, and for eternity: the challenges.
- Reaching youth for Christ in the twenty-first century.
- Making relevant youth ministry in the twenty-first century: Ongoing needs-assessment, goal-setting, functions-adjustments, innovative programming, exciting and inspirational activities.
- Preparing and empowering youth for the twenty-first century: fostering positive self-esteem-enhancing relationships of children and teens with their parents and families, their church school community, and their local church congregations, resulting in youth who are (1) more optimistic about life and healthier, (2) less prone to emotional distress, suicide, violence, substance abuse, and early and out-of-marriage sexual relationships,[9] (3) more resistant to negative peer pressure, (4) more proactive achievers at the elementary, secondary, and tertiary levels; preparing young people to attain their highest good as individuals, socially, occupationally/vocationally, and as significant persons in their communities, contributing to the best good of those communities; empowering young people to live as strong, resilient, self-reliant, spirit-led persons helping youth of all ages to be ready for the events leading up to the glorious return of Jesus Christ.

Training Youth Lay Leadership
- Identifying, equipping, and empowering youth lay leaders.
- Master Guide training for Adventurer and Pathfinder leadership and senior youth involvement in disaster response and relief.

- Senior youth leadership training.
- The youth area coordinators training and program for assisting the conference/mission youth director in youth programs and activities. Area coordinators are to be invested Master Guides and senior youth leaders who have been trained to assist in youth programs and activities, being duly authorized and commissioned by the conference/mission to function in that particular field for a designated renewable period.

Youth Ministry Practicum I

The student is assigned for a given period of time to work in a local church with the leadership of the youth department to develop an action plan, programs, and activities for the youth of the church. The student will be supervised and monitored by the college/university/seminary instructor.

Youth Ministry Practicum II

The student is assigned to work with the conference/mission youth director on a camping, congress, youth revival, Bible conference, Festival of the Word program through the planning, organizing, and implementation stages.

---

[1] *General Conference Commission on Youth Report* (1993), p. 3.

[2] *Ibid.,* p. 5.

[3] Roger L. Dudley and Janet Leigh Kangas, *The World of the Adventist Teenager,* pp. 9-15.

[4] General Conference Youth Department Mission Statement, 1995.

[5] Inter-American Division Youth Council, January 1984, March 1988; *Youth Ministry Handbook.*

[6] Duffy Robbins, *The Ministry of Nurture: How to Build Real-Life Faith Into Your Kids* (Grand Rapids: Zondervan Publishing House, 1990).

[7] Based on Mark Senter III, *The Coming Revolution in Youth Ministry* (Wheaton, Ill.: Victor Books, 1992).

[8] Robbins.

[9] "Reducing the Risk: Connections That Make a Difference in the Lives of Youth," *Add Health* (Minneapolis: University of Minnesota, 1997).

For Further Reading

Allen, Malcolm L. *Divine Guidance or Worldly Pressure?* Silver Spring, Md.: General Conference of Seventh-day Adventists, 1995.

Ashton, Mark. *Christian Youth Work.* Eastbourne, United Kingdom: Kingsway Publications, 1986.

Barun, Ken, and Phillip Bashe. *When Saying No Isn't Enough: How to Keep the Children You Love Off Drugs.* New York: New American Library, 1988.

Baucom, John Q. *Help Children Say No to Drugs.* Grand Rapids: Zondervan Publishing House, 1987.

Benson, Peter L., and Michael J. Donahue. *Valuegenesis: Report I.* Silver Spring, Md.: North American Division of Seventh-day Adventists, 1990.

Brander, Nathaniel. *The Six Pillars of Self-Esteem.* New York: Bantom, 1995.

Burns, Jim. *The Youth Builder.* Eugene, Oreg.: Harvest House Publishers, 1988.

Campbell, Ross. *How to Really Love Your Teenager.* Wheaton, Ill.: Victor Books, 1981.

Cook, David C., ed. *Senior High Pacesetters: The Complete Youth Ministry Resource,* vols.

1-12. Elgin, Ill.: David C. Cook Publishing Company, 1986.

Crawford, Christina. *No Safe Place: The Legacy of Family Violence.* Barrytown, N.Y.: Station Hill Press, 1994.

Dausey, Gary. *The Youth Leaders's Source Book.* Grand Rapids: Zondervan Publishing House, 1983.

DeVries, Mark. *Family-based Youth Ministry: Reaching the Been-There, Done-That Generation.* Downers Grove, Ill.: InterVarsity Press, 1994.

Dudley, Roger L. *Passing On the Torch: How to Convey Religious Values to Young People.* Hagerstown, Md.: Review and Herald Publishing Association, 1986.

———. *Why Teenagers Reject Religion and What to Do About It.* Washington, D.C.: Review and Herald Publishing Association, 1978.

———, and V. Bailey Gillespie. *Valuegenesis: Faith in the Balance.* Riverside, Calif.: La Sierra University Press, 1992.

———, and Janet Leigh Kangas. *The World of the Adventist Teenager.* Hagerstown, Md.: Review and Herald Publishing Association, 1990.

Durfield, Richard C., and Reneé Durfield. *Raising Them Chaste: A Practical Strategy for Helping Your Teen Wait Till Marriage.* Minneapolis: Bethany House Publishers, 1991.

Fletcher, Kenneth R., et al., *Extend: Youth Reaching Youth.* Minneapolis: Augsburg Publishing House, 1974.

Gillespie, V. Bailey. *The Experience of Faith.* Birmingham, Ala.: Religious Education Press, 1988.

Hartley, Fred. *Growing Pains: First Aid for Teenagers.* Old Tappen, N.Y.: Fleming H. Revell Company, 1981.

Johnson, Rex. *Communication: Key to Your Parents.* Irvine, Calif.: Harvest House Publishers, 1978.

Kloss, Walter E. *Addiction: How Christians Can Respond Positively to a Growing Crisis.* Hagerstown, Md.: Review and Herald Publishing Association, 1987.

Lutes, Chris. *What Teenagers Are Saying About Drugs and Alcohol.* Grand Rapids: Zondervan Publishing House, 1990.

McDowell, Josh. *Building Your Self-Image.* Wheaton, Ill.: Tyndale House Publishers, 1984.

———. *Teens Speak Out: "What I Wish My Parents Knew About My Sexuality."* San Bernardino, Calif.: Here's Life Publishers, 1987.

Meier, Paul D., Frank B. Minirth, and Frank Wichern. *Introduction to Psychology and Counseling: Christian Perspectives and Applications.* Grand Rapids: Baker Book House, 1982.

Resnick, Michael D., et al. *Reducing the Risk: Connections That Make a Difference in the Lives of Youth.* Minneapolis: Add Health Project, 1997.

Richards, Lawrence O. *A Theology of Children's Ministry.* Grand Rapids: Zondervan Publishing House, 1983.

———. Youth Ministry: *Its Renewal in the Local Church.* Grand Rapids: Zondervan Publishing House, 1972.

Robbins, Duffy. *The Ministry of Nurture: How to Build Real-Life Faith Into Your Kids.*

Grand Rapids: Zondervan Publishing House, 1990.

Sarafino, Edward P., and James W. Armstrong. *Child and Adolescent Development.* Glenville, Ill.: Scott, Foreman and Company, 1980.

Senter III, Mark. *The Coming Revolution in Youth Ministry.* Wheaton, Ill.: Victor Books, 1992.

Spackman, Carl K. *Parents Passing On the Faith: Establishing a Foundation That Endures.* Wheaton, Ill.: Victor Books, 1989.

Stow, Peter, and Mike Fearon. *Youth in the City: The Church's Response to the Challenge of Youth Work.* London: Hodder and Stoughton, 1987.

Swets, Paul W. *How to Talk So Your Teenager Will Listen.* Dallas: Word Publishing, 1988.

Thomas, E. H. *Integrated Youth Ministries Training Manual,* 1988.

―――. *Operation Return,* 1989.

―――. *Peer Counseling,* 1989.

Veerman, David R. *Youth Evangelism: When They're in Your Neighborhood but Not in the Fold.* Wheaton, Ill.: Victor Books, 1988.

Watson, Robert I., and Henry Clay Lidgren. *Psychology of the Child and the Adolescent,* 4th ed. New York: Macmillian Publishing Company, 1979.

White, Ellen G. *Messages to Young People.* Nashville: Southern Publishing Association, 1930.

Wilson, Earl D. *Try Being a Teenager: A Challenge to Parents to Stay in Touch.* Portland, Oreg.: Multnomah Press, 1982.

Wittschiebe, Charles. *Teens and Love and Sex.* Washington, D.C.: Review and Herald Publishing Association, 1982.

Wright, H. Norman. *Premarital Counseling.* Chicago: Moody Press, 1977.

―――. "Reducing the Risk: Connections That Make a Difference in the Lives of Youth." Add Health Project. Minneapolis: University of Minnesota, 1997.

―――. *Relationships That Work.* Ventura, Calif.: Regal Books, 1998.

―――, and Rex Johnson. Communication: *Key to Your Teens.* Irvine, Calif.: Harvest House Publishers, 1978.

Special Resource Material

A, B, C . . . Z for Youth Ministries, vols. I-III. Silver Spring, Md.: Church Ministries Department, General Conference of Seventh-day Adventists, 1990.

Risk and Promise: Challenges Facing Seventh-day Adventist Education Today. Silver Spring, Md.: North American Division of Seventh-day Adventists, 1990.

Youth Ministry Handbook and Leadership Training Manual. Silver Spring, Md.: Church Ministries Department, General Conference of Seventh-day Adventists.

CHAPTER 35

The Impact of Social Pressures on Youth Ministry

by Antonine Bastien

A S WE BEGIN THE TWENTY-FIRST CENTURY, we realize that we are nearing the close of this earth's history. Our old world, ruined by wars, poverty, and political strife, is suffering an interminable nightmare of catastrophes, spreading terror in every heart. Technological advancements push educational institutions to provide high standards and programs to meet young people's needs. The Internet instantly draws all the world into one room.

In spite of these advances, the family structure is at its lowest degree. Newspapers teem with accounts of murder by teenagers. It seems as though every good instinct of humanity is blotted out. Every day the media testify to the increased insanity in the world. The end-time foretold in the Bible is now.

Because of this, the social pressures that Adventist young people face are stronger than ever. Many are carried out of the church by media, New Age religion, or false literature that sow seeds of skepticism in their hearts. According to surveys conducted by the Adventist Church in 1992, between 1900 and 2000 the church was expected to lose 1 million of its young people.

Malcolm J. Allen, in recounting the history of the youth through the ages, says, "While we can identify providential leading and messages of prophetic guidance that have given the Adventist Church direction in developing youth ministry, the major events of history, the advances of technology, the pressures of society, current customs, trends, fashions, and philosophies, have all impacted, for both good and bad, on our church as they relate to youth and youth ministry."[1]

In this time of trouble, how can a youth leader prepare young people to face social pressures? What strategy should be used to train them for salvation and service? First, we will analyze specific concepts, such as polities, wars, poverty, racism, and race relations, as they relate to youth and youth ministry. Second, we will consider the importance of youth ministry's aim, motto, and pledge. Finally, we will propose some characteristic traits to be developed in young people following Jesus' path.

Political Pressures

Politics, as a science and an art of ruling, deals with material phenomena and creative activity that need experiment, ideas, vision, languages, and history to succeed. A great Haitian leader, François Duvalier, defined politics as "an art, a school of psychology, a laboratory of experiment, that supposes ideas to spread, synthesis to coordinate, a humanism to promote. Politics calls naturally to the power of our youth, their enthusiasm, from the intellectual point of view, like the practical one."[2]

Political parties and leaders around the world discovered long ago that one who wants to influence the world must start with children and youth. They select appropriate, but dishonest, methods to ensure their popularity. They multiply strategies to succeed where others fail.

In the Bible we find in Absalom the type of skillful politician that exists in the world today. He employed every art by which he might win the hearts of the people. Like Absalom, politicians instill in young people a conviction to espouse their cause, to fight for their projects until death.

Impact of Politics on Youth Ministry

Youth ministry leaders need Christian strategies to help Adventist young people espouse God's cause until death. To reach this goal, their program should be planned so that they may be rightly trained to represent the truth, giving a reason for their hope. As Nebuchadnezzar did in the past, committed young people should be chosen to receive proper training in Adventist colleges to become faithful missionaries.

Our universities have the responsibility to provide adequate curriculums for leaders in youth ministry. All entities and institutions should solidly stand together in this project, preparing young Christians to strive against sin.

Like politicians, youth ministers should practice abnegation, patience, courtesy, and righteousness in their relationship with the youth whom they win to Christ. They should be chosen among men of principles, fearing God and as faithful as Daniel in Babylon's palace.

Today the greatest want of the church is the want of leaders to train our children to place salvation and service to others higher than money, luxurious cars, and beautiful houses; leaders who are true and honest, motivating our youth to stand for the right amid the corruption that prevails in the political world. We need Christian leaders who use Christian strategies to lead young people to eternity.

Wars

War is defined as armed conflict between two nations. Tragically, wars and famines have long been recognized as classic scourges of humanity. More than 100,000 died as a result of the two atomic bombs dropped on Hiroshima and Nagasaki in 1945. In spite of the enormous losses in human lives, institutions, and infrastructure, the world is stirred by hate and the spirit of war every day.

Today conflict continues, involving Iraq, Iran, Romania, Algeria, Kosovo, Yugoslavia, and the United States. James W. Sire points out that "beyond the city, the suburbs, and farms, nations battle nations openly and covertly. America supplies arms to Iran and Iraq. Iran and Iraq use them against each other. Terrorists take hostages and assassinate leaders and bystanders alike. This is our world today."[3]

Impact of War on Youth Ministry

War disorientates young people and awakens a feeling of fear about the future that the worst can happen in terms of destruction. What does a youth leader have to do to influence young people positively about war pressures?

First, as young people study their Bibles carefully, they will discover that wars are caused by sin: "From whence come war and fightings among you? come they not hence, even of your lusts that war in your members? . . . Ye fight and war, yet ye have not, because ye ask not" (James 4:1, 2).

We read in Revelation that war began in heaven with the entrance of sin in Lucifer's heart, before the creations of the earth. "And there was war in heaven: Michael and his angels fought against the dragon; the dragon fought and his angels" (Rev. 12:7).

This ideological war that began in heaven has impacted the entire universe. "Satan tempted man to sin, as he had caused angels to rebel, that he might thus secure cooperation in his warfare against Heaven."[4]

Second, leaders have a duty to inform young people that sometimes war comes as God's judgment. "Now therefore the sword shall never depart from thine house; because thou has despised me, and hast taken the wife of Uriah the Hittite to be thy wife" (2 Sam. 12:10).

Third, young people should be taught that war comes also by God's decree: "For he said, Because the Lord hath sworn that the Lord will have war with Amalek from generation to generation" (Ex. 17:16).

Finally, Adventist young people should be taught that "the battles waging between the two armies are as real as those fought by the armies of this world, and on the issue of the spiritual conflict eternal destinies depend."[5]

To help Christians conquer their enemies, the apostle Paul exhorts them to put on the whole armor that God has prepared, to defend his children against cunning attacks that could destroy them. He encourages them to take above all the "shield of faith. . . . to quench all the fiery darts of the wicked" (Eph. 6:16). Otherwise, they court failure.

In Old Testament times, war was necessary, as life is, to teach dependence on God. The instruction to "teach them war" (Judges 3:2) demonstrates that preparation for war was to be part of God's educational program for His children. "God purposed, through the nations that remained in and around Canaan, to repeat the lesson of His former deliverances and of the impotency of heathen gods."[6]

The disastrous effect of war upon the planet and its inhabitants is similar to those of the war between good and evil. Every youth should be taught that the world is a battlefield, that "the struggle for conquest over self, for holiness and heaven, is a lifelong struggle. Without continual effort . . . there can be no . . . attainment of the victor's crown."[7]

Fortunately the final stage of the agelong warfare against Christ and His people now begins. This state is termed "the battle of that great day of God Almighty" (Rev. 16:14). The gospel is the good news that men and women need not die, and that is a welcome word to the warriors facing relentless foes. They stand firm on the knowledge of Christ incarnate, crucified, risen, ascended—the heart of the gospel and the reason for peace.

Poverty

Poverty-struck environments severely limit young people's opportunities to succeed in life. And one of the most serious problems that inner-city neighborhoods face is violence. Poor young people create an unsafe climate of vandalism and extortion against citizens in the streets or in their houses. This is the consequence of a lack of family structure, education, skills, good judgment, and values.

In some countries young people face the day without a piece of bread to eat. In some houses young people are accustomed to drinking salty water for one week, until they find someone to help. These situations push youth in our churches to leave the ranks and to join either the work force or gangs at an early age.

Impact of Poverty on Youth Ministry

Youth ministry leaders need to structure youth programs that can overcome the disadvantages of poverty. In many cases poverty pushes young people to deny their God. They forget that wars, famines, and lack of jobs constitute the fulfillment of prophecy. To obviate this, it is necessary for the church to sponsor vocational programs in areas such as agriculture, cottage industry, cooperatives, and workshops that will develop income-generating projects.

Youth leaders should also encourage young people to learn a trade. Jesus, a carpenter, sets us a worthy example. Young Christians must be encouraged to become financially self-sufficient, doing everything in their power to keep from depending on others. "Work is a blessing; idleness, a curse."[8]

Poverty severely limits opportunities for young people, but it cannot stop them from reaching their ideals. Poor youth in Adventist churches can reach the highest ideal God conceives for His children by working with their hands. Youth ministry leaders must help young people develop the feeling that all children of God are rich people of God's grace. Adventist youth must learn to trust their Master, who provides for everything and gives eternal life.

Racism

Some writers believe it is necessary to distinguish between two forms of racism: the old form and the new one. The old form of racism was based on prejudging all Blacks as somehow inherently undeserving of equal treatment. The new form is more insidious, because it is based on observed sociological data. "The new racist equates the pathology of the poor with race, ignoring the fact that family dissolution, teenage pregnancy, illegitimacy, alcohol and drug abuses, street crime, and idleness are universal problems of the poor. They exist wherever there is economic dislocation and deterioration. They are rampant among the White jobless in Liverpool as well as among unemployed Blacks in New York."[9] Racism has become institutionalized in the functioning of the modern urban society.

The Impact of Racism on Youth Ministry

Youth ministry leaders should teach young people that God is the Creator of all humanity. In Christ there is no superiority of race. Christianity subordinates the role of race and nationality to the principle of the brotherhood of all men. In Christ's kingdom all are covered with the same garment of Christ's righteousness, which they receive by faith in Jesus Christ. "There is neither Jew nor Greek, there is neither bond nor free, there is neither male nor female: for ye are all one in Christ Jesus" (Gal. 3:28).

Whatever their nationality, all human beings are important to God. This is why He calls them to finish the work of the gospel in all the world, even "unto the uttermost part of the earth" (Acts 1:8). Youth leaders must develop the spirit of service in young people. In one part of the world 15 Master Guides, with the help of an engineer, built a depot house for a Baptist orphanage. They were very glad to participate in this joy of service.

Race Relations

The verse that comes to my mind when I consider the pressures of race relations on youth ministry is Acts 17:26: "And hath made of one blood all nations of men for to dwell on all the face of the earth, and hath determined the times before appointed, and the bounds of their habitation." "Paul is stating the historical truth that all men, and consequently all nations, sprang from one common ancestor, Adam. The belief was one that no Greek, and especially no Athenian, was likely to accept. For such, the distinction between Greek and barbarian was radical and essential. The one was by nature meant to be the slave of the other. . . . But there was no place in Paul's theology for a 'superior' race." [10]

The Adventist Youth Society

The Adventist Youth Society objective, "Salvation and Service," reveals the true ideals of youth ministry. The Seventh-day Adventist youth movement has been ordained by God for the salvation of youth and their training in service. Therefore, "all activities and programs must stimulate and capture the youths' attention. Their enjoyment must deepen their relationship with God and focus their attention on Adventism's direction and goal." [11]

The Motto: "The Love of Christ Constraineth Us"

"Love, the basis for redemption and education, is the same to impel young people to sacrifice all they are to please God. The love of Christ is a dominant factor . . . in the Lord's work. The love of Christ constrained young people to stay in the straight and narrow way. The love of Christ added with our response becomes a power to allow young people to reach their aim. . . . The love of Christ in the heart of young people would be like a dynamo whose power never fails." [12]

Young people's response is to love God with all their heart, their soul, their strength, and their mind, and their neighbor as themselves. The biblical concept of divine love works for the very best good of others, even enemies. To love is to know God. To know God is eternal life. (See John 17:3.)

The Aim: "The Advent Message to All the World in This Generation"

To fulfill this aim, the youth and children of the church will need the Holy Spirit. According to Acts 1:8. "You will receive power . . . ; and you will be my witnesses" (NIV). This universal message is contrary to the racist position that prevails in the world today. It is impossible to leave our young people inactive without hope, caught in the nets of political individuals who offer a lot of money for their service. They need to learn from their leaders that the one thing worth living for in this world, the one that will stand forever, is the third angel's message. Therefore, "go ye into all the world, and preach the gospel to every creature" (Mark 16:15).

More than ever Adventist young people need undeviating faith in the specific assurances of success that have been given to the church through the Bible: "Certainly I will be with thee" (Ex. 3:12).

According to Malcolm J. Allen, "the advent message is of infinite value to the world; and those who carry it should obtain the best possible preparation of heart, mind, and life, that in their work they may show themselves approved unto God." [13]

The Pledge: "Loving the Lord Jesus and desiring to be of service in His cause, I associate myself with the young people's society, to take an active part in its work, and by the grace of Christ to do what I can to help others, and to send the gospel of the kingdom to all people, at home and abroad"

The pledge is the youth response to Christ's command to His followers. Those who follow Jesus as Savior engage to enter the service of Christ, to become soldiers of the cross, ambassadors of the gospel. Those who accept the privilege of fellowship with Christ in service receive the only training that imparts a fitness for participation with Christ in His glory.

Characteristics of God's Young Saints

Those young who want to be faithful to God until death should be developing these characteristics:

- The ability to make right choices at any cost (Joshua 24:15).
- The strength to resist social peer pressures when the whole world follows the beast (Rev. 13:3).
- The power to express faith in words and to be channels of truth to others (Rev. 22:17).
- The choice to think positively, speak honestly, and to serve lovingly (Phil. 4:8).
- The ability to be a pattern in love, faith, and clean thoughts (1 Tim. 4:12).
- A firm conviction about values that put service and eternal life ahead of the right to buy and sell (Rev. 13:17).
- The heart to believe in God whatever the circumstances (Dan. 3:17).
- The charisma to receive the latter rain (Joel 2:28).
- The confidence that God has never forsaken His people (Ps. 37:25; Isa. 40:11).
- The conviction that human beings were created to love and serve all (Luke 10:27).

Conclusion

This is a fearful time for the church, and a Christlike character is of primary importance. The last battle is soon to be fought, and that day must find none of our young people sleeping. As good shepherds of the flock, ministers of youth ministry must give themselves to their sacred calling, avoiding competing interests that absorb time and energy that should be devoted to feeding our young Christians for the last crisis.

In the warfare to be waged, all the corrupt powers will be united in opposition to God's people. Leaders and young men and women must be wide awake, as wise virgins having oil in their vessels with their lamps. May God help Christian leaders to prepare Adventist youth to stand the final test in the closing conflict.

[1] Malcolm J. Allen, *Divine Guidance.*

[2] F. Duvalier, *Elements d'une Doctrine,* p. 21.

[3] James W. Sire, *Discipleship of the Mind* (Downers Grove, Ill.: InterVarsity Press, 1990), p. 182.

[4] E. G. White, *The Great Controversy,* p. 505.

[5] White, *Prophets and Kings,* p. 176.

[6] *The Seventh-day Adventist Bible Commentary,* vol. 2, p. 323.

[7] White, *Counsels on Education* (Mountain View, Calif.: Pacific Press Pub. Assn., 1968), p. 243.

[8] *The Seventh-day Adventist Bible Commentary,* vol. 7, p. 280.

[9] Rustin, *Society and Education,* p. 389.

[10] *The Seventh-day Adventist Bible Commentary,* vol. 6, pp. 352, 353.

[11] Allen, p. 11.

[12] *Ibid.,* p. 64.

[13] *Ibid.,* p. 65.

CHAPTER 36

Urbanization and Adventist Youth Ministry

by Gladwin Mathews

THE BEGINNING OF THE TWENTY-FIRST CENTURY brought changes in the political, physical, social, and spiritual world. In the light of these changes, what is the relationship between urbanization and Adventist youth ministry? Before we explore this topic, let us look at the definition of urbanization.

Urbanization is the process of population concentration. Sociologists study it from the point of urban population growth and the forces that encourage the development of urban living. They are interested mainly in urbanism—a distinctive mode of life that is developed in the city but may not be confined there.

India is witnessing urbanization on a tremendous scale. Millions of people from rural areas are migrating to cities. Municipal corporations are under pressure to respond to the demands of citizens but are helpless to do anything. The whole world is experiencing rapid changes. Our church also faces the challenge of a changing world. We need to make changes in our approaches, resources, and training programs for leadership. To cope with this challenge, the church looks to its youth ministry, which is conducted for, with, and by young people.

Our church is a young church—many of our members around the world are in their youth. There are about 2 billion teenagers in the world—including Adventist youth. The Adventist Church has a responsibility to minister to their needs, to provide a Christian education, Christian homes, and Christian atmosphere of love. God's purpose for this church is not yet accomplished. The message of salvation through Jesus Christ has to reach unentered areas. Our young people are full of excitement and energy, and the church needs their enthusiasm to reach the youth of this world. This can be possible only when the church gives the youth a true picture of its vision and commitment and points them in the right direction.

Since our youth are living in this changing, urbanized world, we need to take a closer look at how this impacts our youth ministry.

Characteristics of Urban Life

Decline of Morals

Urbanism as a way of life is generally viewed negatively. Big cities are seen as places of wickedness, corrupters of youth and health, and destroyers of family and community ties. City life is considered to be artificial, glamorous, and impersonal. The headlines are filled with reports of violence, fraud, theft, and rape. This has led to a breakdown of the norms and moral standards of everyday life.

Media-centered Culture

The revolution in communications has made Adventist youth less spiritual and less biblically literate than youth of previous generations. Far more appealing are the attractions provided through modern technology. Today our youth are growing up in a world where media-centered culture has changed the Adventist lifestyle. The idea of family worship is being threatened. Probably only a minority of families gather daily to read a portion of Scripture and pray.

This was not what God had in mind. He has instructed us through his prophet Daniel about the last days and how knowledge would increase (Dan. 12:4). God wants us to use modern technology to prepare ourselves and our youth for salvation and service. We are to be visionaries.

Deterioration of Family Life

Young people living in urban areas formulate view of life, values, and spiritual realities based on the urban lifestyle. In many cities families are suffering. Healthy family life is giving way to broken homes. Young people want to be free from their parents and the traditional values of the church and society. The practice of living together before marriage has brought a destructive influence upon homes and family life—even of Seventh-day Adventists. Our youth need to be reminded of the advantages of a Christian marriage, that "the family ties are the closest, the most tender and sacred, of any on earth."[1]

Other Characteristics

Other distinctive characteristics of urban life may include competitiveness, materialism, noise, crowds, and increasing crime. City dwellers often are afraid to walk alone at night in their neighborhood. As a result, lonely hearts live all around us. Men, women, and youth have been isolated from family, friends, and God. For some, big cities are exciting places to live. People have a wide variety of activities to choose from. It offers more entertainment and other pleasures of life. But these do not offer healing and comfort to many restless youth who are longing for something they do not have.

Youth Ministry in Urban Areas

Though the big cities offer exciting and thrilling experiences, our urban areas are filled with those who are hungry for understanding, fellowship, and love. Is there anything we can do for the youth? Yes. This calls for effective youth ministry in urban areas, which can give purpose. The only remedy for the loneliness of hearts is the presence of Jesus. His presence is needed by those both in and outside of the church. Those who have once known His love but today are strangers to that love also need to be reached.

In the great cities of our countries live thousands who once had received His peace and comfort but are desperately lonely, longing to come back. There are some who have been out of the church for many years and live right near us, but have never been visited. It is for them that youth ministry becomes very important. Ellen White sums up a basic approach to youth ministry: "In our work for the youth, we must meet them where they are, if we would help them."[2] Adventist youth must take the initiative and, with Christian love and a spirit of friendliness, invite the lonely, the discouraged, and those who have not heard about Jesus to come and have a thrilling Christian experience.

Spiritual vision is essential if we are to see the needs of the world as they exist. Paul saw a man calling him to "come over to Macedonia and help us" (Acts 16:9, NKJV). The same call can be heard all about us.

Placed Among Non-Christian Influence

Cities are the centers of popular media, entertainment, competitions, education, industry, and constant migration. Cities are all around us, and millions of people of every kindred, nation, and tongue live in, and are influenced by, these cities. And God has placed us there.

Bruce Moyer, speaking in Prague in 1992 on youth evangelism, stated that there are 330 megacities of more than 1 million population and 45 supercities of more than 4 million people. And the rate of urban growth is twice that of rural growth. Speaking of non-Christian influence, he stated, "Today there are 150 non-Christian megacities and 84 anti-Christian megacities. . . . By the year 2050 four of the five largest cities will be non- or anti-Christian—Shanghai, Beijing, Bombay, and Calcutta."[3] God is interested in young people and these cities. We have been placed in these cities among the non-Christian influence to make an impact as Adventists and transform the cities.

God's Call to Youth

In every age God has called youth to do a special work for Him. He called Jonah and sent him to Nineveh. He called Daniel and sent him to Babylon. Paul was sent to the cities of Asia and Europe and finally to Rome itself. Our Master Teacher, Jesus, ministered in urban settings of Judea, Galilee, Samaria, and to the urban people in Jerusalem. Joshua as a youth was chosen to spy out the land. The Bible records that he went as far north as the city of Rehob (Num. 13:21).

Some might say that our youth are too young to do anything great for God. But the early pioneers of the Adventist Church were young—in their teens or early 20s. John N. Andrews was only 14 when he was recognized as a powerful spiritual leader. James White left school teaching at 21 and joined Millerite preachers. Uriah Smith began to write and edit at the age of 21. Stephen Haskell began to share the light at age 19 and traveled to Africa, Australia, China, and other countries. John Loughborough was a successful preacher at 17 and traveled to England.

Ellen White was chosen by the Lord for a special work when she was 17. Through her inspiring words she challenges the youth and the leaders: "The Lord has appointed the youth to be His helping hand."[4] "With such an army of workers as our youth, rightly trained, might furnish, how soon the message of a crucified, risen, and soon-coming Savior might be carried to the whole world!"[5] "Grave responsibilities rest upon the youth. God expects much from the young men who live in this generation of increased light and knowledge."[6]

God called Jeremiah and told him, "Before I formed you in the womb I knew you;

before you were born I sanctified you; and I ordained you a prophet to the nations." Jeremiah, aware of his youth and inexperience, replied, "Ah, Lord God! Behold, I cannot speak, for I am a youth." But the Lord answered, "Do not say, 'I am a youth,' for you shall go to all to whom I send you, and whatever I command you, you shall speak. Do not be afraid of their faces, for I am with you to deliver you" (Jer. 1:5-8, NKJV). From the very beginning of our work God has called the youth—through the Scriptures and the Spirit of Prophecy.

God has a concern for the cities because a growing number of people in this world are living in urban areas. The message of salvation in Jesus is the same as it was during the time of the prophets. God asks for a willing, committed heart. He says to every youth of the church, "Do not say, 'I am a youth,' for you shall go to all to whom I send you, and whatever I command you, you shall speak" (verse 7, NKJV).

In this final hour of earth's history, our world is sinking in lawlessness, degeneracy, and violence. The call demands commitment, sacrifice, and vision from today's Adventist youth. God has challenged the church to proclaim Jesus to the world, "Go into all the world and preach the gospel to every creature" (Mark 16:15, NKJV). The church has accepted the challenge.

The youth of the Spicer College church took up this challenge. In the past five years 127 new churches were started in the Southern Asia Division; 91 of them have been located in an area where there were no Seventh-day Adventists a few years ago. The youth of Spicer College have felt the importance of youth ministry in urban areas. During every summer holiday they are busy conducting evangelistic meetings in the megacities of Bombay (Mumbai), Madras (Chennai), and Pune. Even the Spicer Pathfinders and counselors are involved; they conducted an evangelistic campaign through "train evangelism" in December 1997 in Pune. The Pathfinders traveled in both local and long-distance trains running between Pun and Mumbai. They presented gospel messages in songs to attract the attention of the passengers, distributed tracts and magazines on health, enrolled passengers in Voice of Prophecy lessons, and distributed stickers with spiritual messages. It was a very successful program.

What Kind of Youth Ministry in Urban Areas?

The cities of the world are crying for help. Ellen White, commenting on a chaotic society, wrote: "Throughout the world, society is in disorder, and a thorough transformation is needed. The education given to the youth is to mold the whole social fabric."[7]

The youth of the Seventh-day Adventist Church have an important role to play in communicating God's message of love to the urban youth through youth ministry. A few ideas, suggestions, and projects are listed below in an attempt to stimulate the mind and to involve our youth and youth leaders in urban ministry. Some projects have been tried and proved successful. Others may need preparation and local adaptation.

1. Hospital and Nursing Home Ministry. Seventh-day Adventists are known for their social involvement and caring touch for those in need. We have Adventist hospitals in many of the major cities of the world. Here are some ways to be involved with them:

- Send patients gifts of flowers and magazines, along with a prayer note for recovery. This will bring them joy and happiness and may even help them to recover sooner.
- Sing gospel songs to patients and pray with them.
- Visit the patients in other hospitals, too. This helps the youth to be compassionate.

- Encourage youth to donate blood. This will help in interaction with non-Christians. Spicer College youth regularly donate blood, and as a result many non-Christian families have expressed their faith in Jesus.

2. Operation Dorcas. During the Christmas season clothes can be collected for the poor. Those who want to do a little extra can bring a smile to some needy ones by taking them shopping. Work this program through AY Societies and Pathfinders.

3. Train/Subway Evangelism. Almost all our cities have subways, shuttles, or local trains running within the city or to the suburbs. Choose teams of Pathfinders or youth to witness to the passengers through song and literature. The Spicer Pathfinders have successfully tried this method of witnessing. The passengers will give you their full attention, as they have nothing else to do. The advantage of this type of witnessing is that you can meet a lot of people in a short time and you will have a multicultural group to witness to.

4. Ministry Through Mission Schools. Seventh-day Adventist schools have brought a tremendous social change. Day schools especially are evangelistic schools of the highest order. They transform the city by transforming the students and their families through worship periods. Spicer Elementary School is the only school in the Southern Asia Division that begins the day with a worship period. And most of the teachers use the Bible as their textbook. Once a Hindu parent borrowed a Bible, read the Creation story from it, and told the story to her child. This school has more than 75 percent non-Christian students.

5. Balloon Evangelism. This is an excellent method of generating excitement and motivation among Pathfinders and youth. Choose a day and time to release the balloons. Invite a group to sing gospel songs and ask some youth to give testimonies. Prepare envelopes with VOP cards, a health lesson card, and a note with a gospel message or a promise from the Bible. Be sure to include an address and telephone number for feedback. Inflate the balloons with helium/hydrogen gas and tie the envelopes to the balloons. Release the balloons in the air after the singing and testimony program. You may want to purchase some inexpensive Bibles as gifts for all those who will receive these envelopes.

6. Vacation Bible Schools. Involve your young people in this easy way to witness to community children. After the VBS, children can be invited to attend Sabbath schools, day camps, or Pathfinder clubs.

7. Day Camps and Overnight Camps. Day camps are an ideal way of reaching unentered areas. Involve youth in this outreach program, which is usually held at a resort area or in nature. The program can include swimming, a moonlight hike, a cookout, campfire programs, devotionals, crafts, and nature activities. Send notes to parents describing the planned campout, and secure written permission ahead of time from parents or guardians.

8. Street Witnessing. This method of witnessing presents the gospel to the youth where they are, using songs, testimonies, and preaching in a city park, street, or square. Young people may go into the streets to share literature, witness to people, and enroll them in Bible lessons. Street plays can be acted out. Be sure to obtain permission from city officials or police before you begin.

9. Temperance and Health Rallies. Pathfinders and young people can use this approach to share with community youth information on smoking, drugs, alcohol, AIDS, etc. Secure information and permission from city officials, then choose a starting point and parade through the streets. You may want to invite public health officials to join you. During this event you can invite people to participate in the Breathe Free smoking-cessation plan. End with a program that includes singing, short messages, testimonies, and an appeal to a better lifestyle.

10. Lifestyle Witnessing. We are to influence the world through "our words, our acts, our dress, our deportment, even the expression of the countenance."[8] This is possible only when our youth are people of deep Christian experience. The Savior declared, "By their fruits you will know them" (Matt. 7:20, NKJV).

Raise the standard of devotion to God. Practice modesty in dress (1 Tim. 2:9). Engage in recreation that uses physical and mental powers to glorify God. Practice self-reliance and self-control, avoiding stimulants or intoxicating drink. Have church-standard social gatherings and musical entertainment. Choose companions who will help in right doing and reject worldly associations that would influence you. Practice Christian courtesy, hospitality, and simplicity—God works through simplicity.

Ellen White admonishes the youth to "follow the example of Jesus in His simplicity" if they are to become "pure in morals."[9] Follow Christ's method. "[This] alone will give true success in reaching the people. The Savior mingled with men as one who desired their good. He showed His sympathy for them, ministered to their needs, and won their confidence. Then He bade them, 'Follow me.'"[10]

11. Community Witnessing. In order to present Christ to the community, you must know your community and its needs. Invite people to community halls and organize lectures and seminars on better health living. Organize Five-Day or Breathe Free plans or Home Health lectures. Distribute health-related literature. Motivate and encourage the young people to dedicate a day to clean streets, parks, and other areas. Organize show programs, street plays, and floats. Conduct Revelation seminars in city community halls.

12. One-to-One Witness. One-to-one witnessing is still the most effective outreach. If every youth of the church witnessed every day to one person, we would reach more people than through all other types of witnessing. The AY2Y (Adventist Youth to Youth) program organized at Spicer College served this purpose in two ways: (1) it trained the Adventist youth of Spicer for one-to-one witness programs and (2) it encouraged them to tell people how they found Jesus and how they also may be helped to find life eternal. Let every Adventist youth's slogan be "Each One Teach One."

13. Operation Telephone Directory. With the revolution in communication media, this method can be very helpful. City life is very busy, and often people have no time to talk to you over the phone. But after work they have time to read magazines or go through the mail. So write the names and addresses of people from the telephone directory on the envelopes. Include an encouraging promise from the Bible or an uplifting message on a sheet of paper and sign: "Your friends, the Seventh-day Adventists." Give your contact address and post the envelope. You can offer a Bible as a gift to anyone who responds to you.

14. Recreational Activities. Many young people can be introduced to Christian atmosphere through social activities organized by Adventist young people. This interaction provides a place to extend an invitation to attend our church services. It is especially effective in cities in which we have Adventist institutions.

15. Musical Groups. Music is a tremendous asset in youth ministry. Many choral groups around the world witness for Christ. Many young people can be involved as you organize youth congresses, street witnessing, hospital ministry, music festivals, caroling at Christmas, concerts, and Sabbath programs.

16. Prayer Groups. Praying for others can be very satisfying. Form a group of interested youth and make a list of specific sick people and non-Adventist friends and relatives who need prayer. Pray for them every day and ask God to show you what you can do to help your prayers to be answered.

Conclusion

This chapter has attempted to challenge and motivate Adventist youth and youth leaders to proclaim the good news of salvation and offer service to the youth of the twenty-first century. It is evident that God "has chosen the youth to aid in the advancement of His cause."[11] We must help the youth to accomplish God's purpose and His goals—salvation and service to all of His young people. May God equip us with the appropriate ideas and plans.

---

[1] E. G. White, *The Ministry of Healing,* p. 356.

[2] White, *Gospel Workers,* p. 209.

[3] *Journal of Adventist Youth Ministry* 3, nos. 1, 2: 41.

[4] White, *Testimonies,* vol. 7, p. 64.

[5] White, *Education,* p. 271.

[6] White, *Messages to Young People,* p. 41.

[7] White, *The Ministry of Healing,* p. 406.

[8] White, *Messages to Young People,* p. 417.

[9] White, *Sons and Daughters of God* (Washington, D.C.: Review and Herald Pub. Assn., 1955), p. 132.

[10] White, *Christian Service,* p. 119.

[11] White, *Gospel Workers,* p. 67.

CHAPTER 37

Youth Apostasy and Recovery of Backslidden Youth

by Barry Gane

Youth, the Church of Today

THE YOUTH OF THE SEVENTH-DAY Adventist Church are its greatest asset and its hope. Consider Ellen White's perspective regarding young people:

"With such an army of workers as our youth, rightly trained, might furnish, how soon the message of a crucified, risen, and soon-coming Savior might be carried to the whole world!"[1]

"Preachers, or laymen advanced in years, cannot have one-half the influence upon the young that the youth, devoted to God, can have upon their associates."[2]

"The church is languishing for the help of [young men and young women] who will bear a courageous testimony, who will with their ardent zeal stir up the sluggish energies of God's people, and so increase the power of the church in the world."[3]

It seems obvious that a church so committed to the Great Commission would put youth at the center of its evangelistic endeavors. Yet most evangelism in the Western church focuses on adults, not young people. As a result, instead of being one generation from the kingdom, we are one generation from extinction.[4]

Being born into an Adventist family doesn't make conversion or baptism automatic. Our own young people need conversion and retention. Today there is an eerie sense that the youth are leaving the church. It's time to face up to the reality and take significant steps to reclaim our lost youth. Determining how many youth really leave the church is difficult. We are hesitant to drop the name of an inactive or missing youth, and the name won't even be recorded until the young person has been baptized—a decision a growing number of youth postpone until late teens.

The first serious attempt to discover how many youth are inactive was a 10-year longitudinal study undertaken by Roger Dudley at the Institute of Church Ministry at Andrews University. Funded by the North American Division, Dudley obtained names and addresses of 1,523 baptized young people, ages 15 and 16. Approximately half attended Adventist academies, with the other half attending public schools.

At the midpoint of the longitudinal study, when the original 15- and 16-year-olds were 20 and 21 years old, self-perceived standing with the Adventist Church showed approximately one fourth as enthusiastic members, one half as so-so members, and the remaining one fourth divided between being on the books but not in heart (16 percent) and dropped out (10 percent).[5] Add to this "inactive" one fourth an estimated half of those who dropped out of the study after the first year. This results in a "guesstimate" of 38 percent dropout during the five years between ages 15-16 to 20-21.[6] (This most accurate statistic to date is still quite nebulous.)[7]

The Valuegenesis study included a projection of one's intension for future church participation. The results indicate that 27 percent of today's 12- to 18-year-olds are not planning to be in the church when they are 40 years old.

Figures for those who leave the church in many congregations and conferences range between 35 and 65 percent. One congregation claimed that generating a list of youth who had left the church would be easy, since they didn't lose many of their youth. After two meetings the youth committee had compiled a list of 135 names of youth who no longer attended church. In this church 40 percent of the youth had left over a five-year period. The time that a young person leaves varies from culture to culture and country to country, but some believe the critical period is at the end of high school, as youth either enter the work force or begin tertiary study.[8] As young people assert their independence, one of the ways they do it is by questioning and often rejecting the values and beliefs of their parents.

Reasons for Youth Leaving the Church

In just the past five years a number of studies have given us an insight into what it is that induces, drives, or just encourages youth to sever their connection with the church. The young adult Valuegenesis results from the South Pacific Division gave us the following reasons (these are in descending order, with the reason most often given at the top and the response that occurred the least at the bottom):

- Adult members are living phony lives.
- The church places too much emphasis on nonessentials.
- The attitudes of older members are critical and uncaring.
- Church leaders are preoccupied with organization and not concerned with people.
- Worship services are dull and meaningless.
- I do not want to be a hypocrite.
- The church is too restrictive.
- I'm attracted to a different lifestyle.
- I do not have any real friends at church.
- The church does not allow me to think for myself.

A simple factor analysis of the data revealed five main factors:

- control: not allowed to think for self, problem with the doctrines, and emphasis on nonessentials
- lack of caring
- lack of meaning and purpose
- personal integrity
- control: discipline, family problems, too restrictive

In 1973 Ila Zbaraschuk's research estimated that 50 percent of Adventist adolescents sever their connection with the church for such reasons as:

- church membership without personal conversion
- impersonal, uncaring attitude on the part of older members
- phony-appearing lives of adult members
- no sense of relevance to needs
- religion not making a difference in own life and not wanting to be a hypocrite
- absence of thinking for oneself
- misplaced emphasis with nonessentials too important
- academy (church school) disciplinary methods
- preoccupation with organization on the part of leaders
- quality of sermons

A comparison between the two sets of results shows that many of the same reasons are given, but there are some major shifts. Many youth cite the fact of a lack of friends at church as a major reason for not wanting to attend—an emphasis on the importance of relationships. Others speak of the irrelevance of the church to their daily lives and also of the meaningless worship rituals. Others experienced trauma or crisis and felt that the church did not respond to their needs. Still others cite the family as being such that they do not want to belong to the church. Many use any or a number of these reasons as an excuse to experiment with the world.

Some studies highlight the family as a key in understanding why young people leave or stay in the church. Brad Strahan has surveyed more than 200 college students in an attempt to see if there is a connection between the relationship that young people have with their parents and their images of God. He is convinced that the quality of the parent-child bond is a more powerful predictor of whether or not there will be a positive faith in the child than the religiosity of the parent. The young person's understanding of God is greatly enhanced when they have a model of God's love demonstrated to them. The most effective parenting style for building the faith and the psychological and emotional health of the youth is one that is high on care (shows affection and warmth) and at the same time allows freedom and empowers youth to be independent.

Many Adventist homes are seen by young people as restrictive and not caring. They feel that their parents view faith as more important than they, the children. Even the temptation to be protective or overly protective, if balanced with warmth and love, can make youth more dependent and less able to make decisions, and affects sons more than daughters. Strahan is convinced that if the parents use religion to control, the young person will use religion to assert his/her independence.

The Attitude of the Local Church

John Savage has studied what happens in the church when someone leaves. Out of the youth's personal anxiety, and perhaps from events even separate from the church, there comes a "cry for help." This can be obvious and audible, but it is often indirect. If the church fails to recognize and respond to the cry for help, the hurting youth begins a predictable dropout track that ultimately leads to a self-protective decision to leave the church. If the church responds at this stage, it may avert the loss; however, the church frequently screens out the cry and the young person. Because of this rejection, the young person stops coming to church.

The church begins to feel the pain of rejection when the young person continues to skip church. In reaction, the church may punish the young person for rejecting it. When this occurs, the young person becomes angry as she/he feels further rejected, hurt, and misunderstood. In the next step, the young person goes into denial, saying that it doesn't matter and acting as if she/he doesn't care.

This whole process can happen in as quickly as six weeks and end in permanent withdrawal or apostasy. If the young person is not visited or if the problem remains unresolved during this time, she/he will feel that the decision to leave the church is a correct one. Savage has shown convincingly that visitation by a person with good listening skills any time in this first six weeks can facilitate the return of the youth to the church family.

Building a Profile of Missing Youth

To reach and reclaim missing youth it is necessary to know who they are! Youth who have not attended for five years or more may prove harder to reach. Start with a list of youth who have left the church in the past five years.

If you have been in a particular youth ministry setting for a number of years, you may already have a good idea of who these people are. However, most local church youth leaders are in the position for only a short period of time, and so the following steps may be useful.

Step 1. Consult the church clerk's records—these should have the names of all baptized youth. Sabbath school record cards may include the names of youth who may not have been baptized. You will need to construct a list of the missing youth. Remember that all youth are not the same and must be seen as individuals.

Step 2. Sell the reclamation concept to your youth team and let them know how many youth already have left. Brainstorm to recall other names that may have been missed.

Step 3. Involve your youth group leadership team in prayer and strategy for contact with missing youth.

Step 4. Contact each missing young person—personal contact is best. Let them know that you are interested in them. Invite them to a fellowship activity first so that relationship can be established. Ensure that their friends at church make contact as well.

The record blank at the end of this chapter will help your leadership team keep up with what is happening and who is being visited.

How Do You Make a Friendship Visit?

Roger Dudley's study has revealed that only about 15 percent of youth who stop coming to church ever receive a follow-up visit or even a call from anyone at church. That means that 85 percent never have anyone visit or say that they cared. Some who decide to return to church find it difficult, if not impossible, to break in.[9]

Before your visit, spend time in prayer for the person you are visiting.[10] Explain that you have missed the person at church and that you and the youth team have decided to visit all the youth who haven't been at church for a while. Your approach may not make much difference if you are praying for the person and if you are sincerely friendly. One important step: before leaving, let the person know that you have enjoyed the visit and that you will be back. Try to work out the best time to get together.

The visit at first should never be more than 30 minutes; 20 minutes is better. Do not do all the talking yourself. Discuss what she/he is interested in, and you will be surprised how soon she/he will bring the conversation to things that have to do with Christ. This isn't a "green light" to initiate a Bible study. The purpose of your visit is to create and interest by your friendship so that she/he will want to come back to church for consistent spiritual involvement.

Developmental Theory

There has been considerable research in recent years into the developmental stages of adolescence, providing an understanding of what is happening in the lives of young people. An adolescent[11] has been described as a person who is no longer a child but not yet an adult. She/he is caught developmentally between the two stages, with all the confusion of not really belonging to either, sometimes wishing to return to childhood and at the same time struggling for independence as an adult.

Erik Erikson, a pioneer in psychosocial development, saw life developing through a series of crises that one must master before progressing to the next. He identified the crisis of identity as being the major issue for adolescents. Erikson saw adolescents as being caught between the sense of competence and achievement of childhood and the crisis of intimacy faced by the young adult.[12]

"Identity" as described by Erikson would give rise to a feeling of inner firmness or of "being together" as a self. It communicates to others a sense of integration or personal unity.[13] The crisis of identity formation involves the adolescent in a number of issues, from gaining a perspective of his/her uniqueness, to a commitment to a sexual orientation and its associated roles, to a primitive ideological position or basic philosophy of life, to a vocational direction.[14] It is part of finding one's own identity that pushes young people to challenge the values of the parents and seek to incorporate a value system of their own. It is clear, however, that many youth who question their parents' values and beliefs ultimately accept them as their own.

John Westerhoff lists four stages of faith, and the primary one that adolescents work through is the third, which he calls "searching faith." This is characterized by doubt and questioning, experimentation with alternate views, and the concept of the need for commitment to people or causes. It comes as no surprise that young people question everything. This can be a particularly hard time for parents and church leaders if they do not understand what is happening.

The young person needs room to move and stretch, to question and challenge, and the church and the home should work in concert to create an atmosphere that will enable this. The young person should feel safe as she/he asks questions and seeks answers. Part of the leader's role is to let youth know that they do not have answers to every question and that sometimes there are no answers, but faith hangs on to the evidence it has.

Religious educator Sharon Parks provides a model that demonstrates cognitive development for higher education that goes beyond the general field of formal operational thinking (à la Piaget). This model presents four stages.[15] Because higher education is driven by a search for truth, questioning is the norm. The model by Parks may not be relevant or helpful for those outside of higher education, but many find it quite descriptive of the higher education experience.

The four stages move from external authority to internal authority. The first stage can be described as "dualistic"—yes and no, right and wrong—with no ambiguity. Truth can always be defined, explained, and applied to every situation. If there are any questions beyond your understanding, a higher (external) authority can provide the correct answer (truth).

Most idealistic college freshmen that hold to this stage soon find their world attacked on all sides. Almost any professor can (and should) challenge such thinking. Most fellow students can provide exceptional situations in which the "correct answers" become inadequate. For example, consider many of the Adventist lifestyle issues. Nonattendance at movie theaters hardly stands up to video usage (sometimes in college classes), campus entertainment, and even evangelistic series conducted in the local theater. Dancing is verboten, but the grand marches and skating sponsored by the college seem similar to some dance forms; gymnastics is a physical education class, plus, the school does recruiting and witnessing with its gymnastic team; and cultural events at the school include folk dances from various countries.

Some try to contort their comfortable dualistic world to meet every exception, but reality soon exceeds the flexibility available. It's no wonder that most collegiates move into the second stage before the end of their first year of school, if not sooner.

The second stage can be described as "questioning." It's a world of relativism. Knowing that exceptions abound, the budding young adult is gun-shy of being certain about anything. The higher education zeitgeist of questioning everything seems far more advanced than the simplistic world of dualism. In fact, answers are no longer important. What really matters is questions. The best way to respond to a question is with another question. The annoying adjective "sophomoric" aptly describes this stage. The inductive method of education has clever appeal.

Looking back to the first stage, a stage-two person has a certain fondness for the "good ol' days" of childhood simplicity mixed with a sense of maturity for shedding that immature skin.

Unfortunately, looking ahead gives a distorted view of reality. Clear perception is only possible looking back. As a result, those still in stage one perceive those in stage two as rebellious humanists who have abandoned the absolutes of the church, Scripture, and even God. From the way they talk and question everything, it appears that they have no faith and already have left the church, or at least the church would be better if they did. It's a major challenge to keep stage-two people involved in the church. They're not looking for answers, only questions. And the questions they ask make everyone in the comforts of dualism uncomfortable. The only Sabbath school class that would welcome them would be the skeptics, if a particular church has such a class. This is the world of the typical collegiate.

After spending a good deal of time wallowing in relativism, real truth seekers eventually tire of the tossing about and instability incumbent to relativism. Having crossed many cognitive seas, they are ready to set anchor in an area in which they can place some confidence, although not to the degree of being absolutely certain. They are aware of other perspectives, but they have enough evidence upon which to make at least some type of commitment. This third stage can be termed "commitment within relativism." From here a stage-three person can look back with a sense of loss to the simple days of childhood in which dualism was adequate. Just thinking of relativism can nauseate them, provided they are fed up enough with it. Yet, they are also grateful that relativism has prepared them to live in the real world rather than denying so much in order to maintain dualism. They appreciate the current peace of making a commitment with the understanding that much is still relative.

For those in stage one the person in stage three seems to be somewhat correct but slipping toward unbelief. If only they wouldn't allow for exceptions they could be "true believers." For those in stage two the person in stage three seems to be in-between stages one and two. They aren't willing to go with each new thought or possibility. Could it be fear rather than exasperation? But neither the stage-one nor the stage-two person realizes that the stage-three person is more mature than either of them.

As the anchor of commitment continues to settle, a person can enter the fourth stage of "conviction within commitment." Here a certainty develops somewhat akin to the stage one dualism. The marked difference is the understanding and appreciation of relativism and the corresponding tolerance for having passed through those stages. There is also an embracing of paradoxes rather than an explaining away of them. It is only by giving a person the opportunity to disagree that they can truly agree. The stage-four person seems at times, a little bit like a mystic. Looking back to stage one, the stage-four person now understands the difference between being childlike and childish. A look to the stage-two person brings reminiscing of self-absorption in counterpoint. The view of stage three seems to signal the possibility of discovering real truth for the heart and soul.

The person in stage one views the stage-four person as a lot like them, only not evangelistic enough and too ethereal. The stage-two person knows a stage-four person has to be wrong, because no intelligent person could be so certain; yet this seemingly unintelligent person always can tease a question beyond the relativist's capabilities. The stage-three person isn't sure if the stage-four person is simply a smart stage-one person or possibly a similar stage-three traveler with greater security.

Sharon Parks' model provides understanding and a clear mandate for significant changes within Adventism. Either we should discourage or discontinue higher education of our young people or else make the concomitant makeover for new wine in new wineskins.

Listening Skills

Because parents and church leaders do not always understand what is happening, youth feel rejected and take their questions elsewhere to be answered. For those involved in reclaiming youth, one of the major skills needed is the ability to listen, and to listen with empathy.

The place to begin is where the young person is. You will need to understand his/her thinking, world, and dilemmas. Tony Campolo warns, "There is no single youth culture in the technological urban industrialized societies of the Western world. Instead, there are a variety of subcultures existing side by side, each with its own language, value system, and worldview."[16] It is best to meet them on neutral ground, and this may mean away from the home or the church. Joseph Aldrich said, "If you are pursuing lost sheep, you must go where they are. You cannot avoid every appearance of evil. Our Lord didn't either. Because of His close proximity to the beer cans and potato chips of His day He was accused of being a drunkard and a glutton. Professional 'weaker brothers,' suffering from hardening of the categories, delight to criticize those who take the Great Commission seriously."[17]

Good communication is dialogue. Often youth leaders want to do all the talking. To reach youth that have severed their connection with the church, you must:

- have a genuine desire to LISTEN
- be willing to read and accept feelings and emotions
- not have the need to always be right
- be accepting, noncritical, and nonjudgmental
- let the young people know that you feel honored to share their story
- be open enough to share some of your journey and even some of your struggles
- be prepared to keep in touch and sacrifice enough to support

It is essential to build a relationship, and this will take time and commitment on your part. Relationships are built on understanding, empathy, and nonjudgmental attitudes. Warm, kind, genuine, and trustworthy people build relationships.

Ask yourself these questions:

- How warm and kind am I?
- How respectful am I of those who act and think in ways that I consider illegal, immoral, or unspiritual?
- How genuine am I?
- Do I feel free to be myself?
- How much of who I am do I hide?
- How trustworthy am I?
- Do I keep confidences?
- How well do I listen?
- Does the other person feel listened to and understood?
- Do I check to see that I understand what is being said and felt?[18]

Empathy is of extreme importance in seeking to understand what is being said. Empathy is not sympathy. "Empathy is the capacity to imagine the teen's experiences . . . as well as to express those experiences to show understanding."[19] In seeking to read the feelings rather than just reflect the words, the acronym SASHET may help, as it stands for the major feelings experienced by youth:

> **S**cared
> **A**ngry
> **S**ad
> **H**appy
> **E**xcited
> **T**ender[20]

You must be prepared to speak the language of the young person and deal with areas of interest to him/her. Listen to his/her concerns and be prepared to explore them a little. Demonstrate that you have higher esteem for people, and don't put anyone or any faith down. At the same time, don't be afraid to challenge the young person's thinking.

When you win trust and youth place confidence in you, they will begin to share, and this sharing will become deeper and more intimate as the relationship grows. Keep a high level of confidentiality, for if you break the person's confidence, you may destroy the relationship and hinder the process of his/her return to the church.

Friendship Evangelism

All young people are searching for meaning or endeavoring to make sense of the world in some way. For some it is the pursuit of pleasure. But for many there is the desire for relationships and spirituality. They want to know where they fit in the scheme of things.

The atmosphere and the attitude of the church are important in bringing youth back to church. There must be a spirit of inclusion as opposed to exclusion. You must be willing to take a risk and know that sometimes these young people will let you down. You must be willing to meet their needs.

Inclusion

Too often our churches appear to be exclusive clubs where those on the inside are looked after and those on the outside are not really welcome and at best only tolerated. This spirit can be seen in such areas as dress and financial support for members. Does your church budget include items to support youth who have not been to church for a while? Are these youth welcome at all events of the church? Is the church and youth hall/center a place in which youth feel comfortable and to which they feel they could invite their friends? Does your church actively seek the return of missing youth through its policies? Is your church actively building a program that will be attractive to missing youth?

Willing to Risk

Are you willing to risk the church facilities and its reputation, or even your own, in an attempt to reach these youth? Think about the people that Jesus mixed with. Ian Thomas makes this powerful appeal:

"I simply argue that the cross be raised again at the center of the marketplace as well as on the steeple of the church. I am recovering the claim that Jesus was not crucified in a cathedral between two candles but on a cross between two thieves, on the town garbage heap, at a crossroad so cosmopolitan that they had to write His title in Hebrew and in Latin and in Greek . . . at the kind of place where cynics talk smut and thieves curse and soldiers gamble. Because that is where he died, and that is what he died about. And that is where churchmen ought to be, and what churchmen should be about."[21]

Is it possible that we are so involved in church work that we forget the work of the church?

Meeting the Needs

What are some of the youth needs that we already know? David Stone highlights what he regards as the five major needs:

1. Self-esteem. An innate need to be important in the eyes of others, especially peers and parents.

2. Self-confidence. A need to know that "I can handle it; you don't have to wipe my nose for me." A sense of knowing that he/she can use his/her ability well.

3. Self-regard. A need to care about how one looks, feels, and thinks in relation to others.

4. Self-worth. A need to know that one's comment, feelings, and thoughts really do count and can make a difference.

5. God awareness. A need to have a power, a force or authority, that is ever present or available to eliminate the caustic, inevitable encroachment of loneliness; a need to believe in a God who is loving and forgiving and always with him/her. Youth need a God who is not a magician but a constant companion whom they can turn to in an emergency situation and who walks beside them or dwells within them as a friend, confidant, and guide.[22] Individual needs will be discovered only in a relationship in which youth trust you enough to tell you what is happening with them.

Church Climate

Because of the challenges young people bring to the Adventist Church, our identity and corresponding church climate must be renovated. Currently it seems that our perspective of being the true church results in a purity-preserving climate. We eliminate questioning, especially outside of acceptable avenues. One needn't be concerned if it hurts or destroys the person, for people who question are destined to hell anyway. They simply had been serving as instruments for the devil to infiltrate the bastion of truth. Some have a perverted sense that as long as the investigative judgment is proceeding in heaven, we might as well keep up-to-date on earth, so that when Jesus comes He will find that judgment already is complete.

The bastion of truth and the hotel for saints are poor models for the church today. Not only are they irrelevant; more important, they are heretically anti-Christian. Organized religion has served more as a citadel for tradition than for truth. And even Jesus, who continues His ministry on earth through His body, the church, came not for the righteous but for sinners. By implementing Christ's attitude, the church will be characterized by the divine characteristics of love, acceptance, and forgiveness.

Unfortunately young people don't perceive it that way yet. Valuegenesis results showed that with academy teens, only 54 percent considered their churches to have an atmosphere of warmth and caring, significantly lower than all six other Protestant denominations that conducted similar studies. When Roger Dudley used the same questions with the 20- and 21-year-olds in his study, the number dropped to 41 percent. The issue of a warm and caring environment is problematic not only of adult attitudes to youth but also of the way young people relate to each other. The cliques among Adventist youth isolate them from caring for people, including their peers.

A similar negative trend could be noted in regard to a church-thinking climate from the teens into the 20s. Valugenesis showed that a paltry 34 percent of Adventist teens consider their congregations to have thinking climates. With Dudley's 20- and 21-year-olds, the number again dropped, this time to 28 percent. This means that while a questioning mind characterizes the collegiate-age category, less than 30 percent of Adventist young people find their churches to be a place conducive for their approach to truth. When they question existing truth, they easily could encounter reactionary insecurity. In reality, they are beginning to internalize their faith, not to give it up. But a remnant theology doesn't permit the luxury of developing faith or processing truth. Questioning is misunderstood as unbelief rather than the pathway to belief. Faced with such options, most young people opt for the integrity of growing in their faith and discovery of truth, even if they are squeezed out of their religion.

Programs to Attract and Incorporate Young People

Many seek that all-encompassing program that will attract and keep young people in their church. No such universal program exists. In fact, what works with one church or one community may fall flat with another. It would be wise to program variety for those within the church and to attract those outside of the church.

Overtly religious programming such as Friday evening vesper programs and weekend retreats will reach some. In North America recreation in the form of volleyball and basketball seem like favorite activities for many, including those wary of religious activities. The need for social activities continues to be strong, especially when young people graduate from Adventist school programming and an increasing number marry later. Service activities are "in," and will continue to have appeal to a number of youth, since these are years of heightened horizontal expressions of spirituality.

Have the young people provide input on specific programming ideas. Be prepared to do something traditional or something totally out of the ordinary. In general, the "three F's"—friends, food, and fun—tend to attract people. Involvement is a key to maintaining interest, but remember that young people, especially collegiate-age, flee commitment. That means that their involvement must be in manageable amounts and backed up by more stable leadership.

A Final Word

If a person has been inactive for a while, realize that to get involved again requires battling a number of fears. Of course, there will be a fear of acceptance. If their current lifestyle isn't completely in harmony with Adventist practices, there may be a fear of behavioral changes, which the person may or may not want to be changed. There is also a fear that should they become involved with the church again, there will be a loss of most of the friends they've made outside the church. At the same time, being fearful that the church hasn't changed much since they left, they probably expect a fair amount of criticism for being away, as well as possibly not fitting in if and when they return.

While no environment is germ-free, a congregation's overall attitude and behavior toward returning young people must be primed periodically. Featuring young people, including returning inactives in the church newsletter or on the platform for various duties or sharing church life can serve as reminders of the church's ongoing ministry to young people. Frequently some of the young people remain in contact with inactive youth. Knowing the church will welcome them back and having something to invite them to equips them to restore the inactive back to the life of the church.

---

[1] E. G. White, *Counsels to Parents, Teachers, and Students,* p. 555.

[2] White, *Messages to Young People,* p. 204.

[3] *Ibid.,* p. 25.

[4] Some of this material was originally prepared by Barry Gane and Steve Case for publication in *Ministry* magazine.

[5] Actual numbers are: enthusiastic member, 27 percent; so-so member, 47 percent; officially a member but not in heart, 16 percent; have dropped out, 10 percent (Roger Dudley, "Why Our Teenagers Leave the Church" [Berrien Springs, Mich.: Institute of Church Ministry, Andrews University, 2000], p. 122).

[6] *Ibid.,* p. 6.

[7] For a more complete review of the first two years of this 10-year longitudinal study, see Roger Dudley and Janet Kangas, *The World of the Adventist Teenager.* Reports for each subsequent year may be obtained from the Institute of Church Ministry, Andrews University, Berrien Springs, Michigan.

[8] Sharon Parks, *The Critical Years: The Young Adult Search for a Faith to Live By* (San Francisco: Harper and Row, 1986), sees this period as crucial in the development of a faith that is owned and lived by.

[9] Roger Dudley shared part of a letter with me that illustrates this point on visitation: "I wanted to write and thank you for allowing me to participate in this survey. I think it is wonderful that people at Andrews are concerned about Seventh-day Adventist youth. Being a participant in this study has meant a lot to me, and I look forward to filling out the questionnaires. So far, you are the only person who has responded to me and my decision to leave the church. I have never been visited by a single person from my SDA church here, nor have I ever been encouraged to return."

[10] The missing youth should be an ongoing part of your prayer list.

[11] Adolescence was identified as a distinct stage of development comparatively recently with the publication of G. Stanley Hall, *Adolescence: Its Psychology and Its Relations to Physiology, Anthropology, Sociology, Sex Crime, Religion and Education* (New York: D. Appleton and Company, 1904).

[12] Erik Erikson, *Identity, Youth and Crisis* (New York: Norton, 1968).

[13] See James W. Fowler, *Stages of Faith: The Psychology of Human Development and the Quest for Meaning,* p. 77.

[14] See Doug Stevens, *Called to Care* (Grand Rapids: Zondervan, 1985), pp. 55, 56.

[15] For a complete presentation, see Sharon Parks, *The Critical Years.* Besides cognitive development, affective and community development are also presented in corresponding stages.

[16] Anthony Campolo, "The Youth Culture in Sociological Perspective," p. 37.

[17] Joseph Aldrich, "You Are a Message," *Moody Monthly,* 1982, cited in Stevens, *Called to Care,* p. 119.

[18] Questions based on those used by David E. Carlson, "Principles of Student Counseling," in *The Complete Book of Youth Ministry,* p. 409.

[19] *Ibid.,* p. 410.

[20] *Ibid.,* pp. 409, 410.

[21] Ian Thomas, cited in Stevens, *Called to Care,* p. 116.

[22] J. David Stone, "Youth Ministry Today; Overview and Concept," in *Complete Youth Ministries Handbook,* ed. J. David Stone (Nashville: Abingdon, 1979), vol. 1, p. 9.

FRIENDSHIP RECORD

Name _____ Age____ Sex____

Address _____

_____

Home phone _____ Cell phone _____

Baptized: Yes ____ No ____   Date attended church _____

Parents: ____   Married ____ Separated ____Divorced ____Single

Mother: ____   Adventist ____   Other ____   Father: ____   Adventist ____ Other

Friends still attending   _____   _____

                            _____   _____

What did he/she enjoy about church?_____

Present relationship to church: _____

Present relationship to family: _____

Work and school_____

Dates of visits

1. _____ 3. _____ 5. _____

2. _____ 4. _____ 6. _____

Comments

CHAPTER 38

Helping the
Wounded Adventist Youth

by Kerry Schafer

Today's Teens

YOUNG PEOPLE TODAY FACE a more uncertain future than any generation before them. The constant threat of nuclear disaster shadows them, along with the certain knowledge that our planet is doomed to destruction if radical environmental changes are not made soon. Their parents are largely absent, either through divorce or the need to work long hours. Youth are surrounded by violence: television and movies glorify violence and weapons, and video games give them practice in the act of killing. The news is full of stories of other teens that have been gunned down in school by fellow students. Many young people live in cities where gangs and street violence are part of daily life. Fear, hopelessness, and lack of purpose are common in those who lack a strong relationship with the Lord. Young as these teens are, many have already been seriously wounded by life.

Although the expression "our youth are our future" has been used often enough to seem clichéd, the truth of it is evident. The teenagers in your youth group today will someday be responsible for the function of the entire church body. Since the church is only as healthy as the body it is made of, the healing of the many wounded youth among us is essential to the survival of the church itself.

By doing this, we are also following the example set by Christ when He lived on earth. Without exception He offered unconditional love, acceptance, and hope to every suffering soul that He met. His rebukes were reserved for those who were striving to be outwardly perfect and did not realize their great inner need. In order to reach the suffering in our world today, we must convey Christ's message to the woman caught in adultery—"Neither do I condemn thee"—before we can move on to "go, and sin no more."

Where Are the Parents?

Teens today lack parental leadership. The cozy, close-knit families of *Leave It to Beaver* and *Happy Days* have become a rarity. In fact, parents of this generation may spend as much as 40 percent less time with their children than their parents spent with them.[1] Young people are likely to build their moral framework around the influences of TV, music, and peers rather than that of their parents, who are conspicuously absent for a variety of reasons.

The incidence of single-parent families in North America has skyrocketed over the past decade, with many studies putting the divorce rate at 50 percent. The number of children living with both biological parents may be as low as 27 percent.[2] Women head most single-parent homes, although more men are beginning to take on the principal parenting role. The majority of children in single-parent homes see their out-of-home parent rarely, and even regular weekend visits don't make the same impact on the child's value system, as does daily contact. A single parent frequently needs to work long hours in order to meet the needs of their family, thus leaving their children to their own devices for long stretches of time. Children and teens left on their own for extended periods often get themselves into trouble.

Homes in which both parents are present are typically dual-income families. Some fathers work two or more jobs to provide the quality of life that they wish for their children; many travel extensively. With the mother also working, the children in these homes have contact with their parents for a few hours a day at most. Consequently their religious and moral systems are also shaped more by peers and media than by family.

Interestingly enough, the highest incidence of juvenile crime occurs not at night, as might be expected, but in the afternoon between the time school lets out and the time parents get home from work. More teen sexual encounters, drug and alcohol use, and acts of violence and vandalism take place during this time period. Unfortunately, innocent youth are also affected as they are likely to get caught in the cross fire when violence erupts.

Violence

It's no secret that we live in a violent society. Check out what's playing at the video store; ask kids about what they are watching on TV; sit in on a video game. High schools frequently have security systems and metal detectors at the front doors, although the recent rash of school shootings makes it clear that these seemingly drastic precautions have not been nearly enough. Teenagers in public schools report a high level of fear of violence.

Studies show that exposure to violence tends to lead to violent actions. Probably, just watching the average teen quota of violent movies is not enough to push a child over the edge. But if the teen lives in an area in which they see violence on a regular basis, if they come from a home in which they witness domestic violence between their parents, or if they have been physically abused, they are at increased risk of acting out the violence around them. The tendency to act out violence is increased when their encounters with violence begin at a young age and are prolonged over an extended time period.

We have had a tendency to believe that youth violence is something that happens in inner-city and gang areas, but the recent explosion of shootings by middle-school teens in small towns has made it clear that no community is immune. Warning signs of violence must be attended to. If a young person makes comments about wanting to kill people, action should be taken immediately. If the teen also has access to a weapon, the situation is particularly critical. In this case, professional help should be sought—child protective services, the police, or a crisis line should be informed at once. It is better to err on the side of caution; one person dead by violence is one too many. In addition, once these youth have crossed the line into serious acts of violence, it is even more difficult to reclaim them.

Other, Less Immediate, Warning Signs of Violence Include the Following:
- cruelty to animals
- frequent outbursts of temper (especially if demonstrated with physical violence)
- preoccupation with weapons
- fascination with death and dying
- withdrawal and antisocial behavior
- serious depression
- detachment from social ties
- history of exposure to violence
- prenatal drug or alcohol exposure (these children have a decreased capacity to understand right and wrong and are much more likely to cross the line)

Although the most successful interventions to prevent teen violence begin with young children, James Garbarino, in his book *Lost Boys,* states that religion has been shown to help these young people, but only if it is love-centered and nonpunitive.[3] Violent teens are hurting teens. Frequently they have been taught to believe that they are bad and unlovable. They are hurt and angry and may have disconnected from society. Just one person, who accepts them, loves them unconditionally, and models a Christian value system can make an enormous difference.

Sexual Abuse

Sexual abuse is a serious and prevalent problem in today's society. About one in four girls will experience some type of sexual abuse before the age of 18. Although there is a myth that boys are immune to this type of abuse, research shows that at least one in six boys will also experience some form of sexual abuse. Researchers believe that both of these statistics are probably low, because of underreporting.

Sexual abuse affects children of all social classes and nationalities. It is most frequently committed not by strangers, but by somebody the young person knows: a mother or father, older brother or sister, close relative, or family friend. Although we would like to believe that the rate must be much lower within the church, sexual abuse may occur with even higher frequency within the homes of strictly religious families. Adventist youth are not exempt, and youth leaders must be aware of the signs of abuse and what to do to help these seriously wounded young people find help and healing.

The young person who has been sexually abused will be seriously damaged psychologically and spiritually. It is nearly impossible for a young person to believe that God is love when the authority figures in his or her life have repeatedly used them to meet the demands of their own twisted desires. Trust is difficult. If the abuse began when the person was young and was committed by a parent, he or she probably never learned what it is to be loved, making it very difficult to love in turn. The feeling of being a worthless object to be used at will and then cast aside may be very strong.

The younger the age at which the abuse begins, the more serious the damage. A child who has been consistently used for sex for as long as he or she can remember tends to become oversexualized at a very early age. The behavior is woven into the moral framework, and it may seem that everybody lives this way. Consequently, even very small children can initiate sexual play with other children around them, and older children and teens may display sexually predatory behavior.

Symptoms of Sexual Abuse Include the Following:
- sexually promiscuous behavior
- compulsive lying and other personality disorders
- sudden changes in personality
- sudden decline in grades
- depression
- low self-esteem
- substance abuse
- delinquent acts such as theft and vandalism
- frequent bladder or vaginal infections for girls
- problems with bowel and bladder control

Remember that it will be very difficult for children to admit that they have been abused. Often teenagers will feel that it is their fault in some way—that they have done something to cause the abuse. Girls often believe that they invited it by their actions or their dress. This perception is even stronger for boys, who sometimes experience arousal and even orgasm during unwanted sex and therefore feel that "since they enjoyed it" they must have consented. In addition to guilt, typically some type of coercion will have been employed to make victims keep the "secret." Silencing tactics range from threats of violence to the teen or their loved ones to an instilled belief that telling will break up their family.

If you seriously suspect that any young person has been sexually abused, seek expert help immediately. In Canada and the United States, people who work with children are required by law to report any suspected abuse to the Department of Social Services. Child protection services workers are specially trained to investigate the situation and protect the young person from further trauma. They are also able to help teens hook up with therapeutic services, such as counselors and support groups.

Youth workers can help by helping the abused teen find a qualified Christian counselor who can help to work through the emotional, moral, and spiritual issues. It is also extremely important to provide acceptance, unconditional love, and companionship.

A note of warning: special precautions must be taken to protect your own reputation when working with these young people. They may very easily mistake a harmless gesture as a sexual one and make damaging accusations. They may also attempt to engage leaders in sexual activity. It is best not to be alone with victims of sexual abuse. For example, keep the door of the study open, rather than closed, when counseling teens.

Job Stress
The teenager who gets good grades, holds down a part-time job, and still maintains an active part in the youth group is generally admired as an example of a well-adjusted young person who has it all together. Unfortunately, this young person may be juggling too many plates and be at risk in a variety of ways, including job stress. Think about it—most young people spend somewhere around 30 hours a week in school. If they work a 20-hour-a-week

part-time job, that adds up to 50 hours. Add in homework, social engagements, and possibly sports or other extracurricular activities, and you have a grueling schedule at a time when physical and emotional energy is typically very low. At this age kids need extra sleep, and may easily be getting less than they should. During a time when a bad hair day is enough to constitute an emergency, they are dealing with a schedule that would make the most energetic of adults collapse in exhaustion. Combining this with the emotional, social, and physical pressures that come with this stage of development can put these young people at serious risk.

Studies show that teens who work 20 hours or more are at higher risk for such undesirable behaviors as substance abuse, violence, and delinquency. They also tend to be less engaged with school. Statistically, the teens that work longer hours are not the underprivileged who need the money. Rather, they are middle-class young people who work in order to earn status symbols: expensive shoes, stereo systems, etc.

As a point of interest, those youth whose jobs are directly related to their future goals are not significantly at risk. Meaningful, productive work that accomplishes a goal contributes to the well-being of teens and adults alike. However, most teen jobs have no connection with any future goals; they are typically menial and meaningless, aside from being a way to make money.

Generally, teens are powerless within the workplace. They have no input and no ability to effect change in their working conditions. If they complain about hours or working conditions, they can very easily be replaced. Often they are undertrained and inexperienced, and can actually be at risk of on-the-job injury because of this.

The youth worker can help by encouraging youth to examine their reasons for working, and help them to set realistic goals. For example, working 10 hours a week, rather than 20, would provide some extra money while still allowing time for homework, sleep, and healthy recreation. Encourage teens wanting or needing work to find jobs that are meaningful to them.

Teen Parents

Most teen parents are single mothers. Research shows that in up to 70 percent of teen pregnancies the fathers are 30 years old or older and are not involved after the birth of the baby. Teenage mothers are often forced to drop out of school in order to care for their baby. Sometimes, leaving school is caused by economic necessity—they need to work, or they can't afford child care. Unfortunately, the dropout rate is increased by the fact that many schools make it clear these young mothers are no longer welcome. Because the types of jobs available to high school dropouts are menial and low-paying, many young mothers end up on welfare. Their babies are at a very high risk for neglect and abuse, and the mothers themselves are highly likely to become pregnant again.

These young parents require massive support, encouragement, and education. Emotionally they are still children, and the demands of a baby (and in some cases also a marriage) are overwhelming. A combination of emotional immaturity and misunderstandings about the nature and needs of babies and small children can lead to neglect and abuse. Teenagers tend to be egocentric. They may expect the child to meet their needs, and react with anger when the child demands to have its own needs met. A baby who cries may be viewed as spoiled and attention-seeking, for example, and be "punished" accordingly. This situation is exacerbated by the fact that teen mothers often do not receive adequate prenatal care and may engage in substance abuse while they are pregnant. Babies who have been pre-natally exposed to drugs or alcohol are very often more difficult and demanding: they may cry more and sleep less. When older, they may show signs of attention deficit disorder or fetal alcohol syndrome. Both of these conditions are challenging for the most experienced of parents to deal with.

In order to be successful, teen parents need nurturing, emotionally supportive people around them. They need to finish school and develop skills that can give them access to a rea-sonable quality of life. The youth ministry can help by providing a loving, supportive net-work, assisting in finding child care during school hours, and possibly setting up a mentoring system with older, more experienced mothers who understand child development and can provide advice and moral support.

Suicide

Probably every youth leader will at some point encounter at least a suicide threat from a young person. Suicide is the third most common cause of death for young people in North America today. Males with access to firearms are most likely to succeed with suicide, al-though girls are twice as likely to make the attempt. Girls tend to be less successful, because the means they use—drugs, for example—work more slowly and increase the chance of dis-covery before death occurs.

Any suicide threat should be taken seriously. The belief that those who talk about suicide don't actually commit suicide is false. If a young person says that he or she wants to commit suicide, take that person very seriously, particularly if he or she has a plan and a means for carrying it out. If the plans have gone this far, action must be taken immediately. Do not leave a suicidal person alone. Listen nonjudgmentally to what the person has to say. Contact a cri-sis line or have the young person admitted to a hospital immediately. This is a situation that cannot wait.

Some young people never tell anybody that they are planning to die, so it is essential to be familiar with the symptoms of suicidal thought. A young person contemplating suicide may exhibit some of the following symptoms:
- depression
- change in sleep patterns (sleeping either more or less)
- changes in eating habits, with weight gain or loss
- carelessness about personal appearance
- hopelessness and sadness
- violence
- delinquency
- withdrawal from social connections
- loss of interest in previously enjoyed activities
- alcohol or drug use
- talking about death
- giving away prized possessions or making a will

Often when an individual has made plans to commit suicide and has made the decision to go ahead with the act, that person will show a dramatic change in mood: from sad and withdrawn to lighthearted and happy. If a young person is displaying any of these symptoms, professional counseling should be sought immediately.

How Youth Leaders Can Help

Whenever possible, it is best to seek professional help for youth who are in crisis. Other suggestions include the following:

1. Prayer. The greatest hope for hurting youth is that of God working in their lives. Regular prayer for them, and if possible with them, opens the door for the working of the Holy Spirit.

2. Love. Many of these young people have not experienced unconditional love. It is difficult for them to believe in the love of God until they experience that love working through other human beings.

3. Acceptance. Accepting these young people with all of their faults and hurts helps them to realize that God also accepts them. This does not mean that unacceptable behavior should be accepted, but if behavior needs to be addressed, it must be addressed with love.

4. Providing a Safe Place. Many youth do not have a safe place to be during the hours between the end of school and the time their parents get home from work. Many youth programs have experienced great success in providing youth programs during this time period.

---

[1] Ron Klinger, "What Can Be Done About Absentee Fathers?" *USA Today* magazine, July 1998, p. 30.

[2] *Ibid.*

[3] James Garbarino, *Lost Boys: Why Our Sons Turn Violent and How We Can Save Them* (New York: Free Press, 1999).

CHAPTER 39

Ministry to Those Who Are Divorced—
Broken Hearts in the Body of Christ

by Jennifer Jill Schwirzer

I CAN RECALL GOING TO THE ice-skating rink as an adolescent and sailing along hand in hand with my boyfriend while the disc jockey from WOKY played Tammy Wynette's hit "Stand by Your Man." It seemed an easy enough thing to do at 13, when going steady demanded little more than wearing a boy's ID bracelet and skating around the rink with him. Another hit Wynette had in 1968 was "D-I-V-O-R-C-E." Ironic how, in the same year, she presented the dark side of the heart's desire for commitment—the fact that sometimes it doesn't last. Wynette may have been the best personification of the dilemma of divorce—the deep longing for stable, enduring love pitted against the poor odds of achieving the same. Herself a four-time divorcée, she married at 17, leaving her first husband while pregnant with their third child.[1] Maybe our relationships have never reached the tabloids, but there are similarities. Like her, we yearn for love and can't seem to hang on to it.

I grew up to become part of the baby boomer generation, a sector of people whose divorce rate skyrocketed beyond previous generations.[2] This trend was felt in the Adventist Church as well, as the divorce rate of people in their 20s and 30s doubled in the 1960s and then increased significantly again in the 1980s.[3] While the rate has decreased in the 1990s, it is by no means low. What we are left with is a large number of divorced persons and, therefore, a rich opportunity for ministry.

What does it take to minister successfully to those who are divorced? Like any problem, the gravity of it must first be understood. Then the reasons for the problem must be explored. Once these first two steps are completed, a biblical solution can be developed. Therefore, we will approach this problem in three steps: assessing the damage, discerning the cause, and finding the answer.

Assessing the Damage

In the general population of the United States there are about half as many divorces every year as there are new marriages. About 26 percent of American adults have divorced, and nearly half of the babies born today will see their parents divorce.[4] Add to this those "divorces" that cannot be computed—the breakup of nonmarried unions and the marriages that remain legally intact while they are emotionally and spiritually fractured—and a grim picture that seems to be a fulfillment of the prophecy "most people's love will grow cold" (Matt. 24:12, NASB) emerges.

At least 272 per 1,000 marriages of Adventists end in divorce.[5] While this may seem to mirror the general population closely, it must be remembered that a percentage of those were divorced before baptism. In one study only one in six Adventists had divorced since they were baptized.[6] This indicates that church membership may help lower the likelihood of divorce.

But the evidence is conflicting. One Adventist conference tracked the divorce rate of its members with the state it was located in for two years and found the rate to be almost precisely the same.[7] Statistics themselves can be misleading for a number of reasons. But whether the church's divorce rate is on par with the world or below, it is most definitely higher than God, who hates divorce (see Mal. 2:16, NASB), would have it.

Why the strong reaction on the part of God to the idea of the breakup of the marriage union? One answer lies in the fact that the bedrock of the church, and therefore the society influenced by the church is relationships of the people within the church. The accomplishment of the purpose for which God raised up the church, to bring the message of the gospel to the world, is contingent upon the demonstration of love found among His followers. Jesus said, "By this all will know that you are My disciples, if you have love for one another" (John 13:34, NKJV).

Another reason God hates divorce is that the children of divorce suffer. A child's primary need is security, which is interrupted by the breakup of the relationship that lies at the foundation of her home. Divorce often presents a demand upon children to place their loyalties upon one of two people, both of whom they love. This dilemma is compounded when parents fight openly and indulge in manipulation of the children in order to "get back" at one another—not an uncommon scenario.

Further difficulty comes when remarriage takes place. In the young mind the stepparent poses as a rival of the absent parent. Constant comparison takes place, and resentment of the stepparent can result. This scenario is of sufficient seriousness to warrant waiting until the children leave home before remarriage. Gary Sprague, founder of Kid's Hope, a ministry to children of divorce, says, "Many studies indicate that kids do better in a single-parent family than in a blended family."[8]

The wounds of the divorced persons themselves can't be ignored. Linda Hunter, editor of Focus on the Family's magazine for single parents, *Single Parent Family,* says that those who desire to minister to those who are divorced must gain access to them within the first two years after the divorce. When crisis comes, healing must follow, or the lives affected by the crisis don't proceed well. Poor choices are made because of extenuating circumstances of various kinds. Financial status is almost always worsened by divorce, and the strain of poverty can add to the emotional load. In addition, loneliness and guilt can compound the stress. Often a new relationship presents itself during this period, like a mirage in the desert, promising satisfaction but providing none. These "rebound" relationships are built upon a false foundation. In fact, the mortality rate of any and all remarriages is about 70 percent.[9]

Divorce is a time of extreme vulnerability. This includes all aspects of life, including the spiritual. Individuals often quit attending church because of this shattering experience. Adventist dropouts are four times as likely as active members to be divorced and single.[10]

Overall, divorced individuals and their children are hurting units that need compassion and support in proportion to their need. But sympathy without knowledge is cheap. These people will best be helped by others who are as informed as they are well-meaning. For this reason it is important that we know something about the cause of divorce.

Discerning the Cause

Why so much divorce? There are two places to which this question must be addressed. One, to the society at large, and two, to the individuals who experience divorce.

The rise in the general divorce rate, and the overall failure rate of marriage as a whole, is very concisely dealt with in several passages of the Bible. According to this source, human beings basically hate one another (see Titus 3:3). However, the God of the Bible does not leave human beings to themselves. He gives the gift of natural affection, which is expressed in such forms as parental, fraternal, and marital love. This natural affection, however, ebbs out of human hearts as time draws to a close. People at the end of time are described as being "without natural affection" (2 Tim. 3:3). The root cause of this death of love is that humanity is "given over" to his or her natural state of alienation without God. His or her affections are then placed upon things that are "unnatural" and "depraved" (Rom. 1:24, 26, 28, NASB). In short, people stop loving what they are supposed to love and start loving that which is forbidden. Apparently human affections have to go somewhere!

The recent rise in divorce in our culture is systemic of the overall decay of the two-parent family structure. From the 1950s to the 1980s the number of children who grew up in a home with two biological parents went from 80 percent to 50 percent. This trend began in the mid-1960s, when the divorce rate went from 10 divorces a year per 1,000 married couples to a sharp increase that peaked at 23 per 1,000 in 1979.[11] "These figures do not account for the number of children born out of wedlock who grow up with a single parent, or for the children of cohabiting couples.

This culture's newfound freedom to love whom we want when we want, which purportedly provides freedom and independence for the adults involved, has resulted in little more than harm to the children. Children in single-parent families are six times as likely to be poor and two to three times as likely to have emotional and behavioral problems. They are also more likely to drop out of school, get pregnant as teenagers, abuse drugs, be sexually abused, and get in trouble with the law.[12] The point is this: God gave us, in the structure of the two-parent family, a haven of well-being and safety. Our deviance from this model shows a lack of regard for the ones most harmed by that deviance—the children. This lack of regard is a result of ungodly principles replacing the biblical principles of unselfishness and sacrifice. Studies show that "fewer than half of all adult Americans today regard the idea of sacrifice for others as a positive moral virtue."[13]

Addressing the question of cause to the individual, we see that Adventists divorce for reasons different from that of the general population. Since adultery is traditionally the only acceptable reason for divorce in Adventism, it is cited as a cause more often than any other. Second on the list is irresponsibility on the part of the spouse. Then come the temperament issues: difficulty getting along, coldness and indifference on the part of one spouse. Lower on the list are such tangibles as alcohol abuse and money problems. Overall, the causes for divorce cited by Adventists were rational rather than material.[14] But we shouldn't overlook the fact that divorce is more common in lower-income families.[15] The stress of poverty can bring out the worst in people.

Finding the Answer

What can be done to heal the wounds of divorce? The answer to this question must come in two phases: prevention and cure. Preventing divorce is the single most effective step in "healing" the would-be victims. Cure entails dealing with the damage that could not, or would not, be prevented. As the healing hands of Jesus, we are called to both.

Some are of the opinion that the increased independence of women is the cause for increase in divorce, tracing this independence back to the equal rights movement and greater opportunities for women in the workplace. The proposed preventative then becomes women staying home with their children and remaining dependent upon their "breadwinner" husbands. There are some elements of truth to this argument, but the fact is that many, if not most, women work because they *have* to. Yes, dependence may prevent divorce in the same way that a chastity belt prevents immorality, but what motives are behind the right behavior? Rather, we should see the increased independence of women as an opportunity for them to stay married for better reasons.

Prevention of divorce within the church starts with church members dealing faithfully and lovingly with those who are at high risk. This entails having a spirit of loving accountability within the church family. If a married member is known to be committing adultery, for instance, that person needs "carefrontation" much more than he or she needs to be ignored. Jesus said, "If your brother sins, go and reprove him in private" (Matt. 18:15, NASB). He went on to counsel us to take another with us if that failed, and then, as a last resort, to take it to the church. In the majority of cases the first step will have the effect of redeeming the brother or sister in the wrong, and no further dealing will be necessary. Although adultery, being the most common cause of divorce among Adventists, will be the thing that most often calls for action, there are other causes that can be addressed, such as abuse and neglect. Obvious signs of these things should never be ignored.

Gary Sprague has suggested that getting married should be harder than it is. This, he believes, would result in few marriages and therefore fewer divorces. He suggests that pastors require eight weeks of premarital counseling before they perform a ceremony. Remarriage, says Sprague, should be even harder. He tells of a remarriage seminar in Fullerton, California, conducted by Pastor Gary Richmond in which 40 percent of the participants decided not to marry after attending.[16] These men are discovering the same fact that Ellen White warned of years ago: "Marriage, in a majority of cases, is a most galling yoke. There are thousands that are mated but not matched. . . . Make haste slowly in the choice of a companion."[17]

Regardless of how successful we are in preventing divorce, there will always be opportunities to minister to those for whom divorce is a reality. This presents a dilemma for Adventists. Often adultery is involved, in which case the guilty party must be disciplined. Because adultery is traditionally the only acceptable reason for divorce, there is a certain amount of pressure to find a guilty party. When the couple divorces for reasons other than adultery, such as abuse, discipline may or may not be called for as well. The church is currently confused as to whether divorce itself constitutes a reason for discipline. Policies differ from church to church, and sometimes from case to case. Divorce within the church can become a whirlwind of side-taking, faultfinding, and condemnation. It is difficult to minister effectively in this environment.

Remarriage presents an even greater problem. Jesus said, "Every one who divorces his wife, except for the cause of unchastity, makes her commit adultery; and whoever marries a divorced woman commits adultery" (Matt. 5:32, NASB). What He meant by this was that people were still married in God's eyes unless their partner committed the marriage act with someone else. Should the church discipline those who marry again after divorce when the divorce was for reasons other than adultery? Apparently so. Because the need for discipline is so intertwined with the need for ministry, ministry to those who are divorced is often fraught with alienation and stress. Yet if discipline is handled correctly, even those disciplined will often admit that it was a blessing from God.

As stated before, many Adventists leave church at the time of divorce. Surveys indicate that there are two factors that cause these dropouts to leave: how church members deal with divorce, and members' attitudes toward single adults.[18] On both fronts a sense of being ostracized can make the church a very uncomfortable place to be.

Regardless of the difficulties that attend divorce, we should minister to those who have fallen prey. The broken pieces of families should be taken under wing. God is "father of the fatherless and a judge for the widows" (Ps. 68:5, NASB). Plenty of victims of divorce are purely *innocent* victims, and even those not innocent should be loved back to right standing with God. The ones who need the most support and care fall into two growing categories: the single parent, and the children of divorce.

Linda Hunter advises, "As soon as a single parent walks through the doors of a church, embrace them, love them, and assess what the needs are."[19] She suggests that a primary factor in their recovery will be the ability to fellowship with other single parents. The magazine *Single Parent Family* is an excellent resource for those who would like to read about the experience of other single parents. These parents often feel isolated, especially in churches that are "couples-oriented." The right resources, including small groups and reading materials, will help diffuse this sense of aloneness.

Hunter also advises that single parents find a ministry of their own. She suggests that this be something that provides a change from the day-to-day scenery. When she was a newly single parent with small children, she admits that "I didn't need to be in the nursery. I got involved in an inner-city ministry. This gave me a sense of being a viable member of the church without being put in leadership right away."[20]

Social events can't be overlooked as a means of facilitating healing in the life of a divorced person, who often feels like a "fifth wheel" at events for married people. But the church should be careful to avoid letting itself become a "couple club" by encouraging families to invite a single parent home for a meal. A well-organized hospitality program is needed, especially in a larger church, to make sure no one falls between the cracks. Often a simple meal, cooked by someone else, and adult conversation will do wonders to boost the morale of someone for whom loneliness is a constant cloud.

Divorced parents can't be ministered to apart from their children. In addition to their own grief and despair, these parents must help their children process theirs. Doesn't this constitute a call to the body of Christ to "bear one another's burdens, and thus fulfill the law of Christ" (Gal. 6:2, NASB)? When one member suffers, do not all members suffer? Shouldn't the overburden of one be the responsibility of another? Much can be done to help a child through the stages of grief and the necessary adjustment to their new life with one parent.

Barbara Schiller, author of the book *Just Me and the Kids,* says the child will pass through two basic stages of grief: early grief, which includes numbness and denial, and acute grief, which occurs when the child comes out of denial, often becoming depressed and emotionally distraught. Finally, after passing through these stages comes the phase of integration of loss and grief when the child is able to talk about the loss and regain self-worth.[21]

Nothing can remove the need for these grieving stages, but programs such as "The Building Blocks of Recovery," put on by Kid's Hope, can help support the child through them. Gary Sprague, who presents the program, helps kids work through the stages of grief, leaving them with the thought that in heaven there will be no more divorce, for God will "wipe away every tear from their eyes; and there shall no longer be any mourning, or crying, or pain; the first things have passed away" (Rev. 21:4, NASB).

We can all look forward to that time. The rending asunder of families in divorce will soon be a thing of the past. But now it is a present reality all around us, a heartache and a challenge, yes, but an opportunity for ministry nonetheless.

---

[1] http://mrshowbiz.go.com/people/tammywynette/content/Bio.html

[2] http://www.cdc.gov/nchs/releases/95facts/95sheets/fs_439s.html

[3] Monte Sahlin and Norma Sahlin, *A New Generation of Adventist Families* (Portland, Oreg.: Center for Creative Ministry, 1997), p. 123.

[4] *Ibid.,* p. 120.

[5] *Ibid.,* p. 121.

[6] *Ibid.*

[7] *Ibid.*

[8] Telephone interview with Gary Sprague, September 1999.

[9] Telephone interview with Linda Hunter, September 1999.

[10] Sahlin, p. 136.

[11] Barbara Dafoe Whitehead, "Dan Quayle Was Right," *Atlantic Monthly,* April 1993, p. 4.

[12] *Ibid.,* p. 1.

[13] *Ibid.,* p. 7.

[14] Sahlin, pp. 128, 131.

[15] *Ibid.,* p. 235.

[16] Telephone interview with Gary Sprague, September 1999.

[17] Ellen G. White, *The Adventist Home* (Nashville: Southern Pub. Assn., 1952), p. 44.

[18] Sahlin, p. 136.

[19] Telephone interview with Linda Hunter, September 1999.

[20] *Ibid.*

[21] Barbara Schiller, "A Grip on Grief," *Single Parent Family,* August 1995, pp. 8, 9.

CHAPTER 40

Ministering to Young Singles

by Regina Reaves Hayden

Y OU'RE THE NEW YOUTH PASTOR, and this is your first Sabbath at your assigned church. Already informed that you have eight senior youth, ages 17-19, in a
quickly dying youth ministry (your goal is to bring it back to life and make it grow),
you've also been given charge to launch a young adult ministry. There are eight young adults
in this small congregation, all single, ranging in age from 21 to 30. Rumor has it that they are
frustrated with the church and feel that it's not meeting their important needs. They feel that
the church does not understand how difficult it is to be a young single Christian in today's
world. The youth group has a similar perspective.

In light of this information and because of the small number of young people in each group,
it seems fitting to combine the classes first, then separate them once the numbers increase.

You breathe a sigh of relief. A problem solved, yes? You feel borderline brilliant until
you start contemplating the various needs of these vibrant young people. How will the two
groups blend? The eight youth are singles, too, but their needs differ from young adult singles. Then there's the age difference. Although the ages seem close enough, some are really
miles apart in personal goals and philosophies, spiritual focus, and maturity. What approach
should you take in ministering to these two similar yet distinctive groups?

But wait, you've overlooked an important bit of demographic information: two of your
young adults are single parents.

One of the biggest factors that draw youth and young adults to church is the social atmosphere. Church for them is a place where they can meet, connect, and network with other
young people. For young singles this networking is more crucial than for couples or those
who have significant family connections in the church. Being single, for some, extends beyond not having a special friend of the opposite sex. Some singles are alone in other aspects—they're new to the area, they haven't accumulated many friends or acquaintances,
their family lives in another state. Although the church is not a dating service, what better
place for Seventh-day Adventist Christian young people to meet other young people who
hold the same religious beliefs and ideals?

What often happens is that not enough programs hold the interest of young singles and
also contain the necessary spiritual emphasis to help root and ground them in their faith. I
could fill this chapter with numerous statistics and philosophical information, but none of that
will assist you in ministering to this special group. You will probably find most of that information in the other chapters of this book. The first step is to find out what young singles want

from the church, how they define church. Once we understand what these young people are really searching for, we will explore solutions for a positive, effective ministry.

Understanding Young Adventist Singles

In a roundtable discussion several youth and young adults share a sampling of the spiritual and social expectations of young Seventh-day Adventist singles.

Young Adventist Singles Want to Be of the Church, Not Set Apart

"Why is it necessary to separate young singles from the rest of the church? I don't understand the purpose of singles ministries. They're just social clubs, and the events make you feel as if you're on an auction block. It can be very embarrassing sometimes."—Carmen, 32.

"I agree. We're looking for the same things as other people in the church. We want to grow spiritually and build a better relationship with Christ. Why should we be made to feel different? If we don't learn to totally love Jesus, we can't effectively love someone else anyway."—Kyla, 18.

Young Adventist Singles Want to Be Actively Involved in Other Ministries of the Church

"Give us opportunities to become actively involved with the ministries of the church. How can we be the church of tomorrow, or today even, if we are not given responsibilities that make us feel like we're a part of our church family? One of the reasons people clamor for singles ministries is for something to do. We want to be active in our church. Select us as deacons, elders, speakers, teachers, and leaders. We don't mind being busy. Some of the loneliness from being single is for lack of having avenues for involvement."—Sean, 31.

"Young people have good ideas and many talents to share. Sometimes the church forgets that. If you want to know how we feel and what our needs are, get to know us individually. I know my pastor personally because he takes the time to talk to me and get to know me as a person. Let young people participate on the church board. Not just one youth representative. Different age groups have different needs. I would suggest selecting from categories of 17-19, 20-25, 26-32."—Toccara, 18.

Young Adventist Singles Want Opportunities to Meet Other Young Singles Through Social Activities

"Singles ministries can provide positive ways for single young people to meet other single young people in a wholesome, safe atmosphere. We want to have fun sometimes, not all church stuff."—Devon, 17.

"Have more singles retreats with good speakers—ones that can hold our attention and who we can relate to, who are down-to-earth. Include planned games for us to interact with each other so we won't isolate ourselves with our own cliques or just hang with people we already know. There needs to be a variety of seminars that will help us develop a closer walk with Christ. And invite other churches to the functions. We get bored hanging with the same people all the time. Sometimes churches act like they're in competition with each other instead of trying to get together and make it a joint effort. We're all after the same thing, aren't we? If other young people are invited to do things with us sometimes, we may not hop around to other churches so much in order to meet people."—Toccara, 18.

"Don't forget about single parents. We want to participate too. Our responsibilities sometimes get in the way of our ability to be involved in some activities, but we have just as much right to be included with singles programs as other singles. People tend to exclude us. Sure, our needs are a little different because of our situations and responsibilities, but we do have needs spiritually and socially."—Sheila, 29.

Young Adventist Singles Prefer That Singles Ministries Focus More on Being a Ministry and Not a Social Club

"What I think is lacking is that singles ministries aren't really ministries. They provide opportunities to just hang out and meet people. Which is good, but we want to be active in other things, too, like evangelism. Being a Christian is more than just socializing. We need to do more ministry things. When you do outreach things together, study together, and pray together, you get to see another side of the person you might be interested in meeting on a personal level."—David, 26.

"I'll tell what we want: more evangelism, more revivals, more Weeks of Prayer. Week of Prayer is usually just once a year when there are 52 weeks in a year to choose from. Have it several times a year. I really enjoy Weeks of Prayer. These types of programs give us more opportunities to evangelize and witness and, of course, *to meet people.*"—Toccara, 18.

Young Adventist Singles Do Not Want to Be Pressured Into Relationships or by Others' Expectations

"I am so glad we're having this discussion. The church does not realize how pressured we sometimes feel being single, especially with some types of singles ministry programs that are planned. One church I visit occasionally actually has a date auction every year. How embarrassing! Once young people become involved in singles ministries, the heat is on. We're expected to find a mate because the stage is set. And if we don't, then there must be something wrong with us. And please, no matchmaking. Let us meet someone on our own; let relationships evolve on their own. Careful consideration is important when planning programs for singles so as not to offend anyone or make them feel uncomfortable."—Carmen, 32.

Young Singles Ministry Solutions

You've heard some of the voices of young singles. This is just a sampling. To know the thoughts and feelings of the young singles in your congregation, ask them. Have a special Sabbath afternoon luncheon or potluck; invite small groups at a time to your home for a meal and/or fellowship; plan a rap session during an AYS meeting on the subject.

Where do we go from here? Ministering to young singles must involve well-balanced programming. It is safe to say that young Adventist singles desire not only a social atmosphere conducive to interaction and networking with other young singles, but also programs and activities with a spiritual emphasis. Here are other suggestions to enhance your ministry to the young singles in your church.

Build an Atmosphere of Acceptance and Respect

People of all ages want to belong and be accepted, whether at school, at work, at church, or in their social environments. They also want to be respected. Make an effort to incorporate acceptance and respect in ministering to all levels of singlehood. As stated earlier, being single entails more than a person's not having a special friend of the opposite sex. There are some singles that enjoy being single and simply maintaining platonic relationships. They may not wish to be in a serious relationship at this stage of their lives. Their needs might centralize on combating boredom or loneliness, having enough involvement in enjoyable activities, finding opportunities to interact and network with others who have similar interests as they, or just wanting to feel needed. The church can help them fill all of these needs.

Helping young people to feel accepted means involving them in all aspects of the church's ministry. Give them positions of leadership in the church. Trust their ideas and gifts, and respect their judgment on issues that directly concern and affect them. When we are involved and busy with God's ministry we seldom have time to feel lonely or bored. "You may never be lonesome, never feel that you are alone, if you will take Jesus as your Companion and your Everlasting Friend."*

Invite Other Groups of Youth and Young Adult Singles to Participate in Your Group's Activities

Some churches are reluctant to advertise the programs and activities of other church congregations for fear it will pull their members away from their programs. Planning ahead can solve this problem. Send a special invitation well in advance to one or more of the Adventist churches in your area to join your singles group in a special social event, evangelistic effort, revival meeting, or Week of Prayer. Your singles will then have the chance to network with other singles in the area.

Take the idea a step further by inviting an out-of-state group to participate in a weekend retreat at your church. Keep it simple and rustic, allowing a relaxed, friendly atmosphere. If the church has a gymnasium, camp out there in sleeping bags. If the weather is nice, camp outdoors at a nearby camping area. Another alternative is for individual families to house the out-of-state singles for the weekend. Provide meals at the church so there is no hardship on the hosting families. Begin the weekend with a Friday night vesper program filled with music, testimonies, and prayer. Invite a guest speaker for Sabbath. Incorporate drama presentations. Spend Sabbath afternoon in such evangelism activities as feeding the homeless, street corner ministry, taking a program to the nursing home or children's hospital, door-to-door evangelism, or passing out tracts. Sabbath evening can be filled with fun activities—e.g., a social or moonlight tour of the nearest city. On Sunday morning hold a prayer breakfast. Set a date to take your group to visit the guest group in their hometown.

Develop Small-Group Ministry Activities and Prayer Groups

Doing things together as a complete group is great. However, consider developing small-group activities. Small-group settings can be more intimate and friendly and provide a less-intimidating atmosphere for those who are shy of crowds. Small-group ministries also give more individuals the opportunity to be heard and acknowledged. The spiritual atmosphere is enhanced as well, because individuals who might not otherwise speak up and share their spiritual thoughts and experiences in a larger group are more comfortable doing so in a small group.

A popular expression states that "a family that prays together stays together." Prayer is important for any ministry and for those involved in that ministry. We can accomplish nothing without it. The church is a family, and young singles are a unit in that family. Young David from our roundtable discussion made an important statement: "When we do outreach things together, study together, and pray together, you get to see another side of the person you might be interested in meeting on a personal level." Young singles are looking for like-minded companions. Small study groups, evangelism groups, and prayer groups allow us to get a closer look at a person's spiritual heart. We can learn things about an individual that may not be shared in another setting, gaining more insight to the person's thoughts and personality. At the same time, there's opportunity for spiritual growth through sharing the Word of God.

Getting young people in the habit of studying and praying together in the church family environment helps to prepare them for continuing the tradition in their future homes when the time comes.

Involve Young Singles in Other Activities in the Church as Part of the Church Family

"For as we have many members in one body, and all members have not the same office: so we, being many, are one body in Christ, and every one members one of another" (Rom. 12:4, 5). If the church, therefore, is a body, the body does not take new cells and put them together somewhere else to develop. The body needs all cells to function. Likewise, the church needs all of the various groups of the church working together to function well. Young singles do not always want to be distinguished as "singles"; sometimes they prefer to be "members" of a family. They are family; we are all family, "members one of another."

Invite the young singles of the church to participate in other activities—spiritual and social—of the church body without the distinguishing title of "singles."

Include Young Single Parents in All Programs and Activities

The number of single parents has escalated worldwide. Separation and divorce have become society's trends for marriages today. When a young person becomes a single parent, regardless of the circumstances that place them in that position, they are still single. So don't leave them out because they have the responsibility of a child or children. Help them to be able to participate by coordinating day-care services for them or by having some events at which children are allowed.

In addition, be aware of other needs and trials single parents face: the feeling of loss if single parenthood is the result of divorce or death; fear of the magnificent responsibility of raising a child alone, managing life alone; recovering from abuse; embarrassment over their situation or being made to feel embarrassed by lack of compassion from others; sadness and hurt.

Some church bodies are reluctant even to acknowledge the single parents in their congregations unless it is through a show of feeling sorry for the individuals. Some feel that if they acknowledge single parents or bring them to others' attention they are condoning their situations. It is not our responsibility to judge another's life. God is judge. A single parent may be a victim of abuse, possibly life-threatening. They may have been abandoned by their spouse. And they may simply have made poor judgments. Our loving Savior's arms are always open to each and every one of us. Regardless of our circumstances or spiritual condition, He—and He alone—can heal and save. So let us be embracing examples of Jesus' unconditional love.

Incorporate workshops on parenting and planning for parenthood that couples, single parents, and those who are *just single* can attend together. We can all learn from each other. Workshops on building healthy relationships are another area that can be shared by various groups in the church.

Have Fun!

Just as a singles ministry should not be all social but include more ministry activities, it should also not be all church and no social aspect. Plan fun activities. You don't always have to be cooped up in a building for a social on Saturday night. Go bowling, roller or ice-skating, spend time sightseeing together in local museums or around your city. Exercise together and play together. Make day trips to other cities together for shopping sprees, dine out, go to Christian concerts and plays together. Singles will have a lot of ideas for activities themselves.

Involve several in the planning and logistics. Don't put all of the responsibility on one person or just a few.

Conclusion

Young singles have spiritual, social, and emotional needs, as do all of us. As youth ministers and leaders we can enhance their experiences in these areas of life through careful and considerate planning. Make church enjoyable. Spiritual activities can be fun, and fun activities can be spiritual. Church is not a dating service, but it can be a place in which young singles feel at home and can meet and network with other like-minded young singles without pressure or stress.

---

* Ellen G. White, *Mind, Character, and Personality* (Nashville: Southern Pub. Assn., 1977), vol. 2, p. 632.

CHAPTER 41

Cyberia:
Youth Ministries' New Frontier

by A. Allan Martin, Ph.D.

S TAR TREK: THE NEXT GENERATION. I became a "Trekker" years ago, but just recently became fully immersed in it by watching all of the episodes during the months
of round-the-clock feeding of our newborn. I especially enjoyed the introduction for
the show, the U.S.S. *Enterprise* zipping through the cosmos and Captain Picard's resonant
voice booming, "Space, the final frontier . . . going where no man has gone before."

What if youth ministry was to do its own spin-off of *Star Trek: NG?* We could call it
YouthWorker Trek. We could explore the "black hole" into which 38 percent of our
Adventist youth continue to disappear.[1] Maybe an exciting episode would even venture to the
edges of the Adventist galaxy; entering the worlds of the unchurched and non-Christian
young person. In what corner of the universe might we find this next generation of youth
without Christ? I would guess our space travel would lead to Cyberia.[2] The intro for
YouthWorker Trek could be something like "CyberSpace, the new frontier . . . going where
few youth ministries have gone before."

Techno Realities of a Cyber Generation

Demographic scanners say they are there in large numbers. Cyberspace is big enough for
them, all 46 million of them, many who are alien to Christianity. Name them "techno
surfers," tag them "screenagers," call them what you will. But know that 70-80 percent of
today's young people, ages 12-24, are in front of a computer every day. Subscriber-based online services, such as America Online, CompuServe, and Prodigy, estimate that 50-60 percent of their user base are families with kids 18 and younger. Many, if not most, secondary
and higher education institutions provide their students with some form of online access.
Teens and young adults comprise the largest age group on the Internet.[3]

The commercial sector is not lost to the fact that this new generation is nearly as avid
about cyberspace as their parents were about television and their grandparents were about
radio. "Kids love the Internet; it's hot," notes Kathleen Criner of the consulting firm Criner-
Wilson. "Research suggests that kids love their computers more than they love their TVs."[4]

"As TV was to the baby boomers, computers are to the Xers," comments Larry Chase,
president of the Online Advertising Agency.[5]

Techno reality clearly points to a young, wired generation populating Cyberia by the tens of millions. Secular corporations have already rocketed into cyberspace, eager to harvest the $100-125 billion young people will spend annually.[6] The nation's largest communication companies are propelling online components onto the Internet to complement their current programming. From cinema to television to radio to magazines to newspapers, almost all have their Cyberian counterpart aimed at reaching screenagers.

Techno reality also says younger generations are hands-on, interactive, and intelligent. Dissatisfied with being passive observers, young people today are looking for involvement and interaction. Compared with other media, cyber communication is more personalized and relational, whether by radio, video, message boards, chat lines, or e-mail. Online services are quickly becoming the telephone of the twenty-first century.[7] And youth are intensely interested in this new technology. They have computer savvy. Screenagers wear their techno intelligence like a badge of honor. The Internet is their social revolutionary platform.[8]

Finally, techno reality reveals screenagers searching for authentic community. With many of them latchkey children, and more than 50 percent of their families experiencing divorce, today's youth seek open, genuine relationships wherever such can be found.[9] Living in a hostile, real-time society often too dangerous, too prejudicial, too superficial, and/or too critical, screenagers are building their own relational communities in cyberspace. Even with the perils of the Internet, many youth and young adults connect with others online, desperately seeking community.

It is clear that secular satellites decorate the cybersky, selling everything from sportswear to sex. Capitalistic corporations enter cyberspace to vie for teen pockets. Educational institutions enter the Internet to capture techno surfer smarts. But what about their hearts? Are screenagers souls doomed to be lost in space?

Connecting With Christ in Cyberspace?

Over the past decade there has been an exponential-type growth of churches that have gone online. From a handful of Christian cyber sites a year ago, there is estimated more than 6,000 churches that can now be found in Cyberia.[10] Cyberspace provides an excellent central location for Christians from all parts of the world to communicate, create cyber communities, coordinate global projects and evangelism efforts. The Internet helps scores of people share/exchange views on Christianity or religion around the globe.

There are thousands of religious Web sites where people congregate to gain knowledge, establish Web traditions, chat, or read about historical and current happenings for their faith community. But interestingly enough, most of those religious sites are not intentionally geared toward youth. Although there are a growing number of cyberlocations created for Christian screenagers, very few places in Cyberia are aimed at introducing new generations to Christ. For those Seventh-day Adventist youth workers who dare enter the new frontier, a substantial challenge and adventure awaits. Given the relative paucity of Internet Web sites for youth and young adult ministry and the enormous population of screenagers in cyberspace, the opportunities are infinite. Adventist youth workers may find the Internet beneficial to their ministry in countless ways; networking, resourcing/planning, research, and evangelism are some of the advantages cyberspace offers them.

Networking

Cyber youth workers find that the Internet allows them to stay in touch with young people and provides avenues through which to support them. Mike Atkinson, Webmaster for the youth ministry publishing company Youth Specialties (http://www.YouthSpecialities.com), asked youth workers how they use the Internet in their ministry. Here are some of the responses he received:[11]

- "I spend extra time with my youth when I help them find information for school papers and projects on the Internet."
- "This is really the spinal cord of our current college ministry, and increasingly the communication network for younger students. E-mail allows instantaneous communication to almost anywhere in the world that has access to the Web. I can send a note to my students here in Houston, or to a college student of mine who is student teaching in Japan within seconds . . . and it is virtually free."
- "I started last year keeping contact with college students away from home. I also send out a general e-mail that includes a devotion and any announcements that might interest them. Online services have enabled me to keep in contact with the college kids like never before. In fact, this is the first time our church has been able to sustain a young adult group for more than one summer. It seems that people (myself included) are willing to send e-mail when they don't feel they have time to write or money to call."

Communication and interpersonal contact are a main stay for any successful ministry, and for the cyber intelligent youth worker, the Internet provides a powerful communication tool.

In addition, cyberspace allows the youth worker to network with peers. Youth leaders around the world can communicate with each other.[12] For example; the Association of Adventist Youth Ministry Professionals is connecting youth workers worldwide via their Web site (www.aaymp.org). Discussion groups can be formed centered on specialty youth ministry issues. With the international availability to talk shop, a global perspective of youth ministry can be gleaned. Communicating via cyberspace can be a source of support, accountability, and inspiration for youth ministers.

Resourcing/Planning

"I am able to get information on lodging, sites to see, directions, ministry opportunities, etc., from the Internet."[13] Given the wealth of information available on the Internet, many youth leaders find that they can plan retreats, access speakers/musicians, order materials, and schedule travel online.

The typical youth worker has very limited time, which often does not include reviewing ministry resources. Some may not even know how or where to access youth ministry catalogs. Cyberspace offers a means by which youth leaders can peruse the latest resources, sample products, and read recent reviews on materials they may purchase.[14]

Research

Clearly, youth culture is continually changing and evolving. The Internet can help youth workers be well versed in the latest trends in youth culture and youth ministry. Here is one example: "Search engines led me to sites and pages with volumes of information helpful in my ministry. For example, I used 'teenagers' as a key word, and came across several outstanding articles on youth gangs: recruitment, colors, dress code, rank, etc."[15]

Media companies are online in full force, eager to entice young consumers online. Right on the pulse of youth culture, media Web sites ranging from movies to music to magazines can educate a youth minister who is willing to surf."[16]

Evangelism

Following Jesus' model of relational evangelism, youth workers, who trek into cyberspace, enter the world of the screenager and can there be used by the Holy Spirit to connect young hearts to Christ. Surfing into cyberspace makes a poignant statement to new generations.

Bill Broadway comments, "Having a Web site proves to the new generation of computer-literate faith seekers that a religious institution is serious about reaching out to them."[17]

But if a youth minister comes off smelling like a cyber televangelist, screenagers will scramble. They can sniff condescension a light-year away. Marketing has largely failed with young adults.[18] Those who try to sell religion will quickly find that screenagers have the option to delete them from the face of their virtual universe. Vendors are a dime a dozen. Screenagers are seeking sincerity in cyberspace. Genuine concern, blind to the trappings of image, can be a compelling evangelistic launch pad.

In many ways cyberspace is blind; blind to age, color, creed, country, social status, and gender. Here youth have anonymity, giving them the chance to explore and grapple with ideas. Ideas are the commodity by which cyber relationships are formed. There can be no assumptions about skin color, gender, or socioeconomic status. The safety of such computer-mediated conversation can reduce self-consciousness and promote brutal, sometimes rude, raw honesty.[19] Cyberspace also fosters community between people who might not otherwise meet or chat. Personal relationships in Cyberia can be based on substance rather than physical appearance, popularity, or power. With a real-time society so caught up with image, the ideal mirages that are impossible to live up to, cyberspace can be a nonjudgmental relational oasis for young people. In such an oasis, relational evangelism can flourish.

Cyber Resources for Youth and Young Adult Ministries

There is a plethora of resources on the Internet that can enhance the ministry of Adventist youth workers. Although the vast network that is the Internet can be rather daunting, skillful use of any search engine will find a wide array of youth ministry sites to surf. Among the more notable engines, cross search (www.crosssearch.com) is a search engine dedicated to locating religious sites. With the list of ministry resources continuing to grow, search engines can help one deal with the information deluge.[20]

With quickly developing technology, the Internet is going beyond mere graphic capability. Other cyber communication abilities are upgrading rapidly. In addition to e-mail, message boards, and online purchasing, many sites now have chat, video, and live audio capabilities. Live video conferencing, distance learning, Webcasting, and other technologies are refining the interactive horizon. Among the best youth ministry resource sites is www.youthpastor.com. In addition, dre.am VISION ministries (www.tagnet.org/dym/) offers a selected directory of Web sites (www.tagnet.org/dym/wildweb.html) that are helpful in youth/young adult ministry.

YO! SaltyFish in Cyberspace

One vision that has emerged from Adventist young people is that of a Web site created by and geared toward youth and young adults. Via cyberspace Adventist youth dream of creating community with their believing peers, but further, look to interact and befriend nonbelieving screenagers. Think of it—a cyber site by Adventist young people, dedicated to worship, community, and reaching out to their online peers who have yet to meet Christ. Sounds like church—cyber church, that is.

Just imagine Adventist screenagers creating a site that can become a regular cyber stop for young people. Ideas would be easily exchanged, youth to youth, youth workers to young person. Youth from Baltimore to Bombay could share conversations and Christ with many others. Student missionaries, with access, would be able to surf the cybersite that would allow them to talk to their friends, share their experiences, and stave off homesickness. Maybe parents could chat with their screenager, too, at a fraction of the regular phone bill. Links to other Web sites could put Christian lifestyle resources at the screenager's fingertips, resources ranging from Home Study International course sites, to mission service sites, to a listing of Christian music concert schedules, to colleges, graduate and postgraduate programs. And in the midst of this cyberspace, Adventist youth workers could be in the mix, encouraging, counseling, nurturing . . . ministering to screenagers.

It's not just a dream—it is reality! YO! (www.youth-online.org)[21] and SaltyFish (www.saltyfish.net)[22] are evidence of dreams and visions coming to fruition! And this is only the beginning of a new millennium of cyber ministries. YO! and SaltyFish not only reach out to non-Christian screenagers, but also empower Adventist youth and young adults to use their talents and build relationships for ministry.[23] In cyberspace youth workers can do ministry with screenagers instead of to them. The vast new frontier calls for team ministry. It calls for community. In cyberspace youth and young adults can realize their role as ministers and join forces with youth workers.

Christless screenagers are looking for genuine people. They are seeking ideas that build relationships, blind faith that heals the heart, and community that is authentic. Cyberspace dares Adventist youth workers to team up with believing screenagers and together fulfill the gospel commission in a new frontier. A cyber universe filled with Christless screenagers awaits. Warp 7 to Cyberia? As Captain Picard would say . . . "Engage!"

---

[1] A. Allan Martin, "The ABCs of Ministry to Generations X, Y, and Z," *Journal of Adventist Youth Ministry,* Winter/Spring 1995, pp. 37-46. A. Allan Martin, Ph.D., and his wife, Deirdre, are cofounders of dre.am VISION ministries, a resourcing agency dedicated to empowering and nurturing young people in Christian lifestyle and leadership. Allan is also a clinical psychologist and serves at the North American Division as the special assistant for young adult ministries.

[2] Cyberia refers to the imaginary, interactive "worlds" created by computers. It is used interchangeably with "cyberspace," "virtual world," or "virtual reality." Cyberia is the interactive environment where the global community of computer-linked individuals and groups live. Cyberia is derived from "cyberspace," a catchword that is now used synonymously with the Internet. This article assumes that the reader has a basic knowledge of what the Internet is. For

those who are clueless, an excellent basic Internet primer is: Q. Schultz, *Internet for Christians: Everything You Need to Start Cruising the Net Today!* rev. ed. (Muskegon, Mich.: Gospel Films Publications, 1996).

[3] These statistics reflect demographic estimates for the United States alone and do not take into account the worldwide youth use of Internet services. The statistics are based on data cited in J. B. Cohen, "Segmenting the Screenager," *Editor & Publisher,* Apr. 27, 1996, pp. 82-84, 98; R. Thau, "Reality Bytes," *Marketing Tools,* January/February 1995, pp. 68-70, 74, 75; I. Woolward, "The Care and Feeding of Screenagers for Fun and Profit," *The Red Herring,* December 1994. Online: www.herring.com/mag/issue16/care.html.

[4] Cohen.

[5] Thau.

[6] Cohen; Woolward, online.

[7] Anyone who has worked extensively with young people or has raised teenagers of their own will attest to the love affair between teens and the telephone.

[8] Woolward, online.

[9] Martin.

[10] B. Broadway, "Flocking to the Web: Religious Groups Great and Small Reach Out to the Believer and the Seeker Through the Internet," Washington *Post,* Sept. 28, 1996, p. B7.

[11] M. Atkinson, "How the Internet Can Help Your Ministry," seminar conducted at the Youth Specialties National Youth Workers Convention, Anaheim, California, Oct. 31, 1996.

[12] "How Youth Workers Are Using Online Services and What the Downsides Are," *YouthWorker,* Winter 1996, pp. 46-50.

[13] Atkinson.

[14] Q. Schultze, "An Internet Primer: Why You Should Get Online, and How to Get There," *YouthWorker,* Winter 1996, pp. 33-44.

[15] Schultze.

[16] *Ibid.*

[17] 1996, in his article "Religious Groups Great and Small Reach Out to the Believer and the Seeker Through the Internet."

[18] Thau; Woolward.

[19] Cohen.

[20] Q. Schultze, *Internet for Christians;* "Web Site Just for You: A Resource List," *YouthWorker,* Winter 1996, pp. 52-56.

[21] Youth Online (YO!) is a cyber arena for Christian teens and young adults to interact with their peers. YO! is also the cyber home for YouthNet, which provides opportunities to serve Christ through mission, social action, and ministry. Finally YO! serves as an informational resource site for the Association of Adventist Youth Ministry Professionals (AAYMP), connecting youth workers, youth pastors, and youth/young adult ministry specialists worldwide. YO! is sponsored by the North American Division Youth/Young Adult Ministries Department of the Seventh-day Adventist Church.

[22] SaltyFish.net is the official Web site of CONNECT, a young adult network of ministries and teams, personally sharing the gospel through communication, empowerment, and community. CONNECT aims to equip young adults for local spiritual impact through discipling, resourcing, and supporting grassroots initiatives. CONNECT is our generation's relational commitment to reveal Jesus Christ to each other and our world.

[23] Martin.

Youth Group Web Page Tips

Here are some tips and suggestions from James C. Moberg to help you start creating an online presence for your youth ministry.[*]

1. Don't use Microsoft Frontpage or Publisher as your HTML editor.

Netscape Composer (part of Netscape Communicator) and AOLPress are both FREE and create more sensible and standardized codes that make for faster loading and better-indexed Web pages. A great non-WYSIWYG recommendation is HomeSite, which comes complete with HTML helps and tag wizards to help you create your page.

2. Don't use your student's full names, e-mail/home addresses, or phone numbers on any Web page.

This could potentially get you into a lot of trouble with parents. There is always the possibility that any sexual predator could use the information from your site to choose his/her next target. Posted e-mail addresses could potentially get added to lots of spam lists, and this would not be good for students who use their parents' e-mail account. Protect your youth by maintaining some anonymity, and use only their first name. (You may use an initial from their last name when two or more youth share the same first name.)

3. Get a separate e-mail account for the youth group's Web page.

Consider the e-mail address similar to a phone number that will not change or be discontinued when students and staff members move. I've found that youth pastors often use their personal e-mail accounts for the Web site, then move to a different church, and the e-mail address on the Web site never gets updated. Get an e-mail address that stays with the local youth group.

4. Don't forget to post your church's address and phone number.

Too often I've read "Come and Join Us!" on a Web page and then haven't had the slightest idea on how to locate or contact the church for more information. A great tool to use when explaining how to get to your church is Maps.Yahoo.com. Fill out your church's address and then copy and paste the URL at the top of the page that displays the map. This way, visitors can enter their personal address and get door-to-door driving instructions. I use this a lot, and it has seldom been wrong.

5. Tell us a little bit about your group.

How often do you meet? What subject material are you currently covering? Do you have a mission statement? Who are the leaders? Can I know a little bit more about them before I allow my kids to attend? What events are scheduled? What type of music does your group listen to together? Do you have photos from any activities? How about posting some testimonies from some of the students? If you have a newsletter, how about publishing it online? What are some links that you and your youth group enjoy visiting?

6. Well, what about graphics?

Use the JPG format for all photos, as this displays 16 million colors and has really good compression. Use GIFs if you want to display graphics that have less than 256 colors or wish to have animation or transparent backgrounds. GifOptimizer.com is a great place to visit if you want to make your GIF images load faster. Try not to use too many graphics or have any graphics wider than 400 pixels, as some visitors may be using older computers or slower connections. *always* enter the width and height in the image tag so that the page loads faster (ex. IMG SRC-"Mygraphic.gif" WIDTH=200 HEIGHT=100 ALT="my graphic'>).

7. Get your youth involved.

Make your group's Web page a ministry to the world at large. Include articles, devotions, testimonies, and artwork that are created by your group in an effort to reach their friends and others. Include photos from mission events. Your students and parents will enjoy inviting their friends and family to visit the Web site to see what God is doing.

8. Don't fill your page up with banners and graphics from other sites.

Keep your pages focused and filled with information pertaining to "your" group. There are a lot of sites that contain very little unique content and seem to be just a collection of links and graphics discovered while surfing. Make your site stand apart by supplying it with unique content generated by your group. Update it periodically and create a page that is dedicated to notifying visitors of new items that have been added.

9. Announce your site!

Join the Youthring! Submit your youth group Web site to the YouthPastor.com Resource Directory. Add your youth group name to the Youthgroup Name Page. Use the All In One Christian Index to submit your site to Christian Web sites. Most search engines allow you to include your Web site for free. You just have to spend a little time entering the information.

10. Do not put all of your information on a single page.

Create subpages and remember to provide links to all of the pages and provide a way to return to the home page. Make sure you have a title for each page, or else it will be listed as "Untitled" in the search engines.

11. Regulate yourself before someone else does.

Some browsers are configured not to allow users to visit Web pages that do not have either SafeSurf or RSACi ratings. Register your site, and you will receive specific HTML codes that you will need to put on every one of your pages.

---

* Used by permission of James Moberg (2000@youthpastor.com), the founder of www.youthpastor.com and the principal designer for JamoDesign.

CHAPTER 42

Crisis Counseling

by Marianne Dyrud

Introduction

IN A CRISIS SITUATION, there are several ways to help:

1. Emotional support. The person in crisis knows that he/she can trust you, and you give empathetic care.

2. Appreciative support. You affirm the person in crisis—affirmation of who he/she is and what he/she does.

3. Informational support. You give practical advice and information about how a certain situation should be handled and solved.

4. Practical advice. You give direct practical help in order to perform a task or solve a problem.

"First aid" in crisis counseling is more effective when you are prepared, oriented about the situation, have a good overview, are updated, are firm, are friendly, set limits, are practical, give hope, accept feelings (in yourself and others), are naturally optimistic, give contact, have compassion, are there (availability).

When it comes to counseling in general, here are some general principles:

- Use active listening—try to understand and empathize with the person.
- Know your personal boundaries and your level of knowledge in counseling situations. Do not be afraid of admitting limitations.
- Refer when in doubt! As a volunteer and youth leader you can be there to provide support and a listening ear. However, when you know that what you are facing is beyond your competence and knowledge, refer the youth to a professional who has expertise in this area.
- Some problems do not have easy answers.
- The best way to offer help in crises is to be there!
- Be someone who can be trusted.

Death of a Beloved

It was Saturday night, and one of the students at the school had just received a phone call: "Your dad is in the hospital. A car hit him earlier this afternoon, and the situation is critical. He might die within the next hour. Please get somebody to take you to the hospital."

Within the next 15 minutes we were on our way. It was an hour before we reached the hospital, and, unfortunately, by the time we arrived, the father was already dead. The student broke down and cried in the arms of his mother. Tears were flowing among those of us who were watching. After an hour our student got to see his father's body. We spent a couple of hours with the family at the hospital, just being together—sometimes in silence and sometimes talking about the accident, as well as praying together.

The days before the funeral were hard. Friends grouped together in sympathy for their friend who had so suddenly lost his father. They wrote cards, called him on the phone, and sent flowers.

What can you do in a situation like this? You can be available, perhaps offering practical help, such as cooking, babysitting, etc. The boy's girlfriend asked me, "What do I say?" I counseled her to just be there for him.

As we see in the Bible, when Job's friends came to be with him they just sat there, without uttering a word, for "they saw that his grief was very great" (Job 2:13, NKJV).

Seven days and seven nights might be unrealistic for us, but the presence of a dear, trusted friend is highly appreciated. After the loss of a loved one, you do not necessarily need to hear a lot of words, but you do need somebody to be there. Perhaps your youth group could organize practical help, such as making food for the family or fixing things around the house. Let the person be able to share his/her grief and sorrow, which will help the pain to dissipate.

Divorce

"It is all my fault!" She was in tears as she came into my office. "My parents left each other, and I am sure it is because of me." Sadly, this is the case for many children whose parents have divorced. The guilt feelings, the sadness, the loss, the grief—all the emotions are there.

At any age, when somebody experiences divorce in the family, it hurts! Teenagers, young people, and children often think it is their fault that their mom and dad are divorcing. "If only I could have done ———," they cry. Or perhaps they feel they have not been good enough, have been a bad child. "It is my fault!" We need to stress that it is not the child's fault! The divorce did not come as a result of the child's behavior.

Stepparent

"I feel like Cinderella! My stepmom is the worst you could think of." Her eyes were dark, and her mouth was tightly closed. No end was in sight for the warlike situation.

In an age in which divorce is as common as staying married, you will encounter in your youth groups people who have problems with their stepparents. The stepparent is not mother or father, but an additional adult that many teenagers and children see as the "bad person." "He/she is not my father/mother! He/she does not have anything to say over me." Or the scenario might be "He/she stole my mom's/dad's place!"

Perhaps good advice would be to look at the stepparent as an adult friend with a special responsibility.

Physical Abuse

"I must be a bad child! My dad beats me with a belt every night so I can learn how to behave."

Unfortunately, in the world we live in, physical abuse of children and teenagers is fairly common. As a youth leader, you might meet kids who have been beaten or are still being beaten at home, although the abuse is not always apparent. It is important for children who have been physically abused to know that they are safe with you. As a youth leader you need to know whom you must notify in these cases—social services, police, etc.—and whom you can refer the child to for help.

Sexual Abuse

She was only 3 years old when her grandfather sexually abused her. She now had problems sleeping at night with the light off. She had a hard time trusting herself in relationships. She would not let people get too close, for fear they might hurt her. She had a hard time setting healthy boundaries.

Sexual abuse affects a person not only physically but also psychologically. Let me give a short description of what sexual abuse is: "Sexual abuse of children consists of activities which expose children to sexual stimulation inappropriate to their age, physical development, and role in the family." *

Sexual abuse happens outside of the family circle as well as within. In 90 percent of the cases it happens with someone the child trusts, which hurts the child deeply. (It can be a father/mother, stepparent, uncle/aunt, grandfather/mother, teacher, pastor, youth leader, etc.)

When someone you trust and care about hurts you, you develop a "shield" of not trusting others, in case you might encounter somebody like that again. Sexual abuse's deep impact on the survivor includes: fear of touching; struggling with self-acceptance and self-image; chronic depression; difficulty maintaining steady relationships (often searching for abusive partners, which is the only "normal" known); problems concentrating; attempting suicide; problems sleeping; boundary issues ("Since my borders were mowed down, I don't have any, and I have a problem respecting others and their borders").

As a youth leader, you may have some in your youth group who have experienced sexual abuse. It is important that you know the laws in your country or local district for reporting sexual abuse. In some countries, if you have a trusted position in the church or school (youth pastor, teacher, etc.), you have a responsibility to report the abuse to the authorities.

The survivor of sexual abuse has problems trusting people in general. Demonstrate that you are a person who can be trusted—someone who will be there to listen and provide support.

Unfortunately, many children have been abused in the name of God, and each child's picture of God has been severely distorted. This needs to be replaced by a realistic picture of God modeled by us in the church, where God's love is portrayed as clean and holy, not dirty, aloof, and abusive.

Rape

In the case of rape the first thing you should do is offer instant help—drive the person to the police, the doctor, or home to parents. Offer a listening ear and practical help in such a shock-inducing experience. In many rape cases the rapist is someone the victim knows and trusts. This makes it even harder to report the case to the police, because many are led to believe that "it was my fault."

In most hospitals there are personnel who can help the victim sort out feelings and reactions after the crime and offer guidance in the next steps. Medical attention is often needed, followed by practical help in contacting the police and finding the person a place to sleep. Eventually the victim will need a lawyer and perhaps a support group for rape survivors. If you are the first person to know about the assault, you are a very important and trusted person.

The person who experiences rape might have nightmares, be afraid to walk alone at night, afraid of being alone, afraid of the darkness, or afraid of people with a certain look. When you counsel someone who has been raped, be patient. Listen to what the person has to say, do not doubt or question her/his experience. Let the person take the initiative as to whether or not she/he wants help. In many places there are special support groups for rape survivors; help the victim make contact.

Suicide

Thoughts of suicide are experienced by many people once or twice during their lifetime. Suicide plans are far more serious than suicidal thoughts and are not as common. The plans are either an appeal or a threat. Threats often are made in difficult life situations and are seen as cries for help. Many who are planning to commit suicide are depressed people.

Suicide attempts are 10 times more common than actual suicides. Most people try an overdose of medicines mixed with alcohol. Ninety percent of them survive and are happy to survive. Suicide attempts are often combined with serious depression, which needs to be treated.

Some facts that are connected with suicide attempts:
- The individual has made previous suicide attempts (look at the seriousness of the attempts).
- The individual has suffered the death or loss of a beloved.
- The individual has revealed a detailed plan of suicide.
- The individual has completed personal business, or made or changed a will.
- The individual lives alone with few or no contacts with people.
- There is a history of suicide in the individual's family.
- The individual has a psychiatric history.
- The individual has a robotic way of acting.
- The individual is suffering from a serious illness, great pain, or depression.
- The individual is abusing alcohol and/or drugs.

A seriously suicidal person should be admitted to a hospital, where he/she can obtain professional help. Your role as a youth leader is to give assurance that the person's life is worth enough for you to help.

The suicidal person may have great guilt feelings about certain things, or feel that he/she will make the world a better place by leaving it. This is where you can help the person see, perhaps through professional help, that life is worth living. In most cases, suicidal people need help fighting against depression, and that help can come through prayer and by talking to a trusted counselor.

Eating Disorders

Eating disorders are often about control or loss of control. When a person has begun to lose control over his or her own body (being unrealistic in body image), the control issue is still there in the form of food intake and doing things "myself." "I want to take control, and I can handle it" is usually the way people react in this disorder.

The stages of eating disorders are often like this:

- Life gets more and more dominated by thoughts about food and body.
- The eating pattern changes and develops into rituals and forced actions, which prohibits normal life.
- The person withdraws more and more from social events and prefers to eat alone.
- The person cannot distinguish between hunger and other forms of needs and emotional needs. It is hard to concentrate on anything.
- The person exhibits depressive traits. Training becomes an obsession.
- Body size has become a part of the person's defense mechanism.
- Physical damage occurs because of insufficient eating, and as the result of eventual throwing up (bulimia), the stomach acid will damage the tissue in the throat and teeth.

It is important for a person who has an eating problem to be accountable to another and have someone follow up. This needs to be done by medical personnel if the eating disorder has come to a serious stage. Otherwise, he/she can be helped by a peer.

It is important for you, the youth leader, to maintain a healthy attitude toward sports, a healthy body, and good self-esteem. Society as a whole puts too much stress on the way we look. Let us celebrate the body as a unique creation of God. Let us also stress the development of a healthy lifestyle, not only for the body, but also for the mind and soul.

Invite people to come to your youth group and talk about their experiences with anorexia and bulimia. Be open about the issue, and make it safe for someone to admit a problem.

Drugs

She was 21, and I had noticed a certain change in her behavior the past couple of months. Her eyes were "swimming" at times when I met her. One day she asked to talk to me: "I need to tell you this when I am not under the influence."

She had been using hash for the past three months in order to forget her past. A couple of weeks after we talked she started seeing a psychologist for therapy and quit using the drug.

Sooner or later you will probably encounter those who have a drug problem. Watch the appearance, hygiene, and behavior. You can look into their eyes and see whether they are on certain drugs; the pupils will be wide or narrow. Obtain brochures, talk to the police, and stay informed.

Observe young people who are depressed, who have had some crisis lately. They are more likely to test drugs if they are desperate to escape the pain in their life. Tell them that the best way of dealing with pain is to go through it. Pain will not kill you; drugs will, eventually. Using drugs is a false escape route, because the pain you are trying to escape will eventually come back to you and perhaps hit harder.

Let your youth group make deals with you for drug-free zones. Involve the parents. Use creative ways to tell young people that you do not need drugs to be cool and strong. Develop small close-knit groups in which people can watch out for each other.

Depression

A depressed person has an obvious sadness that you can observe in speech, facial expressions, and posture. This sadness then develops into an inner tension, reduced sleep and appetite, problems with concentration, lack of initiative, weak emotional reaction (numbness), and depressive thoughts.

In many cases the depressed person has no wish to live, or feels that he/she is of no use in this life. When you recognize the signs, refer the person to someone who can help. Be there with practical help, such as assisting with schoolwork.

Anxiety

Anxiety results most often from traumatic experiences in a person's life (rape, fire, loss of a beloved, abuse, etc.). Perhaps the person has a problem with being alone in the house or is afraid of the dark or of certain people. These phobias are a result of a traumatic experience and require professional help.

You can offer help in practical ways, such as walking someone home at night, being with him/her in the elevator, arranging for a friend to sleep over at the house when parents are gone, etc. Depending on the seriousness of the attacks of anxiety, you can help someone with less-intense problems.

Family Violence

Home is supposed to be a safe haven for children and young people. Unfortunately, this is not always the case. Often family violence is connected with drug and alcohol problems. Your youth group should be a safe haven for someone with problems at home. Perhaps that child or teenager needs to have a place where he/she can hang out, do homework, be safe for a while.

Family violence should be reported to the authorities as soon as possible. Everyone in the family needs to be safe and to have a normal, functional life together, without the threat of a beating from someone. Check with the authorities in your community to find out what you can do. It is necessary to stand firm and to show the child/young person that normal families are not violent; teach him/her how to trust other people again. Offer practical help—perhaps your youth group can provide child care for a crisis shelter for women and children.

Homelessness/Street Kids

Most often street kids have problems at home (alcohol, drug abuse), and the street is a "better" alternative than being at home. On the street the kids find "brothers and sisters," the kind of family feeling that they are missing at home, and the gang often becomes their family.

Your youth group could be involved in centers for these young people, helping them get through school, which will give them a chance at an education and a life away from the streets. Perhaps there are couples in the church that would like to "adopt" a homeless kid, become their "parents" for a while. The Big Brother/Big Sister program, in which young people assist with tutoring, sports, etc., might also help.

*Maxine Hancock and Karen Burton Mains, *Child Sexual Abuse* (Guilford, Eng.: Highland Books, 1993), p. 6.

SECTION 5

Resources for Youth Ministry

CHAPTER 43

Visionary Leadership

by Jennifer Morgan

IT WAS BY THE SIDE of the road, in a parked car and through tear-filled eyes, that Doug Fields began to see God's vision for his ministry. A youth pastor of 20 years, currently ministering at Saddleback church in southern California, Fields describes his Emmaus Road experience in the book *Purpose-driven Youth Ministry.*

"Three main problems haunted me and left me continually frustrated," writes Fields of his early ministry. "I couldn't create attractive programs like those of other churches, I wasn't sure that I was the right person for youth ministry, and I could never do enough to please everyone."[1]

Doug Fields' search for new ideas had him copying everything that looked innovative, exciting, and successful. But Like David in Saul's armor, other people's programs didn't work in his settings. Fields describes the energy boost he used to get from standing in front of a group of students who were excited to be in church. "Their faces said, 'This is going to be good.' But only a few years later, when things weren't going as well, I saw a different look—one that said, 'This better be good.'"[2]

The breaking point came when Doug returned from an attendance-building weekend retreat. He was physically exhausted but spiritually feasting on the praise his church would be rewarding him with. Instead Doug's reception committee turned out to be an irritated administrator with two complaints and an outraged parent phoning to lambaste him. It was while driving away from this onslaught that Doug pulled over so he could weep uncontrollably. There on the side of the road he sensed God saying, "Doug, you'll never be able to do enough to please everyone. Focus on Me. Rest in Me. Abide in Me. When your heart is turned toward Me, we can work together and do some good things."[3]

"My heart had become hard, and I was spending all my time doing the work of God without being a man of God."[4] Doug Fields left behind a program-driven youth ministry and became a spirit-led youth minister. Now he promotes purpose-driven ministry.

Become a Spirit-led Leader

In a book designed for the secular business manager, Burt Nanus describes the success of organizations that catch the vision of their leaders. He cites the influence of Edwin Land on Polaroid, Walt Disney on Disney, and Ray Kroc on McDonald's long after those founders passed leadership on to other hands. Christianity should still be distinguished by the teachings of Jesus. In the Seventh-day Adventist Church we have a unique vision, which was clearly articulated by Ellen White. In her day there was no distinction between "youth ministry" and regular church ministry. But her advice in the books *Education* and *Counsels to Parents, Teachers, and Students* still applies to today's youth leader. Her advice to teachers would have helped Doug Fields: "Before men can be truly wise, they must realize their dependence upon God, and be filled with His wisdom."[5] The psalmist puts it more poetically: "Unless the Lord builds the house, its builders labor in vain. Unless the Lord watches over the city, the watchmen stand guard in vain. In vain you rise early and stay up late, toiling for food to eat—for he grants sleep to those he loves" (Ps. 127:1, 2, NIV).

God's problem is the same as the teacher who found he had a student who finished the teacher's sentences before any assignment was fully explained. Eager to please but bad at listening, the student inevitably had to repeat homework that had been done incorrectly. Henry T. Blackaby and Claude V. King, authors of the workbook *Experiencing God,* stress the importance of nurturing a relationship with God before you decide to throw yourself into your vision of what you think is God's will in your life. The process for determining God's will is God-centered, not self-centered. The central question is not "What is God's will for my life?" or even "What is God's will for my ministry?" but "What is God's will?" If you want to know God's will, you need to know God. "He who loves me will be loved by my Father, and I too will love him and show myself to him" (John 14:21, NIV).

Once you love God, you need to follow Jesus' example: "I tell you the truth, the Son can do nothing by himself; he can do only what he sees his Father doing, because whatever the Father does the Son also does" (John 5:19, NIV). Like Jesus, you should pray and watch to see what God is doing. Blackaby and King predict that you will experience a crisis of faith. Ultimately, if this relationship is important to you, you will adjust your life to fit God's will. Like Peter, Andrew, James, and John, you will leave your nets and follow Him.[6]

"But," you say, "I've already done that! I've left everything, Lord, to follow You. That's why I'm in youth ministry!"

That's what Saul of Tarsus said. He tells us he had devoted his whole life to serving God—from his parents' first dedication to the day he marched to Damascus persecuting God's chosen people. "But whatever was to my profit I now consider loss for the sake of Christ" (Phil. 3:7, NIV). You need to evaluate your mission. Is it for your own profit? Or are you out to help an old friend who loves working with kids? He gets all the credit (and He takes all the blame!). For Doug Fields there are three ways for a youth worker to become dependent on God:

1. Recognize God's power through personal humility.
2. Submit your abilities to God and allow His power to work through who you are.
3. Focus on being a person of God before doing the work of God.

"To know oneself is great knowledge," writes Ellen White. "The teacher who rightly estimates himself will let God mold and discipline his mind. And he will acknowledge the source of his power."[7]

Become a Purpose-driven Youth Leader

When he was teaching youth ministry at the Seventh-day Adventist Theological Seminary at Andrews University, Steve Case was famous for requiring all his students to write a philosophy of youth ministry, which they then had to condense to one sentence. Now,

10 years later, as president of Piece of the Pie Ministries, Steve still stands by his own ministry statement: "Fostering relationships that build responsible student leaders." The mission statement of Piece of the Pie Ministries is "To draw young people to Christ by drawing them into the life of the church."

One of Steve's programs includes conducting training seminars for youth leaders and educators. After 10 years of traveling throughout the United States and Australia, Steve remains disappointed at how few Seventh-day Adventist youth leaders have a mission statement. In September 1999 Steve asked a room of 25 pastors from the Trans-Tasman Union if they could identify their goal for their youth ministry. Not one raised a hand. In a North Pacific Union retreat, three, out of a group of 400 volunteer youth leaders, admitted to having a goal. Only one could state that goal. "And," says Steve, "he couldn't say it in anything less than a paragraph of clichés." For Steve, these two examples are not isolated experiences. "I'm convinced that most people in youth ministry do not know what they are aiming at."

The writer of Proverbs warns us, "Where there is no vision, the people perish" (Prov. 29:18). "Young men should have broad ideas, wise plans," writes Ellen White, "that they may make the most of their opportunities, catch the inspiration and courage that animated the apostles."[8]

"Still," the skeptic will say, "I haven't got a clue what my mission statement is, and my kids love my meetings. We have a huge group that shows up to our Friday night fellowships!"

Burt Nanus repeats a conversation he had with a CEO of a fast-growing food manufacturing company while Nanus was directing University of Southern California's Center for Futures Research. The company was so successful that Nanus wasn't sure why the CEO had come for advice. Every one of Nanus' diagnostic questions were met with glowing descriptions of the company's performance.

"'Look here,' I finally said with some exasperation, 'just what is it that's bothering you?' 'Well,' he explained, 'that's just it. Everything is going so well that I'm getting uneasy. Maybe we've just been lucky until now. Maybe I'm missing something. Or maybe there's something just over the horizon that will clobber us. Besides, when things were tough, I was so busy managing crises that I never had time to think about the future. I used to believe that if everything's going well, leave it alone, or as the old adage says, "If it ain't broke, don't fix it." Now, I know that's wrong. The best time to try something new, to take risks, to move off in a different direction, is in good times, not bad. *Isn't that what leadership is all about—fixing things that aren't broken?*' "[9]

"A leader," says Steve Case, "is a person who has a sense of where to go. A person who knows things that others don't understand, and can see what's happening next. People learn to trust leaders, and so people follow them."

Both Case and Nanus distinguish between a leader and a manager, the latter being a person who maintains successful programs. In Steve Case's estimation the Adventist Church needs more leaders. A manager is a leader without a vision. Without a vision, you don't have any means to evaluate your successes or your failures.

Rick Warren, senior pastor of the Saddleback church and author of *The Purpose-driven Church,* warns churches against relaxing in their successes. Warren advises all churches to rediscover their purposes through Bible study. Study Christ's ministry on earth, the images and names of the church, examples of New Testament churches, and the commands of Christ.

Warren directs the Bible student to ask the following questions:
1. Why does the church exist?
2. What are we to be as a church? (Who and what are we?)
3. What are we to do as a church? (What does God want done in the world?)
4. How are we to do it?[10]

In his book *Visionary Leadership* Burt Nanus distinguishes between a mission statement and a vision statement. A mission statement, according to Nanus, is the purpose for which an organization exists. In contrast, a vision statement is "a realistic, credible, attractive future for your organization."[11] It is an interesting assignment for an Adventist youth minister, using those definitions, to study the writings of Ellen White for mission statements and vision statements.

A mission statement for any youth worker could be the following: "To bring man back into harmony with God, so to elevate and ennoble his moral nature that he may again reflect the image of the Creator, is the great purpose of all the education and discipline of life."[12] A good example of a vision statement would be from *Messages to Young People:* "Christ is calling for volunteers to enlist under His standard, and bear the banner of the cross before the world."[13]

Jesus gave His disciples a mission statement in the great commandment: " 'Love the Lord your God with all your heart and with all your soul and with all your mind.' . . . 'Love your neighbor as yourself.' All the Law and the Prophets hang on these two commandments" (Matt. 22:37-40, NIV). The Great Commission is Jesus' vision statement: "Go and make disciples of all nations, baptizing them in the name of the Father and of the Son and of the Holy Spirit, and teaching them to obey everything I have commanded you" (Matt. 28:19, 20, NIV).

Rick Warren has combined these two quotes into the five purposes of the Christian church:
1. Love the Lord with all your heart.
2. Love your neighbor as yourself.
3. Go and make disciples.
4. Baptizing them.
5. Teaching them to obey.[14]

For Warren, mission and vision statements are combined in his term *purpose statement.*

An effective purpose statement is biblical, specific, transferable, and measurable.[15] Saddleback's purpose statement is: "To bring people to Jesus and *membership* in His family, develop them to Christlike *maturity,* and equip them for their *ministry* in the church a life *mission* in the world, in order to *magnify* God's name." This statement can be further reduced to five key words:

"Magnify: We celebrate God's presence in worship.
"Mission: We communicate God's Word through evangelism.
"Membership: We incorporate God's family into our fellowship.
"Maturity: We educate God's people through discipleship.
"Ministry: We demonstrate God's love through service."[16]

As the youth pastor of Saddleback church, Doug Fields has fully bought into Rick Warren's purpose statement. He has reworded the church's five purposes in more youthful words. As Doug says:

"Reach is our word for evangelism. Connect is our word for fellowship. Grow is our word for discipleship. Discover is our word for ministry. Honor is our word for worship."[17]

You may not enjoy the teamwork that Fields and Warren are experiencing. If your church does not have its own purpose statement, encourage your senior pastor to create a vision team to study Ellen White and the Bible for guidance. If the adults are reluctant, you can still do this in your own youth group and for yourself.

Provide Purpose-driven Programs

Steve Case reports that most youth leaders he talks with evaluate their programs by two main criteria: "People had a good time" and "We had more people than last time."

"OK," says Steve, "if numbers are important, then program for numbers. Hand out $20 to everyone who comes."

Without a biblically based purpose statement, you are programming for a random criteria that may include parental criticism, youth complaints, size of attendance, and maybe some biblical values. Now that you have a purpose statement, you can evaluate your youth ministry by biblically based criteria. Doug Fields grades youth ministries by the five components of his purpose statement. He feels that most youth ministries would get an A+ for fellowship, A for worship, B for ministry, C in discipleship, and D– for evangelism. A quick skim of Ellen White's writings and the Bible, however, shows that evangelism is actually the highest priority of both Jesus and the early Adventist Church.

It is interesting to identify what Nanus calls your "stakeholders," people who have an investment in your organization's future, and invite them to grade your ministry on the basis of your purpose statement. "What are the major interests and expectations of the five or six most important stakeholders regarding the future of your organization?"[18] Fields and Warren name five groups: the core (youth committed to doing ministry), the committed (students who commit to spiritual habits like Bible study and tithing), the congregation (students committed to a small group—a relationship with Christ and other Christians), the crowd (students committed to attending a specific church), and community (students who are committed to not attending any church).[19]

Fields then evaluates each program he is maintaining or initiating by how well it achieves the five purposes in ministry to the five potential audiences. Very few programs will achieve all things—most programs specialize in their purpose as well as their potential audience. But all purposes can be presented to all potential audiences, just in different ways. A basketball game with community students may be a great way to fellowship, but it's a bad time to sit a nonchurched student down for a discipleship Bible study on the health message. But discipleship education can happen during the basketball game when the Spirit leads you into a conversation with a curious visitor about why a pastor also plays basketball. Meanwhile, some small groups decide not to offer food at Bible studies because it distracts from discipleship, but that doesn't mean that students can't hang around afterward for fellowship and refreshments.

You may find that some programs you've been offering don't offer any of your purposes to any of your potential audiences. It may be time to drop those programs. The main thing is that you have a vision to aim at. Without that vision you may be aiming at everything, or nothing; either way the results are the same. If you aim at nothing you are sure to hit it. Likewise, if you aim at everything you are sure to hit something. But you will never hit the target until you identify what your target is.

On March 23, 1989, Ann Landers published the following letter:

"Dear Ann Landers:

"I am a 23-year-old college graduate (business major). I don't presume to speak for my generation, but I know what I feel. People wonder about us. They say we are materialistic, just out for ourselves. They say we are apathetic. It must go deeper than that. Teens are committing suicide in record numbers. What is wrong with us? Just look around.

"The media reach far and wide, bringing stories from all over the world. We have overpopulation, the environment is being destroyed, our natural resources are dwindling. People are oppressed, starving, and killing each other. There are enough weapons to blow up the world we live in 40 times! AIDS continues to spread, and there is no vaccine and no cure.

"On the home front the United States is faltering. The national debt is at an incomprehensible level. Homeless people freeze to death on the streets. Gang violence, alcoholism, and drug use are rampant. Teens are having babies out of wedlock, and many will never get off welfare.

"Not many people my age will be able to own a house, no matter what their educational level or whom they work for. Takeovers and mergers ruin the hopes of job security. Many of us expect to have a lower standard of living than our parents. The U.S. is losing its edge in the world market. It sounds hopeless. But I love this country, and I think there is hope. I don't believe my generation is apathetic. *We just don't know where to start.*

"Waiting for Guidance in California"[20]

Maybe it's time for the church to show people where to start.

---

[1] Doug Fields, *Purpose-driven Youth Ministry,* p. 29.

[2] *Ibid.,* p. 31.

[3] *Ibid.,* p. 33.

[4] *Ibid.*

[5] E. G. White, *Counsels to Parents, Teachers, and Students,* p. 66.

[6] Henry T. Blackaby and Claude V. King, *Experiencing God: Knowing and Doing the Will of God* (Nashville, LifeWay Press, 1990).

[7] White, *Counsels to Parents, Teachers, and Students,* p. 67.

[8] White, *Messages to Young People,* p. 24.

[9] Burt Nanus, *Visionary Leadership* (San Francisco: Josey-bass, 1992), pp. 23, 24.

[10] Rick Warren, *The Purpose-driven Church: Growth Without Compromising Your Message and Mission* (Grand Rapids: Zondervan, 1995), p. 98.

[11] Nanus, p. 8

[12] White, *Counsels to Parents, Teachers, and Students,* p. 49.

[13] White, *Messages to Young People,* pp. 24, 25.

[14] Warren, pp. 103-106.

[15] *Ibid.,* pp. 100, 101.

[16] *Ibid.,* p. 107.

[17] Fields, p. 52.

[18] Nanus, p. 63.

[19] Fields, p. 91.

[20] In Nanus, pp. 186, 187.

CHAPTER 44

Missions

by Kerry Schafer

T HE IDEA OF MISSIONS is certainly not a novel one in our church. Every Adventist has grown up familiar with the command of Jesus to "go ye into all the world, and preach the gospel to every creature" (Mark 16:15). Adults have been working in mission fields for years. More recently people are rediscovering the importance of allowing young people to be immersed in mission experiences. Ellen White wrote a century ago about the need for youth to work for God:

"Every youth should be impressed with the fact that he is not his own; that his strength, his time, his talents, belong to God. It should be his chief purpose in life to glorify God and to do good to his fellowmen. The Bible teaches him that he is a tree, on which fruit must be found; a steward, whose capital will increase as it is wisely improved; a light, whose bright beams are to illuminate the moral darkness that enshrouds the earth. Every youth, every child, has a work to do for God's glory and for the salvation of souls that are ready to perish."[1]

Many youth leaders have witnessed leaps in spiritual growth when young people are actively engaged in outreach and mission activities. In the act of sharing time, possessions, and their faith with others, young people will find a better perspective on both the present world and the one to come, and their relationship with Christ will be strengthened.

In recent years programs designed to give young people the experience of working for others have flourished. Student missionary postings are common, and groups of teens or young adults travel to such places as Mexico or Honduras to complete building projects. Of course, mission trips are not limited to going out of the country; there are plenty of mission fields closer to home. Some young people volunteer time working in the inner-city areas of places like New York, Los Angeles, or Chicago. They work with children in sports and after-school programs, build ministries for gang members, and assist with soup kitchens and homeless shelters. Other youth groups have engaged in such activities as making sandwiches for the homeless or passing out jackets and mittens for cold winter days and nights. The need close to home is often just as great, and the positive effect as profound, as mission work in a foreign country.

These missionary experiences not only help the less fortunate, but make a profound impact on the lives and souls of the young people who give of their time and enthusiasm. Steve Daily comments, "It is my observation that Adventist young people who get involved in mission service and community service have their lives transformed. The kingdom of God becomes an inner reality, and they are never the same again."[2]

This opinion certainly proved to be true for a group of high school students who chose to go on a mission trip to Mexico in place of their usual "fun and games" type of class trip. Their lives were profoundly changed by the experience. They returned home more mature, more serious about the direction their lives were going, and more enthusiastic about God.

In the spring of 1999 the senior class of Cariboo Adventist Academy in Williams Lake, British Columbia, Canada, decided that rather than pursuing their original plan to visit Disneyland, they would like to take a senior trip that made a difference. Plans rapidly fell into place to assist an orphanage in Mexico with some building and maintenance needs.

After an initial call to the orphanage to find out what kind of work needed to be done and what types of supplies were necessary, the students went to work to raise money for the adventure, both for the trip there and for the supplies necessary to do the work after they arrived. They sold fruit donated by an orchard, put on a banquet, and held a silent auction with goods that they solicited from local businesses. In the process they made a positive impact on their own community. It is common for school groups to ask for financial support from local businesses for a variety of school-related projects. To have a group of young people requesting donations of supplies for a mission trip is out of the ordinary.

Teacher Warren Friesen says that although there is considerable work involved in planning your own trip rather than going with an organization that does all the planning for you, there were positive benefits. In the planning and preparation stages the class really pulled together, working hard to make sure that everything was done well. They also had more time to interact with the children in the orphanage than they would have done if they had been involved in a project that was purely work-oriented.

In fact, some of the most profound benefits seemed to come from this interaction with the children. One of the boys came home with barely any clothes in his suitcase—he had given away nearly his entire wardrobe. Another, who had initially objected to the trip, arguing that they could do some service work near home and still go to Disneyland, was so impressed with the experience that he now plans to go back as soon as possible.

Student Christy Hein reports that the benefits of the trip were many. Their class had been growing apart, and the trip taught them to work together and strengthened bonds between them. She says that while in Mexico "we sang together all day and even sang ourselves to sleep at night."

They also experienced miracles. The vehicle in which a group of students were traveling to the airport broke down. This was not a breakdown in the middle of a city with a phone or a police officer close at hand; it was on a highway some distance from any town. The group of young people stood together by the roadside and prayed that God would solve their problem. A short time later the only tow truck in the region "happened" by. The driver explained that he very rarely came through this way and didn't know why he had chosen to do so on this particular day. As a result, the faith of the students was strengthened before they ever got on the plane.

Christy says that they all changed during the experience. It was a real eye-opener having to do work with a bare minimum of equipment, as well as seeing the poverty in which some people live. She says, "I'm not so selfish anymore. I don't take things for granted." The fact that the rest of her class was changed by the experience was proved by the graduation gift they chose to give to the school: a fund of $500 designated for the next senior class to go to the orphanage in their turn.

Monte Torkelson, the associate director of youth ministries in the Oregon Conference, suggests that it is wise to prepare young people before engaging in extended or intensive mission experiences. There are three basic steps to take before committing to anything as intensive as a mission trip to a foreign country.

1. Raise Awareness. Before getting involved in outreach or missions, it is important for young people to understand the needs of people in the world, both in their own country and in foreign places. Monte contributes to raising awareness in Oregon by organizing a mission festival every year. The festival highlights Oregon youth who have been active in prison ministries, church plants, or as student missionaries. The number of groups going on mission trips has increased dramatically since the inception of this program.

2. Gain Local Exposure. Before they make a major commitment, give the young people opportunities to be involved in outreach projects close to home. Visit nursing homes. Help out in soup kitchens. Prepare holiday baskets for the hungry. Engage in other outreach activities such a random acts of kindness campaigns. These activities help to increase young people's spirituality and help them become accustomed to working for others. When the youth group appears to be ready, then it is time to embark upon the third and most intensive stage of mission work.

3. Introduce Larger Time Frame/High-Intensity Experiences. After moving through the two earlier steps, the young people are prepared for more intensive ministry. They are primed and ready to receive the maximum benefit from a foreign mission trip or a long-term project at home. Monte strongly believes that mission trips need to become a ministry experience for young people. It is imperative that they are involved in an integral way and not just as spectators. "They must not just lend a helping hand. They need to stand up and be bold for God."

Sara Hanson is a student at Walla Walla College who stepped out of her comfort zone with lasting effects on her life. At the end of her freshman year Sara still didn't know what she wanted to do with her life. She thought she would like to go on an adventure and take a vacation from school, so she decided to spend a year as a student missionary. The Student Missions Program at Walla Walla helped to arrange all of the details, including obtaining her visa. Sara chose to go to Ecuador. Other students of her acquaintance went to Africa, Peru, Argentina, and the inner city of New York.

In Ecuador Sara and a friend who accompanied her were the only ones in their locale who spoke English. They stayed together in a dorm room on the campus of the academy, where they taught PE, English, and music to students in grades 7-12. Ecuador is notorious for its dangerous highways. Traffic consists almost entirely of buses, and the bus drivers are often drunk and do not adhere to traffic rules. Accidents are common. In addition, the natives showed a definite hostility toward Americans. As if this weren't enough, there were earthquakes, floods, and serious homesickness to contend with.

When asked how the experience changed her, Sara reported that while she grew more mature and independent, she also grew closer to God. Knowing that she faced risks every single day helped her realize her need for God and increased her trust in Him. Sara also feels that she learned something from the local culture, which moves at a much slower pace than ours. The people enjoy life and live in the moment rather than worrying about the future. On returning to the United States, she felt for a while that people were too rushed, and wished that they would slow down. She reports that even though she is now rushing along with everyone else, she retains an awareness of the value of a slower pace of life.

Although mission trips are such positive experiences, both for the youth who volunteer and the nationals who benefit from their services, Carol Moses of Maranatha Volunteers International advises that there are several important things to keep in mind when planning a youth mission trip.

Careful Planning

Leaders need to be certain they have a sense of the big picture. It is essential to understand the needs and culture of the people at the destination site. The work that is planned must be something that will bring pride to the community and not become an embarrassment or an eyesore. Lack of appropriate planning can result in problems. For example, lack of careful planning could result in a group's beginning a project and leaving it unfinished.

A lack of cultural understanding could lead to the expectation that the nationals will be grateful for the work done and finish the project themselves. In this situation completion may never happen, for a variety of reasons. Even if materials are left to finish the job, they may not be sufficient. Alternatively, the nationals may not have the necessary knowledge and skill to continue. Sometimes, if the culture is based on a very relaxed, one-day-at-a-time mentality, the people may just never get around to completing the project. This dilemma can be prevented by careful preplanning. If it seems probable that a group will not have the time to finish a project, they need to be certain that another group will be able to finish in a timely manner what they have started.

Communication and Teamwork

It is also important to work in tandem with the local Adventist union. Suppose, for example, that a group decides that a certain community overseas needs a church. Without thinking to compare notes with the union, the group raises money for the materials, flies to the location, and erects a building. But the union has no money to support a pastor at that location, and the building stands empty. The money and time might have been better spent in a different location.

Gain Experience

Both Carol Moses and Monte Torkelson strongly suggest that a youth leader gain some experience before taking a youth group on a trip on their own. A leader could go on a trip with another experienced person and gain experience. Or the entire youth group could join up with an organization such as Piece of the Pie Ministries or Maranatha Volunteers.

These two organizations organize mission trips for groups of high school students as well as collegiates and young adults. They are also great sources of information and advice. A mission handbook, *Maranatha Guide to Adventure,* is available through Maranatha. Piece of the Pie, headed by Steve Case, offers leadership training for youth leaders.

Although arranging a mission trip requires a significant investment of time and money, the rewards are incalculable. People sometimes have the misconception that it would be more practical in terms of time and money just to send money to the site and hire national workers to complete the project. Although this method is used on occasion, there are a number of reasons it is better to send volunteers. For one, when you send a young person, you are investing in a life—helping to build that person for God. For another, when the project is completed by hired workers rather than volunteers, the nationals at the site miss out on the opportunity to develop relationships with Christians from another country. The camaraderie and teamwork that develop on a project are just as beneficial to the nationals as to the volunteers.

Volunteers also have an evangelistic impact that is missing when nationals are hired to complete the project. The impact on a community can be profound when a group of Christian young people come in to work. The typical view of North American youth is that they are selfish, apathetic, and worldly. When a group of North American youth arrive in a community not to have a good time but to work, people take notice. And when they find out that these young people had to work for the money to come, they are even more impressed. Just the sight of young women doing physical labor catches the attention of the community in places where women do not do this type of work.

As a result, when the new church is completed and holds an evangelistic campaign, the community responds en masse, as their attention has already been captured by the example of young people who are willing to volunteer their time and their money to make a difference.

If your youth group is interested in stepping out boldly for Christ in the area of missions, there are a number of resources available to help you get started. Contact your local conference and speak with the individual responsible for youth ministry. Or get in contact with Maranatha Volunteers International or Piece of the Pie Ministries for information or advice, or to join with them on one of their many adventures.

Maranatha Volunteers International
1600 Sacramento Inn Way, Suite 116
Sacramento, CA 95815
(916) 920-1900
http://www.maranatha.org.

Piece of the Pie Ministries
P.O. Box 2424
Carmichael, CA 95609
(916) 944-3928
Fax: (916) 944-7085
http://www.pieceofthepie.org.

---

[1] Ellen G. White, in *Historical Sketches of the Foreign Missions of the Seventh-day Adventists* (Basel, Switzerland: Imprimerie Polyglotte, 1886), p. 285.

[2] Steve Daily, *Adventism for a New Generation, Portland, Oreg.: Better Living Publishers, 1993)*, p. 250.

CHAPTER 45

Nature and Camping Programs for Seventh-day Adventist Youth

by Gary Thurber

Small Beginnings

THE ADVENTIST CAMPING PROGRAM had its beginnings in the state of Michigan in 1926. Grover Fattic, who was the MV secretary in the East Michigan Conference, had a dream of seeing summer camping become a part of the ministry for the youth in the conference. Time and time again he went to the conference committee for help in seeing this become a reality. Elder Fattic was a persistent man with a big heart for youth. Finally, on his fourth attempt, the conference committee granted him permission to plan for a summer camp program. The only condition was that he would be on his own and would not receive any help from the conference. This did not discourage him at all. With the support of many laypersons, a very helpful Scoutmaster in Detroit, the encouragement and advice of Gordon Smith, the Lake Union MV secretary, and a whole series of other miracles, Elder Fattic was able to secure the funds and find a spot that would be suitable for their camping experience.

At Town Line Lake in Montcalm County, Michigan, summer camp ministry in the Seventh-day Adventist Church began. The cost that summer was $10 for 10 days of camp. The young people stayed in conference camp meeting tents, but that didn't dampen their spirits. As the camp was being prepared, some parents who drove quite a distance to bring their sons to this campsite decided that they couldn't leave their sons. It was too new, untested, and they couldn't be sure it was safe. So they drove home with their sons, much to the dismay of Elder Fattic. But there were 18 boys who did stay, and they made camping history. Many of the first campers at Town Line Lake are still talking about the impact that experience had on their lives. Camp that year was so successful that the next year Elder Fattic organized a camp for the girls as well. Very soon camps sprang up in Wisconsin, California, New England, and eventually all over North America and the world.

Camps today, even though they may look much different from Town Line Lake, have the same kind of impact on our young people. Adventist Camp Ministries (ACM) has thoughtfully prepared a mission statement, philosophy, and goals to help keep the focus of what Christian camping is all about. They are as follows:

Statement of Mission. ACM provides an intentional Christian environment committed

332

to strengthening each camper's relationship with God and all His creation through Scripture, nature, and recreation.

Philosophy. ACM believes that in a camp setting the study of the Bible and nature, in the context of wholesome social relationships and recreation, will place campers and guests in a Christ-centered environment that promotes physical, mental, and spiritual development.

Goals. To be an integral part of the mission and life of the church.

1. To be a servant of the gospel in outreach and to be a resource to the community.
2. To provide programming that focuses on God's creative redemptive love.
3. To recruit and train qualified staff for the camp operation and program.
4. To develop in campers a sense of responsibility for the environment.
5. To maintain a safe, functional, environmentally sensitive, and accredited facility.
6. To encourage networking to enable camps to share resources and information.
7. To provide meeting facilities for conference departmental training seminars and conventions for lay leaders in the local church.
8. To encourage director certification and camp accreditation.

Modern camps offer opportunities for Adventurers (ages 8-9), juniors (ages 10-11), tweens (ages 12-13), and teens (ages 14-16); a wide variety of specialty camps, such as gymnastics, surfing, wake-boarding, rock climbing, and outdoor exploration; and the ever-growing family camps. In addition, most camps operate year-round to provide camping and convention opportunities for Pathfinder groups, church groups, and various other types of conferences and seminars.

Camping Changes Lives

Even though camping has grown tremendously since Town Line Lake, the mission has never wavered. At camp more young people make decisions to accept Christ in their lives than at any other venue. What is the reason for this? What are the factors that bring so much to a young person's life in such a short amount of time? I believe we can readily identify six significant elements about camp that enable this kind of growth to take place.

1. Campers have the opportunity to stay in a Christian community environment.
2. Ministry to the mental, physical, and spiritual components of their lives takes place.
3. Relationships with fellow campers, staff, and God are nurtured.
4. Memories and commitments for a lifetime are created.
5. Leadership skills are taught and learned.
6. Campers see their church reaching out to them and making a significant commitment to them personally. Let's take a closer look at these six elements.

1. Campers Have the Opportunity to Live in a Christian Community

Young people today are growing up in an incredible environment. We hear about the characteristics of the baby boomers, Generation X, and Generation Next and the challenges they face. It is very much a secular world with all kinds of trappings and pitfalls. Camp offers something much different from the normal routine of life. School or home expectations are gone, reputations are largely left behind, peer pressures change, media influence is cut off—all in favor of a special temporary community focused on presenting Christ and nurturing those in the faith toward a maturing walk with God.

The camp uses all its resources of people, environment, and facilities to accomplish its goal. When one is physically removed from their permanent residence and placed in a contrasting Christ-centered loving community, they feel more free to embrace the values and lifestyle of that community. Camp can be a wonderful model to demonstrate how Christians should live.

2. Ministry to the Mental, Physical, and Spiritual Components of Our Lives Takes Place.

Camp is a unique institution because it is able to minister to the "whole person." Many other places can zero in on one or two aspects of a person's growth; however, camp, with its wide range of opportunities, allows for all three components of their lives to flourish.

Through the study of nature, minds are stretched with wonder. The Scriptures and Spirit of Prophecy make it clear that by immersing oneself in God's second book, nature, one can grow intellectually as we come face to face with the wonders of creation.

Camp also offers the opportunity to develop physically. Whether it is horseback riding, waterskiing, swimming, canoeing, hiking, mountain biking, sailing, or climbing the side of a cliff, campers are stretched physically in ways they would normally not be.

Spiritually, there are opportunities for growth at every turn. First, there is the camp council and campfire times, which are spiritually focused at most of our camps. Campers get to experience worship in the great outdoors where they rarely would be able to otherwise. At campfire, meaningful songs are learned and sung. Christ-centered dramas and storytelling take place with the purpose of drawing the camper closer to his or her Creator. There is also the cabin worship time with the counselors. But beyond these opportunities, there is also a Christian staff who through their own relationship with the campers have influence for spiritual growth in the campers.

3. Relationships With Fellow Campers, Staff, and God Are Nurtured

There is no doubt that the activities at camp build social skills. Camp is a highly relational experience. The spiritual mentors talked about in the previous paragraph are always present. They constantly are on alert to build relationships with campers. How to be kind to others when others are unkind to them, how to control anger, how to discipline with love, how to ask for forgiveness, how to grow spiritually, how to deal with temptation, and how to live in a community are all modeled to the camper. Among all of these relationships, the one with Christ is lifted up as the most significant to cultivate.

For many campers, all of this is new to them. Just the experience of living with five to nine other new individuals and needing to function together as a team is quite a feat. Campers run home talking about their counselor. The around-the-clock living arrangement with the counselor in a typical week of camp allows more quality time than a youth pastor has all year. The bonding that occurs by living, playing, worshiping, struggling, and learning together internalizes values taught.

4. Memories and Commitments for a Lifetime Are Made

The short-term stays that most camps offer make a unique experience and a great memory-making opportunity. Because camp is so different from the environment most come from, the campers' senses are heightened and ready to absorb the new stimuli. Therefore, the events at camp become more engaging, alive, and vivid with the energy and focus the camper possesses. Because most camp experiences are beyond the traditional and familiar, they also provide moments that render the camper ready for learning.

At camp, participants sometimes struggle as they experience new and challenging activities. Various camps offer different events, but most have the same philosophy behind them. Whether it is rafting down a white-water river, trying to tackle a 40-foot climbing wall, stepping out on a high-adventure ropes course, going on a wilderness trip, taking aim on an archery range, mounting a horse for the first time, trying to get up on a pair of water skis, jumping onto a 30-foot blob from a 10-foot tower, trying to form a pot out of clay, trying to find raccoon tracks to bring back to the animal-tracking class, dealing with difficult cabinmates, hot or cold weather, disappointments, camp duties, or simply the separation from home and friends—all add to the variety and intensity of the camp experience and bring about wonderful teachable moments. It is at these times that counselors and class instructors have doors of opportunity swung open wide to them where spiritual truths can be presented.

Camp staff have a powerful witness to the campers. In some cases they are only several years older than the camper and are seen as people who love the Lord and are part of an exciting program. Campers tend to make heroes out of the staff, which can be affirming but at the same time carries an incredible responsibility with it.

Spiritual insights at camp flow from many sources: modeling by the counselors and other staff, songs heard and sung at campfires, reflective moments during camp experiences led by the counselors, messages by the camp pastor, friendships with Christian peers, and creative Sabbath programming that makes it the best day of the week. Jesus taught in this manner when He was here on earth. He used special events and situations that prepared His disciples for learning. When He turned water into wine, raised Lazarus from the dead, fed the 5,000, calmed the sea, or healed the 10 lepers, Jesus' messages usually flowed out of the life experiences or felt needs of His students, and then He carefully addressed deeper needs.

When you put together the heightened senses, total engagement, and readiness to learn, along with the spiritual truths attached to these memory-making experiences, camp becomes a life-changing agent in young peoples' lives. Camp is a distinct and intense experience that will forever stand in one's memory. There can be no doubt that the spiritual truths attached to their memorable experiences will stay with them long after they have returned home.

5. Leadership Skills Are Taught and Learned

There is no other venue our church offers for our young adults to learn leadership and team skills that is comparable to camp. Without exception, staff come and learn more about themselves and what it means to work in a team environment. Many of them, who have never been responsible for other peoples' enjoyment, care, and safety, find it much more challenging than they thought. Whether it is leading a cabin of children, teaching a nature class to inquisitive minds, trying to instill calmness in the heart of a camper 25 feet in the air on a ropes-challenge course, or dealing with a homesick camper, a staff member has the opportunity to understand more about life and what it means to be a servant to others. The camp director's greatest joy is to see his or her staff grow in their walk with the Lord. Dependence on Him for strength and wisdom is learned on the job, and when the summer is over, leaders for the cause of Christ have matured greatly.

In a survey commissioned by Christian Camping International (CCI), it was found that more than half of those in full-time Christian ministry had made life-changing decisions at camp as a member of a summer staff. Many camps hold alumni reunions and find that a significant portion of the returning staff point to their experience of being part of a summer camp staff as a major factor in shaping their lives and heading them in the right direction. Camp is a great investment not only for our young people; it is for our young adults as well.

6. Campers See Their Church Reaching Out to Them and Making a Significant Commitment to Them

Robert Folkenberg, during his time as president of the General Conference, proclaimed that we must be sure to give our young people a "piece of the pie." This statement has prompted us to make sure we send our kids the right message about their importance to us as a church.

Camp wonderfully speaks the language of young people. It is filled with all kinds of new adventures and opportunities to which they respond with such enthusiasm. One camper said about his camp, "This place is awesome!" Our young people know that their church built the camp to be a place for them. This is so important, because for many of our kids the church is seen as somewhat cold and distant. To know that you are important enough to your church for it to sponsor this kind of ministry does much to send a positive message to the kids. That is, after all, the truth! Our kids must know that they are paramount to us, and camp is one way that message is sent loud and clear. Camp is a big "piece of the pie"!

Experiencing God's Nature

Camping offers incredible character-building recreation where competition is minimized and personal growth is maximized. It is a place to learn how to interact with many new people and learn how to build a functioning community. It is a place where spiritual truths come out of the woodwork in teachable moments. It is a place with spirit-filled campfires and worships, and to which uplifting music is played and sung. Usually set in an environment that is drastically different from a camper's home life, it is especially a place to which our young people can come and be exposed to God's second book, nature.

Ellen White says: "Nature and revelation alike testify of God's love. Our Father in heaven is the source of life, of wisdom, and of joy. . . . The sunshine and the rain, that gladden and refresh the earth, the hills and seas and plains, all speak to us of the Creator's love. It is God who supplies the daily needs of all His creatures. . . . 'God is love' is written upon every opening bud, upon every spire of springing grass. The lovely birds making the air vocal with their happy songs, the delicately tinted flowers in their perfection perfuming the air, the lofty trees of the forest with their rich foliage of living green—all testify to the tender, fatherly care of our God and to His desire to make His children happy." *

For many kids from the city, to see a deer or a raccoon up close in nature can be a memory in and of itself. Most never have the opportunity to be in the great outdoors where humanity has done little to disturb its natural beauty. The wildflowers, water lilies, birds, horses, and yes, even snakes, all hold countless treasures for our children to discover. This is why it is so important for our camps to have a special focus on getting our kids in touch with God's wonderful nature.

Camps do this in a variety of ways. Many camps require that every camper takes at least one nature class each week. Camps vary in what they can offer depending on the environment that surrounds them. A camp near the coast could easily offer a class on marine wildlife, while a camp in the forest would be well suited to teaching a course on birds or tree identification.

The Adventist Junior Youth honors program followed at many camps offers opportunities to study different aspects of nature, such as animal tracking, rocks, seeds, shells, mammals, reptiles, sands, edible plants, and many others. Kids not only get to learn about these areas; they often are able to earn an honor's patch upon completion of the requirements of the honor. Astronomy is another area of nature that camps are starting to focus on. Several camps now have amateur observatories where campers can study the moon, count the rings of Saturn, or see the beautiful colors of the nebula of Orion. There is a marvelous openness that is created in our young people when they begin to understand the majesty of God's universe.

Camps can offer excellent encounters with creation not only during the summer camp season but year-round as well. Many camps are now beginning to see the importance of being good stewards of the camp environment and using it as a laboratory all year for kids to come and discover their Savior in His handiwork. Curriculum-based outdoor education programs are now being taught at a few of our camps. These programs are geared for the fifth- and sixth-grade level and usually run three to four days. Students who are privileged to be a part of these outdoor schools receive priceless opportunities not only to study but to experience nature at our camps.

For a list of camps that are currently offering outdoor education to schools, simply contact the North American Division Pathfinder and Camping Department. Hopefully outdoor education soon will be the norm in all of our school and camp systems.

At Camp Au Sable, located in the state of Michigan, a beautiful nature center has been established. A quote from Chief Standing Bear, from the Lakota Indian tribe, hangs on a sign outside the nature center: "The Old Lakota was wise. He knew that man's heart away from nature becomes hard. He knew that lack of respect for growing, living things soon led to lack of respect for humans, too. So he kept his youth close to nature's softening influence. Chief father, Standing Bear."

Camp Operation and Support

Today camping is quite a developed profession that requires great care and responsibility for those who become a part of it and give leadership to it. Working with young people in this day and age demands that the programming and events are carried out according to recognized standards for safety and excellence. The Seventh-day Adventist Church has developed a manual on the how to's of camping. This is a must-read resource book for anyone in camp leadership. It covers such topics as programming, risk management, daily schedules, job descriptions, and other pertinent topics associated with a camping program. Camp leaders must also look into the requirements the local government sets for operating camps. In most areas a camp must be licensed by a government agency to accommodate campers. Knowing the requirements and working with the local government inspector is paramount in getting a camp ready for ministry.

During his tenure as NAD camping director, Norm Middag pioneered the Adventist

Association of Camping Professionals (AACP, established in 1995), and it has been growing ever since. It has greatly benefited Adventist camping by bringing it to a new level of excellence—enabling it to impact our young people for Christ even more. The AACP has developed an extensive network of support and even a groundbreaking mentoring program for directors that is essential for anyone new in this ministry. Experienced camp directors are assigned to new directors to help get them established. Camps are a very large liability issue, and to have this kind of training is very important.

The AACP's yearly conventions provide an opportunity to network, plus relevant workshops on various camp topics such as current risk-management issues and the latest innovations in camping. No matter what phase of camping you are involved in, whether it is management, ranger, food service, programming, or even outdoor education, the AACP has a track for you with valuable opportunities for growth. To learn about the association or to become a member, contact the North American Division Pathfinder and Camping Department.

There is a new trend in camping in the Seventh-day Adventist Church. The AACP encourages camps in the United States to become American Camping Association (ACA)-accredited camps. The standards that must be met to accomplish this certification goal are the highest in the camping industry. (For those camps outside of the U.S., similar organizations usually exist and offer the same type of professionalism.) In the U.S., in order to be an ACA-accredited camp, you must be a member of one of two camping organizations: ACA or CCI (Christian Camping International). The AACP encourages membership with CCI because it most closely aligns itself with the mission we have for our camps.

Camping changes people's lives. To be a part of the operating team, or to be a participant, means to come face to face with our Creator in this unique and beautiful setting. May God continue to pour out His blessings on His camps.

---

* E. G. White, *Steps to Christ,* pp. 9, 10.

CHAPTER 46

Nature and Youth Ministry

by Robert Holbrook

A YOUNG WOMAN HALF TURNED in her canoe, looked back toward the leader in his canoe, and sighed, "This was the kind of experience that helps one make the important decisions in life." She was nearing the end of an eight-day canoe trip into Canadian wilderness with a group of Pathfinders and really didn't want the experience to end. That leader had the privilege of baptizing the young woman, performing her wedding a few years later, and then dedicating her first child. In between there were ups and downs, but the "important decisions in life" had been made—while in a very special, intimate relationship with her Creator on His terms, on His turf. She now spends her time showing children the right paths in life.

"If you want to lead young people, you must become an outdoorsman first," Bob Tyson, Nebraska Conference youth director, stated as he began his youth leadership training weekend in the spring of 1962. Tyson never studied biology in a formal setting, never took courses in outdoor education. Yet he was a master of the outdoors and demonstrated an unending ability to relate to the natural world and identify anything youth brought in. His training was based on the folklore of the southern United States, and his stories around a campfire held all spellbound, especially when told in the old rhythmic style known as "ham-boning."

In many ways he was a throwback to the days of Arthur Spalding, Lester Bond, Wilbur Holbrook, and others who pioneered youth work. He wasn't really an entertainer—no big flash, no fancy suit or "with it" garb, no fancy mike system. He didn't speak the hip, cool slang of the youth. He just loved spending time with the kids of his conference—camping on the weekends, talking, listening, giving advice when asked. Small-group campfires were his thing. He smiled a lot, and the kids figured he knew each of them personally. That aspect of his leadership style was typical of leaders from the past: down-to-earth, open honesty, a connection with their Creator that encouraged others to emulate.

The Problem of Technology

During recent years society has made some major shifts in direction that only lead away from God. Technology, originally intended to be a servant of humanity and facilitate its existence, has turned and "bitten the hand" by becoming master and overlord of human beings. It has taken control of life, dominating our existence on a 24-hour-a-day basis. A recent study shows that Internet users now spend an average of three hours per day surfing cyberspace—in addition to the time spent on TV and video programming.[1]

While traveling with a colleague in youth ministry one day, I observed that we could never complete a conversation on any given topic without being interrupted by a phone call. Even driving the car had become a problem to him, and he asked if I could drive awhile. When I commented about his lack of privacy, he responded by rolling his eyes with that look of resigned despair and commented about having no family time and not even being able to sleep at night. If people have a problem, he's their solution—now, whenever "now" is.

I asked to see his business card. After some searching, he found one and handed it to me. Sure enough, he listed on the card his office number, his home number, and his cell phone number. I told him, "You've killed yourself!" He looked at me incredulously. "Your only option for a personal life now is to change your home phone to an unlisted number and change your cell phone to a number only your secretary and wife know and are under severe penalties if released!"

Our rat race has become so intense that A. W. Tozer wrote, "Science . . . has robbed [human beings] of their souls. . . . What was intended to be a blessing has become a . . . curse." Then he goes on to blast our current lifestyle: "One way the civilized world destroys [humans] is by preventing them from thinking their own thoughts. . . . We Christians must simplify our lives or lose untold treasures on earth and in eternity."[2]

That doesn't mean throw out technology; it means regaining control of our lives (which for some that may mean drastic measures). The Spirit of Prophecy continues this same line: "If the frivolous and pleasure-seeking will allow their minds to dwell upon the real and true, the heart cannot but be filled with reverence, and they will adore the God of nature. The contemplation and study of God's character as revealed in His created works will open a field of thought that will draw the mind away from low, debasing, enervating amusements."[3]

Tozer again: "God's word in the Bible can have power only because it corresponds to God's word in the universe. It is the present Voice which makes the written Word all-powerful."[4]

We simply cannot divorce a relationship with God from an understanding of His created world. We cannot expect to have an understanding of salvation nor of God's character through "virtual reality;" we need God's reality. Ellen White reminds us: "He alone who recognizes in nature his Father's handiwork, who in the richness and beauty of the earth reads the Father's handwriting—he alone learns from the things of nature their deepest lessons, and receives their highest ministry. Only he can fully appreciate the significance of hill and vale, river and sea, who looks upon them as an expression of the thought of God, a revelation of the Creator. . . . Nature becomes a key to the treasure house of the Word. Children should be encouraged to search . . . nature. Thus may they learn to see Him. . . . They may learn to hear His voice. . . . And every object in nature will repeat to them His precious lessons."[5]

This brings us back to that opening statement by Bob Tyson: "If you want to lead young people, you must become an outdoorsman first." At a youth leadership seminar in Wisconsin Charles Bradford put it in his own simple, effective way. He said, "You can't teach what you don't know, and you can't lead where you won't go!"

The Way to the Solution

So where do we go from here? I can hear some say, "Since I'm not a naturalist, you're saying I shouldn't be in youth ministry?" "I studied theology" or "I studied psychology" or

"I studied youth ministry"—"None of this was ever presented or deemed necessary." "Our culture is different. That's not where kids are today. We must work with kids where they are."

This may all be true, but it's not God's way. We cannot leave our kids where they are; we must show them something better—God's reality. We must go against the onrushing torrent of current culture if we are to be true leaders of youth. Nowhere in the inspired Word do I find that we are to encourage His followers to continue a status quo "in their sin." Rather, we must turn them toward the true and everlasting light of heaven through the tools God Himself gave us to enable our relationship with Him.

"Even in their blighted state, all things reveal the handiwork of the great Master Artist. Wherever we turn, we may hear the voice of God, and see evidences of His goodness. From the solemn roll of the deep-toned thunder and old ocean's ceaseless roar, to the glad songs that make the forests vocal with melody, nature's ten thousand voices speak His praise."[6] "Let no one make the mistake of regarding himself as so well educated as to have no more need of studying nature."[7]

"Those who sacrifice simplicity to fashion, and shut themselves away from the beauties of nature, cannot be spiritually minded. . . . Therefore their hearts do not quicken and throb with new love and interest, and they are not filled with awe and reverence as they see God in nature."[8]

We have studied many things, we know a lot, we are designated as leaders of the youth of our church. But we cannot stop now and think that we have all the answers, nor do we need to spend time looking for further answers in the mire itself. We need to—we can now begin to—seek answers God's way, from His handiwork. For even though we can't actually see God, we "can understand Him sufficiently" if we "only watch His power and divine attributes at work in nature. It's been that way since the creation of the world." We can understand God's power and goodness by observing what He made, and that leaves us with "no excuse" (Rom. 1:20, Clear Word).

We need to find the time—we need to make the time—as Tozer said, to "simplify our lives," redirect some of our energies, restudy our role as leaders (at all levels within the church "hierarchy"). A statement written by Ellen White to fathers applies to all of us in youth leadership: "In the time that he [the father] would devote to selfish enjoyment of leisure, let him seek to become acquainted with his children—associate with them. . . . Let him point them to the beautiful flowers, the lofty trees, in whose very leaves they can trace the work and love of God."[9]

As we begin our own search process there are some basic principles we must ever keep in mind.

1. "Science is ever discovering new wonders; but she brings from her research nothing that, rightly understood, conflicts with divine revelation."[10]

2. "Is it not the task of the ear to discriminate between [wise and unwise] words, just as the mouth distinguishes [between desirable and undesirable] food?" (Job 12:11, Amplified).

3. Start with the most simple and build toward the more complex as your proficiency improves. Youth are impressed with anything in nature that illustrates God's ways. Use such illustrations as "hill and vale," "forests," "thunder," and "oceans." The Bible also uses some of the simplest illustrations to obtain the deepest meanings. Detailed, intricate things that a naturalist would find are fascinating, but that's not where we start. You'll likely misuse

words and create an illustration out of something that's not accurate (or even fictitious), thus doing more harm than good. Remember, "you can't teach what you don't know."

4. Nature reaches all the senses. If you are using nature to bring home spiritual lessons, be sure that you are allowing nature to make its maximum impact—visual where needed, auditory where needed, etc. Don't just tell about nature; *be in* nature.

The Solution Attainable

Before attempting to create your own lessons from nature, allow the Bible to do it for you. Yes, there are devotional books that use nature as a basis for the lessons taught. But reading something to kids is often the best way to lose their interest. Reliving, visualizing, touching, smelling, hearing—these communicate.

I recall meeting with a group of young people on the beach and talking about sand. God sometimes likes to exaggerate to get His point across. In fact, He uses sand just that way at least 25 times in the Bible. So I took a cup of sand and asked a youngster to count the grains while the group looked at the Bible implications of sand armies, widows, descendants, opposites (foolish and wise). Then we came to Psalm 139:17, 18: "How precious your tender thoughts have been toward me, O Lord. There are so many of them, they never end! If I could count them, they would be more in number than the sands" (Clear Word). Then he closes the psalm with the observation "Search my heart. . . . Let me know if there is any wicked way in me, and then help me to walk the way I should" (verses 23, 24, Clear Word). The next morning kids were sifting sand between their toes and looking first at me, then up toward the sky— and smiling. Remember Ellen White's statement a few paragraphs above, that "nature becomes a key to the treasure house of the Word"?

For some, fashion is everything. Self-worth, personal value, is all based on that which society determines is worthwhile. God's system is quite the opposite. In the Bible He uses a number of examples to get His point across, but I've found few as effective as flowers. Look up those references and see how Jesus makes the applications. Have kids pick a flower and hold it in their hands while out on a walk. At the end of the walk talk about Solomon: These flowers "are more beautiful in their simplicity than Solomon was in all his royal splendor" (Matt. 6:29, Clear Word). What splendor? His annual income was equivalent to US$39,294,000 in gold alone, not counting all the other precious metals, jewels, animals, etc. He had even married the most beautiful women from every country known. Talk about importance! Check out 1 Peter 1: 24; Psalm 103:15, 16; *Early Writings,* page 19; etc. Wilting flowers—just one more very simple lesson God is trying to teach us.

More complicated illustrations will come from extensive reading on all natural history subjects while maintaining the thought in the back of your mind that somewhere in here there's another object lesson. You will find that the bookstores are packed full of fascinating volumes on every subject of God's creation, and lessons will jump out from some of the most unlikely spots. You will find lessons from butterfly wings, from spirals in a sunflower or pinecone, in any and all of the nature honors.

I was searching for answers to the questions in the lichens, liverworts, and mosses honor when I came across a description of the symbiotic relationship between algae and fungi in lichens, which I then used for several years to teach Pathfinders the need for differing talents and use of cooperative effort. Lichens made a really neat illustration, which could be approached very spur-of-the-moment on a Sabbath afternoon nature walk.

Then one day my illustration died. While reading another book dealing with nature in miniature, I found out that the algae and fungi don't exactly "cooperate;" it's more like a tug-of-war! That wouldn't do. Yes, I could continue with my story, but it wasn't true. Even if the kids never found out otherwise, I knew better. The spur-of-the-moment story continued, but now with the "rest of the story" added. Cooperation builds large plants like the tall trees. Turf protection, tug-of-war, creates stagnation, stunted growth, like the miserable little lichens. The lesson is an even better one than I had originally thought of—and makes an even better impact on the listener/observer.

Possible Detours Avoided

Many books we start reading seem to have nonbiblical concepts and theories woven in. These cause concern and even manage to turn some people's ideas away from the plain biblical truths. Some find themselves trying to merge the two opposing concepts by modifying their understanding of the Bible. But remember: "The Bible is not to be tested by men's ideas of science, but science is to be brought to the test of the unerring standard."[11]

I'm quite aware that this is thought to be shallow, narrow thinking by some. After all, the Bible is not a scientific book; it is a book about salvation. True, the Bible does not give many details on some subjects we "nature buffs" would like details on, but that which the Bible does give must be considered as accurate or it invalidates the premise salvation itself is founded on. A clear understanding of three basic concepts are a must: Creation, the Fall, and redemption.

These are absolutes within the Christian worldview, and they provide a foundation on which a solid understanding of nature can be built. The same must hold true for science. Its premises must be accurate, or they invalidate the structure that is built over them. Careful study will show that true science is actually built on principles developed by the Christian worldview.

Now look at an astronomer's opening remarks in a book titled *A Catalogue of the Universe.* "When man views the immensity of the universe, he is awed. In an attempt to ease the nature of the problem, he endeavors to define a small number of labels which he can attach to a large number of objects. . . . *It is reduced to manageable proportions if he can make such untrue statements as.* . . . Try as he might to attach labels to the natural world, man is forever confronted by the infinite diversity of his environment, and is doomed to fail."[12] The need to establish untrue statements is a rather dubious premise on which to build theories about the natural world.

In a fascinating book about whales I found these two sentences in the same paragraph: "All known fossil whales seem to be fully developed aquatic mammals; we do not know the steps that led to their return to the sea . . . . There seems to be no question that the ancestors of whales and dolphins were land-dwelling creatures; the evolutionary development of whales as we know it clearly points to the conclusion."[13] In other words: "What we do not know clearly points to evolution." That's not a very sound premise. Charles Colson said it right: "Only Christianity offers a way to understand both the physical and the moral order.

Only Christianity offers a comprehensive worldview that covers all areas of life and thought, every aspect of creation. Only Christianity offers a way to live in line with the real world. . . . The entire cosmos can be understood only in relation to God." [14]

Michael Behe, a biochemist who has spent a lifetime researching the possibilities of biochemical evolution, states: "Scientists working on the origin of life deserve a lot of credit; they have attacked the problem by experiment and calculation, as science should. And although the experiments have not turned out as many hoped, through their efforts we now have a clear idea of the staggering difficulties that would face an origin of life by natural chemical processes." [15]

"Unbridgeable chasms occur even at the tiniest level of life." [16]

"On the other hand, many scientists think that given the origin of life, its subsequent evolution is easy to envision. . . . Evolutionary biologists make no attempt to test evolutionary scenarios at the molecular level by experiment or calculation. As a result, evolutionary biology is stuck in the same frame of mind that dominated origin-of-life studies in the early fifties, before most experiments had been done: imagination running wild." [17]

The apostle Paul and the psalmist agree in a much less politically correct manner. Paul declares that there have been some who, when they studied God's creation, "still did not give Him credit for His marvelous acts, nor were they thankful for His blessings. They became arrogant and proud of their learning, and their foolish hearts were darkened. They thought they were brilliant, but actually they were fools" (Rom. 1:21, 22, Clear Word). The psalmist seconds the incrimination: "Only a fool says to himself, 'There is no God.' He wants to commit abominable iniquity and not feel guilty about it" (Ps. 53:1, Clear Word). So much for one of the most important premises of all, the chemical mutations necessary to accomplish the neat theories presented.

There are numerous other premises, such as dating methods, that likewise have their Achilles heel when carefully questioned. The facts remain: the naturalistic theories advanced in an effort to explain the facts without recognizing a Designer are to be questioned. For some, the separation between fact and fiction is difficult. We must simply remember that we were not there when matter came into existence. Yet, the *anthropic principle* (the physical structure of the universe is *exactly* what it must be in order to support life) so clearly leads to a logical Designer conclusion that we can stick with the lessons God has for us today and understand that one day we will have the opportunity to relive those incredible acts of creation with the earth made new.

I quote Behe once again: "Biochemical systems were designed. They were designed not by the laws of nature, not by chance and necessity; rather, they were *planned*. The designer knew what the systems would look like when they were completed, then took steps to bring the systems about. . . . The conclusion of intelligent design flows naturally from the data itself—not from sacred books or sectarian beliefs." [18]

The Destination

Nature is truly awesome and inspiring, from the minutest 1-millimeter orchid to the multiple-ton elephant; from the molecular structure of amethyst crystals to the view from the top of the highest mountain. It's God's creation, not humanity's. Therefore, it holds an intrinsic capability of pointing us to our God that nothing else can match. He designed it that way, and if we overlook its potential, neglect it, or give it minimal importance, we can only lose.

Philip Yancey writes about a sermon his pastor gave one day. "My pastor brought in Ralphie, a pet crayfish. 'What do you think about Ralphie?' he asked as the crayfish waved his claws menacingly. The kids responded with gusto: *Cool! Neat! Way cool! Awesome!*"[19]

C. S. Lewis suggests that observing God's creation is a holy calling! Sam Campbell, an early twentieth-century naturalist, once wrote a little piece titled "Dawn." He describes the expectation and suspense while hurrying through the forest in the darkness to reach a certain spot before dawn in an effort to "catch the spirit of the dawn," then the exciting silence as he waits. Then he breaks out in beautiful, descriptive eloquence as he views the coming of the new day across the wilderness laid out before: "Here is an event that even Eternal Hills cannot look upon stoically! *Our thoughts are lifted up in ecstasy—we have caught the spirit of the dawn!*" Then he closes with this thought: "But, pause a moment! Is there not a symbol in what we have seen and felt? Is there not a mental dawn fast trailing the night of human experience? And is there not a spirit—Hope, Faith, Inspiration—which sets the soul to singing and prepares it for the full Day of Revelation? 'Rejoice in the Lord alway: and again I say, Rejoice.'"[20]

Have you had such an experience? Have your youth had such an experience? "You can't teach what you don't know. You can't lead where you won't go."

---

[1] WTOP radio report, Jan. 10, 2000.

[2] A. W. Tozer, *The Best of A. W. Tozer* (Grand Rapids: Baker Book House, 1995), p. 149. (Italics supplied.)

[3] E. G. White, *Testimonies*, vol. 4, p. 581.

[4] Tozer, p. 21.

[5] White, *Education*, pp. 119, 120.

[6] White, *The Ministry of Healing*, p. 411.

[7] White, *Fundamentals of Christian Education*, p. 213.

[8] White, *Testimonies*, vol. 2, p. 584.

[9] White, *Fundamentals of Christian Education*, p. 159.

[10] White, *Education*, p. 128.

[11] White, *Counsels to Parents, Teachers, and Students*, p. 425.

[12] Paul Murdin, *Catalogue of the Universe* (New York: Crown, 1979), pp. 20, 21. (Italics supplied.)

[13] Richard Ellis, *The Book of Whales* (New York: Alfred P. Knopf, 1980), p. 8.

[14] Charles Colson, *How Now Shall We Live?* (Wheaton, Ill.: Tyndale, 1999), pp. xi, xii.

[15] Micael Behe, *Darwin's Black Box* (New York: Free Press, 1996), pp. 172.

[16] *Ibid.,* p. 15.

[17] *Ibid.,* p. 173.

[18] *Ibid.,* p. 193.

[19] Philip Yancey, in *Christianity Today*, April 1997, p. 72.

[20] Sam Campbell, *Nature's Messages of Peace* (Chicago: Associated Authors, 1937), p. 14.

CHAPTER 47

Effective Delegation

by Kim Allan Johnson

ONE OF THE MOST OVERLOOKED and underutilized aspects of effective leadership is the vital subject of delegation. The scriptural counsel "It is more blessed to give than to receive" (Acts 20:35) could apply here. Your ministry will be blessed in proportion to your willingness to give responsibility to others and train them to become effective ministers for God. The following fictional scene illustrates the point.

The kickoff to begin the game sent the football into a long, high arch over the 100-yard field. Coach Joe, the receiver, watched the ball spiral through the air as he squinted into the glare of the bright early-afternoon sun. He could hear the rumble of 11 Goliaths from the opposing team racing to tackle him and pile on. When the ball finally fell into Joe's grasp, he looked ahead, sidestepped one player, spun around another, and was then smothered in a mound of grunting, sweating humanity.

Being the only person on the field for his team, Joe hiked the ball to himself, then ran forward into a solid, impenetrable wall of defenders. He staggered to his feet, hiked the ball to himself again, with the same miserable result. He huddled alone trying to think what to do next. As the rest of the team paced the sidelines, one of them yelled, "Hey, Coach, can we play too?"

Joe shouted back, "Not yet. Things are going great out here so far."

He hiked the ball to himself a third time and was chased backward screaming "Please don't hurt me!" Hit hard, he fumbled the ball to the other team one inch from his own goal.

From the sidelines came another insistent plea: "Coach, you gotta let us play now!"

Joe rubbed the dirt out of his eyes, sucked in a hot, rasping breath, and replied, "I'm doing just fine. So far so good." On the next play the opposing team casually brushed him aside, and their ball carrier danced easily across the line for a much-too-easy score. After two hours of "Joe verses everyone else," the score was everyone else 84 and Joe 0.

This imaginary game is certainly exaggerated, but it's not too far from the truth for too many youth ministries. Joe's biggest mistake was a lack of delegation. Coaches are supposed to equip others to play the game while they give guidance and encouragement. It is not their role to carry the ball all by themselves. So it is in the local church.

Ray Johnston writes, "Delegation is critical because it is almost impossible for an individual to develop maturity, competence, or leadership ability apart from responsibility. Giving teenagers significant responsibility develops these qualities."[1]

John Maxwell, noted trainer of leaders, observes, "Delegation is the most powerful tool leaders have; it increases their individual productivity as well as the productivity of their department or organization." [2]

Barry Gane, an experienced youth leader, counsels, "A spiritually astute minister of youth must realize that the task is far too immense to be attempted alone. The gifts of many persons are needed." [3]

The adage "delegate or die" is certainly true. Lack of delegation is the reason so many church youth leaders get discouraged or burn out. How often have well-meaning adults begun their youth ministry with great optimism only to find, several months later, that they are scrambling to find some magic new program to entertain the 10 to 20, bored, TV-infected teenagers staring back at them on Sabbath morning.

Moses belatedly discovered the importance of delegation when he led the wayward Israelites out of Egyptian bondage (Ex. 18:13-27). I can hear him in the wilderness now: "Do we have any aspirin left? This headache is killing me. Not to mention my sick stomach. I'm beat. Up at 5:00 a.m. every morning and collapsing into bed by midnight. The problems these people have are endless. I can't take this rat race much longer!" Thankfully God sent Jethro with a seminar on successful delegation and saved Moses' ministry.

So now you may be wondering, "If delegation is so important, why do so few leaders practice it? What are some of the roadblocks that keep leaders from giving ministry away?" Here are a few possible answers.

Roadblocks to Delegation

1. Delegation Not Central

Many youth leaders agree that delegation is worthwhile, but fail to put it into practice because they don't see it as central to their purpose. They view it as one direction youth ministry might take among others or as simply another management tool that could be used if needed. In fact, delegation is at the very heart of youth ministry because discipling is at the heart of God's vision for church. The bull's-eye on the leader's ministry target is equipping and building youth to become mature Christians through involvement in meaningful service. The old adage "use it or lose it" is relevant here.

As a parent, nothing gives me more delight than seeing my daughter, who is a junior in an Adventist college, choosing to do ministry for Christ. Along with our own efforts to bring her up in the Lord, the church has helped immensely by getting her involved from her earliest days. She has been asked to give talks, play her oboe, participate in skits, visit the needy, tell stories in primary division at camp meeting, and on and on. Meaningful involvement is a big part of the glue that holds her spiritually close. Youth value what they invest in. They support what they help to create. And at no time in life is the church's role of involving youth more important than during the teen years.

The youth are a critical part of God's plan for saving lost humanity. Paul wrote to Timothy, "Don't let anyone think little of you because you are young" (1 Tim. 4:12, TLB). Ellen White counseled, "With such an army of workers as our youth, rightly trained, might furnish, how soon the message of a crucified, risen, and soon-coming Savior might be carried to the whole world!" [4]

Our role model is Jesus, who made the training of 12 needy people the central focus of His ministry. One of Christ's key followers, the disciple John, was probably not more than 16 when called from his nets. In many ways the beginnings of the Seventh-day Adventist Church itself was a youth movement. Ellen White, John Andrews, J. N. Loughborough, Uriah Smith, and others were teenagers or in their early 20s when tapped by God for weighty tasks. Can the church today afford to do less?

Because youth leaders have limited time, the great temptation is to become program-oriented, with the leader up front and the youth as spectators. Putting on uplifting spiritual programs is important, but that should not become the center of a youth leader's efforts. The acid test of the effectiveness of youth leaders is not how many youth they can get to watch what they can do, but how many young people they can get to do ministry themselves.

2. Lack of Confidence in Youth

Roger Dudley hired a young woman named Vickie to join his summer camp staff. As director he had misgivings because of her emotional immaturity, but chose to take her on nonetheless. During orientation he made it clear how important it was for every staff member to get permission before leaving camp. One night during the first week he asked the nurse to make evening rounds to check that everything was OK. She discovered that Vickie and a girlfriend had secretly sneaked away from camp. After discovering their whereabouts, the director drove out to bring them back.

On the verge of tears, Vickie inquired, "Elder Dudley, are you going to fire us and send us home?"

He replied, "Above everything else, I've got to know that my staff is reliable. I believe that you can be those trustworthy staff members that I can count on."

"You mean you're going to give us a second chance?" Vickie said. "We won't fail you again."

For the rest of camp Vickie proved true to her word. In the years that followed she chose to attend an Adventist academy and college, becoming very active in witnessing activities. Later Dudley read in the *Review* that she had even become an overseas student missionary. He observes, "I leaned back, closed my eyes, and wondered if her story might have turned out differently if I had sent that young non-Adventist girl home from camp. And I thanked God that He had helped me to trust."[5]

Society says we can drive a car, own a credit card, vote for president, and die for our country in the armed forces at age 18. America gives its youth huge responsibilities before they're 20. Should the church not do the same? Youth become leaders by being allowed to lead. They become responsible Christians by being given responsibility. In spite of their flaws, they become trustworthy by being trusted.

"Trust is the highest form of human motivation. It brings out the very best in people. But it takes time and patience, and it doesn't preclude the necessity to train and develop people so that their competency can rise to the level of that trust. "[6]

3. "I Can Do It Better"

I grew up as the kid who held the flashlight. My dad could fix anything from cars to leaky pipes. Unfortunately, he rarely let me help with any actual repairs. "Shine that light over here, son," he would tell me. "No, just a little to the left. That's perfect." As a result of that early training I can now point a flashlight with uncanny accuracy. But I haven't got a clue how to fix very much that goes wrong around me. My dad's considerable mechanical skill kept him trapped in the "if you want it done right do it yourself" mode. His own strengths grew stronger while my weaknesses remained. I love my dad dearly, but I wish he had allowed me to make mistakes and learn under his tutelage.

John Maxwell writes, "It is difficult for people to give up tasks they love to perform. . . . The question leaders must ask themselves is whether the task can be done by someone else. If so, it should probably be delegated. The leader should focus on performing tasks no one else can do, not simply on doing tasks he or she enjoys."[7]

4. "I Don't Have Time"

"I barely have enough time to put together the youth program each week. How am I supposed to find time to train others to do it?" Such a dilemma is very real and can be incredibly frustrating. The solution lies in taking the long view. Suppose, for example, it takes you four hours each week to put together the youth program on your own. That translates to more than 200 hours a year. Now suppose you add an extra hour each week for three months to train others to take over that responsibility. Initially that adds significantly to your load. But if after three months you can delegate that programming to those young people, you have saved yourself a whopping 140 hours in that year alone! In the short term you are busier, but in the long term you are freer to train more people in ministry and expand your team. You can equip youth to plan and lead out in everything from socials to retreats.

The following illustration brings out the point. "John, carrying two briefcases, always arrived late for dinner. One night his 5-year-old daughter asked Mommy why Daddy had to carry two suitcases everywhere. Mommy proudly explained that Daddy was an executive with lots and lots of work to do. More work than he had time to do at the office. The child spoke to the heart of the matter: 'Why don't they just put him in a slower group?' John failed to switch from being a doer to a delegator."[8]

Being too busy to delegate keeps us on a never-ending cycle that is loaded with stress and plagued by limited results. No one on earth has ever been as busy as Christ, and yet He made training and delegation top priority. He laid a foundation on which He could later build a worldwide movement.

So what, then, are some of the principles of good delegation? How can I make delegation actually work?

Principles of Delegation Assess the Person

Delegation is more than simply giving other people something to do. One of the classic mistakes that leaders make is to delegate without carefully considering the talents, personality, and readiness of the other person. The goal is to build disciples, rather than simply using people to accomplish a predetermined task. Don't simply dump your work on others. Start with the person rather than the task.

"Effective delegation begins with careful assessment. Asking the following questions can be helpful: Does he work quickly or slowly? Does he require minimal or maximum direction? Is he organized or disorganized? Does he like working alone or with others? Does he prefer structured work or the opportunity for creativity?"[9]

It is also helpful to consider the "spiritual gifts" of the other person. Youth leaders should become acquainted with the biblical doctrine of spiritual gifts and understand the variety of gifts identified in scripture. Try to match gifts and ministries as closely as possible. Putting round pegs in square holes is just asking for problems and frustration. It is a recipe for procrastination and inadequate performance.

The best way to motivate people is to give them opportunities to minister in ways that are in harmony with their inherent interests. Discovering their "purple passion in life" can provide vital clues as to what type of ministry they would enjoy. Perhaps a young woman has a burden to work with disadvantaged children. Match her up to a VBS program or open the way for her to volunteer periodically in the kindergarten division. If a young man gets excited about cars, give him a chance to make basic repairs for the single moms in your church or community. If several youth love drama, encourage them to put together skits for Sabbath school, vespers, or the worship service.

Give Them Adequate Training

Turning youth loose on a task without adequate training is unfair to both them and the church. Match them up with whoever can provide the best advice and orientation. Have them intern under a more experienced mentor. You can make available books, videos, and audiotapes, and may even find funds to send them to a seminar. Plug them into whatever resources might be needed to accomplish the task. The best training is as personal as possible, built around ongoing, supportive relationships. Jesus, the Master Trainer, didn't simply hand His disciples a manual; He spent time with them, teaching by word and example.

Focus on Results, Not Methods

There is more than one way up a mountain. Clearly describe the task to be accomplished, but allow young people as much latitude as possible in how it is done. Forcing people to use only prescribed methods can sap motivation and destroy creativity.

Stephen Covey advises, "Create a clear, mutual understanding of what needs to be accomplished, focusing on *what,* not *how; results,* not *methods.* Spend time. Be patient. Visualize the desired result. Have the person see it, describe it, make out a quality statement of what the results will look like, and by when they will be accomplished."[10]

Covey illustrates his point by describing the time he delegated the job of mowing their lawn to his 7-year-old son. He took the boy to a neighbor's house and said, "See how our neighbor's yard is green and clean? That's what we're after: *green and clean.*"[11]

Answer the question "How will we both know when the task is accomplished well?" Write it down. With this in place the young person can tackle the job with confidence and ingenuity. Once the delegated task is clearly understood, you can then discuss accountability. How often will they report and to whom? Will they report informally through a phone call or more formally by making out an actual report? If the assignment is large and/or complicated, you may want more frequent checkups. If it is simple and straightforward, an informal report at the end may be sufficient.

Accountability must include specific deadlines for the project. If someone is less experienced, give them simple short-term tasks at first so they can find success, then delegate more challenging long-term activities later.

Give Them Adequate Authority

Effective delegation can easily be undermined by giving young people a task to do without also giving them adequate authority to get the job done. What budget do they have? What decisions can they make on their own? What permissions are needed? What ditches should they avoid? Responsibility without authority will guarantee frustration. You are giving them "limited authority" to work within a certain framework. Such authority should be appropriate to their age and maturity level.

Be on a Constant Talent Search

Youth leaders often complain that they can't find anyone to take on responsibility. John Maxwell writes, "The truth is you must always be looking for people to whom you can give tasks. The times that people will track you down to ask you for something to do will be rare. A leader who can't find people to delegate to may not be looking hard enough." [12]

Throughout the entire process of delegation the young people will need you to be their most avid cheerleader, just as Jesus is for us. Youth can easily get discouraged and need your encouragement on a regular basis. If things go right, give the young people the credit. If things go wrong, take the blame on yourself. That is a sure way to win their loyalty and trust. The youth leader who consistently delegates will certainly meet with difficulties, but will also have the deep satisfaction of knowing they have invested in building young hearts and lives that will bring glory to God throughout all eternity.

---

[1] Ray Johnston, *Developing Student Leaders,* p. 103.

[2] John Maxwell, *Developing the Leaders Around You* (Nashville: Thomas Nelson, 1995), p. 169.

[3] Barry Gane, *Building Youth Ministry,* p. 64.

[4] E. G. White, *Education,* p. 271.

[5] Roger L. Dudley, *Why Teenagers Reject Religion and What to Do About It,* pp. 137-141.

[6] Stephen R. Covey, *The 7 Habits of Highly Effective People* (New York: Simon and Schuster, 1989), p. 178.

[7] Maxwell, p.170.

[8] Carla L. Brown, *Techniques of Successful Delegation* (Shawnee Mission, Kans.: National Press Publications, 1988), p. 170.

[9] *Ibid.,* pp. 20, 21.

[10] Covey, p. 174.

[11] *Ibid.,* p. 175.

[12] Maxwell, p. 171.

CHAPTER 48

The Role of the Pastor in Youth Ministry

by Jennifer Morgan

TANYA DEDE PREACHED HER FIRST sermon in Palo Alto, California, during a youth church scheduled by her pastor, Ifeoma Kwessi. Tanya's sermon was her testimony of the God she'd discovered after growing up in the Seventh-day Adventist Church. Not until a youth pastor at Union College gave her a CD of Jars of Clay did she hear a message that made her think she needed to give Jesus a second chance. "Faith is like skydiving," Tanya told her home church. "You can't experience it if you don't jump out of the plane."

Tanya's mother, Nadine, glows with pride when she talks about her eldest daughter. "People ask me, 'What did you do right?' I tell them, 'This has nothing to do with me!'" Nadine attributes Tanya's spiritual growth to the Holy Spirit.

Tanya's sermon culminated a summer of volunteer youth ministry directed toward her younger sister, Therese, and the other members of the Palo Alto youth department. She had come home to help out at her mother's request. Nadine, the youth Sabbath school teacher, was getting discouraged, and she figured that Tanya, with her fresh ideas, was just the tonic the youth needed. But Nadine will be the first to admit that Tanya's testimony also revitalized her own walk with Jesus.

Now Tanya's younger sister, Therese, is insisting that her mother come to the church's Wednesday night "Experiencing God" workshop. "I'm here because Therese brought me!" confesses Nadine to the other church members. But she seems happy to have her 15-year-old bring her.

Why Should a Pastor Be Concerned About Youth Ministry?

Many pastors freely admit that they are not skilled in youth ministry. But don't let your pastor use this as an excuse to avoid making the youth department one of his or her highest priorities. There are three reasons every pastor needs to be very interested in youth ministry.

The Youth Department Is the Complexion of the Church

In 1 Corinthians 12 Paul describes the church as the body of Christ. The wise pastor will soon realize that the youth department is the epidermis. As an organ the skin is highly underappreciated and often overlooked. However, when the body is sick, where do you look for the first sign? If you've eaten too much sugar or chocolate, where is the first place your excess manifests itself? If you go outdoors and get some exercise, what organ glows an immediate testimonial to your good behavior?

The same is true of the youth department. Structural, social, spiritual—whatever the problem your church has, it probably will show itself first in the youth department. Adults can take months—sometimes years—wondering why they go to church, and slowly drift out the back door. But a teenager will usually bring the problem to the surface. Your teenagers don't bring their Bibles to church? They will tell you directly, "We never need our Bibles in church." The pastor preaches a slow sermon? "Wow, Preacher," the kids will say, "you sure were boring today!" The adults are hiding a sexual sin? Look out! This Vesuvius is sure to erupt in your youth department.

A Youth Department on Fire Will Light Up Your Church

This is the opposite of the first point. Youth don't always reveal all the flaws in the church. A healthy youth department reflects a healthy church. It can also create a healthy church. In the opening illustration, Nadine did not recognize that she needed a spiritual revival. She expressed discouragement about the youth Sabbath school class she was teaching. But it was her daughter's excitement about Jesus that revived Nadine's enthusiasm for church.

Teenagers are called to remind adults about that first-love experience that has gotten blunted throughout the years. They are not afraid to take risks for Jesus and try new things. Ellen White, speaking from personal experience, describes the youth as "an army of workers" who, "rightly trained," will spread the gospel to the world.[1] And to their own families, too. Parents will go to great lengths to save their children's souls and, in the process, will sometimes even be saved themselves. It is important to the whole church to know that this message is timeless and relevant to every generation. Nobody likes to be part of an aging organization.

Crucial Decisions Are Made During the Teenage and Young Adult Years

Tanya Dede accepted Christ when she was away from home and her life was in transition. This is not unusual. This is the time most life decisions will be made, including the young person's relationship with the church. But not all young people will opt for church attendance. In a 10-year study of Seventh-day Adventist 15-year-olds that began in 1987, Roger Dudley, of Andrews University's Institute of Church Ministry, discovered that one out of five teenagers who leaves the church will come back during their young adult years. Dudley predicts that even more of his subjects will return during their child-rearing years, since 88 percent of all respondents wanted their children to be raised in the church. This means that youth ministries is not just leading to youth baptisms, but is sometimes planting the seeds for adult rebaptisms.

But the church doesn't aim for rebaptisms. The church wants young people to give their lives to Jesus and keep their lives in Jesus. Dudley points out the problems of the loss of an estimated 47 percent of his original sampling of 1,523 teenagers, "The disengagement of such a large percentage of well-educated young adults who should now be assuming leadership in the church threatens the future viability of our movement."[2]

The Seventh-day Adventist Church is suffering from the lack of youth ministry, and pastors can help reverse that trend. Of the young Seventh-day Adventists Dudley surveyed, 56 percent reported that a pastor—and 50 percent a teacher in an Adventist school—were a positive spiritual influence.

You may think that this is a bad statistic, but it looks like an improvement over the past 20 years. In 1960 the Robert Johnston Company asked youth to rank the influences in their lives in order of importance. Ministers, priests, and rabbis ranked fourth, with parents being first, teachers second and friends third. In 1980 the same study found that friends ranked first, parents were second, television, records, movies, and radio were third, and teachers were fourth. Ministers, priests, and rabbis ranked number six in teen influences, right after popular sports, music, and cinema heroes.[3] In 1999, with all the other things competing for their attention, if 50 percent Adventist young people credit a pastor or teacher as helping influence them spiritually, that's pretty impressive.

So What Can the Pastor Do to Help the Youth Ministry?

Relate

A skilled youth ministry professional with additional experience teaching ministers how to relate to youth, Steve Case, from Piece of the Pie Ministries, stresses relationship as the center of any youth leader's or pastor's role in youth ministry. Steve's ministry coordinates a lot of mission trips for youth groups, but the trips are designed to establish relationships, and the relationships are used to disciple young people into a deeper commitment with Christ. Youth pastor Doug Fields puts it this way: "I don't want to direct programs; I want to disciple students."[4] But you can't disciple young people until you have established a relationship with them. As David Veerman writes, a "solid and effective ministry must be built on personal relationships, friendships, getting to know young people, and winning the right to be heard."[5]

Veerman calls this process of "winning the right to be heard" building time. There are five steps in Veerman's building time: prayer, planning, coordinating, participating, and affirming. For Veerman, this is an important time not only to model Christian behavior but to learn a lot of information about your youth. "Have fun and be yourself, Veerman advises. "Try to get to know the young person(s), but don't force it."[6]

Most youth leaders understand this instinctively, but some will work with senior pastors who find this first step threatening. Young people are in a distinct culture of their own, and, like any other culture with its own language, dress, and symbols, it is very intimidating to enter. Tim Mitchell, senior pastor of the Sunnyvale Adventist Church (Central California Conference), does not see himself as being naturally talented in youth ministry. He has delegated the direct programming to other lay and professional youth ministers in his congregation. However, Tim definitely sees himself as having a role to play in the lives of his youth.

"You have to minister out of your credibility," says Tim. "Kids don't ask me to come to speak to their chapels—that's not where my credibility is—but they do ask me about basketball. That's where we connect."

When a new pastor arrives at your church, the adults are all waiting to hear the first sermon. This is not true of the typical teenager. Unfortunately, many of our youth see the sermon as something designed for Mom and Dad; they slip in and out of attention during the 11:00 service, not really expecting the preacher to say anything for them. What the teenagers are wondering is "Will the pastor even notice me? Will this preacher joke with me at potlucks? come out to play volleyball on gym nights? sit in on Sabbath school discussions? not be shocked if I speak my mind?"

The vast majority of adult interactions with teenagers are spent in telling them what to do. They already know what the pastor is going to say, and they also suspect that he or she intends to say it in a very long monologue. Encourage your pastor to surprise them. Invite your pastor to come to youth Sabbath school prepared to listen. Ask your youth to preach to the pastor once a quarter. Then encourage the pastor to sit in the pew and listen. (Don't ever miss youth church—that is a cardinal sin for a youth leader or pastor.) Youth leaders and pastors need to drop by school to visit at lunchtime, or sit in on the local academy's assemblies.

In his 300-member church Tim Mitchell doesn't conduct a pastor's Sabbath school class. Instead Tim visits each of the divisions every Sabbath. In the tiny tots he taps the shoulder of at least four parents each week: "Hi, how are you doing?" He kneels with the kindergartners in their prayer corral. The primary children show him their pictures, and he joins right in on the juniors' games, with one or two wisecracks. But in the youth department Tim says, "I go in, and I shut up. Where it's appropriate I laugh and smile."

Tim talks about how much he as an adult, and especially a pastor, wants to moralize to young people. But he advises that adults fight the temptation to preach. He thinks it is critical for pastors to read the movie and entertainment section of the newspaper each week. But this information is so you can understand the culture and their jokes. Tim advises pastors against telling young people what media they should and should not be watching. "If you look at the 10 things a kid can do to get in trouble: going to movies, getting drunk, taking drugs . . . if you moralize about the movies, they're never going to tell you about getting pregnant."

Tim stresses that its not that pastors shouldn't talk about these things to young people. But choose the time, choose the place, and make sure they've laid down a good relationship as a foundation before they criticize anyone on a lifestyle choice. "I only get four times at bat," says Tim, "and I want to do it when the bases are loaded."

"But when thou art bidden, go and sit down in the lowest room; that when he that bade thee cometh, he may say unto thee, Friend, go up higher" (Luke 14:10). "If you come in assuming you have credibility, you've already lost it," says Tim Mitchell. Hang out at the table, circle it, but don't sit down. The youth will tell you what seat to take. When Tim passes a group of teenagers sitting around after church, he will toss out a question or a joke. But if they fall silent after one question, he moves on. "I'm really not welcome in most of their life."

But he is available. And, like Jesus on the road to Emmaus, he is waiting for their invitation to a deeper relationship. It may come in the form of a joke or a nickname: "Hey, Rev!" or "Paaastor Tim." "A nickname is a sign of love," Tim says.

Affirm

Brian Wahl, pastor of Monterey Bay Academy, sums up the role of the pastor in one word: "cheerleading!" Brian's enthusiasm for youth has been a hallmark of his 15 years of youth pastoring in the United States and Canada. But Brian admits to a frustration with this church. Of the five positions where he has youth-pastored, every church Brian has left has decided not to hire another youth pastor. In the absence of any professional mentor, these youth ministries have withered and died.

Brian and his wife, Pam, couldn't understand why talented and dedicated youth volunteers and parents couldn't continue programs they were successfully doing under Brian's supervision. They concluded that the most important thing he and Pam were offering was encouragement. "When you lose that catalyst, it just dies," says Brian.

In the opening illustration the pastor of Tanya Dede's church in Palo Alto, California, is Ifeoma Kwesi. Like Tim Mitchell, Ifeoma does not see herself as gifted in youth ministry. In her 12 years in ministry Ifeoma has only once been a part of a church that has had a youth minister as a paid position. "For a pastor that pastors a congregation that can afford but one pastor and he/she is not particularly gifted in that area," says Ifeoma, "it is important to identify laypeople who have a burden and a great love for young people, and to equip them to serve in that area." She adds that pastors also need "to open up as many areas as possible for young people to serve."

Like most senior pastors, Ifeoma would like to have a full-time professional youth minister on her staff. She points out that in the past often the stress has been on the resources and training of a youth minister, "but the fundamental prerequisite is just a love for and a burden for kids. I think that God can work miracles with that." Kwesi stresses that the mentoring and encouraging of those lay and professional youth workers is essential. She and Tanya Dede were in weekly, sometimes daily, contact during Tanya's summer tenure in the youth department.

Tim Mitchell quotes another pastor from the Central California Conference, Mitch Williams. Before Tim had any children, he asked the older pastor for advice: "What is your secret? How did you raise three such wonderful kids?"

"You know what?" Mitch Williams told Tim. "I take really good care of their mom. If the kids see their mom and dad getting along, they feel safe. And if they see that their mom and dad are happy, they are happy."

If your youth see that you have a team that gets along, they will feel safe in your church. This includes pastors, parents, volunteers, and schoolteachers. Tim admits that he doesn't drop by Mountain View Academy just to see his teenagers, but also to visit with the teachers. "I care about teachers. I consider them my partners in ministry." With the burnout rate that accompanies youth work, it is important, as Tim says, to "pump up the youth staff."

Protect

Along those same lines, the pastor should protect the youth staff. They are like Aaron and Hur holding up the arms of Moses: the youth workers, schoolteachers, youth ministers, Sabbath school leaders, Pathfinder directors, parents. Sometimes these people spend so much time with this age group that they identify more with teenagers than with adults. In adult/teen clashes, a youth minister can find himself or herself in church or school boards trying to plead the cases of young people.

Sometimes teenagers are invited to speak to these small seats of government. Giraffe Ministry is a functioning organization in the Adventist Church. The church needs giraffes—people willing to stick their necks out for youth. Youth workers sometimes feel as though they are out on some limb of the church doing a little-recognized evangelism. Even worse, sometimes there can be church members who appear to be sawing the limb off from the trunk.

Giraffes on decision-making committees will stick their necks out for young people. To switch to a football analogy, the church needs pastors who will run interference for youth ministers. Speak up when church members criticize "today's youth." Be ready with positive examples from the youth department, or local academy, when negative criticism worms its way through the adult division. Encourage church boards to budget for youth evangelism.

Pastors and youth leaders also need to protect our youth. Inevitably, mistakes will happen. A youth worker will show bad judgment. A young person will do something inappropriate. The saints will be shocked. People will look for someone to blame. This is no time to abandon your youth or their leaders. It's also not a time to isolate yourself from the church. You need the pastors support now more than ever. Remind yourself and your congregation that you and they were young once, too. Many of us have unsavory pasts that we know God has forgiven and forgotten. This may be a time for the church to demonstrate to our youth the best asset that God ever gave us: our ability to forgive.

In Pat Wick's Let Me Be a Window she shares a Code for a Safe Place:
- I will not leave or abandon you as a friend.
- I accept you—unconditional love.
- I will not belittle you or reject you.
- You have a right to your own feelings.
- I will not bring up past mistakes.
- I take responsibility for myself.
- I will affirm your right to choose.[7]

This describes the job of the pastor. Churches are often places of criticism and what Phillip Yancey calls "ungrace." We adults need to work together to make churches a safe place for our youth.

Teenagers are scary. It's true. They look like adults, act like kids, and dress like scarecrows. They will seldom say amen without being sarcastic, will not sing when asked to, and will often fill whole auditoriums with their sulky, glowering looks. Or not. They can also be overwhelmingly generous, be the only ones in your congregations who remember your birthday, and have the biggest smiles when you wear that funny Christmas tie. They can hug you when you're least expecting it and get really excited about being asked to preach a sermon. Once in the pulpit, they can say things that will make you worry about losing your job—or they can bring your whole congregation to tears. And your role in all of this is very simple. You are called by God to love them—to cherish them for being just what they are: teenagers.

[1] E. G. White, Education, p. 271.

[2] Roger Dudley, Why Our Teenagers Leave the Church (Hagerstown, Md.: Review and Herald Pub. Assn., 2000), p. 36.

[3] Available at http://www.cyberview.Adventist.org/summer.98/16. Youth Ministry Encyclopedia. (Littleton: Serendipity, 1985), p. 223.

[4] Doug Fields, Purpose-driven Youth Ministry, p. 18.

[5] David R. Veerman, Youth Evangelism: When They're in Your Neighborhood but Not in the Fold (New York: Victor Books, 1988), p. 62.

[6] Ibid., p. 83.

[7] Pat Wick, Let Me Be a Window, p. 67.

CHAPTER 49

Communication With Youth, Peers, and Parents

by Trudy J. Morgan-Cole

COMMUNICATION AFFECTS EVERY ASPECT of your youth ministry. You need to communicate effectively with young people in order to share Jesus' love with them. You need to communicate with the parents of the youth in order to have a successful ministry. And our young people need to learn effective communication skills that they can apply in their own relationships.

Youth ministry author Pat Wick speaks of the "circle of communication: listening, hearing, understanding, responding,"[1] It's vital for us as youth leaders to learn to apply each part of this "circle" as we communicate with our youth and teach them to communicate with others.

Communication With Youth

An effective youth ministry is built on relationships, and relationships are built on communication. As youth leaders, many of us put too much emphasis on planning programs rather than on getting to know our young people..

Communicating with young people takes time. To break down the barriers of mistrust that often exist between youth and adults, we need to spend time with them. This can't be accomplished exclusively in the setting of a Sabbath school class or an AY meeting. "Many teens won't talk on Sabbath morning. Too many people are around, and there's no time to sit and talk. By contacting your youth outside of the church, they have an opportunity in a comfortable, nonthreatening atmosphere to let you know what's on their mind. When youth leaders take time outside of 'church time' to be with youth, a deeper relationship begins to develop."[2]

Try visiting your youth at home or at school. Invite them to your home. Attend their sports events, school splays, music recitals. Let them know that you are interested in them seven days a week, not just on Sabbath. This will open the lines of communication.

As this deeper relationship grows, young people will begin opening up to you. When they talk to you about problems they face at home, at school, and in their developing Christian walk, you have the opportunity to practice that "circle of communication." And it begins with learning to listen. So often as leaders we have the impulse to preach, to jump in with answers and advice, but it's far more important to learn to listen.

Your body language is an important part of communication. As you listen, "face the person, maintain eye contact with them, lean forward."[3] Your posture, as well as your words, should tell the person that he or she matters to you, and that listening to them is the most important thing you have to do right now. "Kids know when your mind is wandering," youth ministry veteran Stuart Tyner points out. "They are fully aware when you'd rather be somewhere else doing something else. And that lack of focus is insulting."[4] Communicate the fact that you're listening verbally as well as nonverbally. Repeat back to the youth what you're hearing. Ask them to clarify things they've said.

"Don't give advice," says Pat Wick. "Remember, you are reflecting back what you hear them saying and what you think they are feeling. . . . Don't tell them what you think they should do."[5] This isn't always easy, but remember that your role is to help the young person move toward finding a solution. Ask such questions as "if you could have any wish you wanted, right now, what would it be?" or "Pretend this problem is solved; what would it be like?"[6] Help the young person to discover and choose the best options. Be willing and available to help, but don't feel you have to provide all the answers or "fix" the problem.

You can help a young person reach a solution to a problem by helping them focus on goals. Long-term goals can be defined by asking questions like "What do you want to do with your life?" "Where do you see yourself in five or 10 years?" When the long-term goals are clear, "help them formulate short-range objectives that will help them arrive at their long-term goals."[7]

Most important, bring an attitude of Christlike acceptance to the conversation. "You create an atmosphere of openness when you communicate unconditional love and when you are willing to listen."[8] The more youth feel loved and accepted, the more willing they will be to share their problems and concerns.

When a young person asks you directly for your opinion on a situation they are facing, youth ministry experts Mike Yaconelli and Jim Burns suggest, "Don't be afraid to tell kids what they don't want to hear." They give the example of a teenage girl who tells her youth leader that her boyfriend is pushing her to become sexually intimate. She wonders how she can "back off" from sexual intimacy without losing the relationship. The honest answer, as most adults will realize, is that "backing off" is almost impossible, and the girl is better off breaking up with this boyfriend. This isn't what she wants to hear, but, say Yaconelli and Burns, "it is what she *needs* to hear." Even if your advice has been requested and you've given an honest answer, "it's unwise to force [youth] to respond the way you want them to respond. Let them hear the hard news and then make the decision on their own."[9]

Remember that your main role as a youth leader, friend, and nonprofessional counselor is not to give advice. It is to listen, to care, and to help the young person discover his or her own solutions to life's biggest questions.

When a young person is in a crisis situation, such as contemplating suicide or dealing with sexual abuse, they should be referred to a professional counselor. This doesn't mean you no longer have a role in the young person's life. You can continue to serve as a friend and support, using all the listening skills discussed above. But don't assume you can handle the problem on your own. If you are not professionally trained in counseling, enlist the help of someone who is. "Remember the first role of counseling: Do No Harm. Please listen and care for the troubled youth, but make sure a trained counselor works through the crisis with them."[10]

The role of the youth worker is different from that of the professional counselor, but it is nonetheless important, and a young person facing a serious crisis will probably need both kinds of help. "Young people in real emotional and psychological trouble will often come to a nonprofessional first because they don't know where else to go or whom to trust. As a non-professional, you can be the bridge between the person in crisis and the professional help, if it's needed."[11]

When we think of helping youth in crisis, the question of confidentiality springs to mind. Young people need to be able to trust that you will not share their problems with anyone else. Always respect the confidence a young person has placed in you by coming to you with their concerns. If there are limits to what you would be willing to keep confidential, be open about that. Remember that in many places the law requires you to inform the authorities if a young person is contemplating suicide or harm to others, or if abuse is occurring. Tell the young person honestly what the limits to your confidentiality are.

Yaconelli and Burns suggest that you could say, "I believe I have an obligation anytime I talk with someone to keep our conversation confidential, but I honestly cannot say that if you were in danger or desperately in need of help, I wouldn't do whatever was necessary to help you."[12] Young people need to feel they can trust you in order to communicate with you, but that doesn't mean you have to be "trapped" into keeping secrets that would endanger the young person. As with all other aspects of communication, honesty is the key. Youth respect honesty, and it keeps the lines of communication open.

Communication With Parents and Families

Parents of adolescents have a tough job. As Jim Burns and Mike Yaconelli point out: "Most parents are afraid—afraid of a lot of things. Especially during their children's adolescent years."[13] They outline some of the major fears parents face: fear of their teenagers' new-found independence; fear that the children will not make up for the parents' failures in life; fear that their children will make life-changing mistakes; fear that they can no longer communicate with their children. Though a youth leader can have a positive impact on a young person's relationship with his or her parents, some barriers will probably have to be overcome. Some parents may initially be wary or distrustful of the church youth leader, or may feel that the youth leader's role excludes parents' involvement. "Sometimes parents perceive youth workers as threats to their relationship with their children because we're adults with whom their teenagers confide," says youth and family minister Tom Lytle. "Adolescence is usually marked by conflict, and many parents experience feelings of failure and guilt because their kids fight with them."[14]

At the same time, it's not unusual for youth pastors and youth leaders to suffer from what author Paul Borthwick calls "parent-noia"—feelings of discomfort around the parents of their youth group members. Borthwick points out that negative experiences in the past may cause youth workers to be afraid of parents, or critical of their parenting skills. A youth leader's pride may make them defensive in the face of a parent's questions. Or youth leaders may just feel apathetic about parents" and feel that they are irrelevant to youth ministry.[15]

You can overcome many of these barriers by making sure that you communicate effectively with parents about their young people and about what is happening in your youth ministry. Keep parents up-to-date and involved with your youth program. Make time to visit with parents and get to know their concerns. Build family activities into your program—a family games night, a family retreat, or a parent-teen discussion session. Recruit willing parents to help with youth activities. Take a few moments at church to chat with parents and give them some positive feedback about their teenagers.

Remember that, as Borthwick points out, "parents hold the ultimate responsibility for raising their children, including their teenagers." Our work will be most effective when we "see ourselves as assistants to the parents as they do their ministry. As one youth leader put it, "I am now going to parents and asking them 'How can I assist you in your ministry with your children?'"[16]

As we improve our own communication with parents, we can help youth and their parents learn to communicate better with each other. "There are two main reasons parents have difficulty talking with their high schooler," Burns and Yaconelli say. "First, *parents have a hard time listening to their children. . . .* Second *. . . parents cannot be neutral* because they are too close to their children and care too much to be neutral.[17]

We can help parents realize that while caring adults such as youth leaders, teachers, and pastors play an important role in listening to and loving their youth, no one can replace the parent. Burns and Yaconelli suggest some ways to help parents and teens work through some of their most common communication problems:

Lack of Trust. Adolescents don't always see the connection between their actions and their parents' inability to trust them. Help them realize that trust must be earned by reliable actions.

Difficulty Expressing Love. As a youth leader, you can encourage both parents and students to be more open in expressing their love for each other. Saying "I love you" verbally is important, but it's not the only way. Doing special activities together, helping one another, writing notes, can all express love.

Lack of Listening Skills. Youth complain, "My parents don't listen to me!" and in the flurry of family life, it's too often true. Share with parents your own experience in developing listening skills.

Parental "Hypocrisy." Parents, like all of us, often fail to practice what they preach. Young people need to recognize that their parents are fallible human beings who deserve compassion and sympathy.[18]

Burns and Yaconelli go on to say that "part of the youth worker's job is to help high school students see that they must assume some responsibility for resolving family conflicts. Getting along is not solely the responsibility of the parents."[19] As we encourage youth to spend time with their parents, understand the parents' perspective, attempt to communicate, and follow the Bible's injunction to "honor and obey," we will help them build stronger bonds within their families.

Communication With Peers

It comes as no surprise to youth leaders that relationships with peers are tremendously important to young people. And, as we all recognize, peer pressure comes in two flavors: positive and negative. Young people can be influenced by their friends to drink, use drugs, have premarital sex, and take part in many other self-destructive behaviors. But Christian youth can also influence their friends to come to church, participate in youth activities, love

Jesus, and serve others. Our goal as youth leaders should be to tap into the power of positive peer pressure: to teach youth to communicate with their friends in ways that will build each other up.

"Wouldn't it be nice if we could walk into the church or the youth group and find no cliques, no competition, no negative vibes?" asks Pat Wick. That, of course, is unrealistic. A church youth group is subject to the same pitfalls that any group of human beings is prey to. But, she points out, as a church "we have a GOAL to be accepting and model affirmation! We want our youth groups to be that safe place for making friends, exploring new ideas and asking questions. We believe that as we get to know other people, we get to know ourselves, and thus we get a clearer picture of God."[20]

The picture of the youth group as a "safe place" is an important one in teaching youth to communicate effectively with their peers. One of our chief goals in planning activities and programs should be to bond the group together, to create a sense of community in which everyone can be accepted as they are.

Most young people are not naturally open and accepting. Adolescence is a difficult time in life, when many people are very self-conscious and deeply concerned about "fitting in" with those they admire. The need to be accepted can often lead them to reject those who are less popular, as if they are advertising, "Hey, I'm not one of *those* nerds . . . I'm one of the cool people!" Youth need to be taught respect for others' feelings. Make it a rule in your Sabbath school or small-group meetings that no one is to criticize or put down anyone else. Give youth plenty of opportunities to affirm each other.

Jim Burns and Mike Yaconelli, after discussing the typical social groupings that occur in high school society (groups such as jocks, brains, nerds, etc.), says that "one of the goals of high school ministry is to create an adolescent community in which these social groupings no longer exist. In school, jocks have nothing to do with nerds. In the youth group, jocks and nerds should be able to be together and not be affected by their social grouping."[21] This is an ideal, of course, and may take a long time, a lot of bonding, and a great deal of spiritual growth for young people to reach. Though we must understand and accept that they have cliques and prejudices, we need to model openness. "It is so easy for the adult leader to fall into the trap of having a little 'gang' of admirers. . . . Is everyone included? Then it isn't much fun for those who are left out."[22]

As we model openness and acceptance and seek to create community among our youth, we can also encourage them to use their peer relationships positively. "High school students themselves are sometimes the best resource for helping another high school student," say Burns and Yaconelli.[23] Peer counseling can be very effective if young people are taught to use their skills to listen to each other and help each other find solutions to problems. Six important qualities youth can use to help each other are "affirmation, to need and be needed, trust, support, recognition of potential, and cohesiveness (unity)."[24] You can pass on the same listening skills and techniques that you have learned to apply in communicating with young people: they can use these skills to help other youth.

It takes time to break down the insecurities and prejudices of adolescent society, but young people can be tremendously powerful helpers and witnesses when they begin accepting and loving one another and using their influence to lead others to Jesus. By learning effective communication skills yourself and sharing them with your youth, you can equip them to minister powerfully with their families and their peer groups.

---

[1] Pat Wick, *Let Me Be a Window,* p. 88.

[2] Jim Feldbush, William Hurtado, and Ron Whitehead, *7 Principles for Youth Ministry Excellence,* p. 52.

[3] Wick, p. 84

[4] Stuart Tyner, "One-on-One Conversations With Youth," in *Project Affirmation: Perspectives on Values,* ed. V. Bailey Gillespie (Riverside, Calif.: La Sierra University Press, 1993), pp. 272, 273.

[5] Wick, p. 84.

[6] *Ibid.*

[7] Feldbush et al.

[8] Mike Yaconelli and Jim Burns, *High School Ministry,* p. 26.

[9] *Ibid.,* p. 50.

[10] Feldbush et al., p. 55.

[11] Yaconelli and Burns, p. 138.

[12] *Ibid.,* pp. 145, 146.

[13] *Ibid.,* pp. 79, 80.

[14] Tom Lytle, "Youth Ministry for the Whole Family," *YouthWorker,* May/June 1996.

[15] Paul Borthwick, "How I Cured My Parent-noia," *YouthWorker,* Spring 1985.

[16] *Ibid.*

[17] Yaconelli and Burns, pp. 80, 81.

[18] *Ibid.,* pp. 83, 84.

[19] *Ibid.,* p. 85.

[20] Wick, p. 55.

[21] Yaconelli and Burns, p. 58.

[22] Wick, p. 58.

[23] Yaconelli and Burns, p. 55.

[24] *Ibid.*

CHAPTER 50

Sports in Youth Ministry

by Manfred Woysch

IN THE FOLLOWING DISCUSSION it will not be possible to go into all the questions that could crop up in a discussion of this topic. In diverse cultures various problems arise within the framework of sports and youth ministry. I hope that my thoughts will be able to contribute something that may bring many a new impulse, or even directly be of some help, in furthering our cause. However, it should be very clear in every reader's mind that sports are not and should not become the most important thing in youth ministry, even though athletic activities are basic for the maintenance of good health. Furthermore, sports can be of great help in perhaps clarifying a problem or to further some other things.

A Philosophy of Sports in Adventist Youth Ministry

We often divide the human being into three parts, classically speaking: the body, the mind, and the soul. Strictly speaking, I am of the opinion that there is no such division, in that our whole being has been affected in each and every situation we have experienced. Let me clarify this: I *am* a body, mind, and soul, rather than I *have* a body, mind, and soul. In the same way, I am a Christian, but do not have only Christian attitudes. As I myself am an athlete as well, let me try to develop some helpful suggestions from this point of view.

If our daily life, for example, seems to consist of a lot of sitting and thinking, with scarcely any physical movement, we are then, to be sure, doing a lot for our minds, but our bodies and souls are, nevertheless, suffering. In this way, our whole being is also suffering. However, it often appears that adults especially have "sat to death" their basic instinct for movement. Their need of movement has been "stunted" or has even become "extinct" through the programming of their daily lives. Completely suppression of movement usually means serious consequences for their health.

Even on the various levels of our Adventist administration it often occurs that the hours and days have been packed full of long sessions without leaving any room for balance. The sessions themselves then become too long, the breaks few and far between, and any movement, especially in the fresh air, has not been planned at all. It seems the simple but oft-quoted statement "Less is often more!" could be applied here. One is not fully aware of how much a healthy body with good blood circulation qualitatively contributes to even better and quicker though processes!

Unfortunately, it has not occurred to anyone to open up the steadfast structures and to prove, through healthy programs, that they can function, that one can think and act much better and more effectively when the blood circulation of the body is continually and thoroughly stimulated. This goal can be achieved much more quickly through frequent, short breaks rather than through long pauses followed by long sessions. There is a lack of courage to integrate reasonably short breaks in the daily agenda of the sessions. Arrangements should be made to provide for reasonable bodily exercise. The earlier that young people become "accustomed" to the fact that their bodies need sensible exercise (not only at school every day, but outside school as well), the more this attitude will be impressed on them.

In many cultures even the athletic programs at the universities come off badly. In most other areas and fields of action outside the school day, a sense for physical exercise has been lost. Nevertheless, the youth are already acquainted with physical exercises and sport activities from school, and these should be appropriated and utilized more intensively.

We have a tremendous chance to anchor the principles about healthy athletic exercise in and around our common activities in our work with young people. Therefore, it is very important that we do not hold only youth programs in which our young people are sitting and listening, sitting and discussing, or sitting and celebrating. No! Get them up out of their "comfortable" armchairs and do something with them. Create a genuine group dynamic through these activities.

It is most important that these activities are many-sided and not just furthering fellowship in the social-cultural aspect. Visiting cultural monuments and programs or even just conducting sightseeing tours is beneficial and appropriate. They bring variety and increase knowledge, but in this context they are, nevertheless, too little. Genuine athletic activities also belong in the program. Perhaps a many-sided, manifold Pathfinder program could serve as an example.

In the discussion being developed here and in the following, one important thing should be kept in mind: Whenever we are talking about activities and athletic exercise in the youth work, this does not necessarily mean that it is everything or the most important thing in this work. Without question the greatest emphasis in the youth work in our congregations should be placed on the spiritual, but it must nevertheless be integrated very well.

In conclusion to this section, let me refer to a Bible text. The human being is composed of moving parts and moved parts. The Bible speaks of the human body as the temple of the Holy Spirit: "Do you not know that your body is a temple of the Holy Spirit, who is in you, whom you have received from God?" (1 Cor. 6:19, NIV). Is it not now time for us to maintain this temple of God in a healthy condition, that is, to use it appropriately?

Noncompetitive Sports

It is important to remember here that with exercise, more than the early-morning walk to the car is meant. The normal daily exercise is not sufficient to create a genuine balance or to keep the body healthy. In order to achieve this, athletic exercise is absolutely necessary. Of course, the daily lives of young people can be quite different. Young people doing manual labor certainly do not need any intensive and strenuous sports, or even professional sports, with its daily training. They need only an athletic exercise that will create a genuine balance. But the many young people still going to school or studying at a university should bring some variety into their often "academic" daily lives. Both groups of young people, however, should be able to find a more relaxing athletic activity on this one level. Competitive sports is therefore not an appropriate athletic exercise for our youth groups.

Nevertheless, a few words about competitive sports should be made here: Competitive sports are also a part of athletics. Much can be learned through competitive sports, through winning and losing, as well. However, it should be accompanied by qualified professionals as a rule. Very few of our youth groups have such qualified professional help; therefore, we should leave competitive sports to the athletic clubs, institutes of training, and associations.

This, of course, does not mean that there are no good or even outstanding athletic teams in our youth groups that are able to compete successfully in one sport or another. But the training of such teams and their activities should in no way be in competition with the youth work itself. There are teams in our youth groups, for example, that play volleyball very well and have rather successfully participated in inner-church tournaments. Sometimes in those youth groups that have been developing over a long period of time there are good athletes in the ranks of the group. From time to time contact has been made with other extra-church teams, and other athletes have been made aware of our "Christian activities" as well. In this way, any sort of competitive sport can be used as a missionary activity.

I have sometimes spoken with other runners about my faith after marathon competitions. However, these are rare opportunities, sent from God, which can hardly be foreseen or even planned. Should an individual young person or youth group find an incentive here, then they should try it out at least once. However, such a thing often includes additional stress and therefore is appropriate for only a few groups!

What Do You Want to Achieve?

In the youth work we should involve such athletic activities taking place outside the competitive field. This certainly includes such activities that (a) strengthen group fellowship or help to solve problems, (b) bring the group closer to nature and in this way to God's creation, and/or (c) be used for missionary activities in the widest sense of the word.

Athletic Activities in Order to Strengthen Group Fellowship

This has to do with simple, easy kinds of sport, chosen by the leaders, that will involve everyone in order to utilize them in youth programs, at conferences, or on trips. In this way the outsider can be integrated into the group, since it sports and games participants can easily come closer to one another. Most of them are any kind of ball games or simple kinds of sport. The rules can be determined by the group or even simplified. It is important that these rules are known to everyone and have been clearly explained so that no tension is brought into the group by such athletic activities. Groups having some kind of open space near their regular meeting place should exercise in the fresh air as often as possible. Many groups have rented a gymnasium in order to become better acquainted through sports and games. These groups have the advantage of offering athletic activities in addition. In this way, even a second meeting can be offered during the week. Consider, however, that this can bring disadvantages as well as advantages. It is very important to see that this does not drive a wedge between an active part of the group and an inactive part.

Furthermore, athletic activities can be a way of using up superfluous energy. It is not important which theory of aggression is represented here, but it is always sensible to discharge some of the bodily stress energy in order to be able to approach a problem more calmly afterward. Or does everything run free of stress in your group, without any quarrels or problems.

Athletic Activities in God's Creation

One can often give a Bible study or study another topic with a group outdoors. This group experience can then be deepened through an enjoyable ball game. The conclusion could then be a picnic together. Of course, there are many other ways to organize such encounters in nature with the group—for example, driving out into the country and organizing a potluck together before having a group study. On such an afternoon an enjoyable ball game could form the conclusion of a deepening encounter. A further example for an alternative youth hour: the youth group could hold an agape celebration outdoors, ending with an athletic activity as the climax.

Above and beyond the normal youth programs, the group leadership should also consider making some trips together, which help a group to grow together as well. Not only do such trips add variety to the maybe already monotonous "daily drag" in a youth group, but the youth are able to become better acquainted with each other as well. It is not very original simply to direct the cars to some predetermined destination. The group's being together alone in one place is already helpful for the group. However, "together on the road" can lead to an unforgettable group experience even more.

As far as it is organizationally possible, an excursion with canoes or bicycles can weld a group together fantastically. It all takes place in God's creation, which often has an even more impressive effect. Even simply hiking can have this effect and can be practiced by groups in every country in the world. All of these examples show that athletic activities can be splendidly integrated into the youth work. It can even help to deepen the group experience and the creation experience.

Athletic Activities With a Missionary Character

Almost every kind of athletic activity can be utilized by our youth groups in order to open them up to nonbelievers or members of other faiths. The exceptions are only those athletic activities needed by the group itself. Here are two samples: athletic activities that a group uses in order to find itself; athletic activities that a group needs in order to relax tensions or to "let off steam." Only those youth programs taking place in the great outdoors can, however, be opened to invited friends and others who are interested. In this way, they are brought into contact with the group, and often this contact can be deepened and one or another of them remain "stranded" with the group.

Even better, canoe tours, bicycle tours, or even hiking tours can be used as adventure tours or experience tours. The public media can be used to advertise such a great tour. Various kinds of invitations can be given personally or in writing. Even the local press can be used to make such a tour known to the public.

We have had manifold experiences in our work with the Pathfinders. The Pathfinders utilize their large camporees in order to take friends and others who are interested with them and to first acquaint them with the Pathfinders. Many of these contacts have already become so involved that these "outside" youth have come into our congregation. Of course, it is important to consider what can be achieved with the group at hand and what the group is capable of doing.

Effective Strategies for Sports in Youth Ministry

Sports must be a regular part of the life of a youth group, because sports can help to strengthen the feeling of belonging together. Once a youth group is consolidated, their meetings should not only become ends in themselves but should also be used to do missionary work. There are many ways the leader of a youth group can utilize the many gifts and talents of the group. That is why it is desirable to attract people's interest in Jesus in a variety of ways. Sports could be one of them, a very attractive way of getting involved in God's work. However, it is important to consider that a group shouldn't demand too much of itself, because fervent missionary zeal could also be detrimental. The first step to a more open attitude should always be a small step.

Sports and the Christian

No youth group should shrink from doing sports. But it is crucial that there is an awareness in advance. The youth leaders must know what they are heading for and why they are offering or doing sports. Finally, I want to add two quotations. Because I think they speak for themselves, I leave them uncommented:

"Proper periods of sleep and rest and an abundance of physical exercise are essential to health of body and mind."[1]

"The human body is created so that it unfolds its full strength only through its permanent use. Obviously the human body is created to be active to its full measure; therefore we should not be astonished that our modern aversion to bodily exercise causes problems."[2]

In the third section of the book *Counsels on Diet and Foods* you can read about Ellen White's opinion concerning the connection of health reform and the third angel's message.

---

[1] E. G. White, *Testimonies,* vol. 7, p. 247.
[2] D. Hawley, *Fang an zu leben* (Hamburg, Germany: 1975), pp. 91, 92.

CHAPTER 51

Small Groups in Youth Ministry

by Hiskia I. Missah

Introduction

SMALL GROUP IS A TERM that is known around the world. It is repeatedly mentioned in the church realm, as well as in the business world. It has various derivatives, such as small company, small community, cell group, group dynamics, group interaction, caring group, support group. It is small in size or quantity, but that does not necessarily mean it is less in power; in fact, it is more powerful because it is cost-effective. As its name implies, it is intended to be small and always remain small, but it does not mean that it will not grow. It is expected to be active and vibrant. A small group has to grow, but when the group grows big, it has to divide into small groups again.

Even though the small group is small in size, it is not small-minded. It does not have a narrow or selfish attitude. It does not think about its own self. It is designed for service. In order for the small group idea to be accepted and supported in our youth ministry, we need to have some sense of what a small group is, who is involved in it, and what its goals are.

The strength and effectiveness of our youth ministry can be tested through the small group in it. As Eliot Porter, an American photographer, said: "Sometimes you can tell a large story with a tiny subject."

In this chapter we will be dealing with the theology of small groups, the rationale for small groups, the kinds of small groups, and utilizing small groups in youth ministry.

A student of accounting in one of the Adventist universities in the Southern Asia-Pacific Division committed suicide by hanging himself in his dormitory room. He was a devoted Seventh-day Adventist youth who read his Bible, attended church services regularly, and had a good outlook on life. What drove him to this untimely death? Apparently he had not found someone to share his problems with. Perhaps if he had found a friend, someone who would pray with him when everything seemed overwhelming, he could have been spared from this tragedy. Loneliness has become an epidemic in this modern society, contributing to the feeling that life is not worth living after all. This can lead someone to end his/her life.

In 1993 a study was done by the Commission on Youth of the Far Eastern Division, together with the theological seminary of the Adventist International Institute of Advanced Studies (AIIAS). For the years 1990-1995, 446,000 out of a total of 892,000 Seventh-day Adventist young people were projected to leave the church, while for the years 1995-2000, 612,500 out of 1,225,000 Seventh-day Adventist youths were declared lost. These figures are very alarming. Some of the reasons for the loss are:

- lack of fellowship in the church
- lack of involvement in the church
- non-SDA friends
- non-SDA fiancé or spouse
- lack of attention

If the above reasons were reversed, they would be as follows:

- lots of fellowship in the church
- lots of involvement in the church
- SDA friends
- SDA fiancé/spouse
- lots of attention

The question now is how to facilitate those better pictures into reality. The answer is through the small group, where friendship and fellowship are formed—a vital tool to make people feel loved and needed.

Theology of Small Groups

The Bible is filled with accounts of small groups. In the Old Testament we find many instances of the presence of small groups. The first small group ever mentioned consists of God the Father, Jesus the Son, and the Holy Spirit. This is a small group with a purpose. Their first mission recorded in the Bible was the creation of the heavens and the earth in six days (Gen. 1). On the sixth day of Creation they met together and made plans to create the first man and woman. "And God said, Let us make man in our image, in the image of God created he him; male and female created he them" (verse 27). This is the best small group that ever existed.

Then we find the organization of small groups formed by Moses in the wilderness. Jethro, Moses' father-in-law, after seeing how Moses sat to judge the Israelites and how the people stood before him all day long, gave his advice to him, recorded in Exodus 18:17-23. His was excellent advice, which was applicable to any organization throughout the ages. It can be summarized as follows:

- What Moses was doing was not good; it would wear away both him and the people.
- It was too heavy a burden for Moses to handle all the problems alone. Responsibilities should be delegated to others.
- Able people were to be chosen as rulers of thousands, of hundreds, of fifties, and of tens. This is an excellent plan for small groups.

Formation of small groups is likened to a journey of a thousand miles. It started step by step, thus breaking an enormous problem into smaller problems. If your problem is as big as an elephant, you cannot eat the whole elephant. You take it segment by segment, bite by bite.

Numbers 13 speaks of the 12 spies. In the New Testament we find a model of a small group formed by Jesus Himself. Jesus chose 12 disciples as an instrument to carry out His mission in the world. He trained them, prayed with them, and made plans with them. He concerted His efforts in training this small group.

Ellen G. White: "The formation of small companies as a basis of Christian effort has been presented to me by One who cannot err. If there is a large number in the church, let the members be formed into small companies, to work not only for the church members, but for unbelievers. If in one place there are only two or three who know the truth, let them form themselves into a band of workers. Let them keep their bond of union unbroken, pressing together in love and unity, encouraging one another to advance, each gaining courage and strength from the assistance of the others."[1] From Ellen G. White's point of view the small group's strategy for evangelism is very important. Every prayer or strategic plan by the church will gain more success if it is implemented by the small group.

Rationale for Small Groups

The number of God's people in the wilderness under the leadership of Moses was huge—there were 603,550 men (Ex. 38:26). Adding women, teenagers, and children, that congregation easily could have totaled 3 million people! What minister today would covet a flock that size? Who could lead or pastor such an enormous assembly? No wonder Moses cried out, "How can I bear your problems and your burdens and your disputes all by myself?" (Deut. 1:12, NIV).

The total number of the Seventh-day Adventist young people around the globe today is more than 7 million. It is a big number compared with the number of world youth leaders (there are three in the General Conference headquarters office and 11 in the divisions). How could these 14 leaders bear the 7 million Seventh-day Adventist young people's burden and strife? It is hard—actually, impossible—for these leaders to help their young people face their problems and difficulties, listen to accounts of their activities, and reach out to them and put their arms around their shoulders. Hence, the small group is the answer for the future's needs. I believe if only there had been small groups in the university in which the student committed suicide, and if only this boy had been one of the members of a small group, and active at that, he would be alive today. Why? Because in the small group members can discuss things together, share their feelings with one another, and pray for one another to find the way out for those who have problems in life.

Another reason for having small groups is that many of our young people can be saved from leaving the church. They can be prevented from using illicit drugs and joining youth gangs. The fact is that many of them feel lonely in the church. No one cares. No one bothers. That is why they leave the church—to find friends "out there." Friends who they think will understand their situation and their problems. Indeed, they crave love, attention, and friendship—the feeling of belonging. They need to know and be known; they need to love and be loved.

Kinds of Small Groups

Our world is divided into nations, kindreds, tongues, and tribes. As a result of these diversities, there are diversities of needs. For this reason small groups have to provide them with an atmosphere in which they can come together and share things together. When Jesus was here on earth, He sent out His disciples by twos. Six to eight people in one company, or even 12—the number of Jesus' disciples—is applicable to the needs. Through these small groups they could feel strength in ministering. As Adventist young people we must follow Jesus' example, that we will be strong in faith and more encouraged to do our task.

There are several kinds or types of small groups that are applicable to young people. The following list is quoted from page 35 of the *Trinity Power Circle Manual:*

Type of Group	Main Emphasis	Other Vital Ingredients	Advantages Strengths	Potential Concerns
1. Nurture	fellowship, caring for church members	prayer, social interaction, relational Bible study	strong bonds develop; closes church's back door	can become self-centered; lack direction and Bible focus
2. Bible Study	discovering truth, learning Scripture	prayer, sharing, outreach to establish the group	inductive Bible study convicts of doctrinal truth	can create a climate of acceptability by conformity or obedience
3. Outreach	growing the groups and the church	prayer, Bible study, sharing, recruiting	the group aids in rapid church growth	can bring an emphasis on numerical rather than spiritual growth
4. Task	planning and preparing for a specific task, e.g., door-to-door witnessing	prayer, worship, Bible study, reporting	support and direction for activities outside the group	task can supersede nurture, nonparticipants may feel unaccepted
5. Support	upholding and encouraging those breaking habits and facing crises	testimonies, prayer, Bible promises	nonjudgmental, strength	can become problem-centered, introverted
6. Intercessory Prayer	uniting in prayer for specific needs	claiming promises, celebrating answers	concentrates Holy Spirit power on situations	may lack incentive for local tasks and outreach

Utilizing Small Groups for Youth Ministry

Our mission today is to save our young people from a dangerous and corrupt world. Rudolfo I. Gratia wrote: "We have to teach and train them well and equip our young people with adequate knowledge, right skills, proper attitude, good habits, and strong values, that they may face the world with confidence and live a life of dignity and peace."

In order for these goals to be accomplished, utilizing small groups is the best alternative. In the small groups the youths can be taught necessary and desirable knowledge, particularly about the Bible. In the small groups they can be trained how to give Bible studies to their fellow young people as well. Through the small groups they can develop their skills and maintain their good habits, as well as become equipped with strong values so that they may have confidence to face the world.

Mrs. White wrote in the *Review and Herald:* "Small companies gathered for prayer and Bible study. All moved forward with harmonious action. Believers went to places where the people have no opportunity to hear the Word of God, and gathered the children for Sabbath school. Efforts were made to help isolated families. Plans were laid for these families to meet with other families for Bible study. Thus, the way was opened for light to shine forth from the Word of God."[2]

The following steps of forming small groups in the church are suggested:

1. Form Adventist Youth (AY) small groups consisting of six to eight members/group with similar interests.

2. Choose a leader of the group.

3. Decide the frequency of meeting (once or twice a week).

4. Plan the activities, such as:
   - prayer
   - Bible study
   - sharing
   - problem solving
   - outreach/inreach
   - social activities

5. Form a "buddy system."
   - Each individual will choose his/her own partner/buddy (by twos).
   - Every "buddy system" member should know exactly his/her buddy's address, phone number, and his/her problems.
   - Each individual is responsible to give report to the group when he/she finds out that his/her buddy is in trouble.
   - The group will decide what they will do in order to help this individual to overcome his/her problems.
   - The whole church or youth society might forget or neglect this individual, but his/her buddy will never forget him/her. He/she will always be caring and sharing.

In some cases in which this has been done, the "buddy system" is really working well in preventing young people from leaving the church.

Conclusion

In a pamphlet entitled *An Appeal for Self-supporting Laborers* we found the following quotation from the pen of Ellen G. White, which will initiate our commitment to this task and service: "Small meetings should now be arranged for, in which two or three workers unite in explaining the truth to the people. Such meetings have been held in many places, and as a result, people have been brought into the truth, and meetinghouses have been built. At first, the work may have to be carried on in a room in a private house. Perhaps, if the weather is favorable, the meeting can be held outdoors. Give a kindly welcome to all who come. Draw near to God and to one another. Let songs of praise be sung. Let the Word of God be simply and clearly explained. Such a service will make a lasting impression."

The objective of small groups in youth ministry is to save our young people from destruction. Through the help of the Holy Spirit such small groups will be a big help and very valuable to meet this objective.

---

[1] E. G. White, *Testimonies,* vol. 7, p. 21.

[2] White, in *Review and Herald,* June 17, 1902.

SECTION 6

Facing the Twenty-first-Century
Youth Ministry

CHAPTER 52

Youth Ministry in the Twenty-first Century—Finding the Lost Generation

by Jennifer Jill Schwirzer

WHEN I WAS THE SAME age as my teenage girls, John F. Kennedy was assassinated, and the country mourned as if for their own brother. Everyone knew JFK was unfaithful to his wife, but no one really talked about it. Things like that were relegated to the unconscious. Likewise, when my friend Sandy's father divorced his wife and married a young dark-haired widow, no one talked much about it. There was enough shame surrounding infidelity to consign it to the silent zone, although that shame was not enough to prevent the problem in the beginning. Everyone knew it was wrong, but no one knew how to stop it.

My children, on the other hand, have little recall of any president but Clinton, whose sexual escapades have nauseated almost every member of his constituency, including those too young to know the meaning of all the graphic terms used to describe his escapades. At least they were too young. Not anymore.

There is pretty serious decadence in our culture these days! But when dealing with the spiritual assault against our youth, a Dr. Laura-esque diatribe isn't enough, because moralism just doesn't fly with most of Generation X. You can't take a slice of our society who work from a framework of postmodernism and tell them something is right or wrong. Postmodernism has taught them that everything is relative, and there are no absolutes—no absolute truth, no absolute moral code. So no matter how well you bolster your argument, the basic premise that there is such a thing as winning an argument about morals has already discredited you. You'll never get past square one.

No right and wrong—just choices with outcomes. Should I abort my unborn child? Should I have sex before marriage? Should I divorce? In the mind of a relativist, the answer is bound up in the answer to another question. Not "Is it right or wrong?" but "Do I feel comfortable with it?" Such is the climate of moral ambiguity our children are subjected to. We watched *Leave It to Beaver;* they have their choice of *Dawson's Creek, Ally McBeal,* and a number of cable shows with almost unprintable content.

What can be done to stop these influences? Well, TVs could be done away with. Everyone could move to northern Saskatchewan, where washing machines must be run off generators. Home school, of course, would be the only way to go, and all friendships would be strictly monitored.

But even that might not do the trick. While sheltering has its time and place, it doesn't work forever. That's because the real enemy is us. Postmodernism lives within us. The human heart minus the Holy Ghost equals amorality.

Consider Lilly. Homeschooled into her teens, she was shielded from "the world" until it was time for college. The first summer she lived away from home, Lilly ended up with an STD. Thankfully, she has recommitted her life to Christ, but she learned that the only lasting shield against sin is an inner one. His name is Jesus Christ.

So, yes, the forces of moral decay have impacted our youth as never before. And yes, because of family breakdown, the instilling of values does not take place at home as it used to. And yes, the media most kids have fed upon has "programmed" them to believe a postmodern pack of lies. But the blood of Christ is still efficacious, God is still alive and well, and the Holy Spirit is still providing power for those who will receive it.

Athens, Past and Present

How do we connect that Spirit to a generation that is unprecedentedly opposed to moral absolutes and organized religion? This question should be the obsession of every minister, Bible teacher, and musician who has been called to "find" those we sometimes call the lost generation.

Let's look at a biblical model, the story of Paul in Athens (Acts 17). There are strong similarities between the moral decadence. Paul met with some failure in his dealings with these people, but also some glowing successes. "Now when they heard of the resurrection of the dead, some began to sneer, but others said, 'We shall hear you again concerning this.' So Paul went out of their midst. But some men joined him and believed" (verses 32-34, NASB). What was this method that brought success where little was expected? First, Paul's "spirit was being provoked within him as he was beholding the city full of idols" (verse 16, NASB). He developed a burden for the people of Athens.

It may seem obvious, but in order to work for Gen Xr's, we must love and care about Gen Xr's. Sergio Manente, a pastor and teacher at Blue Mountain Academy in Pennsylvania, says that the youth have "incredible antennas for hypocrisy."[1] Tim Celek and Dieter Zander, authors of *Inside the Soul of a New Generation,* echo the thought, calling it "radar for phoniness."[2] All three of these front-liners make the point that youth can tell whether you're real or not. And that means they can tell if you love them or not. So "fake it till you make it" isn't an option, because you'll never make it until you *stop* faking it.

Paul's next step is found in verse 17: "So he was reasoning in the synagogue with the Jews and the God-fearing Gentiles, and in the market place every day with those who happened to be present" (NASB). Paul went to the powers that were. First, the Jews, the stolid but faithful churchgoers. Then the God-fearing Gentiles, the upright people of the unchurched community. He attempted to win the support of both church and state for his agenda. In so doing, he honored their position of leadership in the religious and secular community. No doubt some of them were reached with his gospel and became important leaders in the congregation that grew out of his efforts.

The people called Paul a "babbler"—and Paul himself admitted he was not a trained speaker. Evidently polish was not what was needed here. The baby boomer generation has relied heavily on this polish, but not so with the next. Generally speaking, baby busters, as they are called, care more about being able to identify with the communicator than whether he or she can perform well. The emphasis is on not *presentation* but *connection.* So what would normally be considered a liability, such as a stutter or lack of formal education, might actually become a qualification when striving to reach people who are more impressed with "realness" than finesse.

Back in the Athens model, the Greeks were growing more curious by the second. They took Paul to one of their sacred haunts where the god of war was worshiped. The people's ears were itching for something new, and that's exactly what they heard. But first Paul gave them a compliment. "Men of Athens, I observe that you are very religious in all respects" (verse 22, NASB).

Although Paul came preaching a gospel that would automatically rebuke the sinfulness of his target group, he started out by affirming what was good about them. This is common sense that is often overlooked. It's a fact that the gospel, although good news, is cutting truth. Your mother advised, "If you don't have something nice to say, then don't say anything at all," but this isn't good counsel in the realm of Christian witnessing. Many parts of the Christian message don't seem "nice" at all—including blood atonement, divine judgment, and repentance for sin—but it's not ultimately "nice" to leave them out of your ministry. Many people will perish in the lake of fire because someone chose to be "nice" to them rather than give a straight message. But don't fall into the other ditch and forget to treat people with dignity and respect. Give them a compliment to start out with.

Then what are the redeeming qualities of the young generation? Celek and Zander point out again and again how devoted busters are to a sense of community. This comes as no surprise when you remember that approximately 50 percent of them come from broken homes. Their sense of family has been transferred from the nuclear family to the "family" of peers who have similar needs, similar brokenness. One has to admire their survival tactic, as well as their commitment to what is essentially a Christian ideal. Celek and Zander put it this way: "Busters have done away with the autonomous self and have elevated community to a higher value. They realize we can't survive alone; we need each other. Community is supposed to be one of the hallmarks of true Christians, so we have a marvelous opportunity to live out what we believe."[3]

Another buster attitude that seems calculated to invite a Christian witness is the absence of absolute truth in their thinking. Modernism was all the rage from the Enlightenment into the 1960s. It defied reason and claimed that science could figure everything out. But the exaltation of logic had the effect of dethroning faith. Since reality depended upon empirical evidence, things you couldn't see, hear, and scientifically measure entered the realm of impossibility. Out of this came the backlash of relativism, which said, "I create my own reality just by believing it." This, in a sense, gives greater opportunity for the concept of faith to be grasped and utilized. In many ways busters are more willing than the older generations to "believe the unbelievable."

When a buster finally does come to call something "truth," it is usually processed relationally rather than intellectually. These young people are telling us, "Let me see this Christianity." Doesn't the Word advocate that we meet people on this very ground? Paul said, "Be imitators of me, just as I also am of Christ" (1 Cor. 11:1, NASB).

Notice that Paul was acquainted with the Athenian religion. "For while I was passing through and examining the objects of your worship, I also found an altar with this inscription, 'TO AN UNKNOWN GOD.' What therefore you worship in ignorance, this I proclaim to you" (Acts 17:23, NASB).

Today's "objects of worship" might include the pantheon of musicians, movie stars, and athletes who have such a profound impact upon all the culture, especially the youth. Do we know what this generation's influences are? It would be worth our time to educate ourselves. "Jesus found access to the minds of His hearers by the pathway of their familiar associations."[4] It was familiarity with the altar of the unknown god that gave Paul an opening to present the gospel message. He earned their attention by citing a relevant question, one that rattled around their icons as well as in their own heads. Then he answered the question they themselves had raised.

Paul affirmed what was good in the people he desired to reach. He familiarized himself with their culture. Then he brought up a relevant topic—three simple steps into effective ministry. We would do well to imitate him in our efforts to reach today's teenagers.

Bringing the Question Home

To what degree do Adventist youth escape the influences common to their generation? The answer to this differs from family to family, church to church, and area to area. The three institutions designed by God to nurture youth spiritually are, in order of impact, the home, the congregation, and the school. In the Valuegenesis study the highest rate of loyalty to the Adventist Church was found in youth who had effective environments in all three.[5]

Roger Dudley, author of *Valuegenesis: Faith in the Balance,* shows throughout the book that on the whole, Adventist youth do far better spiritually than unchurched youth. This is especially true of Adventist youth who "come up through" the Adventist educational system as opposed to public education. But there are areas of concern. Some of the areas indicate that the ghostly fingers of postmodern despair have seeped through the doors of the church and clutched the hearts of our young people.

For instance, Adventist education did not enhance self-esteem, add purpose in life, or increase the number of Christian friends a young person might have. Just as many youth in the Adventist school system desired to live "by their own rules" as did youth in public education.[6] While Adventist youth, especially those in the church school system, did better in the areas of substance abuse and morality, they were by no means squeaky clean. Depression and suicide were identified as big problems among youth in Adventist schools, with 47 percent reporting depression within the preceding month and 13 percent admitting that sometime in the past they had attempted suicide![7]

Among the suggestions Dudley makes at the end of his book is that we "clarify the gospel," meaning the "righteousness by faith" message God bequeathed to this church in 1888. He laments our lack of clear teaching on this subject:

"Historically, we could look at the struggle of the 1888 General Conference session. Leaders of the denomination, good and faithful men, were afraid the new emphasis on righteousness by faith would blur the distinctiveness of the unique Adventist message. And in spite of Waggoner, Jones, Ellen White, *The Desire of Ages,* and a century of study, preaching, and publication, we haven't gotten it all straight yet."[8]

Dudley goes on to cite several studies that plainly show that our youth have a "law orientation." He says, "The Adventist emphasis on behavioral standards has led the majority to believe that they must somehow do something to merit salvation. It is very difficult for an Adventist adolescent to emotionally accept the fact that his or her salvation rests entirely on the merits of Jesus Christ and that he or she cannot contribute to it in any way."[9]

As a parent with children in Adventist church school, I asked them whether their obedience contributed to their good standing before God. They both answered affirmatively, to my dismay, because I believe strongly that righteousness is by faith alone. I came to the conclusion, as have Dudley and others, that maintaining standards and at the same time conveying a grace-focused gospel is the greatest challenge a parent or educator can face. But it is a worthy pursuit, given the fortification that a true understanding of the gospel can be. If a concerted effort is made to relay it, the natural legalism that pervades the heart can be overtaken by the "much more abounding grace" of God.

In the area of parenting, research indicates that parents who are both affectionate and "strict" have the most well-adjusted teenagers, while permissive ("love" without rules), negligent (no rules and no love), and authoritarian (rules without love) homes tended to produce teens with more development problems.[10] So lowering the standard until it ceases to exist is not the answer. Most child development authorities, and all sane parents, agree that kids need boundaries.

The Adventist Church needs to take another look at the standards issue from two perspectives; consistency and method of implementation. When illogical standards are kept because they are part of the Adventist tradition, consistency becomes a problem. The classic examples are the huge, gaudy brooch that is fine, while a tiny stud earring is not; the Rolex watch perched proudly on the wrist, while the Wal-Mart necklace watch can't be worn; the video at home passing inspection, while the same movie in a theater is off-limits. We need to ask ourselves constantly if the logic behind our rules is . . . well, logical!

And compassionate. Once my daughter came to me with four charm bracelets she had bought. One was for her, two were for her best friends, and one was for her sister. The charms on the bracelet were none other than the Ten Commandments. What would you have said? Or even more important, how would you have said it? Even "illogical" rules can be obeyed from the heart where there is love—a case in point being Abraham and Isaac. When a teen knows that the rule enforcer is someone who loves him or her, they can forgo the reasons, at least for a time. We need to search our hearts and ask ourselves ruthlessly: Have we conveyed love to our youth? Our methods need to align with our message, especially when dealing with the "show me and I'll believe it" generation.

True love is a cure-all. Not sentimental love that would coddle sinners in their sins, but true love that is tough and compassionate at the same time. Rick Trott, who has been in youth ministry for more than 20 years, argues that because most kids have their own "everything"—VCR, transportation, computer, etc.—they don't tend to come out to programs very readily. The one thing they often don't have, however, is someone to truly connect with. "The biggest challenge in youth ministry is to be relevant and still act your age. Students don't want you to be a kid. They just want someone to listen and care. You don't need to know the current slang and have the hippest clothes do that."[11]

Rick sees that God is overcoming evil with good: "If anything, the students we have at

Atlantic Union College are more serious about God than students have been in the past. Many didn't have the tools provided by a stable Christian environment at home, but they are getting it straight from the Lord. In the time of great need God is coming through."[12]

The youth of today are made from the same dough as the rest of humanity—with a little leaven of postmodernism thrown in. Youth leaders should know something about the enemy without fearing it to the point where they lose courage. In *Pilgrim's Progress* Christian trembles in fear at the giants, only to find out that they are easily overcome. In the same way, the greatest threat to our effort to reach today's teenagers will crumble in the hand that reaches out to save.

---

[1] Telephone interview, August 1999.

[2] Tim Celek and Dieter Zander, *Inside the Soul of a New Generation* (Grand Rapids: Zondervan Pub. House, 1996), p. 139.

[3] *Ibid.,* p. 50.

[4] E. G. White, *The Desire of Ages,* p. 476.

[5] Roger Dudley, *Valuegenesis: Faith in the Balance* (Riverside, Calif.: La Sierra University Press, 1992), p. 294.

[6] *Ibid.,* pp. 245, 246.

[7] *Ibid.,* p. 260.

[8] *Ibid.,* p. 98.

[9] *Ibid.,* p. 272.

[10] Mary Pipher, *Reviving Ophelia* (New York: Ballantine Books, 1995), p. 83.

[11] Telephone interview, September 1999.

[12] *Ibid.*

CHAPTER 53

Meeting the Needs of
Twenty-first-Century Youth

by Paul Tompkins

Detached Youth Work

OUR CHURCH—ANY CHURCH—IS structured around meetings. On a regular Sabbath anywhere in the world, you can expect to find at least two of the following: Sabbath school, divine worship, and AYS meetings. During the holidays youth retreats, summer camps, congresses, and a wide variety of other events will be held—all of which will feature a meeting in one shape or form as part of the program. The church is good at organizing meetings.

Now, don't get me wrong; meetings are necessary. Countless young people have made their decisions for Christ when moved by a Spirit-filled presentation. That has always been the case and will continue to remain so. The problem, of course, is that at least sometime in their life not everyone likes to attend the meetings we have so carefully planned. They would rather just hang out, often nearby but not inside. This is usually most noticeable in the teenage years.

My local church has a wall outside one of the side entrances. You can guarantee that during most services a number of teenagers won't get beyond the wall. They've come to church with their parents, but they don't want to come inside. All churches have their equivalent to the wall, and the challenge is what to do with these young people.

This syndrome is often magnified at large conventions. In England, Spring Harvest is a large interdenominational Bible convention, and one of the youth workers has made the following observation:

"Getting them to go to anything is difficult. . . . They often want to major on the site attractions—the go-carting, laser games, or whatever—rather than go to the events organized for them. And they just hang around, like teenagers do." He continued: "Teenagers have this ambivalent attitude—'I don't want to do anything.' Then they realize that's boring, so they find their own routes into things. Whatever structures we create, they'll cut across them and create their own dynamics, within a safe environment."[1]

In a bid to reach these youngsters, the organizers of the event set up their own special youth teams to meet them where they are. In this setting, detached youth workers dress casually, and their job is to make contact with the teenagers and to take time simply to listen to them.

Adventist Youth Are Out There Too

We all know that a significant number of our young people leave the church. Again, this usually happens during the teenage years and is most often not related to a disagreement with our theology. For one reason or another these youngsters have simply stopped even coming and hanging out on the wall or around the site. Often this happens when they are too old simply to be brought to church, and feel that they are now masters of their own destiny.

The truth is, they have not disappeared, and are still out there. This leads us to two conclusions.

1. It is better to reach them while they are still "on the wall."
2. We need to think seriously about developing our own detached youth work teams within the Adventist Church.

When you add to this equation the whole generation of secular kids who are growing up without any knowledge of the Bible at all, then the case for this type of work is overwhelming. They are simply not going to walk into one of our meetings on their own steam.

Making an Impact

Let me first of all look at detached youth work with the unchurched. In recent years I have seen a definite revival in witness programs. Here in the Trans-European Division this has stemmed from the *Impact* Utrecht Field School of Youth Evangelism, run during the time of the General Conference session in 1995. A group of young people were trained in creative street-level evangelistic methods, such as mime, puppets, drama, clowning, and singing. In many ways the old wheel of street witnessing was reinvented.

Since that time a further international event was held in Helsinki, Finland, in 1996. This was probably the most creative of all programs, and our youngsters saw again that there are innovative ways to use their inherent talents in sharing the gospel. Since these events we have run similar events in the British Union in Edinburgh, Scotland; Redruth, England; and Dublin, southern Ireland. Those taking part have found it fun to take part and have also gone back and used the skills they have learned in their own churches.

There is no doubt that our youngsters have greatly benefited, and many have come back time and time again. They have seen that these methods are effective in stopping people on the street, and they enable others to then get alongside them and talk about why they are engaging in Christian street theater. Tracts and invitations are then easily given, and some people have responded by coming into one of our churches, or a neutral venue, for a special event, such as a concert.

In many ways these have been the very best youth programs that we have run over the last few years. To see our youth excited about witnessing is tremendous, but at the same time there is something very important that we must realize. And this is that the most successful *Impact* programs are those that have some form of planned follow-up. Otherwise, we simply go into a city for a week or 10 days, do some eye-catching work on the street but then disappear, not to be seen again.

As one noted Christian youth worker has observed: "Sadly, all too often the well-meaning evangelistic efforts of the church to reach unchurched people is based on a short-term effort. A special mission, a month-long summer club, a week of special events . . . and then, guilt assuaged, the church retreats back into its spiritual ghetto for another year."[2]

In other words, to be really effective in detached youth work—or any youth work, for that matter—we have got to be willing to be there week after week. It is all about building trust and establishing relationships. Here I take my hat off to such groups as the ones I know of in London who have gone into Leicester Square on a continuing basis. Only by meeting the test of time will we really begin to be effective.

Some years ago this was reinforced when I attended a Youth Specialities program in Los Angeles. One of the speakers really grabbed my attention. His name was Bill Wilson, and he had been running a street-level mission among the dropouts, drug addicts, and prostitutes in New York. He had actually lived in the area among all the problems—not retreating to the safety of the suburbs at the end of the day. It certainly takes a special type of person to do that and is not a ministry that many of us could consider. After he had given his presentation he answered a number of questions, one of which was along the lines of "What did you feel was the secret of your success?"

His answer was somewhat surprising. He simply said it was that he had hung in there when others had come and gone. In other words, he had stayed and had built up friendships that had lasted over the years, and he was now trusted because of this.

Understanding the Needs of Today's Youth

Only by passing the test of time will we ever have a chance of really understanding the needs of our young people. This is the same whether they are churched or unchurched, but is shown more sharply in focus with the unchurched. Quite simply, "too few of us really understand the difficulties and problems which face those we seek to evangelize."[3]

Youth culture is both fast-moving and fragmented today. Most of us are probably out of touch with what is really going on in the lives of today's teens. This is quite natural and is not a handicap if we are willing to listen. Too few of us, however, take time to really listen.

The days of the Lone Ranger are long past—and even he had his faithful companion Tonto. It is certainly true that no one person can build a strong relationship with every young person. But someone in a team of workers probably can, and in any form of detached youth work teamwork is essential.

It is also important to realize that we need both male and female in our teem. It is only appropriate for men to work one-on-one with men and women with women. To do any different is both unprofessional and also opens us up to the possibility of accusations that can ruin our reputations as well as our youth ministry. This is so even when working with churched youngsters. All good counseling agencies now stress that it is very dangerous to try to counsel alone a member of the opposite sex.

Relationships Still Count

Now to return to the needs of our churched youth. Sometime ago a young man sat in my office and told me the story of how he had left the church but later returned. He said that he had grown up being taught what was right, but in his teens he had rebelled. Despite his going away from the church, the truth had never left him, and it was always at the back of his mind. the time came when he felt he needed to return; and since then he met an Adventist woman at one of our camps, and I had the privilege of marrying them and later christening their children.

Now, my friend had the courage and strength to return. But the problem is that many do not take this step, and consequently we may never see them again.

The great British leader Winston Churchill once gave a very short address to his men: "Never given in, never give in, never, never, never, never." As *Group* brought out in an article entitled "What Keeps Kid Committed": "That's good advice, as far as your group members are concerned."[4]

If we cannot be involved in detached youth work for the unchurched, we surely must be willing to get out there where our own wounded have fallen. Quoting again from the words of the same article: "We've got to have the guts to keep loving them, to keep after them until they return to their first love."[5]

I was fascinated to read the comments of one of the youngsters interviewed in this article: "Keep inviting. . . . Don't give up and don't assume anything. I have positive memories of the rafting trips and the special events my youth pastor put on even though I hardly participated in the events. They are some the earliest—and now deepest—roots of my Christian life."[6]

The challenge is to build nonthreatening relationships. Not everyone will return—not everyone responded positively to Jesus' contacts (for example, the rich young ruler)—but some will! For others it may take more time.

Some years ago as a young minister I visited the home of two brothers who had grown up in an Adventist home but who had since drifted away. One always seemed warm and friendly, while the other was distant. The friendly one talked of cars, canoeing, and other subjects and slowly built a relationship. Ministry never works in isolation, and at the same time he became interested in a female former student of one of our secondary schools, resulting in their return to church. Because of the relationship we had built up, I had the pleasure of being invited to take part in their marriage service also. The other brother, sadly, has never returned. As I am no longer in the district, we are not in touch anymore, but he is undoubtedly with his brother and sister-in-law, so the contact goes on. Who knows what the future will bring?

Generation X and Beyond

It is undoubtedly true that this generation has to face pressures that most of us never had to deal with at their age. Sometime ago I attended a Critical Concerns course connected to the Youth Specialties National Youth Workers convention. One particular lecture, "Youth Ministry in the Twenty-first-Century," highlighted "Megatrends 2000." The lecturer emphasized how rapid change is part and parcel of today's fast-moving world of technological advancement. This makes most electrical goods obsolete before we buy them in the shops. There is always something with more bells and whistles coming up behind. Apart from the financial concerns that this may cause the purchaser, this syndrome is also causing some other more significant problems.

One of the most pressing of these is the insecurity and depression that this can cause. Some people are bypassed in this technological revolution. Others find their job security threatened. Certainly there is rarely such a thing as a job for life anymore.

In a different vein, but just as important, technological advancement is causing fewer and fewer people to read anything of substance any longer. This is certainly true as far as the

Bible is concerned, and a spiritually illiterate generation has arisen. This trend will countless continue into the lives of the next generation.

A reaction to all of this has already been observed. In Western society the yuppies of the 1980s have been supplanted by bright urban professionals of the 1990s and the new millennium. This group are now turning their backs on the upwardly mobile lifestyle, seeking something personally more fulfilling. This includes more time to enjoy oneself, even at the cost of downsizing in their careers to take on less time-consuming and consequently less stressful jobs.

It is at this point that detached youth work can come into its own. Although the times have undoubtedly changed, people are still basically the same. When the chips are down, the same basic concerns affect us all. By either reacting to today's megatrends or simply by being willing to step off the treadmill, we have a group of young people who are in transition. Church growth exponents have long held that this is the best time to reach people with the gospel message of assurance. To do this, we need youth workers who are able to major on people and reach out to build relationships with them that are long-term and life-changing. To do this, we must be people-centered, not program-driven.

Youth Evangelism Is a Process, Not an Event!

Some years ago I attended a communications lecture in which a BBC radio correspondent shared the following diagram:

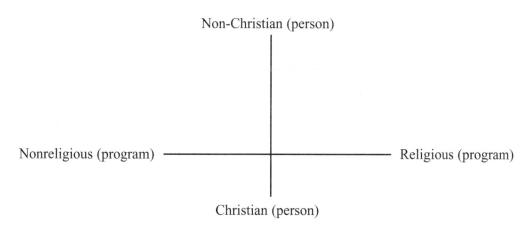

Of the four quadrants in the diagram, we are very comfortable in working in the bottom right quadrant, i.e., an overtly religious program that appeals to Christians. The point is, however, that with both our own youth as well as the unchurched, evangelism rightly understood is a process, not a one-time event. More likely, we need to help youth to be able to move from the other quadrants into this one. Detached youth work is one means of doing this, and it may well take nonreligious contact and content in the initial stages to begin the process.

The important point is that we have youth workers who are out there and in contact with our young people. The Holy Spirit can and will work on their hearts, and I have great hope for so many our youth whom we are tempted to write off. The Lord never gives up on any of us. The challenge is not to look for immediate results but to understand that youth evangelism is a process and not an event. Detached youth work will surely be an increasingly important part of this process in the twenty-first century.

------

[1] "The Youth Are Out There," *YouthWork,* February 1997, p. 18.

[2] John Buckeridge "People, Not Programmers," *YouthWork,* October/November 1995, p. 10.

[3] *Ibid.,* p. 11.

[4] Mike Woodruff, Cathy Jo Gilbert, and Jim Schmotzer, "What Keeps Kids Committed," *Group,* September/October 1998, p. 32.

[5] *Ibid.*

[6] *Ibid.*

CHAPTER 54

Preaching to
Twenty-first-Century Youth

by Siegfried Wittwer

WHOEVER WANTS TO REACH youth needs to know how young people think and feel, what occupies them, what their value system is, and what influences them the most. Therefore, advertising experts study this target group very carefully.

Jesus once said that the "children of this world" are "wiser than the children of light" (Luke 16:8). Maybe He would make this same statement today in reference to youth ministries, because some pastors believe they can preach the gospel to young people the same way they do to adults. If youth are bored, they are totally at a loss. However, pastors can learn not only from advertising experts but also from the apostle Paul. Before conducting an evangelistic campaign in Athens, he took a close look at the city and its inhabitants. Then he began with those questions in which they were interested.

Certainly young people in the diverse countries of the globe are not identical. They are influenced by different political, religious, and cultural trends. Some live in democratic, liberal societies; others live under dictatorships. They may be affected by an atheistic, materialistic society, or they may live with fundamentalists and religious fanatics. Unlimited consumption shapes the everyday life of some; hunger and poverty the life of others. For some a wide variety of educational options are available. Others must be content to learn reading and writing only.

Nevertheless, it is to be expected that during future decades people will become more and more similar. In the years to come, because of the influence of the mass media, especially the music industry and the film industry, as well as through the worldwide connection of computers and the Internet, reasoning and emotions of youth will become alike across political, cultural, and religious lines. By means of colonization the spirit of Europe spread to the other countries of the world (cf. Dan. 2:41-43). Likewise, influential media and economic powers determine the lifestyle of humanity across boundaries.

Of course, in the future there will be numerous countries in which youth feel only a little of this influence because political or religious leaders isolate their people, because the respective society as a whole takes a stand against this influence, or because economic conditions limit it. Likewise, youth in liberal and economically strong countries will take a stand against the manipulation of their minds because the propagated philosophy of life remains unsatisfactory in the end. Moreover, new influences may emerge that drive youth into an unexpected new direction. Nevertheless, even today we notice that our planet is becoming more and more a global village whose inhabitants develop an individualistic-pluralistic philosophy of life. This is true especially for young people.

Twenty-first-Century Youth and Their Problems

Because of political, economical, religious, and cultural influences of the past, the society of most of the Western countries has become pluralistic. Therefore, it is not possible to draw a uniform picture of a typical youth today. Furthermore, many oppose being labeled, and again and again they surprise adults with a shocking individualism and a pluralistic lifestyle. Nevertheless, one can detect a certain tendency in their philosophy of life.

Involvement Is Out; Passively Enjoying One's Life Is In

Previous generations have demonstrated against nuclear power, nuclear waste, deforestation, killing of seals, or oppression of women, but today the fire to get involved has almost been extinguished. Sports clubs, political parties, and churches notice an increasing percentage of older folks because young people stay away. They talk about the "invisible generation" when referring to youth. That does not mean that the ideas of young people have changed. They are still valid, still applauded. However, one does not get involved any longer.

The motto is: "I agree, but I do not participate." Leisure time and pleasure take precedence over religious, political, and social ideas and actions. "I need to have fun" is the slogan of the youth. They are fun-oriented and pleasure-dependent. They often ask the question "How do I profit from it?" To enjoy life determines their behavior to a larger degree than duty, responsibility, codetermination, and cooperation. And they have good reasons for it.

Increasing Pessimism

Young people notice clearly that those generations preceding them have exploited the earth and have polluted nature by means of their consumerism and their philosophy of continuous progress. Water, air, and soil have been poisoned. Precious raw materials have been wasted thoughtlessly. Food supplies have been destroyed while the number of the hungry and malnourished grows. Forests are dying, and the chances to find employment are decreasing. In spite of endeavors and protests of the youth of previous decades, politicians and CEOs continue to lead the world into disaster, because everyone wants to enjoy life and no one is willing to cut back. No wonder youth give up and want to partake in prosperity before everything is gone.

As a result, young people perceive the world pessimistically and do not believe in its future. This is the reason they conduct their everyday lives carelessly, why they seek fun and pleasure and are not interested in accepting responsibility. Further, they criticize those who have carried responsibility so far, and they approach them with mistrust and distance.

Challenging Authorities, Value Systems, and Truths

Formerly God, the Bible, and the church set the standards that determined the lives of humans. After the rise of atheism and liberal theology these authorities have been questioned more and more. Today churches are irrelevant to the majority of the population. When there is no God, when the Bible is only a book of pious legends, then churches, priests, and pastors are only relics of the past that belong in a museum; they have importance only in the history of civilization. The attempts of churches to gain anew the right to existence by means of political activities are often recognized with a mild smile. Only their social involvement (retirement homes, homes for those with disabilities, counseling facilities, community services) is appreciated by the majority of the population.

Christian values, too, lose their importance. For example, theft or adultery are not regarded as really bad. The goal is either redistribution of things to which everyone has a right anyway, or enjoyment of life and independence. If there is no God as the final and highest authority, then all other authorities and standards collapse. There is no absolute truth. Nothing counts any longer, and nothing is obligatory for humans. Everyone can live according to the rules he or she has found to be good, profitable, and right.

Youth's lives center on self-realization, independence, and self-determination. They do not want to be limited by authorities, rules, and laws. They want to do what they like and what brings fun. The laws of a state are observed only when they are perceived as useful or when they are threatened with legal prosecution. These laws are understood as rules created arbitrarily by humans. They are enforced by those in power by means of the police, and they may lose their validity as soon as a change of the political forces takes place. Therefore, even now they are not really valid.

Because the loss of faith in God throws humans back into a cold, empty world and robs them of all personal hope, the question of the meaning of life becomes relevant again. Established Christianity, however, does not profit from this openness. Religion has become a private matter, and the possibilities are endless, from liberal to fundamentalist churches and cults of various kinds. Asian, African, Germanic, and Indian religions, and cults, spiritualistic circles, and occult and esoteric groups, shape the religious scene and offer something for everyone. While searching for "their" religion, youth do not question what is truth, because for them there is no longer absolute truth. What is important for them is that they get something out of it, that they are not limited, and that they have fun.

Pluralism and Individualism

Whenever there are no longer normative values, authorities, and a true philosophy of life, almost everything becomes possible. Therefore, pluralism is the catchword of our time. Nothing is universally valid, nothing uniform and binding. Ideologies, religions, lifestyles, fashion styles, political opinions, stars, and music styles—everything is diverse and has become intricate.

Having so many possible choices, youth support definite individualism. For them, nothing solid is left—only personal experience. They have become their own standard. Whatever fits their immediate horizon of experience is advocated. If what they experience changes, opinions, fashions, music styles, and lifestyles also change immediately.

Because of the multiformity of society, young people oftentimes feel lost and torn. On the one hand, they are looking for something that is stable, and tend to become susceptible to radical nationalistic and fundamentalistic groups that provide clear direction and answers. On the other hand, they drift along and, without scruples, disregard their conscience in matters of principles, guidelines, and laws. Thus, it seems that for modern youth everything is possible. However, they do not always see the chances they have and are often blind with regard to the risks and the consequences of their behavior and their attitude.

Results

The philosophy of life of youth in Western countries will probably spread all over the world because of the media. Later on, we can expect a return swing of the pendulum. Insecurity of one's own life, as well as the endangered future of our planet, will drive humans, as soon as life hits hard, into the arms of authorities that promise security, of religious leaders, and of those who talk about improving the world. First indications can be found today. Until then, we encounter the following problems while working for young people, problems that result from the philosophy of life as we have just described it.

Loss of Orientation. Today, because of the loss of genuine values and securities, many cannot find an answer to the question "Where do we go?" Whoever tries to point out a direction is told that there is no such thing as absolute truth. Young people do not accept something automatically just because God says it, the Bible says it, or the standards of the church say it.

Individualization. There is more liberty; however, there are also more possibilities to choose from and there is more responsibility for one's own life. Limiting rules and authorities—whether they are derived from the Bible or whether they are set up by church and government—are rejected. Human beings are their own standard of good and evil, right and wrong.

Anxiety With Regard to the Future. Although youth are pleasure-oriented, many are afraid of the future. This anxiety is not always caused by life-threatening environmental catastrophes and natural disasters, economic crises, or political misjudgments. Rather, it develops because of the insecurity of youth as they face the complexity of life.

Estrangement and Skepticism. Young people are thorough skeptics concerning authorities, adults, and institutions because often their decisions, views, and "truth" have been proved wrong, harmful, or obsolete. Therefore, they stay away from them. Churches especially notice this estrangement.

Consequences for an Evangelistic Youth Ministry in the Twenty-first Century

Youth ministry has always had to adapt to change. However, the situation as we have described it demands us to consider seriously how we can reach young people with the gospel of Jesus. The following answers are not final, but do relate to their present problems and to their lifestyle.

Truth That Can Be Experienced Instead of Dogmas Unfitted for Life

In the past what has been "sold" to the youth as truth often has proved to be either wrong or unfitted for life. Therefore, youth are no longer willing to follow any dogmas that are not related to their life situation. Their question is: "How do I benefit from it?" If this question is not answered satisfactorily, then they are not interested in the proposed doctrine. They do not believe truth for truth's sake but accept truth that influences their life in a positive way and promises better quality of life.

It goes without saying that truth must be proclaimed in a lively and comprehensible manner for everyone. Dead doctrines in dead worship services cannot persuade anyone. The issue is not simply a new form of proclamation. Each form stays dead if it is not filled with life.

Youth are looking for something they can experience. They want to have fellowship, but also action and fun. Nevertheless, contemporary music and rhetorically excellent sermons are not sufficient to create a lively divine service or an evangelistic campaign.

They do not want a mere copy of a disco. The short-term emotional high and the superficial contacts in a disco leave them empty. In an evangelistic campaign or a worship service geared to youth they expect more than just perfect entertainment on the stage, including sound and smoke. They want to experience Christ. But only those persons who have a living relationship with Christ can help them grasp it.

Whoever proclaims truth must live truth as an example. Young people are more interested in (and accept) persons and models of faith rather than ideas and theories. Humans who live what they confess are more important to them than dogmas and philosophies. They want to notice how truth affects and changes life positively. If truth benefits others, it also can benefit them. If others manifest joy and hope in their lives, then Christian faith could also enlighten their lives.

Lively worship services and evangelistic campaigns are important to reach youth. However, the speakers often keep distant from the audience. What they really think and how they live stays out of sight. They may get the attention of youth for a short period of time, but they cannot change them permanently. In their proclamation youth evangelists must talk about themselves, about their feelings, and about the experiences they have had with Jesus in order to make a lasting impression on their audience. It is even more important to seek personal contact with young people: conversations, group activities, games, and fun. A pastor who plays soccer with them and at the same time models a Christian life rather than using clever arguing, however correct theologically, will be more likely to reach them.

Stimulating Hope for the Future

Youth perceive dark clouds in the horizon of world history. More than that, the intricacy and the incomprehensibility of life frightens them. They do not know where the journey of life will take them, what the consequences of their decisions will be, and which goals it is worthwhile to pursue. Therefore, many try to avoid critical questions. They just drift around without considering the future. And they want to suppress their fear of life.

The proclamation of Christian faith must also be future-oriented. Pessimism is not very helpful. Bad news about the environment and the doom of the world might have awakened former generations, but today's youth have merely filed them away. They do not need the mood of doomsday, since they are already in this mood; they seek action and fun in order to forget it. A message of hope is more important than a description of the hopeless situation of humanity: In the confusion of life and of world history God is in control, He oversees what is going on and He knows where the world is heading. Even more, God works all things for the good. His will is being done. Therefore, we do not need to panic, even if the doors of fate seem to be locked.

Even more important than this global perspective is the message that God also oversees the lives of young people. His commandments are helpful guidelines that help to enhance life and enjoy it. His guidance enables them to reach satisfactory and enjoyable goals. Whoever allows God to control his or her life does not need to be afraid of colliding with an iceberg of fate and drowning. He or she can face the future more calmly.

Furthermore, in the proclamation the different areas of life in which youth are interested should be made more transparent without losing sight of the variety. Structuring complicated facts and connections assists them in discerning the thread that runs through history and also through their own lives. Thus, they see how the Christian faith can help them to develop home and joy and to dispel pessimism and fear.

Strengthening Trust in God as the Authority

Philosophers, liberal theologians, and scientists have declared the death of God. Yet they themselves claim to be authorities whose opinion and teachings should be accepted. Youth, however, are skeptical regarding authorities; they meet them with distrust. This is a chance to rekindle faith in God.

Youth know that humans err again and again. Scientific theories accepted today are obsolete and outdated tomorrow. Indeed, today there are arguments for God that are more plausible than the theory of origin by accident. However, it is not sufficient that youth evangelists talk about scientific, philosophical, and cybernetic facts. Rather, they must proclaim the living God whom everyone can experience. Personal experiences with God are more persuasive than a thousand theories. They need a God whom they can trust, who provides orientation in the perplexities of life, and who is a real authority because His word is true—not only in world history but especially in their own lives. Therefore, whoever talks about God must present clear orientation without being one-sided. Discussing other philosophies of life critically can work out and strengthen these positions and trust in God.

The youth evangelist needs to be trustworthy and reliable with regard to his or her offers and relationships. Youth expect the evangelist's life to prove that God is real and guides us through good and bad days. His word is not ignorant of the world but close to life. Therefore, the evangelist is the first "Bible" that youth read in order to experience God. If his or her words correspond with his or her life, then they are willing to accept God as authority for their lives.

The commandments of God and the truths of the Bible need to be explained to them in a relevant way. God's commandments are, in reality, offers as well as helpful rules in order to conduct one's life more positively. His truths are not meaningless doctrines and dead beliefs; they keep one from deadend roads and false tracks. They help us to reach the goal of our life—to live happily and forever. As soon as youth perceive the doctrines of Holy Scripture from this perspective, they understand how important and helpful it is to accept God and His word as authority.

Leaving Freedom for Self-realization

Having experienced the freedom of a pluralistic and individualistic society, the youth do not find subordinating themselves to a religious or political system governed by rules, regulations, dogmas, and laws very attractive. So far, they could almost do whatever they wanted to do. With their experiences and opinions, they themselves are the measuring rod for good and right or false and evil. Only a few are attracted to groups that regulate and determine the whole life.

Hence, the proclamation of the gospel must be determined by Christian liberty. Freedom and love are two sides of the same coin. The one who destroys one side also makes the other worthless. Because God loves us, He wants to preserve our freedom. He does not force us to believe, follow Him, and accept everlasting life. All of this He offers us as His gifts of love. Humans can freely decide if they want to respond to God's love and live in fellowship with Christ.

Youth value such freedom. Often they know the other side well; they have learned that drugs, occult powers, and sins have made them unfree and dependent. As soon as they see that humans are freed through Christ from their addictions, dependencies, and feelings of guilt and thus can experience self-realization, faith in Christ becomes attractive to them. Furthermore, if they understand that faith does not distort reason, their readiness to trust Christ grows. God is not pleased with marionettes and hallelujah robots, but humans who because of their love have freely decided for Him. The proclamation needs to get this message across to youth.

On the other hand, youth need aids for making decisions. In every new situation of a pluralistic society this will enable them to make right choices. They need to be stabilized so that they can endure contradictions (for example, if the life of the pastor does not correspond with his or her message) and not to lose sight of their future when confronted with new problems. While they work together in groups their independence should be furthered in order for them to learn to make responsible decisions instead of being manipulated by the media, fashions, or those who influence public opinion. In the future we need youth who, in their Christian freedom, follow Jesus in spite of all resistance, because they have made a decision for faith and know by experience that it is worthwhile to live with Christ.

Results

The approach to evangelistic youth ministry described so far does not mean to say that a mere religion of feeling and experience should be communicated to youth, a religion in which everyone can form his or her own philosophy of life. Faced with pluralism, with its manifold offers of philosophies and religions, youth need to discern that there is only one way leading to God, namely, Jesus Christ, and that there is only one reliable foundation of faith, namely, God's revelation in Scripture.

Even if others think that in this world there is nothing that is valid and true, Jesus Christ is the truth in which we can trust. Why? Because He really lives, because He can be experienced, and because He really leads to life. As soon as youth have this experience, they are ready to follow the living Christ in faith, obedience, and love. This is the primary goal of all evangelistic ministry among youth.

Principles of Evangelistic Proclamation for Youth

1. Select Topics That Are Important for Youth

Try to meet their needs, even the needs of which they are not conscious.

2. Connect the Topics With Events and Actions

Youth want to experience the gospel. Example: How the Adventist Church came into existence in "the wild West." Describe the historical situation: the settlers, wars with the Indians, Civil War, inventions, discoveries, new philosophies, etc. Example: Life With Christ: "Tour of Life." Compare it with the Tour de France: without pneuma you are flat. Christians who are stepping on the brakes, cringing before superiors while kicking subordinates, doctrines (spokes of faith, impediments to faith, what makes your life of faith bright, etc.)

3. Clarify the Main Goal of the Series of Discourses

Children believe in God or do not believe in God because adults exemplify it. However, during adolescence they develop their own opinions and philosophies. Therefore, each devotional, each Bible study, and each proclamation will influence their decision and will contribute to their formation of opinion. Present Jesus as one who is loving, trustworthy, and worth imitating. It is not enough to emphasize knowledge. Youth want to know what Jesus is able to do with their lives and what they get from it.

4. Develop Intermediate Goals That Teach an Important Thought or an Enlightening Experience

Written formulations or important sentences help to reach these intermediate goals. Examples: God is able: "Iron can swim!" (see 2 Kings 6:1-7); Communication: "Listen first, then speak!"

5. Develop an Outline

Life is complex enough for youth. This complexity should not be reflected during a sermon by presenting a jungle of ideas, Bible texts, quotations, stories, and different aids. An outline helps to develop a clear line of thought. Youth want to know what is going on. Here's an example:

Introduction: What do human beings need according to the advertisements on TV?

    I. What do we really need? Most of the happy humans on earth did not possess a Sony TV or a Toyota or drink Coca-Cola.

    II. What is absolutely necessary in order to live?

    III. In order to live forever, we only need one thing: John 3:16.

Conclusion: A Toyota can get us to San Francisco or Paris; however, it is only Jesus who leads us to everlasting life. Or: Coca-Cola can quench thirst; however, the thirst for life only Jesus can quench.

6. Speak Briefly and Enthusiastically

Youth do not sit for very long. They enjoy "action and fun." They lose interest if a Bible study or a lecture takes too long, even if it is not boring. Seldom do they manage to listen to a speaker for more than two hours. Do not be deceived. Youth have learned in school how to look interested while their thoughts are elsewhere. Bible studies should last no longer than 30 minutes. They can be interspersed with group activities. Lectures should not exceed 45 minutes, even if they are accompanied by drama and by music. It's better to be hit by one good idea than to drown in a multiplicity of words.

7. Speak Lively and Naturally

Do not talk like a professor or as if you are reading from a sheet of paper. Youth do not like a speaker from the wax figure cabinet, but rather real live persons. Therefore, learn to stress properly. Use your voice. Be outgoing. Take a biblical narrative and try to imagine putting yourself in the shoes of the acting persons. Visualize what they have experienced. Feel what they might have felt and relive their lives. Do not stand stiff. Move your body, your hands, and your arms. Do not overdo; otherwise, the effect of your words will be destroyed.

8. Give Your Audience Visual Impressions and Stimulate Their Imaginations

Because of movies, TV, and computers, youth are used to connecting images with messages. To start with, use *narratives, parables,* or *short stories.* Example: "It was a dark day. Clouds towered high in a threatening way above the town. A gust of wind swept through the streets, swirled around leaves, and propelled an empty cola can over the sidewalk."

Also use *visual comparisons.* Examples: "Like a maniac he sped through the city" (instead of "He was speeding"). "Jonathan was tough as leather." "Saul raged like a demoniac." "The village was like a cemetery."

Use *language pictures.* Examples: A mind sharp as a knife; hair red as fire; baby face.

9. Use Objects, Pictures, and Experiments to Make Bible Study or Proclamations Vivid

Example: Break single matches. They are so weak that even a child can break them. Take a bundle of matches and tape them together. This bundle is stable. If we by means of God's love are connected to each other, then our group, family, or church is strong (see Col. 3:14).

10. Show Youth That You Love Them and That They Are Important

Share your life with them. Take time to answer their questions, and take time for sports and for fun. Be genuine. Live what your are preaching.

CHAPTER 55

AIDS Education in Developing Countries

by Rick Ferret

AIDS Is Here to Stay: What Can You Do About It?

LISTEN TO THESE STORIES:
"I'm 24 years old and have a 4-year-old daughter, Sara. I've been HIV positive for three years. I was a virgin when I married a man whom I loved very much, but he died two years ago of AIDS. Now I need to care for myself, my house, and Sara's future, and I'm all alone. I need to work, but I often suffer from episodic diseases that keep me from the labor market. So I work on a daily basis, cleaning houses" (Brazil).

"I was aware that my husband was having casual sex when not with me, but I was too ashamed to ask him to take precautions. I kept telling myself, next time. My advice to young mothers is 'Don't ever wait for next time.' Now I have big regrets. I'm so lucky that I didn't have any more children after I was infected" (South Pacific).

AIDS: A Deadly Scenario

AIDS and its consequences are just beginning and will continue to be felt for generations to come. There is no cure, and a vaccine for mass distribution will not be ready for several years. At the end of the twentieth century 40 million worldwide were infected by human immune deficiency virus (HIV).

AIDS: A Brief Background

Only 700 years ago plagues moved slowly, inching across the land with the plodding caravans or with the speed of other carriers such as rats and insects. Many forms of plagues are still with us—although now contained by public health measures, vaccines, and cures that are simply taken for granted. Some plagues, such as smallpox, have disappeared forever. In most diseases common symptoms usually appear quickly in someone who has been infected—two or three hours, two or three days, two or three weeks. You and the people around you know when you come down with an illness. Generally you feel ill, take to your bed, and disconnect yourself from everybody else.

But the viruses with long incubation times pose much more difficult problems. The infection may remain dormant, undetected, for years. In the meantime those infected can transmit the infection to others. In 1981 just such a rare virus was suspected in a number of cases of pneumonia and cancer contracted by young men around Los Angeles.

By 1982 the first type of HIV was identified. The human immunodeficiency viruses are the cause of the new plague, whose final toll already threatens to dwarf even the 30 million deaths of the influenza pandemic of 1918-1919. It is a slow plague, but a sure plague.

The average time between initial infection and the collapse of the immune system is about 10 years. Death from once rare but now symptomatic pneumonia, cancers, and brain infections almost invariably follow within three to four years—or only six months if you are a small child.

HIV/AIDS: The Global Epidemic

As of January 1997 more than 8.4 million AIDS cases had occurred since the start of the global AIDS epidemic. However, because of underrecognition, underreporting, and reporting delays, only 1.5 million cumulative cases of AIDS in adults and children have been officially reported to the World Health Organization (WHO) by countries. Because of the long delay between infection with the HIV and the ultimate development of AIDS, a more useful indication of current trends in the global epidemic is the number of new infections with HIV. According to UNAIDS estimates, there were more than 3.1 million new HIV infections during 1996. That is about 8,500 a day: 7,500 in adults and 1,000 in children.

During 1996 HIV/AIDS-associated illnesses caused the death of an estimated 1.5 million, including 350,000 children. Since the start of the global epidemic, close to 30 million people are thought to have been infected with HIV, including children. Of these, an estimated 5 million adults and 1.4 million have already died.

As of this writing, 22.6 million people are estimated to be living with the HIV infection or AIDS. Of these, 21.8 million are adults and 830,000 are children. Approximately 42 percent of the 21.8 million adults living with HIV/AIDS are women, and the proportion is growing. The majority of newly infected adults are under 25 years of age.[1]

HIV/AIDS Regional Statics and Features
(December 1996)

Region	Epidemic Began	Adults and Children With HIV/AIDS	Percent Women	Primary Mode of Transmission
Sub-Saharan Africa	late 1970s, early 1980s	14 million	50	heterosexual
Latin America	late 1970s, early 1980s	1.3 million	20	male-male, IDU,* heterosexual
North American, Western Europe, Australia, New Zealand	late 1970s, early 1980s	1.3 million	20	male-male, IDU, heterosexual
Caribbean	Late 1970s, early 1980s	270,000	40	heterosexual
South and Southeast Asia	late 1980s	5.2 million	30	heterosexual
Central Asia, East Asia, Pacific	late 1980s	100,000	10	IDU, heterosexual, male-male
North Africa, Middle East	late 1980s	100,000	20	IDU, heterosexual
Central/Eastern Europe	early 1990s	50,000	20	male-male, IDU

* IDU: transmission through injecting drug use

HIV/AIDS is not confined to a single country; it is global. Today 14 million in sub-Saharan Africa are living with HIV/AIDS, representing about 63 percent of the world's total. HIV is spreading explosively in some parts of India, Asia, the Ukraine, and the Russian Federation, to name a few. The HIV epidemic has recently developed in Papua New Guinea, fueled in large measure by heterosexual transmission. At the end of 1994 this small island nation of about 4 million people had an estimated 4,000 adults living with HIV, overtaking Australia as the country with the highest per capita prevalence in the Pacific region.

So What Makes HIV Infection Such a Dangerous Disease?
- HIV is a new epidemic.
- It is transmitted from person to person.
- It is transmitted through private sexual activities.
- Millions of people all around the world are already infected.
- The epidemic spreads very rapidly.
- There is no cure or vaccine for HIV infection.
- The long period of time between infection and illness makes the epidemic difficult to see.
- There is a long period of infectivity, when people with HIV are able to transmit the virus to others but may not know that they are infected.
- HIV infection has an unpredictable course; people don't know when or how they may get sick.
- The infection of people in their most productive years intensifies the economic and social impact of the disease.
- HIV is linked to minorities or stigmatized groups in many countries.
- HIV is still the subject of widespread myths.

We are dealing with a mortal disease. On this small planet, where hardly anyone is more than a day from anyone else, we have a new plague.

AIDS Is Here to Stay: What Can You Do About It?

"Barriers to disseminating AIDS information and to people acting on such information are responsible for the lion's share of the estimated 6,000 HIV infections that occur around the world every day."[2]

While there is no ready cure for HIV and AIDS, we are not powerless to do anything. Ways have been found to provide education, care, and support to those living with the virus and to help uninfected people stay free of HIV.

A Christian Response

The Seventh-day Adventist Church is committed to meeting the challenge of AIDS comprehensively and compassionately. Because of its far-reaching ministry in nearly 200 countries, Adventism will encounter many challenges posed by AIDS. Active education for the prevention of the HIV infection is necessary. The AIDS crisis provides the church, pastors, members, chaplains, and health professionals with an opportunity for public dialogue on AIDS, sexuality, marriage, interpersonal relationships, and health practices that provide a barrier against acquiring HIV infection. In advocating behaviors that prevent the transmission of HIV, we can demonstrate the love and compassion of God in our ministry to others.

In response to God's love, Seventh-day Adventists seek to view people suffering from AIDS through the eyes of Jesus. As the epidemic spreads, some people in the world may begin to see its sufferers as lepers were once seen—only as carriers of death, to be shunned and isolated. Jesus set a different example by showing acceptance and treating the people of His day with compassion. Jesus always distinguished between sin, which He never compromised, and care for the sinner, whom He always loved. Adventists are to follow Christ's example in dealing with those who contract AIDS or sickness of any kind.[3]

---

[1] HIV/AIDS: The Global Epidemic. Statistics provided UNAIDS and WHO (19%).

[2] Global AIDSNEWS (WHO, 1995), vol. 1.

[3] *Adventist Professional* 6, no. 1 (Autumn 1994): 10, 11.

Seminar: Living With AIDS in Your Community

The following AIDS seminar can be used in virtually any setting, whether rural or urban, and can be adapted to suit local cultural conditions and languages. Each page can be copied on transparencies and used on overhead projectors.

This seminar consists of four basic sessions that will help the audience understand how you and other people feel about HIV and AIDS. It also provides practical information to help educate people and communities to live positively with HIV and AIDS.

It is vital that the seminar leader understand the following material and is comfortable and relaxed in presenting it to others. Different cultures may demand different approaches when presenting this material; however, the underlying fact is that aids is destructive, and education is not only necessary but vital if behavioral change is to occur.

The majority of this material has been adapted from *Living With AIDS in the Community: A Book to Help People Make the Best of Life,* published by the World Health Organization in 1992. Any of the following seminar material may be copied, reproduced, or adapted to meet local needs without permission from the authors or publisher, provided the parts reproduced are distributed free of cost—not for profit.

**The material on the following pages has been arranged for use
with an overhead projector. To make your presentation more appealing,
you may retype this material using larger type and more space
between sections. Adding appropriate illustrations will help
keep your audience's attention.**

Session 1: HIV and AIDS

What Is HIV?

HIV is a very small germ called a virus. HIV makes the body weak and less able to fight sickness and disease. People with HIV in their body go on to become sick with AIDS. The following is a simple way to understand what HIV does in the body:

- The body is normally protected by white blood cells.
- White blood cells fight disease and protect the body.
- Strong diseases can make one sick during the fight, but white blood cells usually win in the end.
- HIV is a very strong germ. If HIV gets into a human body, it attacks the white blood cells.
- After a long fight, HIV makes the white blood cells weak. The body then has very little protection.
- Without white blood cells, diseases can attach and kill.

How Is HIV Spread?

HIV is found in the blood and in the sexual fluids (semen in men, vaginal secretions in women).

This means that HIV is spread in three main ways: sex, infected blood, mothers to babies.

- **Sex.** Most people get HIV by having sex with someone who already has HIV.
- **From Infected Blood.** People get HIV when HIV-infected blood enters their blood. This infected blood can come from a blood transfusion. It can also come from a needle or cutting blade that has been used on a person with HIV and not sterilized afterward.
- **Mothers to Babies.** Mothers with HIV can pass it to their babies. The baby becomes infected while in the mother's womb or as it is being born. As soon as HIV enters your body, you become infectious; that is, you can infect other people with HIV.

How HIV Is Not Spread

- You cannot give or get HIV by sharing food, touching, hugging, shaking hands, crying, sitting close to other people, or holding and touching people in other normal ways.
- You cannot give or get HIV by sharing combs, clothes, sheets, towels, soap, or eating utensils. Sharing the same toilet is also safe.
- You cannot get HIV from mosquitoes, bedbugs, head lice, or any other insect or animal.

How HIV Infection Can Be Prevented

- Do not have sex until you get married, and then stay faithful to your partner.
- If you know you are uninfected and already sexually active, have sex only with a mutually faithful partner who is also known to be uninfected.
- In all other situations, a condom should always be used during sex.
- Women with HIV should seek advice before getting pregnant, because they may pass HIV to their baby. Pregnancy can be avoided by using condoms and/or other family-planning methods.
- Avoid the need for blood transfusions. Seek proper medical treatment (especially for malaria) before you become anemic (have a shortage of blood).
- When you cannot avoid a blood transfusion, insist on having blood that has been tested for HIV.
- When you cannot avoid such skin-piercing instruments as blades, needles, and syringes, insist on having sterilized instruments.
- Don't share razor blades, because they might come into contact with blood from cut skin.
- Cover cuts and wounds with bandages or a clean cloth.

The HIV Test

Most people with HIV feel healthy. They don't know that they have HIV. If you are healthy, the only way to know if you have HIV is to have a special blood test. If you take this blood test, you may be told that you are HIV positive. This means that you have HIV in your blood.

If the test cannot find any signs of HIV in your blood, you will be told that you are HIV negative. But you should know that it takes time for the signs of HIV to show in your blood. If you have avoided unprotected sex and have not been exposed to blood during the three months before your test, you probably will not need to be retested.

The people who give you the HIV blood test can advise you whether you need to take the test more than once. If your test is negative, it does not mean that you will be protected in the future, unless you follow the advice for HIV prevention.

More About the HIV Test

If you want an HIV test, discuss this with a doctor or health-care worker who can tell you if it would be useful and, if so, where to go. You might choose to get an HIV test:

- if you are concerned you might be infected
- if your partner is infected
- if you are thinking about getting married
- before you decide to have a baby

But remember, it is up to you alone to decide if you want an HIV test. No one else has the right to force you to have an HIV test if you are not ready to know the result. This is why it is important to talk to someone before the test, and to make sure someone is there to talk to you after the test.

When You Have an HIV Test:

- a small amount of blood is taken from you
- the result may take several weeks to arrive
- the result is private
- there should be someone there to help you think about how you will cope with the result of the test

Important Information for Couples About the HIV Test

It is possible for one partner to have HIV while the other partner does not. This means that there is still time to protect the partner who is not infected. So if you find that you have HIV, your partner may also want to be tested. It can be difficult to tell your partner that you have HIV. But it may be important because:

- you may then be able to talk more freely with your partner about such things as using condoms to make sexual intercourse safer
- you can openly do things to help yourself live longer
- your partner will know better how to help you
- you will be able to plan for the future together

If you are worried about telling your partner that you have HIV, ask a health-care worker or counselor to help. With time, your partner will be grateful that you told him or her.

What Is AIDS?

AIDS is the group of sicknesses that come after HIV has made the body weak. People with AIDS get such sicknesses as fever, rash, and diarrhea. They also lose weight.

At the moment there is no known cure for AIDS. But people with AIDS and HIV should be comforted by the fact that there are medicines that can help them to fight off the sicknesses that come with AIDS. Antibiotics and other medicines can help people with AIDS feel much better and live longer.

AIDS is a new and serious disease, so there have been false rumors and misunderstandings about it. But AIDS is just a disease, like cancer or polio. It is not a curse or a punishment.

HIV Can Progress to AIDS Quickly or Slowly

Some people develop AIDS a few years after becoming infected with HIV. Some people can be infected with HIV for 10 years or longer without developing AIDS. However, most people will not know when they become infected. They will realize they are infected only when they become sick. It is believed that everyone who has HIV will eventually go on to develop AIDS.

It is now known that if you take care of your health, it can help you live for a longer time with HIV before you develop AIDS. It is also known that if you look after your health, you have a greater chance of living longer after you have developed AIDS. Later on we will discuss how you can take care of your body and mind if you have HIV or AIDS.

Talking to Someone About HIV and AIDS

People with HIV and AIDS need to talk to someone about how they are feeling. They also need information about what to expect and what they can do to help themselves. There are many people to talk to. A religious leader can give spiritual comfort. Doctors, nurses, health-care workers, and counselors can give useful facts and support.

These people are trained to listen to your problems and experiences with HIV and AIDS. They can help you understand your feelings, sort out your problems, and make decisions for yourself, either individually or within your family or small group.

Session 2: Feelings About HIV and AIDS

HIV and AIDS are basically new and serious problems. It is natural for people to have strong feelings about them. Most people are frightened of HIV and AIDS. People who know that they have HIV or AIDS feel many different emotions. Some feel shocked. Some feel angry.

Shock

- No matter how much you prepare, it is a shock to learn that you have HIV or AIDS.
- You may feel very confused and not know what to do. It is good to be with someone you can trust at this time.
- The feelings of people with HIV or AIDS change often. One day they may feel rejected and lonely. The next day they may feel hopeful. This is normal.

Denial

- At first some people cannot believe that they have HIV or AIDS. They say: "The doctor must be wrong." "It can't be true. I feel so strong."
- If you have been told that you have HIV or AIDS, a counselor can help you understand what this means.

Anger

- Some people get very angry when they find out they have HIV or AIDS.
- They blame themselves or the person they think gave them HIV. Some may even blame God.
- Anger is normal, but it is not helpful. Talking to a counselor or a friend can help you through the feelings of anger.

Bargaining

- Some people try to bargain. They say to themselves: "God will cure me if I stop having sex." "The ancestors will make me better if I make a sacrifice."
- People with HIV or AIDS need to be helped to get through the feeling of bargaining.

Loneliness

People with HIV or AIDS often feel lonely. If you have HIV or AIDS, remember, you are not alone. Many other people have HIV or AIDS. If someone you know has HIV or AIDS, give them companionship. Take away their loneliness.

Fear

People with HIV or AIDS fear many things:

- pain
- losing their job
- other people knowing that they are infected

(continued)

- leaving their children
- death

It is frightening to have HIV or AIDS, but you may find that your fear lessens when you talk to someone who understands. You may also find that you are worried about things that you do not need to fear. For example, you may find that when other people learn you have HIV, they show you great love and kindness.

Self-consciousness

Some people with HIV or AIDS think that everyone is looking at them or talking about them. This makes them want to hide. Sometimes they feel rejected by other people, or they reject themselves. Sometimes they feel guilty.

- If you have HIV and AIDS, don't hide.
- Try not to feel discouraged if people talk about you.
- Stay active in your village or community. By staying active, you can show your community that people with HIV and AIDS are valuable members of society, just like anyone else.
- If you have HIV or AIDS, try to think well of yourself. Be proud of yourself. You are still you. You are still important.

Depression

Some people with HIV or AIDS feel there is no good reason for living.

- They feel useless. Sometimes they stay at home, not eating, not talking to anyone.
- Depression can make you weak in mind and body, so it is important to try to overcome depression.
- If you have HIV or AIDS, don't give up. Put on your nice clothes. Visit your friends. Keep busy. Do something that helps others. If you have children, think about them; they still need you.
- Health-care workers may help if you feel depressed. Do not hesitate to visit one if your depression is very deep or long-lasting.

Acceptance

After some time most people with HIV or AIDS accept their situation. This is helpful. They often feel more serene (peace of mine). They often feel able to begin to think about the best way to live. They think:

- *What can I do to make the best of the rest of my life?*
- *What foods should I eat to help me stay healthy?*
- *What plans shall I make so my children are provided for in the future?*
- They might also think: *Let me be grateful for every day. Let me appreciate my friends and family.*

(continued)

Hope

People with HIV or AIDS can hope about many things:

- that they will live a long time
- that a cure will soon be found
- that the doctor will be able to treat each sickness as it comes
- that they are loved and accepted for who they are
- their beliefs

It is important to have hope. Hope lifts your spirits and gives you strength to face each situation. Hope can help you fight HIV and AIDS and live longer. Remember: even if you have hope today, it is possible to feel angry or depressed tomorrow. This is normal. The important thing is to try to regain the feelings of hope again and again.

Session 3:
Living Positively With HIV and AIDS

Hope and acceptance can help you to live positively with HIV and AIDS. But what does living positively mean? It means:
- making choices in your life that are good for your health
- making the best of your life as a person with HIV and AIDS
- living as normally as possible
- looking after your spiritual and mental health

The Importance of Family

Families are very important for people with HIV or AIDS. The family home can be a shelter in which:
- someone can rest assured he or she is loved and accepted
- someone doesn't have to be brave or hide his or her feelings.

If someone in your family has HIV or AIDS, you can help this person in many ways:
- You can help them to rest by doing their household jobs for them.
- You can help them to eat nutritious foods by going to the market or gardens and cooking for them.
- You can help to dispel fear by making them feel loved and welcomed.

If you have HIV or AIDS, it is usually good for your family to know that:
- they can give you love and support
- you can make plans for the future
- they can share the financial burden
- it will be easier for you if you do not have to hide your situation

If someone in your family is sick with AIDS, you can:
- bring them food and drink
- wash their clothes and sheets
- nurse them

Remember, if you have HIV or AIDS, you can use the knowledge you have to help others. You can teach your family how HIV is spread and how it is not spread. You can help them to avoid HIV. This is one of the most loving contributions you can make.

Don't Let HIV or AIDS Divide Your Family

Sometimes when a husband knows that his wife has HIV or AIDS, he sends her away from home. Sometimes it is the wife who abandons the husband with HIV or AIDS. Abandoning your partner can cause problems and add to the pain. The children will certainly suffer. They need love and guidance from both their parents.

Such separation can spread HIV. For example, the husband may also have HIV. But he will want to take a new wife. The new wife may then become infected with HIV. It is better to stay together and work out the future together.

Sometimes families argue about who is to blame for bringing HIV into a marriage. This can cause great unhappiness. It can make positive living difficult.

(continued)

Some people believe that the person who falls sick first is the one who got infected first. This is not always true. Of course, it is natural to think about who brought the infection. But thinking or talking about it too much will cause more pain. It is much more helpful:

- to forgive
- to support each other
- to plan for the future by making a plan to provide for your children and partner
- to care for your children
- to enjoy the remaining days together

Going Back to the Village

Some people with HIV or AIDS want to go back to the village. They may find better food there. The extended family may be able to give them more attention than they would receive in town. Village life may be better for them.

But some people with HIV or AIDS do not want to go back to the village. Their village relatives may be very poor. They may feel that because they cannot care for themselves, they will be neglected. For some people, village life may be worse.

People with HIV or AIDS should be allowed to decide for themselves about returning to their village. It is better if it is their choice and not the choice of their elders, parents, or partner. Remember: people with HIV or AIDS need medical treatment to feel better and live longer. Is there a doctor or medicine in the village? Town life may be very poor for some people.

Husbands or other relatives who remain in town can still support a family member who returns to the village. They can send money and medicine. They can visit. But town life may be better for others. If a wife goes back to the village, she should take the things that belong to her and that she bought with the money she earned in town.

Friends

If you have a friend who has HIV or AIDS, you should be supportive and kind. You can learn from your friend. Your friendship can even grow. You can also help your friend to live positively. You can meet your friend at a place where you can drink tea or soft drinks, not alcohol. You can go to ball games and other events together.

And remember, if you have HIV or AIDS, your friends still need you. Don't cut yourself off from your friends. You are still worthy of friendship. You are still the same person.

If a friend seems to reject you, try not to feel hurt. It may be that they are not rejecting you. You may be imagining it and worrying for nothing. It may be that they don't know what to say. They may also be ignorant. Or they may fear that they also have HIV.

Like anyone else, people with HIV or AIDS can make new friends. Often, they like to make friends with other people with HIV or AIDS. They find them more understanding about the frustrations and challenges. If you have HIV or AIDS, you may find new friends at AIDS support groups, or you could start one.

(continued)

Neighbors or Villagers

Neighbors can help a family that is affected by AIDS. They can
- collect water
- go to the market
- cook food
- care for the children
- help in the garden
- wash clothes

They can also spend time with the family. Often this is the most important thing neighbors can do. Their concern will help those with HIV or AIDS feel that they are still part of their community.

It is good if a community feels free to talk about AIDS, just as it talks about any other sickness. Then the people who want to gossip in an unkind way will find themselves isolated and with nothing to say.

Remember: "Today it is me, tomorrow someone else."—Philly Bongeley Lutaaya, popular Ugandan songwriter, who died of AIDS.

Some Traditional Customs That Can Spread HIV

Some traditional customs are now risky because of HIV. Customs that involve having nonregular partners are risky. Any custom that involves sharing cutting instruments is also risky.

Risky customs include:
- wife sharing and wife inheritance
- circumcision with unsterilized knives or blades
- scarification with unsterilized knives or blades

You cannot know who has HIV. And AIDS is found both in villages and towns. So it is much safer to modify dangerous practices in order to make customs safe.

Session 4: Caring for Yourself if You Have HIV or AIDS

- Get medical help whenever you feel unwell.
- Eat nutritious food.
- Practice good hygiene.
- Take plenty of rest.
- Keep active and busy.
- Avoid heavy smoking and alcohol.
- Use condoms.

Caring for yourself is part of living positively.

Getting Medical Help

If you have HIV or AIDS, your resistance to infection is weakened. You will fall sick more easily. It is very important to go to a doctor as soon as you feel sick. Most of the sicknesses that come with HIV or AIDS can be treated. Getting prompt treatment will help you to live longer. For most problems, doctors can give you medicine that will:

- make you feel better
- keep the problem from becoming more serious

So if you have a bad, persistent cold or cough, go to the doctor. Don't let it develop into something serious, such as pneumonia or tuberculosis. And if you have a cut, cover it and seek treatment. Don't let it become infected.

It is important to get treatment from qualified health workers. You can get treatment from your doctor. You can also go to a clinic or hospital. If someone you love has AIDS and seems to be getting weak, don't despair. Encourage them to go to the doctor or hospital. Treatment can make them much more comfortable and give them a feeling of well-being.

Eating and Drinking

Your body needs food to build it up, give it energy, and protect it from infection. You should try to eat even when you do not feel hungry. You can take small meals and eat them more often.

If solid food is difficult to eat, make it into liquid form. Eat what you can tolerate. Drink milk or juice instead of alcohol. Drink plenty of water.

You may have sores in your mouth that stop you from eating. Mouth sores can be treated, so take liquid food and go to see a doctor.

If you have diarrhea, you will need to drink a lot. It is good to take an oral rehydration drink that can be made with packets, as follows:

- Measure one liter of drinking water into a clean container.
- Open the packet of oral rehydration salts and empty it into the water.
- If you do not have ORS in packets, you can make SSS (salt, sugar solution) as follows: Pour 1 liter of clean water into a container. Add one (1) teaspoon salt and eight (8) teaspoons sugar. Stir SSS until the sugar and salt have dissolved.

If you do not have oral rehydration salts, drink plenty of clean water, tea, juice, milk, or other liquid. Drink one full cup or more every time you have diarrhea.

(continued)

Nutritious Foods

You should try to eat from each of the following groups at every meal. This does not have to expensive. You can choose the cheapest food from each group, and most of the foods are grown in your own gardens or are easily available.

1. Body-building foods: peas, beans, soya, lentils, groundnuts (especially peanuts, which are plentiful in the highlands), eggs, milk, meat, and fish
2. Energy-giving foods: sweet potatoes, rice, bread, bananas, etc.
3. Foods that protect the body from infection (vitamins): all fruits and vegetables

Cigarettes, Alcohol, and Bui (Betel Nut) Are Harmful

It is harmful for anyone to smoke. Smoking damages the lungs and many other parts of the body, and allows infections to enter the body more easily. Chewing bui is known to cause cancer and is not a healthful habit.

Drinking too much alcohol also hurts the body, especially the liver. Just as important, alcohol can make you disorganized and forgetful. You may forget to have safe sex. Remember, even if you have HIV now, it is possible to get other sexually transmitted diseases, which will make your body weak.

Cigarettes, alcohol, and betel nut are expensive. You could spend your money better on nutritious food. Good food strengthens your body and will help you live longer.

Rest and Relaxation

Your body needs extra rest. Try to sleep for eight hours every night. Rest on weekends and whenever you are tired. It is also good to relax whenever possible. You can listen to music, read, or do whatever makes you relax. You can relax with people you love. You can spend time relaxing with your family.

Work

It is good to work for as long as you can. Work earns some money and keeps you active. You see your friends at work. Being around them and working helps you to forget your worries. If you start to feel too tired to do your normal duties, you may need to change jobs or reduce your working hours, if possible.

Message to Employers: If one of your workers has HIV or AIDS, try to be understanding. They can still do valuable work.

Safer Sexual Practices

HIV is passed mainly through sexual intercourse. The only way to be absolutely sure you are not going to infect someone else is by not having sexual intercourse. If you already have HIV, it is risky for you to be exposed to other sexually transmitted diseases.

But it can be difficult to give up sex. So what can people with HIV or AIDS do?

(continued)

- They can use a condom every time they have sex. Condoms used correctly can reduce the risk of passing on HIV or getting other sexually transmitted diseases.
- It is very important to use the condom correctly. If you do not know how, have a health worker instruct you.
- If you decide to use condoms, you will need to discuss it with your partner first. Do not force the other person to do what you want. It is better to discuss the risks and advantages together.
- You can buy condoms very cheaply from the chemist or get them from a health clinic or the hospital.

Remember, if you have another sexually transmitted disease, you should seek treatment immediately.

Other Ways to Show Love, Affection, and Caring

Sexual intercourse is not the only way to show love and be intimate. If you have HIV or AIDS, it is safe to:
- hug
- hold someone in your arms
- touch
- kiss (if you do not have cuts or sores in your mouth)

You can also think about other ways of showing love. You can:
- help your partner
- remember the special things that he or she likes
- listen to what he or she says
- spend time together
- comfort and console each other

Pregnancy

If you have HIV or AIDS, you should seek advice from your health-care worker or doctor before deciding if you want to become pregnant.
- Your baby may be born with HIV, even though many children born to HIV infected parents are not infected.
- A baby needs healthy parents to raise him or her.

Some husbands get angry and violent with their wives if they don't produce children. Some leave their wives. But an understanding spouse will help a partner make decisions regarding pregnancy if either one has HIV or AIDS. They will want to stay healthy for as long as possible. They will not want the sadness of being the parents of a baby with HIV or AIDS.

Often health-care workers and counselors can be helpful in discussing the issues surrounding pregnancy and HIV infection, and can help you come to a decision that is right for you.

(continued)

Children With HIV or AIDS

Most children with HIV become infected while they are still in their mother's womb or as they are being born. However, in the first year of a child's life the commonly available tests cannot tell if an HIV infection has been passed on or not. Most babies with HIV develop AIDS before the age of 2. But some can remain healthy up to the age of 6. Children with HIV or AIDS need:

- love and attention
- nutritious food
- a hygienic environment

They should be taken to a doctor whenever they seem unwell. It is completely safe to hold or hug a child with HIV or AIDS. HIV cannot be spread by children's urine, saliva, feces, or vomit. A child with HIV cannot infect others by playing with them or sharing toys.

Breast-feeding. Breast milk is almost always the best food for babies. It is the baby's best protection against diarrhea and many other diseases. Breast-feeding is recommended even if the mother or the baby or both have HIV, unless your doctor or health worker give you special reasons not to do so. Women who know they are infected with HIV should consult their health-care worker for advice about feeding their babies.

Immunization. Immunization is important. If your child has HIV or AIDS, he or she should be taken to the hospital for immunization.

Healthy Children in the Family Affected by HIV or AIDS. Parents with HIV or AIDS may have several healthy children. These can be children who were born before the mother became infected with HIV. Or they can be children who were born after the mother became infected with HIV but who did not become infected themselves.

These healthy children need a lot of love, care, and attention. One or both of their parents will eventually die. They will become orphans. Parents with HIV or AIDS can help their healthy children by:

- spending time with them and giving them care and guidance
- making proper arrangements for relatives to look after them in the future
- making arrangements, if possible, for future financial commitments
- protecting their family and property for their children

Relatives and other concerned people in the community need to mobilize to help children who are orphaned by AIDS. Various social, religious, and health organizations can help, but they cannot take on the whole responsibility.

Blood Transfusions

People should know that they cannot get AIDS by donating blood. But if you know that you have HIV, you should not donate (give) blood. This is because your blood will be tested and then rejected.

When you cannot avoid a blood transfusion, insist on having blood that has been tested for HIV.

If you have HIV or AIDS and you need blood, you may still receive tested blood from people without HIV.